THE
READER'S DIGEST ILLUSTRATED

BOOK OF DOGS

Second Revised Edition

Published by The Reader's Digest Association, Inc.

PLEASANTVILLE, NEW YORK • MONTREAL

The Reader's Digest Illustrated Book of Dogs

Editor: Patricia Sylvester
Art Supervisor: Diane Mitrofanow

Contributing Staff
A. R. Byers, Michèle McLaughlin,
Philomena Rutherford, Andrée Payette, Francis Legge

Consultant: Sarah Marshall Diamond
Cover Design: John McGuffie
Cover Illustration: Philippe Saunier

The publisher also acknowledges the contributions of
Barbara Black, John Gilmore, Natalie King, Joan Morden,
Allan Reznik, Mary Shaw, Billy Wisse, Sally Dennet,
Vere Dodds, Shelley Gaffe, Frances Gallagher,
Peter Macnaughton-Smith, Kelly Ricard, Luc Granger

Staff for the Second Revised Edition
Editors: Tim Nicholson, Philomena Rutherford
Art Supervisor: John McGuffie   **Designer:** Lucie Martineau
Research Editor: Wadad Bashour
Copy Editor: Joseph Marchetti
Coordinator: Susan Wong   **Production:** Holger Lorenzen

CAVEAT

THE READER'S DIGEST ILLUSTRATED BOOK OF DOGS is not designed
to supplant professional diagnosis and treatment of canine
disorders: if your dog is ill, take it to a veterinarian.
Furthermore, veterinary practices may vary among regions;
so information here may sometimes conflict with
recommendations of other experts. In such cases,
follow your veterinarian's advice.

The credits and acknowledgments that appear on page 384 are hereby
made a part of this copyright page.

Based on the book first published in France as **Guide des chiens**
Copyright © 1982, Sélection du Reader's Digest, S.A.

SECOND REVISED EDITION

Copyright © 1993 The Reader's Digest Association, Inc.
Copyright © 1993 The Reader's Digest Association (Canada) Ltd.
Copyright © 1993 Reader's Digest Association Far East Ltd.
Philippine Copyright 1993 Reader's Digest Association Far East Ltd.

Canadian Cataloguing in Publication Data
Main entry under title:
The Reader's Digest illustrated book of dogs

2nd rev. ed.
Based on the book first published in France as Guide des chiens.
Includes index.
ISBN 0-88850-205-2
1. Dog breeds. 2. Dogs. I. Sylvester, Patricia.
II. Reader's Digest Association (Canada).

SF426.R42 1993   636.7   C93-090088-X

Printed in the United States of America
Second Printing, April 1994

Introduction

For thousands of years dogs have kept humans company with single-minded devotion. As undemanding partners they have contributed to our welfare in a host of far-reaching ways: hauling supplies across polar ice-fields; rescuing drowning people; ferreting out avalanche victims; pulling in fishermen's nets; herding sheep and cattle; protecting homes from intruders—the list could go on. They act as our eyes, our ears, our police, our playmates, and even our confidants.

The fact that there are nearly 160 million dogs in the world today would seem to attest to the dog's widespread popularity. Man's abiding interest in the selective mating of canines has resulted in the establishment of some 400 distinct breeds—'standardized' animals that superbly perform their pre-ordained tasks. A large number of these breeds are represented in this book. They were selected from kennel club registries in Australia, Canada, Great Britain, and South Africa, as well as from the registries of the more than 30 member-countries of the Fédération cynologique internationale. The animals were chosen variously for their popularity, rarity, beauty, working skills, hunting abilities, or simple uniqueness. Since many pure-bred dogs are not registered with kennel clubs by their owners, it is impossible to estimate how commonplace a particular breed is. We have assessed the relative popularity of pedigreed dogs, however, by referring to tabulations compiled by the largest canine organizations in the English-speaking world: the Kennel Club of Great Britain and the American Kennel Club.

Because nomenclature—the naming of breeds and the spelling of those names—differs from country to country, we have included a short index at the back of the book. By consulting it, you can quickly determine the alternate names by which a particular breed is known. A convenient glossary, also located at the back of the book, explains the meaning of the various technical terms used herein. Measurements are rendered both in the imperial and in the metric system.

—The Editors

Table of Contents

Dogs and Civilization

The First Dogs **9**
   Prehistory 10
   Transformation of the Wolf 12
   Dog Migrations 12
   Breeds and Possible Parentage 14

Early Domestication of Dogs **16**
   Mesopotamia 16
   Asia 17
   Egypt 18
   Greece 20
   Rome 21

The Socialization of Dogs **24**
   The Middle Ages 24
   The Renaissance 26
   Dogs for Royalty and Citizens 28
   The Industrial Age 30
   The Twentieth Century 31

Identifying Dogs

Physical Characteristics **34**

Classifying Breeds **42**

Album of Dogs

Preface to Album **44**

Featured Breeds, from Affenpinscher to Yorkshire Terrier . **45**

Unofficial Breeds **282**

Mongrels **284**

You and Your Dog

Choosing a Dog 286

Sleeping Quarters 290

Feeding 292
Basics of Canine Nutrition and Proper Diet 292
Staples in Canine Diets 293
How to Feed Your Dog 295

Hygiene and Grooming 298
Keeping Your Dog Clean 298
Grooming 301

Canine Psychology 303
Territorial Instincts 303
Canine Hierarchies 304
Sexuality 306
The Maternal Instinct 307
Language 308
Intelligence 311
Puppy Psychology 312

Education and Training 313
Basic Education 313
General Training 314
Training Guard Dogs 320
Training Hunting-dogs 322
Special Training 323

Health

Your Dog's Anatomy 326
Skeleton 326
Muscles 327
Digestive System 327
Respiratory System 329
Urinary and Genital Systems 329
Circulatory System 330
Nervous System 331
Sensory Organs 331

Your Dog's Physiology **332**
    Digestion 332
    Reproduction 332
    Circulation and Respiration 335
    Thermoregulation 335
    Seeing, Hearing, and Smelling 336
    Gait 337

Medical Care **338**
    Your Veterinarian and You 338
    Emergencies 341
    Surgery 343
    First Aid 344
    Diseases 349

Kennel Clubs

Overview of Kennel Clubs **368**

Fédération cynologique internationale **369**

Australian National Kennel Council **370**
    New Zealand Kennel Club 370

Canadian Kennel Club **372**
    American Kennel Club 373

Kennel Club (Great Britain) **374**

Kennel Union of Southern Africa **376**

Glossary **378**

Index **382**

Credits and Acknowledgements **384**

Dogs and Civilization

The First Dogs
9

Early Domestication of Dogs
16

The Socialization of Dogs
24

An artist's reconstruction of Pseudocynodictis (upper illustration). This early member of the Canidae family lived in North America more than 25 million years ago. It was an ancestor of the Tomarctus (lower illustration) which in turn gave rise to the genus Canis. The earliest known example of Canis in the Old World dates back six million years. Its descendants were forbears of a number of species, including Canis lupus (wolf), which goes back 300,000 years and is widely believed to be the forerunner of modern-day dogs.

The First Dogs

Dogs are members of the order *Carnivora*, a group of mammals with origins in the Tertiary era, about fifty-five million years ago. The earliest fossils of ancestors of this order, the *Miacoides*, predate that distant time. These animals varied in size, from about the length of a weasel to that of a wolf, and had the characteristic teeth of present-day carnivores. The upper jaw held six small incisors, two large canines shaped like daggers, and six molars. The lower jaw held six incisors, two canines, eight premolars, and six molars. The first molars, larger than the others, developed into what are called 'carnassials.'

Nowadays the order *Carnivora* embraces such widely differing animals as the hyena, the marten, and the jennet, and also the family *Canidae*, which includes dogs, wolves, jackals, and wild dogs proper.

The first of the *Canidae—Hesperocyon*—originated about twenty-five to thirty million years ago. Its earliest members were born in what is now North America. Later, *Canidae* spread westward across the Bering Strait, which was not then covered by sea. Some *Canidae* advanced southward, into South America, where they evolved into foxes.

Because dogs first came into being in prehistoric times it is almost impossible to reconstruct the process by which men of about twenty thousand years ago developed the ancestors of the faithful companions of today. The dog, widely believed to be descended from the wolf, is a domestic animal which would never have existed had it not been for the intervention of humans. Over thousands of years it has undergone an evolution—directed by man—that doubtless virtually transformed its wild, ancestral nature.

Ever since man first conceived of trapping young wolves and raising their offspring in captivity, he has been altering the course of their evolution. Domesticating the wolf meant isolating wild representatives of the species in an artificial environment, under conditions very different from those provided by nature. In the natural state there were many wolves and the environment was more or less constant. But the number of individual animals raised by man was limited; their offspring, therefore, possessed highly individualistic genetic traits, and passed these 'mutations' on. This phenomenon was accompanied by the loss of some hereditary wolf-like characteristics. As selective pressures increased, new genetic stock evolved over generations into animals hardly resembling their ancestors. As with all domestic species, the selective pressures were not due to 'natural' causes which act upon wild species, but to man, who chose for breeding just those animals with qualities he wished to perpetuate.

It seems likely that humans in different areas of the world have attempted selective cross-breeding since the days when dogs were first domesticated. Certainly, different breeds are known to have existed from earliest times. Modern breeders have benefited from this trial-and-error selection carried out over the course of time and under the joint influence of natural and human environment. Unsuitable dogs were eliminated before reaching the age of reproduction, and thus different breeds were gradually developed: large, heavy

Lower jaw of Cynodictis. *The carnassial tooth (the first of the six molars) and the fang are typical of the jaw of a dog.*

ANCIENT FORMS OF THE DOG

The story of the *Canidae* family begins in the Northern Hemisphere during the late Eocene and early Oligocene epochs. On each side of what is now the Atlantic Ocean there lived two closely related animals: *Cynodictis* in Europe and *Pseudocynodictis* in North America. The European animal died out in the Oligocene epoch (35 million years ago) through competition with the more highly evolved *Ursidae*. The North American species survived, later giving rise to what we now recognize as the dog. *Pseudocynodyctis* was a low-slung and very long animal with a long muzzle. Evolution led to the lengthening of its legs.

Following *Pseudocynodictis* in North America carne *Mesocyon*, with a skeleton similar to that of a present-day wolf. Its descendant was *Cynodesmus* (early Miocene epoch, 25 million years ago) which thereafter gave rise to *Tomarctus*, known to have existed in the middle and late Miocene epoch. Shortly before the beginning of the Pliocene epoch (10 million years ago) the genus *Canis* appeared and migrated into what is now Eurasia. Its earliest representative in the Old World, *Canis cipio*, was discovered in the deposits in Concud, near Teruel, in Spain. It lived about six million years ago. The genus evolved through different species up to the *Canis lupus*, or wolf, which dates back approximately 300,000 years.

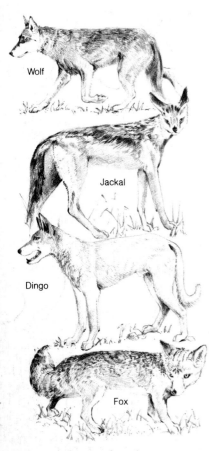

Among these four animals,
the wolf (Canis lupus) is
generally regarded as the dog's
most likely ancestor.

mountain dogs, slender dogs of the steppes, small forest
dogs. Each of these breeds was further subdivided—to
obtain different types of coat, for example, or ways of
carrying the ears or tail, or for such qualities as keen-
ness of hearing or scenting.

Most of today's breeds were established around the
turn of this century; only a few date further back than the
eighteenth century. But the main types—sheep-dogs,
hunting-dogs, guard dogs, and pets—were known to
the ancient Egyptians, among others, long before then.

Prehistory

If the early stage of the dog's evolution seems straightforward, the sequel is considerably more obscure, even
though we are dealing with a relatively recent period,
starting only about fifteen thousand years ago.

The wolf, jackal, and fox have all been claimed as direct ancestors of the dog. It has also been suggested that
the dog is descended from another line of yet undisco-
vered ancestors. This last claim, voiced during the
eighteenth century, is not supported by any evidence
worthy of mention.

The fox can be crossed off the list of claimants right
away. Its form is too different from the dog's and it has
fewer chromosomes. Its eyes have oval rather than
round pupils; its head is very long and pointed, with no
dip ('stop') where the cranium meets the muzzle; lastly, its bushy tail is carried well behind it. It is also
worth noting that foxes, unlike dogs and wolves, never
live in packs or bands.

For similar reasons, the wild dog has also been eliminated by virtually every palaeontologist who has studied the origin of the dog.

Of the remaining possibilities—the wolf and the
jackal—it is the wolf that is favoured by the specialists
of today. Indeed, from one to three species are said to be
the ancestors of the dog, depending on whether one accepts a single or several lines of descent.

While the jackal is easy to tame and likes to live near
human habitation, it dislikes dogs intensely. This fundamental enmity between the two animals suggests a
lack of affinity. In support of the jackal, on the other
hand, it has been pointed out that wolves distrust humans and flee from them; are hard to tame; and howl
but do not bark. These arguments, however, are regarded as inadequate.

The long spiral tail of this
primitive dog suggests an
affinity with such sight hounds
as the Sloughi that live in desert
regions today. Rock painting at
Tassili n'Ahaggar (Algeria).

This depiction of dogs pursuing wild sheep reveals what must have been the earliest vocation of the dog: hunting. Rock painting at Fezzan (Libya).

In favour of the wolf hypothesis, it is clear that the wolf has special hierarchical behaviour and also has instincts that prevent mortal combat between members of the same pack. Wolves are also a highly adaptable species, capable of adjusting to entirely different environments. Before man decimated their populations there were wolves in every country—but wolves which nevertheless showed marked differences from their counterparts in other regions.

As a side-note to this discussion it is also worth mentioning the work of Konrad Lorenz, the Austrian behavioural scientist. He has divided dogs into two classes according to their psychological make-up: 'wolf-dogs,' which keep a certain distance from man (sheep-dogs, for example) and for whom hierarchy is very important; and 'jackal-dogs,' which spend their lives closer to man, like some hunting-dogs and pets. These distinctions, however, tell us little about the origins of this domestic animal.

Over the years, the work of certain zoologists has led to the hypothesis that dogs were domesticated in several separate areas of the world, towards the end of the Palaeolithic and up to the start of the Neolithic period, some seven to fifteen thousand years before the Christian era. But with which subspecies of wolf did domestication originate? Was it with the grey wolf of the North which, by living around human settlements, had its young raised by man, becoming gradually accustomed to his presence? Or was the first domesticated

THE WOLF HIERARCHY

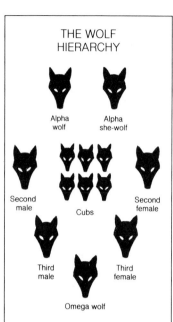

Alpha wolf   Alpha she-wolf

Second male   Cubs   Second female

Third male   Third female

Omega wolf

The pack, or family group, is composed of about six members. It has a fairly rigid structure, and nearly always includes a dominant male, his female and cubs, and several other adults and young. At the lowest level is the Omega wolf. This animal, male or female, lives on the fringes of the pack and is a victim of constant harassment. For reasons still not clear, wolves need this underdog. If he or she dies, another low-status animal takes over the role. The whole group apparently benefits from this; it reduces their ever-present latent hostility. The dominant male often shows authority by threatening to bite the neck or back of a subordinate. The latter, ears down, head and tail low, adopts the humble, subservient pose typical of lower-status wolves.

A high tail is a sign of dominance. Likewise, a low, aggressive growl is a dominant wolf's threatening warning to subordinates. The Alpha wolf's independent decisions—when to rest, when to hunt, whether to pursue prey—are usually followed by the other wolves. But the leader may change a course of action if his companions seem hesitant or fearful. Lower-ranking wolves always welcome the dominant male, greeting the leader with respect and affection. They surround him, and each one tries to touch him, to lick him, to nibble at his jowls. The ritual resembles the behaviour of cubs expecting food as the pack wakes up or the Alpha wolf approaches.

dog actually the Indian wolf (*Canis lupus pallipes*), originally raised as livestock destined to be eaten?

Among other subspecies of wolf which may have been antecedents of the dog, the desert wolf of the Middle East is sometimes mentioned; and so is the woolly wolf of Tibet and northern India, an animal so sensitive to cold that it may have drawn close to the fires of human settlements.

Transformation of the Wolf

It is conceivable that our Stone Age ancestors, when they squatted around the fire after a hunt, were not particularly disturbed by the presence of wolves eyeing them hungrily in the flickering light. The fire would protect them, just as it still protects some primitive tribes today.

In those early times, fear of not having food was what drove man to become a hunter—to eat as much as possible at a single sitting to stave off the hunger that would inevitably follow feasting. Often, however, man killed animals far bigger than he could possibly devour in one go, and the remains were left to rot around the edge of the encampment. Doubtless the wolves lurking nearby looked after the job of cleaning up, much as hyenas do today in parts of Africa.

Because of this some experts theorize that the earliest dogs were household hangers-on—dogs that followed man and later helped with hunting and the guarding of flocks. Domestication could thus have taken place when man lived by hunting and food-gathering. Following this line of reasoning, it is plausible that *Canis lupus pallipes* was the direct ancestor of the dog. However, in spite of all the studies made so far, the origin of 'man's best friend' remains unclear.

By the Bronze Age there were definite types of dogs, which eighteenth-century zoologists divided into five primitive categories: *Canis familiaris palustris*, the so-called Tourbières Dog and ancestor of the spitz breeds; *Canis familiaris metris optimae*, forerunner of the sheep-dogs; *Canis familiaris inostranzevi*, forbear of the mastiffs, originally from northern India; *Canis familiaris intermedius*, a more recent arrival, ancestor of the pointers; and *Canis familiaris leineri*, from which come the greyhounds. This classification remains widespread but is disputed.

Dog Migrations

Once dogs became domesticated—or at least closely associated with people—they accompanied migrating civilizations around the world. One explanation for the development of specific breeds is based on these canine movements. Many experts believe that the animals that accompanied migrating people had been carefully preselected for particular characteristics: draught animals had to be sturdy and capable of great endurance; military dogs had to be ferocious, yet responsive to their trainers; guard dogs had to be fierce and threatening. As long as one type of dog was kept isolated from other types, its genetic traits remained pure.

The earliest peoples of Western Europe did not have dogs—at least, no evidence to this effect has been found. They were trappers and food-gatherers. It is thought that only when traders and invaders from the East arrived were dogs introduced to the region. Some authors believe that Celtic Greyhounds (if they existed

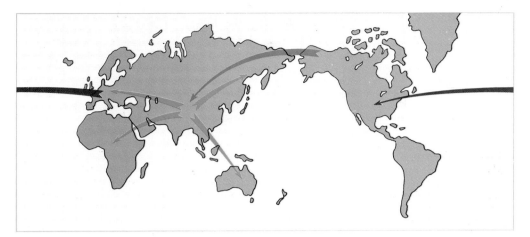

at that time) may have interbred with the greyhounds brought in by Phoenicians and Arabs. Other breeds were introduced by the Romans, who brought with them their famous military dogs, large mastiffs that had originated in the Orient.

Other dogs, notably northern breeds descended from the Tourbières Dog, interbred with those from the East. These may have given rise to dogs of the spitz type, indigenous to Scandinavia, Russia, Japan, and Greenland. Certainly, these dogs went south where, despite their dislike of mild climates, they shared territory with many other dogs of eastern origin.

There is no evidence, though, that any northern dog originated in the south. Those that came from North Africa (Egypt and the Maghreb) were from the Middle East, and they followed the movements of various civilizations around the Mediterranean.

When Christopher Columbus discovered America in 1492, there were already dogs in the New World, dogs that had most likely come from China by way of an isthmus that today is the Bering Strait.

Carnivorous ancestors of the dog came from America across a land bridge (now the Bering Strait) and settled in Eurasia. As true dogs, they began to range across Asia, Europe, and Africa. Some went East, accompanying invaders, and others roamed back to America.

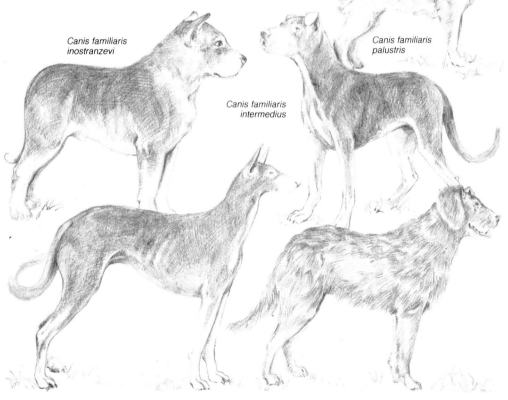

Canis familiaris
inostranzevi

Canis familiaris
intermedius

Canis familiaris
palustris

Canis familiaris leineri

Canis familiaris metris optimae.

Breeds and Possible Parentage

Most books about dogs display genealogical trees depicting the majority of present-day breeds together with their supposed lines of descent. Yet these lineage trees vary greatly from one author to another. The fact is, there are not sufficient archaeological or historical records to allow us to trace, with assurance, the history of different breeds, and where they branch out from their common origins.

Archaeological excavations have unearthed a few skulls of the earliest dogs in various parts of the world. Some archaeologists have described these dogs, furnished them with Latin names, and suggested—without further evidence—that each of these skulls represented the only type of dog living in that region at that time. By comparing the skulls with modern ones, the archaeologists have hypothesized long lines of descent for the modern breeds. We have illustrated such a system below to show this line of thought. As one of many variations, this chart con-

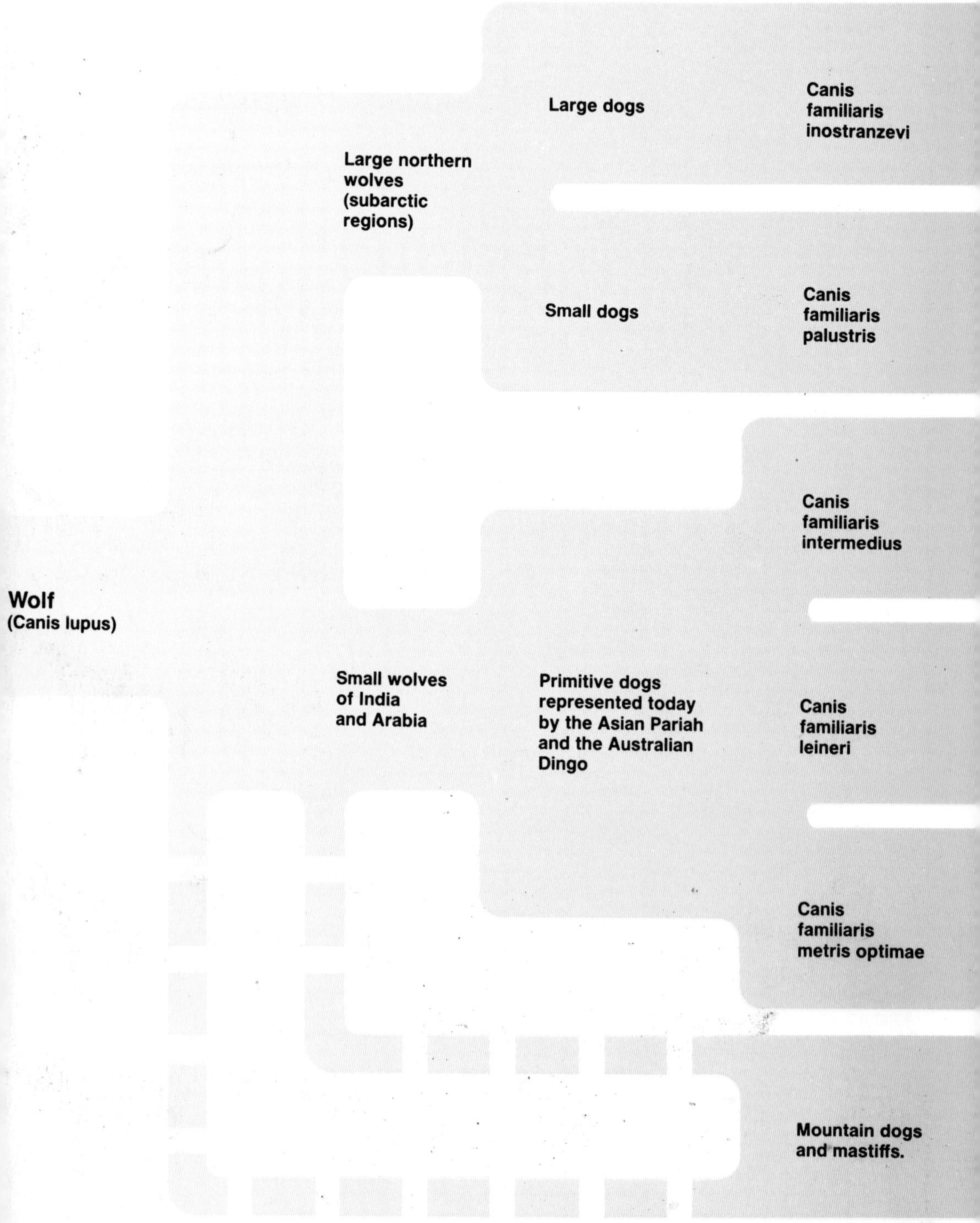

Wolf
(Canis lupus)

Large northern wolves (subarctic regions)

Large dogs — Canis familiaris inostranzevi

Small dogs — Canis familiaris palustris

Canis familiaris intermedius

Small wolves of India and Arabia

Primitive dogs represented today by the Asian Pariah and the Australian Dingo

Canis familiaris leineri

Canis familiaris metris optimae

Mountain dogs and mastiffs.

tains lines of descent that are disputed among canine experts.

Nowadays it is commonly believed that in the Quaternary period (12,000 to 600,000 years ago) there were two sizes of wolves that were the forerunners of most modern breeds. Near the ice-cap which covered northern Europe and Asia, large wolves well adapted to a harsh climate may have been the ancestors of a series of breeds, some of which became dwarfs. All other dogs may be descended from much smaller wolves suited to temperate climates. Wolves of this type still exist in India.

The Dingo gives us a picture of what the first true dogs in temperate climates may

have been like. Its erect ears are a primitive mutation which remained unchanged for millennia, appearing long before other ear types had developed—some so large that they hung down. Humans noticed the differing abilities associated with bodily variations and were able to select breeds particularly suited to hunting or guarding.

In spite of a widespread opinion to the contrary, it is unlikely that all large breeds of mountain dogs share a common ancestry. More probably, early groups of humans who settled in mountain regions bred oversize dogs as a defence against marauding bears and other sizeable animals, starting each time with local breeds.

Akita Alaskan Malamute Elkhound Samoyed Siberian Husky Keeshond

Chow Chow Eurasier Finnish Spitz Pomeranian Bull Terrier

Basset Hound Beagle Bloodhound German Short-haired Pointer Braque Français Poodle Cocker Spaniel

Pharaoh Hound Deerhound Greyhound Irish Wolfhound Afghan Hound Saluki

German Shepherd Berger Picard Collie Beauceron Briard Old English Sheepdog

Pyrenean Mountain Dog Dogue de Bordeaux Komondor Leonberger Mastiff

Early Domestication of Dogs

Virtually wherever history has been recorded there have been dogs represented in writings and on pictographs. Evidently, the domestication of dogs and the civilization of man occurred at the same time.

Mesopotamia

In the Middle East (Assyria, Persia) and as far away as India, dogs existed at least six thousand years before Christ. In fact, two distinctly different types of dog are known to have remained unchanged from Sumerian times up to the time of Darius (4000 to 500 B.C.). There were other types of dog too, in Nineveh and Babylon (2100 to 689 B.C.), but of these we have only' vague descriptions to go by.

The first Mesopotamian dogs on record were greyhounds. Fragments of 8,000-year-old pottery found in the Kurdistan region show these animals hunting gazelle. These findings indicate that greyhound breeds originated in the Tigris-Euphrates valley, rather than in Egypt, as is commonly believed.

Mastiff-type dogs were domesticated during the Stone Age by the inhabitants of what is now Iran. They doubtless found these dogs in the Tibet region, and the dogs stayed with them during their wanderings. Being raised in packs and often trained for battle, these dogs were highly prized by the Babylonians, the Assyrians, the Medes, and the Persians, who later introduced them to Greece. The dogs were used in combat and also to guard temples and large estates, as well as for hunting boars and lions. In some periods they were used as executioners: Condemned prisoners were eaten alive by mastiffs that had been deliberately starved in preparation for the event.

Although the ancient Aryan peoples kept flocks, shepherding was a minor activity that was usually left to children. Thus it is unlikely that mastiffs were ever used for this purpose. (Specialized sheep-dogs were probably not bred until much later, in Europe, once the northern dogs had migrated south.)

In addition to greyhounds and mastiffs there were the pariah-dogs, living on the fringes of society. Despite their low status as scavengers, many of these dogs were depicted on the bas-reliefs (low-relief sculptures) of the region.

A lion hunt. Huge mastiffs enjoyed attacking large wild animals. Hittite bas-relief from Malatya, ninth century B.C.

A mastiff walking in a royal park. Detail from an Assyrian bas-relief from the palace of Nineveh, built by Assurbanipal about 649 B.C.

A watch-dog. Chinese enamelled terracotta from the Han dynasty, third century B.C.

Asia

At a time when the Chinese already had sophisticated knowledge of worldly things, it appears that they knew little about dogs. Though seemingly strange, this is quite understandable. China is a land of intensive agriculture where every patch of fertile soil is used for growing crops. Hunting is therefore seldom practised, and animal husbandry is almost wholly limited to pigs, which can be fed on left-overs. As a result, dogs were of little practical use in China and Japan, except for the spitz types employed for draught and hunting purposes in northern Asia.

Yet dogs, as the West transformed them, made precious gifts to be offered to emperors. A book by Chu-King which describes the exploits of the emperors says that some specimens were imported for the imperial collections. Also, according to historical records, about 3450 B.C. Fo-Hi was thinking of breeding tiny dogs to slip into his sleeves to keep his fingers warm in winter. Emperors of the Chow dynasty (1050–249 B.C.), a well-documented period, commanded the ambassadors of their distant provinces to provide them with hunting-dogs. Evidently, even though the peasants did not hunt, the emperors relished this sport. They also received dogs to keep as pets.

When Tibetan Mastiffs were introduced to China, they were used for the hunt, in battle, and for food. They were very popular in the Han dynasty (206 B.C.– A.D. 220). The first real food-dog, however, was a spitz-type dog from the north. When it was exported to Europe much later, it became known as the Chow Chow. The Chinese also seem to have used greyhounds, for hunting boars and even tigers, in the third or fourth century B.C.

Lap dogs given to the emperors were, for the most part, put on strict diets to influence their growth. This, combined with almost haphazard cross-breeding, produced dogs with deformed legs. When these dogs were crossed with other small dogs, such as those received from Constantinople by the emperor Kan-Tzu, a breed of small dogs with bent legs and squashed faces was created. By the seventeenth century this breed had become established as the true Pekingese. Lhasa Apsos, given to emperors of the Manchu dynasty (1659–1840) by Tibetan lamas, were known as 'lion-dogs' because they roamed inside imperial palaces, standing guard lion-like against intruders who might somehow manage to slip past the guardian mastiffs. It is said that

Tibetan Mastiffs were often used as palace guard dogs in ancient China.

Because of their rarity in ancient China, dogs were recognized as unique and fitting gifts for the emperors of that country. For hundreds of years the animals were ensconced in the Forbidden City. Sculpture from the Sung dynasty (eleventh and twelfth centuries).

Anubis, the Egyptian god of the dead, with a dog's or jackal's head. Bronze statuette, period of the Lower Kingdom (3400–3200 B.C.)

these diminutive dogs could be terrifying—even more so than the mastiffs.

As early as the seventeenth century, a few small Chinese dogs had been introduced into Britain. But this trend did not last long, and no more were brought in until the 1860s, during the surge in popularity of dog shows. When the Chinese Empire fell, in 1912, nearly all the dogs in the royal breeding establishments were slaughtered. A few of the animals were saved, however, and merchants sold them to those renowned dog lovers, the British.

Much like China, Japan had little use for dogs. Its dense island population left virtually no space to accommodate them (except for the spitz breeds living in the north, used for draught purposes). However, small dogs known as Chins were raised there from the seventh century on. These dogs originated as gifts to the Japanese emperor of that time. When the Japanese Chins were introduced to the West much later, they became known in some countries as Japanese Spaniels.

Though dogs were rare in Japan, they occupied a place in the religion of that country. Omisto, the god of suicide, was depicted as having a dog's head. Anyone killing himself in the name of that god was promised eternal joy in the hereafter.

Egypt

The Egyptians of antiquity valued dogs from the earliest times. Indeed, they recognized the importance of these animals in their culture, being hunters who eventually turned to raising livestock.

The Egyptians deified the falcon, the ox, the cat, and the dog—the dog being the symbol of Anubis, god of the dead which guided human souls into the afterlife. Although some authors claim that Anubis did not have a dog's head but rather a jackal's or a wolf's, it is generally agreed that its head is like that of a wolf-dog.

Even before this, around 4500 B.C., the Egyptians worshipped another god that had the form of a dog. Seth (Set), the god of evil, was represented as a greyhound with erect ears and a forked tail. Thus it has been suggested that Egypt is the home of the modern English Greyhound, whose ancestors may have come from Mesopotamia, but more probably from Ethiopia. In the tomb of a certain Pti (circa 2600 B.C.) we can see a representation of a dog of this type. The greyhound is yellowish, has erect ears, and is engaged in hunting.

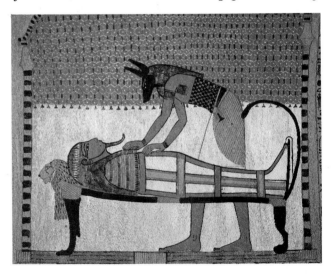

Anubis preparing a mummy. In ancient Egypt this god presided over the embalming of the dead. From the necropolis at Thebes.

From the inception of their civilization, Egyptians included in their tombs likenesses of the settings, objects, people, and animals that had surrounded them during their lives. The stele (memorial stone) of Antef II (circa 2000 B.C.) forms, in a sense, the first list of breeds of dogs. By the side of the Pharaoh we see two greyhounds and a dog which might equally well be an Australian Dingo or a German Shepherd. Above these there is a long-loined dog, possibly an ancestor of the Dachshund and the Basset Hound.

At the beginning of the Middle Kingdom (circa 2050 B.C.) Egyptians crossed greyhounds with bloodhounds, producing greyhounds with drooping ears. In time, the dogs became smaller and were adopted as domestic

A Pharaoh hunting ostriches with fast-running greyhounds. The Egyptians deified dogs, yet used them regularly for hunting. Ceremonial fan of the Eighteenth Dynasty (1530 B.C.).

Seth, god of evil (often shown with the body of a greyhound), and the goddess Nephthys, a friend of the dead, at their judgement. Egypt (1250 B.C.).

These two greyhounds and the dog with erect ears suggest that different breeds existed in the Egypt of the Pharaohs. Stele of Antef II (Eleventh Dynasty).

19

pets. Then, around 1800 B.C., Aryan hordes from what is now Syria established themselves in Egypt. They brought with them mastiffs and greyhounds that resembled Salukis. Both these breeds remained in Egypt after their masters had been expelled and were doubtless used for warfare. Ancient depictions show Tutankhamen, the child-Pharaoh of the Eighteenth Dynasty, pursuing Nubians, accompanied by mastiffs wearing collars bristling with iron spikes.

It is unlikely that the ancient Egyptians used mastiffs to guard their flocks—there were no large predators in the region. By the beginning of the New Kingdom (circa 1550 B.C.), these dogs had lost all practical importance. Greyhounds, however, continued to be highly regarded. Corporal punishment was meted out to anyone found mistreating one of these dogs, and the animals were still being mummified along with their owners. Greyhounds had a new status—as pets.

Two dogs confront each other. From earliest times, men organized these combats for pleasure. Bas-relief from the Acropolis, Athens (510 B.C.).

Greece

Hercules leading three-headed Cerberus away from the entrance to the underworld. Attic amphora (fifth century B.C.).

The ancient Greeks had dogs from the earliest days, but until the classical period these were wild wolf-dogs, with erect ears, of the type found throughout prehistoric Europe. With time, however, dogs became domesticated and accompanied the Greeks on their daily rounds, especially to the hunt. In the rough and hilly terrain of northern Greece, hunting-dogs were particularly prized. Dogs of Indian origin, which barked when they located game, were commonly used. Greyhounds, with their sleek lines, were also popular.

Mastiffs were first brought into Greece as the spoils of victory, after the defeat of Xerxes I, a ruler of Persia, in 480 B.C. Alexander the Great had these same dogs brought in from India, where they originated, and used them in battle to wreak havoc among his enemies.

The Greeks also valued watch-dogs, which guarded the temples of Asclepius. It is said that the guard dogs could distinguish true Greeks from the barbarians who attempted to enter the temples of Minerva. During the Peloponnesian wars watch-dogs are reputed to have saved the city of Corinth from surprise attack. Forty-nine of the fifty mastiffs guarding the city were slaughtered by the enemy, according to legend, but the fiftieth managed to raise the alarm. Grateful residents built a monument to their four-footed defenders, and the survivor received an inscribed, silver collar.

Dogs were common in the literature as well as in the life of the ancient Greeks. In the *Odyssey* (ninth century B.C.), Homer pays tribute to the unshakeable loyalty of dogs. When Odysseus returns home after an absence of 20 years, only his dog, Argos, recognizes him. Worn out by emotion, it dies on the spot.

Dogs also play a role in many of the fables of Aesop (sixth century B.C.). Two centuries later, Xenophon wrote a treatise on hunting with dogs. Even Aristotle saw fit to write about dogs. His *History of the Animals* mentions a number of breeds, and also discusses canine reproduction and illnesses. Alcibiades, a friend of Socrates who was noted for his excessive behaviour, purchased a Bichon-type dog for 7,000 drachmas, a ridiculously high price in those days. In a further fit of outrageousness, he had the dog's tail lopped off.

In Greek mythology, dogs occasionally stray into the picture. Cerberus, a three-headed dog with a dragon's tail and serpents' heads on its back, was the monster that guarded the gates of the underworld.

Cerberus, the fearsome three-headed dog of Greek mythology. Vase from a Greek tomb in Italy (fifth century B.C.).

Actaeon, the mythical Greek hunter of Boeotia, was eaten by his own hounds after being turned into a stag because he accidentally saw the goddess Artemis bathing. From the Greek temple at Selinunte (Selinus).

This expressive dog is a bronze sculpture found during excavations of Roman ruins at Sierre, Switzerland.

Rome

Dogs were present in Rome from the earliest times, a legacy from the Greeks. Indeed, if one accepts the story about Romulus and Remus, it is conceivable that the city itself was founded by a primitive form of dog—a she-wolf or, possibly, a wolf-dog of the type that roamed prehistoric Europe. If the pups had accidentally died or been killed, the two brothers may have replaced the offspring.

In Rome, and later throughout the Roman Empire, dogs could be seen virtually everywhere. They were used in hunting, of course, for the Romans had inherited this passion from their Indo-European forbears, and from the Greeks upon whom they patterned themselves to a great extent. Bloodhounds and greyhounds were the dogs most popular for hunting. Smaller dogs, however, were used for pursuing small game. These were easier to handle than the fleet greyhounds, and eventually they developed into pointers.

Large mastiffs known as *Molossi* were considered ideal fighting dogs and were used in the arenas during gladiator shows. They were also used in warfare. Ac-

21

Boar-hunting. Mosaic from a hunting lodge. Roman villa at Casale, France (third or fourth century A.D.).

Head of a mastiff. Mastiffs were highly prized in Imperial Rome. They took part in circus games, worked alongside the Roman legions to guard camps and to drive cattle, and accompanied well-to-do Romans on hunting expeditions. Detail of a mosaic, Roman villa at Casale, France (third or fourth century A.D.).

Gallic dog with erect ears. By the end of the Roman Empire, dogs had joined households to become pets. White terracotta from l'Allier, France.

cording to the Greek historian Polybius, who lived in Rome during the second century A.D. and who was an expert on military tactics, these dogs had three separate functions: to attack the enemy, to defend the camps, and to carry messages. As message-carriers the dogs were forced to swallow copper capsules containing secret documents, then required to slip, or fight, through enemy lines. The messages were recovered by putting the dogs to death.

The dogs bred for attack and defence were almost certainly descended from Sumerian Mastiffs that the Greeks had captured from the Persians, and their prowess in battle was legendary. One Roman general, it is said, equipped his dogs with flame-filled saddle-pots and directed the animals to run into the midst of the foe, searing the underbellies of the enemy horses.

Roman dogs were also used widely and successfully to guard public monuments and towns. On one historic occasion, however, they were upstaged by a flock of geese, when the Gauls made a night attack on the Capitol. Geese, it seems, were commonly used to raise the alarm in districts where people could not afford to keep their own watch-dogs.

We know how important watch-dogs were in patrician homes because in Pompeii mosaic depictions of dogs were placed at the entrance to houses along with the words *Cave canem*—'Beware of the dog.' These dogs, too, are thought to have descended from Sumerian Mastiffs.

In Rome we see the beginnings of 'dog loving' as we know it today. Bas-relief and mosaic depictions attest to this, revealing a number of different types and breeds of dog. Dogs are also mentioned in early literature. Varro (first century B.C.) writes about a sheep-dog in his book, *Rerum rusticarum libri*. He warns readers not to buy a dog from a butcher, for it will attack the flock; nor from a huntsman, for it will be easily distracted from guarding the flock if a hare or fox should chance that way. Columella, in the first century A.D., describes watch-dogs—particularly their colourings—at great length in his *De re rustica*. A century later Arrian, a Greek historian living in Rome, gives advice on buying dogs for hunting small animals (hares, foxes, and so forth). Ovid, in his lyrical *Metamorphoses*, describes a

Cave canem ('Beware of the dog').
This sign was very common at
the entrance to Roman houses.
Sometimes there was a picture of
a dog as well. Mosaic from
Pompeii (first century A.D.).

greyhound chasing a hare and struggling swiftly and
passionately with it. The poet Virgil, in his book *Buco-
lics*, writes that Romans frequently cut the ears and
tails off their sheep-dogs—not for aesthetic reasons but
to avoid having these body parts grabbed and chewed
by wolves and foxes.

Patrician families were greatly taken by lap-dogs
during the long wars of the Republican and Imperial
times. Certainly Julius Caesar came under the spell of
these little dogs. He may have developed an attachment to them during his contacts with Cleopatra in
Egypt and Bythinia, since it seems that these dogs were
highly popular among inhabitants along the banks of
the Nile. Small Bichon-type dogs and forerunners of
the Italian Greyhound were particularly in vogue during those times, and wealthy Romans bedecked their
precious pets with jewels and even built elaborate
tombs for them. Actually, some experts believe that
the expression 'beware of the dog' is an admonition not
to step on the household's lap-dog.

Dogs accompanied the Roman legions on their conquest of Gaul. The Celts had occupied northern Europe
and the British Isles since the fifth century B.C. They
had come from the shores of the Caspian Sea, up the
Danube and across present-day Germany, bringing
along horses and dogs, which they used in battle.
When the Romans crossed into ancient Britain, they
encountered Celts determined to defend themselves—
and dogs determined to protect their keepers. In one
battle, it is said, the Roman army took less than a day to
defeat the Celt warriors. They spent two more days,
however, trying to overcome the Celt dogs guarding
their slain masters' chariots and supplies—such was
the ferocious loyalty of the animals encountered.

It is questionable whether the Celts had greyhounds,
for hunting in their time had given way to agriculture.
These dogs had most likely become rare in Gaul as well
as in what is now Spain and the British Isles. It is possible, of course, that the dog had become more of a household animal among the Celts than among the Romans.
Curiously, the Gallo-Romans developed more highly
specialized breeds—a clear separating of sheep-dogs,
hounds, and pets—that would still be found, almost
unchanged, at the end of the Dark Ages.

*This small greyhound has
succeeded in seizing a hare.
Gallic knife-handle in bronze,
from Mâcon, France.*

*Dogs, especially small ones,
share their masters' lives
completely, like this one lying at
the feet of the* Bordeaux Lovers.
Gallo-Roman terracotta.

The Socialization of Dogs

Saint Roch is said to have been fed by his dog when he was lost in the desert. Church of Saint Junien, Haute-Vienne, France (fifteenth century).

DOGS AND RELIGION

Primitive man lived in constant fear of wild beasts. Because he could not easily defend himself against them, he revered them as gods in the hope of appeasing them. Some religious sects even kept domestic animals in their temples. The ancient Egyptians represented Anubis, god of the dead, as a man with a dog's head. When a domestic dog died, its Egyptian owners would shave their heads as a sign of mourning.

The mythological god-dog Anubis had a close counterpart in ancient Greece, where it was widely believed that the gates to Hades were guarded by Cerberus, a three-headed dog with the tail of a serpent.

In the Christian West, dogs fared both well and badly at the hands of the Church. In its intent to suppress pagan idols, the Church looked askance at dogs (and at animals in general). However, it was also the Church that made Saint Cosmas and Saint Damian the patrons of sick animals, while the treatment of rabies was reserved for Saint Hubert. Rogation litanies still preserve this connection between pets and the pulpit, as do such customs as the Mass of Saint Hubert, at which packs of hounds are blessed.

Although the Middle Ages began badly for dogs, the situation changed dramatically by the beginning of the Renaissance, by which time dogs were a thoroughly domesticated species. Industrialization in the 1800s introduced a new leisure-time activity: the showing of dogs. By the twentieth century, dogs had become integrated into the human social fabric.

The Middle Ages

The deposition of Romulus Augustulus in A.D. 476 marked the end of the Western Roman Empire. It also initiated the arrival of barbarian hordes who destroyed virtually all traces of urban and even rural life. Peasants took refuge in the local forests, and their dogs followed them.

Thus, by the beginning of the Middle Ages, dogs had reverted to the habits of their ancestors. Half-wild, they roamed in savage packs, covering vast areas and probably spreading many diseases, including rabies. Widespread famine drove many of these dogs into their former role as scavengers around settlements, feeding on carrion and even on buried bodies. The presence of feral dogs on the periphery of encampments fostered epidemics of fear and superstition.

The Gallo-Romans came to regard dogs as demonic creatures—'hell-hounds.' Indeed, it took many centuries before this image fully vanished. During this time, the human imagination created werewolves, 'snake-dogs,' and *Cynocephales*—dog-faced monsters much feared at the time.

Most people, in any event, could not afford to keep animals, even small ones. They caught birds with rude lines and traps, while the nobility increasingly began to acquire sophisticated packs of hunting-dogs. Greyhounds were cross-bred with mastiffs and kept well protected from the savage, starving dogs that roamed the European countryside.

By the year 1000, the nobility had come to regard their hunting rights and privileges with even greater proprietorship, and they took no small interest in the quality of their dogs. Dog breeding revived, and sheepdogs were once again in demand. But the distinction between hunting-dogs and shepherd dogs was blurred.

Attacking the quarry. In the early days of large packs, mastiffs were becoming more lightly built, greyhounds sturdier.

To clarify the situation, Canute (or Knut), who variously ruled Denmark, England, and Norway, issued a decree in 1016: All peasants' dogs living within at least ten miles of his hunting lands should have the tendons of their hocks cut. This barbarous custom spread quickly across Europe and was still practised in the eighteenth century.

At the time of Canute's decree, dogs were categorized according to their uses: pointers flushed game, hounds drove stags into the open for other dogs to chase, greyhounds were employed for hunting hare and deer, and mastiffs were used to bring down large quarry. Forerunners of the terrier family tracked down rodents, while various other dogs trailed game birds.

Towards the end of the Middle Ages some nobles began to record their experiences with hunting-dogs. Among the first was the German emperor Frederick II of Ancona (reigned 1220–50), who produced a treatise titled *De arte venandi cum avibus*, which dealt mainly with falconry. In the fourteenth century, however, a French count named Gaston Phoebus (or Phébus) wrote his famous *Traité de la chasse* ('A Treatise on Hunting'). It is said that the count never travelled without the company of his sixteen hundred dogs. In his treatise he reviews the breeds of dogs, describes cross-breeding, and discusses how to attend to dogs kept in kennels, from how to train them to how to feed them—something revolutionary in those days.

A white greyhound and, behind it, an early ancestor of the Bloodhound. To the left of these are griffons, already used in hunting. From the Grimani Breviary, Venice (1515).

A hunting-dog with drooping ears, and a wolf. From a fourteenth-century illuminated manuscript of Aesop's Fables.

Hunting with falcons and dogs was a major perquisite for the aristocracy of the Middle Ages. Detail from the Bayeux tapestry.

In China, dogs were used to patrol and protect the province of Kwei-Chou when it was overrun by mountain lions. Illustration from The Book of the Marvels of the World, *by Marco Polo (fifteenth century).*

'How the good huntsman must pursue his prey and seize it by force.' The Traité de la chasse *of Gaston Phoebus, Compte de Foix, provides a fascinating fourteenth-century look at raising and training dogs.*

Saint Eustace, accompanied by small pointers, a large greyhound, and a small greyhound with erect ears. Etching by Dürer (1471–1528).

Pisanello's painting of Saint Eustace portrays greyhounds, mastiffs, and spaniels; it is an important Early Renaissance depiction of dogs.

Life had thus, once again, become relatively civilized. Gentility returned to European households. With this came a resurgence of appreciation for domestic dogs. Consequently, small pets, such as some greyhounds, began to find a place in the home once more.

The Renaissance

The Renaissance brought a spirit of freedom to the West. Italy, being the country closest to the source of ancient values that inspired this renewal in art and secular life, was home to artists who were at the forefront of the movement. Yet even then, Gothic artists such as Pisanello had already portrayed dogs, usually greyhounds, in their works. These dogs were frequently shown as companions of saints.

At the beginning of the Renaissance the archetypical dog was the hunting-dog, the pride of the aristocracy. Much was written about it. In 1492 Guillaume Tardiff produced his prestigious *Art de fauconnerie ou des chiens de chasse* ('Art of Falconry and Hunting with Dogs') at the request of Charles VIII of France. In 1590 a book appeared in England dealing with such topics as the 'choosing, hygiene, and sicknesses of dogs,' a forerunner of present-day dog manuals.

Classification of dogs continued into the sixteenth century, but by now the categories were more refined. There were still the swift greyhounds, but there were also pointers and terriers. Mastiffs and other large dogs, however, continued to be regarded as being solely for military purposes.

By this time dogs were no longer strictly the preserve of the aristocracy; the merely well-to-do could also afford to have their faithful companions included in portraits. This was particularly true of Flemish merchants, for they lived in a society whose artists had studied in Italy. These artists produced a wealth of paintings depicting celebrations, bazaars, meetings of municipal bodies, and gatherings of fraternal orders, and in many of these works the merchants were grouped with their dogs in attendance. These were not hunting-dogs; they were 'ratters' for the most part, dogs that would protect a merchant's goods from rodents. Women of affluence, on the other hand, were portrayed with frail toy dogs the size of cats.

In almost all the works of the painters, sculptors, and engravers of this time, the mastiff lost ground to that

most elegant of dogs, the greyhound. An etching by Dürer, the famous German artist of this period, shows no fewer than five distinctly different types of greyhound, all endowed with different abilities.

Among the most popular of all greyhounds was the variety known today as the English Greyhound. This dog, which dates from the Roman occupation of Britain, had always been prized as a hunting-dog, but soon it became recognized as a racing dog. It was named Greyhound, experts agree, not because of its colour, but because of its presumed origin in Greece—that is to say, a 'Greek hound.' (Another theory, however, traces the origin of the word greyhound back to the Celtic *greg* or *grech*, meaning, simply, 'dog.')

For centuries there were five categories—one could almost call them breeds—of dog in Great Britain: Greyhounds, Terriers (which would soon crop up as a number of new varieties), Slowhounds (a now-extinct specialist in hunting over marshland), Large Hounds (mastiffs), and Bulldogs. This last type was used to bait bulls, a popular sport that remained legal until 1835.

In the sixteenth century British breeders developed a number of different breeds from these five varieties of dog, beginning with sheep-dogs and watch-dogs called Bandogges and Tynkers, and Mooners (which evidently had a tendency to bark at the moon). The hunting-dogs included Bloodhounds, Gazehounds, Lymeers, Tenneblers, Harriers, and a number of terriers. Various types of spaniels and setters were sent to track, flush, and retrieve game birds. The English also had pets and 'luxury' animals such as Warners (or Roquets) and Tornspits.

In the sixteenth century, spaniels were used to retrieve birds, and were valued as pets. As such, they were much in fashion. Anonymous watercolour.

Two women at a balcony. Renaissance women took a great interest in miniature dogs, which had already been developed by this period. Painting by P. Veronese (sixteenth century).

This dog, somewhat like a Bichon Frise, was the faithful companion of Saint Jerome. Detail from Saint Jerome in his Cell, *painted by V. Carpaccio (end of fifteenth century).*

Great Britain quickly became what it has remained to this day—the world's foremost exporter of dogs. The Tudors, in the 1500s, set aside an entire island—the Isle of Dogs—as a place to install sumptuous kennels. The Stuarts, who inherited the kennels, modernized them to meet the demand of the European market: Francis I of France and the Duke of Milan wanted hunting-dogs, while Philip I of Spain wanted fighting dogs. And pets in general, of course, were becoming more and more popular.

Understandably, there was some resistance to this sudden monopoly of the dog world. The French aristocracy—and especially the monarchs—could not tolerate the notion that the splendour of their hunts depended solely on their British suppliers. Thus they developed the *Blancs de Roy* ('King's Whites'), a superb breed of dog that remained famous until the French Revolution. Nonetheless, the French continued to replenish their packs from Great Britain, particularly from breeders in Scotland.

Diana the huntress. The goddess is accompanied by a greyhound. School of Fontainebleau (sixteenth century).

The *Blancs de Roy* were regarded as being without peer by their French owners, and were coveted accordingly. At Chambord, a prime hunting area, local commoners were once again forced to cut their dogs' tendons or to hang large blocks of wood around the animals' necks—all to stop 'ordinary' dogs from spoiling the fruits of the hunt for the king's finest.

French noblewomen of the time favoured miniature spaniel breeds and Italian Greyhounds. Indeed, Henry III of France appointed keepers and set aside the lavish sum of 100,000 gold crowns to ensure a luxurious life for his packs of miniatures.

England and France, thus, were prominent among European countries for their promotion of dogs during the Renaissance. But it was left to the Italians— particularly to the artists in the rival cities of Venice and Florence—to record these dogs on canvas for posterity.

Dogs for Royalty and Citizens

By the Late Renaissance, the popularity of dogs had extended to nearly all social classes. The kings of England, France, and Spain maintained large packs of hunting-dogs. Their queens, on the other hand, favoured small dogs, as pets.

The wealthy citizens kept 'affordable' dogs—animals that were not so large or specialized as to require expensive upkeep.

At the low end of the scale were the common people, who kept mixed breeds—mongrels that had to have their tendons cut according to the law of the day. Thus mutilated, these dogs were incapable of hunting.

Louis XIII of France maintained no fewer than four lieutenants to look after his packs. In turn, these officers were assisted by four mounted kennel masters and another four on foot. These officials had charge of eighteen keepers of the hounds and four servants of the kennels. Each had to prove that he was 'of good family, sober, and God-fearing.'

Under Louis XIV the same royal kennels were expanded. The dauphin and other noblemen also maintained large packs, and until the French Revolution hunting remained the privilege of the nobility. Most was done on horseback, although there was some falconry. The best packs for horseback hunting continued to be composed of *Blancs de Roy*, but other packs were established, using breeding stock sent from England.

In England at this time, hunting had become more widespread than ever and there were considerably more hunters. They pursued small game such as foxes and birds, and thus needed compact, independent dogs that were easy to maintain. As a result, there was an increase in the number of small hunting-dogs. These were mainly terriers, spaniels, and scent-hounds, all of which were exported widely.

The fashion among royalty for keeping dogs as pets originated on the Continent with Henry III of France. At council meetings the king would surround himself with miniature spaniels—his *Papillons* ('Butterflies'), as he called them. What was perhaps even more startling in those days, however, was the common knowledge that he permitted the animals into his bed, the ultimate sign of royal approval.

In Britain, the fashion caught on during the reigns of Charles I and Charles II. Their preferred court dog was what is now known as the Cavalier King Charles Spaniel, a small black and flame or white and orange breed that through the years has gained popularity.

Portrait of Madame de Porcin. In the eighteenth century, noblewomen and rich commoners favoured little dogs. Painting by Greuze.

Dog guarding game (detail). The royal packs in France consisted of Blancs de Roy. *Painting by A. F. Desportes, École française.*

The royal dogs, as well as various other types of pet dogs, notably Maltese and Bolognese Bichons, could be found in the salons of the ladies of the court. These breeds were also common in the homes of wealthy citizens. Other dogs that might be found in homes of affluence—especially among the far-travelling merchants of Flanders—were Pugs and Schipperkes, and Brussels and Brabançon Griffons.

By the eighteenth century, hunting had become noticeably democratic in Britain. Bloodhounds and mastiffs had virtually disappeared because of the lack of large game, but spaniels and setters and, above all, pointers had replaced them.

The character of traditional French hunting packs changed somewhat with the large-scale introduction of pointers from England and Italy. In the course of this introduction, the number of different pointing varieties increased, the most famous new breed being the Braque Saint-Germain.

Hunters of that time also used a small dog to catch waterfowl: Its long, thick coat protected it from the cold but had to be cut short at the back to prevent the

The Prince Imperial and his dog Nero. French princes were devoted to their hunting-dogs (in this case a pointer).

The English Terrier was an excellent hunting-dog and highly prized as such. Portrait of Joseph Greenway, by Jens Juel.

Hunting on horseback in the forest of Fontainebleau. After the French Revolution large packs were built up once again, but they no longer consisted of Blancs de Roy. *Painting by Carl Vernet (1756–1836).*

Above right: the seduction of Layla on the domed balcony of her house. Persian miniature (end of seventeenth century).

Voltaire in the morning. This energetic, faithful spaniel shared every moment of Voltaire's life. Painting by Jean Huber (beginning of eighteenth century).

dog from being dragged underwater and drowned. One day, a bitch of this breed gave birth to four puppies with extremely beautiful, black, curly coats. These were the forerunners of the Poodle.

In Russia at this time, the wolf was still hunted, for the animal had not yet disappeared from western and central Europe. Aristocratic families in that country raised packs of long-haired greyhounds for these wolf-hunts. The dogs are now known to us as Borzois.

The Industrial Age

The industrial revolution of the nineteenth century brought increased mechanization, and the dog's working talents were less valued. Emphasis was placed on its friendliness and appearance.

And dog lovers were becoming organized. The first dog show was held in 1859, in Britain, and it caused a considerable stir. Within twenty-five years, Australia, Canada, France, and the United States were hosts to shows that have since become annual events.

The lack of judging guidelines at the early shows inspired a London doctor, J. H. Walsh, to publish in 1867 a book entitled *The Dogs of the British Islands* which included detailed descriptions of thirty-five breeds—thereby developing the concept of breed standards by which dogs are judged everywhere today.

In 1873, the British created a national society to improve, maintain, and even reconstitute British dog breeds, and to acknowledge the foreign breeds which could be used to perfect British stock. This was the Kennel Club, an organization that was to spawn similar societies in other countries by the end of the century. The Fédération cynologique internationale, the only kennel society to operate internationally, was founded in 1911, in Brussels.

The first of what was to become the world's most famous dog show was staged in Britain in 1891. Later named the Crufts Show after its originator, Charles Cruft, it earned swift popularity thanks to royal patronage and the presence of exotic breeds.

Meanwhile, the number of breeds was growing. In August of 1897, the Count of Bylandt published two large volumes, entitled *Les Ra es de Chiens*, in Brussels. In them, he described 274 dog breeds.

DOGS IN NORTH AMERICA

North American Indians attached their sled dogs to 'toboggans' made of thin planks and fitted with handles. Although seemingly unwieldy, the vehicles were efficient.

The dog in North America was never really a fighter. It was, however, an invaluable draught animal. While rivers were the main arteries for transportation in summer, they were often frozen in winter, particularly in Canada. Thus white men depended to a great extent on dogs for hauling, even after the introduction of the horse to the North American continent in 1680.

In order to obtain a heftier breed of dog, small, local northern dogs were crossed with mastiffs, sheep-dogs, and other large breeds imported from Europe since the mid-1660s. The result was a sturdy animal—commonly called a husky—that became the trusty dog of all trades for the early settlers. In summer and autumn it guarded flocks and herds and raised the alarm when warlike native bands approached. In winter it pulled sleds. In spring it helped with the sap round-up in the sugar-maple forests.

In 1675 the dog turned its talents, as it were, to building, when it helped in transporting the bricks

Again, it was largely due to dog teams—composed of Eskimo Dogs—that Robert E. Peary was able to reach the North Pole, on April 6, 1909. (His sled was also equipped, however, with a sail and an auxiliary motor.)

Dogs among North American Indians

North American Indians used dogs for hunting and for keeping guard, and certain tribes used them for transport. In winter the dogs were harnessed to lightweight 'toboggans' made of one or more thin planks of wood and fitted with two handles for the driver to grip. To stop the dogs the driver simply tipped the vehicle on its side. When wood was scarce a toboggan might be made of frozen meat, whalebone, or even a block of ice. The harness was of strips of caribou hide.

Spanish conquerors throwing Indians to mastiffs. Detail from an engraving by Theodore de Bry (end of sixteenth century).

Peary and his Eskimo Dogs. The American explorer was the first man to reach the North Pole.

used in the construction of Québec City. Indeed, throughout New France at this time, these indefatigable labourers were used to haul wood in winter, ice in summer, and bread all year around.

The Royal Canadian Mounted Police also made good use of these huskies. Dog-sled patrols were instituted in 1872 and continued until 1969, when snowmobiles rendered them obsolete. Even during the gruelling saga of the Klondike gold-rush, the dogs earned their keep. They carried supplies and baggage over treacherous terrain for prospectors heading into the Yukon, and they served as invaluable protectors of whatever fortunes these adventurers brought back.

Dog fanciers took to importing breeds from other countries to improve their own stock and to develop new breeds. The Chinese Spitz outside its native land became known as the Chow Chow around 1880. A dog discovered in Africa in 1895 was one of the last breeds to slip into Britain before the 1901 quarantine restrictions. This breed was later named the Basenji.

Nationalism stimulated each country to develop its own breeds. In the latter half of the nineteenth century, the French 'created' a Bulldog, and in the United States the Boston Terrier—a cross between the English Bulldog and the Bull Terrier—appeared. By 1903 the Australian Cattle Dog was recognized in Australia, some twenty years before South Africa was to register its native breed, the Rhodesian Ridgeback.

The Twentieth Century

More than 15,000 dogs were called into service by the Allied forces during the First World War, and almost a third of these were killed or lost in action. Their tasks ranged from guard duty and patrol to carrying messages, munitions, and medical supplies to the front lines. Some were even used to catch trench rats.

During the Second World War, the Russian army employed dogs in true kamikaze fashion. The dogs were deliberately kept starved, then trained to enter armoured vehicles to obtain food. Borrowing from the techniques of their famous countryman Ivan Pavlov, the Russians used conditioned reflex to get the same dogs to enter enemy vehicles, again in search of food. This time, however, electromagnetic mines were strapped to the dogs' backs.

In the 1960s dogs were used in Vietnam by the United States Army to flush the enemy out of cover and to detect hidden mines. The dogs could locate both buried mines and explosive devices concealed up to two metres (six feet) above ground. In disasters, such as the 1985 earthquake in Mexico City, specially trained dogs led rescuers to victims buried in the rubble.

Mostly, however, dogs live less exciting and relatively comfortable lives. Today grooming salons for animals can be found in most cities. Health care is so sophisticated that veterinarians specialize. There are pet psychologists available to dogs, elaborate burial services, canine couturiers and fashion boutiques, and even specialized restaurants that cater exclusively to patrons of the four-footed kind.

Television and cinema, too, have drawn the canine world sharply into focus. Recognized 'stars' include Lassie, Rin-Tin-Tin, and the Littlest Hobo—and, of course, Mickey Mouse's amiable sidekick, Pluto. Perhaps the most prestigious role of all, though, was the real-life performance of a small Russian dog, Laika, which in 1957 preceded man into space.

Through such organizations as The Seeing Eye, Guide Dogs for the Blind, and Leader Dogs for the Blind, sightless people have become considerably more independent. An even newer idea is the Hearing Ear programme, which trains dogs to recognize sounds and alert deaf people to them. Such dogs can be taught to distinguish between the cry of a baby, the whine of a smoke alarm, and the ringing of a doorbell.

In the final analysis, though, dogs are simply good company. Indeed, it is an acknowledged fact that a dog, as a pet, helps to alleviate stress, reduce loneliness, and counteract nervousness and depression. It is small wonder that so many people lavish attention on their canine companions.

A bronze sculpture of a greyhound, created by François Pompon (1932).

This painting by Francis Barraud achieved enormous popularity as the trademark of R.C.A. The inquisitive Fox Terrier has appeared on millions of record labels.

THE DINGO

The Dingo is one of the last dogs in the world to be domesticated. In its native land, Australia, it verges on being formally recognized as a breed though many people regard it with suspicion. Indeed, some canine authorities say the dog is not trustworthy.

Even so the Dingo has played a major role in the development of Australian working dogs. Used as a stud, it gave herding dogs more stamina and cunning. With official kennel club recognition should come breed refinements, and the Dingo's characteristic slyness may be bred out. Contrary to popular belief, Dingoes do bark. But the noise is more high-pitched than a normally resonant bark.

Identifying Dogs

Physical Characteristics
34

Classifying Breeds
42

Physical Characteristics

Just as people are identified by appearance and race, so are dogs similarly classified: by build and breed. This section describes the body shapes that distinguish one class or type of dog from another. Details of physical features—from the teeth to the tail—indicate differences among breeds and individual dogs.

Body

Proportions vary greatly from one breed of dog to another, but the general physiology is the same, whether Chihuahua or Greyhound.

A dog's height is measured from its withers, the highest part of the shoulders; height is the distance from the withers to the ground when the dog is standing. The loin and the back form the topline, that part of the dog's outline from just behind the withers to the root of the tail. This may be arched, as in the case of the Borzoi, or nearly level, as for the German Shepherd. It should never be concave. The croup is the rear part of the back, from the pelvis to the tail.

A good chest should be broad, high, and deep, and its circumference well developed. The belly should not be large, the flanks neither bulging nor hollowed. A male dog has two rows of nipples on its belly; a female, two rows of teats. Also on the belly of the male is a sheath protecting the genital organs. At the anus are glands which secrete a substance with a distinctive odour. Dogs recognize each other by their individual scents and use this secretion to mark territory.

Build

On the whole, dogs come in three sizes: toy, medium, and large. Their profiles are defined more precisely.

Dogs of medium height, such as the English Springer Spaniel, are said to be eumetric. The very tall dogs—Great Danes, for example—are classed as hypermetric. Toys are called elliptometric.

When the height is the same as the body length, as measured from the front of the breast bone to the tail root, a dog is said to be 'square,' or mediolinear. If the height is clearly greater, the dog is longilinear. Dogs whose bodies are long for their height are said to be brevilinear.

In addition to classification by proportion and size, dogs are categorized according to the shape of the head.

Rectilinear dogs, such as setters and spaniels, have a foreface parallel to the skull and a slight stop. (The stop is the 'step up' from foreface to skull.)

POINTS OF THE DOG

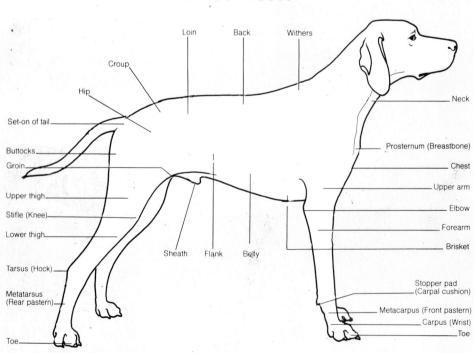

Mediolinear proportions: German Shepherd

Longilinear proportions: Borzoi

Brevilinear proportions: French Bulldog

Convexilinear breeds, such as Greyhounds, Bull Terriers, and Bedlington Terriers, have no stop; the skull is rounded, and the foreface turns down towards the tip of the nose.

Concavilinear breeds, such as Bulldogs, have a very prominent stop, which sometimes causes respiratory problems. The foreface is compressed, and the cranium is arched.

Head

No matter what its shape—whether coarse or delicate, heavy or light, big-boned or finely chiselled—the head always has the same basic anatomy. The top of the head is termed the skull. Some breeds have a pronounced bone near the back of the skull, called the occiput, while in others this bone does not show. The front of the head, from skull to nose tip, is the foreface. (A foreface that is darker than the rest of the head is called a mask.) Separating the skull from the foreface is the stop. Like the occiput, the stop is more noticeable in some breeds than in others, and some breeds have virtually none.

A pale patch on otherwise dark noses is considered in most breeds an aesthetic fault and a sign of degeneration.

The lips close the oral cavity (mouth); they should fit together reasonably closely. Some breeds have a pendulous upper lip

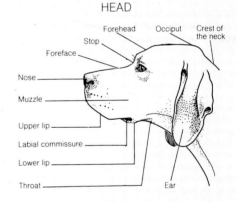

HEAD

Forehead · Occiput · Crest of the neck · Stop · Foreface · Nose · Muzzle · Upper lip · Labial commissure · Lower lip · Throat · Ear

Rectilinear profile: Collie

Concavilinear profile: Boxer

Convexilinear profile: Bull Terrier

Lupoid: Belgian Shepherd Dog

Braccoid: Weimaraner

Molossoid: Dogue de Bordeaux

Graioid: Afghan Hound

ears that hang. The muzzle is short, the lips thick and long. These dogs run the gamut from giants to toys. They can be hypermetric (Saint Bernards), eumetric (Boxers), elliptometric (Bulldogs), or even superellipto-metric (Pugs). Yet they are all concavilinear and brevilinear. Also in this family are the Pyrenean Mountain Dog, the Briard, the Dobermann Pinscher, the Schnauzer, and various mastiff breeds.

• *Graioids* have elongated, cone-shaped heads, without a visible stop. The ears are small, and lie back or stand up. The muzzle is prominent, also angular; the lips are thin and close-fitting. The legs are slender and the belly 'well tucked up'—that is, quite arched. Graioids are rectilinear or slightly convexilinear, yet always longilinear, and, sometimes, hypermetric. These are most greyhounds: some eumetric, such as the Sloughi, some elliptometric, such as the Italian Greyhound. The Collie and the Shetland Sheep-dog also belong to this family.

There is yet another classification of dogs, based not upon their build but on their purposes. Kennel clubs classify dogs into one of two divisions: sporting or nonsporting. These divisions are further subdivided into groups (see p. 42).

(see p. 42)

Ears

The carriage of the ears is a fundamental breed characteristic. When a puppy is born, its ears are small and closed. At three weeks they open and take a semi-erect position; only in later months do they take their final form.

Dogs' ears have different shapes and pos-

that causes the corners to droop in what are called flews. Bloodhounds have characteristically long flews. The palate can be pink or mottled, like the tongue, which must be completely pigmented. Coloration depends on the breed, however. In the case of the Chow Chow, the palate is black.

In spite of, or perhaps because of, the great diversity in the shape of dogs' heads, some experts rely on these characteristics in classifying dog breeds:

• *Lupoids* (from the Latin *Lupus*, meaning wolf) have a pyramidal, slightly concave head, erect ears, a long muzzle, and thin, close-fitting lips. These dogs are eumetric, rectilinear, and brevilinear. Among the lupoids are the Keeshond, the Chow Chow, and the Pomeranian. Although the German Shepherd definitely belongs to this family, it is not at all representative. In many ways it is of much farther descent from the wolf than are the other three breeds.

• *Braccoids* have prism-shaped heads and muzzles as wide at the end as at the root. The stop is pronounced. The ears hang, and the lips are long and well-flewed, the upper lip overhanging the lower jaw. These animals are eumetric, concavilinear, and mediolinear. The braccoids include two types of dogs: scent hounds and gun dogs (pointers, setters, and spaniels).

• *Molossoids*, because of their small stops, have massive, rounded heads and small

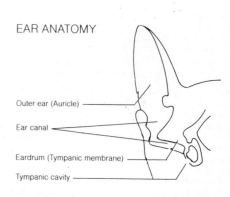

EAR ANATOMY

Outer ear (Auricle)

Ear canal

Eardrum (Tympanic membrane)

Tympanic cavity

EAR CARRIAGE

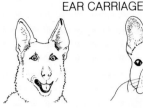

Erect ears, pointed: German Shepherd, Akita, Alaskan Malamute

Bat ears, set on high: Boston Terrier, Welsh Corgi, French Bulldog

Erect ears, blunt-tipped: Chow Chow

Drop ears, folded: Weimaraner, Bloodhound

Rose ears, well set back: Whippet

Drop ears, hanging flat: Poodle

tures. The German Shepherd's ears are erect isosceles triangles, whereas the Chow Chow's are equilateral triangles. The Belgian Shepherd Dog has pointed ears. The French Bulldog has 'bat ears,' the semi-erect ears of some terriers are bud-like 'button' ears, while the Fox Terrier's erect ears are bent over in a V. Hanging ('pendent') ears may be heart-shaped, as in the case of the Pekingese; lobular, as for the Sussex Spaniel; rolled, as for the Bloodhound; and flat, as for the Pointer.

The dog is said to be badly or well 'covered' according to how high the ears are set on the head. The ear counts as large if, when pulled forward, it reaches the tip of the nose. With some breeds in some countries, it has long been customary to crop a part of the lobe. This causes the ear to stand erect when otherwise it would fold. Where not banned, this practice is falling out of favour.

On a dog of a breed with erect, or prick ears, cocked ('semi-prick' or 'semi-drop') ears are regarded as a fault by show judges. By the same token, erect ears on a dog of a breed with semi-erect ears are also considered faulty. Surgery can sometimes correct these faults, but this is not allowed if the dog is to appear in the show ring.

Eyes

For a domestic animal, the dog has eyeballs that are disproportionately large for its body weight. The eyeball is proportionally larger in small breeds than in big ones. The eyeball tends to bulge in concavilinear breeds. Dogs have relatively poor eyesight, the pupil being usually dilated. Some breeds see best at night.

The colour of the iris is yellowish or brownish, although many Siberian Huskies have blue eyes. Some dogs have eyes of two different colours. 'Eye type' refers to the shape of the eye as outlined by the rim. Almond eyes are oval and bluntly pointed at both corners, characteristic of the Borzoi and German Shepherd. Eyes showing a haw, typical of the Bloodhound, display an abnormally large amount of conjunctiva because the lower eyelid droops. Oval, or oblong, eyes have rounded corners and are long for their height; most dogs have this eye type.

The eye should be bright and clear; the eyelids should be fine and distinct; and the conjunctiva, which is pink, should not show, except for dogs expected to display the haw.

EYE ANATOMY

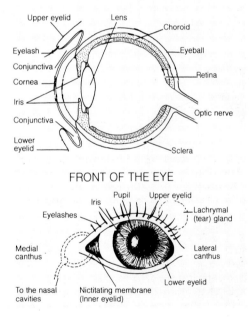

Upper eyelid — Lens — Choroid
Eyelash — Eyeball
Conjunctiva — Retina
Cornea
Iris — Optic nerve
Conjunctiva
Lower eyelid — Sclera

FRONT OF THE EYE

Pupil — Upper eyelid
Iris — Lachrymal (tear) gland
Eyelashes
Medial canthus — Lateral canthus
Lower eyelid
To the nasal cavities — Nictitating membrane (Inner eyelid)

Dogs with eyes of different colours are often allowed in competition, depending on the breed.

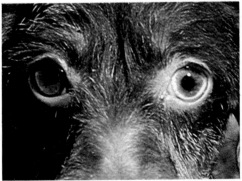

DENTITION

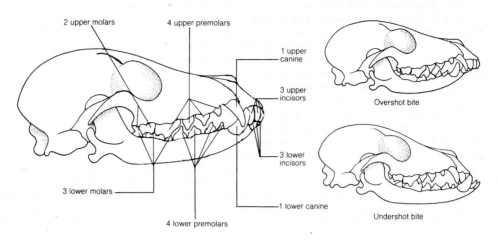

2 upper molars

4 upper premolars

1 upper canine

3 upper incisors

Overshot bite

3 lower incisors

3 lower molars

1 lower canine

4 lower premolars

Undershot bite

Teeth

Puppies are born without teeth. Within five weeks, they will have cut their full complement of deciduous (milk) teeth. This 28-tooth set consists of the following:
– 12 incisors, for biting
– 4 canines (eye-teeth), for grasping and tearing
– 12 premolars, for crushing

AGE AND TEETH

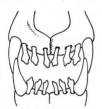

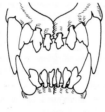

At 2½ months: milk-teeth only

At 7 months: complete set of permanent teeth

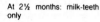

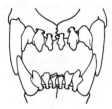

At 1½ years: lower middle incisors are worn down

At 2½ years: all lower incisors are worn down

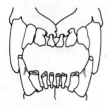

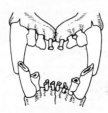

At 6 years: all teeth are worn and yellowed

At 10 years: teeth may be worn down to the roots

Permanent teeth start to push out the milk-teeth when the puppy is four months old, on average. This gradual process lasts several months and is generally completed by the time the puppy reaches seven months of age. A complete set of teeth is composed of the following:
– 12 incisors
– 4 canines
– 16 premolars (an addition of 4)
– 10 molars (additional crushing teeth)

The full dentition of 42 teeth, while desirable in a show dog, is not essential to a dog's health or appearance. Many dogs have missing teeth, mostly premolars. In fact, premolars are often absent from the mouths of the Chinese Crested and Mexican Hairless dogs.

Characteristic of dogs is the systematic wear on the incisors. If the dog has been correctly fed, and if its bite is not faulty, its age can be determined quite accurately by the degree of wear on these teeth. At four years, the upper incisors are levelled off. Between seven and eight years, the crowns of the teeth have become very worn, to the extent the canines are blunted. In addition, more and more tartar collects on the teeth.

The condition of a normal, healthy dog's teeth depends to a great extent on the size of the breed. Large dogs have few problems and are relatively old before tartar collects. By contrast, most of the small dogs require dental attention regularly— at least twice a year.

The efficiency of a dog's bite is essential to its comfort and, in some cases, its working ability and even its survival. The type of bite varies according to breed. A level, or pincer, bite is one where the upper and lower incisors meet edge to edge when the mouth is closed. In a scissor bite, the upper teeth overlap the lower teeth so that they just touch each other back to front. A dog is said to be overshot when the upper incisors overlap the lower ones without touching them, and undershot when the lower incisors overlap the upper ones.

Whatever the bite (which depends on the breed of dog), canine teeth are intended to eat meat: to tear, to bite, to chew and grind and crush. The canines enable a dog to bite down on its prey and to hold the quarry fast. The incisors tear at skin and eviscerate the game. The premolars and molars can crush bones. The enamel of these back teeth is exceptionally hard.

Tail

When 'well carried,' the tail is an ornament that emphasizes the elegance of the body. Tail carriage is also a distinctive breed characteristic. Pointers carry their tails straight and horizontal; Chow Chows have curled tails, set high and carried well over the back; Basset Hounds and German Shepherds have sabre-like tails that curve gently either upwards or downwards. Above all, the tail assists in locomotion. With the neck it acts to balance the dog and is especially important when the dog is running, jumping, or swimming.

In competitions, the tail is a measure for the judge. It indicates the strength of the dog's pelvic muscles, and thus the efficiency of the dog's hindquarters. Tail carriage is determined by three muscles: two upper and one lower. If the muscle tone is poor, the tail will be carried improperly.

Some dogs, such as the Old English Sheepdog and the Schipperke, are born without tails. Ultrabrevilinear dogs have naturally short tails (Bulldogs). The tails of some breeds are traditionally docked (Boxers, Dobermann Pinschers, and most terriers). Greyhounds have long tails that reach to the hock, while hounds and setters have medium-length tails.

The shape and curvature of a dog's tail is a breed characteristic, too. Labrador Retrievers have 'otter tails,' that is, thick, densely coated tails that taper towards the tip. The Chihuahua's tail is flattish, slightly broader in its middle than at its root and pointed tip. The Shih Tzu's tail, beneath its plumes, is called a 'pot-hook' tail for its high arc. The Pekingese's plumed tail, on the other hand, nearly lies flat over the topline, hence its name, 'squirrel tail.'

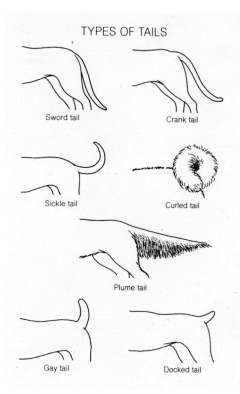

TYPES OF TAILS

Sword tail

Crank tail

Sickle tail

Curled tail

Plume tail

Gay tail

Docked tail

Stance

The quality of a dog's stance (the orientation of the limbs) is more than a matter of appearance. Proper angulation of the shoulder and leg joints—the bones should meet at correct angles—can play a significant part in assuring efficient movement.

If angulation is correct, the legs will be generally parallel, viewed from the front or back. In other words, the distance between the shoulders will equal that between the elbows, and the distance between the tips of the buttocks will equal that between the hocks. When a dog's angulation is proper for its breed, that dog is said to be 'well turned' or 'well angulated.'

Poor angulation can occur at any of the leg joints—hocks, stifles, shoulders, wrists, or elbows. Pasterns that are too long or short, too sloping or else upright, also throw a dog off from its appropriate stance.

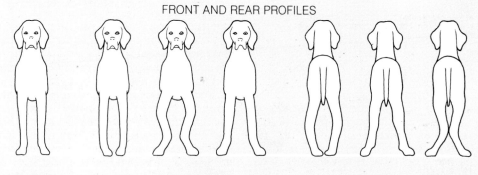

FRONT AND REAR PROFILES

Normal front   Pigeon-toed   Fiddle front   East-west front   Bandy legs   Hocking out   Cow hocks

SIDE PROFILES

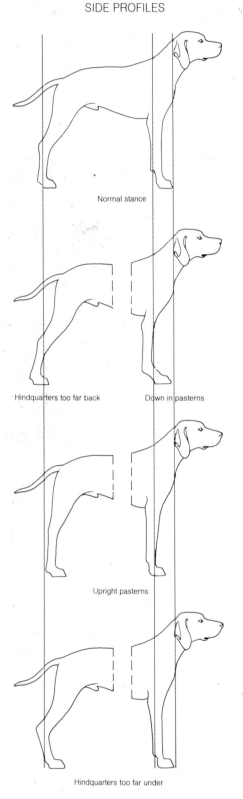

Normal stance

Hindquarters too far back

Down in pasterns

Upright pasterns

Hindquarters too far under

In the illustrations on page 39, the pigeon-toed dog suffers from weak pasterns and wrists. Weak pasterns are also the cause of the splayed legs of the dog with the east-west, also called French, front. Elbows too wide apart, with forearms sloping inwards, create the violin-like shape of the fiddle-front dog.

The dog with bandy rear legs (also referred to as barrel legs or barrel hocks) owes this condition to outward-turning hocks. Over-angulated stifles, that is, stifles more straight than bent, can produce the excessive leg spacing of the wide-hocked ('hocking out') dog. Inward-turning hocks produce what are called cow hocks, an affliction that causes the rear pasterns to brush against each other when the dog is in motion.

Even when the joints do not turn in or out, a dog can have a poor stance, as seen in the illustrations to the left. When the rear pasterns slope too far forward and the stifle is over-angulated, the hindquarters are said to be 'too far back.' Weak front pasterns ('down in pasterns') cause the dog's forequarters to be slightly recessed; and front pasterns that are upright ('over-angulated') also create that condition. Upright rear pasterns produce straight legs that fail to absorb shocks adequately. Whether pasterns are down or upright, the dog so formed tires more easily than sound dogs with properly sloping pasterns. Hindquarters are said to be 'too far under' when weak pasterns slope rearward to excess and fail to do their share in holding up the body—another reason for premature fatigue.

Coat

Length and colour are perhaps the most significant characteristics of a dog's coat.

Some dogs are long-haired with rough coats (terriers and griffons); some have a medium-length coat of silky, wavy, or woolly hair (spaniels and setters); others are short-haired (mastiffs and pointers). There are even dogs with no hair at all (Mexican Hairless). Some parts of a dog's coat are longer than others, producing a characteristic 'ruff,' 'plume,' or 'culottes.' Some coats are naturally tufted; some are specially clipped.

The coat is said to be self-coloured when it is of a single colour. Many dogs have coats comprising two colours of hair. Orange roan, for example, is a mixture of red and white hair. When black is finely mixed with white, the coat is grey; blue is a variant of this. Ticking is a mixture of colours (usually two) in individual hairs. A brindled coat has stripes of black hair on a lighter base. The pied coat is white with patches in another colour. A harlequin coat is usually pied, with large black spots on a white background. A wild boar, or quail, coat is pied with brindled patches. Among three-colour mixed coats, roan is a fine mixture of black, white, and red hair; dapple-grey has tan, black, or white spots on a grey background. The tricolour (hound-marked) coat is a pied coat—thus, predominantly white—with both black and tan patches. Parti-coloured coats are patched with at least two colours.

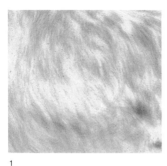

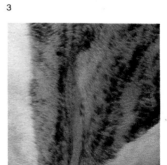

1

2

3

COAT COLOURS

1. Orange roan
2. Black and tan
3. Black pied
4. Parti-colour
5. Wild boar
6. Brindled
7. Ticked
8. Tricolour (Hound-marked)

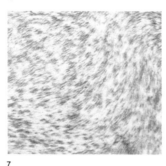

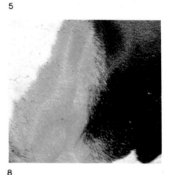

4

5

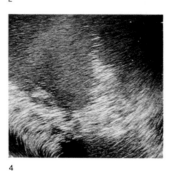

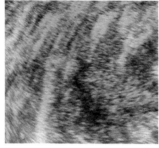

6

7

8

Some dogs change colour, the Yorkshire Terrier for example. Dalmatians acquire their spots as they grow. Too much sunlight tends to redden black hair. Scarring tends to produce black or white hair.

Some coats grow continuously and need regular clipping (Poodles), while others grow intermittently.

Feet

The forefeet (paws) have five toes, and the hind feet four. Shape varies with breed. The foot can be round—this is known as a cat-foot—as with the Fox Terrier or Schnauzer, oval (Pyrenean Sheep-dog), or long (Greyhound). This last is called a hare-foot. A flat foot with open, spreading toes is called a splay-foot. Webbed toes are commonly found on water dogs.

Age

Besides the state of a dog's teeth, there are several means of judging its age. One sign of ageing is the greying of the hair around the nose and eyes and on the forehead. Also, old dogs' eyes seem to sink into their sockets as pads of fatty tissue build up around them. Furthermore, elbows and hocks in many older dogs become calloused at points of contact.

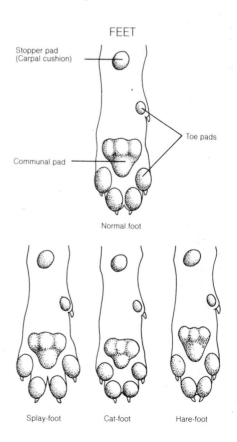

FEET

Stopper pad (Carpal cushion)

Toe pads

Communal pad

Normal foot

Splay-foot   Cat-foot   Hare-foot

Classifying Breeds

Kennel clubs everywhere classify dogs on their breed lists into *groups*, largely for the purpose of organizing dog shows. These groups—based loosely on the common ancestry, function, or physical build of a given set of dogs—provide the framework for judging at championship shows.

The grouping system evolved over the years as kennel clubs increased their recognition of breeds. Faced with a growing number of dogs at their shows in the late 1800s, the Kennel Club of Great Britain had to develop a system to streamline the judging process: hence, the grouping of breeds. Initially, the Kennel Club created two groups: Sporting Dogs and Non-sporting Dogs. Over the years, however, the number has grown to six, a scheme followed basically in Canada, Great Britain, and South Africa. Australia and New Zealand have seven groups.

On the whole, the English-speaking countries use the same groups, with slight variations in nomenclature. Australia and New Zealand, Canada, South Africa, and Britain all have groups named Hounds, Toys, and Working Dogs. What Canada calls Non-sporting Dogs are generally termed Utility breeds in Britain. Canada's Sporting Dogs are referred to in Australia and Britain as Gun Dogs. (For a listing of each country's breeds categorized by group, see pp. 370–377.)

Hounds in all countries are hunting dogs that trail by sight or by scent. Their ranks include such scent hounds as the Beagle and Elkhound and such sight hounds as the Borzoi and Irish Wolfhound.

Retrievers, pointers, setters, and most spaniels belong to the Gun Dog, or Sporting, group. These dogs generally accompany hunters after feathered game. They track their quarry and either point at the bird, flush it, or retrieve the dead prey. (The name of a Gun Dog breed is no clear indicator of the dog's particular hunting prowess. An English Setter, for instance, is a spaniel that serves as a pointer and, often, as a retriever as well.)

What Canada, Britain, and South Africa call Terriers are termed Sporting Terriers in Australia. Terriers are diggers. They were originally bred to ferret out such animals as badgers, otters, and vermin that burrow underground. But having terrier in its name does not automatically relegate a dog to this group. Australian Silky Toy Terriers and Yorkshire Terriers are Toy Dogs in all English-speaking countries. The Boston Terrier is a Utility dog in Britain and a Non-sporting breed in Australia and Canada.

The Working group in all countries includes sheep-dogs, guide-dogs, and watch-dogs. These are the Collies, German Shepherds, and Australian Cattle Dogs, among dozens of others, that herd cattle and sheep, draw sleds, or guard homes and businesses. Australia's Working group, however, excludes some 20 of Canada's, Great Britain's, and South Africa's working breeds—notably Boxers, Dobermanns, and Saint Bernards—classifying them in its Utility group.

Dogs in the Toy group are pets, bred to be appealing rather than functional. Chihuahuas, Pugs, Pomeranians, and Pekingese are among the best-known Toys.

The Non-sporting classification—the Utility group in Britain and South Africa—embraces dogs that fit into none of the other groups. They are considered pets, although some have worked for their keep. The Dalmatian, Poodle, and Lhasa Apso represent the diversity of this group.

Album
of Dogs

Preface to the Album of Dogs

This illustrated album describes 175 breeds of dog. Virtually all these breeds are recognized by one or more of the following kennel clubs: Australian National Kennel Council, Canadian Kennel Club, Kennel Union of Southern Africa, Kennel Club (Great Britain), and the Fédération cynologique internationale (F.C.I.). An entry on breeds that lack widespread recognition, 'Unofficial Breeds,' and one on mixed breeds, 'Mongrels,' complete the album. For each dog highlighted you will find the following information:

• A heading, often accompanied by alternate names for the dog. Alternate names are indexed on pp. 382–383.

• A colour illustration and, in some cases, drawings.

• Text describing the dog's habits and nature.

• An historical note, 'Origins,' tracing a breed's evolution.

• A box indicating in which countries the featured breed is registered. The following abbreviations are used: AUS. for Australia, CAN. for Canada, S. AF. for South Africa, U.K. for the United Kingdom, and F.C.I. for the Fédération cynologique internationale.

• A 'Characteristics' box describes the physical features required of a good show dog. (The descriptions combine the breed standards of the national kennel clubs. However, standards vary from country to country, despite attempts by the clubs to make them match, and they are also under constant revision. For up-to-date standards of a specific breed, readers should contact their national kennel club.) Note that a dog's height is measured from the withers. If only one figure for height or weight is given, it is that of the male (referred to as the 'adult dog'). Qualities that are listed under 'Faults' would lessen a dog's competitiveness at a show, if not disqualify it. Canine terminology is defined in the Glossary, pp. 378–381.

• Practical information, a section that advises on daily care, grooming, diet, exercise, and diseases or conditions most likely to affect the breed. Quick-reference symbols rate the dog's exercise, grooming, and diet requirements:

Exercise is represented by a dog running. A white symbol means that minimal daily exercise is needed; a light grey one, that the dog requires regular exercise. The dark grey silhouette signifies that this is a breed which must have extensive exercise, or is suited to living outdoors.

Grooming requirements are presented in a similar manner, ranging from simple brushing (light symbol) to difficult and demanding grooming sessions (dark symbol).

Diet symbols are read as follows: a white bowl means that the dog requires some 500 grams (1 pound) or less of canned food per day; a light grey bowl, as much as 1 kilogram (2 pounds); a dark grey bowl, more than 1 kilogram daily of tinned food.

These are, of course, general suggestions. Requirements vary considerably according to the age and life-style of the individual dog.

Affenpinscher

Monkey Dog, Monkey Terrier

AUS.	CAN.	S. AF.	U.K.	F.C.I.
●	●	●	●	●

The wiry-haired little Affenpinscher derives its name from its resemblance to the monkey (*Affe*, in German) and its kinship to the Pinscher. Related they may be, but the Affenpinscher can hardly be confused with the Pinscher, a miniature replica of the Dobermann. Indeed, with its small, impish head, it most closely resembles a non-relative, the Griffon Bruxellois.

Apart from its value as a show dog, the Affenpinscher is a likeable and lively companion. Extremely curious, exuberant but obedient, it is also a brave and alert watch-dog. In addition, it is a determined rodent hunter and in the country can track quail and rabbits.

ORIGINS

Some people claim that the Affenpinscher is descended from the Griffon Bruxellois, while others vehemently insist that it was the other way around—that the Affenpinscher actually originated the Griffon Bruxellois line. In fact, both breeds could have descended from an extinct German Pinscher.

Characteristics

General appearance: small, stocky. Trotting gait.
Height: 22.8 to 28 cm (9 to 11 in.). Under Canadian standards, no more than 26 cm (10¼ in.).
Weight: 2.7 to 4 kg (6 to 9 lb). Under F.C.I. and Canadian standards, not specified.
Head: rounded but not too heavy, full. Domed forehead. Short, blunt muzzle. Black nose and lips. Can be slightly undershot but teeth must not protrude.
Eyes: deep, round, sparkling, prominent but not bulging, surrounded by a ring of shaggy hair.
Ears: set high, upright, or neat drop ear. Under F.C.I. and Canadian standards, may be cropped.

Body: square. Level back. Short, straight back. Barrel-shaped chest.
Tail: not docked in Australia. Usually docked short and carried high elsewhere.
Forequarters: legs straight, elbows close.
Hindquarters: Hocks set well under the body. Legs well balanced below croup.
Feet: small, round, compact. Toes tight and arched. Hard, dark, strong pads.
Coat: stiff and plentiful. Shaggy around the face, giving monkey-like appearance.
Colour: preferably black.

Practical information: The Affenpinscher is uncomfortable in very warm homes and tends to lose its coat. Vitamins and daily brushings minimize its discomfort. Eyes should be checked regularly. Before the dog is ten days old, the tail should be docked to two-thirds its length. If the ears are to be cropped, the dog should be between eight and ten weeks of age.

Afghan Hound

Tazi

AUS.	CAN.	S. AF.	U.K.	F.C.I.
●	●	●	●	●

The Afghan Hound's striking appearance has long commanded attention. Its supple, majestic gait, proud and noble head, and long, silky coat give the dog an air of elegance and nobility. It is also a runner of great speed and a hunter that fears neither rain, snow, nor rough terrain. In Afghanistan, it is a valued companion of nomad chieftains, tracking deer or wild goats, even wolves and snow leopards. Shepherds prize it as a herder and watch-dog. In the Middle East, so the story goes, Afghan Hounds were so valued by members of the nobility that foreigners were prohibited from obtaining dogs to take home.

The Afghan's long seclusion as a hunter in wild, mountainous terrain is largely responsible for its handsome coat, necessary to protect it from frigid temperatures. The dog's wide-set hip bones enable it to twist, turn, and leap around and over the rocks and ravines that make up much of Afghanistan's countryside. Its tail, carried high with a curve at its tip, alerts hunters to its whereabouts when it is charging through heavy brush.

Like all oriental dogs, the Afghan has a very independent character; it is impossible to make a servile dog of this hound. With strangers, or anyone outside the immediate circle of family and friends, it keeps its distance. Among friends, however, it is a lively and spirited companion, craving and delighting in lavish affection. Thanks to an uncanny instinct for comfort, it can be relied on to choose the best armchair. Outdoors, however, it harks back to its origins, giving itself up to the pure joy of running, or barking playfully after butterflies and falling leaves.

The Afghan has been highly regarded in Britain since the turn of the century. Its more recent popularity has been phenomenal.

ORIGINS

The roots of the Afghan, as of most hounds, reach far into ancient times. Cave drawings dating back more than 4,000 years have been found in the Balkh region of north-western Afghanistan, showing dogs which closely resemble the breed known today. Evidence of its existence has been found in Greece on pictorial fabric believed to have been created in Athens in the sixth century B.C. An Egyptian papyrus from the fourth century B.C. mentions the Afghan. The first Afghan to reach Europe was imported into England at the end of the last century. In 1907, the dog was exhibited in London under the name Oriental Greyhound; it met with immense success. It was also in England that the first Afghan Hound club was founded, in 1926. That same year the breed was granted official recognition by the British Kennel Club.

Characteristics

General appearance: very tall, impressive, and aloof in manner, the Afghan hound has a characteristically supple and elastic gait.

Height: 68.6 to 73.7 cm (27 to 29 in.) for the adult dog; 63.5 to 68.6 cm (25 to 27 in.) for the bitch. Under Canadian standards, 66 to 71 cm (26 to 28 in.) for the adult dog; 61 to 66 cm (24 to 26 in.) for the bitch.

Weight: under F.C.I. standards, 25 to 30 kg (55 to 66 lb) for the adult dog and 20 to 25 kg (44 to 55 lb) for the bitch. Under Canadian standards, 27.2 kg (60 lb) for the dog and 22.7 kg (50 lb) for the bitch. Elsewhere, not specified.

Head: skull long, not too narrow, with prominent occiput. Long muzzle. Powerful jaws. Abundant topknot.

Eyes: slanting slightly upward from the inner corner towards the outer corner. Preferably dark.

Ears: long, set low and well back, the tip level with the corner of the mouth. Covered with long, silky hair.

Neck: long and strong. Head carried erect.

Body: flat, muscular back of moderate length; a slight knot of muscles at the loin. Deep chest. Loin rather short and strong. Prominent hip bones, wide apart.

Tail: not too short, ending in a ring, sparsely feathered, carried high.

Forequarters: long and sloping, well laid back, elbows tight. Legs straight and well boned.

Hindquarters: powerful, long, and well angled to the hock. Great length between the hip and hock. Pasterns long and springy. No dewclaw.

Feet: covered with thick, long hair. Forefeet strong with large, arched toes. Hind feet long and broad and covered with thick hair.

Coat: thick, long, and silky, falling flat along the body except on the back saddle where it is short and close in mature dogs. From the brow backwards, the long, silky hair hangs in bangs; the hair is short on the forehead.

Colour: all colours.

Faults: a heavy appearance. Large skull. Short muzzle. Eyes large and round. Thick, short neck.

Practical information: This hardy dog is able to tolerate heat, cold, and rain. It needs space and must be able to run itself out at least once a day. Its sumptuous coat requires a good deal of upkeep; it is best to have the dog groomed regularly. It must be thoroughly brushed every two days, shampooed once a month. Handle an Afghan Hound gently; it is sensitive.

Airedale Terrier

AUS.	CAN.	S. AF.	U.K.	F.C.I.
●	●	●	●	●

ORIGINS

The Airedale was developed around 1850 by cross-breeding the English Black and Tan Terrier (now extinct) with the Otterhound. From the former, it inherited excellent hearing and eyesight. To the latter it owes its keen nose, its strength, and its prowess as a swimmer. First called variously the Waterside, Bingley, Warfedale, or Working Terrier, the breed was officially recognized in 1879 under the name Airedale. After the Second World War, the Airedale's popularity declined, no doubt because of its size. In recent years, however, the breed has come back into favour not only in Britain, but in Germany, Canada, and the United States.

The Airedale is too big to qualify as a dog that goes to ground: it cannot slip down into the narrow tunnels of weasels and rabbits. Yet it can hunt larger game—indeed, it is adept at tracking deer, wild boar, even bear. Formidable as a badger hunter, the Airedale makes a speciality of otter, the reason for its 'invention' as a breed. The terrier owes its name, in fact, to a small otter river near Leeds, England. Tracking down this clever little water mammal—whose capacity for fish was the bane of fishermen—required a good swimmer that was also happy charging round the marshes and exploring the otters' open-ended burrows. Hence the origin of the Airedale.

This versatile terrier with its supple and elegant lines is an animal of many talents. It was one of the very first canine recruits for the British and German police forces. During the First World War, it took to the vast mire of battlefields as if they were a giant burrow made to order. Agile and tireless, threading its way through trenches and shell craters, it was used by Germans and Allies alike to carry messages and detect approaching enemies. Upon its 'discharge' it resumed its hunting activities and became a guard and even a guide dog. Its easy, straightforward nature and disarming innocence make it a lively and fun-loving pet. Occasionally gripped by its 'terrier complex,' a natural unruliness, it will take to tracking an imaginary badger lurking under a chair. Like other terriers, the Airedale needs a forceful master who will keep it affectionately but firmly in line from an early age.

GROOMING THE AIREDALE TERRIER

The Airedale's grooming is similar to that of the Wire-haired Fox Terrier, with a few exceptions. To emphasize the slender, elongated line of the head, the ears are shaved both inside and outside. The top and sides of the skull, the cheeks, and under the jaw are closely cut. The beard is left on the corners of the mouth and the muzzle and combed forward. The eyebrows are left rather bushy. The neck is layer-cut so that the dog appears narrow from the front; the back should be very smooth so as to look straight. The rib area is lightly trimmed, also in layers. In order to 'shorten' the dog as much as possible, the back of the thighs and the buttocks are shaved carefully, rounded on the sides. The tail should be trimmed regularly in good proportion to the body.

Characteristics

General appearance: alert expression, rapid movement. Body is well proportioned and symmetrical.

Height: 58.4 to 61 cm (23 to 24 in.) for the adult dog; 56 to 58.4 cm (22 to 23 in.) for the bitch.

Weight: not specified.

Head: long and flat skull, not too broad between the ears, narrowing to the eyes. Elongated muzzle. Barely visible stop. Flat cheeks, tight lips. Powerful, strong, and muscular jaws, vice-like, but not excessively developed. Strong teeth. Black nose.

Eyes: dark, small, not bulging. Intelligent and alert in expression.

Ears: small, V-shaped, and carried to the side of the head, not pointing to its eyes. Topline of the folded ear extends above the skull. The tip falls forward to the top of the eye.

Neck: lean, muscular, moderately long and thick, widening at the shoulders. No loose skin.

Body: short, strong, straight back. Muscular loin. Prominent ribs, with little space between the ribs and hips. Chest deep but not broad, reaching to the elbows. Shoulders long and sloping to the back; shoulder blades flat.

Tail: set high, carried gaily but not curved over the back, of good substance and fair length.

Forequarters: legs perfectly straight with good bone. Elbows close to the body, working free of sides.

Hindquarters: legs long, strong, with a muscular second thigh. Stifles well bent. Hocks well let down, parallel when viewed from behind.

Feet: small, round, compact. Toes slightly arched, not turned in or out. Thick pads.

Coat: stiff, dense, and wiry, lying close and covering the dog well over the body and legs. Not ragged; sometimes slightly wavy and crinkling. Shorter, softer undercoat, dense and not curly.

Colour: tan on the head and ears, except for dark markings on each side of the skull; the ears a little darker in tone. Tan feet, up to the thighs and elbows. The body is black or dark grizzle.

Faults: curly or soft coat. Hound ears. White feet. Poor bite. Light or bold eye.

Practical information: This sturdy terrier adapts to any climate and is rarely ill. Its only weak point: a tendency to gastro-enteritis. Indoors, it could show a tendency to eczema, so inspect its skin regularly. Its rough, thick coat is difficult to groom unless dead hair is regularly removed with the fingers or a comb. Clippers should not be used because they cut too close and ruin the texture and colour of the coat. If this is neglected, the dog quickly takes on the appearance of a woolly bear-cub. For dog show competitions, the Airedale requires professional grooming.

Akita

Japanese Akita
Akita Inu
Akita Prefecture
Shishi Inu

Courageous, strong, and spirited, the Akita is the most beautiful of Japanese dogs. An excellent hunter of deer and wild boar, the Akita in times past would readily attack the black bear of Hokkaido Island. Used in dogfights for nearly three centuries in feudal times, the breed almost disappeared because few dogs survived these spectacles. Today, dogfights are prohibited and the Akita, considered Japan's national dog, is most often used as a police and guard dog. Despite its strength, this is a docile and affectionate animal that makes a fine, highly prized house-pet.

AUS.	CAN.	S. AF.	U.K.	F.C.I.
●	●	●	●	●

ORIGINS

The Akita is one of three spitz-type dogs native to Japan. At one time, only the Japanese aristocracy was permitted to own the formidable hunter. The breed has changed little since the seventeenth century.

Characteristics

Height: 66 to 71 cm (26 to 28 in.) for the dog; 61 to 66 cm (24 to 26 in.) for the bitch. Under F.C.I. standards, 63 to 69 cm (24⅞ to 27⅛ in.). Under South African standards, 51 to 69 cm (20 to 27⅛ in.).
Weight: under F.C.I. standards, 40 to 50 kg (88¼ to 110¼ lb). Elsewhere, not specified.
Head: broad, flat, and heavy, forming a blunt triangle. Well-defined stop. Strong, short muzzle. Black nose.
Eyes: small, deep-set, triangular, dark brown.
Ears: small, triangular, carried erect.

Body: broad and deep chest, thick, muscular neck, level back, muscular loin, well-rounded ribs.
Tail: thick, carried high and curved over the back of the dog.
Forequarters: strong and powerful shoulders. Legs heavily boned. Elbows close to the body.
Hindquarters: muscular. Bone comparable to forequarters. Hocks less angular than other breeds.
Coat: stiff outer coat; fine and thick undercoat.
Colour: all colours.

Practical information: The Akita is an athletic dog that requires a great deal of exercise if it is to be a good pet. It is robust, and rarely ill. During its first year, growth should be monitored to ensure it is adequately fed: the Akita needs fairly large meals. The coat is easy to care for, requiring regular brushing but only infrequent baths.

Alaskan Malamute

Malamute

This large, powerful spitz-type dog has long been used by North American Inuit to hunt polar bears and wolves and to guard caribou herds. Arctic explorers teamed Malamutes to haul sleds on expeditions to the North Pole. In summer, the Malamutes were saddled with packs weighing as much as 22.5 kilograms (50 pounds), which they carried as far as 32 kilometres (20 miles) a day. Though the snowmobile has reduced the usefulness of the Malamute, the dog remains a beloved family pet and guard dog.

AUS.	CAN.	S. AF.	U.K.	F.C.I.
●	●	●	●	●

ORIGINS

The Alaskan Malamute is believed to descend from the boreal wolf. The pure strain of Malamute would have become extinct if not for the efforts of a few determined breeders.

Characteristics

General appearance: hardy, compact, well-built.
Height: under F.C.I. standards, 55 to 67 cm (21½ to 26¼ in.). Elsewhere, 58.4 to 71 cm (23 to 28 in.).
Weight: under F.C.I. standards, 29 to 35 kg (64 to 77 lb). Under Canadian standards, 38.6 kg (85 lb) for the adult dog; 34 kg (75 lb) for the bitch. Elsewhere, 38.6 to 56.7 kg (85 to 125 lb).
Head: large, well proportioned. Broad skull, slightly rounded between the ears. Broad, thick muzzle. Black nose. Strong jaws. Broad, strong teeth. Scissor bite.

Eyes: large, almond-shaped, dark, slanting.
Ears: small, wide-set at back of head, triangular.
Body: powerful, well-developed, deep chest, straight back sloping gently to hips, very muscular loin.
Tail: full, carried curved over the back.
Forequarters: legs strong, straight, and muscular.
Hindquarters: broad and very muscular thighs. Strong, well-balanced hocks.
Coat: thick, coarse outer coat; woolly undercoat.
Colour: usually light grey or black and white.

Practical information: A hardy dog, rarely ill, the Alaskan Malamute needs exercise and prefers to live outside. It must be brushed and curried several times a week (daily when shedding). Training must be strict and consistent, without sacrificing encouragement and affection. The Malamute prefers the cold, but it can live in a temperate climate.

Anglo-Français

An eager hunter with a keen sense of smell, the Anglo-Français is the most popular pack hound in France, though it is seldom found elsewhere. The dog excels at hunting boar: With near reckless abandon it charges into thorny, dense thickets in pursuit of wild pig. As a pack dog, the Anglo-Français needs canine company. Otherwise it is restless and may even wander.

The name Anglo-Français reflects the dog's parentage. English Foxhound blood accounts for its endurance; genes of the Poitevin (a rare French breed) account for its courage.

AUS.	CAN.	S. AF.	U.K.	F.C.I.
				●

ORIGINS

Excessive inbreeding very nearly wiped out the Anglo-Français. But breeding with the English Foxhound subsequently fixed a healthy strain of hound noted for its speed, vitality, intelligence, and courage.

Characteristics

General appearance: solid, distinctive-looking.
Height: 58.4 to 68.6 cm (23 to 27 in.).
Weight: not specified.
Head: rather long, relatively narrow. Well-defined occiput. Barely visible stop. Muzzle medium long. Prominent nose.
Eyes: large, expressive.
Ears: semi-long, thin, slightly turned, set fairly low.
Body: long, thin, muscular. Muscular back. Very deep chest, higher than it is wide. Long and rounded ribs, slightly raised flanks.
Tail: thin, not bushy, set high and curved.
Forequarters: straight and muscular. Legs stand wide apart.
Hindquarters: muscular. Low, slightly bent hocks.
Coat: short and glossy hair.
Colour: tricolour (white, black, and orange); white and black; white and orange.

Practical information: This dog is particularly susceptible to leptospirosis, an infection carried in the urine of rodents. During hunting season, the Anglo-Français needs high-energy food. After the hunt, it must be protected against cold and humidity and examined for wounds and parasites. Pack dogs do not need to be bathed; their coat tends to clean itself.

Australian Cattle Dog

Blue Heeler, Queensland Heeler, Australian Heeler

The Australian Cattle Dog was developed to be a strong biting dog, one able to drive wild cattle over long distances. Its speckled coat camouflages it when nipping at the bovines' legs. Its punishing jaws are essential to a cattle dog in mustering and moving wild livestock. Protecting its master's family and home is a responsibility the Australian Cattle Dog takes as seriously as squiring cattle.

AUS.	CAN.	S. AF.	U.K.	F.C.I.
●	●	●	●	●

Characteristics

General appearance: sturdy, compact, symmetrically built.
Height: dogs 45.7 to 50.8 cm (18 to 20 in.); bitches 43.2 to 48.3 cm (17 to 19 in.).
Weight: under F.C.I. and Canadian standards, 15 to 23 kg (33 to 51 lb). Elsewhere, not specified.
Head: blunt, wedge-shaped, with broad skull. Strong underjaw.
Eyes: alert, oval-shaped, medium size, brown.
Ears: medium size, broad, muscular, pricked.
Body: back strong. Shoulders broad, muscular. Ribs well sprung.
Forequarters: strong, round, straight legs.
Hindquarters: legs broad, strong, muscular; thighs well developed.
Coat: straight, weather-resistant outer coat; short, dense undercoat.
Colour: blue or red, with or without markings.

Practical information: Bred to withstand the rigours of the Outback, its weather-resistant coat needs only routine brushing. But as an energetic working dog, the breed does require plenty of exercise.

ORIGINS

When Australian stockmen required a herding dog to help control the half-wild cattle and sheep, they set out to breed one. The process began in the 1830s when a stockman named Timmins crossed a Smithfield, a tough but noisy working breed, with a Dingo. The resulting Timmins Biter had the Dingo's silent ways but proved difficult to manage. A further cross with Collies enhanced tractability, but barking became a problem once more. Again, the Dingo was used. Later, to improve temperament, Dalmatian stock was introduced. To further develop working ability, the Australian Kelpie was interbred. This final cross produced just the versatile canine the stockmen were searching for. Their creation, the Queensland Heeler, later renamed Australian Cattle Dog, possessed stamina, reliability, and uncanny intelligence.

Australian Kelpie

Kelpie, Australian Collie

I n Scottish folklore, a kelpie is a water sprite capable of transforming itself into a horse. The name is apt for this agile, hard-working Australian sheep-dog. An excellent herder, the Kelpie works tirelessly, often without supervision. On its own, it can separate 50 to 100 head of sheep and lead them to water, all the while keeping an eye on the rest of the flock. It is said that this dog can perform the work of several men and travel more than 60 kilometres (almost 40 miles) in a day.

Active, independent, and difficult to control, the Kelpie thrives in wide-open spaces and is the most common working sheep-dog in Australia and New Zealand.

AUS.	CAN.	S. AF.	U.K.	F.C.I.
●		●	●	●

ORIGINS

No doubt the blood of the Dingo, as well as that of the smooth-coated Collie, flows in the veins of the Kelpie. One champion of the breed, Coil, won two Australian national championships in 1898 despite a leg injury—definitive evidence of the Kelpie's fortitude.

Characteristics

General appearance: average size, robust, lively, hard-working.

Height: under Australian standards, 43.2 to 50.8 cm (17 to 20 in.). Under F.C.I. standards, 50 to 58 cm (19½ to 23 in.). Elsewhere, dogs 45.7 to 50.8 cm (18 to 20 in.); bitches 43.2 to 48.3 cm (17 to 19 in.).

Weight: under F.C.I. standards, 13 to 15 kg (28½ to 33 lb). Elsewhere, not specified.

Head: long and narrow, wide between the ears. Slightly rounded head. Definite stop. Scissor bite.

Eyes: dark, almond-shaped, very expressive.

Ears: medium, pricked, carried very straight.

Neck: moderate length, powerful, slightly arched.

Body: deep chest. Straight back, loin well developed. Ribs well sprung.

Tail: medium length, set low.

Forequarters: straight and muscular.

Hindquarters: large, muscular thighs. Legs straight and parallel from hocks to feet.

Feet: short, compact. Arched toes. Hard pads.

Coat: short, double-coated, smooth. Dense undercoat.

Colour: black, black and tan, red, red and tan, fawn, chocolate, or blue.

Practical information: This hardy country dog does not tolerate living indoors.

Australian Terrier

Aussie

Low-slung, sturdy, and shaggy, this little dog seems almost to skim the ground. Like all terriers, it is lively, bright, and brave. It was bred by Australians to hunt rabbits and rats. The dog is also adept at killing snakes by leaping into the air and pouncing on the reptile from behind.

The Aussie is playful and loyal. It is a beloved and faithful house-pet.

AUS.	CAN.	S. AF.	U.K.	F.C.I.
●	●	●	●	●

Characteristics

General appearance: rather squat, sturdy, compact, and vivacious.
Height: 25.4 cm (10 in.).
Weight: under F.C.I. standards, 4 to 5 kg (9 to 11 lb). Elsewhere, 6.3 kg (14 lb).
Head: long. Flat skull. Slight but definite stop. Long and strong jaws.
Eyes: small, alert, dark.
Ears: small, erect, pointed, set high, no long hairs.
Body: rather long. Well-sprung ribs. Level back. Deep flanks.
Tail: customarily docked. Set high, erect but not over back.
Forequarters: legs perfectly straight, well-boned.
Hindquarters: legs sturdy, parallel. Hocks well bent and well let down. Stifles well turned.
Coat: straight, stiff, dense outer coat; soft undercoat.
Colour: blue or silver grey, tan on the feet and muzzle, blue or silver topknot. Under Canadian standards, clear sandy or red.

Practical information: With insufficient exercise, the Aussie could become unruly. It is susceptible to eczema.

ORIGINS

A combination of British terrier stock—probably a mix of the Cairn, Dandie Dinmont, Irish, Yorkshire, and Scottish terriers—resulted in this intrepid working dog. The breed appeared at a dog show for the first time in 1899, in Sydney, although it had been a mainstay of Outback stations for some 20 years before. The first dogs exported to Great Britain, in 1906, aroused little interest. In 1921, Lady Stradbroke, wife of a former governor of the State of Victoria, imported several Aussie specimens to breed with existing stock, thereby improving the strain found in Britain. The same year, the Australian Terrier Club was formed and the breed's first standard established. The most important contributing factor to this dog's popularity in England was the adoption of an Aussie by the Duke of Gloucester during his stay in Australia. The breed was officially recognized by the Kennel Club in 1936.

Basenji

Congo Terrier, Barkless Dog

The Basenji is a queer specimen indeed: It does not bark. Instead, it emits a sound resembling a yodel. Furthermore, it cleans itself like a cat and trots like a thoroughbred horse.

A peculiarity in the dog's larynx is believed to be responsible for the Basenji's lack of bark. Yet the dog is far from mute. It expresses itself with a variety of noises, including its characteristic 'chortle' that is half-way between a joyous laugh and a Tyrolean yodel. Versatility as a hunting-dog—it can point, retrieve, drive game, and pick up a scent 75 metres (250 feet) away—assured its respected position among the tribes of central Africa, its land of origin.

Europeans knew nothing of the Basenji until the 1870s, when English explorers discovered the dogs in an area of Africa still relatively unknown, between the Congo River and Sudan. The dogs had been carefully bred; they served as bush-trackers and watch-dogs.

The breeding of Basenjis outside Africa proved difficult, with foundation stock regularly dying of such diseases as distemper. It was not until 1936 that an imported brace, *Bongo of Blean* and *Bokoto of Blean*, produced a healthy litter. These puppies were shown at the world-renowned Crufts Show, in 1937. They generated such excitement that guards had to be called in to control the enthusiastic crowds.

The Basenji has a happy temperament and punctuates its peculiar conversation with gay tail-wagging. At the slightest incident, it is on the alert, both ears pricked and the skin on its skull wrinkled to produce that irresistible look of surprise that is so characteristic of the dog.

AUS.	CAN.	S. AF.	U.K.	F.C.I.
●	●	●	●	●

ORIGINS

This ancient breed originated in central Africa, in an area bounded by Zaire, formerly the Belgian Congo. It has remained a pure breed, merely refined by selective breeding. The difficulty and expense of importing dogs from Africa cannot be underestimated. First, some worthy specimens must be found: an arduous trial-and-error experience in a landscape that is rough and peopled by primitive tribes. Then the dogs must survive an air or sea voyage. In their new countries, the canines must be supremely healthy to resist diseases unknown in their native land. Much credit for the sturdy Basenji of today goes to Veronica Tudor Williams, who travelled through the remotest areas of Africa in search of specimens to better the strain. One of those dogs, Fula, was a superb bitch that contributed much to the breed.

Characteristics

General appearance: rather high on its legs, yet well-balanced, the Basenji has an alert appearance and an alluring way of cocking its head to the side.

Height: 40.6 to 43.2 cm (16 to 17 in.).

Weight: 9.5 to 11 kg (21 to 24 lb). Under F.C.I. standards, not specified.

Head: of medium breadth, narrowing at eye level, carried high. Flat skull. Fine, profuse wrinkles on forehead. Muzzle narrows from the eyes to the nose; is shorter than the skull. Level teeth. Nose black.

Eyes: small, almond-shaped, deeply set, dark.

Ears: small, pointed, erect, of fine texture, set well forward on top of head.

Neck: medium long, well set into shoulders. Fairly full at the base, with a muscular crest.

Body: oblique shoulders well set in. Medium-wide, deep chest. Prominent ribs. Level back. Short loins with sharply defined waist.

Tail: set high, curling tightly over the back once or twice.

Forequarters: legs level. Clean bone structure with well-defined tendons. Pasterns fairly straight, flexible, and of good length.

Hindquarters: sturdy, muscular legs. Long thighs. Hocks well let down, not turned.

Feet: small, narrow. Well-arched toes. Deep pads.

Coat: short, silky hair; very pliant skin.

Colour: chestnut with white markings, white at the tip of the tail, feet and chest. The darker the chestnut, the smaller the white markings. White and black; white, black, and tan coats are also found.

Practical information: A fastidious dog, the Basenji cleans itself with its tongue. Groom it with a semi-hard brush; to make the coat shine, rub the dog every day with a horsehair glove. This breed is sometimes susceptible to respiratory problems.

Basset Hound

The Basset Hound is sometimes said to be half a dog in height, but twice a dog in length. With its wrinkled forehead and long, drooping ears, the breed is hard to resist. Cleo, the Basset Hound television star, charmed millions of Americans with her low-slung profile. Advertisers took advantage of the breed's appealingly lugubrious expression when they used a Basset—one of Cleo's relatives—to launch the 'Hush Puppies' line of casual shoes.

Affectionate and gentle, extremely devoted, the Basset Hound makes a good, calm pet that never expends energy unnecessarily. It is serene and well-behaved. It never jumps up on the laps of guests, for instance. Instead, it approaches them inconspicuously, sniffs politely, then returns to its place. On the other hand, behind the guise of a solemn and melancholy old judge lurks a sporting temperament. Young or old, this is definitely not a sedentary dog. It needs to use up its energy. The back garden is not sufficient for exercising a Basset—fields are what it requires.

The Basset Hound is first and foremost a hunting-dog, one well qualified to follow a trail over difficult terrain, especially when the quarry is hare. Despite its bulk, it can manoeuvre through thickets with surprising agility. And its nose is nearly as accurate as the Bloodhound's. Endowed with exceptional physical stamina and perseverance, it is a formidable and relentless foe of the deer, hare, or rabbits it trails.

AUS.	CAN.	S. AF.	U.K.	F.C.I.
●	●	●	●	●

ORIGINS

According to some authorities, the Basset Hound descends from ancient, extinct French hunting-dogs, perhaps the Basset d'Artois, or the low-set Saint Hubert. The Basset Hounds may have been dwarfs among normal litters of either breed that were retained as curiosities, though subsequently bred to develop a pure strain. Others ascribe oriental origins to the Basset Hound—it may have been brought to Europe from Constantinople during the Crusades. In any case, the Basset is truly an oddity as a universally known hunting hound in that it is neither British nor American in origin. The first Bassets in England were named Basset *and* Balle, *bought by Lord Galway in 1866 from the Comte de Tournon. A subsequent breeder, Sir Everett Millais, added the Bloodhound strain to his Basset stock to create a distinctively British breed—a dog that is longer in the head than its Continental counterpart.*

Characteristics

General appearance: disproportionately short legs and heavy bones for its height. Of considerable substance, while well balanced. Smooth, free action with the forelegs extending well forward and the hind legs thrusting backwards powerfully.

Height: 33 to 38 cm (13 to 15 in.). Under Canadian standards, not specified.

Weight: under F.C.I. standards, 23 kg (51 lb). Elsewhere, not specified.

Head: broad and well proportioned. Skull narrow and dome-shaped, of good length, the occiput prominent. Loose skin, falling in deep folds above the eyebrows when the head is lowered. Dark nose, preferably black, with large, wide-open nostrils. Muzzle deep, heavy, not pointed. Teeth large, solid, and regular; scissor bite. Dark lips; flews of the upper lip overlap the lower.

Eyes: brown to hazel, lozenge-shaped. Set in slightly, with some haw showing.

Ears: extremely long, narrow, set low. When drawn forward, they extend to the nose tip. Velvety. Hanging in loose folds, curling slightly inward, set far back at the base of the skull.

Neck: strong, of good length, well arched. Pronounced dewlap.

Body: long, smooth ribs carried far back; well rounded and sprung. Level back. Deep brisket. Prominent sternum. Shoulders well back and strong, but not heavy. When seen from behind, croup and legs appear heavily muscled for a round, barrel-like shape.

Tail: well set on, rather long, tapering. Carried high and sabre-fashion over the back when in action.

Forequarters: legs short, solid, very heavy. Wrinkled skin between knees and feet. Loose elbows, well muscled, standing out well.

Hindquarters: Hocks low, turning neither in nor out. Stifles well bent. Dew-claws may be removed. Thighs full of muscle.

Feet: thick and solid. Heavy, well-rounded pads.

Coat: short, smooth, dense, free from feathering. Skin loose and elastic. Wrinkles of skin between knee and foot.

Colour: any hound colour; generally black, white, and tan or lemon and white.

Faults: flat ears, set high. Cow hocks, straight hocks, or weak hocks. Roach back. Stiff shoulders, narrow front. Out at elbows. Flat ribs. Long coat. Showing too much leg. Razor back. Slackness of loin. Ears too short. Stiff movement. Dragging toes. Snipy muzzle. Underdeveloped flews. Knuckling over.

Practical information: Because the Basset Hound is constantly sniffing the ground, it can easily pick up parasites, bacteria, and certain viral diseases. Regular stool analysis by a veterinarian is necessary. Do not leave dangerous objects within a pup's reach, as it will swallow anything put in front of it. The ears are quite delicate and must be examined regularly; clean them with a cotton swab, dry or dipped in a weak solution of hydrogen peroxide. Special deep, narrow dishes, available in pet stores, are advisable for a Basset so that its ears will not fall into the food. Primarily a hunting-dog, this hound needs a great deal of exercise and is not content confined indoors.

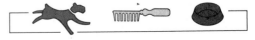

Beagle

'No good hound is a bad colour.' This maxim among hound devotees is especially true of the Beagle, with its superb black, white, and tan coat. Looking like a smaller version of the Foxhound, this dog is endowed with a surprisingly melodious bark. As for the name, it is thought to derive from the Celtic *beag*, meaning 'small'—for this hunter is the smallest of the English hounds.

The Beagle is a tireless hunter, excellent in the pursuit of both large and small game. Sometimes accompanying mounted hunters in a pack, it most often travels alone or in a brace, with a single hunter following on foot.

At one point the breed was small enough to fit into the pocket of a hunting coat. Up to a dozen Beagles were said to fit into saddle baskets strapped to a rider's mount. Since then, Beagles have grown somewhat. Oversize varieties found in some tropical countries would seem to be a different breed of dog entirely, for rather than track the nervous hare or cottontail, they are set loose to corner formidable leopards and jaguars.

An agreeable temperament makes the Beagle a good pet. Unfortunately, it is highly prized by medical research laboratories because the breed is uniformly small.

AUS.	CAN.	S. AF.	U.K.	F.C.I.
●	●	●	●	●

ORIGINS

Some authorities claim that the Beagle originated in Greece. Certainly small dogs hunting in packs were found in Greece as far back as 400 B.C. The dog was later employed in France as a courser of hare, then brought into England during the Norman Conquest (1066). For the next few hundred years breeders developed two sizes of Beagle, the largest referred to as a vache, the small type known as a 'pocket Beagle,' a variety that has ceased to exist.

THE BEAGLE-HARRIER

Once, the Basset, Beagle, Harrier, and the Foxhound offered hunters a fine and adequate range of size and scenting skills from which to choose their hounds. But no, a fifth type was deemed necessary—hence the development of the Beagle-Harrier. Recognized as a breed in France, though not in English-speaking countries, this cross-bred dog is endowed with the Beagle's keen nose and the Harrier's speed. The first Beagle-Harrier litters were lacking in homogeneity, but the later Beagle-Harriers have measured up to their breeders' expectations: They excel at hunting hare and are a worthy match for boar.

Characteristics

General appearance: well proportioned, as long as it is tall. Compact, muscular, vivacious, and active, exuding strength and energy.
Height: 33 to 40.6 cm (13 to 16 in.). Under Canadian standards, no more than 33 cm (13 in.) for the small variety, and 33 cm (13 in.) to 38 cm (15 in.) for the large variety.
Weight: not specified.
Head: large, broad, dome-shaped skull, flattened on top. Well-defined stop. Narrow muzzle. Lips covering lower jaw. Black nose. Strong, broad nostrils.
Eyes: large, round, deep-set or prominent. Dark brown or hazel, often ringed with black. Alert and sensitive expression.
Ears: long, flat, set low, carried forward, fine texture.
Neck: strong, not too short. Sometimes slight dewlap.
Body: slightly oblique shoulders. Ribs well sprung. Chest well let down. Short, straight, muscular back. Loin supple, powerful, extending well back, without excessive cut up. Muscular thighs. Hocks well let down.
Tail: moderate length, set high, carried gaily but not curled over the back. Fairly thick base, tapering to a thin tip, with longer hair on the underside with brush.
Forequarters: legs perfectly straight, strong, muscular. Short, strong pasterns. Elbows firm.
Hindquarters: legs well muscled. Hocks firm, well let down, parallel.
Feet: round. Toes tight, strong, and well arched. Pads hard, compact and very developed.
Coat: short, dense and weather-resistant.
Colour: any hound colour except liver. Top of stern white.
Faults: narrow head. Roman nose. Stop too pronounced. Heavy muzzle. Short or high-set ears. Wavy or V-shaped ears. Eyes small, too close together, or heavily rimmed with black. Thin neck. Weak back. Long loin. Tail too long, too thick, or bent.

Practical information: A Beagle bred as a pack hound requires canine companionship and lots of exercise. These hardy dogs need special care only for their long ears, which must be cleaned regularly. The coat needs a thorough brushing, once or twice a week, to rid it of dust and dead hair.

Beauceron

Berger de Beauce

The elegant and powerful Beauceron is an ancient French breed that some call the 'king of sheep-dogs.' A good herding dog is not trained to round up sheep; it does so instinctively. But because a dog's herding and hunting instincts are intertwined, a sheep-dog is likely to handle its flock roughly—as prey—unless trained otherwise. The Beauceron's hunting instinct is particularly fierce and close to the surface, and that is why a well-trained Berger de Beauce makes a superlative shepherd: with no hesitation it takes the offensive against straying sheep or encroaching strangers.

The Beauceron is mainly found in Continental Europe where, during the last century, it was responsible for containing sheep within pastures and for herding them along roads. Since only two dogs were necessary to control 200 to 300 sheep, they were indispensable on farms where manpower was limited. Since then, industries have spread to the countryside, claiming large chunks of open pasture, and animal husbandry has become scientific. Today, the Beauceron's job as a sheep-dog is limited to escorting flocks from one fold to another.

The dog's hunting instincts are increasingly valued, however. With its quick reflexes, readi-

AUS.	CAN.	S. AF.	U.K.	F.C.I.
		●		●

ORIGINS

Contrary to widely held opinion, the name 'Beauceron' does not mean that the breed originated in the Beauce region of France, any more than the name 'Briard' specifies Brie as that sheep-dog's place of origin. Both of these dogs—one short-haired, the other long-haired—belong to an ancient family of shepherding dogs once found throughout France. Although separate breeds, each of long and pure lineage, the Beauceron and Briard were considered virtually the same animal until the late 1800s, when a commission of scientists and veterinarians differentiated between them. The names were arbitrarily conferred at that time.

ness to attack, and deep-seated mistrust of strangers, it is an ideal guard dog. Not even another dog should stray into its territory—the Beauceron will lunge at its throat.

But such spontaneity and natural aggressiveness—some say viciousness and brutality—are tempered by unconditional loyalty to its master and an aptitude for obedience. The trick is to train this intelligent dog carefully. Its independent disposition makes it very difficult to control, and it does not readily accept changes of hand. Some Beaucerons, if poorly handled or unloved, can prove extremely dangerous, and no amount of discipline or affection can condition this dog to accept city life. Yet if raised at the same time as the master's children, a Beauceron can prove to be an affectionate and protective pet.

Characteristics

General appearance: solid, powerfully built, muscular but not heavy. Supple and relaxed bearing. This tough, intimidating sheep-dog bears some resemblance to the Dobermann Pinscher.
Height: 61 to 70 cm (24 to 27½ in.).
Weight: not specified.
Head: long, flat or slightly rounded skull. Barely defined stop. Slightly convex muzzle neither narrow nor pointed. Tight, highly coloured lips. Strong, well-formed teeth in scissor bite. Nose well developed, never split, always black.
Eyes: horizontal, round, dark, but may be lighter in pale dogs.
Ears: set high. Rather flat and short. Under F.C.I. standards, may be cropped and carried erect, pointing slightly forward.
Neck: muscular. No dewlap.
Body: oblique, medium-long sloping shoulders. Broad, deep brisket. Level back. Broad and taut loin, croup slightly sloping.
Tail: carried low, falling at least to the point of the hock, slightly hooking at the tip.
Forequarters: legs muscular and trim, well balanced.
Hindquarters: legs well balanced. Strong hocks. Double dew-claws.
Feet: strong, round, hard. Flexible pads. Black nails.
Coat: very short on head, a bit longer on the back. Strong, thick, dense, and flat on the body. Undercoat very short, fine, dense, downy, preferably mouse-grey.
Colour: black with tan (squirrel red) markings below the eyes, on the muzzle, chest, throat, feet, and under the tail. Also black, red, grey, or grey and tan.
Faults: skull flat or too round. Stop too pronounced, or no stop. Head too small or too heavy. Eyes too light. Poor ear carriage. Incomplete set of teeth. Brisket too cylindrical. Short or curled tail. Coat too short or too long. Squat feet. Single dew-claws. Extensive white markings on the upper chest; tan markings too plentiful or poorly distributed.

Practical information: The Beauceron is temperamentally unsuited for urban life, though it seldom suffers from health problems. Check to make sure the dew-claws do not become ingrown. A dog that lives outdoors should be brushed briskly every day; if it is damp, dry the dog with a towel and brush again. The Beauceron is slow to mature, and training will, therefore, be ineffective if it is begun before the dog is two years old.

THE DOUBLE DEW-CLAW
The dew-claw is the fifth toe of the dog. Located on the inside of the paw, its position corresponds to that of the human thumb, although it is virtually useless. As a general rule, there is always a dew-claw on each foreleg. Some dogs may not appear at dog shows unless their dew-claws have been removed. By contrast, the Beauceron has a *double* dew-claw on its hind legs, or six toes in all. Characteristic of the breed, these dew-claws must never be removed if the dog is to be shown.

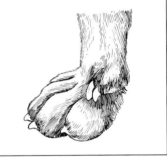

SHEEP-DOG TRIALS
One of the best-known organizers of sheep-dog trials is the International Sheep-dog Society, founded in Scotland in 1906. Representing countries in the United Kingdom, the group oversees a series of national trials that culminate in an international championship contest.

These performance tests are work-related, and they involve several stages. The degree of difficulty posed by a course depends upon its championship level. A typical event requires a dog to herd 25 sheep as fast as possible from one pen to another along a winding obstacle route. Dogs must not harm sheep, and biting brings disqualification. The handler accompanies his dog, giving orders by voice, whistle, or hand. Prizes go to the most intelligent, energetic, and obedient dogs.

Sheep-dog trials are popular wherever sheep are raised, though the contests vary greatly from place to place. In France, the Beauceron is a regular sheep-dog champion, yet it seldom appears at trials outside Continental Europe.

Bedlington Terrier

Gypsy Dog

With its pear-shaped head, its curly coat closely trimmed like a poodle's, and its odd but not inelegant lines, this dog bears a clear resemblance to a lamb. The Bedlington's fragile appearance is, however, deceptive. In earlier days, when it was known as the Rothbury Terrier, this strongly built dog had shorter legs and was used to hunt not only such vermin as mice, rats, and badgers, but also foxes and, perhaps, even wolves.

In the late eighteenth and early nineteenth centuries, miners in Northumberland used the Rothbury underground to rid their mine tunnels of rats. Later, they crossed it with the Whippet, among others, and produced a longer-legged, more refined Bedlington Terrier, without sacrificing the breed's original qualities. The new breed's terrier endurance and racing-hound speed made it a long-standing companion of poachers, hence its nickname, Gypsy Dog. An all-purpose animal, it could go after an otter, run down a rabbit, and hold its own in a dogfight.

Gradually, it became valued as a companion dog. Modifications in breed type were made and the Bedlington Terrier was transformed into the charming and comfort-loving creature known today. Artistic trimming and barbering give the dog its distinctive, lamb-like silhouette.

Although the Bedlington is, at times, fairly stubborn and often very aggressive towards other dogs, it does show a great deal of affection and absolute loyalty to its family.

AUS.	CAN.	S. AF.	U.K.	F.C.I.
●	●	●	●	●

ORIGINS

Basically British, this breed probably hails from Northumberland, although its exact origin remains a mystery. It is certain, however, that the Dandie Dinmont Terrier is one of its ancestors, and that a cross with the Whippet helped to refine its lines. Some authorities attribute the Bedlington's shape and physique to the presence of Poodle genes. While this hypothesis is intriguing, it is disputed. The first officially listed Bedlington Terrier is a male, Old Flint, that belonged to a certain Squire Trevelyan. It was whelped in 1782. Documents trace Old Flint's descendants as far down as 1873. However, the first 30 Bedlingtons registered with the British Kennel Club possessed no pedigree; in fact, the parents of only 11 are mentioned. For this reason, therefore, it is impossible to establish conclusively whether they descend from Old Flint.

Characteristics

General appearance: graceful, agile. Fully arched back gives impression of delicacy and strength. Especially talented at coursing. Light and flexible gait.

Height: 38 to 40.6 cm (15 to 16 in.). Under Canadian standards, 42 cm (16½ in.) for the adult dog; 39.4 cm (15½ in.) for the bitch.

Weight: 7.7 to 10.4 kg (17 to 23 lb).

Head: narrow, rounded skull, covered with a full, nearly white, silky topknot. No stop; unbroken line from occiput to nose. Tight lips, no flews. Black nose with blue or blue and tan coat; brown nose with liver or sand coat. Broad nostrils. Jaws long and tapering. Level bite.

Eyes: small, shiny, well set in. Dark to light hazel depending on coat colour.

Ears: medium size, filbert-shaped, set low, falling close to the cheek. Covered with fine short hair, with a fringe of whitish, silky hair on the tips.

Neck: long and tapering. No dewlap. The head carried rather erect.

Body: muscular, but extremely flexible. Flat ribs and deep, rather broad brisket. Roached back. Very arched loin. Slightly curved croup. Flanks tucked up.

Tail: medium length, thick at the base, tapering towards the tip. Slightly curved, set low but never curled over the back.

Forequarters: legs straight, wider at the brisket than at the feet. Pasterns long and slightly sloping.

Hindquarters: legs medium size and muscular; because of the arched loin, they appear longer than the forelegs. The hocks should be strong and well let down.

Feet: long, hare-footed. Pads thick and tightly closed.

Coat: thick and linty, with a tendency to curl, particularly on the head and face. Woolly undercoat.

Colour: blue, blue and tan, liver, or sandy. Dark shades are preferred by breeders.

Practical information: This terrier enjoys good health but, given its fighting instinct, keep a first-aid kit on hand. Clean its delicate ears regularly with a dry cotton swab. Its coat requires clipping about every month and a half. Because grooming this dog is difficult, anyone attempting it for the first time should seek instruction from a specialist. Between clippings, a light daily brushing is sufficient.

GROOMING THE BEDLINGTON TERRIER

To accentuate the distinctive silhouette of the animal, start by thinning the coat. Then clip the body hair (1) to about a 1-centimetre (½-inch) length, accentuating the curve of the back so that it has the required rise. Next, remove the hairs between the toes (2). The hair on the tail should be clipped short (3) but left thicker at the base. Groom the head to emphasize its oval shape (4): trim the curls on the top of the skull and on the nape of the neck. Shave the upper chest, neck, and throat, as well as part of the head (5) up to the horizontal line that starts at the top of the ear and goes to within 1 centimetre (½ inch) of the outer corner of the eye. Shave the ears, too (6), leaving a tassel of hair at the tips. The areas near the neck and shoulders should be layered (7) to blend with the shaved area.

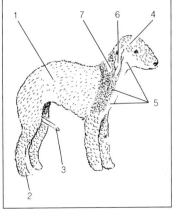

Belgian Shepherd Dog

Belgian Sheep-dog

Groenendael

For ages, closely related types of herding dogs guarded the flocks in Belgium and other European countries, until fenced lands, railways, and motor vehicles put them out of work late in the nineteenth century. Fearful that these dogs might disappear completely, breeders got together to determine which qualities were worth preserving in a breed to be officially named the Belgian Shepherd Dog. They agreed on everything except the type of coat and its colour. So four varieties—the long-haired Groenendael and Tervuren, the short-haired Malinois, and the rough-coated Laekenois—survived. These are generally recognized as one breed except in the United States, where the first three are considered separate breeds (known as the Belgian Sheep-dog, Belgian Tervuren, and Malinois respectively). The rare Laekenois is not recognized in the United States.

Bright and athletic, the Belgian Shepherd has excelled in police and war work. Used as a guard dog in bars, it never bothers customers; but once the establishments close for the night, intruders risk a vicious attack. Yet the dog can also be an endearing family pet—as long as this intelligent, sensitive animal has an owner who understands its nature and is willing to train it patiently.

AUS.	CAN.	S. AF.	U.K.	F.C.I.
●	●	●	●	●

ORIGINS

The Belgian Shepherd Dog is descended from an ancient and numberless variety of herding dogs. Fifteenth-century drawings show ancestors in the company of the dukes of Bourgogne and Hapsburg. In 1897, Belgium's national kennel club recognized three varieties: the Groenendael, the Tervuren, and the Malinois. The Laekenois owes its existence to enthusiasts in France and Holland. After the First World War almost destroyed the breed, most fanciers concentrated on the black Groenendael, deciding it would be the only long-coated variety. Despite this, some enthusiasts revived the fawn-coloured Tervuren dogs. The breed almost died again in the Second World War, but a few survivors rebuilt it once more.

Tervuren

Characteristics

General appearance: well proportioned, elegant, and hardy.

Height: 61 to 66 cm (24 to 26 in.) for the adult dog; 56 to 61 cm (22 to 24 in.) for the bitch.

Weight: under F.C.I. standards, 30 kg (66 lb). Elsewhere, in proportion to height.

Head: clean-cut, strong, lean, chiselled, long. Muzzle tapering towards nose. Well-balanced bridge. Slight stop. Narrow cheeks. Tight, wide, black lips. Even or scissor bite. Black nose, flared nostrils.

Eyes: medium size, slight almond shape, neither deep nor prominent. Brown, the darker the better. Lids ringed with black. Lively and intelligent expression.

Ears: set high, triangular. Stiff, straight external ear rounded at base.

Body: long, oblique shoulders. Chest not too wide, but deep and low. Level back, broad and muscular. Moderately wide croup, slightly sloping. Stomach gracefully curving from the chest.

Tail: firmly set on, medium long. At rest hanging down, the tip curled slightly backwards. When in motion lifted.

Forequarters: strongly boned with lean, powerful muscles; legs long and muscular. Pasterns medium long, strong, and slightly sloping.

Hindquarters: powerful, but not bulky. Thighs wide and very muscular. Legs long, wide, muscular, angled to the hocks without excess. Hocks well let down, wide and muscular. No dew-claws.

Coat: long-haired varieties (Groenendael and Tervuren) have short hair on the head, outside the ears, and on the lower part of the legs. Long fringes down the backs of the forearms. Long, smooth hair on the rest of the body. Long and abundant hair around the neck and chest forms a ruff. Cluster of hair inside the ears. Croup covered with long hair, forming a culotte. Plumed tail. Short-haired Malinois has comparatively short, straight hair with dense undercoat. Longer neck hair forms ruff. Rough-haired Laekenois has rough, dry, harsh hair with a thick, woolly undercoat.

Colour: Groenendael, black; small white markings permissible. Malinois, shades of red, fawn or grey with black overlay. Tervuren, red, fawn, or grey with black overlay. Laekenois, reddish fawn with black shading.

Practical information: These are healthy, robust dogs that easily adjust to inclement weather. All varieties need lots of exercise or they will gain weight. Given adequate time outdoors, the Tervuren calmly accepts the confines of an apartment or flat, whereas the Malinois is best suited to country life. The long-haired Groenendael and Tervuren require daily combing and brushing. Special attention must be given to their undercoats during the shedding season—dead hair can mat their coats, particularly the culottes and ruffs. It is also advisable to pluck excess hair from their inner ears and to clip long hair from the outer ears and from between the toes.

Berger Picard

Picardy Sheep-dog

AUS.	CAN.	S. AF.	U.K.	F.C.I.
				●

Rugged in appearance, of medium build, energetic yet dignified, this shaggy-haired sheep-dog has earned its reputation as a reliable worker. Beneath well-arched eyebrows, its intelligent, wide-awake eyes dart back and forth in lively fashion, alert to everything around it. In days gone by, no sheep could stray beyond the dog's scan, no predator move in unnoticed or unchallenged. Today, farm machinery and modern transportation are eliminating more and more of this guardian's ancestral duties. Nevertheless, the breed still takes well to training and participates eagerly in working and defence trials, where it can display its skills with competence and style.

The Berger Picard's rough, dry outer coat, together with its fine and dense undercoat, provide waterproof protection against the worst weather conditions. The breed is loyal, stubborn at times, and spirited when the situation calls for it. It has always been a favourite in the pastures of northern France. When the task was to protect the flocks, the light-coloured Berger was especially valued, because it was easy to distinguish from predators at night. The breed has gradually been transformed into a companion dog, though its tough past as a sheep-dog hardly prepared it for domestic life. Yet it does adapt easily and makes a calm and well-mannered house-pet.

ORIGINS

The Berger Picard is descended from ancient sheep-dog breeds known in France for many centuries. Paintings and engravings from the Middle Ages depict medium-size, well-built dogs with hard, long hair, which greatly resemble the present Berger Picard. However, the history of this dog remains unclear. It is known only that the present type was perfected by breeders who retained the essential characteristics of the ancient sheep-herders. The Berger Picard was first shown in 1863. Selective breeding began after 1898, but the Berger Picard nearly disappeared during the First World War. It was officially recognized in 1925 and, by 1948, breeders had again established a fixed type.

TRAINING SHEEP-DOGS

The qualities of a good sheep-dog like the Berger Picard are, to a great extent, inherited. Generally, a puppy born of dogs working with sheep—parents themselves descended from generations of working dogs—will likely carry on the family tradition and become a reliable sheep-dog. But its innate potential must be developed through training, which begins as soon as the pup is from six to eight weeks old. At this age, the apprentice is taught to bite a piece of sheepskin without tearing out any tufts of wool. According to tradition, if it passes this first test the dog will almost certainly succeed in its life-work and guard its beloved flock with courage and care.

In the beginning, the young pup is held on a lead to watch the work of experienced dogs and learn to imitate them. It will observe, for example, that rather than biting its charges, a good sheep-dog will just nip at the sheep.

When a French shepherd takes his flock to graze, he designates a specific area, allowing about one square metre or yard per head. Each animal must eat its plot bare, and at one feeding, because a sheep will not graze where it or another sheep has trodden. Using his heel, the shepherd traces the outline of the grazing area in the grass and has his dog sniff the boundary line. The flock must remain within this boundary. Should a sheep attempt to stray outside its territory, the dog must immediately bring it back. Again, the dog works on a lead at first, and is not set free until it has properly learned to do what its master wishes.

Depending on the dog's talents, the shepherd will train it either to work closely and only on command, or to work on its own, well apart from the shepherd. In the latter case, the fully trained sheep-dog patrols the far side of the flock, some 300 metres (or yards) away from the shepherd.

Training a dog to take initiative and act independently takes about three years. The result is a singularly reliable working animal.

Characteristics

General appearance: lively, well built, elegant.
Height: 60 to 65 cm (23½ to 25½ in.) for the adult dog; 55 to 60 cm (21½ to 23½ in.) for the bitch.
Weight: not specified.
Head: well proportioned. Slight stop. Well-arched brows do not cover the eye. Slightly arched forehead. Fairly round cheeks. Muzzle strong, not too long. Black nose. Lips tight and lean. Slight moustache, small beard. Powerful, well-developed jaws.
Eyes: medium size, almond-shaped, not prominent. Dark, never lighter than hazel.
Ears: medium size, broad at the base, set fairly high, always erect, the tips slightly rounded.
Neck: strong and muscular, good length, clearing the shoulders well, carrying the head proudly.
Body: brisket deep but not lower than the elbow. Level back. Solid loin. Belly slightly raised. Shoulders long, oblique, muscular.
Tail: hairy, hanging. At rest, slight curve at the tip reaches the hocks.
Forequarters: legs well balanced, lean.

Hindquarters: long, well-muscled thighs. Solid, supple legs. Hocks slightly bent. Leg bones are hardy and lean.
Feet: rounded and short, well closed, arched. Nails strong and short. Pads firm.
Coat: hard, semi-long, rough and brittle outer coat; neither curly nor flat. Insulating undercoat of fine, dense hair.
Colour: grey, grey-black, grey with black highlights, grey-blue, grey-brown, light or dark tawny, or a mixture of these shades.
Faults: head disproportionate, lacking definition, insufficient or over-abundant hair. Skull flat or dome-shaped. Sloping forehead. Cheeks too full, flaccid. Muzzle too long, too thin, or too thick. Drooping flews. Poor bite. Ears too big, set on too low, or too close together; badly carried. Expression tired or evasive. Tail carried low or missing. Coat too long or too short, curly or very flat, soft or woolly. White, black, pied, or excessive white markings on the chest or feet are unacceptable.

Practical information: In the city, the Berger Picard is susceptible to chronic eczema. Dogs ten years of age and older may also be plagued by advanced osteo-arthritic problems. Companion dogs should be groomed daily with a hard brush and a large-tooth comb. Do not comb the coat when it is wet as this might rip out tufts of hair.

Bernese Mountain Dog

Swiss Mountain Dog

Long considered lowly farm animals, Swiss Mountain Dogs were, until relatively recently, treated with indifference by canine experts. Today, it is agreed that the important features of this handsome family should be recognized, and breeders are working hard to maintain the distinctive characteristics of the four varieties.

The Bernese Mountain Dog, the only long-coated member of the quartet—and thought by many to be the most beautiful—was first recognized in 1892. It is the best-known variety outside Europe and in English-speaking countries. The Greater Swiss Mountain Dog, a larger relative of the Bernese, had a fixed breed type by 1905. The curly-tailed Appenzell, as its name indicates, hails from the canton of Appenzell. The Entlebuch is the smallest of the group.

All four varieties share many sterling qualities that make them excellent guardians and companion dogs: unwavering loyalty, an affectionate nature, superior intelligence, and a remarkable memory. It is said that, as cattle dogs, they can recognize each animal in the herd they are tending. In his book, *Die Schweizer Hunderassen* (Swiss Dog Breeds), Hans Räber mentions the characteristics so highly valued by Swiss farmers: 'A dog is good when it is watchful and lively ... does not run into the crops, protects its master in difficulty ... and does not poach or wander....'

AUS.	CAN.	S. AF.	U.K.	F.C.I.
●	●	●	●	●

ORIGINS

The four types of Swiss Mountain Dog are believed to have descended from the Tibetan Mastiff. According to experts, Switzerland had no mastiff-like dogs in prehistoric times. The first such animals were imported from Asia by Xerxes, and later introduced into Europe by the Phoenicians and Greeks. At the time of the Roman conquests, these burly dogs accompanied the herds of livestock that were destined for consumption by the legions. One of the major army routes to Transalpine Gaul passed through Saint Gotthard, and these mastiff-like canines remained in that area. The ancestry of today's Swiss Mountain Dogs can be traced to these travellers of antiquity.

FOUR MOUNTAIN DOGS, MANY ADMIRABLE QUALITIES

Nicknamed the 'bear cub,' the Bernese Mountain dog—the 'most beautiful dog in the world,' according to at least one canine authority—is very similar to the Greater Swiss. However, the Bernese coat is long and wavy, while that of the Greater Swiss is short and close-fitting.

An excellent draught and guard dog, energetic and ever-willing, the Bernese knows how to keep the most obstinate cow in line. This dog's temperament requires firm but gentle handling; harshness accomplishes little, if anything. Although it learns very slowly, the Bernese retains everything it is taught. In Switzerland, it belongs to the sporting group of breeds and fares well in defence and life-saving trials. The Romans used it as a fighting dog, sending it into battle wearing a protective collar studded with iron spikes.

The Greater Swiss performs almost the same functions as the Bernese. It has been known in the cantons since the twelfth century and, in the fourteenth, accompanied soldiers to war. In 1489, an edict issued by Hans Waldman, the burgomaster of Zurich, ordered that this dog be exterminated because it was harming game and the vineyards. However, farmers refused to part with their faithful companions, and the edict was never heeded. An easily trained draught and guard dog, the Greater Swiss also makes an affectionate pet.

The Appenzell, with its distinctive tail curled tightly over its back, can withstand the bitter cold of the mountain winter as well as the intense summer heat. Tireless and always active, it demonstrates its intelligence by its ability to maintain order in a herd of several hundred animals. This is a most affectionate dog, deeply attached to its master.

The Entlebuch is the smallest of the four Swiss varieties, originally from the cantons of Lucerne and Berne and born, strangely enough, without a tail.

Characteristics

General appearance: a self-confident and good-natured breed, the active, sturdy Bernese Mountain Dog is slow to mature. Vigorous, solidly built.

Height: under Canadian standards, 62 to 70 cm (24½ to 27½ in.) for the adult dog and 58 to 66 cm (22¾ to 26 in.) for the bitch. Elsewhere, 64 to 70 cm (25 to 27 in.) for the adult dog and 58 to 66 cm (23 to 26 in.) for the bitch.

Weight: under F.C.I. standards, 40 kg (88 lb). Elsewhere, not specified.

Head: skull flat and broad with slight furrow. Stop well defined. Muzzle strong, straight. Lips black, slightly developed.

Eyes: dark brown, almond-shaped. Showing no haw.

Ears: medium size, set high, triangular shape. Lying flat in repose. When alert, the ears are brought slightly forward, and raised at the base.

Neck: strong and muscular, medium long.

Body: compact rather than long. Broad chest with good depth of brisket reaching at least to the elbow. Well ribbed. Strong, muscular loin. Solid and level back. Broad and strong croup. Rump smoothly rounded.

Tail: bushy, falling to the hocks, then curving up slightly. When the dog is alert and on the move, the tail may be raised, but it is never curled or carried above the level of the back.

Forequarters: legs straight and strong. Shoulders long, strong, and sloping. Pasterns flex slightly.

Hindquarters: long, strong thighs. Stifles well bent. Hocks strong, well let down, and turning neither inward nor outward. Dew-claws should be removed.

Feet: short, rounded, and compact.

Coat: soft, silky, long and slightly wavy, but should not curl when mature. Bright sheen.

Colour: jet black with brown-red on the cheeks, legs, the brisket, and over the eyes. White markings on head and brisket are essential. White paws and tip of tail preferable.

Faults: eyes too light. Ears or tail badly carried. Faded or impure colours are unacceptable. White neck ring. Markings absent.

Practical information: Swiss Mountain Dogs are a particularly hardy breed and rarely ill. However, they need a good deal of space. Although these dogs can be reliable guardians and workers, they do not take well to a change of ownership after they have reached 18 months of age: health problems may develop, or they may become too aggressive to manage. Their coats need vigorous brushing from time to time. The dew-claws should be removed at birth.

Bichon Frise

Teneriffe, Bichon Frisé

Since the fourteenth century, when it was brought to Europe from the Canary Islands, this playful powder-puff has charmed countless generations with its tricks and its lively, almost human expression. Very much in vogue in sixteenth-century France, the Bichon Frise paraded happily through the royal apartments together with another highly prized *bichon* (French for lap-dog), the Maltese. When it was no longer a court favourite, it pranced with equal zest in the circus ring. Today the breed is especially popular in Italy, France, Great Britain, and throughout North America.

AUS.	CAN.	S. AF.	U.K.	F.C.I.
●	●	●	●	●

ORIGINS

The Bichon first appeared during the fourteenth century, a cross between the Maltese and the Poodle. In spite of its alternate name, the Teneriffe, the dog has no Spanish breed's blood; it has been officially recognized as Franco-Belgian.

Characteristics

General appearance: proud, alert, sturdy.
Height: under Canadian standards, 22.8 to 30.5 cm (9 to 12 in.) for the adult dog and 24 to 26.6 cm (9½ to 10½ in.) for the bitch. Elsewhere, 22.8 to 28 cm (9 to 11 in.).
Weight: not specified.
Head: skull longer than the muzzle. Nose rounded, black. Fine lips, fairly tight. Muzzle not thick or snipy.
Eyes: dark, with dark rims. Fairly round, not too large.
Ears: narrow and delicate, hanging close to head, well covered with long, finely curled hair.

Body: chest well developed, deep brisket. Flanks well raised at the belly. Shoulders rather sloping. Loin broad, well muscled, slightly rounded.
Tail: usually raised and curved, but never curled.
Forequarters: legs straight, well balanced, fine-boned. Pasterns short and straight.
Hindquarters: broad and well-muscled thighs.
Coat: double coat. Fine, silky hair, which is very loosely curled, not flat or twisted, 7.6 to 10 cm (3 to 4 in.) long.
Colour: pure white. Dark skin desirable.

Practical information: The Bichon Frise's coat needs very special attention. It must be groomed daily with a stiff brush, and the dog bathed once a month. Runny eyes are a recurrent problem—due to obstructions in the tear ducts—and must be cleaned regularly with a cotton swab dipped in a special lotion; consult your veterinarian.

Billy

This French hound was named after the small village in Poitou where the breed was developed a century ago. The Billy's ancestor is the King's White Dog, which made up the royal packs in France for centuries prior to the French Revolution. The packs were disbanded around 1725, and the King's White gradually disappeared, but not before it passed its genes to the Billy and, possibly, the Harrier in Britain.

The Billy's inherited instincts and quick reflexes make it an excellent small-game hunter. Blessed with great stamina as well, the Billy can gallop long distances in pursuit of quarry.

AUS.	CAN.	S. AF.	U.K.	F.C.I.
				●

ORIGINS

During the late eighteenth century, a French breeder named de Céris interbred King's Whites with some small Swiss hounds to obtain a new breed: the Céris. The present-day Billy was the result of a cross between a Céris and a de Montemboeuf.

Characteristics

General appearance: well built; lightweight yet strong. Large forequarters in proportion to body.
Height: 60 to 70 cm (23½ to 27½ in.) for the adult dog; 58 to 62 cm (23 to 24½ in.) for the bitch.
Weight: not specified.
Head: fairly slim, fine, medium long. Forehead slightly rounded, not very broad. Prominent occiput. Nose rather squared off, muzzle rather broad and straight, slightly rounded, moderately long. Nose black or rusty brown. The upper lip covers the lower, which is often visible at the corners of the mouth.
Eyes: alert, dark, ringed with black or brown.

Ears: medium size, rather flat, slightly curled.
Body: back rather broad, strong, slightly convex. Brisket deep and fairly narrow. Ribs flat. Flanks rather long and slightly raised. Broad loin, slightly harp-shaped. Shoulders rather long and close to the body.
Tail: long and strong. Sometimes slightly hairy.
Forequarters: legs strong and flat, straight.
Hindquarters: thighs moderately muscled, hocks slightly bent, broad and strong.
Coat: skin flexible, thin, usually white. Hair short, stiff.
Colour: white, light tan, white with markings, light orange, or lemon.

Practical information: This dog must not be exposed to severe cold or it may contract bronchitis.

Bleu de Gascogne

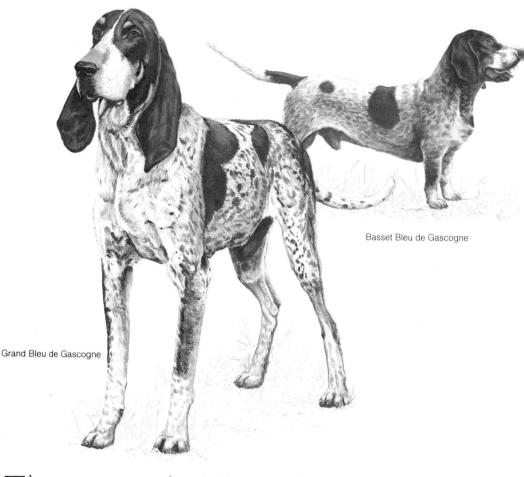

Basset Bleu de Gascogne

Grand Bleu de Gascogne

There are no more wolves in Gascony and, therefore, no more Grands Bleus and Petits Bleus—or precious few.

In its early days, the courageous Bleu de Gascogne hunted wolves and all manner of big game, winning the admiration of many for its spirit and sporting ability. However, despite its prowess in coursing hare as well as deer, the breed has nearly disappeared along with the big-game hunting packs of France.

Although it resembles the American Bluetick Coonhound, the Bleu de Gascogne, with its slate-coloured coat, noble-looking head, and melancholy expression, is an ancient and distinct breed. Its ancestry can be traced to a Bloodhound brought back to fourteenth-century France from the Ardennes. Gaston Phoebus, Count de Foix, returned from war on the banks of the Rhine with the ancestral dog in tow. From the Bloodhound the Grand Bleu acquired its solemn expression, keen sense of smell, and powerful voice.

An excellent but rather plodding hunter with an incomparable nose and a distinctive sound, the breed earned a place of honour in the royal packs

AUS.	CAN.	S. AF.	U.K.	F.C.I.
			●	●

ORIGINS

The Grand Bleu de Gascogne is descended from Bloodhounds that were probably crossed with local hounds in Gascony. The breed may have acquired its blue coat as a result of the hot, dry climate in southern France. By judiciously selecting suitable stock, breeders produced finer hounds with each new generation. The Grand Bleu de Gascogne itself figured prominently in the development of several breeds of large dogs such as the Français Blanc et Noir. Bred down from the Grand Bleu, the Petit Bleu is the product of careful mating done by the huntsmen of the Midi. They chose the smallest offspring from each litter and bred them together.

of Henry IV of France. After countless generations, however, its lines softened and became more refined. With its long, strong limbs, today's Grand Bleu de Gascogne is a taller, more slender hound than its forbears were.

As for the Petit Bleu, this proud and daring hound is capable of great speed and excels at hunting hare. A first-class baying dog, solidly built and always dependable, it also possesses the same expert trailing and hunting qualities as the Grand Bleu.

Characteristics

General appearance: an ancient French breed of proud bearing. Distinctive blue cast on coat. Petit Bleu, shorter, more compact than the Grand Bleu. Although the Petit Bleu de Gascogne was highly regarded as a hunting-dog in France earlier in this century, it has become rare nowadays.
Height: for the Grand Bleu, 63.5 to 68.6 cm (25 to 27 in.). For the Petit Bleu, 50.8 to 58.4 cm (20 to 23 in.).
Weight: not specified.
Head: elongated, rather large, covered with fairly loose skin, with one or two wrinkles along the cheeks. Head of Petit Bleu is more refined, rather long, somewhat light. Skull a little rounded, fairly prominent occiput, with a barely visible stop in the Grand; lean and slanted in the Petit. Both have a long muzzle, the flews falling rather heavily, covering the lower jaw. Nose is black. Black palate.
Eyes: dark chestnut, with thick rims lined in black, allowing a little of the haw to show, not prominent. Sad, trusting expression.
Ears: fine, set low, curled inward. Ears of Petit Bleu less wavy than those of the Grand Bleu.
Neck: medium long, rounded at the top. With dewlap.
Body: brisket well formed and deep. Back rather long, well supported. Ribs slightly rounded. Loin a little flat in the Grand, slightly harp-shaped and compact in the Petit. Prominent haunches. Croup sloping.
Tail: well set on, fairly long, carried out and up in a semicircle.
Forequarters: legs well muscled, forearms strong.
Hindquarters: broad and well muscled. Thighs long. Hocks low and not compact.
Feet: oval. Long, deep and well padded.
Coat: skin is black or heavily patched. Mucous membranes and genitals black. In the Grand Bleu de Gascogne, hair is fairly thick, not too short, and plentiful. In the Petit Bleu, hair is semi-thick.
Colour: black on a white ground, having a slate-blue cast. Tan markings above the eyes, on the cheeks, jowls, feet, and under the tail. In the Petit, the coat is blue with tan markings on the head, inner ear, and legs.
Faults: in the Grand Bleu de Gascogne, short head, skull too flat. Ears short and set high. Light-coloured eyes. Spindly legs. Slouching croup. Absence of tan markings. Off-colour coat. Down in the pasterns. In the Petit Bleu de Gascogne, skull too large. Light-coloured eyes. An off-colour coat is unacceptable.

Practical information: The Grand Bleu de Gascogne needs too much exercise to be happy living indoors. Around the age of 11 or 12, it has a tendency to develop osteo-arthritis, with the possibility of paralysis. With its gentle and affectionate nature, the Petit Bleu makes an ideal companion dog. Its eyes are susceptible to conjuctivitis, caused by various irritations. Its long ears must be carefully checked.

THE BASSET BLEU DE GASCOGNE

The origin of the Basset Bleu de Gascogne is highly controversial. Some claim it descends from a mutant in a nineteenth-century pack of Grand Bleus, an ancestor that would account for the Basset Bleu's colour, voice, and keen scenting ability. Others, such as canine historian Gaston Dhers, maintain that this Basset, in spite of its name, is not originally from Gascony. Finally, according to a Major Malric, an important breeder of this hound during the First World War, the Basset Bleu de Gascogne is just a Basset Artésien-Normand, and its blue coat a mere quirk of nature.

Whatever its origins, the Basset Bleu is an excellent little hunting-dog, especially for hare and deer. It is full-voiced, and some even say that four Bassets can make as much noise as a whole pack. Because it does not tire easily and is naturally obedient and easy to train, hunters favour it over many other dogs. The breed makes up for a certain slowness by its great confidence and remarkable hunting ability. The Basset Bleu de Gascogne has a gentle expression and a shy manner, making it a pleasant companion dog despite its frequent baying.

This dog stands between 34 and 42 centimetres (13½ and 16½ inches) and weighs about 15 kilograms (33 pounds). Its blue coat has black markings more or less all over, with traces of tan accents on the cheeks and muzzle and inside the ears and legs. Its coat is not too fine. The skin may be dark or light, and is marbled with black patches. The slim head has an elongated S-shaped profile. The Basset Bleu's dark brown eyes have a kind but sad expression. Sometimes the lower lid, slightly drooping, reveals a little of the haw. The ears are long, fine, and set on low, highlighting the skull. The nose is black, with broad nostrils.

Bloodhound

Saint Hubert

Although known world-wide by an English name, the Bloodhound is nonetheless a Belgian. It is, in fact, the Saint Hubert, the great pack hound raised in the Ardennes since the beginning of the Middle Ages, and preserved and selectively bred by the British after the eleventh century. It was then that it was given the name Bloodhound. In 1553, Dr. Johannes Caius, the physician and canine expert, gave this explanation of the name: 'It is well known that [Bloodhounds] follow their prey not only while alive, but also after death when they have caught the scent of blood.' However, this interpretation has been contested: some believe that 'blood' signifies a pure-bred dog or a nobleman's dog, much as 'blood horse' refers to a thoroughbred. Whatever the derivation of the name, William the Conqueror valued the animal enough to decide that on his lands, other breeds of dogs must have three toes amputated so as not to compete with the Bloodhound for game.

Powerful and solid, the Bloodhound moves with great dignity. The head, with its wrinkled brow and distinctive jowls, its long ears and drooping eyes, resembles the Basset Hound's. But the Bloodhound's expression is more solemn. Its skull is long and narrow, and the occiput well developed, forming one of the Bloodhound's more noticeable features. Endowed with the keenest sense of smell of any domestic animal, it is reputed to be the best of all trackers.

AUS.	CAN.	S. AF.	U.K.	F.C.I.
●	●	●	●	●

ORIGINS

Arrian of Nicomedia, the second-century Greek historian, described a hound called the Segusium in Cynegeticus, a treatise on hunting. The Saint Hubert probably descends from this Segusium of the Celts and Gauls. The Saint Hubert was established around the eighth century at the Abbey of Saint Hubert in the Ardennes of Belgium. Each year the monks sent six of the most attractive new members of the breed to the king of France on his birthday. The court lavished attention on these prized dogs, even assigning valets to look after their every need. During the Crusades, the Saint Hubert temporarily lost ground to the Saint Louis Grey Dog, brought to France from the East. Faster, but more impulsive and disobedient, the Grey enjoyed only a brief moment of glory before the Saint Hubert reclaimed its place in the royal packs. It held this honoured position until 1570 when Charles IX of France replaced it with the King's White Dog, itself descended from white Saint Huberts. The Saint Hubert breed died out at the beginning of the French Revolution in 1789. Fortunately, in the eleventh century, some black Saint Huberts had crossed the Channel with William the Conqueror. In England, the Duke of Normandy refined the breed in his kennels and, in effect, founded a new line, the Bloodhounds. In those days monasteries, too, had their kennels, and clerics rode to hounds. Churchmen deserve as much credit as the nobility do for developing the Bloodhound and maintaining its purity down through the centuries. The breed has been recognized and shown in Britain since the earliest dog shows.

Characteristics

General appearance: solid, dignified, with a measured gait. Movement is elastic, swinging, free.

Height: about 64 to 69 cm (25 to 27 in.) for the adult dog; about 58 to 64 cm (23 to 25 in.) for the bitch.

Weight: about 40 to 50 kg (90 to 110 lb) for the adult dog; about 36 to 45 kg (80 to 100 lb) for the bitch.

Head: characteristically large and long, but narrow. Loose skin hangs in deep folds. Nostrils large, open. Jaws long and broad near the jowls; hollow and thin under the cheeks. Jowls are long and drooping, continuing into the folds of the neck. Scissor bite.

Eyes: medium size, fairly well set in, deep hazel or brown, depending on coat colour. Should be free from interference by lashes.

Ears: long and set low, thin, soft, covered with silky hair, falling in graceful folds. Lower parts curling inwards and backwards.

Body: deep brisket. Broad and deep back. Solid loin. Belly slightly arched. Shoulders sloping and muscular.

Tail: long, carried elegantly above the topline, set high, not curled.

Forequarters: legs straight, strong, rounded bone structure. Pasterns strong.

Hindquarters: legs very sturdy. Hocks bent and let down.

Feet: round, cat-footed, strong, and well knuckled in.

Coat: smooth, short, dense, and weather resistant.

Colour: black and tan, liver and tan, red, tawny. The black must extend on the back, loin, top of the neck, and top of the head. A little white on the chest, legs, and top of the tail permissible.

Practical information: Exercise is absolutely vital for the Bloodhound. When confined indoors, it becomes restless. It is preferable to feed this hound in the evening; in fact, it tends to suffer from stomach cramps, and activity after meals is not advised.

Border Terrier

P rimarily a working dog, the tough little Border Terrier is able to keep pace with a horse despite its small stature—it is no bigger than a Pug. It takes its name from the area where it was originally bred and where it thrived long before it became known by the rest of the world: the border between Scotland and England. The region, located at the base of the Cheviot Hills, also lent its name to another versatile little working breed, the Border Collie.

In this hilly area where farms were widely scattered and difficult to protect, the Border Terrier proved its worth by disposing of the hill foxes that had acquired a taste not only for poultry, but also for sheep and newborn calves. Undaunted by rain and inclement weather because of its double covering—a dense and wiry coat over a thick undercoat—the little Border would uncomplainingly spend days on end in this damp, cold countryside. To run for long hours and long distances behind a mounted hunter, a dog had to be light and long-legged enough so that it would not tire too quickly. This dynamo, with its exceptional endurance and spirit, summoned up enough energy after running the fox down to boldly attack it—even if the quarry had managed to take refuge underground in its lair. Patient, even obstinate, its small size an advantage, the Border Terrier would remain alert near the foxhole, waiting as long as was necessary to trap the prey in its solid jaws and finish the job.

Owners of this able, reliable dog were perversely pleased that it was not quite as elegant as some of its show-dog relatives. So it is not surprising that some fanciers were upset when the British Kennel Club recognized the Border Terrier in 1920. They were fearful that breeders would try to prettify the dog and, in so doing, diminish its grit and stamina. Their fears were unfounded: the Border Terrier has remained game and agile, still able to follow a horse all day if necessary.

Its working manner is very similar to the Lakeland Terrier's. In fact, there has always been great rivalry among hunters who own dogs of either breed. The Border Terrier is not satisfied with just hunting fox. Nimble and sturdy, it will also track badger, marten, and otter.

With its highly sociable character and its ability to adapt to small quarters, the Border Terrier has today become a valued companion dog.

AUS.	CAN.	S. AF.	U.K.	F.C.I.
●	●	●	●	●

ORIGINS

Although terriers resembling the Border type appeared in paintings of the late seventeenth century, this specific breed's origins cannot be reliably traced before the mid-nineteenth century, when it was apparently known in both Westmoreland and Cumberland, where it was used to go to ground in traditional terrier fashion. Earlier records show only the jumbled, collective history shared by all the terrier breeds. It can be confirmed that there was an ancestor common to the Lakeland, Bedlington, Dandie Dinmont, and Border Terriers. Also, the Redesdale—a completely white terrier now extinct—was another progenitor, responsible for the white markings occasionally found on some puppies. The name of the breed was fixed in 1880; before then, it bore such names as Reedwater Terrier and Coquetdale Terrier. In 1913, Mosstrooper, owned by Miss Mary Rew, became the first Border Terrier registered by the British Kennel Club, in the classification reserved for little-known and foreign dogs. It was only seven years later, in 1920, that the breed was officially recognized, after it had been exhibited in numerous shows. Not well known outside Great Britain, the Border Terrier has nevertheless become popular in Sweden, and is now fairly well established throughout the English-speaking world.

Characteristics

General appearance: essentially a working terrier with characteristics of gameness, speed, and hardiness.

Height: not specified.

Weight: 6 to 7 kg (13 to 15½ lb) for the adult dog; 5.2 to 6.4 kg (11½ to 14 lb) for the bitch. Under F.C.I. standards, not specified.

Head: resembles an otter's. Skull moderately broad. Muzzle short and strong. Nose preferably black, but paler nose is permissible. Scissor bite.

Eyes: dark, hazel, with keen expression, neither prominent nor small and beady.

Ears: small, V-shaped, of medium thickness and falling forward close to the cheek.

Neck: medium long, muscular, clean.

Body: narrow, deep, fairly long. Ribs well back but not over-sprung. Strong loin, underline fairly straight.

Tail: moderately short and fairly thick at the base. Tapering. Set high and carried gaily, but never curled over the back.

Forequarters: legs are straight, bone structure not too heavy.

Hindquarters: round thighs. Hocks well let down. Stifles well bent.

Feet: small, with thick pads.

Coat: rough and dense with a thick, close undercoat. The terrier's skin must be thick. Wiry, broken topcoat.

Colour: red, wheaten, grizzle and tan, blue and tan.

Faults: aggressiveness towards other dogs. Light eyes. Straight stifles. Tail long and thin or curved over the back. Excessive white markings. Poor bite. Curled or wavy coat.

Practical information: This is one of the few terriers that does not need clipping or trimming more than once a year. An older dog is susceptible to glaucoma as a result of another eye problem: luxation of the crystalline lens. A bluish cast visible in daylight, a white film, or one eye larger than the other are warning signals that must be heeded. The Border adapts readily to city life, but still requires regular exercise. Because it has a hearty appetite, its meat should be chopped very fine to prevent choking if the dog gulps too quickly.

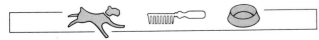

FOX-HUNTING

Trapping, poisoning, smoking out the foxhole, hunting—these are the methods used to destroy the much hated fox, which has earned its nasty reputation with many farmers by stealing poultry and other small animals. Traditional fox-hunting, with its view halloos and colourful riding habits, is still practised—amid much controversy—in Great Britain and in several provinces of France. But the fox is also tracked by hunters with guns, who lie in wait near the animal's lair. Trailed by Dachshunds or by such terriers as the Border, the fox—unlike the badger that will immediately fight any dog chasing it—tries to avoid all contact with its pursuer. Its first reaction is to take refuge in the nearest hole, whether an actual burrow or merely a hollow in a tree. The barking dog hurries after it, forcing it to flee through another opening, where the hunters are waiting for it.

If the fox is cornered, with no way to escape, it then must face the dog. In this situation, the Border fully displays its hunting abilities. It grabs its enemy by the throat to choke it, and then pulls it out of the burrow. This style of hunting, with fox and dog in close contact, is discouraged in areas where rabies is prevalent.

79

Borzoi

Russian Wolfhound

Tall, slender, haughty-looking—the Borzoi is a study in elegance and nobility. For three centuries before the 1917 revolution this magnificent member of the greyhound family was used in Russia for wolf-hunting, understandable in a country overrun with these predators. Prominent families set up kennels to raise their own packs. The tsars' imperial kennels were started in 1613. The best at that time belonged to the Grand Duke Nicholas: it had no fewer than 150 dogs.

Eventually, the rest of Europe was attracted to the Borzoi and it was found gracing salons and drawing rooms throughout the continent, where its exquisite lines and quiet conduct won it a host of enthusiastic admirers. It became the faithful companion of royalty and was entered in prestigious dog shows. By the 1840s, Queen Victoria had Borzois and soon, following her example, so did most of the British aristocracy. Tsar Alexander II presented Edward VII's future queen with a superb pair of Russian Wolfhounds. The male, entered in numerous dog shows, remained an undefeated champion.

AUS.	CAN.	S. AF.	U.K.	F.C.I.
●	●	●	●	●

ORIGINS

Some canine authorities claim that the Borzoi is descended from the greyhounds of ancient Egypt that eventually found their way into Russia. There, various greyhound types were supposedly developed, including the existing Borzoi, the product of a cross with a long-haired Russian sheep-dog. Others maintain that after Ivan the Terrible captured Kazan in 1552, he exiled all noblemen to the upper Volga, where these princely Tartars then crossed their Asian greyhounds with indigenous dogs to develop the first strain of Borzoi. In any case, it is generally accepted that the Borzoi breed was fixed in Russia around the sixteenth century.

80

Characteristics

General appearance: imposing stature and harmonious lines. Handsome, luxurious coat. Elegant and dignified.

Height: 73.7 to 81.3 cm (29 to 32 in.) for adult dogs; 68.6 to 76.2 cm (27 to 30 in.) for bitches. Under Canadian standards, 71 to 81.3 cm (28 to 32 in.) for adult dogs; 68.6 to 76.2 cm (27 to 30 in.) for bitches.

Head: fine, long, narrow, lean, well formed, tapers towards the nose; in proportion with body length and breadth. Bones and principal veins clearly seen. Jaws long, deep, and powerful. Skull slightly domed. Nose black, relatively large. Scissor bite.

Eyes: dark, almond-shaped, set obliquely, placed well back. Expression keen, alert, intelligent. Eye rims black.

Ears: set high and back. Small, fine, narrow, pointed.

Neck: long, well muscled, slightly arched. No dewlap.

Body: back rises slightly at loin to form a wide arch. Long, broad, muscular croup. Brisket is deep, with narrow, oval ribs. Belly well tucked up, not too developed.

Tail: long, set low, sickle-shaped from the level of the hocks, well feathered, not ringed.

Forequarters: legs straight, long.

Hindquarters: legs straight and parallel, broader and more muscular than the forelegs. Thighs broad and lean. Hocks well let down.

Feet: front feet narrow, oval. Hind feet, harelike. Toes tight.

Coat: skin fine, taut. Long hair, wavy, silky, never woolly. Short and smooth on head, ears, and front legs; the frill on the neck profuse and curly. Forelegs and chest well feathered. Hindquarters and tail, long and profuse feathering. Quality of coat determined by maturity and seasonal changes.

Colour: any colour or pattern acceptable.

Faults: tan marks too noticeable. Light eyes. Legs too short.

Practical information: To ensure the Borzoi does not develop stomach cramps, divide its daily rations into two or three separate meals. Vary the dog's diet, ensuring that it eats plenty of meat. Although well suited to domestic life, the Borzoi must run and take long walks. Its coat must be brushed and combed regularly. Pups must be closely watched: their growth can be so rapid that they need calcium supplements. This breed has a tendency to suffer leg fractures.

Boston Terrier

Round Head

The Boston Terrier was indeed born in Boston, but if one judges by looks it seems to be more Bulldog than terrier. In fact, some mistakenly call it the Boston Bull or Toy Bulldog. It may have inherited the terrier's great fondness for play and activity, but it has little of the hunter in its make-up and is much less noisy than other members of the terrier family. The Bulldog blood has contributed an obedient, protective, and gentle nature to the breed. The Boston is boisterous, bright, alert, and exceptionally affectionate, if a trifle pigheaded. Although it was originally developed for fighting, it is now a peaceful dog. Clean, well-behaved, likeable, and with a pair of exceptionally expressive eyes, the Boston Terrier makes an excellent pet.

AUS.	CAN.	S. AF.	U.K.	F.C.I.
●	●	●	●	●

ORIGINS

The Boston Terrier was originally bred for dogfighting, until recently a popular activity in Boston and throughout the United States. Breeders first crossed Bulldogs and Bull Terriers. The offspring of these matings were selectively inbred, and there were probably subsequent crosses, most likely with the French Bulldog.

THE BIRTH OF A BREED

There was once in Boston, around 1870, a dog called *Judge*. In 1875 it was renamed *Hooper's Judge* after its new owner, Robert C. Hooper, a local breeder. According to the story, this dog had more Bulldog than terrier in its background. It was well built, weighing about 15 kilograms (33 pounds), and dark brindled with a blaze on its heavy, squarish head.

This male was bred to *Burnett's Gyp*, a much smaller white bitch that weighed only 9 kilograms (20 pounds), but had an equally squarish head and a relatively short tail. From this union came *Well's Eph*, which was mated in turn with *Tobin's Kate*, a small, short-headed, golden brindled bitch. Thus was born *Barnard's Tom*, the canine patriarch of the Boston Terrier breed as we know it.

Around 1889, about 30 Boston breeders organized the American Bull Terrier's Club and began showing their dogs. Breeders of actual Bull Terriers did everything in their power to discourage them. However, the 30 breeders persisted and, in 1891, founded the Boston Terrier Club of America. Finally, in 1893, the American Kennel Club recognized the breed. These dogs still did not look exactly like the present-day type, and selective breeding was necessary to create more elegant specimens.

The Boston Terrier is one of only a dozen or so species bred and developed in the United States, where it ranks among the 25 most popular breeds. In fact, after 1920, it was so fashionable that it represented between 20 and 30 per cent of dogs entered in shows. Though its heyday has passed, the breed is still well liked in many countries, whether for showing or for enjoying as a pet.

Characteristics

General appearance: well built, with a confident, graceful gait. An intelligent expression is characteristic of this dog.

Height: not specified.

Weight: less than 11.3 kg (25 lb).

Head: flat skull, squarish. No wrinkles. Cheeks flat, broad, and square. Forehead straight. Stop well defined. Muzzle short, square, broad; no longer than one-third the length of the skull. Nose black, broad, with a distinct groove between the nostrils. Bite level or slightly undershot. Chin very square, not sloping. Jowls deep, not pendulous; covering the teeth.

Eyes: wide apart, large, round, dark, square in skull. Alert and intelligent expression.

Ears: small, fine, carried erect. Set on as near the corner of the skull as possible. Under Canadian and F.C.I. standards, ears may be cropped.

Neck: fair length, slightly arched, neatly set in shoulders, carrying head gracefully.

Body: shoulders sloping. Chest very broad. Ribs deep, prominent. Short back. Loin short and muscular. Croup slightly rounded.

Tail: set low, short, fine and tapering. Straight or screw. No feathering, no hard hairs. Not carried above the topline.

Forequarters: legs straight, well muscled, fairly wide apart. Elbows close. Pasterns short, strong.

Hindquarters: legs strong, well balanced. Thighs very muscular. Bent stifles. Hocks well let down.

Feet: round, small, compact, straight. Toes arched.

Coat: short, shiny, fine, smooth in texture.

Colour: brindle with white markings. Black with white markings permissible, but brindle with black markings preferred, with brindle even and regular. Ideal markings for the dog are white muzzle, even white blaze over head, collar, breast, forelegs, and on hind legs below the hocks.

Faults: skull domed or inclined. Forehead sloping. Eyes small, sunken, prominent, light. Muzzle clamped shut. Protruding teeth. Neck too short, wide. Dewlap. Back roached. Tail too long. Coat completely white; absence of white marks; hair too long or rough. Coat black, black and tan, liver, mouse grey. Tail docked. Butterfly nose.

Practical information: The Boston Terrier is a hardy dog and adapts perfectly to domestic life, but it must have regular exercise. Several peculiarities should be noted: If it is too active and gets overheated, it has difficulty breathing, which could strain its heart. Like Bulldogs and all breeds with flat faces whose salivary-gland passages are shortened, it tends to drool, especially if excited. But not every Boston drools uncontrollably. Also, bitches have problems whelping: Boston Terrier puppies have sizable heads that with difficulty pass through the birth-canal. As a preventative measure, the pups are generally delivered by Caesarean section, and thus must be bottle-fed. In North America, the ears are often cropped to a sharp point and carried erect. In those parts of the world where ear-cropping is banned, natural ears are standard. The Boston's short-haired coat does not need much grooming, and a daily brushing and rub-down with a chamois will keep it clean and shiny. No other special care is required, beyond routine inspections for external parasites.

Bouvier des Flandres

With its powerful body, its rough, dishevelled coat, and its bushy eyebrows, beard, and moustache, the Bouvier des Flandres can seem intimidating to anyone unfamiliar with the breed. Yet the Bouvier is a very calm, quiet, even-tempered dog, totally faithful to its owner. In short, it is a gentle giant with a soft heart. To be convinced, merely look into its deep, intelligent, kind eyes: the cast of friendliness therein is unmistakable.

This breed has had many names in the past, but its current name most accurately describes it. *Bouvier* means cowherd or ox drover; *des Flandres* indicates it came from the east and west provinces of Flanders, an area that once covered parts of the Netherlands and France, as well as the present Belgian provinces.

The Bouvier des Flandres is without question one of the finest of the European cattle dogs that were once commonly found driving herds of beef from grazing grounds to butchers' pens—just as sheep-dogs once escorted flocks. Well into the last century, a cattle drover walked his animals to the slaughterhouse along lonely country roads, assisted only by his droving-dog. The drive often took several days in miserable weather, and it

AUS.	CAN.	S. AF.	U.K.	F.C.I.
●	●	●	●	●

ORIGINS

The Bouvier's origins are the subject of considerable speculation. Some people say the dog was the product of a cross between a Beauceron and a griffon breed. Other hypotheses mention the Berger Picard and Deerhound as its forbears. Early in this century, there were several types of cattle dogs in the Flanders region, including the Bouvier des Flandres and the Roulers. The breed was practically destroyed during the First World War and was left to die out until 1923, when Flemish breeders began to work with several surviving dogs. To silence arguments over whether the Bouvier is of French or Belgian origin, canine authorities have agreed to consider the dog as Franco-Belgian.

was the Bouvier des Flandres that took on much of this gruelling work. The drover depended on his dog—and it rarely let him down. With instinctive initiative the Bouvier went about its tasks single-mindedly, without waiting for orders from its master. It would even work alone if the drover went away for a short time. Using its bulk and strength to redirect straying animals, it would nudge them back onto the road and prod them towards the rest of the herd without having to nip at their heels.

This breed possesses above-average scenting ability, along with exceptional bravery and physical strength. During the First World War it carried messages under fire and helped army medical units locate the wounded. But its participation proved costly: its courageous indifference to gunfire and cannonry meant that the breed was almost decimated. Twenty years later, the Second World War was almost as devastating for the remaining Bouviers des Flandres.

Today, the Bouvier's field of expertise has expanded into new areas that capitalize on the dog's rare courage and sense of initiative. It is an excellent watch-dog for both city flats and large estates. Its intelligence and aptitude for training qualify the Bouvier as a fine guide dog. Many police rate the former cattle dog as a first-rate tracker.

EAR-CROPPING

The Bouvier's ears used to be cropped to protect them from damage in the line of duty. Today, in Canada, the United States, and in other countries that permit the practice, ear-cropping is primarily a matter of aesthetics. But as more and more owners show their dogs with natural ears, conceptions of beauty will likely change. Beautiful or not, the Bouvier below seems friendlier than the fierce-looking dog illustrated on the opposite page.

Characteristics

General appearance: compact, stocky, powerful but not heavy. Intelligent expression. Energetic, enthusiastic, and brave.

Height: 62 to 68 cm (24½ to 26¾ in.) for the adult dog; 59 to 65 cm (23¼ to 25½ in.) for the bitch. Under Canadian standards, 59 to 70 cm (23¼ to 27½ in.) for the adult dog; 57.5 to 63.5 cm (22⅝ to 25 in.) for the bitch.

Weight: 35 to 40 kg (77 to 88 lb) for the adult dog; 27 to 35 kg (59½ to 77 lb) for the bitch. Under Canadian standards, not specified.

Head: solid appearance emphasized by the beard and moustache. Head well sculpted and well proportioned. Carried proudly. Stop shallow. Brow noticeably arched. Muzzle broad and powerful, bony, tapering towards the nose. Nose black, broad, well developed. Nostrils wide open. Jaws well developed. Teeth strong, white, healthy. Canines set wide apart, incisors in scissor bite. Lips dry and tight fitting.

Eyes: average size, neither protruding nor sunken. Dark but not black. Slightly oval. Expression frank and alert. Haw reversible.

Ears: Rough coated, set high; in proportion to the head. Very flexible. Under F.C.I. and Canadian standards, may be cropped to a triangle and carried erect.

Neck: strong and muscular. No dewlap.

Body: strong, squarish. Back broad and short. Ribs curved. Brisket descends to elbows. Short flanks. Loin short and muscular. Level croup. Shoulders long, muscular, slightly sloping.

Tail: docked to about 10 cm (4 in.), set high and carried up.

Forequarters: strong bone structure, legs well muscled and straight. Elbows tight to the body.

Hindquarters: legs strong, muscular. Thighs broad. Hocks broad and strong, well let down. No dewclaws.

Feet: short, round, and compact. Toes tight and well arched. Nails strong and black. Pads thick and hard.

Coat: profuse. Hair rough to touch, about 5 cm (2 in.) long; dishevelled but not woolly or curly. Shorter on the head, hard and rough on the back. Undercoat fine and dense. Moustache and beard ample. Skin dark.

Colour: from black to fawn, often brindled or shaded. White star on the chest permissible.

Faults: hair soft, woolly, too long or too short, silky. Narrow muzzle. Eyes light or with a wild expression. Ribs flat or too round. Wall-eyes. Spotted, pink, or brown nose. Poor bite. Coat too brown or too white.

Practical information: The Bouvier is a sturdy dog suited to living outdoors. The tail is customarily docked at birth and, in those countries that allow it, the ears are often cropped at the age of two to three months. The rough, dry outer hair and the fine, dense undercoat must be stripped regularly. Baths, however, should be infrequent, unless the dog lives indoors. This powerful animal has a hardy constitution and is rarely ill.

Boxer

F ew people realize that the Boxer was virtually unknown outside Germany until four decades ago. At the end of the Second World War, returning British and American soldiers brought the dogs home with them and the breed's popularity soared within a few years.

This handsome athlete of the canine world— muscular, fiery, and determined—requires a sports-minded owner who enjoys long walks and will share the dog's great love of play, for the Boxer is one of the most active breeds in the world. Even at an age when other dogs are seeking peace and tranquillity, the Boxer is still ready for roughhousing. It is this boundless energy that makes it an ideal companion for children, whom it adores.

Happy, affectionate, but a little stubborn, the Boxer can be an exuberant handful if it does not receive firm and thorough training. Its owner must adopt a gentle but no-nonsense approach to bring out the enjoyable qualities of this intelligent and sensitive dog.

The Boxer, completely devoted to its loved ones, makes a superb watch-dog. It will defend its family and their property with courage and spirit. In fact, the Boxer is a particularly well-balanced guard dog, demonstrating both courage and control. Nowadays, however, the Boxer is gaining prominence as a companion dog. It is clean, not too noisy, and a docile house-pet if properly trained.

AUS.	CAN.	S. AF.	U.K.	F.C.I.
●	●	●	●	●

ORIGINS

The Boxer's two ancestors, the Bullenbeiszer and the Barenbeiszer, lived in Germany. They were originally trained to hunt bear and boar, and then were used as cattle dogs. These breeds closely resembled the Mastiff, with which they were housed in Bavarian kennels during feudal times. Around 1850, German breeders crossed the Bullenbeiszer with the Bulldog. After careful selection, and the introduction of additional Bulldog blood, they finally succeeded in developing a new breed that possessed the traits of the present-day Boxer.

EAR-CROPPING: NECESSARY OR NOT?

In those countries that neither ban nor frown on ear-cropping (including Canada and the United States), most owners and breeders adhere to local standards, which generally stipulate that the Boxer must have erect ears cut to a point and not too long. Supporters claim that this minor operation, when performed on a very young dog under general anaesthetic, is no more disabling or uncomfortable than the removal of a child's tonsils. The practice of ear-cropping originally spared fighting dogs from getting their hanging ears torn in battle. Today, this operation is done only for convention's sake.

Characteristics

General appearance: average size, smooth coat, solid, muscular body, with no fat. Exceptionally faithful, protective, and courageous.

Height: 57 to 63.5 cm (22½ to 25 in.) for the adult dog; 53.3 to 58.4 cm (21 to 23 in.) for the bitch. Under Canadian standards, 55.3 to 59.7 cm (21 to 23½ in.) for the bitch.

Weight: 30 to 31.7 kg (66 to 70 lb) for the adult dog and 25 to 27.2 kg (55 to 60 lb) for the bitch. Under Canadian standards, not specified.

Head: well proportioned, not too slight or too heavy, as lean and square as possible. Cheeks not full, rather lean, no wrinkles except when it pricks its ears. Dark mask on well-developed muzzle. Skull slightly rounded. Stop well defined. Jaws strong and broad, obviously undershot though teeth are not visible. Flews thick and black. Nose broad and black.

Eyes: dark brown. Frank and intelligent look.

Ears: moderate in size, thin, set high, lying flat and close to the cheek when in repose. Under F.C.I. and Canadian standards, may be cropped to a point, not too broad, and carried erect.

Neck: well proportioned, round, fairly long.

Body: square. The thorax descends to the elbow. The height of the brisket is equal to half the dog's height. Ribs are curved but not cylindrical. Back short, straight, broad, and well muscled. Croup broad and rounded. Flanks short, taut, and tucked up. Belly forming an elegant curve towards the rear of the dog.

Tail: set high, usually docked, and carried erect.

Forequarters: legs straight and parallel.

Hindquarters: legs well angulated; parallel when seen from behind. Thighs broad and round.

Feet: small, compact, cat-footed. Pads hard, black.

Coat: short, shiny, and hard hair, very flat on the body.

Colour: fawn and brindle, with shades of fawn ranging from light yellow to dark red. White markings on muzzle, neck, chest, and feet or legs.

Faults: lack of distinguished bearing or expression. Solemn face. Head too light. Bulldoggish appearance. Teeth and tongue visible when muzzle is closed. Eyes light, haw visible. Roach back; swayback. Narrow croup. Tail set low. Hare-footed. Discoloured nails. Coat white or black. Stilted gait.

Practical information: This sturdy dog does have some physical vulnerabilities. Do not hesitate to consult the veterinarian if, during brushing, you discover lumps, abrasions, or large pimples on the skin. Skin tumours occur often on Boxers, and while some are benign, potentially malignant ones must be removed at an early stage. The Boxer's teeth and gums also require regular attention. Often rheumatic, this breed ages quickly and rarely lives more than 12 years. It is susceptible, more so than other dogs, to cerebral haemorrhage—usually after the age of nine.

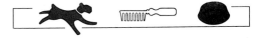

Bracco Italiano

Italian Pointer

The history of this 'noble Bracco Italiano,' as its admirers sometimes refer to it, is indeed an impressive one. This dog has existed for as long as man has hunted. Like the *Chiens d'Oysel* (Bird Dogs) described by Gaston Phoebus in the fourteenth century, it accompanied net hunters of the Middle Ages. Later it was teamed up with falconers, who used it to flush the falcon's quarry.

Noblemen as well as crowned heads of Europe—including such French kings as Louis XII and Francis I—developed a passion for this Italian pointing dog. Today, pointers from other countries have surpassed the Bracco in popularity.

AUS.	CAN.	S. AF.	U.K.	F.C.I.
				●

ORIGINS

Ancestor of all European pointers, the breed itself was the product of a cross between an Egyptian coursing hound and an ancient Assyrian mastiff in the fifth century B.C. Over time, two sizes of the breed evolved.

Characteristics

General appearance: robust and graceful, with a powerful appearance. Serious, sensitive expression.
Height: 55 to 67 cm (21½ to 26½ in.).
Weight: 25 to 40 kg (55 to 88 lb).
Head: angular, lean. Occiput well defined. Nose straight or slightly hooked and protruding; pink or brown. Pendulous jowls. Jaw strong. Scissor bite.
Eyes: neither sunken nor protruding. Yellow or ochre.
Ears: set well back. Well developed, hanging.

Body: chest well let down. Ribs arched. Back broad and muscular. Croup short and sloping downwards. Shoulders strong, sloping.
Tail: thick at the base; docked.
Forequarters: legs well balanced.
Hindquarters: muscular legs, long thighs.
Coat: short, lustrous coat.
Colour: white, white with orange, amber, or brown marks. White flecked with orange or brown. Roan.

Practical information: This energetic sporting dog is best suited to living outdoors. A well-balanced diet is essential. Feed the large Bracco variety generous amounts of food; the smaller variety needs proportionately less. The Bracco's wrinkled ears are longer and more sensitive than those of other pointers and require regular attention.

Braque d'Auvergne

No matter where this breed is put to work searching for partridge and woodcock—on the plains or in the mountains or forests—it performs with equal *élan*. Seemingly unmindful of weather conditions, it puts up with humidity, rain, cold, and ice. The Braque d'Auvergne is a tireless, methodical hunter. But its excellent pointing instinct shows up rather late: not until the female is a year, and the male 18 months old.

Characteristics

General appearance: strongly built yet elegant, not heavy.
Height: 57 to 63 cm (22½ to 24¾ in.) for the adult dog; 55 to 60 cm (21 to 23 in.) for the bitch.
Weight: 22 to 25 kg (48 to 55 lb).
Head: long. Muzzle square. Skull oval at the back. Nose black. Lips fairly thick. Jaws large and of equal length. Scissor bite.
Eyes: dark hazel. Rims black. Candid look.
Ears: set low, at eye-level, fairly well back.
Body: chest medium size, well let down. Back short and straight.
Tail: docked by two-thirds.
Forequarters: legs straight, forearms strong and muscular.
Hindquarters: thighs muscular, well shaped. Powerful hocks.
Coat: short hair neither too fine nor too hard; lustrous.
Colour: white with black or charcoal patches.

Practical information: Do not overfeed this dog, whose appetite is voracious. The tail should be docked at birth.

AUS.	CAN.	S. AF.	U.K.	F.C.I.
				●

ORIGINS

The history of this dog is not well known. Some say it was brought to France during the Middle Ages by the Knights Templar; others contend that it arrived with the Knights of the Order of Malta who, after the Napoleonic wars, emigrated to Auvergne. Still others maintain that it results from crossing the Braque Français with a Pointer. Purists believe that the Pointer traits were eliminated during subsequent selections. In any case, by the nineteenth century, the Braque d'Auvergne was noticeably different from the Pointer: its bone structure was more substantial, and it worked more slowly. Although the Braque d'Auvergne was nearly decimated during the Second World War, dedicated fanciers took up its cause and eventually restored its ranks.

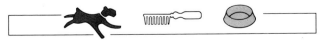

Braque Français

French Pointer

T he Braque Français was a fashionable dog in France up until the last century. It was popularly known as the Braque Charles X. Eventually, the British setters and pointers came into vogue and lured away many of the Braque's admirers.

Two varieties exist: the large one, called 'Gascon' or 'de Gascogne,' and the small one, called 'des Pyrénées.' The smaller of the two regained public favour because of its talent for hunting on any terrain (some say it is born trained), its small size, and its versatility.

AUS.	CAN.	S. AF.	U.K.	F.C.I.
				●

ORIGINS

The breed originated in seventeenth-century France and may be descended from the Spanish Pointer. Some experts maintain, however, that its ancestor is the Bracco Italiano.

Characteristics

General appearance: powerful, but not heavy.
Height: for the Gascon, 56 to 65 cm (22 to 25½ in.). For the des Pyrénées, 50 to 55 cm (20 to 21½ in.).
Weight: for the Gascon, 25 to 32 kg (55 to 70½ lb). For the des Pyrénées, 17 to 25 kg (37½ to 55 lb).
Head: large but not massive. Skull slightly rounded. Stop moderate, muzzle broad and rectangular. Nose brown, nostrils wide. Flews fairly full. Scissor bite.
Eyes: well open, brown or dark yellow.
Ears: medium size, set at eye level.
Neck: good length, slightly arched, rather thick.

Body: brisket broad and deep. Back straight. Loin short, slightly arched. Croup short and sloping. Flanks flat. Shoulders well muscled and straight.
Tail: docked to half its length.
Forequarters: legs straight, pasterns strong.
Hindquarters: thighs strong. Hocks broad and well let down.
Feet: almost round. Nails strong. Pads thick.
Coat: thick, dense hair, finer on the head and ears.
Colour: white with brown markings, with or without brown patches or ticking; brown with ticking.

Practical information: This breed is hardy and easy to rear. It needs exercise and daily walks.

Braque Saint-Germain

Similar to the Pointer both in silhouette and hunting ability, this is the most elegant of all French *braques* (pointers). It is not widely found, however, even in France, though it is an excellent hunter of pheasant as well as rabbit, and has even demonstrated a talent for flushing large game. The Braque Saint-Germain adapts well to any terrain, but it works in forests more successfully than in marshland. This able worker can point and retrieve quarry efficiently—minimizing the distances covered. The breed is easily trained.

AUS.	CAN.	S. AF.	U.K.	F.C.I.
				●

ORIGINS

In 1830, in France, Baron de Larminat of Compiègne bred a Pointer bitch to a Braque Français. The puppies were eventually taken to the Saint Germain woods, hence the name.

Characteristics

General appearance: elegant, well proportioned. Bone structure finer than the Pointer's.
Height: 56 to 62 cm (22 to 24½ in.).
Weight: 20 to 25 kg (44 to 55 lb).
Head: skull slightly rounded. Stop less pronounced than the Pointer's. Muzzle straight or slightly convex. Nose dark pink or fawn. Thin lips.
Eyes: golden yellow, deep-set.

Ears: set at eye level. Long, pendent, supple.
Body: brisket broad and deep. Ribs long. Short loin. Croup bony. Shoulders long, sloping.
Tail: set low. Thicker at the base. Not docked.
Forequarters: legs straight, strong.
Hindquarters: thighs muscular.
Coat: hair fine and short.
Colour: flat white with bright orange marks.

Practical information: This is a hardy sporting breed that does not require special care. Give the dog calcium supplements until it has reached the age of six or seven months, and include fresh vegetables and a little vegetable oil in its diet. The coat will need grooming once or twice a week. Check the ears and feet after hunting expeditions.

Briard

With its coarse, rough coat, its distinctive beard and moustache, and its dark eyes hidden by tufts of hair, the Briard is a handsome and rugged working dog. Few can resist its intelligent and loving expression, its playful disposition, and its reassuring 'teddy bear' look.

The Briard's energy and sprightliness made it, years ago, a superior sheep-dog and guard dog, respected for its courage, authority, and initiative. Two or three dogs were enough to watch over vast flocks of 600 or 700 sheep. They usually managed to accomplish this task without having to nip at sheeps' hocks or to attract the shepherd's help.

The dog is a superb runner, able to cover 80 kilometres (50 miles) in a day. It is a pleasure to watch a Briard taking off across a field—trotting, sprinting, turning, and galloping in great, graceful strides.

The versatile Briard served France well in the First World War. It carried ammunition and other equipment, located wounded soldiers, and patrolled the front lines to warn of surprise attacks. Although the breed has fewer and fewer opportunities these days to tend flocks, the dog is widely used as a guide dog, and in police, life-saving, and security work.

The Briard is a very sensitive animal. Handled with affection, it will become a tractable, devoted family pet.

AUS.	CAN.	S. AF.	U.K.	F.C.I.
●	●	●	●	●

ORIGINS

It is believed that Charlemagne owned a Briard at the beginning of the ninth century. In his fourteenth-century treatise on hunting, Gaston Phoebus described a white dog very similar to the Briard. A century later, Andrea Mantegna included two Briard look-alikes in his painting of the martyrdom of Saint Sebastian. It is likely that, down through the ages, some cross-breeding has changed the Briard's appearance. During the last century the short-haired Beauceron and the long-haired Briard were considered to be one breed, although one Abbé Rozier distinguished between those two French sheep-dogs for the first time in 1809. Both were exhibited at the Paris dog show of 1863. In 1896, the two were officially recognized as separate breeds.

Characteristics

General appearance: well proportioned, very intelligent. Supple, muscular, active. Alert, lively, and fearless.

Height: 58.4 to 68.6 cm (23 to 27 in.) for the adult dog; 53.3 to 63.5 cm (21 to 25 in.) for the bitch. Canadian standards for the bitch, 56 to 64.8 cm (22 to 25½ in.).

Head: large, fairly long. Visible stop. Long hair forming beard and moustache. Eyebrows slightly covering the eyes. Muzzle square, very long, neither narrow nor pointed. Stop clearly defined. Lips black. Teeth strong and white. Scissor bite. Nose black, large, and square.

Eyes: horizontal, well open, rather large, dark. Gentle expression. Eye rims always black.

Ears: set high, covered with long hair, not too flat against the head. Under F.C.I. and Canadian standards, may be cropped.

Body: chest broad and deep. Back level. Croup slightly sloped.

Tail: long, carried low, well feathered, curling at the tip.

Forequarters: well muscled with strong bone structure. Shoulders laid back, well angulated.

Hindquarters: legs, and especially the thighs, well muscled. Double dewclaws.

Coat: slightly wavy, not less than 7.6 cm (3 in.) long, dry, stiff and strong, goatlike.

Colour: all solid colours except white. Dark colours preferred.

Practical information: The Briard is a vigorous sheep-dog that can live happily indoors only if it is given sufficient and regular exercise. Its coarse, rough coat is considered self-cleaning because it retains neither mud nor moisture. Outdoor dogs seldom need bathing. However, house-pets and show dogs should be brushed regularly—to remove any dead undercoat—and given an occasional bath.

CROPPING THE BRIARD'S EARS

To meet the requirements of some standards, the Briard's ears are oftentimes cropped, although natural ears are generally permitted as well. Many people see this operation as unjustifiably cruel because it serves no useful purpose; others consider it necessary for the animal's health and appearance.

In fact, the controversial practice is a very old one. Originally, herding dogs' ears were cropped so that there would be as little lobe as possible to grasp when the dogs fought each other or battled wolves while defending their charges.

Although the argument for appearance is not very convincing—the Briard is equally likeable and pleasant to look at with its ears left hanging naturally—the contention that ear-cropping is essential, justified for health reasons, has convinced some Briard owners. They claim that the practice helps prevent ear infections and keeps out mites, burs, and other foreign matter.

93

Brittany

Brittany Spaniel, Breton Spaniel

Many believe that setter blood courses through the Brittany's veins. How else can one explain its excellent pointing abilities? This alert, intelligent dog is the smallest, best-known, and most popular of the French spaniels. Because it can point game as well as retrieve it, the Brittany is favoured by many hunters, who find it a manageable, good-natured field dog, as well as a pleasant companion at home.

The breed is endowed with a remarkable sense of smell, and it has all the qualities of the finest bird dogs. Its tenacity and single-minded approach to work have wrongly earned it a reputation for being stubborn, even pigheaded. In reality, however, the Brittany has just the opposite characteristics.

Reliable and hard-working, it can spend an entire day hunting in cold weather or in the rain without losing strength or spirit. If it must plunge into an icy pond after a fallen duck, it will—readily and boldly. Although its favourite quarry is woodcock, it is equally competent hunting partridge and pheasant.

This combination pointer-retriever hunts with its nose to the wind and its head raised, within easy range of its owner. Its small size enables it to slip easily through undergrowth, thicket, or thorny brush. However, despite its passion for locating game, the Brittany is willing, on command, to give up the point.

Such all-purpose hunting skills, which firmly established the Brittany in France and the rest of Europe, have earned this spaniel respect throughout the English-speaking world, where it is now the most popular pointer for bird-hunting, surpassing even the German Short-haired Pointer.

AUS.	CAN.	S. AF.	U.K.	F.C.I.
●	●	●	●	●

ORIGINS

The Brittany's most likely ancestor is the Chien d'Oysel (Bird Dog) which, used for many cross-breedings, also contributed to the development of other spaniels and setters. One variety of spaniel offspring, scattered throughout France during the sixteenth century, became the Épagneul Français; it was later renamed Épagneul Breton, or Brittany Spaniel. Certain seventeenth-century paintings by Rembrandt depict this tailless dog with a more pointed muzzle than is found today. Early in the last century, cross-breeding—mainly with English Setters, but also with Pointers—produced a slightly heavier and taller animal, with a keener sense of smell. At this time, a small spaniel called the Épagneul Fougères is said to have been interbred to refine the dog's lines. The first official Brittany standard was established in 1907.

HOW THE SPANIEL GOT ITS NAME

There is little doubt that the English word 'spaniel' and its French equivalent, *épagneul*, derive from the same Old French word. But just which Old French word is a matter of dispute in France.

Hunters in the Middle Ages called their bird dogs *chiens couchants* (lying dogs) to distinguish them from *chiens courants* (coursing dogs). When the *chien couchant* scented game birds, it would lie flat so the hunter could throw the net over both dog and bird. Some believe that these dogs were the *Chiens d'Oysel* described in Gaston Phoebus's fourteenth-century treatise on hunting—the same bird dog that begat the Brittany and other spaniels. Therefore *épagneul* may come from the Old French verb *s'espanir* or *s'espaignir*, meaning 'to stretch out' or 'to lie down.'

It is much more likely, however, that *épagneul* is a corruption of the Old French *espaignol* meaning 'Spanish,' since spaniels, as well as pointers and setters, probably originated in Spain.

Characteristics

General appearance: small, elegant dog, with an intelligent expression. Vigorous and energetic. Having the appearance of agility and ruggedness.
Height: 43.2 to 50.8 cm (17 to 20 in.). Under Canadian standards, 44.5 to 52 cm (17½ to 20½ in.).
Weight: 15 kg (33 lb) for the dog; 13 kg (28½ lb) for the bitch. Under Canadian standards, 14 to 17.7 kg (31 to 39 lb).
Head: round. Skull of average length, rounded, slightly wedge-shaped, lateral walls well rounded. Stop well defined, not too deep. Muzzle shorter than the large axis of the skull, straight or very slightly curved. Nose fawn, tan, brown, or deep pink, depending on coat colour. Nostrils open, well shaped. Lips thin, tight, slightly raised, the upper lip extending a bit beyond the lower lip. Scissor bite.
Eyes: well set in head. Dark amber to dark hazel, blending with the coat. Alert and expressive.
Ears: drop ears, set high. Fairly short, set above the level of the eye. Slightly rounded, slightly fringed though covered with straight hair. Should lie close to the head.
Neck: of medium length, clean and well set.
Body: deep chest, fully let down to elbows. Ribs well sprung, rounded. Shoulders sloping and well muscled. Back is short, but never swayback. Loin is short,

broad, and strong. Hindquarters are lower than the withers, prominent. Croup slightly sloping.
Tail: Naturally short. If the dog has a tail, it is usually docked to 10 cm (4 in.).
Forequarters: legs very straight, carpal bones slightly sloping, thin, and muscular. Feathered.
Hindquarters: thighs broad, very muscular. Hocks moderately short. Stifles well bent. Carpal bones well balanced. Feathered to mid-thigh.
Feet: toes tight, not heavily feathered.
Coat: fine, dense hair, rather flat or slightly wavy.
Colour: white and orange, white and brown, white and black, liver and white, tricolour or roan. Some ticking permissible.
Faults: too large or too small. Off-coloured. Nose narrow, divided. Lips thick, sagging. Tight nostrils. Drooling. Muzzle too short or too long. Skull squared, slanted, narrow, round, too straight. Eyes too light, prominent. Mean or aggressive expression. Ears set low, hanging, broad, or very curly. Neck too long, too thin. Back long or hollow. Chest narrow, shallow. Ribs flat. Loin long, narrow. Croup too narrow, too straight, or too sloping. Falling pasterns. Flanks heavy and falling. Tail long, bare. Thighs straight, no fringe. Feet broad, long, thick, too round, or open. Skin thick or too loose. Coat curly or too silky.

Practical information: The Brittany is susceptible to ear infections; check and clean the ears daily. Train the dog for hunting at one year of age and condition it before each season starts. Even for the dog that does not hunt, exercise and frequent walks are essential. Females living indoors may be subject to false pregnancies. Grooming a Brittany consists of bathing it several times a year and brushing it regularly, at least once a week.

Bulldog (English)

British Bulldog

This awkward, oddly built beast with its enormous wrinkled head and distorted face was obviously never bred for beauty and symmetry. One nineteenth-century writer saw it this way: '... the head is very large, almost appearing as of disproportionate size to the body. The forehead sinks between the eyes, and the line of the nose rises again at a considerable angle; the lower jaw projects beyond the upper, often showing the teeth, which altogether, with the frequent redness about the eyelids, produces a most forbidding aspect ....'

Despite its 'forbidding aspect,' this compact, muscular, low-slung athlete has attracted a host of admirers who consider it the most distinguished—and most British—of all canines. Indeed, the British chose the Bulldog to symbolize the qualities Britons display in their finest moments—courage, tenacity, equanimity.

Today, Bulldog owners praise the dog's loyalty, reliability, and gentleness. But it was not always so gentle. One of its ancestors, the Alaunt, hunted wild boar and drove beef cattle. The early Bulldog was a fighter that was pitted against bears, badgers, bulls, and, occasionally, other dogs.

Since Roman times, the baiting, or tormenting, of animals was a popular pastime in Britain, as it was in other parts of Europe. Bull-baiting set dogs against bulls. Since entertainment was scarce, the bloody confrontations attracted as many villagers as city dwellers, as many lords as commoners. Patronized by royalty as well as the nobility, bull-baiting thrived. And attempts to develop a better

AUS.	CAN.	S. AF.	U.K.	F.C.I.
●	●	●	●	●

ORIGINS

The distant origins of the Bulldog are uncertain. It probably descended from the Molossus, a mastiff which Phoenicians introduced to the British Isles around the sixth century B.C. A Molossian offshoot was trained to battle wild animals and gladiators in Roman Britain's arenas. Although writers from as early as the thirteenth century referred to dogs that fought bulls, and a letter from 1631 mentioned 'Bulldogs' as a distinct breed, it is unlikely that these animals resembled today's breed. Until little more than a century ago, the Bulldog probably looked more like the Staffordshire Bull Terrier. The massive head, flattened muzzle, and upturned lower jaw were unanticipated mutations that were maintained through selective breeding in the last century. The Bulldog was officially recognized by the British Kennel Club in 1873.

canine bullfighter intensified. What fanciers wanted was a barrel-chested dog with a wide stance, light, muscular hindquarters, and a short but massive jaw—a dog that could fasten onto a bull's head and bring it down, fending off the bull's frantic attempts to shake loose or kill its tormentor. Breeders eventually produced a Bulldog similar to the one of today.

Public opinion, however, finally condemned bull-baiting. In 1835, legislation put an end to this cruel spectacle, and erstwhile fans lost interest in their favourite dog. Concerned breeders, however, aware that the Bulldog faced extinction, hoped to preserve its many fine qualities while eliminating its ferocity. So they attempted to transform the pugnacious brute into a peaceable companion—and they succeeded. Today's beloved Bulldog is a remarkably sweet-tempered animal.

Characteristics

General appearance: stocky, heavy, rather low, very compact dog, conveying an impression of strength. The head, bold and massive, is rather broad in proportion to the dog's size.

Height: under F.C.I. standards, 30 to 40 cm (12 to 16 in.). Elsewhere, not specified.

Weight: under Canadian standards, 23 kg (50 lb) for the adult dog and 18 kg (40 lb) for the bitch. Elsewhere, 25 kg (55 lb) for the adult dog and 23 kg (50 lb) for the bitch.

Head: short, covered with loose skin forming heavy wrinkles. Skull very broad, forehead flat, face fully lined with wrinkles. Stop strongly defined. Circumference of the head must equal the height of the dog at the shoulder. Muzzle short, broad, and turned up. Nose black, broad, large, set back deeply between the eyes. Jowls thick and hanging, entirely covering the teeth. Jaws broad and square, the lower extending greatly beyond the upper, and curving upwards. Cheeks round, full.

Eyes: set low, wide apart, far from the ears, round in shape, of average size, very dark, no haw.

Ears: quite far apart, set high. Small, thin rose ears.

Neck: moderate length, very thick, deep, strong. Well arched at back.

Body: medium size, thickset, fairly low, strong, pear-shaped. Back short and strong, broad in the shoulders, narrow towards the loin, slightly arched or rounded. Chest capacious, broad, deep, thick, ribs well rounded. Belly tucked up. Shoulders muscular, heavy, well separated, broad, sloping.

Tail: straight or screw, short, set low and carried downwards. Never curved or curly, or with coarse or fringe hair.

Forequarters: legs straight, well boned and strong, set wide apart.

Hindquarters: legs strong, muscular, longer than the forelegs. Hocks well let down, slightly bent.

Feet: medium size, round, compact, straight or slightly turned outwards.

Coat: fine, short, close, and smooth.

Colour: red brindle, all other brindles, pure white, red, beige, pied. Sometimes black mask or muzzle.

Practical information: This very hardy dog has few health problems except that it can develop breathing difficulties. The Bulldog is a drooler. Its head is shorter than that of other dogs, which affects the development of the salivary glands and shortens their passages. If drooling is excessive, your veterinarian can take steps to reduce it.

THE ROSE EAR

To quote the British breed standard, the Bulldog's rose ear 'folds inwards at its back, the upper or front edge curving over outwards and backwards, showing part of the inside of the burr.'

Bulldog (French)

Frenchie, French Bulldog

To watch a sensitive French Bulldog romp with children or snuggle up quietly beside an elderly master, it is difficult to believe that its ancestors were battling with bulls in England as recently as 150 years ago. The heftier British Bulldog was bred for its aggressiveness and courage, and its bloody forays in the bull-baiting rings thrilled commoners and nobility alike. Queen Elizabeth I apparently enjoyed the sport so much that she organized private spectacles for visiting ambassadors.

When a parliamentary decree put an end to bull-baiting in 1835, the British Bulldog was quickly adopted as a companion dog. It thrived especially in the English Midlands, where lace-making flourished as a local industry. Attracted by better jobs, many lace-makers moved to France around the middle of the nineteenth century, taking their Bulldogs with them. There, according to one version of the French Bulldog's ancestry, the British breed was crossed with other dogs, became smaller and more docile, and by the end of the nineteenth century was known as the *Bouledogue Français*, a breed that briefly reached the height of canine fashion. Some authorities, on the other hand, refer to an ancient bronze plaque dated 1625 that shows a bat-eared dog bearing a close resemblance to the French Bulldog. The plaque is inscribed 'Dogue de Burgos, España.' Burgos is the home of bullfighting. From the bullrings, it is believed, the dogs went to France where they were used to fight donkeys prior to becoming fashionable and miniaturized.

AUS.	CAN.	S. AF.	U.K.	F.C.I.
●	●	●	●	●

ORIGINS

Modern Bulldogs and Mastiffs can be traced all the way back to the ancient Tibetan Mastiff. A descendant of the Tibetan dog is believed to have been brought to ancient Britain from Macedonia by Phoenician traders. In time, generations of crossbreeding with terriers reduced its size and weight. The British Bulldog that resulted became, in turn, the breeding stock from which several other types of 'bull' dogs were developed, including the French Bulldog. American breeders were responsible for putting the finishing touches on the French Bulldog's bat ear, an improvement over its ancestors' typical rose ear. Somewhat ironically, the eventual introduction of the French Bulldog into Britain is credited with strengthening the British breed.

The English were at first indignant over what they regarded as stealing the name of Bulldog, the proud symbol of the British Empire. But the popularity of the 'Frenchie' quickly spread and the British Kennel Club officially recognized the breed in 1902.

This compact, muscular dog makes an ideal family pet. Highly responsive to affection and caring, it adapts itself to those around it: children love its energetic playfulness, while elderly people are comforted by its devotion.

Characteristics

General appearance: medium or small, muscular build, intelligent, with a compact frame and solid bone structure. The French Bulldog has a short, smooth coat.
Height: not specified.
Weight: 12.7 kg (28 lb) for the dog; 11 kg (24 lb) for the bitch. Under Canadian standards, less than 10 kg (22 lb) for the lightweight variety; 10 to 12.7 kg (22 to 28 lb) for the heavyweight variety.
Head: large, broad, square. Domed forehead. Skin forms almost symmetrical folds and lines. No occipital crest. Nose black, broad, very short, and turned up, with nostrils wide open and a well-defined line between. Jaws are square, broad, powerful, slightly undershot, well turned up. The thick upper and lower lips cover the teeth completely. The muscles in the cheeks are well developed, but not prominent. Stop is well defined below the broad, almost flat skull.
Eyes: under arching brows are dark, round, fairly large and prominent. Set low on skull, wide apart, neither sunken nor bulging. Neither haw nor white should show when eyes are looking forward.
Ears: broad at the base, rounded at the tip, medium size, set high on the head, carried erect. Bat ears. Skin soft and fine.
Neck: well arched, short, thick, slightly narrowing, then widening. Loose skin at the throat, but no dewlap.
Body: short, well rounded, chest broad. Brisket cylindrical, barrel-shaped. Back is broad and muscular. Loin short and stocky; croup slanting. Belly and the flanks are tucked up.
Tail: very short, set low, close to the thighs, thick at the base, straight or screwed and tapering at the tip.
Forequarters: legs short, set wide apart, straight-boned, muscular.
Hindquarters: legs a little longer than forelegs; strong and well muscled. Hocks well let down. No dewclaws.
Feet: small and round, especially the forefeet. Cat-footed, well positioned on the ground, turned slightly outwards. Nails short and thick.
Coat: hair short, fine, dense, lustrous, soft. Skin soft and loose, wrinkling especially on the head and shoulders.
Colour: brindle, some white on the chest and head permitted; or fawn or pied. Canadian standards permit white, and brindle and white.
Faults: tail curving up, too long or not visible. Long hair. Coat ticked or too black. Ears not erect. Eyes light or wall-eyes. Teeth and tongue visible. Nose any colour but black. Too heavy or too light in weight. Harelip. Tail docked. Tan, mouse, or grey-blue coat.

Practical information: The French Bulldog cannot tolerate high temperatures and is susceptible to sunstroke. It must have at least three daily outings and one long walk a week. Brush the coat every day when the dog is shedding, and bathe it every two months. The eyes are prone to glaucoma and should be checked regularly. Whelping is sometimes difficult due to the puppy's large head; Caesarian sections may be called for. In this instance puppies will have to be bottle-fed. Snorting is common only among those dogs whose noses do not meet the breed standard.

THE TALE OF THE BULLDOG'S TAILS

A distinctive feature of the French Bulldog, as with its English cousin, is the tail. For most dogs there is but one ideal tail for show purposes. In the Bulldog's case, however, the standard permits three types: the straight, kinked, or screwed tail. The kinked and screwed tails must never be curved or curly, a distinction sometimes difficult to make. Twists and angles should be abrupt, even knotty. The straight tail must be cylindrical in contour.

All three types, nonetheless, must be short. Although the lengths can vary slightly, as pictured below, the tails must never reach the hocks. They are set, furthermore, low on the dog's croup, beneath the topline, their thick roots tapering to a thin tip. A Bulldog's tail is never docked.

One curious aspect of the kinked tail, illustrated here, and the spiralled screw tail is that the bends and angles are, in fact, deformities. In some dogs, foreshortened tendons on one side cause the tail to hook sideways. In others, the bends result from congenitally deformed vertebrae. Vertebrae that have been broken or separated in accidents contort the Bulldog's tail.

The kink and screw tails are prevalent among Bulldogs regardless of the reason for the twists, and are not considered faults at dog shows.

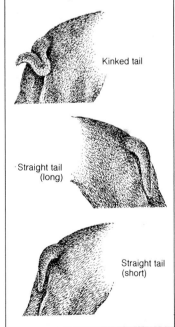

Kinked tail

Straight tail (long)

Straight tail (short)

Bullmastiff

The Bullmastiff's melancholy expression, enhanced by a black mask around its dark eyes, hides a spirited and intelligent character. Whether used principally as a guard dog or as a companion dog, it thrives on attention and discipline, and responds with loyalty.

The Bullmastiff was developed in England at the end of the nineteenth century to fulfill a specific need for an aggressive and powerful guard dog. It was during this period that poaching was rampant, to the extent that gamekeepers feared for their lives. Their solution was to develop a breed of dog that was big, agile, and fast. This Bullmastiff has inherited the best characteristics of its two principal ancestors, the British Bulldog and the Mastiff. The breed combines the tenacity, courage, and ferociousness of the smaller Bulldog with the speed, strength, and excellent sense of smell of the larger Mastiff. Police forces and armies have taken advantage of these qualities, enlisting the Bullmastiff as a guard dog. The animal requires careful training at an early age, however, if its inherent skills are to be properly developed. Even if it is adopted as a household pet, it needs obedience schooling to curb its naturally impetuous behaviour.

Despite its imposing size and weight, the Bullmastiff can be an affectionate and calm companion dog, and is suprisingly patient with children. But this loyal, intelligent animal demands considerable attention. Left alone for long periods, the Bullmastiff quickly becomes bored and will spend much of its time sleeping.

AUS.	CAN.	S. AF.	U.K.	F.C.I.
●	●	●	●	●

ORIGINS

British gamekeepers had a dangerous job at the end of the nineteenth century. Poaching was punishable by death, and lawbreakers would kill a gamekeeper rather than risk being caught. Gamekeepers needed a special breed of dog to accompany them on their late-night rounds—an obedient dog with a well-developed sense of smell, an animal that was aggressive enough to attack on command and knock a poacher down without mauling or biting him. The 'gamekeeper's nightdog,' as the Bullmastiff became known, was created by crossing two breeds in exact proportions: 60 per cent Mastiff and 40 per cent Bulldog. The resulting breed was one of the first dogs to be developed deliberately, and then stabilized. In 1924 the British Kennel Club officially recognized the Bullmastiff on condition that only dogs with three generations of pure breeding behind them could be registered. In this way, continued crossbreeding between the Bulldog and the Mastiff was stopped.

TRAINING THE GAMEKEEPER'S ASSISTANT

Though the Bullmastiff was ideally suited to assist nineteenth-century gamekeepers in their dangerous work, it had to have considerable training to prepare it for its professional life. Gamekeepers needed a dog that could help them find a poacher, remain silent as the intruder approached, attack only on command, then knock the surprised victim to the ground and pin him without biting him.

With this goal in mind, trainers kept only the strongest puppy from every Bullmastiff litter. The youngster was pampered for four months with good food and no special training routine. Then, gradually, it was taught to accept the presence of other household dogs but to maintain a distance from them. This achieved, the process was repeated with poultry and cattle until the trainer was certain the dog would not be distracted by other animals.

Then it learned to listen to rifle shots without flinching, to scale walls, jump ditches, and even swim rivers. At eight months it was muzzled and set loose in the countryside to chase a man. Welcomed with blows from a club, the dog quickly learned that it must knock the man down if it did not want to be hit. With each lesson, the pursued man put up more resistance and the dog had to work harder. After 18 months, the Bullmastiff was trained.

Characteristics

General appearance: powerful, symmetrical build, exceptionally strong, but not ungainly.

Height: 63.5 to 68.6 cm (25 to 27 in.) for the adult dog; 61 to 66 cm (24 to 26 in.) for the bitch.

Weight: 50 to 59 kg (110 to 130 lb) for the adult dog; 45.4 to 54.4 kg (100 to 120 lb) for the bitch.

Head: large and square. Wrinkled when dog is attentive, not when resting. Muzzle short. Black mask. Lower jaw broad. Nose black, broad with wide-open nostrils, not pointed or turned up. Flews must not hang below base of the lower jaw. Stop well defined. Jaws of equal length. Canine teeth strong and well separated.

Eyes: dark or hazel, medium size, set apart the width of the muzzle, with a furrow between them.

Ears: V-shaped, folded back, set high and wide at the occiput level, giving a squarish look to the skull. Small, darker than the body. Tip must be level with the eye when the dog is alert.

Neck: well arched, moderate length, well muscled.

Body: chest compact, deep, and wide, well let down between forelegs. Shoulders well laid back, strong but not overdeveloped. Back short and level. Loin broad and muscular. Flanks fairly deep.

Tail: set high, thick at the base and tapering, reaching to hocks. Carried straight out or curved up.

Forequarters: legs straight, powerful, wide apart. Pasterns straight and strong.

Hindquarters: legs strong and muscular. Hocks slightly curved.

Feet: well arched, cat-footed. Pads strong. Toes well rounded. Dark nails.

Coat: hair short and dense, very close to the body.

Colour: all tones of red, fawn, or brindle, but uniform. Muzzle black, fading towards eyes, with dark markings around them, giving characteristic expression.

Faults: eyes light or yellow. Rose ears. Teeth irregular. Camel back or swayback. Cow hocks. Down on the pasterns. Split or crank tail. Coat long, silky, or woolly. Stilted gait. Weaving or rolling action.

Practical information: The Bullmastiff lives an average of 12 years, which is somewhat longer than the life span of the Mastiff. It has a reputation for good health and stamina. Brush the Bullmastiff's coat for 15 minutes every day, and clean the folds of its skin with a cotton swab dipped in a solution of warm water and bicarbonate of soda. If the dog lives indoors, a bath every three months is usually sufficient. However, if the dog is active in the countryside, more frequent baths may be required. Give your Bullmastiff a moderate amount of exercise, but do not tire the dog unduly.

Bull Terrier

Once known as the gladiator of the canine world, the Bull Terrier is now regarded as a true gentleman. Its transformation from fierce warrior to agreeable companion started early in the last century with the banning of bull-baiting in Britain. The abolition of this cruel spectacle led to the creation of another—dogfighting—to satisfy the appetites of bloodthirsty fans. The massive, slow-moving Bulldogs that had fought bulls were now pitted against each other.

Handlers soon realized they needed a faster, more agile breed, one as strong and vicious as the dog they had but with a longer muzzle to inflict more damage. So they crossed their Bulldogs with terriers to produce what was known simply as a 'bull and terrier dog.' Later crosses eventually yielded today's remarkably benevolent pet.

Though the Bull Terrier has lost virtually all of its bellicose temperament along the evolutionary road, it has lost none of its courage and quick instincts. Less reckless than its ancestors, it is no less alert and lively. The frightening tenacity with which it confronted bulls, badgers, and other dogs in the past is seen today only when it goes after rats. Its newly developed even temper has turned it into a companion dog.

Almost from birth, the Bull Terrier must be raised with a firm hand. It craves attention and can be persistent in demanding it. While its devotion to its master is unquestionable, it sometimes becomes belligerent with strangers. Nevertheless, it can be a loyal sidekick for a growing, boisterous youngster.

Cartoonists have always enjoyed exaggerating the Bull Terrier's egg-shaped head and piercing, narrow eyes. The all-white, glossy coat—initially the only recognized colour of the breed—was developed through patient and careful crossings with white terriers and Dalmatians.

AUS.	CAN.	S. AF.	U.K.	F.C.I.
●	●	●	●	●

ORIGINS

When the British Bulldog was crossed with terriers, the result was a relatively nondescript 'bull and terrier.' Subsequent crosses of this offspring with the Old English Terrier, the English Toy Terrier, and the Whippet delivered a formidable fighting dog, but one of inconsistent shape and colour. These experimental types were closer to the modern Staffordshire Bull Terrier than to the Bull Terrier. Dogfighting was eventually banned, and British breeders turned their attention to other qualities in the breed, emphasizing the terrier traits. Around 1860, James Hinks, a Birmingham dog dealer, successfully bred a dog with a smoother head, shorter legs, and whiter coat than its predecessors—the forerunner of the Bull Terrier. Because ear-cropping had been banned in Britain, dog breeders also worked on developing the small, fine, and erect ears found on today's dogs. The Bull Terrier Club of England was formed in 1888 when the breed was officially recognized.

THE MINIATURE BULL TERRIER

The Miniature Bull Terrier has evolved from the selective cross-breeding of small Bull Terriers—produced in the last century when the Bull Terrier breed was being developed—with the old Toy Bull Terrier. The first progeny were so delicate that breeders soon stopped producing them. Revived interest in a small Bull Terrier replica prompted new experimentation in the 1920s, and gradually the dog's weight was increased. Recognized by the British Kennel Club in 1943, the Miniature Bull Terrier is now about 9 kilograms (20 pounds), with a height of no more than 35 centimetres (14 inches). With the exception of size, the breed standard is the same as that for the Bull Terrier.

Characteristics

General appearance: strongly built, well proportioned, muscular, and alert, agile, with a spirited expression. Very determined and courageous. The Bull Terrier has an easy, nimble, efficient gait. Its legs move in parallel, seen head-on or from the back.

Height: under F.C.I. standards, 30 to 45 cm (12 to 18 in.). Elsewhere, not specified.

Weight: not specified.

Head: long, strong, and deep to end of muzzle. Oval, almost egg-shaped, well filled out, no hollows or indentations. Forehead flat. The face, longer than the forehead, is very full. Cheek muscles are not prominent. Upper part of the skull almost flat, from ear to ear. Profile sloping gently downwards from the top of the skull to the tip of the nose, which bends downwards. Nose black, with well-developed nostrils. Muzzle shows great strength, not pointed. Jaws strong and deep. Teeth healthy, clean, strong, good size, perfectly regular. Upper incisors must fit exactly in front of the lower, scissor bite. Lips thin and tight.

Eyes: deeply sunken, black, or as dark as possible, with a piercing glint. Small, almond-shaped or triangular, set closer to the ears than to the nose, and slanting.

Ears: small, thin, close together, set high and carried erect.

Neck: very muscular, long, arched, tapering from the head to the shoulders. No dewlap.

Body: brisket broad and deep. Back short and well muscled with a level topline that arches slightly at the loin. Ribs round, deep, and well sprung. Shoulders flat and well muscled. Great depth from withers to brisket, which is nearer to the ground than is the belly. Broad chest.

Tail: short, set low, carried horizontally, thick at the base tapering to a fine point.

Forequarters: legs straight with heavy, round bone structure of average length, perfectly parallel, providing for dog's solid stance. Elbows well placed, straight. Pasterns strong and upright.

Hindquarters: legs very straight, thighs heavily muscled with second thigh well developed. Hocks let down, with the bone to the foot short and strong. Stifles are well bent. Legs parallel when viewed from behind.

Feet: round and compact with well-arched toes.

Coat: short, flat, uniform, harsh to the touch and lustrous. Skin fits the body tightly; it is never loose or wrinkled. A soft textured undercoat may be present in winter.

Colour: white, can have coloured markings over eye or ear. Pigmentation of the skin and markings on the head do not constitute faults. Brindle, plain or with white markings. Blue or liver markings, tick markings on white.

Faults: Deafness and, according to the standards in some countries, blue eyes.

Practical information: This short-haired dog must be groomed every day, using a brush with medium-hard bristles. Every other day rub the dog down with a horsehair glove to shine its coat. It may need a bath every month if it lives outdoors, but probably no oftener than every three months if it lives indoors. A hardy, athletic animal, rarely ill, the Bull Terrier nevertheless needs long walks to maintain physical fitness and an even temperament.

Cairn Terrier

This mischievous little companion dog with its shaggy, weather-resistant coat is one of the most popular of a group of terriers that originated in Scotland around five centuries ago. The Highlands are dotted with piles of stones known as cairns, which mark the graves of ancient Romans. As these burial grounds fell into disrepair, they became overgrown with brambles and overrun with small, destructive animals. The Scottish chieftains set their terriers to control the vermin, and it was here, amid the crumbling cairns, that the Cairn Terrier earned its keep and, ultimately, its name. These doughty little dogs went after rodents, otters, weasels, foxes, and even wildcats with a fierce determination.

Precious little is known about the Cairn's background beyond the fact that Martin's *History of the Dog* described the breed accurately some 70 years before it was first shown, in 1909. A fifteenth-century writer, John Leslie, alluded to a small breed of terriers—probably the ancestors of the Cairn and the Scottish Terrier—used in hunting fox and badger. A portrait painted by Jan van Eyck in 1434 included a small, dark dog bearing a distinctive resemblance to the Cairn Terrier found today.

These hunting terriers were highly valued in Scotland. James VI, son of Mary Queen of Scots, sent six Cairn-like terriers to the King of France as a gift, around 1600. So concerned was he about the risks of the ocean voyage that the dogs were divided into two groups of three and sent on separate ships.

Though the Cairn Terrier wasn't granted official recognition by the British Kennel Club until 1912, it is widely believed to be one of the oldest terriers of pure British stock. Centuries after its ancestors were hunting amidst the cairns, this dog continues to enjoy burrowing in the earth in search of vermin, much to the annoyance and dismay of gardeners.

Equally adaptable to city and country living, the Cairn has a cheeky, sometimes exasperating, character. It is a restless dog, curious about the slightest disturbance. Unlike most terriers, it will not start a fight, but if it is attacked it will respond pluckily. Affectionate, its devotion to its owner sometimes borders on jealousy, especially if a baby comes into the house. Yet its fox-like expression can be a source of constant amusement.

AUS.	CAN.	S. AF.	U.K.	F.C.I.
●	●	●	●	●

ORIGINS

Though its origins are obscure, most experts trace the Cairn Terrier's ancestors to the Isle of Skye, off the north-west coast of Scotland. The oldest kennel known to have bred Cairns was set up in Dunvegan Castle by one Captain McLeod, who devoted himself to improving the breed for some 70 years. The best of today's Cairns descend from his stock. When the dog was first shown in Inverness, it was called a Short-haired Skye Terrier. Not surprisingly, this choice of name greatly upset owners of the distinct Skye Terrier. After a lengthy dispute the dog was renamed the Cairn Terrier in 1910. Two years later, thanks to the efforts of a Mrs. Campbell and the Honourable Mary Hawke, the British Kennel Club recognized the breed. The American Kennel Club registered the Cairn in 1913.

MAINTAINING THE BREED

For a while after the Cairn Terrier was officially recognized as a breed, some people continued to cross Cairns with West Highland White Terriers. In the litters that resulted, puppies with lighter coats were registered as West Highlands, while those with darker coats were accepted as Cairns. Left unchecked, this practice would have eventually blurred the distinction between the two breeds. In 1924, the British Kennel Club decided to fix the Cairn breed by refusing to register the offspring of crosses.

Characteristics

General appearance: well supported by the forefeet. Very free in movement. Strong and compact.

Height: 28 to 30.5 cm (11 to 12 in.). Under Canadian standards, 25.4 cm (10 in.) for the adult dog; 24 cm (9½ in.) for the bitch.

Weight: 6.4 to 7.3 kg (14 to 16 lb). Under Canadian standards, 6.4 kg (14 lb) for the adult dog; 5.9 kg (13 lb) for the bitch.

Head: small, well proportioned. Muzzle powerful. Strong, level jaws.

Eyes: wide-set, medium size, dark hazel, slightly sunken, with bushy eyebrows.

Ears: small, pointed, carried erect.

Neck: well set on, but not short.

Body: compact. Level back, of average length. Ribs deep, well sprung. Shoulders sloping. Strong, supple loin.

Tail: short, well covered with hair, not feathered, carried gaily.

Forequarters: legs of medium length, good bone structure; straight, covered with harsh hair. Elbows tight.

Hindquarters: legs very strong. Hocks well let down.

Feet: forefeet larger than hind, slightly turned out, pads thick.

Coat: thick, harsh but not coarse. Undercoat short, soft, and dense.

Colour: cream, wheaten, red, sand, grey, brindle, or nearly black.

Faults: jaw undershot or overshot. Eyes protruding or too light. Ears too large, rounded at the tips, or too hairy. Coat silky or curly (a slight wave is permitted). Nose flesh-coloured or light. Resemblance to Scottish Terrier. Solid black, white, or black and tan colouring.

Practical information: While the Cairn adapts well to life in cramped quarters, its nails must be clipped regularly to prevent them from becoming ingrown.

GROOMING THE CAIRN TERRIER

The workmanlike, unkempt appearance of the Cairn's coat is misleading: it requires regular, careful grooming. Brush the dog two or three times a week, but be careful not to remove too much of the soft undercoat. Bathe the dog once a month, and brush the coat while it is drying. The hair must be thinned regularly to keep it in good condition. Pay particular attention to the neck and ears, where dead hair must be cut short with scissors and then removed. The tail should be left bushy, but not feathered.

Chesapeake Bay Retriever

The Chesapeake Bay Retriever has never been a pampered darling of the show ring. From the beginning, this American creation was valued as a superior water-dog, bred for versatility rather than for elegance.

A rough-and-ready specimen, the Chesapeake takes to the great outdoors much more eagerly than to the kennel. One admirer, writing more than a hundred years ago of the dog's work with duck hunters, compared its hardy manner with that of a shivering setter and a wet, uncomfortable-looking spaniel. He went on to describe the Chesapeake's seeming disdain for comfort this way: '. . . the shaking he has given his coarse, oily coat has freed it entirely from ice and water; he cannot be enticed into a kennel, but must sit out on the frozen shore, rain or shine, and watch as well as the gunner.'

During the late nineteenth century when the breed became famous for its prowess in the icy waters of Chesapeake Bay, Maryland, the dog was often called upon to retrieve 200 to 300 ducks a day. Today, hunters speak in glowing terms of the Chesapeake's remarkable endurance and boundless enthusiasm. In the minds of many, the breed is without peer in rough water.

The Chesapeake Bay Retriever's coat and colour are two of its most distinctive characteristics, and

AUS.	CAN.	S. AF.	U.K.	F.C.I.
●	●	●	●	●

ORIGINS

In 1807 a British brig was shipwrecked off the coast of Maryland. Among the survivors were two Newfoundland puppies, a light rust male named Sailor and a black female that was named Canton in honour of the American ship which rescued them. These two dogs were bred with American retrievers to create the Chesapeake Bay Retriever. Among the new breed's ancestors are the Curly Coated Retriever and the Irish Water Spaniel. The standard was established in 1885 and a club for the breed was formed in 1918 at Albert Lea, Minnesota. Selective inbreeding has emphasized the dog's hunting skills, its powerful musculature, and its water-resistant coat.

both serve a vital purpose. Because the breed often works in ice and snow, proper coat texture is essential. The oil in the harsh outer coat and the woolly undercoat keeps cold water from reaching the dog's skin and also helps in quick drying. When the dog emerges from the water and shakes itself, the coat should not retain any water, but merely be moist.

In colour, the Chesapeake varies from a dark brown to a faded tan or 'deadgrass.' Since the breed is used for duck-hunting, the coat colour should, ideally, match the local surroundings. Interestingly, the deadgrass colour was developed in the midwestern United States, where the breed became popular shortly after the Civil War.

For all its endurance, the Chesapeake seldom garners top awards at field trials. The swifter Labrador Retriever is the most consistent victor at these competitions. Chesapeake fanciers maintain that the trials simply do not present the breed with enough of a challenge.

However, when it comes to the dog's courage and devotion to family, especially children, there is no debate: it will guard its loved ones tenaciously. More than one drowning youngster can attest to the Chesapeake's bravery and intelligence.

Characteristics

General appearance: well proportioned, good musculature, intelligent expression.
Height: 58.4 to 66 cm (23 to 26 in.) for the dog; 53.3 to 61 cm (21 to 24 in.) for the bitch.
Weight: 29.5 to 34 kg (65 to 75 lb) for the dog; 25 to 29.5 kg (55 to 65 lb) for the bitch.
Head: skull broad and round, medium stop. Muzzle short, pointed, but not sharp. Lips thin, not pendulous. Scissor bite.
Eyes: medium size, set well apart, very clear yellowish colour.
Ears: small, set high, and hanging freely.
Neck: medium length, well muscled, tapering from head to shoulders.
Body: medium size, somewhat hollow. Deep, wide, strong chest, flanks well tucked up. Back powerful, well-sprung ribs. Shoulders well laid back. Powerful, free movement.
Tail: medium length, straight or slightly curved, fairly thick at base. Moderate feathering permissible.
Forequarters: legs straight, powerful. Well-angulated shoulders of good bone and musculature. Pasterns slightly bent.
Hindquarters: well coupled, powerful. Medium hocks. Well-rounded toes (hare-footed), webbed feet. No dewclaws.
Coat: not more than 3.8 cm (1½ in.) long, thick, straight. Harsh, oily, weatherproof. Undercoat dense, fine, woolly. Tends to wave on shoulders, neck, back, and loin.
Colour: preferably solid-coloured, varying from dark brown to dark tan to deadgrass.

Practical information: An outdoor dog, the Chesapeake Bay Retriever must swim regularly and get plenty of other exercise to maintain its stamina and ideal weight.

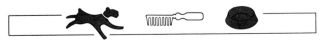

Chihuahua

Long-coat Chihuahua

Smooth-coat Chihuahua

AUS.	CAN.	S. AF.	U.K.	F.C.I.
●	●	●	●	●

The smallest breed of dog in the world was discovered by tourists in the Mexican state of Chihuahua near the end of the last century. Written accounts from as early as 1850 described tiny dogs with both long and short hair living in Mexican-American border towns. James Watson, a Chihuahua expert, wrote that he had been buying such dogs in Texas since 1888.

Long thought to have been a true native of Mexico, this diminutive dog has left no archaeological evidence that its ancestors were part of Aztec life before the Spanish conquest in the sixteenth century. Scientists have never found true dog remains in Aztec graves or other archaeological digs. Creatures pictured in Aztec art and reported in early writings to be the Chihuahua are probably some kind of rodent.

The Spanish invaders were far from being natural-history experts. Many of the strange Mexican life forms they encountered—coatimundis, opossums, raccoons, and gophers—probably resembled animals they knew at home. When they saw something that looked like a dog, they called it a dog. But the various tree climbers and tunnel dwellers they described were certainly not dogs. It is much more likely that the Chihuahua's forbears landed in Mexico before the conquest and survived the destruction of the Aztec nation long enough to catch the eye of American dog fanciers.

The Chihuahua is one of the most readily recognizable breeds in the world, and it continues to

ORIGINS

Dog historians are quick to argue about the distant origins of the Chihuahua. Some say it evolved in Egypt and found its way to the Mediterranean countries, from where it was taken to Mexico during the Spanish conquest of 1519. Another theory says that four breeds of dog— one resembling the Chihuahua—were domesticated in Mexico long before the conquest. Aztec sculptures from northern Mexico, where the state of Chihuahua is located, depict a little animal with big ears that was thought to be an ancestor of the Chihuahua breed. Counter-arguments maintain that just as many of today's domestic animals—cows, goats, horses, pigs, and sheep—were not indigenous to Mexico when the Spaniards arrived, neither were dogs. Yet another theory has it that traders carried the Chihuahua to Mexico from China more than a hundred years ago. But whatever its past, the breed's forerunners were brought into the United States well before the turn of the century and crossed with terriers such as the Black and Tan Toy to produce the modern Smooth-coat breed.

amaze people with its size. The most valued dogs weigh less than 1 kilogram (2¼ pounds), while the largest of the breed are just double that weight. Easily carried in one hand, the Chihuahua has been a popular companion dog for decades. Yet, as irresistible as they are to carry, the Chihuahua needs a surprising amount of exercise and should therefore be encouraged and allowed to move around on its own.

Loyal by nature, at times even jealous, the Chihuahua is not totally comfortable with strangers. It pays strict attention to its owner's every move and hates to be left alone; in fact, it welcomes the company of another dog, and will play happily with a fellow Chihuahua. This intelligent animal responds enthusiastically to training.

Characteristics

General appearance: alert, vivacious, and graceful.

Height: under F.C.I. standards, 16 to 20 cm (6 to 8 in.). Elsewhere, not specified.

Weight: under F.C.I. standards, 1 to 3.5 kg (2¼ to 7½ lb). Elsewhere, 1 to 2.75 kg (2 to 6 lb).

Head: apple head with lean cheeks. Stop well defined. Occipital bones prominent. Muzzle short and slightly pointed. Jaws strong, scissor bite. Black nose valued. In blond and light types, nose can be pink, light, or black. In taupe, blue, or chocolate types, the nose is the same colour as the coat.

Eyes: bright, full, round, not too prominent, set wide. Dark; light eyes are permitted with blond coats.

Ears: large, flaring, and well separated. Carried erect when dog is in motion and set at a 45-degree angle when at rest.

Neck: medium length, slightly arched, sloping into shoulders.

Body: deep brisket; short, level back. Well-sprung ribs. Shoulders well laid back.

Tail: long, full when plumed, set high and curved over the back. Never carried between the legs. Furry, flattish, broadening slightly in centre and tapering to a point. No tail or natural bobtail acceptable.

Forequarters: legs straight, elbows flexible and long, brisket well defined, fine and flexible pasterns.

Hindquarters: legs muscular, hocks wide, straight, well balanced.

Feet: small and dainty, toes separated but not widely spaced. Thick pads, nails long and curved. Harelike or catlike foot highly undesirable.

Coat: in Smooth-coat breed, short and dense, lustrous. Small ruff desirable. In Long-coat dog, hair is long, silky, well feathered. A slight wave is permissible.

Colour: all colours and mixtures of colours. Most sought after are tawny, brown, chocolate, white, cream, grey, black, black and tan.

THE LONG-COAT CHIHUAHUA

The Long-coat breed is believed to have been developed in the United States by crossing Smooth-coat Chihuahuas with other miniature breeds—the Papillon, the Pomeranian, the Pekingese, the Yorkshire Terrier, and the Toy Poodle have been put forward as possibilities. The Long-coat is identical in almost every respect to the Smooth-coat, except for its soft and abundant hair, which covers it from head to toe. Still considered a rarity in many parts of the world, the Long-coat is bred mainly in Great Britain, Canada, and the United States.

Practical information: Exercise the dog regularly and feed it lightly. Check its teeth for tartar deposits and brush them occasionally; have a veterinarian check them twice a year. The eyes are susceptible to drying of the cornea, or hypertrophy (secondary glaucoma). Clean the Smooth-coat with a wet cloth or glove. Bathe the Long-coat once a month and dry it thoroughly. Keep the dog off freshly fertilized grass and away from sprayed bushes. Don't let it lick or eat toxic products used in treating it for parasites.

Chow Chow

AUS.	CAN.	S. AF.	U.K.	F.C.I.
●	●	●	●	●

ORIGINS

The Chow Chow is a direct descendant of the Canis palustris, *the probable ancestor of all spitz-type dogs. The Chow Chow's structure and form is similar to that of the oldest fossilized dog—several million years old—found in the United States. The Chow Chow arrived in China with the first immigrants from northern Asia. The British improved the breed by careful selection, transforming the Hong Kong strain into the modern Chow Chow by correcting its physical imperfections, balancing its proportions, and minimizing the less attractive elements of its character. Organized breeding of the Chow began in Great Britain in 1887. The breed was recognized by the Kennel Club in 1894.*

A delightful teddy bear when a pup, the Chow Chow grows quickly into a powerful dog with a superb mane that gives it the look of a miniature lion.

Clean and well behaved, courageous but less ferocious than it looks, the Chow Chow has a strong personality and a will all its own. This proud, independent animal is not easily mastered. Breeders recommend adopting it as soon as it has been weaned and raising it lovingly and patiently, but with a firm hand.

Its aloof, almost cat-like character has given it an undeserved reputation for unpredictability and even treachery. It does not take easily to strangers and is sometimes unfriendly or aggressive towards them. But it will never attack without warning, preferring to display any hostility openly. The Chow Chow is simply a one-owner dog. As Chow owners can testify, the dog is loyal, devoted, and completely predictable to those it likes. Some say it would die for its human family. Though it seems discreet, almost shy, in the way it demonstrates affection, the Chow Chow is full of warmth. All in all, this dog is both an ideal household pet and an effective guardian.

The West knew nothing of the Chow Chow until the late eighteenth century, though the dog has been known in China for at least two thousand years. Detailed drawings in Chinese iconography indicate that the breed remained pure down through the centuries. Chow Chows probably first arrived in the British Isles around 1780. They apparently had the blue-black tongue and leonine head of the modern Chow, as well as the same general silhouette.

THE CHOW CHOW IN CHINA

In China long ago, Chow Chows guarded herds, sampans, and junks, and hunted sable and other animals. This hard-working dog hardly resembled the well-groomed Chow Chow of today. Harnessed to carts or sleds, the strongest dogs could haul heavy cargo despite a meagre diet.

In Cantonese, the word *chow* means 'food.' The forerunner of the Chow Chow was considered a delicacy by some Chinese, and on certain farms it was fattened to be eaten when it was between ten months and one year old. The Chow Chow's furry hair trimmed the coats of many a wealthy Chinese gentlewoman.

Characteristics

General appearance: compact body. Perfectly balanced. Massive, cobby, and powerful. Shining coat. Dignified, distant bearing. Stiff gait. Blue-black tongue, flews, and roof of mouth, unusual in other dogs.

Height: 48.3 to 55.9 cm (19 to 22 in.) for the dog; 45.7 to 50.8 cm (18 to 20 in.) for the bitch. Canadian standards not specified.

Weight: under F.C.I. standards, 20 to 25 kg (44 to 55 lb). Elsewhere, not specified.

Head: flat and broad. Stop well defined. Fullness under eyes. Muzzle medium long, broad to the tip. Large, broad nose, usually black. In white and cream dogs, a light coloured nose is permissible; in blues and tawny dogs, a nose the same colour as the coat is permissible. Teeth strong and level; scissor bite. Lips and palate black, gums preferably black.

Eyes: dark and small, preferably almond-shaped. In the blues and the tawny, light coloured eyes are allowed. Clean eye free from entropion.

Ears: small, thick, slightly rounded at the tip. Carried stiff and erect, set well in front, above the eyes, and spaced wide apart, creating the 'scowl' that is characteristic of the breed.

Neck: strong, full, well set on the shoulders.

Body: chest broad and deep. Back short, level, and strong. Loin powerful. Shoulders muscular.

Tail: set high and carried well over the back.

Forequarters: legs perfectly straight, of medium length, good bone structure.

Hindquarters: legs muscular, hocks well let down and perfectly straight, essential to the stiff gait characteristic of the breed.

Feet: small, round, cat-footed. Thick pads.

Coat: in rough-coated variety, coat is abundant, dense, and straight. Outer coat harsh, undercoat soft, woolly. In smooth-coated varieties, coat is abundant, dense, short, and plushy in texture.

Colour: solid-coloured black, red, blue, tawny, cream, or white, often shaded, but the coat must not have any defined markings and must not be more than one colour. The underside of the tail and brace of the thighs are often light coloured.

Faults: drop ear or ears. Tongue red, pink, or obviously spotted with red or pink. Tail not carried over the back. Nose wrongly coloured. Coat that has been clipped or is of several colours.

Practical information: The Chow Chow is susceptible to eczema, so its hygiene must be supervised all its life. The joints are delicate. It suffers frequently from entropion, an eye disease in which the lid turns inward against the haw. The lashes eventually irritate the haw, causing conjunctivitis and ulceration of the cornea. Usually congenital, entropion can be treated surgically. Thin the Chow Chow's coat thoroughly from time to time, particularly during shedding periods, to remove dead hairs. Use a steel brush. The mane should be groomed every day. Bathing is not recommended; if the dog is very dirty, however, it can be bathed once or twice a year, at most.

Clumber Spaniel

A sturdy, low-slung body, square head, and heavy muzzle are characteristic of this dog, which bears little resemblance to other spaniels. Its name comes from Clumber Park, the Duke of Newcastle's estate. The duke set up a kennel there in the late eighteenth century to breed spaniels given to him, so the story goes, by French aristocrats newly arrived in England. Whatever the origins of the breed, it prospered in England, reaching the height of its vogue in the nineteenth century, then diminishing in popularity after the Second World War.

The Clumber has a reputation for silence in the field. In earlier days a pack hound, it now works alone or in small groups. This playful, calm, good-natured animal makes a charming companion.

AUS.	CAN.	S. AF.	U.K.	F.C.I.
•	•	•	•	•

ORIGINS

Practically nothing is known of the Clumber Spaniel's origins. Some experts say it belonged to an ancient French line, raised in the kennels of the Noailles family, who gave some of the breed to the Duke of Newcastle. For many years, Clumber Spaniels were much sought after by the British aristocracy. The breed has changed little since the late nineteenth century.

Characteristics

General appearance: very sturdy, active. It has a rolling gait and a thoughtful expression.

Weight: dogs about 36.3 kg (80 lb); bitches, 29.5 kg (65 lb). Canadian standards: dogs 25 to 29.5 kg (55 to 65 lb); bitches, 16 to 22.7 kg (35 to 50 lb).

Head: massive, square, solid. Occiput prominent. Heavy eyebrows. Stop well defined. Muzzle heavy, lips well developed. Nose flesh-coloured.

Eyes: clear or dark amber, haw slightly visible.

Ears: large, vine-leaf shaped, covered with straight hair, dropping slightly forward.

Neck: thick, powerful, fairly long, well feathered on the underside.

Body: long, low, and heavy. Chest deep, well-sprung ribs. Back level, broad, and long. Loin powerful. Shoulders very strong, sloping, muscular.

Tail: set low, feathered, level with back.

Forequarters: legs short, straight, thick, and strong.

Hindquarters: thighs powerful, hocks well let down, stifles well bent.

Coat: abundant, silky, straight. Legs well feathered.

Colour: white with lemon or orange markings.

Practical information: The Clumber Spaniel is a robust dog and needs plenty of exercise. It is best suited to life in the country. Its long, dense coat needs thorough and regular brushing, especially if the dog lives indoors. After hunting, check carefully for parasites, thorns, or brambles. Check and clean the ears carefully and regularly.

Cocker Spaniel (American)

A great charmer, thanks to its splendid coat and beautiful head, the American Cocker is smaller than its English counterpart. Although they shared a common ancestor, the English and American Cockers had become so different by the 1930s that a movement got underway to recognize two distinct breeds. This was achieved after the Second World War. By then, the American Cocker was the most popular dog in North America. Although it is now considered a pet and show dog, the American Cocker has lost none of the hunting instincts typical of all spaniels. It still flushes game with obvious ease, skill, and delight. Beneath the Cocker's air of sophistication lurks a real athlete that needs regular exercise. At home, the Cocker makes an ideal pet.

AUS.	CAN.	S. AF.	U.K.	F.C.I.
●	●	●	●	●

ORIGINS

In 1882 the English Cocker was exported from Britain to the United States. Through rigorous selection, American breeders produced a smaller dog with longer legs, while retaining the finely chiselled head with its square muzzle and deep stop. The American Cocker was introduced to Europe in the middle of this century.

Characteristics

General appearance: a sturdy, compact, well-balanced dog with a refined head.
Height: 35.6 to 38 cm (14 to 15 in.). Under Canadian standards, 36.8 to 39.4 cm (14½ and 15½ in.) for the adult dog; 34.3 to 38 cm (13½ to 15 in.) for the bitch.
Weight: not specified.
Head: well developed and rounded. Eyebrows and stop well defined. Forehead smooth. Muzzle broad. Jaws square. Nose black or brown, depending on coat colour. Black dogs must have black noses.
Eyes: slightly almond-shaped; iris dark brown.
Ears: long, covered with silky hair.

Body: compact, robust. Back short, strong, sloping.
Tail: customarily docked by three-fifths. Set on and carried in line with top of back or slightly higher. In motion, merry tail action.
Forequarters: shoulders deep, clean-cut, and sloping. Legs straight, strong-boned, and muscular. Elbows close, turning neither in nor out. Pasterns short.
Hindquarters: legs strongly boned and muscled with good angulation at stifle. Hocks strong, well let down.
Coat: silky, flat, or slightly wavy.
Colour: jet black, and other solid colours; may include tan markings. Also, parti-coloured.

Practical information: Sensitive eyes, prone to watering, are the only weakness of this generally healthy dog. Clean the eyes regularly. Bathe often, shampooing the coat well and drying it thoroughly. Then use a hard brush to clean the mane, being careful not to tear out the long, silky hair. The Cocker's superb coat can become so tangled in brambles that the dog may be unable to free itself. Avoid walking the dog through thickly wooded areas.

113

Cocker Spaniel (English)

AUS.	CAN.	S. AF.	U.K.	F.C.I.
●	●	●	●	●

The English Cocker Spaniel is a tireless, enthusiastic hunter. Its small size allows it easy access everywhere so it can methodically explore terrain and discover game where other dogs cannot. Unmatched in hunting woodcock or pheasant, the Cocker can also flush out partridge and will wade fearlessly into a marsh to pick up a duck or goose. It is an excellent and willing retriever.

The Cocker has also become a popular companion dog, admired for its size, elegance, soft coat, and beautiful head framed by long, dangling ears. It is gentle, playful, even impish at times. Naturally fastidious, it spends long periods cleaning its coat, somewhat like a cat.

Curious about the world around it, submissive but not slavish, this dog takes an active interest in its owner's life and is a devoted pet. Rudyard Kipling once called his English Cocker his greatest fan, pleased and amused that it loved him without ever having read a word he had written.

Despite the Van Dyke painting from 1630, which shows the children of Charles I of England with two spaniels that resemble the modern English Cocker, this dog cannot tolerate the awkwardness and teasing of young children.

The English Cocker is independent and intelligent, and has a strong personality. It must, therefore, be raised with a degree of firmness.

ORIGINS

The Cocker Spaniel, along with other members of the spaniel family, may have originated in Spain. In the fourteenth century, Gaston Phoebus, Count de Foix, wrote a treatise on hunting. The chapter devoted to chiens d'oysel *(bird dogs) referred to* Espainholz, *a likely Spanish ancestor of the Cocker. Another hint at Spanish origins occurs in the writings of Dr. John Caius, who, in 1576, said: 'The common sort of people call them by one general word, namely spaniells [sic] as though these dogs came originally and first of all out of Spain.' The word 'spaniel,' probably derived from the Old French word* espaignol, *simply meant 'Spanish dog.' By the seventeenth century there were all kinds of spaniels—big and small, long and short, fast and slow. Some were used in France and Britain for hunting with nets. Eighteenth-century England had two distinct varieties of spaniel: the larger Springer, highly valued in hunting waterfowl, and the Cocker, used for hunting woodcock. The Cocker, therefore, may have been named for its ability to 'cock' or flush game. The dukes of Marlborough bred Cockers and, by adding strains of the King Charles Spaniel, changed the line completely. The breed was definitely established late in the last century.*

Characteristics

General appearance: merry, alert, well built, the Cocker Spaniel must compensate for its small, heavy appearance with boundless energy and stamina. A thoughtful expression indicates exceptional intelligence.

Height: 38 to 43 cm (15 to 17 in.). Under Canadian standards, 40.6 to 43 cm (16 to 17 in.) for the adult male; 38 to 40.6 cm (15 to 16 in.) for the bitch.

Weight: 11 to 15.4 cm (24 to 34 in.) Under Canadian standards, 12.7 to 15.4 kg (28 to 34 lb) for the adult male; 11.8 to 14.5 kg (26 to 32 lb.) for the bitch.

Head: not heavy or solid. Long, lean, with well-defined lines. Skull and forehead well developed. Occiput moderately prominent. Eyebrows shielding most of the eye. Muzzle square, powerful, straight, solid, and broad. Stop well defined. Lean cheeks finely chiselled. Lips neither pendulous nor limp. Full jowls. Strong jaws. Scissor bite. Nose broad, nostrils well developed.

Eyes: dark, filling the sockets but not protruding. Alert, bright, and intelligent. Showing no haw. The axes of eyes must be exactly parallel.

Ears: lobular, set low. Broad, thin, and flexible, they are covered with a layer of silky, thick hair. They hang flat, close to the cheeks, nicely framing the head.

Neck: moderately long and muscular, well set on the shoulders, slightly arched. Clean in throat; no dewlap. Abundant ruff.

Body: compact and well coupled, conveying concentrated strength and vigour. Back short, strong, and compact, slightly sloping downwards towards the tail. Shoulders very long and well angulated. Chest broad, deep, well down. Ribs well sprung. Loin very powerful, short, muscular.

Tail: set slightly below topline, docked two-thirds of its length, carried in line with back. Tail-wagging is typical of the breed.

Forequarters: good bone structure. Legs straight, powerful, fairly short, amply feathered, not too close together or too far apart. Paws strong, feathered.

Hindquarters: very powerful, broad, well rounded, very muscular. Thighs well muscled. Hocks long and well let down, not turned inwards or outwards.

Feet: solid, cat-footed. Pads very hard.

Coat: all the same texture, flat, silky, never stiff or wiry, with ample, straight feathering. Hair flat, thick, dense, never woolly or frizzy.

Colour: All colours. Also parti-coloured blue, liver, red, orange and lemon, black and tan. Solid-coloured must have no markings except for a little white on the chest, which is permissible.

Faults: large skull, too flat, or too rounded. Light bone structure. Coat too curly, soft, or wiry. Excessive angulation. Barrel ribs. Dewlap. Exaggerated tuck up. Conspicuous haw. Ears insufficiently feathered. Tail carried gaily. Stop not well defined. Light eyes.

Practical information: The Cocker Spaniel is susceptible to ear infections. Clean excess wax from the inside of the auditory canal regularly. If the dog is in pain, or if there are traces of congealed blood in the ears, consult a veterinarian. The Cocker gains weight easily. Feed it moderately, depending on the exercise it gets. An average diet consists of 650 to 800 grams (23 to 28 ounces) of meat and vegetables or grains. Cheese and peeled, fresh fruit can replace some of the meat. If the Cocker does not get enough exercise it may become nervous or even aggressive. It must be taken for long, daily walks as well as weekly runs in the country.

Collie

For centuries Collies were little known outside the Scottish Lowlands, where they guarded the large flocks of sheep that roamed freely over the heath. Then, in 1860, Queen Victoria took a holiday at Balmoral Castle and, charmed by the breed, brought several Rough Collies back with her to Windsor Castle. Helped by a hint of snobbishness, the Collie fad was launched; both Britons and Americans fell madly in love with the rough-coated beauties.

Easy-going indoors, the Collie brims with exuberance the moment it gets outside. Sometimes, responding to an ancestral urge, it will crawl along the ground as if trying to approach a sheep without frightening it.

Highly strung, sensitive, and anxious to please, the Collie mistrusts strangers but grows deeply attached to its owner and family. It is affectionate with children, and its keen sense of belonging makes it an effective watch-dog. Intelligent and easily trained, it also possesses all the necessary qualities of a good police or guide dog.

AUS.	CAN.	S. AF.	U.K.	F.C.I.
●	●	●	●	●

ORIGINS

The Collie's ancestors were probably an ancient breed of dog indigenous to the northern British Isles and a breed of sheep-dogs which arrived in Britain with the Romans, about 500 B.C. Somewhere along the way it was probably crossed with the Newfoundland and the Deerhound. At the beginning of the last century selective breeding began to produce an efficient herding Collie that was crossed with the Borzoi around 1830. The result was a streamlined dog with a more elongated head and more beautiful coat.

OTHER COLLIE BREEDS

Many people, when they think of the Collie, immediately visualize the Rough Collie, perhaps unaware that there are two other distinct breeds: the Bearded and the Border Collies. (The rarely seen Smooth Collie is like the Rough Collie except for a short coat.) The Bearded Collie resembles the Old English Sheepdog. The Border Collie is bred as a sheep-herder and is popular in Australia. The Shetland Sheepdog (see p. 253) is a miniature of the Rough Collie.

Bearded Collie

Border Collie

Rough Collie

Characteristics (Rough and Smooth Collies)

General appearance: dog of great beauty, dignity, and grace.
Height: 50.8 to 61 cm (20 to 24 in.). Canadian standards: 61 to 66 cm (24 to 26 in.) for dogs; 55.9 to 61 cm (22 to 24 in.) for bitches.
Weight: 18 to 28.6 kg (40 to 63 lb). Under Canadian standards, 22.7 to 29.5 kg (50 to 65 lb).
Head: skull flat, broad between the ears, gradually tapering towards the eyes. Muzzle follows an almost straight line towards the nose. Stop not well defined. Nose must be black.
Eyes: medium size, slightly oblique, almond-shaped.
Ears: moderately broad at base, set not too close together at top of skull. Semi-erect with tip folded forward.
Neck: muscular, strong, good length, well arched.
Body: rather long. Ribs well sprung, brisket deep. Well-muscled loin.
Tail: long, reaching at least to hock, carried low when passive, tip slightly turned up when active.
Forequarters: legs well balanced, straight and muscular.
Hindquarters: muscular; thighs, lean and sinewy.
Feet: oval, well padded. Toes arched, close together.
Coat: in Rough Collie, very dense, long, stiff; the undercoat soft, thick, and dense. Mane and collar abundant. In Smooth Collie, short, hard, dense, flat hair; abundant undercoat.
Colour: sable and white, tricolour, and blue merle. Under Canadian standards, sable and merle, and predominantly white.
Faults: head length out of proportion with body; shaped like the Borzoi's. Eyes with poor expression. Tail carried over back.

Practical information: Good tolerance for cold and rain, but not for heat and inactivity. The Collie must have daily exercise. Indoors, it tends to lose its hair.

THE COLLIE IN HOLLYWOOD

With the release of the first Lassie film in 1943, the already popular Collie breed expanded its circle of admirers. And the Rough Collie that played Lassie became a celebrity even though most adoring fans were unaware that the star of *Lassie Come Home* was, in fact, a laddie named Pal.

Metro-Goldwyn-Mayer hired Pal, born near Hollywood in 1941, after it outperformed hundreds of other dogs in a screen test that required candidates to ford a river and collapse, convincingly exhausted, on the other side. Because *Lassie Come Home* was enormously successful, M.G.M. awarded Pal a lucrative multi-year contract. The canine star had its own house, studio, and stand-ins for difficult scenes. Pal worked only about five years and was then retired to a life of ease on a ranch where it died at the age of 19. The canine actors that carried on the Lassie legend lived, worked, and were retired in the same pampered, luxurious fashion.

Curly Coated Retriever

The Curly Coated Retriever is the oldest of the English retrievers. The breed is instantly recognizable among retrievers for its tightly curled, black or liver-coloured coat. These astrakhan curls insulate the dog against the elements and equip it especially well for swimming in cold water at any time of year. Widely used in the last century, the dog is still considered by many sportsmen to be the best for duck-hunting in wetlands. Independent by nature, the Curly Coated Retriever is sometimes unfriendly, even hostile, towards other dogs.

AUS.	CAN.	S. AF.	U.K.	F.C.I.
●	●	●	●	●

ORIGINS

The Curly Coated Retriever was created in the last century. According to one authority, it is the product of a cross between the Newfoundland and the Irish Water Spaniel.

Characteristics

General appearance: elegant, flexible, steady on its feet. Smart, active, hard-working.
Height: 63.5 to 68.6 cm (25 to 27 in.).
Weight: 31.7 to 36.3 kg (70 to 80 lb).
Head: skull long, well proportioned, flat. Jaws strong and long. Scissor bite. Nose broad, black or liver.
Eyes: large, but not protruding. Black or dark brown.
Ears: rather small, set low, close to head.
Neck: moderately long, no dewlap.
Body: well-sprung ribs, brisket broad, not long in loin, and well tucked up.

Tail: medium, carried straight, tapering towards the point.
Forequarters: shoulders very deep, muscular, and oblique.
Hindquarters: legs muscular, sturdy, moderately long. Hocks well let down and well bent.
Feet: round, compact. Toes well arched.
Coat: mass of tight, crisp curls over whole body.
Colour: black or liver. A few white hairs permissible.
Faults: broad skull. Eyes light. Gay tail. Saddle back. Patches of straight hair.

Practical information: The Curly Coated Retriever needs plenty of exercise, including a regular swim.

Dachsbracke

Drever

Dachsbracke

Except for its longer legs, the Dachsbracke resembles its relative, the Dachshund. This flexible, sure-footed dog has a keen sense of smell. Although it has been around since the 1600s, the Dachsbracke is not very common today. German royalty, in times gone by, favoured this hound for its hunting abilities. At the beginning of this century, the Danes and the Swedes adopted the dog and cross-bred it to start two new breeds. One of these breeds, the Drever, is a popular dog in Sweden, and it has also been recognized by the Canadian Kennel Club.

AUS.	CAN.	S. AF.	U.K.	F.C.I.
		●	●	●

ORIGINS

The Dachsbracke may be the cross-bred result of matings between Dachshunds and Basset Hounds. There are two types of Dachsbracke: the Alpine Montano and the Westphalian Basset.

Characteristics (Dachsbracke)

General appearance: resembles a large Dachshund.
Height: under F.C.I. standards, 30 to 42 cm (12 to 16½ in.). Elsewhere, not specified.
Weight: under F.C.I. standards, 15 to 25 kg (33 to 55 lb). Elsewhere, not specified.
Head: slightly convex. Slight stop. Muzzle almost straight, and nose not too large. Lips well closed.
Eyes: medium size, round, generally dark brown.
Ears: medium length, broad, pendent.
Body: brisket ample, well let down. Topline level, firm, long. Croup rounded. Belly tucked up.

Tail: medium long, broad at the base, tapering towards the tip.
Forequarters: legs hardy, muscular, almost straight.
Hindquarters: legs lighter, very angular.
Feet: forefeet better developed than hind feet, well closed. Pads large and firm.
Coat: hair short, dense, hard but flexible. Little or no undercoat.
Colour: black with rust or brown markings, red with pale tan markings, or white patched with several colours (all reds are permissible).

Practical information: Not well suited to indoor life. Check the ears regularly.

Dachshund

Teckel

T his dog is a bundle of contrasts. Its stubby
legs are out of all proportion to its long body.
It is a mischievous, affectionate companion dog,
yet it displays extraordinary courage and endurance as a hunter. And its bark—ferocious enough
to frighten off a prowler—is gargantuan in comparison to its diminutive size.

Dachshund is the German word for 'badger dog,'
a dog that 'goes to earth.' Despite the English mis-
translation of the word *hund* as 'hound,' the Dachshund is arguably a terrier—a dog that can go to
ground and crawl into an animal's lair and drag its
prey out. True to its name, the Dachshund will
never hesitate to attack the sharp-clawed badger
with an audacity unusual for such a small dog.
Many a zealous dog has been known to plunge into
a tunnel after quarry—only to get stuck inside.

Neither brush nor thicket can stop this tireless
animal as it forges ahead, baying while it tracks.
It is remarkably adept at finding wounded prey,
thanks to its well-developed sense of smell. The
French have nicknamed it *chien rouge*, or 'red-
hot dog,' because of its reputation for tracking a
wounded boar or stag for up to two days after having sniffed only a few drops of the quarry's blood.

Many kennel clubs recognize six breeds of
Dachshund: three of standard size named according to their coats—the Smooth-haired, Long-
haired, and Wire-haired Dachshunds—and three
miniaturized versions of the standard sizes.

Any Dachshund is generally good-humoured
and a bit of a show-off, though it can also be cunning and somewhat stubborn. It will try to train
its owner rather than allow itself to be trained.

AUS.	CAN.	S. AF.	U.K.	F.C.I.
●	●	●	●	●

ORIGINS

*The Dachshund's distant past
remains a mystery. Dachshund-
like dogs were depicted in
ancient Egyptian temples and
tombs, and in carvings from
Mexico. Some authorities believe Dachshunds existed in
South America hundreds of
years before Europeans arrived.
Whatever its earliest ancestor,
the Dachshund probably descended from the French Basset
Hound, or both descended from
a common forbear, along with
the Dachsbracke. The Dachshund was known in Germany
in the early 1700s. In 1833,
Queen Victoria referred to her
'Dash' in a diary entry. The British first showed the breed in the
1870s.*

Smooth-haired Dachshunds

Long-haired Dachshund

Miniature Smooth-haired
Dachshund

Wire-haired Dachshund

Miniature Long-haired
Dachshund

Characteristics

General appearance: low to ground, short legged, long bodied and compact, head held proudly. Miniature breeds are replicas of the standard breeds.
Height: not specified.
Weight: from 4.5 to 11.8 kg (10 to 26 lb), depending on variety. Under Canadian standards, miniature breeds, ideal weight 4.5 kg (10 lb); standard breeds, more than 5 kg (11 lb).
Head: long, tapering towards the muzzle, which is long and narrow. Nose black or brown according to coat colour, Roman nose. Well-defined eyebrows. Skull slightly arched, without prominent stop. No furrow. Lips covering lower jaw without flews. Well-developed jaw, strong canines, scissor bite.
Eyes: almond-shaped, brown, set obliquely, varying from reddish brown to dark brown; dark preferred. Intelligent, lively, friendly expression.
Ears: set high towards occiput, moderately long. Flat and rounded at the tips, dropping close to cheeks.
Neck: good length, muscular, dry, no dewlap.
Body: powerful, prominent sternum, thorax broad and long. Loin short and slightly arched. Belly tucked up. Oblique shoulders. Back level. Rump broad.
Tail: set high, not curved, carried level with back.
Forequarters: muscular, well-developed legs, good bone. Forearm short, carpus broad and thick, metacarpus short and strong.
Hindquarters: parallel, seen from behind. Thighs round and muscular. Legs robust and well muscled. Good angulation. Hocks well let down.
Feet: front feet, large and round. Hind feet, smaller, narrower. Toes tight and arched.
Coat: the smooth-haired breeds have dense, smooth, short coats. Wire-haired breeds have short, rough coats with finer, shorter hairs distributed among the coarse hairs. Long-haired breeds have soft, straight, silky hair, slight wave permitted. Abundant feathering behind the legs, and on tail.
Colour: whole and two colours of red, black, tan, silver, blue, brown. Brindled, tiger-marked, or dappled.
Faults: poor temperament. Broken tail. Coat all white or black without tan points. Lack of deep keel.

Practical information: The Dachshund is a big eater and tends to become overweight, particularly in old age. A combination of exercise and attention to its diet will keep its weight under control. Check for hereditary eye problems, such as atypic pannus. This dog often develops paralysis of the hindquarters brought on by a herniated disc.

Dalmatian

Coach Dog, Firehouse Dog

AUS.	CAN.	S. AF.	U.K.	F.C.I.
●	●	●	●	●

Though the black-spotted Dalmatian has been a symbol of elegance for more than 300 years, no one can accurately trace its history. One theory says that, in the Middle Ages, gypsies from India or the Middle East carried the dog into Dalmatia, now a region of Yugoslavia. Later, upper-class Englishmen on their grand tours, perhaps attracted to the spotted dogs by their bizarre appearance, may have brought them back to Great Britain.

The Dalmatian resembles the Harlequin Great Dane in colour, but that is as far as the resemblance goes. It is more closely related to the Braque Français, and some believe it is a descendant of the Bengali Braque. Although its name would suggest some link with Dalmatia, experts believe its bloodline is only remotely connected with that country through the Istrian Pointer, a possible ancestor whose silhouette is similar to the modern Dalmatian's. The Dalmatian probably earned its name during the Balkan Wars of 1912 and 1913, when it was used as a messenger, especially in Dalmatia. But its talents do not stop there. For centuries it has been used equally well as guard dog, draught dog, herd dog, sled dog, and hunter. It was also used in bygone years to reduce the rat and vermin population of London's stables and fire stations.

Paintings from the seventeenth century show that the Dalmatian was a favourite of royalty. It was always portrayed in the company of horses. The British nicknamed the Dalmatian the 'Coach Dog' because it loved to accompany carriages, trotting beside the horses and even threading its way neatly among the horses' hooves without disturbing them. But the dog could also remain motionless for many hours, regardless of cold or fog, to guard the coach and horses. In the nineteenth century, it was fashionable in England and France to enhance one's horse and carriage by adding some Dalmatians. The height of chic was to co-ordinate the harnesses with the colours of the dog's coats.

Now a companion dog, the Dalmatian demonstrates great patience and gentleness. Obedient, while distant with strangers, it is an excellent and courageous guard dog and a remarkable guide dog. It loves children and plays with them willingly. British children have nicknamed it 'Plum Pudding,' imagining the markings on its coat to be the raisins in that favourite cake.

ORIGINS

There is a great controversy over the Dalmatian's origins. Some say it comes from the Orient, and indeed, antique frescoes and paintings discovered in Egypt and Greece depict dogs similar to the Dalmatian. Others think it may have descended from the Bengali Braque, now extinct, and was then crossed with the Bull Terrier and the Pointer. There is even a theory that the Dalmatian descended from the Great Dane, but there is little evidence to support this contention.

101 DALMATIANS

The 1959 Walt Disney film *101 Dalmatians*, adapted from a British novel by Dodie Smith, was a dazzling success and contributed to the breed's popularity. Before the Disney studio began creating this animated film, Walt Disney and a team of technicians travelled to a breeding kennel near Paris. There they filmed and photographed Dalmatians in all possible positions. Thanks to this research, *101 Dalmatians* faithfully captures the expressions and movements of the real dog.

The breed was aptly chosen to tell the story of an extraordinarily large dog family. Dalmatians make excellent mothers, and usually have six to eight puppies in a litter.

Characteristics

General appearance: strong, active, muscular, well balanced, good temperament.

Height: dogs 56 to 61 cm (22 to 24 in.); bitches 53.3 to 58.4 cm (21 to 23 in.).

Weight: under F.C.I. standards, 22 to 25 kg (48½ to 55 lb). Elsewhere, not specified.

Head: good length, skull flat, stop moderate with no wrinkles. Muzzle long and powerful, never snipy. Lips clean. Jaws strong. Nose black in the black-spotted variety, brown in the liver-spotted type.

Eyes: medium size, round, alert, set well apart, brilliant. Expression intelligent. Dark in black-spotted, amber in liver-spotted type.

Ears: set high, of average length, tapering. Fine in texture.

Neck: long, well arched, light and tapering, no dewlap.

Body: shoulders moderately laid back. Chest not too broad; deep and ample. Ribs well sprung. Back strong and level. Loin strong, lean, and muscular, slightly arched. Shoulders oblique.

Tail: thick, tapering towards the tip, slightly curved, never curled.

Forequarters: legs straight, strong, round bone structure.

Hindquarters: rounded, lean muscles. Well-developed stifles, hocks well turned.

Feet: round, compact. Toes well arched, cat-footed. Rough pads.

Coat: short, hard, fine, and dense. Smooth and lustrous.

Colour: white, spotted with well-defined black or liver markings.

Practical information: This hardy dog is rarely ill, but needs exercise. Brush it every day with a medium-hard brush. It is prone to congenital deafness and bladder stones.

THE DALMATIAN'S COAT

A litter of new-born Dalmatians can be a shock to an inexperienced breeder: six to eight all-white puppies, without a spot on them! A visible mark on a new-born Dalmatian is considered a fault. Only after the second week should the nose and the eye rims become pigmented and spots begin to appear on the coat. The markings will not be fully developed until the dog is about one year old.

Dandie Dinmont Terrier

The Dandie Dinmont Terrier is a curiosity not only in name but also in physique. Unlike most terriers with their squat, square features, the Dandie Dinmont has a long body, an arched back, and a tail shaped like a scimitar. Beneath a silky topknot and an abundant crop of bushy hair, its large, round, hazel eyes express dignity, intelligence, and great determination. Though it has been popular for centuries with hill farmers along the border between Scotland and England, it is still rarely seen outside the British Isles.

Originally, the Dandie Dinmont was bred to destroy farm vermin such as rats, stone martens, and field-mice. It later proved to be equally adept at hunting rabbits, otters, and badgers. After its sudden climb to popularity in Britain in the last century, breeders began emphasizing its domestic qualities and unusual, but appealing, appearance.

The modern Dandie Dinmont makes an excellent companion dog. It is happy, affectionate, and loyal, and loves to play with children and other dogs. Easy to transport, it adapts readily to almost any living condition and can be as content to live on a boat or in a tent as it would be in a large house. It is a strong-willed dog, however, and requires a firm owner.

The Dandie Dinmont's extreme loyalty also makes it an excellent guard dog. Reserved when introduced to strangers by its owner, it is also highly suspicious of unannounced intruders and warns of their presence with loud, resonant barking that is startling for a dog of this size.

AUS.	CAN.	S. AF.	U.K.	F.C.I.
●	●	●	●	●

ORIGINS

The Dandie Dinmont Terrier's ancestry has never been firmly established. Most people believe it originated in Scotland, where it may have descended from the Skye Terrier, which used to have droopy ears like the modern Dandie Dinmont. Some experts also see links with the Border Terrier, the Cairn Terrier, and the Scottish Terrier. It may have been crossed with the Bedlington Terrier and the Otterhound. There is even a theory that one of its ancestors may be the Basset Hound, which William the Conqueror brought to England from Flanders. What is known for certain is that in the seventeenth century a dog resembling the modern Dandie Dinmont lived in the border country between Scotland and England. It was first noted as a distinct type at the beginning of the eighteenth century, and around 1820 acquired its unusual name. The Dandie Dinmont Terrier Club, founded in 1876, drew up the initial breed standard. That standard has changed little over the years.

Characteristics

General appearance: hardy, long, low-slung.

Height: 20.3 to 25.4 cm (8 to 10 in.). Under Canadian standards, 20.3 to 28 cm (8 to 11 in.).

Weight: 7.7 to 11 kg (17 to 24 lb). Under Canadian standards, 8 to 11 kg (18 to 24 lb).

Head: large and strong. Jaws well developed. Skull broad between the ears. Forehead well rounded. Head covered with soft, silky hair. Nose black. Teeth very strong, especially the canines; scissor bite. Interior of mouth black, or a dark colour.

Eyes: large, round, not protruding, set wide. Bright and prominent. Dark hazel. Expression sad.

Ears: pendent, hanging flat to the cheek, set well back, wide apart, and low, with slight feathering of light hair.

Neck: well developed and strong, very muscular.

Body: long, strong, flexible. Ribs round, well sprung. Back rather low at the shoulder. Brisket well developed with good depth.

Tail: rather short, 20 to 25 cm (8 to 9¾ in.), covered with stiff hair, darker than the body hair, nice feathering of about 5 cm (2 in.).

Forequarters: legs short, muscular, strong bone structure, feathered.

Hindquarters: legs a little longer than the forelegs, set rather wide apart. Thighs well developed. No feathering, no dewclaws.

Feet: round, well padded. Hind feet smaller than forefeet. Nails dark, varying in coloration according to the shades of the coat.

Coat: Double coat. Hair about 6 cm (2½ in.) long, from the skull to the base of the tail; mixture of stiff and soft hair feeling fuzzy to the touch, not wiry. The hair must not be too stiff. Hair on underside of the body is lighter and softer than on top.

Colour: pepper or mustard. Peppers vary from dark bluish black to light silvery grey. Body colour extends under shoulders and hips and merges into the colour of the legs. Mustards vary from reddish brown to pale tawny, with the head creamy white. Paws and feet darker than the head. Usually a little white on the chest. A few have white toes. White feet are a fault.

Practical information: This strong, healthy dog needs two walks daily and a lean diet to prevent obesity. Brush it daily with a medium-hard, long-bristle brush. Clean the eyes with a cotton swab dipped in water that has been boiled and cooled. Cut the hair around the eyes regularly. Check the nails often, clipping and filing when necessary.

In the seventeenth century, families living along the border between Scotland and England kept terriers. The head of one of these families was Willy 'Piper' Allan of Northumberland, a musician. His particularly fine pack of terriers so charmed the duke of Northumberland, according to legend, that he offered Willy a farm in exchange for just one of his dogs. But Willy the Piper had no interest in becoming a farmer, and he refused repeated offers from the duke. After Willy's death in 1704, several generations of Allans kept the strain alive and occasionally traded dogs for favours.

The story goes that James Davidson, a border farmer, had a pair of Allan dogs, which he bred, and that he named them and their offspring *Mustard* and *Pepper*, according to their colours. Sir Walter Scott knew Davidson and his dogs. When Scott wrote his novel *Guy Mannering* he created a character named Dandie Dinmont, a gentleman farmer who, like the real-life Davidson, never left home without his pack of mustard and pepper terriers. The six fictional dogs were called *Auld Pepper*, *Auld Mustard*, *Young Pepper*, *Young Mustard*, *Little Pepper*, and *Little Mustard*. The hugely successful novel spread the terrier's fame throughout Britain, and owners of similar dogs started calling them Dandie Dinmont's terriers.

Deerhound

Scottish Deerhound

The Deerhound has hardly changed in more than a thousand years. A fast, powerful, and fearless dog, it was raised to hunt deer and stags in the Highlands and is still sometimes called a Scottish Deerhound. Originally, it was almost indistinguishable from the Irish Wolfhound, but it now more closely resembles the Greyhound.

Favoured by Highland chieftains for centuries, the Deerhound was once known as the 'royal dog of Scotland.' Anyone below the rank of earl was forbidden to own one. So valued were the dogs as hunters that the Picts and the Scots were known to battle bloodily over a stolen Deerhound.

The breed's privileged existence came to an end in the eighteenth century, when the clan system collapsed in Scotland and deer hunting ceased to be an exclusive right of nobility. Better firearms also reduced the dogs' role to simply finding wounded animals. At one point the breed was in danger of extinction. When deerstalking was revived as a sport in the last century, breeders once again turned their attention to the Deerhound. The first breed standard was set in 1892.

Like the Greyhound, the Deerhound eventually became a companion dog, a role for which it has proven well suited. It is intelligent, calm, and gentle, and shows great affection for its owner. Its enormous size and energy, however, call for plenty of open space.

AUS.	CAN.	S. AF.	U.K.	F.C.I.
●	●	●	●	●

ORIGINS

When and how the Deerhound's ancestors arrived in Scotland is a mystery. Phoenician traders are believed to have brought greyhounds with them to Britain about 1000 B.C., and as the dogs moved north to Scotland they may have developed a rough coat as protection against the environment. The Celts may also have brought an ancestor of the Deerhound when they invaded Britain in the fifth century B.C. Stone carvings from A.D. 800 portray a rough-coated hound. Some authorities think the Deerhound is a descendant of the Irish Wolfhound, while others believe the Deerhound preceded the Wolfhound. The first standard for the dog was set in 1892. The Deerhound is most popular in Australia, North America, and parts of Europe.

A FAMILY THREATENED WITH EXTINCTION

The greyhound family of dogs is one of the oldest on the planet, but many breeds are now extinct. Human negligence, whims of fashion, and poor adaptation have combined to slowly undermine the diversity of those breeds which survive.

The Deerhound is a striking example of this loss of diversity. Early varieties came in several colours, including yellow, rust, and wheat. Short-sighted selective breeding has left us with only blue-grey.

The Galgo, a Spanish greyhound, has disappeared as a distinctive breed through centuries of careless crossing with other greyhounds.

The Borzoi lost much of its original character when it became a popular salon dog in England around the beginning of the twentieth century. When the fad passed, extinction loomed, until the Russians resumed breeding it for hunting.

Faddishness affected the Afghan Hound as well. Careless breeding to meet a sudden rise in public demand in the 1970s has weakened some of this greyhound's characteristics.

The equally elegant Saluki, once near extinction, is quickly becoming a popular companion dog, and care must be taken to ensure that irresponsible breeding doesn't weaken it as well.

The Pharaoh Hound and the Ibizan Hound were both near extinction in Mediterranean countries when Westerners began breeding them in earnest.

The Sloughi, a short-haired hound, is still in danger, despite rescue programmes launched recently.

Of all the greyhounds, the small Italian Greyhound, also known as the *Piccolo Levriero Italiano*, seems to have adapted best to domestic life, and this breed, at least, remains strong and healthy.

The common Greyhound, which once roamed the English countryside by the thousands, now owes its survival to dedicated breeders keeping it alive as a pet, show dog, and racer.

Characteristics

General appearance: characteristic greyhound lines. Hardy, tall, with rough, long, dry hair.

Height: 76.2 to 81.3 cm (30 to 32 in.) for the adult dog; 71 cm (28 in.) and upwards for the bitch.

Weight: 38 to 48 kg (84 to 106 lb) for the adult dog; 30 to 36.3 kg (66 to 80 lb) for the bitch. Under Canadian standards, 38.5 to 50 kg (85 to 110 lb) for the adult dog; 34 to 43 kg (75 to 95 lb) for the bitch.

Head: broad skull, tapering towards the eyes. Muzzle pointed, skull flat, no stop, slightly aquiline. Nose black (blue in the blue-fawns). Scissor bite.

Eyes: gentle, dark. Rims black.

Ears: soft, lustrous, as small as possible, black or dark, set high, folded towards the back in repose.

Neck: long, very strong, able to hold a deer. Throat lean, and of good length. Nape prominent, no dewlap.

Body: shoulders well laid back. Chest deep, flat, not too narrow. Loin well arched. Hips set well apart.

Tail: long and thick at base, straight or curved, covered with thick stiff hair, longer on the upper side.

Forequarters: legs broad, flat, balanced, straight.

Hindquarters: legs long, muscular. Hocks broad, flat.

Feet: close, compact. Nails strong.

Coat: shaggy; hair thick, dense, stiff or crisp to the touch, 8 to 10 cm (3¼ to 4 in.) long on the body, neck, and legs, much softer on the head, brisket, and belly. Slight fringe on inside of legs, but not long enough to resemble feathering.

Colour: grey-blue; preferably dark. Also, brindle, grey, yellow, sandy rust, or tawny rust with black points. White chest and toes are permissible. A slight white mark near the tail is tolerated.

Faults: light eyes. Ears erect, thick, or falling close to the head, or thickly covered with hair. Shoulders full and straight. Cow hocks. Straight back. Tail curled or ring. Pasterns weak. Stifles straight. Feet turning outwards. Coat woolly. White; white blaze on the head, white ruff.

Practical information: Like any hunting-dog, the Deerhound is not well suited to life in the city. It feels cramped indoors and requires open spaces where it can run at full speed and at length. Do not be alarmed by its cry, which is the Deerhound's way of expressing need or impatience. A hardy outdoors dog, equipped with a heavy, weather-resistant coat, it is undaunted by cold or rain. Feed it high-quality foods, especially when it is young and growing fast.

Dobermann Pinscher

The Dobermann Pinscher deserves the respect it commands. Its legendary character inspired many tall tales. One improbable story has it that a particularly fearsome beast in the United States won Best in Show three times before any judge had enough courage to examine its mouth. The fourth time around, a foolhardy judge pried the dog's mouth open and discovered teeth missing, an obvious fault.

Quick, intelligent, strong—aggressive, even, when encouraged to be so—the Dobermann is a born guard dog. It is not unusual for a two-month-old puppy to growl and bare its teeth in a display of domination. Nevertheless, given an owner capable of both commanding its obedience and winning its love, the Dobermann Pinscher can be a stable, devoted companion dog.

Created late in the nineteenth century in Germany, where the word *Pinscher* means 'terrier,' the dog was received with something less than enthusiasm. The first examples of the breed were looked on as coarse, ill-tempered ruffians. According to Swiss breeder Gottfried Lietchi, 'They were certainly robust, had absolutely no fear, not even of the devil himself, and it required a great deal of courage to own one.' By the turn of the century a breed club had been formed, and the dog was entered in a dog show for the first time, attracting the attention of those who wanted an alert security dog. The Dobermann was quickly adopted for police work, and by the time of the First World War it was serving as a patrol and guard dog at the German front lines. Blinded soldiers also used it as a guide dog.

Two world wars drastically reduced the numbers of Dobermanns. But after 1945 the breed was built up again in Europe, and more dogs were shipped to North America.

AUS.	CAN.	S. AF.	U.K.	F.C.I.
●	●	●	●	●

ORIGINS

The Dobermann Pinscher is named after its developer, a German tax collector called Louis Dobermann. A skilled dog breeder, he set out, between 1865 and 1870, to create a large, alert, and aggressive terrier to protect him while he made his rounds. As keeper of the local animal shelter, Dobermann had access to a variety of dogs for his experiments, and while no records were kept of his work, experts believe he used the Pinscher, the Rottweiler, the Manchester Terrier, the Beauceron, and the Greyhound. By 1899, Dobermann was satisfied that he now had the dog he had set out to breed. Another breeder, Otto Goeller, helped refine the species and added Pinscher to the name. He also drafted the first standard and won official German kennel club recognition for the dog in 1900. Examples of the breed were taken to the United States soon after, and breeders there are credited with further developing the Dobermann Pinscher's qualities.

Characteristics

General appearance: medium build, hardy and muscular, elegant, bold, alert, compact. Gait must be elastic, rather feline, when moving slowly. The Dobermann is intelligent, loyal, and obedient. Squarely built, it is capable of great speed.

Height: 63.5 to 68.6 cm (25 to 27 in.). Under Canadian standards, ideal weight for adult dogs, 70 cm (27½ in.), and for bitches, 64.8 cm (25½ in.).

Weight: under F.C.I. standards, 20 to 26 kg (44 to 57 lb). Elsewhere, not specified.

Head: long and lean, shaped like a truncated triangle. The stop is barely visible, the cheeks are flat. The jaws are deep and broad and the lips tight. Scissor bite.

Eyes: almond-shaped, average size, must be as dark as possible. Lively, alert expression.

Ears: small, neat, set high, normally dropped but may be erect. In some countries, cropped to a point.

Neck: long, lean and muscular, rising in a graceful curve from the thorax and shoulders. No dewlap.

Body: square, shoulders well defined. Back firm and short. Croup slightly rounded. Withers strongly defined. Brisket broad and deep, good tuck up.

Tail: usually docked at first or second vertebra.

Forequarters: legs straight and parallel.

Hindquarters: thighs broad and muscular, hocks well developed.

Feet: well arched, compact, and catlike.

Coat: short and thick, flat and smooth.

Colour: black, red, fawn, brown or blue with well-defined red-rust markings.

Faults: build heavy and massive. Head short and thick. Muzzle pointed. Hesitating gait. Fearful or nervous temperament; skittishness. Weak or knuckled-over pastern.

Practical information: Like all short-coated dogs, the Dobermann is prone to intestinal diseases particularly in cold weather, and to skin diseases. Outside, in bad weather, keep the dog moving at all times; dry it thoroughly when it comes back indoors. Rigorous daily brushing removes dead hair from the coat, soothes the muscles, stimulates the circulation, calms the nervous system, and aids digestion. The young Dobermann is especially susceptible to a skin parasite called demodectic mange which shows up as greyish bald patches around the eyes and on the elbows and body. This disease must be treated by a veterinarián. Inspect the dog regularly for staphylococcus; this bacterium produces clusters of blisters, especially between the toes. In North America, the Dobermann's ears are frequently cropped; this should be done when the dog is 10 to 12 weeks old.

Dogue de Bordeaux

This rare French mastiff, with its deeply lined face, resembles a tired, ageing prize-fighter. The comparison is fitting because the Dogue de Bordeaux was once used as a ferocious fighting dog, trained to attack bulls, bears, and other dogs. Although today's breed appears as intimidating as its ancestor, it is a calm and gentle creature, loyal to its master and patient with children.

During the Middle Ages, the Dogue de Bordeaux was considered a brutal and expendable beast. Gaston Phoebus, a fourteenth-century French writer, described the dogs as follows: '... with their thick heads, thick lips, and large ears, they are well suited to hunting bear and pigs because they are stubborn. But they are heavy and ugly and, if a wild boar were to kill them, it would be no great loss.' The early contempt for the Dogue de Bordeaux survives in some everyday French phrases. In France, people still say 'une humeur de dogue,' when referring to a bad temper, and use 'l'air de dogue' to describe an unpleasant expression.

By the end of the Middle Ages, the formidable Dogue de Bordeaux had acquired a new—and more respectable—occupation as a working dog. Butchers used the breed to drive their cattle to market. This role earned the Dogue de Bordeaux its lasting nickname as 'the butcher's dog.'

From the lowly meat-seller's shop, the Dogue de Bordeaux ascended to the estates and mansions of the wealthy and the aristocratic. The rich prized the dogs as protectors whose vigilance and courage deterred thieves and intruders. This patronage may have salvaged the breed's reputation, but it almost brought about its extinction. When the French Revolution came in 1789, many of these faithful and ferocious guard dogs perished with their masters.

Fortunately, the butcher's dog survived in sufficient number to permit the breed to continue. Until recent years, the competition from other more popular watch-dogs, such as the Boxer and the Great Dane (which is a member of the same ancestral family as the Dogue de Bordeaux), kept its number extremely low.

Today, however, the Dogue de Bordeaux is enjoying a revival in popularity, thanks to a growing recognition of its gentleness and devotion. The breed is well established in France, and its reputation is spreading elsewhere.

AUS.	CAN.	S. AF.	U.K.	F.C.I.
				●

ORIGINS

Among the ancestors of the Dogue de Bordeaux are the Tibetan Mastiff and the Molossus of Epirus, now both extinct. The origins of the Tibetan Mastiff can be traced back five thousand years. The Molossus of Epirus, which came from the Greek–Albanian border region, was known as early as the fifth century B.C. and was famed as a dog of war. Legend has it that Alexander the Great sent his terrified enemies to flight by turning these mastiffs loose among the victims' battle ranks. Roman gladiators prized the dogs for bloody amphitheatre sports. The earliest Dogue de Bordeaux was as fierce as its forbears. After the French Revolution, the breed almost vanished, except in the region for which it is named. Conscientious breeders kept the strain alive, introducing it to dog shows in the late nineteenth century. They reduced the breed's size and eventually crossed it with the British Bulldog to change its blood line. The present-day specimen first appeared at the turn of this century.

Characteristics

General appearance: powerfully built, pugnacious mastiff, with a muscular, well-balanced body.

Height: 60 to 68 cm (23½ to 26¾ in.) for the adult dog; 58 to 66 cm (23 to 26 in.) for the bitch.

Weight: at least 50 kg (110 lb) for the adult dog; 45 kg (99 lb) for the bitch.

Head: very full, angular, broad, and fairly short, lined with symmetrical wrinkles on each side of the median groove. Stop well defined. Muzzle powerful, broad, thick, rather short. Nose broad with wide nostrils, black or brown, depending on the mask. Mouth undershot; when shut, incisors and canines must not be visible. Jaws broad, very powerful. Teeth very strong. Lips thick, moderately pendulous. Cheeks prominent.

Eyes: oval in shape, set wide apart. Hazel or deep brown. A light colour is permissible in dogs with a red mask.

Ears: relatively small, fall close along the cheeks. Set high, slightly rounded at the tip.

Neck: very strong, muscular, almost cylindrical. Skin loose and supple. Dewlap prominent.

Body: chest powerful, deep. Broad shoulders quite strong with prominent muscles. Back broad and mus-cled. Withers well defined. Loins broad, rather short, sturdy. Croup slightly sloping.

Tail: tapering, not reaching past the hock, drooping, turned up when the dog is moving.

Forequarters: legs well muscled with strong bone structure. Elbows turned neither inward nor outward.

Hindquarters: thighs thick, very well developed. Hocks short and taut. Legs parallel.

Feet: strong, toes tight. Nails short and strong. Pads well developed and flexible.

Coat: hair fine, short, and soft.

Colour: solid-coloured fawn or in the tawny range. White marks not too widely spread are permitted on the chest and feet. Black or red mask strongly accentuated.

Faults: head too small. Elongated, narrow skull when viewed from the top; skull too round or too oval when viewed from the front. Muzzle too long or too short. Nose too narrow, multi-coloured. Jaws in pincer bite. Lips too long or flaccid. Cheeks soft, wall-eyes, loss of pigmentation in eye rims. Rose ears. Brisket narrow. Tail twisted, docked, curled. Solid white coat. Hair thick, rough, long, wavy. Dew-claws on the hind feet.

Practical information: The Dogue de Bordeaux makes an excellent guard dog, or a companion, if owners ensure that it has an active, outdoor life. At birth, a veterinarian may have to perform a Caesarian section due to the large size of the pups' heads. To control any aggressive instincts, particularly towards other canines, start training the dog at an early age. Brush its hair occasionally to remove dust and dead hair. Feed the dog a mixed diet, with plenty of meat.

Elkhound

Norwegian Elkhound

This Scandinavian hound, a member of the spitz family of dogs, is compact, solidly built, and wolf-like in appearance. With its grey coat, the Elkhound is perfectly suited to its natural habitat, the rugged landscape of Norway.

Although ancestors of the Elkhound can be traced back thousands of years, the dog has changed remarkably little through the ages. It has always shown exceptional courage at confronting prey. As early as 800 B.C., Scandinavian peoples used the hounds to hunt wolves and reindeer.

The Norwegians have relied on the Elkhound's superior scenting ability to find the elusive elk. But it is equally skilled at tracking badger, bear, deer, lynx, rabbit, and other wild game. Moreover, the dog has the stamina and agility to keep hostile or skittish quarry cornered until the hunters arrive to make the kill.

Like other spitz dogs, the male Elkhound can be teamed to pull sleds—as long as it is paired with a female of the same breed. The best sled teams are made up of male and female pairs which work together regularly. Male dogs are best kept away from each other; if harnessed too closely, they are likely to fight.

The Elkhound makes a good family dog, although its independent temperament can try one's patience. When called to 'come,' it will obey—in its own time. It rarely wanders away from home or out of earshot. Thanks to a highly developed sense of its own territory, it performs well as a watch-dog, and also as a herder.

In Norway, the Elkhound is considered the national dog. Throughout Scandinavia and elsewhere, it is now gaining popularity as a house-pet.

AUS.	CAN.	S. AF.	U.K.	F.C.I.
●	●	●	●	●

ORIGINS

Skeletons of Stone Age dogs almost identical to that of the modern Elkhound have been found in Scandinavia. This confirms the place of origin and the ancestry of hounds which, a thousand years ago, accompanied Norse explorers on their far-ranging North Atlantic expeditions. The Elkhound has hardly been changed over the centuries. Subsequently, selective breeding honed its hunting skills and produced the rustic, yet elegant, present-day type. Despite its impressive ancestry—few dogs have such unmixed lineage—the breed was not officially recognized until the mid-1870s, when it first appeared at dog shows in Oslo.

IN PURSUIT OF THE ELK

With its keen scent, the Norwegian Elkhound can detect prey which may be several kilometres away. When the elk is sighted, the hound will drive it into a trap and send up a cry to alert the hunter. While waiting for its master to arrive, the Elkhound holds the quarry at bay. Although the hound is smaller than the elk, it will attack the animal brazenly, nipping at its heels.

The elk, as fearsome and fearless as its pursuer, is far from defenceless. Like a bull, the elk lunges at the hound and tries to spear the dog with its antlers. The agile, tireless Elkhound can dodge the horns and wear out the enemy. If harassment fails and the elk escapes, the hound keeps on its trail, announcing with new cries that the chase is on again.

Unfortunately for the Elkhound—but mercifully for its prey—elk-hunting is limited to a short season in most countries. Today the dog rarely has a chance to expend all its energy on the pursuit of its traditional prey. But it has found another tough and tenacious opponent—the badger. This creature is active at night, the best hunting time for the Elkhound. The day-blind hound finds its way more easily in the dark than in the light.

Characteristics

General appearance: this dog has a compact, relatively short body. Its coat is thick and abundant, but not bristling. The tail is carried well curled over the back. Proud carriage.

Height: 50.8 cm (20 in.) for the adult dog; 48.3 cm (19 in.) for the bitch. Under Canadian standards, 52 cm (20½ in.) for the adult dog; 49.5 cm (19½ in.) for the bitch.

Weight: 23 kg (51 lb) for the adult dog; 20 kg (44 lb) for the bitch. Under F.C.I. and Canadian standards, not specified.

Head: wedge-shaped, broad between the ears. The forehead and back of the head are slightly arched. The stop is clearly defined. The muzzle, broad at the base, tapers gradually. Not pointed. Jaws strong. Lips tightly closed. Scissor bite. Tight-fitting skin on head.

Eyes: dark brown; their expression is frank, fearless, friendly.

Ears: small, set high; firm, erect, pointed, and very mobile.

Body: powerful, back short and strong. Chest broad and deep with well-rounded ribs. Loin muscular. Very little tuck up.

Tail: set high, tightly curled over the back. Hair thick and coarse.

Forequarters: legs firm, straight, powerful, and steady.

Hindquarters: powerful, with a little bend at stifle and hock.

Coat: close, abundant, weatherproof. Soft, dense, woolly undercoat, coarse, straight outer coat.

Colour: different shades of grey with black tips where hair is longest; lighter on the brisket and belly.

Faults: there should be no dewclaws on the hind legs. Any distinct variation from a grey coat; colours too light or too dark.

Practical information: This hound can withstand cold and snow, but may find intense heat unbearable. It is not really a suitable dog for city life, particularly not for apartment dwelling, because it needs open space for exercise. The Elkhound gains weight quickly, and must not be overfed, even after strenuous activity. Give its thick, coarse coat a good brushing occasionally to remove dead hair.

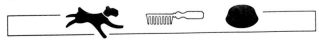

English Setter

Laverack Setter

Sleek and good-natured, the English Setter is one of the most appealing breeds, both in temperament and in appearance. These dogs are fond of children and are fine pets for the family. A gently wafting tail signals the dog's calm, affectionate disposition. Its limpid eyes gaze with longing for attention.

The English Setter is a good hunter—an outdoors animal that will pursue game for its master virtually anywhere and any time of year. With its long stride and elegant gait, it will race through underbrush and over fields in search of game birds, and it is always ready to plunge into reedy waters to retrieve downed prey. Hunters use the thick-coated English Setter in the wintertime because it can withstand the cold weather which short-haired dogs find unendurable.

The English Setter's name derives from its work as a hunter. By 'setting,' or positioning its body with the head towards the game, it prepares the prey for the sportsman's gun—and, in earlier times, for the net. After holding a point, the dog advances stealthily towards the quarry until the hunter gives the command to flush the game birds and put them to flight.

AUS.	CAN.	S. AF.	U.K.	F.C.I.
●	●	●	●	●

ORIGINS

The English Setter descends from an ancient line of sporting dogs, possibly of Spanish origin, known in Britain as early as the fourteenth century. Originally referred to as spaniels, these sporting dogs were later recognized as a distinct canine group and identified as 'setters.' Subsequently, separate breeds—notably, English, Irish, and Gordon setters—were established. The early English Setter was neither as elegant nor as graceful as the present-day dog. Credit for developing the modern breed—with its handsome, sleek appearance—goes to the British breeder, Sir Edward Laverack. In 1825, Laverack bought a pair of the setters—Ponto and Moll—and, by following a careful breeding programme, established the English Setter's lineage. Laverack spent fifty years of intense effort improving the breed's virtues and reducing its faults. In the early 1870s, Laverack published a book on the English Setter. It was so widely read that the breed became identified with him— hence, the popular name, the Laverack Setter. Another enthusiastic breeder, Sir Purcell Llewellin, also refined the Setter, but preserved its sporting qualities. Laverack and Llewellin are responsible for producing the two distinct strains of English Setter—one for showing, the other for hunting and field trials.

Characteristics

General appearance: of medium height, clean outline. Elegant, friendly.

Height: 63.5 to 68.6 cm (25 to 27 in.) for the adult dog; 61 to 63.5 cm (24 to 25 in.) for the bitch.

Weight: 27 to 30 kg (59 to 66 lb) for the adult dog; 25 to 28 kg (55 to 62 lb) for the bitch. Under Canadian standards, not specified.

Head: long and lean. Skull oval from ear to ear. Well-defined occiput. Pronounced stop. The length of the skull is equal to that of the muzzle. Muzzle fairly square. Wide nostrils. Nose black or liver according to the coat colour. Lips not to be pendulous. Jaws of equal length.

Eyes: oval, bright, gentle, intelligent. Hazel and dark brown.

Ears: moderate length, set low, landing in neat folds next to the cheek. Velvety tip, upper part covered with fine, silky hair.

Body: moderate length, deep chest. Rounded, prominent ribs. Straight, moderate back. Broad loin, slightly arched, strong and muscular. Shoulder oblique, well laid back.

Tail: set almost in line with the back, medium length, slightly curved or scimitar-shaped. Well feathered. No tendency to turn upward.

Forequarters: muscular, solid. Forearms big with rounded bones. Elbows well let down. Pasterns strong, short, round.

Hindquarters: thighs long, stifles well bent. Loins wide, strong, slightly arched.

Coat: long, flat, and silky. Slightly wavy from the back of the head. Thighs and legs well feathered almost to the feet.

Colour: black and white, lemon or orange and white, liver and white, tricoloured black, white, tan. Ticking preferred to large spots.

WOODCOCK HUNTING

The woodcock is one of the most challenging game birds to hunt. It has two outstanding natural advantages over any pursuing dog. First, it has a brown and grey plumage which blends into the landscape and camouflages its whereabouts. Second, its large eyes, placed high in the head, permit clear vision in all directions. But the English Setter has traits which are useful for trailing the bird successfully. With a highly developed sense of smell and a virtually silent footfall, the dog can scent and locate the woodcock before its own presence is felt. When the dog nears the bird's hiding place in the undergrowth, it alerts the hunter by pointing its tail.

Practical information: The English Setter is a robust creature which grows restless indoors and needs daily outdoor exercise. Examine its long ears regularly. If kept in the house, the English Setter may develop eczema. The bitch is subject to false pregnancies.

English Springer Spaniel

This strong, agile, medium-size sporting dog takes its name from its use by hunters for 'springing' forward to drive game out into the open. It is the oldest of the spaniel stock and is probably the forbear of most spaniel breeds, as well as other kinds of field dog. One of its closest offshoots is the smaller Welsh Springer Spaniel.

The English Springer is considered the most robust of all the spaniels, and it is thought to have the pleasantest disposition, too. As a breed, the Springer resembles the Cocker Spaniel, although it is much larger. Its coat is soft, short, straight, and water-repellent. Coat colours are usually white with black or liver markings.

The English Springer Spaniel is prized by hunters because it can take on many different hunting roles. A keen and active creature with a good nose, it works well both on land and water, as well as in any weather. It excels at hunting in the thick cover of the woods and underbrush, and is vigorous and intelligent in its search for prey. One of its greatest skills is flushing woodcock from the undergrowth. Moreover, this spaniel points well and is a superb retriever. It plunges without hesitation into deep, marshy waters to recover downed birds for its master.

The English Springer Spaniel is ideal for sportsmen who, by inclination or necessity, prefer to hunt alone. It is quick to learn, obedient, easy to train, and eager to please. It enjoys the company of a family and is patient and affectionate with children. Somewhat reserved with strangers, the Springer makes a good watch-dog.

AUS.	CAN.	S. AF.	U.K.	F.C.I.
●	●	●	●	●

ORIGINS

Spaniels have been known in England since the Middle Ages. In the sixteenth century, Dr. Johannes Caius, the first chronicler of dog breeds, wrote that the dogs originally came from Spain—hence the name 'spaniel.' Caius also divided the spaniels into two groups—those that hunted on land and those that worked in water. Until the early nineteenth century, however, little or no distinction was made among the different spaniel types. At that time, though, breeders began the intensive development of a land spaniel which had been used for springing game for hunters. By the 1850s, the forerunner of the present-day breed was well established and was given the name 'Springer' because of its special sporting skill. The first club of the breed was created in 1885, and the breed itself was officially recognized in Great Britain in 1902. The English Springer Spaniel was introduced into North America in 1907. It was registered in Canada and the United States within ten years.

Characteristics

General appearance: well-balanced, compact, strong, steady dog, built for endurance and movement.

Height: 51 cm (20 in.) for the adult dog and 48.3 cm (19 in.) for the bitch.

Weight: under Canadian and F.C.I. standards, 22 to 25 kg (49 to 55 lb). Elsewhere, not specified.

Head: face broad and high, of medium length, well chiselled below the eyes. Skull of average length, fairly broad, the skull slightly rounded. Stop divided by fluting between the eyes. Cheeks flat. Nostrils well developed, liver-coloured or black. Flews squarish and slightly pendulous. Jaws strong, square, lean, and even. Scissor bite.

Eyes: dark hazel, average size, almond-shaped, well set in, and set well apart, not showing haw. Kind, alert expression.

Ears: set at eye level, close to the head, lobular, of good length and width. Slightly arched, tapering towards head.

Neck: moderately long, strong and muscled, gradually blending into sloping shoulders. No dewlap.

Body: strong and well proportioned. Brisket well let down. Ribs well sprung and tapering towards the back. Loin muscular, strong, and slightly arched, close coupled. Shoulders sloping and well laid.

Tail: set low, well feathered and wagging actively. Never carried above level of back. Customarily docked.

Forequarters: legs straight and well feathered. Elbows strong and set well to body.

Hindquarters: legs muscular, well let down from haunch to hock.

Feet: tight, compact, well rounded, well arched. Pads strong, full.

Coat: close, flat, water-repellent but never coarse. Moderate feathering on ears, forelegs, body and hindquarters.

Colour: Liver and white, black and white, or one of the two with tan markings are preferable.

Practical information: This robust, healthy dog needs plenty of space for exercise. Brush its hair often and briskly. After hunting, inspect the coat for parasites. Check the insides of the ears carefully.

English Toy Terrier

Black and Tan Toy Terrier
Toy Manchester Terrier

Since 1960, this breed has been called the English Toy Terrier, but in North America it is known as the Toy Manchester Terrier. The forbears of this small dog were the Black and Tan Terriers, famed for centuries as rat fighters in the north of England. In the nineteenth century, the Black and Tan Toy was adopted by fashionable society. But this popularity was almost the undoing of the breed. Public demand for tiny specimens produced stunted, sickly creatures. Since the 1950s, breeders have improved its health and appearance.

A lively dog, the English Toy Terrier is an ideal pet for an apartment or flat. Loyal and affectionate, it uses its piercing bark to sound an alarm.

AUS.	CAN.	S. AF.	U.K.	F.C.I.
●	●	●	●	●

ORIGINS

The English Toy Terrier, like the larger Manchester Terrier, descends from the old English Black and Tan Terrier. Nineteenth-century breeders created this unusually tiny dog by repeatedly inbreeding small Manchester Terriers. The 'manufacturing' of miniature dogs has ended, and breeders have now established robust English Toy Terriers.

Characteristics

General appearance: small, compact, well balanced, and elegant.
Height: 25.4 to 30.5 cm (10 to 12 in.). Under F.C.I. and Canadian standards, not specified.
Weight: 2.7 to 3.6 kg (6 to 8 lb).
Head: long, narrow, wedge-shaped. Skull flat and narrow. Muzzle long, delicate, wedge-shaped. Level bite, tight-lipped jaws. Nose black. Slight stop.
Eyes: small, dark to black, almond-shaped.
Ears: candle-flame shape, slightly pointed.
Body: compact, shoulders clean, well laid back. Chest deep, narrow. Well-sprung ribs. Back short

and slightly arched at the loin. Buttocks well rounded.
Tail: moderately short, thick at base, tapering to a point, carried low in a sabre-type curve.
Forequarters: legs quite straight, well under the body. Fine-boned, clean line.
Hindquarters: hocks well let down. Cat-footed.
Coat: dense, shiny, close, short and smooth hair.
Colour: black and tan clearly outlined. Tan colour over the eyes, on the muzzle, inside the ears, on the chest, legs, and underside of the tail. Throat marked with a distinctive tan V. Outside of hind legs should be black. No white hairs forming a patch.

Practical information: This dog has a modest appetite and a trouble-free coat. It requires little exercise.

Épagneul de Pont-Audemer

From French ancestors the Épagneul de Pont-Audemer has inherited its tracking and pointing abilities. Its swimming skills come from another forbear, the Irish Water Spaniel. With powerful muscles and broad, webbed feet, the Pont-Audemer swims rapidly and retrieves downed birds with ease. A thick coat provides a protective covering against icy marsh water. Like all spaniels, the Pont-Audemer is companionable, intelligent, and easy to train. The dog is favoured by sportsmen who enjoy hunting game birds in the marshy regions of north-western France, but it is rarely found outside its country of origin.

AUS.	CAN.	S. AF.	U.K.	F.C.I.
				●

ORIGINS

The ancient ancestors of the uncommon Épagneul de Pont-Audemer were Chiens d'Oysel *(bird dogs) and the Normandy Spaniel, now extinct. It was developed from the Irish Water Spaniel and possibly the French and Picardy Spaniels in the late nineteenth century.*

Characteristics

General appearance: stocky and vigorous dog.
Height: 52 to 58 cm (20½ to 23 in.).
Weight: 25 kg (55 lb).
Head: skull rounded, occiput prominent. Very curly topknot on the skull. Muzzle long, sloping a little. Nose brown, rather pointed. Lips lean.
Eyes: small, dark amber or hazel.
Ears: set a little low, moderately thick, flat, long, with curly hair.
Neck: rather thin, slightly arched, well muscled.
Body: brisket broad. Ribs long. Back straight, loin short. Croup sloping. Shoulders strong, oblique.
Tail: average length or docked by one-third. Slightly curved. Carried rather straight.
Forequarters: legs well muscled.
Hindquarters: thighs well let down, straight, muscular, well shaped and filled out. Hocks straight, broad. Buttocks prominent. No dew-claws.
Feet: round. Toes webbed, well furnished with hair.
Coat: thick, slightly oily, curly on the body.
Colour: brown, brown and grey, variegated.
Faults: no topknot. Coat black or black and white.

Practical information: This robust dog needs exercise, but little care beyond regular brushing. Never bathe the dog during the season when it hunts in the marshes. Even a mild detergent can destroy the oily layer which protects the coat and skin when the dog swims. Examine the ears and the spaces between the toes and pads for cuts and parasites.

Épagneul Français

French Spaniel

With a keen sense of smell, the Épagneul Français hunts under the gun and never strays too far from its master while searching for game birds. A calm and methodical hunter, this dog advances with its nose up, zigzagging along so quickly that sportsmen have to make sure it hunts upwind. It is willing to work on land and water, even in the most inhospitable conditions.

The French Spaniel points with awesome proficiency. The skill is so natural that, from the age of three months, it will point at a hen or a sparrow. Easy to train as a hunter, it is loyal, gentle, and friendly as a companion.

AUS.	CAN.	S. AF.	U.K.	F.C.I.
	●			●

ORIGINS

The Épagneul Français was a favourite with hunters of game birds until the eighteenth century, but it was overshadowed in popularity by English dogs. During the next century, French breeders developed the present-day type and saved its inherited hunting skills.

Characteristics

General appearance: large, strong dog with no heaviness; has a proud bearing.

Height: 56 to 61 cm (22 to 24 in.) for the adult dog; 53.3 to 58.4 cm (21 to 23 in.) for the bitch.

Weight: 20 to 25 kg (44 to 55 lb). Not specified under Canadian standards.

Head: large but not heavy, elongated. Skull long, not quite flat. Stop defined, but not too sharply. Muzzle slightly convex. Nose broad, well open, brown.

Eyes: medium size, dark amber. Haw not visible.

Ears: set low and relatively far back, long, rounded, covered with silky, wavy hair, rounded tip.

Neck: moderate length, muscular, slightly arched, in proportion with head and body.

Body: brisket deep. Back long. Loin straight. Croup sloping. Flanks raised. Shoulders long, well laid back.

Tail: set low; fairly long, feathered.

Forequarters: legs straight, muscular.

Hindquarters: legs straight, muscular. Thighs well let down and feathered. Hocks slightly bent.

Feet: lean and oval. Toes arched. Pads hard.

Coat: hair long and supple, fine, clean, and glossy. Wavy on the ears, neck, feet, and tail.

Colour: white, marked with brown.

Practical information: The French Spaniel is a robust hunting-dog which requires a great deal of regular daily exercise. If it leads a quiet life, it should be given a moderate diet. When the dog is used for hunting, however, it needs substantial nourishment. Watch for skin problems which may develop if the animal is exposed to dry, indoor air. Brush the coat regularly.

Épagneul Picard

Picardy Spaniel

The athletic and hardy Épagneul Picard, the tallest of the French spaniels, has an air of serenity and strength. A highly skilled hunter, it adapts to virtually any kind of environment, whether forest, field, or marsh.

This spaniel has a remarkable sense of smell, and can hold a perfect point without difficulty until its master arrives ready to shoot. Robust, intelligent, and sturdy, the dog works well in marshland and is particularly adept at hunting wild duck. It is easy to handle, obedient, and greatly valued by sportsmen who want to use only one dog when hunting.

The Picardy displays loyalty, gentleness, and sensitivity as a companion dog.

AUS.	CAN.	S. AF.	U.K.	F.C.I.
				●

ORIGINS

The Picardy was once favoured by hunters in north-western France. The breed declined in number during the nineteenth century. It was rediscovered at a Paris dog show in 1904, when prized specimens, the results of a long breeding process, were presented.

Characteristics

General appearance: strong and sinewy limbs.
Height: 55 to 62 cm (21½ to 24½ in.).
Weight: not specified.
Head: large, round skull, well-defined occiput. Distinct, oblique stop. A long, fairly wide muzzle.
Eyes: dark amber, wide open. Straightforward look.
Ears: set low, framing the head well.
Body: deep, fairly broad chest. Back medium length.

Very straight loin, not overly long, broad, or thick. Slightly sloping and rounded croup.
Tail: two slight curves. Silky haired.
Forequarters: legs straight, well furnished.
Hindquarters: straight and muscular thighs with furnishings.
Coat: hair coarse, slightly curly.
Colour: ticked grey with brown patches on the body.

Practical information: The Picardy Spaniel was bred for fresh air and open spaces. It is easy to train as a hunter. However, if it is kept as a house-pet, it should be taken out for exercise several times a day. Regular brushing is essential to remove dirt and dead hair. Examine the long ears carefully and ensure they are kept properly clean.

Eskimo Dog

Canadian Eskimo Dog, Grönlandshund

A powerfully built, medium-size native of the Canadian Arctic, the Eskimo Dog is prized for its stamina and vigour. One of its striking traits is the ability to endure below-freezing temperatures for long periods of time with very little to eat. Even on the coldest winter night, the creature needs only its warm, thick coat for shelter. It sleeps curled up in a ball, with its muzzle tucked under its fluffy tail.

The Eskimo Dog shares the life and hardship of its master. Man and beast are fashioned by the same harsh environment. Both form an inseparable year-round team. In winter, the people of the North use the dog to pull their sleds. To this task, the tough, hard-working Eskimo Dog brings energy and enthusiasm, often covering vast distances on limited rations or without any food at all. In summer, the dog acts as a pack animal to transport small loads. Throughout the year, the Eskimo Dog is an indispensable hunting partner which can ably locate seal breathing holes, or hold musk-ox and polar bear at bay.

The Eskimo Dog is an independent creature which is fond of open spaces. It reacts forcefully to almost every activity—working, playing, and fighting. The mature animal can be gentle and affectionate. It may show either friendly curiosity or indifference towards strangers. Although it is not an ideal companion dog, it can become one with proper supervision.

AUS.	CAN.	S. AF.	U.K.	F.C.I.
	●	●	●	●

ORIGINS

The Eskimo Dog belongs to the spitz group of Northern dogs, which includes the Alaskan Malamute, the Siberian Husky, and the Samoyed. Between one and two thousand years ago, it was being used by the Inuit who lived along the coast and on the islands of what is now the Canadian Arctic. Before that, the dog may have been brought by Mongolian races which migrated from Asia to North America. Some experts believe that, at some point, Inuit cross-bred the dog with the wolf. During the 1920s, there were 20,000 pure-bred Eskimo Dogs in the Arctic but, within five decades, this number had fallen to below 200. The decline followed replacement of the sled by the snowmobile. Efforts to re-establish the breed were undertaken in the 1970s with the assistance of the Canadian Kennel Club.

THOSE AMAZING SLED DOGS OF THE CANADIAN NORTH

The toughness of the Eskimo Dog is legendary. One Arctic explorer once reported using a six-dog team to haul a 320-kilogram load (roughly 700 pounds) over a thousand kilometres in two weeks.

The training of an Eskimo sled dog begins at the age of four months, when it is harnessed close to its mother. For journeys across the Arctic wastes, each dog is equipped with a brace which is looped twice around its shoulders.

The sled team, consisting of nine dogs tethered together at the braces, is organized in a flexible, fan-shaped arrangement. While travelling, the dogs can quickly assume loose or tight formations according to the changing surface of the land. Tethering the team also helps when a dog falls into an icy crevasse. The combined strength of the team may be needed to pull the animal out of the hole.

To direct—and sometimes to reprimand—the team, the sled driver uses a whip about eight metres (25 feet) in length. To make the team turn right or left, the driver hits the ground on the desired side of the sled. He will crack the whip above the dogs' heads to increase speed or in front of them to bring them to a halt. Cracking the whip is accompanied by shouted orders. The command to depart, for example, is the shout 'kra!'

In recent years, Eskimo Dogs have been harnessed by chains. In the past, however, dogs were tethered by seal-skin lines. To prevent the dogs from chewing through these lines, the Inuit cut or broke the animals' canine teeth. This practice presented problems. The drivers had to cut or grind up seal meat for their voracious dogs. On one occasion, an Arctic explorer cut up 29 kilograms (65 pounds) of meat and fed it to his 29 dogs. They devoured it all in less than a minute.

Characteristics

General appearance: sturdy, built for hard work.

Height: 58.4 to 68.6 cm (23 to 27 in.) for the adult dog; 50.8 to 61 cm (20 to 24 in.) for the bitch. Canadian standards, 58.4 to 70 cm (23 to 27½ in.) for the male; 49.5 to 59.7 cm (19½ to 23½ in.) for the bitch.

Weight: 34 to 47.6 kg (75 to 105 lb) for the adult dog; 27.2 to 40.8 kg (60 to 90 lb) for the bitch. Under Canadian standards, 30 to 40 kg (66 to 88 lb) for the adult dog and 18 to 30 kg (40 to 66 lb) for the bitch. Under F.C.I. standards, not specified.

Head: broad, wedge-shaped, skull strong and flat. Stop moderate, medium-length muzzle tapering gently toward the nose. Nose and lips black. Lips thin and tight. Teeth large, strong, and uncrowded. Strong scissor bite.

Eyes: dark, brown or tawny. Slanting, small.

Ears: small, triangular, erect. Set well apart, facing forward.

Body: strong, well muscled. Chest and shoulders very wide. Loin straight and well developed. Croup slightly sloping downward. No tuck up. Level back.

Tail: thick, bushy, and rather large, set high and curled loosely over the back, falling either side.

Forequarters: legs straight and muscular, heavy-boned, elbows close.

Hindquarters: legs straight, stifles well bent, hocks broad and strong, heavy bone structure. Thighs broad, heavily muscled.

Coat: thick double coat, soft undercoat. Outer coat dense, straight, long, stiff and rough, shorter on the head and legs, longer on the neck and the body.

Colour: all colours accepted.

Practical information: Like most Northern canines, the Eskimo Dog is capable of adapting to a milder climate than the one for which it was bred. However, owners of the Eskimo Dog may find that this active dog is not suitable for urban living, particularly if it is kept indoors. If the Eskimo Dog is a house-pet, it must get several hours of exercise daily.

Eurasier

The Eurasier, a newcomer among dog breeds, was developed by scientists and researchers working in Germany during the early 1950s. Its name evokes its European and Asiatic ancestry—the Wolf-Spitz and the Chow Chow—and it combines many of their qualities.

Like the Wolf-Spitz, a close relative of the Keeshond, this dog is elegantly but solidly built, and has a sumptuously rich coat in red to sand, pale yellow, black, or grey. The eyes, set in a fox-like head, have a frank, intelligent expression.

From the Chow Chow, the Eurasier inherits a tender and affectionate nature. It is a clean and quiet dog. It makes an ideal companion dog and is well suited to family life. It enjoys children and adopts a paternal attitude with infants, never displaying the slightest jealousy towards them. Because the Eurasier needs company, it may refuse to be excluded from the household—to be put in a kennel or tied up outdoors.

The Eurasier seems to have a sense of humour, especially during its mischievous first few months. When the dog matures, it becomes more reserved and equable in temperament. Nevertheless, adult dogs can still be extremely playful.

The Eurasier is very loyal to its mate, and it is friendly with other dogs. It is something of a charmer with cats. Even the most timid felines can rarely resist its attraction.

Easy to train, the Eurasier is an attentive, vigilant guard dog when protecting its human family. It barks only when necessary, but hardly ever attacks. When provoked, it emits a deep growl similar to that of its earliest forbear, the wolf.

AUS.	CAN.	S. AF.	U.K.	F.C.I.
				●

ORIGINS

The Eurasier originated centuries ago among tribes living in central Siberia. These remote Russian peoples domesticated primitive dogs, descendants of the Wolf-Spitz and Chow Chow, which they named the Laika. The present-day Eurasier is similar to the Laika. During the 1950s, when the export of Soviet dogs was prohibited, German scientists, led by Professor Konrad Lorenz, decided to revive the breed by crossing a female Wolf-Spitz with a male Chow Chow. The actual developer of the breed, Julius Wipfel, named the offspring Eurasier. This new species, now well established, was recognized by the Fédération cynologique internationale in 1973.

HOW SCIENTISTS REGENERATED AN ANCIENT RUSSIAN BREED

The Eurasier breed was developed through the efforts of German scientists and researchers working at Gottingen University and at the Max Planck Institute in Heidelberg. In the 1950s, the two groups, headed by Professor Konrad Lorenz, joined forces to restore the Laïka, an ancient Russian dog breed unavailable in Western Europe at that time. Extensive studies and experiments in genetics and animal psychology had to be carried out before the teams succeeded in their objective.

The scientists matched a female Wolf-Spitz with a male Chow Chow. The first offspring resembled the mother. While trying to improve the selection process, scientists limited cross-breeding to specimens of the same generation to ensure a proper balance between the physical and psychological qualities of the parents. To avoid great disparities in the offspring, the same sires were used, but the females were changed often. Any offspring which resembled the Chow Chow or the Wolf-Spitz too closely, or over-reacted to their surroundings, were excluded from the breeding experiments. Breeders kept only the specimens which represented the best blend of the two species. Careful selection eventually produced the Eurasier—a dog with well-proportioned physique and stable character.

Characteristics

General appearance: longer than it is wide, the Eurasier is of average height. The head of this dog is shaped like that of a wolf.

Height: 52 to 60 cm (20½ to 23½ in.) for the adult dog; 48 to 56 cm (19 to 22 in.) for the bitch.

Weight: 25 to 30 kg (55 to 66 lb) for the adult dog; 20 to 26 kg (44 to 57 lb) for the bitch.

Head: wedge-shaped, muzzle medium length, not foxy. Skull flat, with a pronounced stop widening slightly towards the skull. Nose medium size. Jowls flat, not pendulous, with black pigmentation, which is also found on the mucous membranes, eyelids, and nose. Strong scissor bite.

Eyes: dark, not deep-set, almond-shaped. Dignified appearance.

Ears: average size, erect, not far apart.

Neck: head held high and attached to the shoulders by a muscular, well-set-on neck.

Body: muscular shoulders. Well-curved, deep chest. Curved ribs. Solid, straight back extended by a long, wide croup; pelvis is angled to the hindquarters. Chest deep, with gradual tuck-up.

Tail: reaching hocks while at rest, it curls up on the back and sideways when the dog is moving.

Forequarters: forelegs perfectly straight and stiff down to the feet.

Hindquarters: muscular thighs, hocks well let down, perfectly straight.

Feet: strong; cat-footed. Toes arched and close. Thick, heavy-duty pads.

Coat: the entire body of the Eurasier is covered with a short, dense undercoat and a medium-length outer coat. Long hair on the tail, rump, and forelegs. The mouth, jaw, and under-side have short hair. The coat around the neck is slightly longer than on the body, although it should not resemble a mane.

Colour: red to sandy shades or pale yellow, grey-black and black with fainter markings around the eyes and on the rump and tail.

Faults: head too heavy or pointed. Hind legs too rigid, making the dog seem to be 'walking on stilts.' Undercoat too thick, making the coat too dense. Jaw and upper part of the face forming a snipy muzzle. Eyes too light or too dark. Ears too far apart or too small. Brindle coat. A dog which is aggressive, fearful, or overly nervous.

Practical information: This vigorous dog is rarely ill and adapts easily to different environments. The Eurasier requires minimal exercise. With appropriate affection and care, the Eurasier lives happily within the human family circle. Unlike the Chow Chow, it is unaffected by seasonal changes, and it rarely suffers from eczema. Bathe the dog several times a year. Its coat, particularly the long hair on the tail, rump, and forelegs, requires regular brushing.

Finnish Spitz

The *Suomenpystykorva*, known in English as the Finnish Spitz, is found virtually everywhere in its native land. In the city, it plays the part of a companion; in the country, it is still a working dog. The Finnish Spitz has a friendly disposition and is loyal and faithful to its owner. It is very playful, particularly with children. A vigilant guard dog, it will alert its master to the least suspicious noise.

Experts believe that, for thousands of years, the Finnish Spitz existed as a hunting-dog in Lapland, which covers the northern regions of Norway, Sweden, Finland, and Russia. The breed eventually travelled southward and became particularly numerous in Finland.

Towards the end of the nineteenth century, the Finns became alarmed at the effects of indiscriminate cross-breeding between the Finnish Spitz and other Scandinavian dogs. The breed was disappearing, and its hunting and working qualities were deteriorating. The Finns decided to revive the breed and sent expeditions to northern Finland to find pure-bred dogs. Those specimens that were brought back provided the basis for the present-day breed.

Originally, the Finnish Spitz was prized as a hunter of all varieties of game, from bears to squirrels. The present-day breed is strictly a bird dog which is used particularly for flushing wood grouse. The breed is tireless in the pursuit of its prey. With a rousing bark, the tenacious dog marks the position of the wild bird for the hunter. The trait has earned it the appropriate nickname, 'the barking bird dog.'

Every year, in Finland, there is a competition to crown a champion Finnish Spitz. The winner of the contest is the dog that displays the finest hunting qualities.

AUS.	CAN.	S. AF.	U.K.	F.C.I.
●	●	●	●	●

ORIGINS

After a long period of decline, the Finnish Spitz was rescued from further deterioration in abilities and number during the late nineteenth century. In 1892, Finland's kennel club established a standard for the present-day Finnish Spitz. It was many years before the dog became well known outside its own country. In 1927, Sir Edward Chichester imported a pair of Finnish Spitzes into England, and the breed was recognized by the British Kennel Club in 1935. One of the pioneer British breeders, Lady Kitson, called the dog 'Finkie'—a nickname still popular with many of the breed's fanciers.

Characteristics

General appearance: body almost square, proud, lively. The Finnish Spitz is famed for its endurance, caution, courage, and fidelity.

Height: 43 to 51 cm (17 to 20 in.) for the adult dog; 39 to 45 cm (15 to 18 in.) for the bitch. Canadian standards: 44.5 to 49.5 cm (17½ to 19½ in.) for adult dogs; 39.5 to 44.5 cm (15½ to 17½ in.) for bitches.

Weight: 14 to 16 kg (31 to 35 lb) for adult dogs; 10.5 to 13 kg (23 to 29 lb) for bitches. Under F.C.I. standards, 23 to 27 kg (50¾ to 59½ lb).

Head: foxlike, average size, clean-cut. Forehead slightly arched. Skull a little domed. Muzzle narrow, evenly tapered, moderate stop. Nose pitch black. Thin, black, tight lips. Scissor bite.

Eyes: medium size, vivid, preferably dark, almond-shaped, slanting.

Ears: small, pricked, pointed, very mobile. Fine in texture.

Body: back, almost square in outline, short, level, and strong. Chest deep. Slight tuck up. Shoulder fairly straight.

Tail: plumed, curved in a vigorous arch from the root. When straightened, it reaches the hock joint.

Forequarters: legs straight and strong.

Hindquarters: strong, hocks of medium size.

Coat: double-coated, short and close on the head and front of legs; hair is longer and straight on the body, more rigid on the neck and back, semi-erect and coarser on the shoulders, dense and long at the back of the thighs and on the tail. Undercoat short, soft, tight, lighter in colour. No trimmings.

Colour: red-brown or red-gold on back, lighter inside the ears, on the cheeks, under muzzle, chest, stomach, inside of legs, back of thighs, and under-side of tail.

Practical information: The adult dog is robust, but at birth the delicate puppies need attentive care. Brush the coat regularly and vigorously. If this thick-coated dog is over-exposed to dry, indoor air, it may develop skin diseases.

Flat-Coated Retriever

The Flat-Coated Retriever resembles its ancestor, the Newfoundland dog, but it is smaller in size. It is more outgoing than other dogs of similar size and traits—for example, the Golden Retriever and the Labrador. With proper training, this bright, active dog can become a first-class retriever of waterfowl.

As a pet, the Flat-Coated Retriever is affectionate, patient, docile, and companionable with family and friends.

AUS.	CAN.	S. AF.	U.K.	F.C.I.
●	●	●	●	●

Characteristics

General appearance: medium size, very active.
Height: dogs 58.4 to 61 cm (23 to 24 in.); bitches 56 to 58.4 cm (22 to 23 in.).
Weight: dogs 25 to 35 kg (55 to 77 lb); bitches 23 to 34 kg (51 to 75 lb). Canadian standards are 27.2 to 31.8 kg (60 to 70 lb).
Head: skull flat, moderately broad, slight stop. Jaws strong, long.
Eyes: medium size, dark brown or hazel with intelligent expression.
Ears: small, well set on, close to side of head.
Body: chest broad, deep. Back short, square, well ribbed up.
Tail: short, straight, carried gaily, but never above level of the back.
Forequarters: straight.
Hindquarters: muscular, hocks slightly bent and well let down.
Coat: dense, of a fine to medium texture. Flat.
Colour: black or liver.

Practical information: This sporting dog needs regular exercise.

ORIGINS

The evolution of the Flat-Coated Retriever occurred in England during the last two centuries. Breeders began the development with Newfoundland dogs brought to British ports by Canadian seafarers. Later, Collie blood was added to increase working strength, and setter blood to enhance scenting abilities. The first specimen was shown in Britain about 1860, but the type was only established twenty years later. From the end of the last century until the beginning of the First World War, the Flat-Coated Retriever enjoyed success as a show dog and as a sporting dog. Later, it was passed over in favour of more popular sporting dogs such as the Labrador and the Golden retrievers. Today, the Flat-Coated Retriever is somewhat rare. But new interest in the breed was sparked in 1980, when one was chosen Supreme Champion at Crufts.

Foxhound

English Foxhound

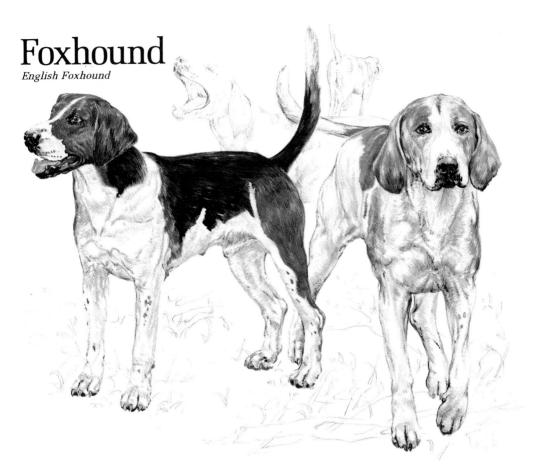

The Foxhound is an eager and obedient field dog, with a commanding bark and keen scenting ability. This pack dog has the stamina to follow a trail all day and in any weather, and it can run for hours at speeds which would exhaust other pure-breds. The Foxhound was bred strictly for the hunt. In Britain, where there are some 200 packs of trained scent hounds, it remains a pure working breed, and rarely appears in recognized dog shows.

In the mid-1600s the English Foxhound was imported into North America, where it was crossed with French and Irish hounds to produce the lighter, swifter, American Foxhound.

AUS.	CAN.	S. AF.	U.K.	F.C.I.
●	●	●	●	●

ORIGINS

By the eighteenth century, fox-hunting replaced stag-hunting as the sport of English gentry, and hunters needed faster dogs. Foxhounds evolved by crossing Staghounds with Bulldogs, and various greyhounds and terriers. Breeding is now supervised by the masters of hounds, who lead the fox-hunts.

Characteristics

General appearance: muscular and heavy-boned.
Height: not specified.
Weight: not specified.
Head: tapered. Skull broad. Stop hardly noticeable. Nose long, black. Thick, slightly drooping chops.
Eyes: fairly large, round, brown.
Ears: set low, short, lying close to the cheeks.

Body: massive chest. Level, wide back, tapering. Shoulders well sloped. Ribs very deep.
Tail: well set on, carried gaily, never over back.
Forequarters: muscular. Elbows and legs straight.
Hindquarters: very strong, solid, straight stifles.
Coat: short-haired, dense, hard, and glossy.
Colour: any hound colour.

Practical information: The Foxhound is a robust and sturdy hunter, and its upkeep is easy. Like all pack dogs, however, this hound craves the company of its own kind and the noisy excitement of the chase. These natural inclinations make it a poor pet, particularly for city dwellers, who might find the dog difficult to keep exercised and under control.

Fox Terrier

Smooth-haired Fox Terrier

Wire-haired Fox Terrier

T here are two breeds of Fox Terrier—the Smooth- and the Wire-haired. Although the two types do not appear to be similar, the only difference between them is the texture of the coats. They have the same lively—and, some might say, pugnacious—disposition. Physically, they are the same. Indeed, with the exception of the coat, they are judged by the same set of standards at dog shows.

The early history of the Fox Terrier is unclear. Some experts believe the wire-haired type is the older form, but an opposing claim is made for the smooth-haired type. There can be no doubt, however, that both these small and sturdy breeds derive from terrier stock known in Britain since the fifteenth century, and from hunting-dogs.

Fox Terriers first made their mark in the eighteenth century when fox-hunting became widespread in England. The smooth-haired variety was introduced to the general public at a Birmingham dog show in the early 1860s and quick-

AUS.	CAN.	S. AF.	U.K.	F.C.I.
●	●	●	●	●

ORIGINS

The Wire-haired Fox Terrier was developed in the early 1800s for fox-hunting. Little is known about its history. One of its forbears was a famous Smooth-haired Terrier, called Jack, *whose mate was* Trap, *a rough-haired Black and Tan Terrier bitch. The Wire-haireds are reputed to have the blood of Beagles, Bulldogs, Greyhounds, and other terriers. The distinction between the Wire-haireds and the Smooth-haireds was made in the 1870s. The present-day Wire-haired was bred about 1900. It had a peak period of popularity in the 1920s.*

ly became a popular favourite. The wire-haired variety, which looks appropriately Victorian with its stylish whiskers, made its debut a decade later.

The standard for the breed, prepared in the nineteenth century, is still applicable today: 'The terrier should be alert, quick of movement, keen of expression and on the tiptoe of expectation at the slightest provocation. Character is imparted by the expression of the eyes, and by the carriage of ears and tail.' Elsewhere in the standard, the Terrier is described as 'a well-made hunter' with 'a general gay, lively and active appearance.'

Although originally a hunting-dog, the Fox Terrier is now chiefly a companion animal. It can adapt to city or country life. As long as its human family is near, the dog will be happy. It is devoted, loyal, and an excellent watch-dog.

Characteristics

General appearance: lively dog, intelligent looking, alert to the slightest movement, ready to charge at any provocation. Disposition of both smooth-haired and wire-haired varieties is the same.
Height: under F.C.I. and Canadian standards, 30 to 39 cm (12 to 15½ in.). Elsewhere, not exceeding 39 cm (15½ in.).
Weight: 7.3 to 8.3 kg (16 to 18 lb) for the adult dog; 6.8 to 7.7 kg (15 to 17 lb) for the bitch.
Head: skull flat, moderately narrow, decreasing in width towards the eyes. Slight stop. Little difference in length between the skull and the muzzle. The nose should be black. Cheeks rather lean. Strong muscular jaws. Scissor bite. Not much falling away under the eyes.
Eyes: dark, moderately small, not prominent, full of fire and intelligence; circular. Rims dark.
Ears: small, V-shaped, moderately thick, flaps neatly folded over and close to the cheeks.
Neck: clean and muscular, of fair length, gradually widening at the shoulders, presenting a graceful curve.
Body: chest deep, not too broad. Back short, straight, and strong. Shoulders oblique, well laid back, slender at the points, well defined at the withers. Powerful, very slightly arched loin. Fore-ribs moderately arched, back-ribs deep.
Tail: set high, carried erect, neither over the back nor curled, of good strength and fair length. Customarily docked.
Forequarters: strong bone structure. Legs straight, solid.
Hindquarters: strong, muscular, and straight. Thighs long and powerful. Hocks well bent and parallel when seen from behind.
Feet: round, compact, and not large. Small, tough, thick pads. Toes moderately arched, turning neither inward nor outward.
Coat: wire-haired variety: dense, very wiry; undercoat of short, softer, broken hair. Smooth-haired variety: straight, flat, smooth, dense, and abundant.
Colour: predominantly white. Brindle, red, or liver markings very undesirable. Otherwise, colour not overly important.
Faults: nose white, cherry, or very spotted. Ears straight, tulip, or rose. Mouth much undershot or overshot. Light eyes.

Practical information: The Fox Terrier needs a great deal of exercise. If kept indoors, it tends to develop eczema. This aggressive terrier is often bitten in fights with other dogs. Have disinfectant and bandages on hand for its wounds. The female has a tendency to have false pregnancies.

Français Blanc et Noir

AUS.	CAN.	S. AF.	U.K.	F.C.I.
				●

This is one of the finest hunting-dogs in France. The Français Blanc et Noir is prized for its endurance and its keen scent. It comes from a long line of French hunting hounds. From its different forbears, it inherited a tall, muscular frame, but with a refining blend of elegance and finesse. Among its other distinctive features are the large patches of black or dark blue on its coat, and the small grey spots on its legs.

ORIGINS

The Français Blanc et Noir is descended from two rare French breeds, the Saintongeois and the Gascons, but it also has a dash of English hunting-dog blood. The standards for this breed were established in 1957.

Characteristics

General appearance: tall, dignified, stable-looking.
Height: 65 to 72 cm (25½ to 28¼ in.) for the adult dog; 62 to 68 cm (24 to 26¾ in.) for the bitch.
Weight: not specified.
Head: rather large, elongated, expressive. Skull narrow, slightly rounded. Occipital protuberance. Slight stop. Nose black, nostrils wide. Jowl covering lower lip, though not pendulous.
Eyes: dark, intelligent, trusting expression.
Ears: set at eye level, slightly turned.
Neck: fairly long, strong, slight dewlap permissible.

Body: shoulders clean, long, oblique. Chest deep. Straight, long back, loin muscular.
Tail: long, thick at the base.
Forequarters: strong, straight. Elbows held close to the body.
Hindquarters: thighs long and muscular. Large, powerful hocks.
Coat: short, close, dense, and strong hair. Skin same colour as the hair covering it. Subcutaneous blue patches on stomach, insides of thighs.
Colour: black and white.

Practical information: Systematic vaccinations are essential for a pack dog like the Blanc et Noir.

Galgo

Spanish Greyhound

Once used only for hunting, the Galgo was renowned for endurance, agility, and perseverance. This lean and elegant dog was the companion of the Spanish nobility, who kept the breed pure for hundreds of years.

Early in this century greyhound racing enthusiasts decided to develop this hunting-dog· for their sport. By the 1930s, the 'Galgo Greyhound' had replaced the hunter. Today, this racing variety is well regarded and popular in Spain. It has become an affectionate, faithful—if somewhat possessive—companion dog.

AUS.	CAN.	S. AF.	U.K.	F.C.I.
				●

ORIGINS

Experts claim the ancient Canis Gallicus, *and the Sloughi, and, possibly, the Ibizan Hound, as ancestors of the Galgo. In the 1930s, the purity of the Galgo was debased when it was bred with the English Greyhound.*

Characteristics

General appearance: tall, strongly boned, very muscular, fast, and tenacious when racing.
Height: 65 cm (25½ in.) for the adult dog; 60 cm (23½ in.) for the bitch.
Weight: 25 to 30 kg (55 to 66 lb) for the adult dog; 20 to 25 kg (44 to 55 lb) for the bitch.
Head: elongated. Stop not too defined. Prominent nose. Powerful jaw, lips thin, teeth strong, scissor bite.
Eyes: large, dark, and fiery.
Ears: delicate, partially hanging, set high and positioned towards the back of the head.
Neck: long and slender, muscular, held high, slightly flattened.

Body: chest deep. Ribs well rounded. Back strong, muscular. Croup rounded. Belly well tucked up. Shoulders oblique.
Tail: long, thin, carried straight down with a curl near the hocks.
Forequarters: long, lean, straight, and muscular.
Hindquarters: muscular. Hocks well let down.
Feet: nearly round, compact.
Coat: two varieties, one short and soft; the other hard and glossy.
Colour: cinnamon, auburn, black, rust, white or a blend. Often brindled on fawn background with white patches on head, neck, and feet.

Practical information: This hardy, robust dog needs exercise, but little upkeep. Brush it regularly.

German Shepherd Dog

Alsatian, Alsatian Wolf Dog

AUS.	CAN.	S. AF.	U.K.	F.C.I.
●	●	●	●	●

One of the most popular breeds in the world, the German Shepherd is a large, strong, and well-muscled dog whose intelligence and resourcefulness are greatly admired. Since the 1920s, when the breed first attracted attention outside Germany, it has generated good as well as bad publicity. Enthusiasts who feel that the German Shepherd is the finest of all breeds cite its remarkable contributions to human society as a sheep-dog, a companion dog, guard dog, guide dog for the blind, and as an army and police dog. The widespread acceptance of the Shepherd as a multitalented working dog is a tribute to its exceptional character and skills.

Detractors of the breed point to incidents involving attacks by German Shepherds. The reputation of the breed was damaged by inept handling and indiscriminate breeding in the past, particularly after it was introduced into Britain during the 1920s. In most cases of savagery, the master is at fault for failing to control the dog's aggressiveness. If properly trained when young, the German Shepherd will be loyal, faithful, and obedient when mature.

The versatile German Shepherd can be trained for almost anything, even home life. It fits well within the family circle and can be an ideal companion, respectful of family, friend, and stranger.

ORIGINS

Originally, the German Shepherd was used for herding, guarding, and farmwork. Its early ancestors may have been wolves (or have had wolf blood), but the matter is debatable. The present-day dog was bred in the 1880s by a German cavalry officer. The first society for the breed was founded in 1899, and it remains one of the largest clubs of its kind in the world. During the First World War, German Shepherds were used as army dogs, whose valour and versatility impressed Allied soldiers. During the 1920s, despite strict quarantines, great numbers were imported into Britain and the Commonwealth. Until the 1970s, the dog was called the Alsatian, or Alsatian Wolf Dog in Britain to avoid arousing anti-German sentiment.

THE MANY ROLES OF THE GERMAN SHEPHERD

The German Shepherd is easy to train because it is intelligent and has highly developed senses. Specialists can prepare the individual dog to take on one role from a wide range of possible parts: defender, drug dog, guard, life-saver, sentry, tracker, army or police dog, dog to lead the blind or to rescue victims of earthquake and avalanche.

The training of the German Shepherd begins when it is only ten weeks old. At this stage, it takes part in walks and games, during which it learns to respond to its name when commanded by its trainer, to accept the collar and leash, and finally to walk leashed or free.

At the age of eight months, a trainer teaches the Shepherd how to guard, jump, search, track, refuse bait, and retrieve. Its 'vocabulary' is extended to include an understanding of such commands as 'go,' 'stay,' 'get up,' and 'lie down.'

The last, difficult training stages are for German Shepherds being educated as defenders or guards.

They are taught to deal with intimidating situations, such as threatened beatings, and to become used to the sound of gun-fire. Each animal goes through attack-training. During carefully simulated encounters, the dog is ordered to attack an intruder, which may be a dummy or, in some cases, a properly protected instructor. Once attack-training is completed, the defending or guard dog is assigned to its own handler and attacks only on his command. The training of an army or police dog is based on these principles. Duties may include patrolling, tracking, detecting mines, and protecting military bases.

German Shepherds were first trained as avalanche dogs in 1970. Their highly developed sense of smell and their tough, weather-resistant coats make these dogs the most effective and rapid rescuers of victims of these natural disasters. Other Shepherds are now used to save human lives wherever earthquakes, explosions, floods or other catastrophes take place.

Characteristics

General appearance: robust and supple, this slightly elongated dog is all muscle. Its dignified bearing and courageousness command respect.

Height: 63.5 cm (25 in.) for the adult dog; 58.4 cm (23 in.) for the bitch.

Weight: under Canadian standards, 34 to 38.5 kg (75 to 85 lb) for the adult dog, and 27.2 to 31.8 kg (60 to 70 lb) for the bitch. Elsewhere, not specified.

Head: in proportion with the body, clear-cut, fairly broad between the ears. Stop barely defined. Muzzle long and strong. Lips are clean, tight. Nose black, muzzle straight. Teeth sound and strong, scissor bite.

Eyes: medium size, almond-shaped, slightly slanting, not protruding, dark brown preferred. Expression alert, highly intelligent and self-assured.

Ears: medium size, broad at the base, set high, carried erect and pointed forward. The ears of young dogs sometimes hang until the sixth month or later, becoming erect with the replacement of the milk teeth.

Great care should be taken not to break the cartilage.

Neck: fairly long, strong, well muscled.

Body: chest deep, capacious, but not too broad. Ribs long and well sprung, not too flat. Belly firmly held, not paunchy. Back straight. Flanks broad, strong, and well muscled. Croup long and slightly sloping. Shoulders long, oblique, well laid back. Loin broad and strong.

Tail: bushy, set low rather than high.

Forequarters: legs straight, elbows neither wide apart nor sloping.

Hindquarters: thighs broad, muscular. Hocks bent, firm, and vigorous.

Coat: an outer and inner coat, both thick. Stiff, thick, flat, coarse hair. Breeching near the thighs. Hair length varies.

Colour: black with brown markings, tan, light grey with black and dark saddle. Small white markings on the chest or inside of legs are permissible.

Practical information: The German Shepherd needs daily brushing and only one or two baths a year. It may suffer from chronic eczema, keratitis (inflammation of the cornea), and hip dysplasia (malformation of the hip joint), a hereditary affliction which becomes apparent about the age of four months. To avoid buying a sickly dog, always go to a reputable breeder.

German Short-haired Pointer

Kurzhaar

AUS.	CAN.	S. AF.	U.K.	F.C.I.
●	●	●	●	●

O ne of the best all-purpose hunting-dogs, the German Short-haired Pointer can track all manner of game. It works as well in open fields and marshes as it does in woods and on the mountains. It is particularly excellent as a hunter of grouse and pheasant in upland areas.

This medium-size pointer, known in Germany as the *Kurzhaar* ('short-hair'), pursues its quarry with spirit and energy, has great stamina, and can withstand cold weather. Unfortunately, its abilities are not at their best in warm weather. Moreover, the breed is slower on the open field than setters or other types of pointers. But this is not a drawback for the solitary sportsman who likes to follow a dog on foot.

In the seventeenth century, the German Short-haired Pointer was prized both by German nobles and poachers for its skills as a night hunter. During the last century, breeders added English Pointer blood to improve scenting ability and running style. They succeeded in making the dog lighter and more flexible, and endowing it with an elegant and noble air.

The German Short-haired Pointer is ready—and usually eager—to start training by the age of eight months. If the programme is ineffective or undemanding, however, this intelligent dog may attempt to dominate its master.

Although the German Short-haired Pointer has a strong personality, it is amiable and adapts well to family life. This pointer is full of energy. Like so many other hunting-dogs, it may get out of control and act foolishly if it is confined for long periods and lacks opportunity for exercise.

Today, its popularity is on the increase in Britain and North America.

ORIGINS

It was during the 1600s that breeders in Germany crossed imported Spanish Pointers with Bloodhounds to produce the Kurzhaar. The early German Short-haired Pointer was a little heavier, broader, stockier, and less elegant than the present type. It was skilled at pointing, retrieving, tracking day and night, as well as hunting various game. It was also valued as a watch-dog and as a companion. During the nineteenth century, the present-day breed started to evolve when breeders decided to enhance its hunting qualities. They added English Pointer blood to improve its slow and heavy gait as well as its inferior sense of scent. The years between 1860 and 1880 saw the emergence of a new type which was thinner and speedier, had a better 'nose,' and was a better tracker and retriever. The first German Short-haired Pointer was initially registered by the German Kennel Club in 1872. By 1911, the breed had been standardized. It was introduced into North America around the mid-1920s.

THE SKILL OF THE POINTER

Pointing is an ability of a specific group of lean and muscular hunting-dogs, which take their name from a shared instinct. The pointer hunts by scent. When the dog locates game, it signals this discovery to the hunter by assuming a rigid stance known as the 'point.' There are three basic features to a pointer's stance. The dog's nose is held high in the wind, its foreleg may be raised, and its tail is elevated.

The last physical sign is important, because it distinguishes the point from a momentary pause in the tracking of the prey. When the pointer has a keen scent, the dog's whole body—particularly the tip of its nose—trembles. The hunter must not disturb the point. When the hunter puts the game birds to flight, the dog relaxes its position. If the bird continues to hide in the tall grasses, the dog itself will glide along, still in pointing position, and force the game to take flight.

Another remarkable ability of these dogs is that they can point almost simultaneously. The second dog will take the same position as the first, after a delay of only a second.

Characteristics

General appearance: a sturdy and speedy dog.

Height: 58.4 to 63.5 cm (23 to 25 in.) for the adult dog; 53.3 to 58.4 cm (21 to 23 in.) for the bitch.

Weight: 25 to 31.8 kg (55 to 70 lb) for the adult dog; 20.4 to 27.2 kg (45 to 60 lb) for the bitch. Under F.C.I. standards, not specified.

Head: clean-cut, neither too light nor too heavy, well chiselled and well proportioned. Skull broad, slightly rounded. Stop not too defined. Muzzle long and strong, not pointed. Jaws powerful. Teeth sound and strong, in a scissor bite. Nose solid brown with wide, soft nostrils.

Eyes: medium size, dark brown, not protruding or set too deep.

Ears: set high, broad at the base and rounded at the tip. Carried flat against the cheek.

Neck: muscular, of average length, slightly arched.

Body: shoulders sloping and muscular. Brisket powerful, deep. Ribs deep and well sprung. Back short, firm, and level. Loin wide, short, muscular, slightly arched. Croup wide, long, not sloping.

Tail: set high, thick at base, tapering towards tip. Usually docked. Carried horizontally or slightly raised.

Forequarters: legs straight, lean and muscular. Elbows well laid back. Pasterns sloping slightly.

Hindquarters: thighs powerful. Hips broad and wide. Hocks square with body. Pasterns nearly upright.

Feet: compact, close-knit, and round to spoon-shaped. Toes arched, heavily nailed. Pads hard and strong.

Coat: short, flat and coarse; very thick on the brisket, finer and shorter on the ears and head.

Colour: solid liver, liver and white, liver- and white-spotted and ticked, liver roan, black and white.

Practical information: Brush the dog once a week and bathe it every two or three months. Clean the ears regularly. Check for fungus or eczema between the toes. With these conditions, red patches appear, and the dog licks its paws often. This active hunting-dog can be quite happy in a rural or suburban setting, but it is essential that its owners keep it well exercised.

German Wire-haired Pointer

Drahthaar

AUS.	CAN.	S. AF.	U.K.	F.C.I.
●	●	●	●	●

T his dog has exceptional hunting skills, a striking appearance, and a strong character. Its
German name comes from one of its most notable
and important features—the wiry coat (*draht*,
wire; *haar*, hair) which resists cold, damp, and injury. The versatile German Wire-haired Pointer
is able to point and to retrieve on land or in water.

ORIGINS

*During the late nineteenth cen-
tury, German breeders combined pointers, terriers, and
other breeds, notably Poodles, to
produce this remarkable variety of hunting-dog.*

Characteristics

General appearance: medium size, sturdy, dignified,
intelligent expression.
Height: 61 to 66 cm (22 to 26 in.) for the adult dog: 56
to 61 cm (22 to 24 in.) for the bitch. Under Canadian
standards, not less than 56 cm (22 in.).
Weight: 25 to 34 kg (55 to 75 lb) for the adult dog;
19.5 to 29 kg (43 to 64 lb) for the bitch. Not specified
under Canadian standards.
Head: average length. Skull broad. Occiput not
prominent. Muzzle broad and fairly long. Stop medium. Nose liver or black. Nostrils well open. Jaws
strong. Scissor bite. Lips close, with beard.

Eyes: dark brown, average size, bushy eyebrows.
Ears: of average length, set high, hanging close.
Body: shoulders sloping and muscular. Chest wide
and deep. Ribs well sprung. Back short, firm, and lev-
el. Loin well muscled. Croup long, wide, and slightly
sloping. Bone solid, strong. Good tuck up.
Tail: tapering. Customarily docked. Never held high.
Forequarters: legs straight and lean, elbows tight.
Hindquarters: thighs strong and muscular, stifles
well bent and hocks well let down.
Coat: rough, thick, medium length; dense undercoat.
Colour: liver, liver and white, black and white.

Practical information: Brush this dog's coat once or
twice a week, and thin it in spring and autumn. Clean
and check the ears regularly.

Golden Retriever

This is a hardy, well-built dog with a golden, wavy coat. It was bred to retrieve waterfowl. A truly superior hunting-dog, the Golden Retriever has a highly developed scenting ability and great intelligence which makes it easy to train. It retrieves as naturally as it breathes, and will leap eagerly into water to recover downed birds. It is happiest when fetching and carrying and, in a show of affection, it will look for an opportunity to bring things to its master. The Golden Retriever is also an effective gun dog which can systematically track prey in the field.

Its calm, gentle, and loyal nature makes the Golden Retriever an ideal family companion.

AUS.	CAN.	S. AF.	U.K.	F.C.I.
●	●	●	●	●

ORIGINS

The public once believed that Golden Retrievers were descended from performing Russian circus dogs. But research in the 1950s showed that the Golden Retriever was initially derived from a Flat-Coated Retriever and a yellow Tweed Water Spaniel. The new retriever was granted breed status in 1913.

Characteristics

General appearance: active and solid.
Height: 50.8 to 61 cm (20 to 24 in.). Canadian standards: 58.4 to 61 cm (23 to 24 in.) for the adult dog; 54.6 to 57 cm (21½ to 22½ in.) for the bitch.
Weight: 29.5 to 34 kg (65 to 75 lb) for the adult dog; 27.2 to 31.8 kg (60 to 70 lb) for the bitch.
Head: skull broad. Muzzle pointed, deep, wide. Strong jaws and teeth. Scissor bite. Defined stop.
Eyes: set wide apart, dark, brown, dark rims.
Ears: medium size, well proportioned, well set on.

Body: well balanced, short coupled. Ribs deep, well sprung. Level topline. Strong, muscular loin. Shoulders long, wide, well laid back.
Tail: neither curled at the end nor carried gaily.
Forequarters: legs straight with good bone.
Hindquarters: legs strong, muscular. Stifles well bent. Hocks well let down.
Coat: waterproof, flat or wavy, with good feathering. Dense undercoat.
Colour: any shade of gold or cream.

Practical information: This energetic dog needs lots of outdoor exercise. Brush the coat regularly.

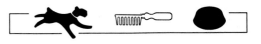

Gordon Setter

The Gordon Setter is the largest and most powerful of the three setter varieties. This handsome dog was built for strength and endurance rather than for swiftness. An early description of the Gordon is still accurate today: 'They are not fast dogs, but they have good staying power and can work steadily from morning until night.'

The Gordon excels at hunting on land or water, no matter what the weather. Hunters use this setter on stubble-covered fields because the dog has solid pads on its paws, which are impervious to thorns and twigs. The Gordon is better than most dogs at tracking for long periods of time without getting thirsty. As an early writer observed, 'Their noses are first-class and they seldom make a false point.' They spot prey quickly and retrieve instinctively. Their favourite game birds are partridge, pheasant, and woodcock.

The shiny, silky coat of a Gordon in good condition imparts a stylish air. Even so, some hunters shy away from the Gordon because its coat blends too well with the natural background.

Although active, the Gordon Setter makes an agreeable companion dog because it is gentle and affectionate. Its even-tempered disposition is closer to that of the English Setter than that of its other cousin, the Irish Setter. It is loyal to its immediate human family, but tends to be somewhat reserved with strangers.

AUS.	CAN.	S. AF.	U.K.	F.C.I.
●	●	●	●	●

ORIGINS

This field dog, once known as the Black and Tan Setter or Scottish Setter, dates from the early seventeenth century, in Scotland. Around 1800, the Duke of Gordon developed the present type from his own Black and Tan strain. This heavier and stronger dog was so highly regarded, not only in Britain but also abroad, that it was named after Gordon. One was judged best of all setters at the world's first dog exhibition, held in England in 1859. During the nineteenth century, it was a favourite in Britain and North America. But in this century, the numbers fell drastically. In Great Britain there were only 28 Gordon Setter registrations in 1962. Since then, interest in the breed has revived.

A COLLIE ANCESTOR

The Gordon Setter once had a tendency to circle rather than to point the game. This odd quirk was attributed to a dash of Collie blood in the dog's veins. It has been suggested that a Collie bitch belonging to the Duke of Gordon's shepherds may have been a founder of this setter breed. The bitch had an excellent nose and a skill—astonishing in a herding dog—for hunting game. When the Duke became aware of these abilities, he used the herder-turned-hunter for this purpose. Later, he cross-bred the bitch with the setter sires of his kennel. Although there is some reasonable doubt about this story, Collie ancestry was cited as a way of explaining the Gordon Setter's odd trait. The 'eccentricity' was eventually suppressed by deliberate and careful breeding.

Characteristics

General appearance: stylish appearance. Its conformation is perfectly symmetrical.

Height: 61 to 68.6 cm (24 to 27 in.) for the adult dog; 58.4 to 66 cm (23 to 26 in.) for the bitch.

Weight: 25 to 34 kg (55 to 75 lb) for the adult dog; 20.4 to 29.5 kg (45 to 65 lb) for the bitch.

Head: deep rather than broad. Skull slightly rounded, well developed between the ears. Clean stop. Muzzle fairly long, with almost parallel lines. Cheeks narrow. Nose big, broad, black. Nostrils open. Tight lips. Flews not pendulous. Level jaws. Scissor bite.

Eyes: of fair size, neither too deep nor prominent. Sparkling and dark brown. Intelligent expression.

Ears: set low, medium length, fairly large yet thin, lying close to the head.

Body: medium length. Ribs well sprung. Chest not too wide. Deep brisket. Back short, strong, and straight. Loin broad, slightly arched. Croup almost horizontal. Long, oblique shoulders.

Tail: rather short; straight or slightly scimitar-shaped, tapering. Must not reach below the hocks. Carried horizontally or under the line of the back. Long, straight feathering, growing shorter to the point.

Forequarters: big, flat-boned, and straight. Elbows well let down. Strong, upright pasterns.

Hindquarters: from hip to hock, long, wide, and muscular; from hock to the feet, strong and short. Stifles well bent. Hocks straight, well let down.

Coat: short, fine hair on the head, and on front of legs; medium length and straight on the rest of the body, as flat as possible, without curl even in the feathering. Nice feathering on the stomach, which may extend onto chest and throat. Long, silky hair on the ears, long and fine at the back of the hind legs.

Colour: dark, shining coal-black without any rust, with tan markings of a vivid reddish brown, or rich chestnut, or mahogany. The tan marks are clearly outlined over the eyes, on each side of the muzzle, on the throat, the chest, on the inner face of the hindquarters and thighs, on the forequarters, and under the tail. A very small white patch is permissible on the chest.

Faults: the 'Bloodhound' appearance, with a heavy head. The Collie-type, with pointed muzzle and curved tail. Pointed head. Eyes too light, deep-set, or prominent. Ears heavy and too wide. Neck thick and short. Hair curled, woolly, dull. Black and tan colours not clearly defined. Back and shoulders irregularly formed. Limbs crooked. Chest too broad. Tail hooked at the end. Flat feet. Toes spread. An overall impression of stupidity.

Practical information: After a hunt, dry the dog if it is wet, and give it a moderate amount of water to drink. Examine the coat for wounds and parasites, and check the ears carefully. Eight to ten days before the hunting season, strengthen the sole pads by submerging the paws for five minutes a day in a pharmaceutical solution recommended by your veterinarian.

Great Dane

It is doubtful whether this majestic dog originated in Denmark. Yet, George Buffon, the
eighteenth-century French naturalist, evidently
thought so when he called it the *Grand Danois*.
The English accepted the name, and 'Great Dane'
has stuck throughout the English-speaking world.

The Germans, however, use the name *Deutsche
Dogge* (German Mastiff), which is closer to the
truth because the present-day dog was developed
by German breeders during the nineteenth century. The Great Dane was first displayed at a
Hamburg dog show in 1862. German enthusiasm
for the Great Dane led to its selection as the national dog in 1876. The German Chancellor, Bis-
marck, appropriately chose the dogs for pets and
bodyguards. British fanciers of the Great Dane
founded the first speciality club in 1882.

AUS.	CAN.	S. AF.	U.K.	F.C.I.
●	●	●	●	●

ORIGINS

*Egyptian hieroglyphics dating
from 3000 B.C. seem to depict
dogs similar to the Great Dane.
Some canine experts claim that
Phoenician traders spread the
mastiffs throughout the Mediterranean. The Germans, however, believe that invading
Roman legions brought the forerunner of the Great Dane to
their country in the first century. During the Middle Ages,
German noblemen used Great
Danes for hunting boar.*

Great Danes were first exhibited in North America in the late 1870s. The new arrivals acquired a reputation for ferocity but, within 20 years, North American breeders had created docile and protective specimens.

The Great Dane is a giant of the canine world. It displays affection towards its master, patience with children, loyalty to friends, and restraint with strangers.

Characteristics

General appearance: large and muscular, with an elegant form and graceful gait. Courageous, friendly, and dependable.

Height: at least 76.2 cm (30 in.) for the adult dog; 71 cm (28 in.) for the bitch. Under Canadian standards, the preferred weight for the adult dog is 81.3 cm (32 in.); for the bitch 76.2 cm (30 in.).

Weight: at least 54.4 kg (120 lb) for the adult dog, and at least 45.4 kg (100 lb) for the bitch. Under Canadian standards, not specified.

Head: elongated, expressive, finely sculpted. Stop well defined. Forehead parallel to the nose. Muzzle and skull equal in length. Pendulous jowls. Nose large and black. Bridle of nose very wide, with slight ridge where cartilage joins bone. Lips hand squarely in front. Teeth level. Scissor bite.

Eyes: medium size, preferably dark. In the Harlequin type, light or differently coloured eyes permitted but not desirable.

Ears: triangular, medium in size, set high and folded forward. Under Canadian and F.C.I. standards, ears may be cropped.

Neck: long, well arched, clean and free from loose skin. Held well up; well set on shoulders.

Body: deep and broad with well-sprung ribs. Brisket descending to the elbows, deep and well drawn up. Back short and firm. Croup full. Loins pulled in and strong. Belly arched. Shoulders long and sloping.

Tail: set high, just reaching the hock. Thick at the base, tapering to the tip, carried in straight line, level with back, when dog is moving.

Forequarters: strong and muscular, well-sloped back. Elbows well under the body. Forelegs straight with big, flat bones.

Hindquarters: thighs broad and extremely muscular. Hocks and stifles well bent, hocks well let down. Full croup, slight droop to tail root.

Feet: cat-footed. Nails well arched, close, strong, dark.

Coat: short, thick, glossy, never inclined to roughness.

Colour: for brindles, all shades of fawn, with black stripes. Fawn dogs: lightest buff to deepest orange, with black mask. Blue dogs: steel blue with no trace of yellow, black, or mouse grey. Black dogs: glossy black. Harlequin dogs: white with irregular black markings well distributed over the body. Boston or Black-Mantled dogs: black and white with the black mantle extending over the body.

Faults: head round, apple- or wedge-shaped. Poorly defined stop. Muzzle snipy. Eyes too light, slanting, with visible haw. Poor ear carriage. Short neck. Dewlap. Swayback or camel back. Tail too long, or ringed. Cow-hocked. Shelly body. Straight shoulders. Out at elbows. Hare-footed. Dewclaw on hind leg. Coat long, dull, or off-colour.

Practical information: This outdoors dog needs a great deal of exercise, particularly when it is a pup. Its growing period lasts 20 months. Check-ups are essential between two and eight months. If necessary, have the ears cropped between the ages of two and three months. The Great Dane requires a concave cut, and splints or a cap may be necessary for several weeks after the cropping. For a daily diet, the young Great Dane needs more food per unit of body weight than the adult dog. Meat, rice, carrots, green vegetables, and cheese are acceptable foods. Bathe the animal several times a year.

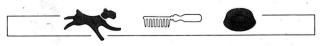

Greyhound

English Greyhound

The Greyhound has always been prized as a hunting-dog capable of outpacing such quarries as stag, fox, and hare. Probably the fleetest dog in the world, it is capable of reaching speeds of 70 kilometres (43.5 miles) an hour. Monarchs throughout the ages have admired its silhouette of pure, long lines, and its elegant bearing. During the sixteenth century, the English chose the Greyhound for 'coursing'—a sport that pits one animal's speed and skill against another's in pursuit of a live hare. Many people now regard this as a cruel sport that should be banned.

Greyhound racing was introduced in the late nineteenth century as a more humane alternative to coursing. Today, such racing is widely enjoyed by enthusiasts in Australia, Britain, and the United States, and to a lesser degree in Canada. But some North American humane societies, citing abuses in training and mass killing of non-racing specimens, denounce the sport's dark side.

In Great Britain, the Greyhound is still chiefly bred as a racer and as a show dog. In Canadian shows, the breed is among top contenders in the Hound Group. Like most racers, the Greyhound is a proud and intelligent creature, but it keeps its distance from strangers. If properly exercised, this dog can be a quiet and agreeable house-pet.

AUS.	CAN.	S. AF.	U.K.	F.C.I.
●	●	●	●	●

ORIGINS

The Greyhound is one of the oldest pure breeds in existence. It is often depicted in Egyptian engravings and sculptures dating back five thousand years. Originating in the Middle East, the Greyhound was probably brought to Europe by Phoenician traders. Medieval noblemen would often present the dog as a gift to their hosts. The origin of the name is difficult to ascertain. Some believe that it derives from gradus *meaning 'rank.' Others claim that the name can be traced to* grach, *the Old English word for 'dog,' or to* Grais *meaning 'Grecian.' Surprisingly, the form and function of this dog have altered little since the days of antiquity.*

TRAINING A FIRST-CLASS RACER

Greyhounds course hares, but they also race on oval tracks where they pursue an electrically operated, mechanical lure. The speed of the lure is increased as the hounds close in. Although the first recorded race with a rabbit 'decoy' occurred in England in 1876, greyhound racing originated in the United States, where it became popular during the early 1920s. Britain's first track opened at Manchester in 1926. A year later, a track race was held in New South Wales, Australia.

Today greyhound racing is the leading spectator sport in Britain, which has roughly 50 licensed tracks and a larger number of unlicensed ones. It is also taking off in Australia, is making some inroads in Canada, and has become a billion dollar industry in the United States. Except in Canada, where wagering is limited to horses, large sums are placed on the hounds at the tracks and winnings can be substantial.

Training a future champion begins when the Greyhound is six months old. The pup is housed in a box stall, fed top-quality food to ensure proper muscular development, and walked daily on hard surfaces and over considerable distances to strengthen its feet. A Greyhound with weak feet can never become a racer because it loses precious distance at the start of any race.

To improve the gait of the hound, a trainer may use a bicycle to exercise it. At this early stage of development, the trainer will not encourage the Greyhound to trot or gallop. Galloping without a leash is an exercise separate from walking and is used to develop lung power. It is, however, dangerous to overdo this form of exercise when the Greyhound's bones are still fragile. At 15 months, the Greyhound begins short racing trials at the tracks, but it will not participate in obstacle races until the age of two.

Meantime, many people are troubled by reports of live lures being used by disreputable trainers. Other concerns are the fate of greyhounds that fail to reach champion status, or outgrow it. Animal lovers are aware that greyhounds are sometimes destroyed inhumanely and in large numbers. Various organizations now exist to find homes for dogs who have finished their racing careers. Even for top champions, this can be as young as four years of age.

Characteristics

General appearance: strongly built, well outlined, powerfully muscled.

Height: 71 to 76.2 cm (28 to 30 in.) for the adult dog; 68 to 71 cm (26¾ to 28 in.) for the bitch. Under Canadian standards, not specified.

Weight: under Canadian standards, 29.5 to 31.8 kg (65 to 70 lb) for the adult dog; 27.2 to 29.5 kg (60 to 65 lb) for the bitch. Elsewhere, not specified.

Head: long and narrow, moderately wide between the ears. Slight stop. Clean bridge of nose. Muzzle long and narrow. Nose black and pointed. Jaws strong and powerful. Strong teeth. Scissor bite.

Eyes: oval, bright, set obliquely. Preferably dark. Intelligent expression.

Ears: small, finely textured, rose-shaped.

Body: tall and elegant. Deep, wide, well-developed chest. Ribs well sprung, deep, carried well back. Flanks well cut up. Broad, muscular, well-arched back. Powerful, arched loin. Shoulders well laid back, good angulation and muscular. Narrow and clearly defined at top.

Tail: long, set rather low, strong at the root, tapered, carried low, slightly curved upwards.

Forequarters: long and solid. Legs are straight. Elbows are free and well set under the shoulders. Elbows and pasterns should turn neither outward nor inward.

Hindquarters: long, well coupled with the body, powerful. Thighs and second thighs wide and muscular. Hocks well let down, turning neither outward nor inward.

Feet: moderate length. Compact toes, well knuckled. Strong pads.

Coat: fine, close hair.

Colour: black, white, red, blue, fawn, fallow, brindle, or one of these colours with white.

Practical information: The Greyhound should be neither too thin nor too fat. Watch its weight and diet carefully, particularly if the hound is a racer. Give the dog thick, solid food, including semi-fat meat. Avoid liquid or fatty mash, and starchy foods. Two or three light meals a day are preferable to one heavy one. The diet should be rich in calcium, vitamins, and minerals.

Use a soft brush on the coat. To give the coat a lustre, use a piece of chamois. Take the Greyhound for daily walks on a leash or, better still, use a bicycle. Let the mature Greyhound gallop freely once or twice a week.

Griffon Bruxellois

Brussels Griffon

Petit Brabançon

The Griffon Bruxellois is so similar to its cousins the Griffon Belge and the Petit Brabançon that the three are often categorized under one heading. This may be because they differ only in the colour and texture of their coats. There are two coat textures: the rough-coated (the Griffon Bruxellois and the Griffon Belge) and the smooth (the Petit Brabançon). The Griffon Bruxellois and the Griffon Belge, with wiry hair, sport little beards and moustaches. Admirers think that the Petit Brabançon with its smooth coat has almost human features, but its detractors say that the dog looks like a monkey.

Originally, the Brussels Griffon was used to catch rats in stables where hansom cabs were kept. Coachmen would ride about the city with these little dogs perched beside them. From this elevated position, the Griffons assumed the role of watch-dogs and attracted attention as they rode by barking at people in the street.

Towards the end of the nineteenth century, the Brussels Griffon won the favour of the royal Belgian court and attracted British interest. The first Brussels Griffon was registered in Canada just before the First World War.

Griffons are inquisitive, at times impertinent, but always watchful. They make charming companions.

AUS.	CAN.	S. AF.	U.K.	F.C.I.
●	●	●	●	●

ORIGINS

The earliest ancestors of the Griffons were first described in medieval French writings. German breeders, however, have put forward the claim that the Brussels Griffon can be traced to the Affenpinscher—a dog with monkey-like features similar to those of the Griffon. Today, it is accepted that the modern Brussels Griffon is descended from dogs which were once kept as ratters in stables. The Brussels Griffon, the Griffon Belge, and the Griffon Brabançon are Belgian dogs which were developed by crossing the 'stable' Griffons with English Toy Terriers. The breed was registered in 1863, and the definitive type was established in 1905. The dogs were almost annihilated during the First World War, but breeding with a few specimens began to revive in Belgium during the late 1920s.

Griffon Bruxellois

Griffon Belge

Characteristics

General appearance: stocky, short. Terrier-like temperament.
Height: not specified.
Weight: from 2.3 to 5 kg (5 to 11 lb), depending on whether small or large class of dogs. Diminutiveness is most desirable. Canadian standards: for small-size dogs and bitches, no more than 3 kg (7 lb) . For large-size dogs, no more than 5 kg (11 lb); for large bitches, 5.4 kg (12 lb).
Head: large, rounded, wide between the ears. Wide muzzle, neat lips with good turn-up. Black, short nose with large, open nostrils.
Eyes: very large, dark, round, clear, alert, well spaced.
Ears: small, set high, semi-erect. Under Canadian and F.C.I. standards, may be cropped.
Body: short, level back. Deep, well-sprung ribs, short, strong loin.
Tail: carried high, two-thirds docked at right angle from topline.
Forequarters: legs of average length, straight, very solid.
Hindquarters: muscular thighs, stifles bent. Hocks low to ground.
Feet: short, thick, catlike. Pads black. Nails black.
Coat: Griffons Belge and Bruxellois, harsh and wiry. Petit Brabançon, short and tight. Free from curl. Preferably with undercoat.
Colour: rust, black, black and tan, black and rust, tan, or clear red, depending on the variety.

A RARE BREED

Griffons Bruxellois are rarities outside their native Belgium because they reproduce seldom and only with extreme difficulty. Bitches come into heat irregularly and often do not become pregnant after mating.

To promote successful reproduction, a breeder matches the small male Griffon with the largest available female. In any case, delivery may be difficult due to the bulky, round skulls of the puppies. Caesarian birth is often required. Litters are small, and often only one puppy is produced. During the first three weeks of life, the puppies are very delicate. Even with the best of care, the mortality rate is high.

Practical information: The Griffon's coat requires no special grooming, but it is essential to remove excess hair with a hard brush or a fine-tooth comb. The eyes may 'weep' and can be cleaned with a cotton swab saturated in boiled water. The tail must be docked between the eighth and fifteenth day after birth.

Griffon Fauve de Bretagne

The Griffon Fauve de Bretagne is a medium-size, muscular and well-boned hound. The colours of its coarse coat—fawn with shades of gold and reddish brown—blend with autumnal hues that provide camouflage during the hunting season. This hunting-dog has a character as tough as its wiry hair. It is extremely tenacious and more than a little stubborn. Even in the family circle, the Griffon Fauve de Bretagne tends to remain somewhat distant and aloof. Its short-legged cousin, the Basset Fauve de Bretagne, is recognized in some English-speaking countries.

AUS.	CAN.	S. AF.	U.K.	F.C.I.
				●

ORIGINS

The Griffon Fauve de Bretagne is the descendant of the Grand Fauve de Bretagne and other famous French breeds of the past. Although this hunting-dog is prized in France, it is little known elsewhere.

Characteristics

General appearance: this vigorous dog with its hardy appearance is recognized solely by the F.C.I.
Height: 50 to 55 cm (19½ to 21½ in.) for the adult dog; 47 to 52 cm (18½ to 20½ in.) for the bitch.
Weight: not specified.
Head: skull rather long, flat, tapering. Arch of eyebrows not pronounced. Bridge of nose long, straight, slightly hooked, with a stop only slightly pronounced. Nose black, or dark brown. Muzzle without flews. Nostrils well open.
Eyes: dark, bold.
Ears: set well, level with the eyes; medium, tapering, covered with fine, soft hair.
Body: deep, wide chest. Well-rounded ribs. Short,

wide back. Loin short coupled. No tuck-up. Shoulders are well laid back.
Tail: rather small, well proportioned, carried well, hanging down and tapering.
Forequarters: muscular.
Hindquarters: sturdy thighs.
Feet: tight, lean, hard.
Colour: fawn, golden wheat, or vivid reddish brown.
Faults: spindly, delicate appearance. Skull too wide or too narrow. Arch of the eyebrows too pronounced. Muzzle pointed, short, with flews. Ears set on too low, too short, too long, or covered with curly hair. Belly tucked up. Thighs too round. Soft, wide feet. A white or charcoal coat is undesirable.

Practical information: Brush the coat regularly. Inspect the dog's ears and feet.

Griffon Nivernais

Once used for wild boar hunting, the Griffon Nivernais is active and untiring in its relentless pursuit of prey. As a hunting-dog, it is valued for its tenacity, strength, and endurance, rather than for its speed.

The Griffon Nivernais has a powerful, muscular body and a waterproof coat which enables it to cross marshland in search of quarry. The dog has a somewhat sad and dreamy expression in its sombre eyes. An affectionate animal, the Griffon Nivernais has a rough appearance which some find unattractive in a pet.

AUS.	CAN.	S. AF.	U.K.	F.C.I.
				●

ORIGINS

The Griffon Nivernais takes its name from the region in France where it is reputed to have originated. Among its ancestors are the Ségusien, the Bleu. de Gascogne, the Griffon Vendéen, and the Foxhound.

Characteristics

General appearance: this relatively large dog, with lean limbs and muscles, has a supple and elegant gait. It is recognized only by the F.C.I.

Height: 55 to 66 cm (21½ to 26 in.).

Weight: not specified.

Head: light, medium long. Skull almost flat. Bridge of nose straight. Stop slightly defined. Arch of eyebrows accentuated. Black nose and lips. Small beard.

Eyes: lively, penetrating, dark.

Ears: quite wide, rather long, soft; turned slightly backwards, set high.

Neck: rather light, lean. No dewlap.

Body: lean shoulders, close to the body, slightly inclined. Deep chest, quite narrow. First ribs rather flat, last ribs more rounded. Long back, well-supported loin. Flank slightly raised.

Tail: medium length, carried like a sabre.

Forequarters: legs are lean, very solid. Pasterns are well supported.

Hindquarters: lean thighs, rather flat. Hocks well let down, slight angulation.

Feet: slightly long. Solid toes.

Coat: wiry, dense, long hair; tousled, bushy, tough, neither woolly nor curled.

Colour: preferably wolf-grey, blue-grey; also steel-grey; fawn with black and white hair; blackish or black, flecked with tan on the cheeks, over the eyes, inside the legs, and at the back of the limbs.

Practical information: This robust dog should have its ears checked regularly.

Griffon Vendéen

R obust and well proportioned, the Grand Griffon Vendéen is a French hunting-dog. It is
the largest of the four types of Vendéen Griffons,
whose name is derived from the French department of Vendée. The Grand Griffon Vendéen is an
athletic creature with an elegant physique and
gait and a vivacious air. Powerfully built, this dog
tracks prey over the most difficult terrain but, in
its zeal for hunting, it can tire quickly. English-
speaking countries recognize the smallest variety, the Petit Basset Griffon Vendéen, although
the dog is rarely shown.

AUS.	CAN.	S. AF.	U.K.	F.C.I.
				●

ORIGINS

*The ancestry of the Grand Grif-
fon Vendéen may include the
Chien Gris de Saint-Louis, the
Bloodhound, the Griffon Fauve
de Bretagne, and the Bracco Italiano. The Second World War
almost destroyed the breed.*

Characteristics

General appearance: solid, robust, light. The Grand
Griffon Vendéen is solely recognized by the F.C.I.
Height: 60 to 65 cm (23½ to 25½ in.).
Weight: about 35 kg (77 lb).
Head: long, rounded skull, not too wide between the
ears. Black nose. Long hair on lips like a moustache.
Eyebrows pronounced, but not covering the eye.
Eyes: large, vivid black.
Ears: narrow, delicate, slightly oval, and turned in at
the tip; with long hair, set low.
Neck: light, no dewlap.

Body: medium, deep chest. Ribs slightly rounded.
Tail: set high, carried like a sabre. Thick at the root
and tapering.
Forequarters: straight, well-boned. Elbows close.
Hindquarters: long, muscular thighs. Wide hocks,
well let down, turned neither in nor out.
Coat: long, bushy, coarse, wiry hair. Dense undercoat. Well-haired belly and interior thighs. Skin not too
delicate.
Colour: two or more shades of tan, fawn, white, grey,
and black.

Practical information: As hunting-dogs go, this dog
tires easily. As a result, it is a breed best used by
sportsmen who want to hunt only for short periods of
time—a half day or so. The dog's paws should always
be examined for any injuries after hunting. When the

animal begins to shed, remove excess hair with a
hard brush or comb.

Hanoverian Schweisshund

Sportsmen value the Hanoverian Schweiss-hund for its keen scenting ability. It is generally used in packs for leading hunters to wounded game and to underbrush where prey has taken refuge. Intelligent, courageous, and vigorous, the Hanoverian Schweisshund is also an excellent tracker for boar. It still works in packs, but it may also be leashed on a long lead and used in a solitary fashion. Its quiet and tranquil character makes it a good companion dog. Although this hound is descended from some of the great European dogs of the distant past, it is unknown outside Germany.

AUS.	CAN.	S. AF.	U.K.	F.C.I.
				●

ORIGINS

The earliest ancestors of the Hanoverian Schweisshund are the Canis bracco celticus, *a French-Swiss hound from the region between the Rhône and the Rhine rivers, and the Bloodhound. The present-day breed was developed during the last century.*

Characteristics

General appearance: an active dog that is powerfully built and relatively short.
Height: approximately 56 cm (22 in.).
Weight: approximately 35 kg (77 lb).
Head: average, skull slightly domed, forehead slightly furrowed. No stop. Prominent eyebrows. Nose black, nearly straight and broad. Muzzle same length as skull. Lips pendulous. Jaws strong, scissor bite.
Eyes: dark brown. Haw not visible.
Ears: long, broad, rounded. Tips set high.
Neck: long, strong, no dewlap.
Body: brisket broad, deep. Back slightly roached to-wards the loin. Croup sloping. Shoulders sloping.
Tail: long, thick at the base, tapering at the tip.
Forequarters: strong and muscular. Pasterns strong and straight.
Hindquarters: muscular. Thighs strong, long, sloping, covered with thick hair. Hocks almost straight with slight outward turn.
Feet: solid, round. Toes curved. Pads thick.
Coat: thick, ample, nearly smooth, supple and glossy.
Colour: dark grey or tawny, with tan marks over the eyes, ears, and muzzle.
Faults: white, or light yellow markings on the coat.

Practical information: This outdoors dog needs little special care.

171

Harrier

Although this breed resembles the Beagle, it is larger and more elegant. Strong and light, the Harrier has a highly developed sense of smell and a commanding bark. Smooth-haired and medium-sized, it has a coat that is short, hard, and close. The Harrier is swift and shows great stamina. It hunts best on open fields.

The Harrier was bred specifically for hare coursing. Some claim that the name is derived from the word 'hare,' but others believe that the name comes from the Norman-Saxon 'Harier' which means a general hunting-dog.

Hunting hare is an ancient sport. Hunters on foot used a pack of dogs to follow the prey. The Harrier, with its exceptional sense of smell, was ideal for the task because it could outwit the manoeuvres and tricks of the quarry. The Greek historian, Xenophon, described a small hound similar to the Harrier as early as 400 B.C. The Greek hounds may have been introduced into Britain by the Romans. The earliest British reference to the breed appears in the Middle Ages.

In the eighteenth century, hare-hunting began to resemble fox-hunting. Hunters on horseback who enjoyed a cross-country gallop wanted a faster dog to keep the hare running along a straight path. This need led to the creation of the modern Harrier, which was developed by adding Foxhound blood to the breed. Today, hare-hunting is rare, but the Harrier is still used to hunt fox.

AUS.	CAN.	S. AF.	U.K.	F.C.I.
●	●			●

ORIGINS

The Harrier has been known in Britain since the Middle Ages. It may have been brought there by the Romans and, throughout the centuries, then undergone changes as it was crossed with other breeds. Some experts believe that the earliest Harriers may have been mixed with the now extinct Talbot hound, the Bloodhound, and the French Basset. The first pack of Harriers is described in a document dating from 1260. Further mentions of hunters on foot using Harrier packs to track appear later in the same century. The modern Harrier was first identified in the late eighteenth century. It was introduced into North America at this period.

Somerset Harrier

Harrier

Characteristics

General appearance: strong and distinguished, the Harrier has a supple and sure-footed gait.

Height: 48.3 to 53.3 cm (19 to 21 in.).

Weight: not specified.

Head: expressive, rather wide. Muzzle relatively long, pointed rather than square. Good, bold forehead. Occiput slightly pronounced. Flews covering the lower jaws. Well-developed black nose.

Eyes: dark, medium size, not too round. Never prominent.

Ears: V-shaped, almost flat, slightly turned. Quite short, set rather high. Mobile and expressive.

Body: shoulders oblique, muscular. Chest more deep than wide. Ribs well sprung, running well back. Straight, muscular back. Loin strong and slightly arched. Flank neither too full nor turned up. Hips strong and well attached.

Tail: medium size, slightly curved and carried controlled.

Forequarters: good, straight, with plenty of bone.

Hindquarters: thighs long and well let down. Hocks neither too straight nor too angled. Legs and back stand square.

Feet: round, catlike, close, toes turning inwards.

Coat: smooth, flat hair, not too short.

Colour: all shades from black to orange, usually on a white background with black stripes.

Faults: loin long and soft. Thighs spindly. Nose without pigmentation. Poor bite. Testicles discoloured.

Practical information: The Harrier enjoys robust health. It is first and foremost a hunting-dog and, despite its friendly character, it is not a suitable house-dog. Like the Beagle and the Foxhound, the Harrier prefers pack life. In Great Britain, attempts at placing Harrier puppies in private homes have been unsuccessful. After hunting, the nails must be examined to ensure that they have not been torn or broken off by stones. Injured nails often take a long time to heal. Brush the coat of smooth flat hair regularly.

SOMERSET HARRIERS: ENGLISH HUNTING-DOGS WITH FRENCH ANCESTORS?

The Somerset Harrier, a hunting-dog that is bred in Devonshire as well as Somerset, is also known as the West County Harrier. Experts insist that it was created by cross-breeding Foxhounds with a pack of *Chien Blancs du Roy*, which were brought to England at the beginning of the French Revolution in 1789. Some dog historians, however, claim that the Somerset Harrier is descended from the Porcelaine, a French hunting-dog with a white and orange coat. According to another group of experts, the Somerset Harrier comes from the English Staghound.

Closely related to the Harrier, the Somerset Harrier is a solid, elegant dog, with a supple, rapid gallop, and a happy and spirited nature. Like the Harrier, it has a subtle sense of scent. Moreover, it is capable of outhunting the Harrier on uneven ground. An efficient tracker, the Somerset Harrier detects fox, hare, and rabbit with astonishing acuity.

Astute and rather docile, this animal is easy to train. It is a gentle, lively, affectionate creature, one that can be relied upon.

Ibizan Hound

Charnique, Podenco Ibicenco

The Ibizan Hound is believed to have originated on Ibiza, one of the Balearic Islands off the Mediterranean coast of Spain. Although the breed thrives everywhere on the Balearics, the best examples as well as the greatest number are found on the neighbouring island of Majorca.

The Ibizan Hound has an astute and vigilant air. Its head is long and narrow, its ears are erect, the colour of the eyes is clear amber. The coat is white, red, or fawn, or different combinations of these shades.

This Spanish greyhound, with its exceptionally fine sense of scent, is used to hunt hare and rabbit, as well as fox, partridge, and other game. It is able to track on virtually all types of terrain, even in thick underbrush, and barks only at the scent of game. When the hound sees or hears prey, it points, and holds its position with ease. It is also an excellent retriever.

Spanish hunters work with packs of Ibizan Hounds consisting of ten females and one male. The disproportionate number of females in the pack is due to the quarrelsome nature of the male hounds. Two males have only to meet for a fight to erupt. Under these circumstances, it is highly unlikely that they can be transformed into compatible hunting partners.

Apart from this problem, the Ibizan Hound has

AUS.	CAN.	S. AF.	U.K.	F.C.I.
●	●	●	●	●

ORIGINS

The Ibizan Hound is one of the most ancient breeds in the Mediterranean region, and its history reaches back to the days of the Pharaohs. An image of the dog appears on a dish dating from the First Dynasty (3100 to 2700 B.C). It is possible that the ancestors of the Ibizan Hound were imported into Spain by Phoenician traders.There is another historical claim that the hounds were introduced much later by the Saracens and the Moors. Even if the importers are unknown and the period of arrival is uncertain, the Ibizan Hound has maintained its purity through the centuries, because the geographical isolation of the Balearic Islands has protected the dogs from external contacts and inter-breeding. The breed is becoming popular in Australia as well as in Great Britain, Canada, New Zealand, and the United States.

another bizarre characteristic. After pursuing rabbit and other game all day, some dogs inexplicably lose interest in the chase, and nothing will induce them to return to it until they have had a long rest. Spanish hunters have a word for this display of boredom. They call it 'over-rabbiting.'

Some Ibizan Hounds have another serious flaw. Although the animals are intelligent creatures and are highly prized as hunters, there may be training problems in cases where the hounds are unusually aggressive.

The Ibizan Hound is also known as the Podenco Ibicenco and the Charnique, but its real name is *Cà Eivessenc.* Also simply called the Podenco, it should not be confused with the Portuguese Podengo Hound.

Characteristics

General appearance: elegant, agile, tall, and narrow. Robust bone structure and muscularity. This greyhound bears a close resemblance to the Pharaoh Hound.

Height: under F.C.I. standards, 60 to 65 cm (23½ to 25½ in.) for the adult dog and 57 to 63 cm (22½ to 25 in.) for the bitch. Under Canadian standards, 61 to 68.6 cm (24 to 27 in.) for dogs; 58.4 to 66 cm (23 to 26 in.). for bitches. Elsewhere, 56 to 73.7 cm (22 to 29 in.) for dogs; bitches, as in Canada.

Weight: under F.C.I. standards, 22.5 kg (49½ lb) for the adult dog and about 19 kg (42 lb) for the bitch. Elsewhere, 20.4 to 25 kg (45 to 55 lb) for dogs; 18 to 22.7 kg (40 to 50 lb) for bitches.

Head: long and narrow, with prominent occipital bone. Skull long and flat. Stop not well defined. Narrow forehead. Slightly convex muzzle. Nose flesh-coloured in harmony with the coat. Open nostrils. Jaw strong and lean. Lips thin and tight. Even, white teeth. Scissor bite.

Eyes: almond-shaped, large, round, not prominent. Clear amber to caramel colour. Very intelligent expression.

Ears: rigid, mobile, thin, rather large. No hair on the inside.

Neck: very lean, rather long, muscular and slightly arched.

Body: level back. Narrow, deep, and long chest. Flat ribs. Oblique shoulders. Loin arched, medium width. Short-coupled with well tucked up waist, breastbone very prominent.

Tail: long, thin, set low. When the dog is at rest, tail is carried low in a natural way. In action, it is sometimes carried high, but never curled over the back.

Forequarters: strong and tight. Erect pasterns of good length.

Hindquarters: long, lean, straight; strong thighs.

Feet: well-arched toes. Nails long and tight, very strong, light coloured. Abundant hair between toes. Pads very hard.

Coat: either smooth or rough, always dense and hard. Hair longer at the back of the thighs and lower part of the tail than on the head and the ears. Often with a generous moustache.

Colour: white, chestnut, lion, or any combination of these.

Faults: drop ears. Dark eyes. Sternum not defined. Wide loin. Large hips. Thighs rounded, wide, with veins sticking out. Forelegs too wide spread with feet turning out.

Practical information: This sporting animal thrives in the countryside. The Ibizan Hound is highly prized in its native land as an astute and intelligent hunter of small game and wild birds. It is capable of weathering storms, and extremes of heat and cold. This hound should be given a lot of regular exercise, but it needs little particular care. Ensure that the dog is brushed regularly.

Irish Setter

Red Setter

The Irish, or Red, Setter is a popular show dog, but it began as a hunting-dog. The earliest Irish Setters were used by sportsmen for falconry and for netting game. The present-day dog appeared in the mid-nineteenth century, when its beauty as a show dog was over-valued at the expense of its importance as a hunting-dog. Today, the balance has been redressed among enthusiasts of the Irish Setter who recognize its dual role as a field and show dog.

The Irish Setter is treasured world-wide by sportsmen who enjoy strenuous hunting and have the stamina to follow its relentless pace. The dog is a fast tracker which hunts effectively, either on the open field or in the woods. Its ideal territory is the Yorkshire Moors, where it developed the ability for tracking over long distances, well in advance of the hunters. It weaves rapidly from right to left to ensure that a maximum area is explored. This technique leaves ground game little chance of escape.

The Irish Setter was once used to stalk grouse and woodcock. Today, sportsmen prefer its skills as a pointer, ideal for hunting duck, partridge, pheasant, and teal. A highly developed sense of scent enables the Setter to hold a long point. When pointing, the Irish Setter has a good silhouette, although the Pointer is obviously its superior in this respect. The Irish Setter has the advantage, however, of being an excellent retriever for recovering downed game birds from marshes, and it will plunge into water without hesitation in search of its master's prize.

Energetic and tenacious, the Irish Setter has a keen mind. It is, however, a spirited and high-strung creature with a marked propensity for independence. These characteristics may make the training of the breed difficult.

If an Irish Setter is well trained, it can be an asset to the hunter. If the animal is not properly controlled, its restless behaviour can cause problems. This dog was bred for the open countryside, and some specimens may be unsuitable for city life. An excitable, house-bound Setter is often tagged as a 'crazy dog' simply because its owners, who think of it only as a companion, neglect to give it the right amount of exercise. A properly kept Irish Setter can be an agreeable companion for both young and old, and it will show affection and loyalty to its master.

AUS.	CAN.	S. AF.	U.K.	F.C.I.
●	●	●	●	●

ORIGINS

The Irish Setter is a descendant of the old Irish Spaniel which, in turn, came from the Continental Spaniel. It was modified by rigorous selection and cross-breeding with the English and Gordon Setters, the Water and Springer Spaniels, and the Pointer. At the beginning of the nineteenth century, there were a number of varieties, including the Red and White. Nineteenth-century British breeders decided to perfect this variety. In attempting to produce a beautiful dog, some fanciers introduced Borzoi and Newfoundland blood into the breed. Fortunately, these experiments were stopped. Eventually, breeders succeeded in eliminating the white areas, and a solid-coloured Red Setter developed. The founding father' of the present-day Irish Setter, Palmerston, was born in County Tyrone, Ireland, in 1862.

THE SETTER AND ITS COAT OF FIERY COLOUR

The extraordinary colour of the Irish Setter, which is unique in the canine world, is judged by rigorous standards. The bright, glossy red coat should shine. The lighter-coloured undercoat has copper highlights. The overall shade must be uniform all over the body. A slight gradation of colour on the feathering of the stomach and back portion of the animal is acceptable. Silky silver-grey hair may appear behind the ears and in the feathering of the hindquarters of dogs aged 12 to 20 months. This is a sign that the dogs will have a rich red coat at maturity, when the silver-grey hair disappears.

Characteristics

General appearance: racy but substantial in build. Dignified stance. Kindly expression.

Height: under Canadian standards, about 68.6 cm (27 in.) for the adult dog; 63.5 cm (25 in.) for the bitch. Elsewhere, not specified.

Weight: under Canadian standards, about 31.8 kg (70 lb) for the adult dog; 27.2 kg (60 lb) for the bitch. Elsewhere, not specified.

Head: long and lean, muzzle moderately deep, chiselled, rather square. Oval skull, occiput well defined. Stop highlighted by pronounced eyebrows. Drooping flews. Mahogany, dark walnut, or black nose. Jaws of nearly equal length, flews not pendulous. Scissor bite.

Eyes: dark to medium brown, medium size, almond-shaped.

Ears: moderate size, fine in texture, set low, well back, hanging neatly folded close to the head.

Body: long, oblique shoulders. Deep chest, well down, rather narrow. Well-sprung ribs. Muscular, slightly arched loin.

Tail: medium length, tapered, set low, carried level with the back, or below the back.

Forequarters: straight and sinewy, elbows free, well let down.

Hindquarters: long and muscular from the hip to the hocks; strong and short from the hocks to the heels. Joints well angulated.

Coat: fine, short hair on the head, front of legs, and tips of the ears; elsewhere, medium long and flat. Long, silky feathering on the ears, at the back of the limbs, on the stomach and tail.

Colour: rich chestnut. White markings on chest and toes are tolerated.

Practical information: The Irish Setter is a hardy dog. Examine its ears regularly for inflammation caused by ear mites. Brush the coat once or twice a week. After hunting, the dog must be rubbed down and brushed carefully.

Irish Terrier

A close relative to the Wire-haired Fox Terrier, the Irish Terrier is a spirited daredevil whose courage verges on recklessness. Its boldness and the all-red colour of its coat have earned it the nicknames 'red devil' and 'wild Irishman.' Although it is quarrelsome with fellow canines and was once used as a combatant in dogfights against adversaries bigger and heavier than itself, the Irish Terrier is companionable with humans. It is devoted and even gentle with its owner and, as a guard dog, it will rush to his or her defence.

The Irish Terrier is excellent at flushing rabbit, and it is also a good soft-mouthed retriever of game from the marshes. It was built for running and has a reputation for tracking over incredible distances. Another early name, 'Irish Sporting Terrier,' seems well deserved. According to one late nineteenth-century fancier, a certain Mr. Krehl, the Irish Terrier was as valiant as the ratter, and a hunter of hare, fox, badger, and otter. This enthusiast claimed that the dog entered thickets like a spaniel does, retrieved like a Labrador, and covered terrain like a pointer or setter. Moreover, according to Krehl's account, the Irish Terrier had courage, was trainable and fearless, and was gifted with a wonderful character. While Mr. Krehl might be accused of exaggerating, there is also some truth in his praise. From its first appearance in the 1870s, the Irish Terrier attracted fanciers in the British Isles, where it is still in demand today. It is sometimes seen in the Commonwealth countries.

AUS.	CAN.	S. AF.	U.K.	F.C.I.
●	●	●	●	●

ORIGINS

The first image of the present-day Irish Terrier appears in a painting dating from the eighteenth century. However, it is generally felt that the breed was developed in Ireland centuries before. Red is the preferred shade of this solid-coloured dog. This colouring—a mark of its Irish background—is also found on the Setter and on Irish horses. Although the Irish Terrier may share common ancestry with the Wire-haired Fox Terrier, its roots are uncertain. It is difficult to say, for example, which of the two races comes first in lineage. Breeding has evidently centred on the dog's colour. The Irish Terrier made its public debut at a Dublin dog show in 1875. The following year, it appeared officially in England at the Bristol Dog Show. The terrier was again shown at Glasgow in 1879.

Characteristics

General appearance: good-tempered, sturdy, strong, plucky.
Height: about 48 cm (19 in.) for dogs; 46 cm (18 in.) for bitches.
Weight: about 12 kg (27 lb) for dogs; 11 kg (25 lb) for bitches.
Head: long, flat skull, rather narrow between the ears, free from wrinkles. Stop hardly noticeable except in profile. Jaws strong and muscular, of good length. Delicately chiselled muzzle. Black nose. Lips well fitting, almost black. Wiry hair, rather long on the muzzle, with beard. Strong, even teeth. Jaws strong. Scissor bite.
Eyes: dark, hazel, small, not prominent, full of life and fire.
Ears: small, V-shaped, moderately thick, well set and dropping forward close to the cheek. Hair shorter and darker than on the rest of the body; no feathering. Tip of folded ear well above level of skull.
Neck: fair length, gradually widening towards shoulders.
Body: shoulders fine, long, well laid back. Deep, muscular chest neither full nor wide. Moderately long body. Back strong and straight. Loin muscular and slightly arched. Well-sprung ribs.
Tail: generally docked at three quarters of its length. Without feathering, but well covered with rough hair. Set high and carried gaily, but not curled.
Forequarters: moderately long, perfectly straight, very muscular.
Hindquarters: strong, muscular. Thighs powerful, hocks well let down. Legs must move in a straight line. Stifles moderately bent.
Feet: strong, round, moderately small. Toes arched. Nails black.
Coat: hard, wiry hair having a broken appearance. Softer undercoat.
Colour: bright red, wheaten red, golden- or yellow-red. A small white patch on the chest is permissible. Black shading undesirable.

Practical information: If the Irish Terrier is kept as a house-pet, it should be given a lot of outdoor exercise. Daily brushing prevents its undercoat from matting, and its nails must be cut regularly. It can be groomed in the same way as a Fox Terrier. Always have medication on hand to tend its wounds.

A COMMOTION AMONG CANINE ENTHUSIASTS

In 1875, a few Irish Terrier fanciers decided to introduce the breed to the public and to publicize it outside its native land. A major dog show was organized in Dublin and brought together about 50 entrants.

The rules governing the exhibition were unorthodox. As a result, visitors saw dogs of all shapes, sizes, and colours. Not all the entrants were pure-breds or hunters. Although the best specimens in this incongruous assembly were appreciatively noted, the exhibition caused a commotion among some enthusiasts who subsequently banded together to form the first speciality club and draft the standards that have remained in force to this day. Within a few years, the Irish Terrier became a widely popular dog. It was first registered in Canada in 1888–89.

In the years between the World Wars, the breed fell from favour. Gordon Selfridge attempted unsuccessfully to revive flagging public interest by holding a special Irish Terrier exhibition in one of the departments of his London store. Today, the Irish Terrier is once more much in demand, especially as a companion dog.

Irish Water Spaniel

T he Irish Water Spaniel has a striking appearance—a frizzy bang over its forehead and a mass of tightly curled, liver-coloured ringlets covering its body and tail. It is hard to believe that it is a spaniel because it is so large and so different in shape and disposition from other spaniels. Some canine experts have pointed out its resemblance to the Poodle, but few authorities can agree on the origins of this dog.

No one, however, is in dispute that nature equipped the Irish Water Spaniel for water-retrieving. Well protected by a short, dense, oily coat, the dog will plunge into frigid waters day or night. An additional characteristic contributes to the dog's assurance in water: webbed toes. When swimming, the dog can increase the surface area of its toes and use them like paddles.

Like the Poodle, the Irish Water Spaniel is adept at hunting wild duck in marshes and lakes. Its infallible sense of smell helps it track wounded prey through reeds and bullrushes. Its tenacity is legendary. No hunt, either on water or land, seems too arduous for the animal.

Although this dog was bred for living outdoors, it is an excellent companion dog and was much in demand in the 1920s and 30s. After the Second World War, its popularity plummeted. Interest in the breed has revived since Irish Water Spaniel won Best in Show at the 1979 Westminster Kennel Club show in New York.

AUS.	CAN.	S. AF.	U.K.	F.C.I.
●	●	●	●	●

ORIGINS

The Irish Water Spaniel may have developed from a mixture—of Poodle and Irish Setter. Some dog historians believe that it was developed from a combination of Poodle and Curly Coated Retriever. One fact seems certain: The present-day dog started in 1834 with the birth of Boatswain, a dog that lived 18 years and left its mark on subsequent generations of the breed. The Irish Water Spaniel was first presented in 1862 at the Birmingham Dog Show, and the first club was founded in 1890. Another club, the Irish Water Spaniel Association, joined forces with the former in 1926, and their combined efforts helped to popularize the breed. The 1920s was the period of greatest enthusiasm for the Irish Water Spaniel. In Great Britain, registration with the Kennel Club climbed steadily until the Second World War, but declined thereafter.

Characteristics

General appearance: strongly built, with a characteristic gait.
Height: under Canadian standards, 56 to 61 cm (22 to 24 in.) for the adult dog; 53.3 to 58.4 cm (21 to 23 in.) for the bitch. Elsewhere, 53.3 to 58.4 cm (21 to 23 in.) for the adult dog and 50.8 to 56 cm (20 to 22 in.) for the bitch.
Weight: under Canadian standards, 25 to 29.5 kg (55 to 65 lb) for adult dogs; 20.4 to 26.3 kg (45 to 58 lb) for bitches. Elsewhere, not specified.
Head: relatively large and long. Domed skull. Muzzle rather square, long and strong. Graduated stop. Large, dark, liver-coloured nose. Skull covered with long loose curls forming a pronounced topknot.
Eyes: almond-shaped, alert, and keen. Under Canadian standards, hazel; elsewhere, medium to dark brown.
Ears: long, lobular, set low, hanging close to the cheeks and covered with long, twisted curls.
Body: back and ribs carried well back from the shoulder, giving a barrel-shaped look. Chest deep, but not too wide. Back short, wide, and level. Loin deep and wide.
Tail: short, straight rat tail, peculiar to the breed, thick at the root and tapering to the end. Tight curls cover root, ending abruptly; remainder bare, or covered with fine, straight hairs. Low set, below back level.
Forequarters: well boned, straight, solid. Forelegs well down.
Hindquarters: powerful, long stifles. Hocks well bent and set low.
Coat: densely covered with tight, crisp ringlets, oily, but not woolly. Forequarters covered with curly feathers to the feet. Hindquarters smooth in front, feathered behind down to the feet.
Colour: dark liver with a purple tint or bloom, peculiar to the breed.

Practical information: Brush the coat as little as possible. When it is necessary to do so, use a scrubbing brush. Shampooing with detergents is inadvisable because the oily hair must stay greasy. The Irish Water Spaniel usually cleans itself by rolling in grass or straw.

Irish Wolfhound

Wolfhound

AUS.	CAN.	S. AF.	U.K.	F.C.I.
●	●	●	●	●

This majestic dog was once, as its name suggests, used to hunt wolves. Its powerful jaws and impressive muscular structure made it highly suitable for strenuous sport. Yet, despite its colossal height and its energetic nature, the Irish Wolfhound can be docile and quiet.

This handsome breed is undoubtedly of very ancient origin. Two thousand years ago, the Greek historian Strabo described the export of large dogs similar to the present-day Wolfhound from the British Isles to Rome.

In pre-Christian Ireland, a large, rough-coated canine giant, known as the *Cu*, was used to hunt elk, wild boar, and the wolf. The Cu was ferocious in battle, but a docile and trustworthy defender of hearth and home. Only kings, poets, and noblemen were permitted to own a dog of this kind. Early descriptions of the Cu suggest that it was the forerunner of the modern breed.

Wolfhounds were held in such high esteem that they were given as gifts to foreign sovereigns, ambassadors, and other dignitaries. In 1652, Oliver Cromwell was forced to prohibit the export of Wolfhounds from the British Isles because the hounds were becoming rare and were needed to hunt the wolves that infested England.

By the 1800s, the extinction of the wolf population led to a drastic decline in the use and number of Wolfhounds. At the end of the nineteenth century, however, intensive breeding had helped to restore the breed again.

ORIGINS

There are conflicting stories about the origin of the Irish Wolfhound. Some historians say that it was produced by cross-breeding the Irish Sheepdog with the Sloughi, which was brought to Ireland centuries ago. Other experts believe that it was bred by combining these two dogs with Scottish Deerhounds. Regardless, by the late eighteenth century, the breed had almost vanished. In 1862, a British army officer, Captain George Graham, began efforts to revive the breed. Graham contended that, although the breed had deteriorated, it still existed. For almost 20 years, he obtained stock related to the ancient Wolfhound and carefully restored the breed to its early vigour. Thanks primarily to Captain Graham's efforts, the breed was successfully reintroduced. The first Irish Wolfhound was registered in Britain in the 1880s and, again, in 1909. Today, the breed is well established.

TAKING FULL MEASURE
OF A CANINE GIANT

The Irish Wolfhound is one of the largest dogs on earth. Comparing this canine giant, whose average weight is more than 50 kilograms (110 lb), with a small Italian Greyhound, which weighs only 3 kilograms (6 lb), gives a striking indication of the differences in physical size in the canine world.

In the past, the stories about the size of the Irish Wolfhound were probably exaggerated. The medieval Italian explorer, Marco Polo, reported that, on his travels, he had seen Wolfhounds as big as donkeys. The eighteenth-century writer, Oliver Goldsmith, described hounds which were 1.2 metres high (48 in.). Both descriptions sound far-fetched, because the average hound usually stands about 90 cm (roughly 36 in.).

In recent times, *Floyd av Krooden*, a champion born in 1968, has been widely regarded as one of the most impressive of all Irish Wolfhounds, with a height of 98 cm (38 in.) at the withers and a weight of 86 kilograms (189 lb).

Characteristics

General appearance: very tall and muscular, strong, but gracefully built. Resembling the Greyhound, but heavier. Combines speed, strength, and keen vision.

Height: under Canadian standards, a minimum height of 81.3 cm (32 in.) for the adult dog; 76.2 cm (30 in.) for the bitch. Elsewhere, at least 78.7 cm (31 in.) for the adult dog and 71 cm (28 in.) for the bitch.

Weight: under Canadian standards, a minimum 54.4 kg (120 lb) for adult dogs; at least 47.6 kg (105 lb) for bitches. Elsewhere, at least 54.4 kg (120 lb) for adult dogs; a minimum 40.8 kg (90 lb) for bitches.

Head: long, frontal bones slightly raised, small indentation between the eyes. Skull not too broad. Long, moderately pointed muzzle. Nose and lips black.

Eyes: dark, oval and full. Eyelids black.

Ears: small, rose-shaped. Greyhound-like in carriage.

Neck: rather long, strong, and muscular; well arched. No dewlap.

Body: chest very deep and wide. Back long rather than short. Loin arched. Belly well tucked up. Shoulders muscular and oblique.

Tail: long and slightly curved, moderately thick, well covered with hair, carried low.

Forequarters: strong and straight, very muscular.

Hindquarters: thighs muscular, long, and strong, stifles well bent. Hocks well let down and turning neither outward nor inward.

Feet: relatively large and round. Toes well arched and closed. Nails very strong and curved.

Coat: rough, harsh hair, especially wiry and long over the eyes and under the jaw.

Colour: grey, brindle, red, black, pure white, fawn, or steel grey.

Practical information: The mature Irish Wolfhound has a robust constitution. The whelp, whose rearing can be difficult, must be watched attentively. Until the age of three, when its body is fully developed, the dog needs a diet rich in meat and calcium. Give the rough coat of the Wolfhound regular brushings with a metal comb or hard brush.

Italian Greyhound

This delicate creature, a model of grace and elegance, is a miniature, or toy, Greyhound. It has pure lines, a perfect bone structure, and a solid build. In spite of its small size, this dog has no dwarfish traits, and its frail appearance can be deceptive. Its frequent trembling is rarely caused by cold or fear, but rather by emotion. This pure-bred shivers at the slightest upset. A caress usually dispels the agitation.

If the Italian Greyhound is trained at a young age, it becomes a fearless sporting dog which can endure cold and blustery weather. Like the Whippet, it can reach 60 kilometres an hour (about 40 miles an hour) in sudden bursts of speed. And as a hunter, it can catch hare on the run and loves to flush partridge and pheasant from the undergrowth. But the ideal role for the Italian Greyhound is as a house-pet. It can be easily carried anywhere by owners because of its low height and weight. Outwardly playful, vivacious, and charming, the Italian Greyhound is inwardly calm. Its posture is naturally graceful and, even while sleeping or lying down, it takes the elegant pose that has been captured by artists in paintings and sculptures.

Owners of an Italian Greyhound should not count on it to sound an alarm or protect the house. As one nineteenth-century writer observed, it is destined for such comforts of the living room as the tea service, the rug by the fireplace, the soft sofa, and the attentions of its owner.

AUS.	CAN.	S. AF.	U.K.	F.C.I.
●	●	●	●	●

ORIGINS

The origin of the Italian Greyhound, as with all greyhounds, goes back to antiquity. Its ancestors were widely admired by the ancient Egyptians and the Romans. In Europe, the popularity of the Italian Greyhound lasted from the Middle Ages to the late nineteenth century. The peak of its fame was at the royal courts of Italy and Spain during the sixteenth century. By 1900, fanciers wanted only an abnormally small Italian Greyhound. It became short-legged and never measured more than 25 centimetres (10 in.). Breeders tried to arrest the dwarfing, but their first efforts failed. Not before 1968 were the proper characteristics of the Italian Greyhound successfully restored. That same year the official standard for the breed was established in Italy.

Characteristics

General appearance: silhouette similar to a miniaturized Greyhound, though more slender. Agile, elegant, and affectionate.

Height: Under F.C.I. standards, 32 to 38 cm (12½ to 15 in.). Under Canadian standards, 33 to 38 cm (13 to 15 in.). Elsewhere, not specified.

Weight: about 2.5 to 4.5 kg (5½ to 10 lb). Not specified under Canadian standards.

Head: skull long, narrow and flat, occipital crest not very prominent. Stop slightly defined, muzzle long and fine. Nose bridge pointed. Prominent nose, dark or black. Level jaw. Scissor bite.

Eyes: large, round, and expressive, neither protruding nor deep-set. Under F.C.I. standards, the iris must be dark; the eyelids darkly pigmented.

Ears: small, delicate, placed well back. Soft and fine, not pricked. Rose-shaped.

Neck: long, lean, slightly but gracefully arched, equal in length to the head. No dewlap.

Body: its length must be equal to or shorter than its height. Chest narrow and deep. Ribs slightly arched. Loin very round, blending with the topline and the croup. Back slightly arched over loin. Croup tucked up. Belly cut up. Shoulders long and sloping.

Tail: set low, delicate, tapering, covered with fine hair, carried low, half straight, half curved, reaches hocks.

Forequarters: straight, light bones.

Hindquarters: long, lean thighs, well-bent stifles. No dewclaws.

Feet: long, hare-footed. Small, lean hind feet, less oval than forefeet. Toes well arched. Nails black or dark.

Coat: short, fine, glossy hair. Skin fine and supple.

Colour: all shades of black, fawn, red, cream, blue, or any of these colours broken with white.

Faults: blue or black with tan markings.

Practical information: Walks are essential for the Italian Greyhound. The dog is inured to cold weather and rain, and needs no special covering. Give it two light meals daily. Its satiny coat requires no upkeep, but a rubdown with a piece of chamois improves its sheen.

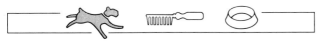

Italian Spinone

Italian Griffon, Spinone, Italian Pointer

AUS.	CAN.	S. AF.	U.K.	F.C.I.
●		●	●	●

R uffled, moustached, and bearded, the Italian Spinone is a solid, hardy, and instantly likeable member of the griffon family. It is one of the oldest griffon varieties in existence and is descended from an ancient hunting breed found in the Piedmont region of Italy.

This tall, muscular dog resembles the German Wire-haired Pointer (*Drahthaar*), and is considered equivalent to the Wire-haired Pointing Griffon in sporting skills.

The Italian Spinone has a hunter's temperament and all of the qualities found in the old French griffons. Ardent and fearless, it can hunt on open fields and in forests.

The Italian Spinone is also used by marshland hunters because it is an excellent swimmer. In winter, its thick, wiry, slightly curled coat protects it from brambles and thickets, as well as from freezing water.

In summer, when its rough coat becomes thinner, it hunts well on the arid, rocky terrains in its own country.

Easy to train, the Italian Spinone is considered to be one of the best pointing griffons. It can retrieve wild game with ease because of its subtle sense of smell. The Italians use it more than any other type of hunting-dog.

Apart from its sporting qualities, the Italian Spinone is intelligent, companionable, and affectionate. It lives happily within the family circle and adores children. Courageous and faithful, the Italian Spinone will brave any danger to defend its master.

ORIGINS

Experts consider the Italian Spinone to be the founder of the Wire-haired Pointing Griffons. During the nineteenth century, there were two varieties: the Cane de Pelo Duro *(wire-haired) and the* Cane Griffone *(long-haired). The latter resulted from cross-breeding the old wire-haired Italian Spinone with the French long-haired Griffon Boulet, which was introduced into Italy in 1809. During the nineteenth century, the Italian Spinone received pointer blood. Later, the breed split into two varieties: a heavy type similar to the Griffon Boulet, and a lighter type which is the Italian Spinone of today.*

HOW THE POINTER TRAPS ITS PREY

Through careful selection, breeders have been able to fix one of the Italian Spinone's chief characteristics—its ability to point before attacking game birds. A good hunting-dog, particularly in mountainous terrain, it can point for up to half an hour while waiting for its master to join it.

This pointer usually traps the game bird in a hiding place where the bird's only escape route leads to inevitable capture. The prey flattens out on the ground hoping to remain unnoticed. If it shows itself in the open, it has little chance of evading the powerful jaws of the pursuer. This instinctive defence is an effective tactic.

Some experts claim that a bird trapped by a pointer can control the emanation of its odour to avert detection by the dog's sense of smell. However, no scientific confirmation of this ability has so far been produced.

In all likelihood, the bird plays dead to protect itself. Before pointing, the dog always sniffs for the breath of its quarry. However, if the prey can hold its breath long enough, the dog becomes confused and may hesitate before attacking, if not abandon the spot to search elsewhere.

Pointers were once trained to trap game on the ground by stalking the prey silently. Hunters used a net, shaped like a funnel and weighted on the inside rim, which was thrown over the game, and even the dog. In Italy, the pointers were once called *cane de rete*—'net dogs.'

Characteristics

General appearance: vigorous, heavy-boned, but rather slender dog. Trotting gait. Solid, hardy, intelligent and companionable.

Height: 59.7 to 70 cm (23½ to 27½ in.) for the adult dog and 58.4 to 64.8 cm (23 to 25½ in.) for the bitch.

Weight: under F.C.I. standards, 32 to 37 kg (70½ to 81½ lb) for the adult dog and 28 to 32 kg (62 to 70½ lb) for the bitch. Elsewhere, dogs 31.8 to 37 kg (70 to 82 lb); bitches 28 to 32.2 kg (62 to 71 lb).

Head: long, strong, flat, occiput well developed. Bridge of nose straight or slightly hooked. Slight stop. Lips rather thin. Strong jaws. Solid teeth. Large nose with wide-open nostrils. Scissor bite.

Eyes: large and wide open. Neither deep-set nor protruding. Lower eyelid must never turn outward. Dark yellow iris for white or white and orange dogs; ochre for reddish-brown dogs. Expression very gentle.

Ears: set on level with the eyes. Relatively long, but no more than 5 cm (2 in.) longer than the jawline. Somewhat triangular, drooping, slightly rounded tips. Covered with thick, short hair mixed with long hair.

Neck: strong and muscular. Slight dewlap.

Body: shoulders well laid back, strong, and muscular. Chest wide, open, ample. Ribs well rounded, oblique. Length of body equals height at withers. Back straight, rising slightly towards the loin. Croup wide, robust, muscular, and sloping. Belly slightly raised. Brisket reaching at least to level of elbows.

Tail: set level with croup. Thick at the root. Carried horizontally or low. Customarily docked 15 to 20 cm (6 to 8 in.) from the root.

Forequarters: straight, heavy-boned.

Hindquarters: thighs long, wide, muscular.

Feet: round, close. Toes tight, arched. Pads lean and hard. Nails strong and curved. Hind feet slightly more oval than forefeet. Dewclaws on all four feet.

Coat: rough, thick skin. Hair wiry, thick, slightly curled, and rather close to the body. From 4 to 6 cm (1½ to 2½ in.) long on the body, less on the legs and feet. Longer, rough hair on frontal parts; long but less rough on the cheeks.

Colour: white, white with orange markings; white uniformly spotted with orange with a reddish-brown tint, with or without brown markings.

Practical information: This hunting-dog enjoys robust health. However, during its first six months, the growing dog needs minerals and vitamins to prevent rickets. Its thick, wiry coat requires regular, vigorous brushing, particularly during winter. Check its ears regularly. After hunting, examine its paws for cuts and abscesses, and provide appropriate medication.

187

Jack Russell Terrier

Parson Jack Russell

A hunting terrier, the Jack Russell was developed in the nineteenth century by Parson Jack Russell, a fox-hunting Devon clergyman with strong views on what he wanted from a working dog. The longer-legged variety is known as Parson Jack Russell. The Jack Russell is still used to hunt small vermin, run with foxhounds, and unearth foxes. A lively, alert dog with a fearless and confident temperament, it has become a popular companion and family dog. It requires early training and lots of exercise to prevent it becoming hyperactive. Nowadays the term 'Jack Russell Terrier' is used incorrectly to describe a wide range of small, white terrier types. Most are not true Jack Russell or Parson Jack Russell terriers and would not meet the breed criteria for registration.

AUS.	CAN.	S. AF.	U.K.	F.C.I.
●		●	●	●

ORIGINS

One morning in 1819, while an undergraduate at Oxford University, Jack Russell was walking to college when he saw a milkman on his rounds accompanied by his white terrier, 'Trump.' Russell was so struck by the terrier's appearance that he bought it, and 'Trump' became the foundation bitch of his line of white, rough-coated fox terriers.

Characteristics

General appearance: strong, active, and well-built, with a keen, intelligent expression.
Height: 33-36 cm (13-14 in.). In Australia the smaller, 25-35 cm (10-12 in.) type is also recognized.
Weight: not specified except in Australia, where it is 5-6 kg (11-13 lb).
Head: flat, moderately broad, narrowing to eyes. Shallow stop. Black nose.
Eyes: dark, almond-shaped. Deep set.
Ears: small, V-shaped, falling forward close to head.
Neck: powerful, not too long.
Body: moderately deep chest. Slightly longer than tall. Level back. Ribs well sprung. In Australia, the Jack Russell Terrier should be short in the loin.
Tail: strong, straight, and set high. May be docked to allow tip to be level with ears.
Forequarters: shoulders well sloped back. Legs strong and straight. Elbows set under body.
Hindquarters: strong, muscular. Stifles well angulated and hocks set low.
Feet: round, hard pads. Toes moderately arched.
Coat: smooth, broken or rough. Weatherproof.
Colour: white, or predominantly white with tan, lemon or black markings.

Practical information: Adaptable to country or city life. Requires only minimum grooming.

188

Japanese Chin

Japanese Spaniel, Tchin

Protected by its sumptuous coat, the high-stepping Japanese Chin moves with grace and considerable elegance. Its noble bearing recalls an ancient past when it was the favourite of the Japanese Imperial court.

Merry and affectionate, the Japanese Chin plays boisterously and continuously until it drops from exhaustion. Two Chins raised together will chase each other through the house, with cat-like nimbleness, never upsetting or breaking anything. The Chin is the perfect pet, intelligent, full of charm, very gentle and clean.

AUS.	CAN.	S. AF.	U.K.	F.C.I.
●	●	●	●	●

ORIGINS

In the eighth century B.C forbears of the Chin were introduced into Japan. For centuries, they were the pampered pets of the Imperial court. The Chin became known in the West in the 1860s.

Characteristics

General appearance: small, dainty, lively dog with a stylish, high-stepping gait. Compact carriage and luxurious coat give an air of elegance and distinction.

Height: approximately 30 cm (12 in.) for the adult dog under F.C.I. standards. Bitch slightly smaller than the adult dog. Elsewhere, not specified. Generally, the smaller the better.

Weight: 2 to 6 kg (4½ to 13 lb) under F.C.I. standards. Elsewhere, approximately 1.8 to 3 kg (4 to 7 lb). Generally, the smaller the better.

Head: large in proportion to body. Skull broad and rounded in front. Forehead very rounded when viewed straight on. Stop well defined. Snout and muzzle very short. Nose black or dark flesh colour, matching coat colour. Jaws broad and short.

Neck: moderate length, carried proudly.

Eyes: large, dark, rather prominent. Set well apart.

Ears: small, V-shaped, well feathered, set high, carried slightly forward.

Body: square, compact. Back short and straight. Loins broad, slightly rounded. Chest broad and deep. Belly tucked up.

Tail: set high, luxuriously feathered. Close curled or plumed, falling to one side.

Forequarters: straight, fine, well feathered.

Hindquarters: well positioned, amply feathered.

Coat: long, silky fur, profusely covering the whole body, except on the head. Hair long, flat, free from waves or curls. Neck, thighs, and tail feathered.

Colour: black and white or red and white.

Practical information: This toy dog snacks rather than eats, and delights in sharing tasty morsels from its master's plate. To prevent tangles in the Chin's fine hair, brush and comb the dog every day. Complete the grooming by spreading the coat out flat over the body with a horsehair glove. Wash the delicate eyes regularly with a cotton swab dipped in boiled water.

Keeshond

Dutch Barge Dog

I ntelligent and easy to train, the Keeshond (pronounced 'kayshond') has played a part in history. The name of this popular dog is derived from Cornelis ('Kees') de Gyselaer, the leader of Dutch rebels who rose against the ruling House of Orange during the late eighteenth century. Because the royalists already had the Pug as their mascot, de Gyselaer selected the little spitz as a symbol of resistance for the opposing rebel party. The dog was given the Dutch leader's nickname and became known as 'the dog of Kees' or Keeshond.

The breed received a setback when the House of Orange was restored to power. The Keeshond disappeared from cities, but could be found in the countryside and on the canals. Captains whose barges plied the waterways of Holland valued the Keeshond as a guard dog and, as a result, it acquired its other name—the Dutch Barge Dog.

In the late nineteenth century, the Keeshond was restored to public favour. Although it has recently been removed from the Dutch list of purebred dogs, it remains a favourite in the Netherlands. The Wolf-Spitz, which closely resembles the Keeshond, is popular in Germany, where it is still considered a pedigree dog.

The present-day Keeshond was first exhibited at a Dutch dog show in 1891. It made its British debut in 1923 and was imported into North America in the late 1920s.

AUS.	CAN.	S. AF.	U.K.	F.C.I.
●	●	●	●	●

ORIGINS

Spitz is the term used to describe a category of northern dogs that includes the Siberian Husky, the Japanese Spitz, the Norwegian Elkhound, and even the miniature Pomeranian. The Keeshond, the Wolf-Spitz, and the Grand Spitz are also members of this canine family. Centuries ago, the Finnish Spitz was imported into north-eastern Germany, where it was used for herding and pulling carts. The Wolf-Spitz, the German cousin of the Keeshond, was well known by 1700, and the German Wolf-Spitz Club was established by the end of the nineteenth century. The ancestors of the Keeshond may have come to Holland from Germany.

THE GRAND SPITZ

This spitz dog is known under different names: Grand Loulou in France, Volpino in Italy, and Laïka in the Soviet Union. The F.C.I., however, has officially adopted the name 'Grand Spitz.'

One of the characteristics distinguishing the Grand Spitz from the Keeshond and the Wolf-Spitz is the difference in the colours of their coats. The Grand Spitz is black, white, or brown, while the Keeshond and the Wolf-Spitz have wolf-grey or, more precisely, silver-grey coats.

The Keeshond and the Wolf-Spitz surpass the Grand Spitz by several centimetres in height. The Keeshond is usually from 45 to 55 centimetres (about 18 to 20 inches) high, but it sometimes reaches 60 centimetres (about 24 inches).

With those the animal knows and likes, the Grand Spitz is calm, companionable, and unfailingly dependable. It falls into a category of 'wolf-dogs,' identified by Konrad Lorenz, the Austrian ethologist famed for his study of animal behaviour, which are faithful to only one master.

This attractive creature loves family life and never shows unwarranted aggressiveness. It is good-tempered, intelligent, and devoted to children. While it is extremely attached to the family home, which it considers as its own personal territory, it distrusts strangers, particularly any trespasser unfortunate enough to cross its path. Courageous and vigilant, the Grand Spitz has a well-justified reputation as an excellent guard dog which barks in alarm at the slightest disturbance.

Unfortunately, the Grand Spitz finds the presence of other animals intolerable and can make itself sick with jealousy. When confronted with an intruding canine, it will launch an attack even if the other dog is larger and stronger.

Keeshond

Grand Spitz

Characteristics

General appearance: a handsome, compact dog, with an intelligent expression and a well-balanced carriage. Luxurious coat, richly plumed and curled tail. Head, like that of a fox; small, pointed ears. Lion-like mane.

Height: 45.7 cm (18 in.) for the adult dog; 43 cm (17 in.) for the bitch.

Weight: not specified.

Head: well proportioned, wedge-shaped when seen from above. Profile exhibits definite stop. Deep muzzle, medium length, neither coarse nor snipy. Characteristic 'spectacles'—a black line slanting upward from corner of eye to lower corner of ear; distinct markings and shading form eyebrows. Jaws strong. Scissor bite. Nose and lips black.

Eyes: dark, medium size, obliquely set.

Ears: small, ivy-leaf in shape, set high, carried erect. Dark, covered with thick, velvety, short hair.

Body: length of back from withers to croup equals height. Short, straight back sloping towards hindquarters. Deep, strong, well-ribbed chest. Shoulders well sloped. Belly moderately tucked up.

Tail: set high, moderately long, tightly curled; double curl at end desirable. Black tip, light-coloured plume where curled. Carried closely at all times.

Forequarters: feathered, straight.

Hindquarters: profusely feathered down to hocks, not below. Hocks only slightly bent. Cream in colour.

Feet: well padded, round, catlike, tight.

Coat: dense, harsh, long outer coat standing out from thick, downy undercoat. Dense ruff. Profuse 'trousers,' with soft, thick undercoat. Leg hair smooth and short, except for feathering. Head hair smooth, soft, short.

Colour: Mixture of grey and black. Undercoat very pale grey or cream. Outer coat tipped with black.

Practical information: Give the dog's double coat a daily rub-down with a rigid, short-bristled brush to prevent matting. After brushing, comb against the grain to air the coat. Untangle knots with a metal comb with long teeth. Bathe the dog two or three times a year.

The dog prefers meat to other foods, but the pup should be trained to eat rice, noodles, and vegetables.

Kerry Blue Terrier

Irish Blue Terrier

AUS.	CAN.	S. AF.	U.K.	F.C.I.
●	●	●	●	●

With its bushy beard and moustache, the stylishly trimmed Kerry Blue Terrier of the dog shows looks like a dandy—a role remote from its origins as a herder and a hunter. The colour of its silky, thick, curly coat, flecked with shades of silver and steel, varies from dark to pale blue. Its expression radiates the best traits of other terriers—intelligence, vivacity, and good humour.

The origin of the dog is rooted in the farms of south-western Ireland. Legends about its ancestors abound. According to one story, it may have descended from dogs that survived the wreck of Spanish ships off the coast of Ireland in 1588. The Spanish dogs swam ashore and imposed the right to establish their own breed by killing all the male canines in County Kerry.

According to some experts, the Kerry Blue has a touch of the Irish Wolfhound in its make-up. Irish peasants were forbidden by their overlords to own pure hunting-dogs, but the clandestine mating of the farmers' terriers with the lordly Wolfhound continued.

The truth of the matter, however, is that dogs of the Kerry Blue type were indigenous to Ireland. They have traits similar to those of the Irish Terrier and other Irish breeds.

By the early 1800s, a breed of silver-blue terriers was being used by farmers for fighting, hunting, ratting, guarding herd and hearth, and even churning butter. During the late 1880s, the breed was well established in Ireland, where it was known under different names—the Silver-haired Irish Terrier, the Irish Blue Terrier, or the Blue Terrier. Its present name was adopted in the 1920s.

The year 1922 brought international recognition for the Kerry Blue Terrier. It was presented at the Crufts Show in Great Britain and introduced in the United States. The breed was officially recognized by the American Kennel Club in 1924. The first Canadian registrations were recorded in 1924–25. The first champion, a female named *Martells Sapphire Beauty*, named for her sapphire-coloured coat, was born in Ireland on June 22, 1920. At present, the Kerry Blue is well represented in Great Britain, the United States, and the Netherlands.

Through breeding, the Kerry Blue has become an agreeable, if somewhat stubborn, companion. Although it may quarrel with fellow dogs, it is affectionate and gentle with man.

ORIGINS

Forbears of the Kerry Blue may include the Bedlington Terrier, Dandie Dinmont Terrier, and Irish Terrier. The introduction of Bedlington Terrier qualities probably influenced the texture and colour of the coat. The coat may have originally been black, but the blue colour was produced by selective breeding. The puppies and young dogs are black until the age of 18 months, but some fully grown animals never acquire the desired blue shade. The present type was established in the late nineteenth century. Oddly enough, County Kerry never claimed the dog which bears its name. The only connection between the Kerry Blue and the county was one of its pioneer breeders, Mrs. Casey Hewitt of Tralee, who improved the strain and set the standards for the dog in 1922. She also introduced the animal into Britain.

Characteristics

General appearance: compact, powerful, muscular, well proportioned. A graceful, disciplined dog of alert determination.

Height: 45.7 to 48.3 cm (18 to 19 in.) for the adult dog; bitches measure slightly less. Under Canadian standards, 45.7 to 49.5 cm (18 to 19½ in.) for the adult dog; 44.5 to 48.3 cm (17½ to 19 in.) for the bitch.

Weight: 15 to 16.8 kg (33 to 37 lb) for the adult dogs; 16 kg (35 lb) for the male is ideal. Slightly less for the bitch. Under Canadian standards, 15 to 18 kg (33 to 40 lb) for dogs.

Head: quite long and lean, with a slight stop. Flat top of skull. Foreface and jaws very strong, deep, and solid. Black nose, open nostrils. Teeth level. Scissor bite. Gums and roof of mouth are dark.

Eyes: as dark as possible. Small to medium size, keen expression.

Ears: small to medium size, V-shaped. They are carried forward but not too high.

Neck: strong and reachy, running into sloping shoulders.

Body: short coupled with good depth of brisket. Ribs well sprung. Deep chest. Topline level. Flat shoulders well laid back.

Tail: set high and carried erect. Customarily docked.

Forequarters: flat shoulders with elbows close to the body. Legs straight, powerful. Front straight, neither too wide nor too narrow.

Hindquarters: hind legs large and well developed. Stifles well bent. Hocks well let down.

Feet: small and round. Heavy boned. Black nails.

Coat: soft, silky, thick, wavy.

Colour: blue-grey, with or without black hair. A hint of tan permissible in puppies, as is a dark colour until 18 months old. Small white patch on chest admissible.

Faults: coat wiry or woolly. Bumpy cheek-bone. Poor bite. Rose-ears. Eyes pale and round. Roach or hollow back. Stilted or cow-hocked in action. Snipy foreface.

Practical information: Prevent skin problems by a diet of vitamins and careful maintenance of the coat. Groom the dog's coat thoroughly every two weeks.

HOW TO 'BARBER' THE KERRY BLUE

Skilful trimming and careful presentation have transformed the Kerry Blue from a herder and a hunter into an elegant show dog. With the exception of the Poodle, this terrier is the most 'barbered' of all dogs.

Exhibitors groom the Kerry Blues to point up the jaw, the depth of the chest, and the powerful limbs. Other accentuated features include: long, thick eyebrows reaching to the bridge of the nose; short hair on the skull and ears; a luxuriant beard and moustache; and abundant, stylishly combed hair on the legs. At the neck, as well as on the croup and tail, the hair is kept short. Owners try to get flat shoulders and well-outlined thighs, and to maintain a muscular look.

The grooming of the Kerry Blue, just like that of the Wirehaired Fox Terrier, starts with the stripping away of excess hair, followed by trimming or shaping of the coat to highlight the silhouette of the body. Exhibitors aim for a head contour similar to that of the Fox Terrier.

When trimming a Kerry Blue, use thinning shears. Never work with a razor or a knife. This harms the hair, causing it to stiffen and grow back in its initial colour.

King Charles Spaniel

English Toy Spaniel

King Charles
Spaniel

This small spaniel, sometimes called a Carpet Spaniel or Charlie, was long a favourite of European royalty. The breed, which probably originated in China or Japan, was well established in France before appearing in England in the 1500s. It is believed to be the 'Spaniell Gentle, otherwise known as the Comforter,' described by Dr. Johannes Caius, physician to Queen Elizabeth I. Ladies of the court are said to have sought winter warmth by keeping the little animals hidden under their enormous skirts. One of the breed also comforted Mary Stuart during her last days, clinging to her even after her death on the scaffold in 1587. Her loyal pet was one of a pack of sporting dogs she had brought with her from France, when returning as Queen of Scotland.

The breed achieved its greatest popularity during the reign of Charles II (1660-85). The king kept a large number as pets and brought them everywhere with him. This passion not only gave the dogs their name but seems to have incensed Samuel Pepys. The diarist wrote in his famous *Journal* that the king amused himself with his dogs, instead of attending to his royal duties.

The monarch's pets were known as Black and Tans. Three other varieties were developed later— the tri-colour Prince Charles; the Ruby, a solid chestnut red; and the Blenheim, a red and white.

Whichever coat it wears, the King Charles is affectionate, intelligent, and an excellent pet for a family with small children. It is no longer used as a sporting dog.

AUS.	CAN.	S. AF.	U.K.	F.C.I.
●	●	●	●	●

ORIGINS

Most authors agree that the King Charles originated in Japan or China. The breed has been produced in four colours for centuries, and credit for one of these colour variations, the Blenheim, is generally ascribed to John Churchill. In 1702, he became the first Duke of Marlborough and made Blenheim the Marlborough family seat. Here he is said to have produced the chestnut red and white variety, hence the name. Sporting instincts made the King Charles popular at woodcock shoots in the 1800s, but cross-breeding gradually caused the sporting qualities of the breed to disappear.

Cavalier
King Charles Spaniel

Characteristics

General appearance: stocky, compact, well proportioned body.
Height: under F.C.I. standards, 26 to 32 cm (10¼ to 12½ in.). Under Canadian standards, 30.5 to 33 cm (12 to 13 in.). Elsewhere, not specified.
Weight: under Canadian standards, 4 to 5.4 kg (9 to 12 lb). Elsewhere, 3.6 to 6.4 kg (8 to 14 lb).
Head: massive skull relative to height, dome shaped, full over the eyes. Short, black, turned-up nose. Wide lower jaw, lips well fitting, cheeks well cushioned up. Tongue not protruding. Well defined stop.
Eyes: very large, dark, set wide apart. Eyelids square to line of face.
Ears: set low, drooping, very long and feathered.
Neck: medium length, arched, giving proud carriage of head.
Body: chest wide, deep; back short, level. Shoulders well laid back.
Tail: well flagged and feathered, lower than the topline.
Forequarters: short and straight. Close elbows.
Hindquarters: straight, pasterns firm, hocks well let down.
Coat: long, silky, straight, well feathered. A slight wave is tolerated.
Colour: Black and Tan type: rich, glossy black with mahogany tan markings on muzzle, ear linings, chest, feet, over the eyes and under the tail. Tri-colour type: pearly white ground, well-distributed black patches; bright tan markings on the cheeks, ear linings, over the eyes, under the tail; white blaze between the eyes and up the forehead. Blenheim type: pearly white ground with well-distributed chestnut patches; wide, clear blaze with the chestnut 'lozenge spot' in centre of skull. Ruby type: uniform, rich chestnut red.
Faults: white patches on Black and Tan or Ruby dog. Curly coat.

Practical information: The long coat and feathering must be brushed and combed each day. The ears must be cleaned regularly with a cotton wad soaked in mild soapy water and all dead and matted hair must be removed. Clean the eye rims with boiled water.

THE CAVALIER KING CHARLES SPANIEL

Roswell Eldridge, an American dog fancier, visited Britain in the 1920s looking for King Charles Spaniels. Those he found were quite unlike their namesakes as depicted by Gainsborough, Rubens, and Rembrandt: over the years, the animals had become smaller, snub-nosed, and round-headed. In a bid to re-create the original characteristics, Eldridge offered prizes at London's Crufts Dog Show for the dog and bitch best resembling those in the Old Masters' paintings. Breeders responded and the new breed was recognized in 1945 by Great Britain, at first, and subsequently by other kennel clubs. Aside from the word Cavalier, the handsome newcomer is distinguished from the King Charles Spaniel by a flatter skull and longer muzzle. The Cavalier's eyes are not prominent, its ears are set high, it has a scissor bite and a slight stop. It has recovered its hunting instincts and is taller and somewhat heavier than the King Charles. But inherited characteristics, notably the four coat variations, remain alike in the two breeds.

Komondor

AUS.	CAN.	S. AF.	U.K.	F.C.I.
●	●	●	●	●

Solid and impressive in its thick, white, corded coat, the muscular Komondor has a graceful gait. In snowy regions police have used these dogs as trackers but their principal role has always been to protect livestock. For centuries Hungarian shepherds have relied on the breed to protect their flocks from bears, wolves, and brigands. Some U.S. ranchers now use Komondors to fight off coyote packs that kill as many as a million sheep a year. The Komondor, a loyal pet, is wary of strangers, yet gentle with children.

ORIGINS

The Komondor, largest of Hungary's herding breeds, is known as 'the king of the working dogs.' But the title has less to do with stature than with the animal's fiercely protective nature. The breed first came to Central Europe during the Mongolian invasions of the thirteenth century. Admiring the Komondor's vigilance and courage, the Magyars used other dogs for rounding up the herds and looked to the Komondor for protection only. Komondors, immensely popular in Eastern Europe, are gaining popularity in Canada and the United States.

Characteristics

General appearance: very tall, powerful dog.
Height: about 63.5 to 80 cm (25 to 31½ in.) for the adult dog; 59.7 to 69.9 cm (23½ to 27½ in.) for the bitch.
Weight: about 50 to 61.2 kg (110 to 135 lb) for the adult dog; 36.3 to 50 kg (80 to 110 lb) for the bitch.
Head: Short but delicate, covered with abundant hair. Arched skull. Moderate stop. Broad, coarse muzzle, not snipy. Black nose. Scissor bite. Tight lips.
Eyes: as dark as possible. Eye rims grey or black.
Ears: set high, hanging, U-shaped, medium size.
Neck: medium length, muscular. No dewlap.

Body: level back, broad, deep, muscular chest. Rump broad, belly arched up, well-laid shoulders.
Tail: set slightly low, reaching to hocks.
Forequarters: straight, well boned and muscular.
Hindquarters: strong, wide apart, well angulated.
Feet: firm, elastic pads. Strong nails.
Coat: long, coarse outer coat, curly or wavy, with softer undercoat. Hair clings together like tassels giving corded appearance.
Colour: white; skin should be grey, pink acceptable.
Faults: spotted feet. Cow hocks. Erect ears. Short tail. Coat shaded or multi-coloured. Blue-white eyes.

Practical information: This dog requires exercise and must run long distances each day. The coat must be brushed and combed daily to avoid matting. If the coat is intended to cord naturally, it should neither be brushed nor combed—just washed and dried naturally. (You can also use a hair dryer if you wish to dry the dog's coat more quickly.)

Kuvasz

Hungarian Kuvasz

Solidly built and with a majestic gait, this large herding dog exudes strength and dignity. Its name, from the Turkish *kawasz*, means 'guard' or 'protector,' and indeed this dog was originally used to defend both sheep and nobleman. In view of its stamina—a Kuvasz can trot non-stop for up to 30 kilometres (20 miles)—it is not surprising that it also served as a hunting-dog. Intelligent, courageous, and suspicious of strangers, Kuvaszok are fine guard dogs and, as such, are used by military and police. These docile dogs are easily trained, make playful, faithful pets, but are not very affectionate.

AUS.	CAN.	S. AF.	U.K.	F.C.I.
	●	●	●	●

ORIGINS

The Kurds are said to have introduced the Kuvasz to Hungary in 1100. By the fifteenth century the dogs were highly prized in Hungarian royal circles. The Kuvasz may be related to both the Maremma and the Pyrenean Mountain Dog.

Characteristics

General appearance: the Kuvasz is well proportioned. Movement is smooth and effortless.
Height: under Canadian and F.C.I. standards, 71 to 75 cm (28 to 29½ in.) for adult dogs; 66 to 70 cm (26 to 27½ in.) for bitches. Under South African standards, at least 58 cm (23 in.) for adult dogs; 51 cm (20 in.) for bitches. Elsewhere, not specified.
Weight: under Canadian and F.C.I. standards, about 40 to 52 kg (88 to 115 lb) for the adult dog and 30 to 42 kg (66 to 93 lb) for the bitch. Elsewhere, not specified.
Head: well-defined skull. Muzzle tapers gently.

Eyes: oblique, almond-shaped, as dark as possible.
Ears: rather small, V-shaped, set high, pendent.
Neck: medium length, muscular. No dewlap.
Body: deep chest. Oblique shoulders. Medium back.
Tail: set low, reaching down to the hocks.
Forequarters: straight and solid.
Hindquarters: muscular. Hocks long and powerful.
Feet: round, tightly closed. Well padded, firm.
Coat: short, straight hair. Weatherproof.
Colour: white, ivory permissible.
Faults: long neck, straight ears, yellow eyes, wiry or felt-like hair, curled tail. Coat not white.

Practical information: This robust dog is hardly ever sick. Coat must be brushed daily.

Labrador Retriever

Sturdy and compact, Labradors are loved and respected world-wide for contributions as war dogs, police dogs, and guides for the blind. And with their satin-smooth coats, Labradors are as magnificent in appearance as they are courageous and hard-working.

These powerfully built dogs are also mighty swimmers and will plunge into even ice-cold water. In fact the Labrador, also known as the St. John's Dog, was once a valued crew member of every Newfoundland fishing boat. These dogs were trained to jump overboard when the boats neared land, gather the ends of the fish-laden nets in their mouths, and swim ashore where other members of the fishing team emptied the catch. British sportsmen who heard about these retrievers of fish wanted some as retrievers of game. So Newfoundlanders who took their catch to British ports sometimes ended up selling their dogs as well as their fish.

The Earl of Malmesbury was one of these buyers. In describing his purchases, he wrote in an 1870 letter: 'We always call them Labradors.' The name stuck.

Newfoundlanders stopped raising Labradors in the late 1800s, partly because of a stiff local dog tax and partly because British quarantine laws cut off their profitable sideline. By then, however, the breed was firmly established in Britain.

Labradors make splendid retrievers and can be trained as early as six months of age. They are as much at ease in water or marsh as they are in woods or on level ground, and they are particularly good at trailing wounded animals.

Exceptional patience, intelligence, and gentleness make Labradors prized pets the world over. Always popular in Britain, they are now much appreciated in Australia and are a favourite hunting-dog in the United States.

AUS.	CAN.	S. AF.	U.K.	F.C.I.
●	●	●	●	●

ORIGINS

Labrador Retrievers, as we know them today, were developed in Britain from the excellent water dogs of nineteenth-century Newfoundland. English sportsmen saw the breed's possibilities and they imported many of the dogs. One such sportsman, a Colonel Hawker, noted that they were 'by far the best for any kind of shooting ... extremely quick running, swimming, and fighting ... and their sense of smell is hardly to be credited.' By the late 1800s, new breeding stock was difficult to find and the Labradors were crossed with other sporting breeds—the Flat-coated Retriever, the old Tweed Water Spaniel, and the Curly Coated Retriever. In time, the Labrador became Britain's favourite gun dog, a position it still holds. It is particularly prized for its 'soft' mouth: the jaws will not damage game in their grip. Dogs with yellow coats are preferred to the black-coated variety.

A NOSE FOR NARCOTICS

Labradors do not follow game directly but rely rather on an excellent nose and memory. These attributes, particularly the acute sense of smell, are valuable in many areas of police work, especially in narcotics detection. Every year, helpful Labradors sniff out about 1,000 large caches of illicit drugs for the U.S. Bureau of Narcotics alone.

Dogs are trained for this work by a series of ball games. First they have to identify which of several balls thrown to them contains drugs; later they must track down the ball hidden in a suitcase or desk drawer. Training for identifying hashish or marijuana takes about eight weeks; other drugs may require longer training periods.

Characteristics

General appearance: strongly built, short coupled, and solid. Very active with a brisk gait.
Height: under Canadian standards, 57 to 62.2 cm (22½ to 24½ in.) for the adult dog and 54.6 to 59.7 cm (21½ to 23½ in.) for the bitch. Elsewhere, 54.6 to 57 cm (21½ to 22½ in.) for the adult dog and 53.3 to 56 cm (21 to 22 in.) for the bitch.
Weight: under Canadian standards, 27.2 to 34 kg (60 to 75 lb) for the adult dog and 25 to 31.8 kg (55 to 70 lb) for the bitch. Elsewhere, not specified.
Head: clean-cut. Wide skull. Defined stop. Medium-long, powerful jaws. Sound, solid teeth. Wide nose. Nostrils well developed. Scissor bite.
Eyes: brown or hazel, intelligent expression.
Ears: neither large nor heavy. Set rather far back and hanging close to the cheek.

Neck: powerful and strong, clean-cut.
Body: deep, wide chest. Ribs well sprung. Back short and level. Long, oblique shoulders. Wide loins.
Tail: tapers from very wide base. Covered in short, thick, dense coat, giving rounded appearance.
Forequarters: straight from the shoulder to the ground, well boned.
Hindquarters: well developed. Hocks well let down.
Feet: round and compact. Toes well arched.
Coat: short and dense, without curl or feathering and quite hard to the touch. Weatherproof.
Colour: wholly black, yellow, or liver and chocolate. A small white patch on the chest is permissible.
Faults: poor bite. No undercoat. Feathering. Snipiness. Ears wide or heavy. Cow hocks. Tail curled over the back. Dudley nose.

Practical information: This robust dog has excellent health. Its short, dense coat with very tight hair must be brushed once in a while to get rid of dust and dead hair that would otherwise form mats in the coat. The Labrador must get enough exercise, or else it gains weight. This can easily happen since the dog has a voracious appetite.

Lakeland Terrier

The Lakeland Terrier has a fearless, yet friendly demeanour and can be an amusing companion. Its acute hearing and alert nature make it an excellent watch-dog for small quarters.

The Lakeland was bred to kill foxes and other vermin that preyed on farmers' lambs and poultry. Its nimble body enabled it to squeeze through rocks and into burrows and scrap with foes in their mountain lairs. Often these terriers would follow the prey considerable distances underground, even to the point of becoming trapped.

The breed has swept top honours at many of the world's most prestigious dog shows.

AUS.	CAN.	S. AF.	U.K.	F.C.I.
●	●	●	●	●

ORIGINS

The Lakeland hails from the north of England. Several terriers—the Bedlington, the Border, the Fox, the Dandie Dinmont, the extinct English Black and Tan, and even the Otterhound—have been cited as playing a role in the development of this protector of the sheepfolds.

Characteristics

General appearance: small, squarely and sturdily built. Friendly and self-confident manner. Lithe and graceful movement.

Height: 36.8 cm (14½ in.). Canadian standards permit a 1.3 cm (½ in.) variation for the the adult dog and 2.5 cm (1 in.) for the bitch.

Weight: dogs 7.7 kg (17 lb); bitches 6.8 kg (15 lb).

Head: well balanced, rectangular. Skull flat on top and moderately broad, cheeks almost straight-sided, stop barely perceptible. Broad muzzle.

Eyes: dark or hazel, somewhat oval.

Ears: small, V-shaped, carried alertly.

Neck: reachy and of good length, refined but strong.

Body: approximately square in overall length-to-height proportion. Chest relatively narrow but deep.

Shoulder blades sloping, well laid back. Ribs well sprung, moderately rounded. Back short, strong.

Tail: set high, customarily docked so that tail tip is approximately level with skull; gay or upright carriage but not over back or curled.

Forequarters: strongly boned, clean, absolutely straight when viewed from front or side.

Hindquarters: strong and sturdy.

Feet: small, round; toes compact and well padded.

Coat: double, weatherproof. Outer coat hard and wiry, undercoat soft. Furnishings on muzzle and legs plentiful.

Colour: blue, black, liver, black and tan, blue and tan, red, red-grizzle, grizzle and tan, or wheaten.

Faults: soft outer coat, no undercoat, slanting eyes.

Practical information: The Lakeland is a hardy dog, not subject to any particular medical problem. Its exercise needs are moderate but its wiry coat calls for considerable stripping and styling. Some owners may be able to handle the grooming themselves, others will need the help of a professional. Being a terrier, the dog may have a stubborn streak.

Leonberger

AUS.	CAN.	S. AF.	U.K.	F.C.I.
		●	●	●

This big mountain dog has the thick, fawn coat and the mane, and might of a lion—but the resemblance between the two animals stops there. The Leonberger is affectionate, gentle, and very protective towards children.

These majestic dogs are devoted to their masters. Intelligent and fearless, they make fierce watch-dogs of home or business, yet are not given much to barking. Leonbergers need freedom.

ORIGINS

Some writers say the Leonberger dates from the fifth century. Others say it was bred in the 1840s in Leonberg, Germany, by cross-breeding Newfoundlands and Saint Bernards.

Characteristics

General appearance: muscular.

Height: 71 to 80 cm (28 to 31½ in.) for the adult dog and 63.5 to 73.7 cm (25 to 29 in.) for the bitch. In South Africa, at least 76 cm (30 in.) for the adult dog and 69 cm (27 in.) for the bitch.

Weight: not specified.

Head: skull slightly rounded, more deep than broad; moderately domed. Jet black nose. Scissor bite.

Eyes: medium size, dark, frank expression.

Ears: set high, close to head, rounded at tips.

Neck: medium strong, muscular, no dewlap.

Body: deep oval chest. Back rather short, wide, straight, and muscular. Loin short and slightly arched.

Tail: set low, strong, long and bushy.

Forequarters: muscular, straight and well boned.

Hindquarters: long thighs, moderately built hocks.

Feet: tight, round, and webbed. Black pads.

Coat: thick mane and trousers. Woolly undercoat.

Colour: light yellow to red-brown with dark mask. Black or dark points on coat permissible.

Practical information: This breed needs a lot of exercise and must be brushed once a week.

Lhasa Apso

Tibetan Apso

The Lhasa Apso is a small, clever dog with an impressive coat, and eyes hidden behind a cascade of hair. For centuries the breed was almost unknown outside Tibet, where it was bred by Lhasa's lamas and nobles. Originally the dogs were cherished as harbingers of good luck, were never sold, and only males were given as gifts.

The origin of the Apso portion of the name is uncertain. It may be from the Tibetan word *rapso* for goat-like, a possibility in view of the dog's thick, golden coat. But it more likely was derived from the animal's nickname, *Apso Seng Kye*, which means Barking Lion Sentinel Dog. The breed was said to symbolize the lion, the protector of Buddha. (Indeed one legend holds that Lhasa Apsos are reincarnated lamas who have not yet reached Nirvana.) Certainly, intruders who got past the Tibetan Mastiff, said to have mounted guard outside every monastery and royal household, stood little chance of slipping by the little Lhasa Apso standing sentinel within.

Lhasa Apsos can endure high altitudes and are reputed to sense avalanches before they occur. Sherpa guide Tenzing Norkay was a breeder of the dogs. Norkay, who conquered Mount Everest with Sir Edmund Hillary, obtained his first stock from a Tibetan monastery.

Lhasas first came to Britain in the 1920s, and the breed was recognized by the British Kennel Club in 1933. North Americans received their first Lhasas that same year—the Dalai Lama gave them as presents to friends.

Lhasa Apsos have particularly acute hearing, are hardy, easily trained, responsive to kindness, obedient to those they trust, intelligent, and alert. They cannot bear to be left alone and they abhor changes in routine. The Lhasa is also an attentive mother. During weaning, the bitch predigests food, then regurgitates it to feed the pups.

AUS.	CAN.	S. AF.	U.K.	F.C.I.
●	●	●	●	●

ORIGINS

The Lhasa Apso is believed to be one of the world's most ancient breeds. Some authorities claim it dates back to 800 B.C., when it was developed from the Tibetan Terrier and the Tibetan Spaniel. For centuries the dog was bred exclusively in Tibet, which has been inaccessible and unwelcoming of foreigners throughout much of history. Rarely were Lhasa Apsos permitted to leave their homeland, and the few that were given to honoured guests, mostly Chinese, were male. In this way, reproduction of the species remained in Tibetan control. Such dogs as did leave the country were gifts: Buddhism, the religion of most Tibetans, prohibits the trading of living things. The first Lhasas in Britain were originally gifts to a member of the Indian Medical Service, who in turn gave the dogs to the wife of a British official. Breeding in North America began with dogs presented by the Dalai Lama to a New Jersey couple.

A SACRED DOG?

For centuries the lamas of Tibet preserved the purity of the Lhasa Apso breed, surrounding it with attention that bordered on reverence. The dogs not only guarded the monastic treasures, they also participated in religious ceremonies, during which they sat enthroned on silk cushions. Surrounded by such a wealth of solemnity, they may well have been regarded, as legend claims, as reincarnated lamas who were unable to ascend to Paradise.

Aside from the lamas, only Tibet's dignitaries and highest-ranking army officers could own Lhasas. To give a Lhasa was to bestow great distinction. It was an honour reserved for only the most esteemed of foreigners.

Characteristics

General appearance: compact and well balanced with a profuse, long coat. By temperament, alert and assertive, wary of strangers.

Height: 23 to 28 cm (9 to 11 in.). Under Canadian standards, 25.4 to 28 cm (10 to 11 in.), but up to 29.2 cm (11½ in.) is permissible; bitches slightly smaller.

Head: heavy, with abundant hair falling over the eyes. Dark beard and moustache. Narrow, rather flat skull with medium stop, straight foreface. Muzzle about 4 cm (1½ in.) long. Black nose. Level jaw.

Eyes: medium size. Not large or full, small or sunken. Dark, frontally placed.

Ears: drop, heavily feathered. Dark tips an asset.

Neck: strong. Covered with dense mane, more pro-nounced in the male than in the female, well arched.

Body: long for its height. Ribs well sprung. Strong loin. Well balanced and compact. Level topline.

Tail: well feathered, often ending in a kink. Carried over the back.

Forequarters: straight. Very hairy.

Hindquarters: well-developed thighs.

Feet: round, cat-footed, well feathered. Thick pads.

Coat: thick, straight, rough hair of good length. Moderate undercoat.

Colour: under Canadian standards, all colours. Elsewhere, golden, sandy, honey, dark grizzle, slate, smoke, parti-colour, black, white, brown.

Faults: square muzzle. Tail carried low. Large skull, dome- or apple-headed. Woolly or silky coat.

Practical information: The Lhasa Apso is a robust dog. Tearing is inherent to this breed, however, so some attention must be given to the eyes. Clean the eye contours with cotton swabs dipped in either boiled water or in a commercial isotonic product and remove any sticky matter. If tearing is abundant, consult a veterinarian. The condition may result from an eye infection or an obstruction of the tear ducts. The Lhasa's opulent coat also calls for attentive care. Brushing, combing, and untangling must be done daily. Occasional baths may be in order for Lhasa Apsos exposed to urban grime: ordinarily, this dog should not be bathed more than two or three times a year. Dirt can also be removed with powdered chalk, talcum, or one of the preparations available at most pet-supply stores. Simply rub into the coat and brush out thoroughly.

Maltese

Melita

For thousands of years this small dog with its long, lush, white coat has been depicted on art objects; and for centuries it has reigned in elegant salons world-wide. Beauty, however, is but one attribute of the Maltese. It is also intelligent, affectionate, a good watch-dog, and strong and hardy.

Authorities disagree on the origin of the breed's name. Some claim it is named for the Island of Malta; others say that the honour belongs to the Sicilian town of Melita. But all agree that the breed was widespread in Mediterranean countries from the earliest times. One theory is that the dogs were items of barter and were exchanged for goods along the old trade routes.

No one can be sure when the Maltese first arrived in Britain. The breed may have been brought in as early as 55 B.C.—the time of the Roman invasion. A more widely held view—and a more likely time frame—is that the dogs were brought home by returning Crusaders. By the late 1500s the animals were 'chiefly sought after for the pleasure and amusement of women, who carried them in their arms, their bosoms, and their beds,' wrote Dr. Johannes Caius, personal physician to Elizabeth I.

Artists down the years, including Goya, Titian, and Sir Joshua Reynolds, have included the Maltese in their paintings. Sir Edwin Landseer entitled his 1840 representation of a Maltese *The Last of the Race*. His foresight, fortunately, was faulty and the breed continues to thrive, particularly in North America.

AUS.	CAN.	S. AF.	U.K.	F.C.I.
●	●	●	●	●

ORIGINS

No one has conclusively determined the exact birthplace of the Maltese. It is known that the breed existed in ancient Egypt: small statues of Maltese have been found in the tomb of Rameses II, who ruled from 1290 to 1223 B.C. Phoenician traders may have brought the dogs to Malta and the surrounding Mediterranean countries. Publius, a first-century Roman governor of Malta, is known to have owned a Maltese. The breed has remained very pure through the centuries and present-day specimens match exactly the descriptions of their ancestors. A Maltese was first shown in Britain in 1862 and appeared at its first North American show in 1877. The breed is now widely distributed and there are excellent breeding kennels in most countries.

Characteristics

General appearance: small, thin, well balanced, sprightly, and elegant. Covered with long, bright white, silky, glossy mantle. Intelligent, alert, a fearless demeanour, affectionate towards its master; a popular pet world-wide, but particularly in North America.

Height: 20.3 to 25.4 cm (8 to 10 in.). Not specified under Canadian standards.

Weight: under F.C.I. standards, 3 to 4 kg (6½ to 9 lb). Under Canadian standards, 1.8 to 2.7 kg (4 to 6 lb). Elsewhere, not specified.

Head: in proportion to size of dog; skull slightly rounded, rather broad between the ears, and moderately well defined at the temples. Well-defined stop. Fine, slightly tapered muzzle, not snipy, firm underjaw. Large, black nose with well-open nostrils. Thin, black lips covered with long hair. Scissor bite.

Eyes: oval, dark, alert, well open, of good size. Black around the rims of the eyes.

Ears: flat, almost triangular, set wide and high. Well feathered with long, thick, straight hair reaching to the shoulders.

Neck: medium length, no dewlap. Carriage erect as if the head were thrown back.

Body: square. Straight topline, muscled loins. Full brisket let down slightly below elbows; rounded ribs. Belly rather low, well-defined hollow in the flank.

Tail: well set on, thick at the base and thin at the tip, carried in a large arch, the tip folding over the back.

Forequarters: vertical, fully covered with hair; lean muscles, strong bone structure. In stride, forelegs reach forward straight and free from the shoulders, elbows close.

Hindquarters: muscular thighs, well-boned legs. Hocks perfectly balanced when viewed from behind. In stride, hind legs move in a straight line with good driving action.

Feet: round. Toes close and arched, covered with long, thick hair, including between the toes. Pads and nails dark.

Coat: very long, dense, silky, glossy, heavy, straight. Average length 23 cm (9 in.), entirely covering the body and falling heavily to the ground on either side of a parting that runs from the tip of the nose to the tip of the tail. No curls or tufts. No undercoat.

Colour: pure white. Slight lemon or beige markings permissible.

Faults: ambling gait. Resemblance to the Pekingese. Nose any colour but black. Muzzle over-long or snipy. Jaws too short or too long. Wall-eyes, pink eye rims. Gay tail. Coat any colour but white or pale ivory. Curly or woolly coat. Cow hocks. Eyes too prominent. Poor bite. Undercoat.

Practical information: One of the hardiest of the toy breeds, Maltese—unlike many of the smaller dogs—make fine pets for families with young children. These dogs are seldom ill although their eyes tend to 'weep' from time to time. But considerable time must be spent on grooming, if one is to do full justice to this dog's beauty. It must be brushed and combed daily and both tasks must be done very gently, lest the animal's silky coat be damaged. You will need special brushes, combs, rakes, and other tools. These, and specific grooming instructions, are available at most pet-supply shops. Keep in mind that the coat must hang flat on either side of the centre parting, which should run from the tip of the nose to the tip of the tail.

If the coat is inclined to break, you can roll the hair onto cloth or paper curlers. The hair should be rolled close to the skin on either side and can remain in curlers for up to three days. To avoid crimping, make sure the dog's coat is perfectly dry before rolling into curlers. The rich 'mane' of the Maltese may either be left hanging, or dressed by knotting it once or twice high on the head. Bathing need only be done occasionally. Even this can be simplified by using one of the commercial products designed to eliminate tangles. The ears should be cleaned regularly.

Manchester Terrier

This short-haired dog with the long, handsome head has a small but loyal following. Originally, the Manchester Terrier was much sought-after as a sort of 'do-it-all dog.' A descendant of the Black and Tan Terrier, it was developed in the north of England, mostly in Lancashire, for rabbiting and ratting. It was not only charged with ridding homes and warehouses of rodents but was a rat-pit favourite as well. Dogs' ears were cropped for this sport to protect them from rat bites. Britain banned ear-cropping in 1895, however, and now these terriers are shown with natural ears in Britain, Australia, and South Africa.

AUS.	CAN.	S. AF.	U.K.	F.C.I.
●	●	●	●	●

ORIGINS

This terrier was developed in the eighteenth century by Manchester breeder John Hulme. It was born from a cross-breed of the now extinct Black and Tan Terrier, the Whippet, and probably the West Highland White Terrier.

Characteristics

General appearance: compact, with a good bone structure.
Height: 40.6 cm (16 in.) for the adult dog and 38 cm (15 in.) for the bitch. Under Canadian and F.C.I. standards, not specified.
Weight: under F.C.I. standards, 8 kg (17½ lb). Under Canadian standards, 5.4 to 10 kg (12 to 22 lb). Elsewhere, not specified.
Head: long, level, and wedge-shaped. Slight stop. Tapering, tight-lipped jaw. Scissor bite.
Eyes: small, almond-shaped, moderately close, dark.
Ears: small, V-shaped. Carried high above the head.

Neck: rather long, slightly arched, tapering towards the head. No dewlap.
Body: short, slightly arched. Ribs well sprung. Shoulders clean-cut and very oblique. Narrow chest.
Tail: short, thick, tapering.
Forequarters: straight, well proportioned.
Hindquarters: very solid. Well-bent stifles.
Feet: small, strong. Toes well arched and black.
Coat: dense, short, smooth, glossy. Firm texture.
Colour: jet black and mahogany tan, well outlined. Tan on muzzle, lower jaw, throat, below the knee, inside the hindquarters.

Practical information: Brush the coat each day. If it is a house dog, cut its nails.

Mastiff

Old English Mastiff

An excellent guard dog, the Mastiff (also known as the Old English Mastiff) must be handled firmly: otherwise it can become dangerous. Aggressiveness, after all, is at the core of this line of warriors. Phoenician traders probably brought the dogs to Britain in the sixth century B.C. In 55 B.C. Mastiffs were pitted against Roman legions (who later took some to Rome). There they were matched against bears, bulls, lions, tigers, and even gladiators. The dogs' pursuits in Britain were no less bloodthirsty—wolf-hunting, dog-fights, bear- and bull-baiting. The breed was known as Molossus, Alan, Alaunt, Dogue, Tie-Dog, Bandog, and—from the sixteenth century on—Mastiff. Today there are more Mastiffs in the United States than in Britain.

AUS.	CAN.	S. AF.	U.K.	F.C.I.
●	●	●	●	●

ORIGINS

Most English Mastiffs today are from lines bred at the Duke of Devonshire's kennels at Chatsworth and from the Lyme Hall kennels outside Stockport in Cheshire. The Lyme Hall strain goes back to a bitch that defended its fallen master at the Battle of Agincourt (Oct. 25, 1415) in France.

Characteristics

General appearance: massive, symmetrical.
Height: under Canadian standards, at least 76.2 cm (30 in.) for the adult dog and 70 cm (27½ in.) for the bitch. Elsewhere, not specified.
Weight: not specified.
Head: short, square-cut muzzle. Well-defined stop.
Eyes: small, widely spaced. Dark hazel-brown.
Ears: small, widely spaced, set high.
Neck: rather long, slightly arched, very muscular.

Body: shoulders slightly oblique, heavy, muscular. Wide chest. Arched ribs. Deep flanks.
Tail: set high, wide at the root, tapering.
Forequarters: straight, strong, wide apart.
Hindquarters: broad, muscular. Hocks well let down.
Feet: wide and round. Toes arched. Black nails.
Coat: short, dense, close lying.
Colour: apricot-fawn, silver-fawn, fawn, dark fawn-brindle. Muzzle, ears, and nose black.

Practical information: This short-haired dog is easily cared for. It needs only to have its hair brushed.

Mexican Hairless

Chinese Hairless, Xoloizcuintli, Xolo

In pre-conquistador Mexico, the Mexican Hairless was prized by Aztec and non-Aztec alike. The Aztecs revered it as Xoloizcuintli or Xolo, the earthly representative of Xolotl, the god charged with escorting the dead to the next world. But to the non-Aztec tribes, the animal was a much sought-after source of gourmet fare.

By the nineteenth century the *Pelon* (Bald) dog, as it was then called, was being credited with curative powers. Some fanciers claimed that asthma, malaria, and rheumatism were 'drawn away' when the animal was held close.

The folk-tale, which persists today, is probably related to widespread beliefs that the body temperature of the Mexican Hairless is consistently higher than that of other breeds. True, the dog is warm to the touch but this is simply because it has no coat. The skin looks like elephant hide but it is actually soft as a baby's cheek.

This dog is intelligent, quiet, and extremely sensitive. One should always address it softly, even in reprimand.

Most Mexican Hairless litters contain one 'powder puff,' a puppy with hair.

AUS.	CAN.	S. AF.	U.K.	F.C.I.
●	●	●	●	●

ORIGINS

Although hairless dogs are found in China, Mexico, Turkey, and elsewhere, their obscure origins have long been debated. Some experts believe all hairless dogs are the offspring of a common ancestor, while others claim the dogs are merely derived from local breeds.

A CAP FOR THE EARS

The standard for the Mexican Hairless requires that the animal's large, delicate ears be carried erect. One must prepare for this when the dog is two months old. First, place a cone-shaped wad of cotton-batting inside each ear; then, beginning at the base of the ear, wrap an elastic bandage three-quarters of the way up each ear. Next, tie both bandaged ears together with a third bandage, forming a figure eight. Leave this 'cap' on for about ten days, adjusting it at intervals to make sure the ears are in the right position.

Mexican Hairless

Chinese Crested Dog

Characteristics

General appearance: well balanced and graceful. Thin and well-proportioned feet. Hairless skin, warm to the touch.

Height: under F.C.I. standards, 30 to 50 cm (12 to 19½ in.). Under South African standards, about 28 cm (11 in.). Under Canadian standards, not specified. Elsewhere, 28 to 33 cm (11 to 13 in.) for the adult dog; 23 to 30.5 cm (9 to 12 in.) for the bitch.

Weight: Under Canadian standards, not specified. Elsewhere, not exceeding 5.4 kg (12 lb).

Head: skull rather broad. Long, tapering muzzle. Stop barely defined. Scissor bite. Dark nose, sometimes pink or brown.

Eyes: medium size, neither sunken nor protruding, slightly almond-shaped. Yellow to black, the darker the better.

Ears: expressive, large (up to 10 cm or 4 in.) on the side of the head, set low, erect, and at an angle when the dog is active.

Neck: carried high, long, lean, flexible, slightly arched, no wrinkles.

Body: rather long. Back straight, supple. Croup well rounded. Brisket deep, fairly narrow. Belly muscled and well tucked up. Breastbone prominent, chest broad and deep.

Tail: set high, smooth, rather long, thin at the tip.

Forequarters: straight, well proportioned, elbows tight.

Hindquarters: straight; solid and muscled thighs.

Feet: hare-footed, with retracted toes. Nails any colour.

Coat: smooth skin, as warm as 40°C (104°F). Tuft of short, stiff hair on the skull. A few frizzy hairs on the tip of the tail.

Colour: any colour or combination of colours.

Faults: ears not quite erect. Hair anywhere but the places mentioned. A lot of discolouration. Skin too loose. Dewclaws. Ears hanging. Tail docked or broken. Albino.

Practical information: This hardy dog can be raised in any climate, without special care. It can be bathed occasionally and does not get ticks, fleas, or other parasites, which afflict breeds with coats. It can go without a jacket in winter but, if you want to provide some winter protection, avoid woollen garments that irritate its skin. Use cotton instead. Unlike most other breeds, the Mexican Hairless breathes through its skin, and thus never pants.

THE CHINESE CRESTED DOG

This dog, occasionally referred to as the Chinese Hairless Dog, is said to have existed as far back as 1000 B.C. Common in China in the mid-1800s, the breed has been extinct there for half a century, although it is making healthy progress in Britain and in North America.

The tiny, svelte, Chinese Crested is active, affectionate, clean, and odourless—a splendid pet for adults. It is finely boned and graceful with one outstanding characteristic: a flowing crest of silky hair crowning its fine-muzzled head. Its large, thin ears, sometimes feathered, are carried erect.

Like the Mexican Hairless, the skin of the Chinese Crested is smooth, soft, and warm to the touch. Unlike the Mexican Hairless, though, the skin can be any colour or mix of colours: blue, grey, gold, pink—either as solids or patched with white. And the dog changes colour with the seasons. Tones are usually darker in summer than in winter. Also, its delicate skin is easily irritated, and even contact with clothing can provoke skin lesions. Not surprisingly, this unusual, little dog is extremely sensitive to cold.

The Chinese Crested Dog has long, narrow paws, each shaped somewhat like a hare's foot and covered with tufts of hair. As happens with the Mexican Hairless, 'powder puffs,' or pups with coats, occur in Chinese Crested litters. These coats consist of short, downy-soft undercoats overhung with long, veil-like overcoats.

Powder puffs are not bred. Their occurrence is believed to be nature's way of keeping the hairless puppies warm until they can move around and keep warm on their own. The smaller the Chinese Crested, the more it appeals to its fanciers.

Neapolitan Mastiff

Mastino Napolitano

AUS.	CAN.	S. AF.	U.K.	F.C.I.
		●	●	●

F rom its distant past as a fighting dog, the Neapolitan Mastiff has retained its athletic build—its weight often surpasses 100 kilograms (220 pounds). All muscle under a short-haired coat, usually black or grey, it walks with a lumbering gait, its head nodding gently. Yet it can seem quite majestic when trotting, loping along with mighty strides, rarely galloping.

Though most Neapolitan Mastiffs seen today appear docile, it should never be forgotten that this breed has an extraordinary combative nature combined with exceptional courage. This dog can be dangerous when trained to attack and it is vital that its master be able to control the animal. Otherwise some innocent intruder may end up clamped in the dog's powerful jaws.

Some authorities believe that the Mastino Napolitano owes its name to Mastineria, a type of farm in the south of Italy, which the dog guarded. Dogs so employed spent their lives chained to a tree or to a ring bolted into a wall.

Though the Neapolitan Mastiff remains one of the most fearsome guard dogs, it can be an excellent pet, loyal to its master and good with children that it knows well. The female of the species makes the better pet, being more sensitive and more submissive to its master.

The Italian police and armed forces have long used the Neapolitan Mastiff as a guard dog. Even so, the breed was hardly known outside Italy a decade ago. Now, however, it is becoming increasingly popular throughout Europe.

ORIGINS

The Neapolitan Mastiff dates back some 25 centuries. Assyrian bas-reliefs depict the dog much as we see it today: the same impressive bulk, the same fighting stance, the same powerful, wrinkled head. This breed is descended from the Molossus, a mastiff raised in Greece and exported to Rome for use in the circus games. The Romans, being great enthusiasts of bloody spectacles, were more concerned with their dogs' build and 'bite' than with their beauty. Through breeding and cross-breeding they produced many Neapolitan Mastiffs that were real 'killers.' Later the dogs left the arenas for the farms and eventually the species declined. It almost disappeared completely during the Second World War. Interest in the Mastiff was rekindled, however, the number of dogs increased, and by 1949 the breed was formally recognized. Today, the breed is flourishing in France, Germany, and the Netherlands, as well as in Italy.

CROPPING THE EARS

The ears of Neapolitan Mastiffs are cropped in some countries. The practice dates back to the days of the Roman arena when the dogs fought in the circus games. The ears were removed then so that their antagonists could not bite them off.

Cropping today is partly for aesthetic purposes and partly because of tradition. The shortest of all crops now practised, it is done when the pup is two to three months old.

The surgery is performed with the animal under a general anesthetic. The ear is cropped close to the head, around the auditory canal. Cutting begins just above the skull and continues almost straight down, completely removing the lobe. Once cut, the ear must form an equilateral triangle.

Characteristics

General appearance: agile despite its substantial bulk.
Height: 63.5 to 73.7 cm (25 to 29 in.) for the adult dog; 58.4 to 68.6 cm (23 to 27 in.) for the bitch.
Weight: 50 to 70 kg (110 to 154 lb).
Head: large, flat skull. Rounded occiput. Short muzzle. Large nose. Well defined stop. Large upper lip overlaps lower. Robust jaws.
Eyes: dark, rather large, deep set; lively and expressive.
Ears: small, set forward. Under F.C.I. standards, may be cropped.
Neck: stocky, strong, muscular. Much dewlap.
Body: wide, muscular shoulders. Well-developed chest. Full dorsal line. Upper back round, well shaped, lower slightly sunken.
Tail: robust and tapering. Should be docked by one-third.
Forequarters: muscular. Pasterns slightly sloping.
Hindquarters: long, wide, muscular thighs. Long, strong legs.
Feet: big, oval, compact. Toes well arched. Strong nails. Pads thick:
Coat: short, thick, even, fine, hard texture, good sheen, no fringe.
Colour: black, blue, grey, brindle, fawn. White patches sometimes on the chest and toes.

Practical information: With proper and sufficient training, this can be a splendid house dog. The male is considerably more aggressive than the female. Whatever the sex, the coat requires regular brushing and dew-claws should be removed. Eyelids should be inspected regularly for any signs of infection.

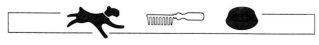

Newfoundland

Landseer

This large dog with its massive head and gentle eyes personifies loyalty and protection. In fact the Newfoundland stands for devotion and courage world-wide.

During the nineteenth century this gentle dog became something of a status symbol in many European countries, especially England. Then, as now, it was surrounded by a rich history of service—carrying lifelines to stricken vessels, aiding drowning victims, helping fishermen with their nets, saving children from harm. Its popularity was further enhanced when Sir Edwin Landseer featured a black and white Newfoundland in his painting, *A Distinguished Member of the Humane Society*. The two-colour variety of the breed has since been known as the Landseer.

Around the turn of the century, the Newfoundland was often used as a draught dog on the island for which it is named. Harnessed to a sled, it transported mail to remote areas of Newfoundland. Elsewhere in Canada the animal was—and of course still is—appreciated as an all-purpose dog: it can hunt, guard flocks and houses, and pull a wagon occupied by a child.

Newfoundlands make excellent rescue dogs and training is simplified because of the breed's intelligence and love of water. A dog so trained will respond to a call for help from a drowning victim or, on its master's command, return the person in difficulties to shore. It shows no more reluctance to dive off a boat than it does to swim out from land and it has even been known to tow distressed vessels to safety.

For all its bulk a Newfoundland is a docile, easy-going pet, as much at ease with other pets as it is with members of the household. It is not unusual to see it affectionately licking kittens under the watchful eyes of mother cat. It does not bite and does not bark unnecessarily, yet makes a good guard dog.

The Newfoundland's loyalty is unwavering. Indeed this dog becomes so deeply attached to its master that it cannot bear to be separated, much less change owners. A playful dog, it gets along splendidly with children of whom it is the traditional playmate and protector. It is therefore not surprising that the traits of a Newfoundland named *Boatswain* inspired Lord Byron to extol its character as having 'all the virtues of man without his vices.'

AUS.	CAN.	S. AF.	U.K.	F.C.I.
●	●	●	●	●

ORIGINS

The Newfoundland is one of the few dogs native to North America. Some authorities claim it is descended from the large, black 'bear dogs' that accompanied Norse settlers to Newfoundland late in the tenth century. Others believe that its ancestors were a European breed that inhabited the Canadian Arctic in prehistoric times: bone fragments recovered from ancient burial grounds seem to be from Newfoundland dogs. Yet a third view is that the breed resulted from the mating of local Labradors with dogs introduced by the European fishing fleets of the eighteenth century and that the Newfoundland is related to the Leonberger, the Saint Bernard, and even the Pyrenean Mountain Dog. In the late 1800s, when a distemper epidemic all but wiped out the famous Alpine rescue dogs of the Hospice of Saint Bernard, Newfoundlands were brought in to re-establish the Saint Bernard kennels.

THE CHARACTERISTIC WEBBED FEET

The Newfoundland's paw has an intertoe membrane that ends at the second phalanx. This membrane or webbing enables the dog to paddle through water with ease. Substantial webbing of the toes is present in all Newfoundland dogs and is evident even in the fetus. But the Newfoundland is not the only dog to possess this peculiarity: other water dogs, such as the Labrador, are similarly endowed. It is thought that all European dogs with webbed feet contain some genes of the Newfoundland dog.

Characteristics

General appearance: massive; moves freely and loosely.
Height: 71 cm (28 in.) for the adult dog and 66 cm (26 in.) for the bitch.
Weight: 63 to 68 kg (139 to 150 lb) for the adult dog; 50 to 54.4 (110 to 120 lb) for the bitch. Under Canadian standards, the average weight is 68 kg (150 lb) for adult dogs and 54.4 kg (120 lb) for bitches.
Head: wide and massive. Well-developed occiput. Short, rather square muzzle. Slightly defined stop. Soft, well-covered lips.
Eyes: dark brown, small, rather deep and wide-set.
Ears: small, well set, very close to the head.
Neck: strong, well set into the shoulders and back.
Body: deep chest, rather wide, well covered with hair. Powerful ribs. Wide back. Strong and muscular loin.
Tail: medium length, fairly thick, well covered with hair.
Forequarters: straight; muscular, elbows well down.
Hindquarters: very strong. Dew-claws must be removed.
Feet: wide and well shaped. Cat-footed. Webbed.
Coat: double, flat, dense, strong hair; slightly oily. Waterproof.
Colour: black, brown, white with black markings (Landseer). Tinge of bronze or splash of white on the chest and feet is permissible.
Faults: weak or saddle back. Weak loin. Cow hocks. Splayed feet.

Practical Information: The Newfoundland is very robust and needs to run and swim at will. It does not like heat. Brush its coat with a curry-comb; shampooing is not recommended. A puppy's bone development should be monitored carefully.

THE NEWFOUNDLAND RESCUE DOG

The Newfoundland, an exceptionally gentle and docile animal, is also gifted with incredible strength, great intelligence, and superior swimming skills. These qualities make it an excellent rescue dog.

Training for such work includes exercises in endurance and obedience. Little by little the dog is taught to swim more rapidly and to become more proficient in water. In response to its trainer's command it first 'rescues' a lifebuoy, then a canoe, later a weighted canoe, and finally a human 'victim.' Training is usually completed when the dog returns to shore towing the 'victim' by the arm.

The breed's best rescue dogs act on their own initiative. Such dogs will automatically take the shortest route to shore, for example, without being commanded to do so by their masters.

Norfolk Terrier

The Norfolk is every bit as feisty and sturdy a working terrier as its sister breed, the Norwich. In fact, for three decades preceding 1965—when it was granted status as a distinct breed—the Norfolk was the drop-eared variety of the Norwich Terrier.

Though not a noisy animal, the Norfolk will bark warnings of strange noises and people. The breed makes an ideal companion for those who appreciate the jaunty terrier personality but do not relish hours of grooming. The Norfolk's hard and close coat does not collect dirt and requires little trimming.

Breeders have worked to preserve the breed's true terrier character and spirit. It is robust, good-natured, and at home in town or country.

AUS.	CAN.	S. AF.	U.K.	F.C.I.
●	●	●	●	●

ORIGINS

Norfolk and Norwich Terriers share a common ancestry—Irish, Border, and Cairn Terriers. For years both were known as Norwich, were interbred, and were shown under the same breed classification. Eventually it became evident that two distinct types of terrier were emerging and, in 1965, the British Kennel Club granted separate breed status.

Characteristics

General appearance: a small, low, compact, and strong dog. May display scars from fair wear and tear.
Height: 25.4 cm (10 in.).
Weight: not specified.
Head: skull wide, slightly rounded. Strong, wedge-shaped muzzle. Well-defined stop. Scissor bite. Strong jaw. Tight-lipped. Strong, rather large teeth.
Eyes: dark, oval, deep-set, alert, keen.
Ears: medium size, V-shaped but slightly rounded at tip, dropping forward close to cheek.
Neck: medium length and strong.
Body: short and compact; level topline; well-sprung ribs; clean and powerful shoulders.
Tail: medium length, may be docked.
Forequarters: short, powerful, and straight.
Hindquarters: well muscled. Good turn of stifle.
Feet: round with thick pads.
Coat: hard, wiry, and straight, lying close to body. Longer and rougher on neck and shoulders. Hair on head and ears short and smooth, except for slight whiskers and eyebrows.
Colour: all shades of red, red wheaten, black and tan, or grizzle. White marks or patches permissible but undesirable.

Practical information: The Norfolk enjoys unlimited exercise but can be content with a run in the park.

Norwich Terrier

AUS.	CAN.	S. AF.	U.K.	F.C.I.
●	●	●	●	●

Sturdy and lively, the little Norwich Terrier is both shaggy and short-legged. One of the smallest of the working terriers, it can go in and out of burrows easily. This breed excels at flushing a quarry, yet makes a charming pet.

Norwich Terriers have been shown regularly since 1932. Originally, there were two varieties: the drop-eared and prick-eared specimens, but judges consistently chose the prick-eared. Supporters of the drop-eared dogs finally sought separate recognition. In 1965 the Kennel Club of Great Britain decided that the prick-eared should be known as Norwich and assigned the name of Norfolk to the drop-eared variety.

ORIGINS

The Norwich is believed to have descended from small Irish Terriers—known as Cantab Terriers—that were much sought-after by Cambridge undergraduates of the 1870s. Some Cantabs were crossed with other hard-working terriers such as the Bedlington and Staffordshire Bull. The progeny was known in some parts of Britain as Trumpington Terriers; in other parts, and in North America, they were called Jones Terriers. By 1923 the breed had been stabilized and nine years later the British Kennel Club recognized the Norwich.

Characteristics

General appearance: small, low, compact.
Height: 25.4 cm (10 in.).
Weight: not specified.
Head: wide, slightly rounded skull. Strong, fox-like muzzle. Well-defined stop. Tight lips. Strong jaw.
Eyes: small, oval, dark, lively, brilliant, expressive.
Ears: erect, set well apart, pointed tips.
Neck: strong, of good length.
Body: short, compact. Well-sprung ribs. Shoulders well laid back. Level topline. Short loin.
Tail: may be docked.

Forequarters: strong, solid, short.
Hindquarters: solid, muscular. Well-turned stifles.
Feet: rounded, thick pads.
Coat: hard, wiry, straight hair. Long and rough on the neck and shoulders; short and smooth on the head, ears, muzzle. Distinctive whiskers and eyebrows.
Colour: red, wheaten, black and tan, grizzle. White patches and marks are undesirable.
Faults: small boned. Long or weak back. Poor bite. Long, narrow head. Cow hocks. Pale or yellow eyes. Coat soft, curly, wavy, or silky.

Practical information: The tail should be docked at the fourth vertebra within a few days of birth. Docking, however, can be done up to the second week of the pup's life. The Norwich Terrier's coat should be brushed and combed daily and, unless the dog is getting a lot of exercise, its nails should be clipped. Norwich Terriers may occasionally show battle scars.

Old English Sheepdog

Bobtail

O ld, in this context, is probably a term of endearment, for this prototype of English
sheep-dogs is only about 200 years old. Large,
square, and agile, the breed is distinguished by its
coat of long grey-blue or white and black hair. At
least, show dogs of the species are—some of the
breed's working dogs are relieved of their overcoats at sheep-shearing time. Warm sweaters and
blankets that are reputedly indestructible are
sometimes fashioned from the shearings.

This breed's physique inspired many British
artists. An Old English Sheepdog is easily recognized alongside the Duke of Buccleuch in Gainsborough's portrait. Philip Reinagle (1749-1833)
immortalized the breed with a painting that is
said to be the finest of the artist's dog portraits.

The Old English Sheepdog was developed by
sheep farmers in the English West Country and
by the mid-nineteenth century the breed was
widespread in rural areas. The dogs were mostly
used as drovers—driving livestock to market—
and, as working dogs, were exempt from taxation.
To prove their occupation the dogs' tails were
docked, a custom that produced both the present
practice and the nickname 'Bobtail.' The popular
belief that the docking of old produced a breed of
tail-less dogs is pure myth.

The Bobtail's massive size and strength deterred predators of old and today makes the breed

AUS.	CAN.	S. AF.	U.K.	F.C.I.
●	●	●	●	●

ORIGINS

*The Bobtail, believed to be
descended from a crossing of
several working breeds, was
founded in Great Britain, where
it is regarded as the oldest indigenous sheep-dog. The West
Country farmers who developed
the dog wanted an animal that
was agile, hardy, and intelligent. To get it, they mated indigenous breeds, such as the
Bearded Collie, with imported
stock. Today's Bobtail is probably related to several European herding breeds, including
the Russian Owtchar, the Hungarian Puli, perhaps even the
Briard. Three unimpressive Old
English Sheepdogs were shown
in Britain in 1873, the first time
the breed was exhibited. Yet in
time, the Bobtail gained in popularity and numbers and today
it is in demand the world over.
Since the turn of the century
breeders have focused mainly
on aesthetic characteristics.*

a valuable guard dog. If anything, it tends to be overly possessive of what it perceives as its territory or property. And its bark tends to be loud with a peculiar sonorous quality—not unlike that of a cracked bell.

Walking or trotting, this dog looks like a bear, with its great hairy body and peculiar ambling, or pacer, gait. (Both legs on the same side move forward simultaneously.)

This boisterous dog is extremely affectionate, loves playing with children, and watches over them with the care it once lavished on flocks. This, and performances by an Old English Sheepdog in stage presentations of *Peter Pan*, has inspired its nickname—Nanny Dog.

To be a good drover, the Bobtail had to anticipate the sheep's movements and nudge any strays back to the flock. This instinct can be seen at work today whenever its owners, out for a walk, drift apart. The Bobtail will continue running from one to the other until they reunite.

Characteristics

General appearance: strong, compact, muscled and symmetrical. Able-bodied and alert. No legginess. Profusely coated all over. Loud, peculiar bark. Elastic gallop; ambling walk and trot.

Height: Under Canadian standards, 56 cm (22 in.) and upwards for dogs; slightly less for bitches. Elsewhere, dogs at least 61 cm (24 in.); bitches 56 cm (22 in.).

Head: large, rather square-shaped skull. Well-arched eyebrows covered with hair. Long, strong, square, truncated muzzle. Well-defined stop. Broad, black nose. Strong, broad, well-formed, level teeth.

Eyes: brown or wall-eyes; blue eyes permissible. Set well apart.

Ears: small, moderately coated, and carried flat against the side of the head.

Neck: fairly long, gracefully arched, well coated.

Body: rather short and compact. Brisket deep and full. Strong, slightly arched loins. Sloping shoulders.

Tail: short; missing or docked at first joint from the body.

Forequarters: very straight, well coated all around, strong bone structure.

Hindquarters: round muscled. Hocks well let down. Hams densely coated with a thick, long jacket.

Feet: small, round. Well-arched toes. Thick, round pads.

Coat: abundant, hard texture, not straight but shaggy and free from curls. Undercoat should be a waterproof pile, when not removed through grooming or shearing.

Colour: grey, grizzle, blue, or blue merle, with or without white markings.

Faults: long, narrow head. Softness or flatness of coat and all shades of brown or fawn.

Practical information: Faithful and easily trained, the Bobtail needs plenty of open space. This athletic dog really needs to run. It is a sturdy animal but becomes quite uncomfortable in hot weather. Ears should be swabbed clean regularly and all tangled hair should be removed with extreme care. Twice-weekly brushings should keep its coat from matting. Dust does not cling to this dog's hair so bathing is seldom necessary. The Bobtail has a tender mouth and can be trained as a retriever.

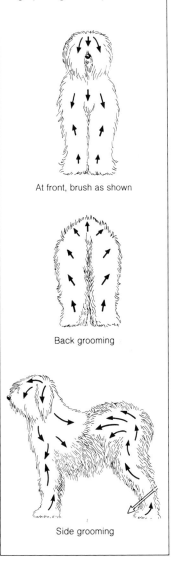

For grooming the Bobtail, use a brush with hard bristles and brush in the directions indicated by the arrows in the illustrations below. When grooming the face and head, brush forward so that the hair encircles the face, as shown in the sketch.

Body hair should be brushed from head towards tail at the shoulders, and hair at the rear should be brushed forward until it looks like a thick puff. Brush the legs from bottom to top.

Finally, using deft light strokes, brush down the curls on the hind legs (see light arrow).

At front, brush as shown

Back grooming

Side grooming

Otterhound

AUS.	CAN.	S. AF.	U.K.	F.C.I.
•	•	•	•	•

Back in the twelfth century, these rough-coated hounds accompanied monarchs on the hunt and were highly regarded by the aristocrats who maintained the packs. Every master was singularly proud of his Otterhounds, but authorities concede that the best-trained pack that ever hunted in England belonged to Squire Lomax of Clitheroe. The squire's pack reached its zenith around 1868 when, it is said, the hounds would respond to the most casual wave of their master's hand.

Otter-hunting remained popular until after the Second World War. Then the otter population all but disappeared. Otters were declared a protected species in 1978 and shortly after that the Otterhound Club of Great Britain was formed.

When the first standards for the breed in Britain were drawn up, the Otterhound emerged as a show dog, which brought protests from those who believed the breed should remain a pack and kennel dog. Up till then, the only Otterhounds exhibited were the occasional specimens sent forth by the major pure-bred packs. Impeccable breeding, however, was quickly appreciated by knowledgeable dog fanciers and the Otterhound soon found its way into the winner's circle.

The Otterhound came to North America in 1900. It was soon recognized by the American Kennel Club and exhibited for the first time in 1907. Although never used on otter, the breed has been employed with great success hunting mink, raccoon, cougar, and bear. Even though the breed has never gained widespread popularity among North Americans and is seldom seen at dog shows, Otterhounds have still managed to win handsomely in prestigious, all-breed competitions. Interestingly, several North American breeders have imported hounds from the remaining British packs as foundation stock for their kennels.

The Otterhound is a handsome dog with a massive head, deep-set eyes, and a wise expression. Its distinctive coat is crisp, hard, fairly long, and oily enough to withstand immersion in water. Any true hound colour is acceptable, and these vary from grizzle, sandy, and wheaten, to blue and tan, black and tan, and black and cream.

The Otterhound has a powerful bay, and gives a musical chase. There is universal praise for the animal's working ability, unflagging loyalty, and engaging personality.

ORIGINS

The Otterhound, one of the most ancient of the British breeds, was greatly favoured by the nobility. As water dogs with exceptional swimming ability, Otterhounds were used in packs to kill the otters that robbed rivers of their fish. The first-known pack belonged to King John (1199-1216). Edward II (1307-27) was the first Master of Otterhounds, and since then many British monarchs have kept their own packs. Elizabeth I (1558-1603) was the first Lady Master of Otterhounds. The Otterhound's exact origins are not known but it is commonly believed that the Bloodhound, together with the old Southern Harrier and various European griffon breeds, played a part in its development. Though never a major sport in Britain, otter-hunting has nevertheless existed since earliest times. It reached its peak early in the 1900s, when nearly two dozen packs hunted regularly through the season. The period between the world wars saw continued sport but then times, and public opinion, changed. Pollution poisoned the streams and rivers, fish died, otters all but disappeared, and the hounds—which conservationists blamed for the otter's sudden decline—dwindled in number. Indeed many fine hounds were destroyed in 1978, when the otter became a protected species. Fearing that all pure-bred hounds would be lost, the two remaining pure-bred packs, Kendal and Dumfriesshire, containing some 100 hounds between them, determined to keep the breed alive. Following a campaign in the pages of Our Dogs, *the British Kennel Club accepted registrations and the Otterhound joined the ranks of the show dog.*

Characteristics

General appearance: symmetrical, strongly built, great endurance, with unfailing powers of scent. Rough-coated and majestic, with free-moving gallop and loose, long-limbed stride.

Height: about 68.6 cm (27 in.) for adult dogs and about 61 cm (24 in.) for bitches. Under Canadian and F.C.I. standards, not specified.

Weight: not specified.

Head: large, imposing, deep rather than wide. Forehead high. Strong, deep muzzle. Wide nostrils. Jaws strong. Large scissor bite.

Ears: long, thin, and pendulous, fringed with hair.

Neck: long, powerful, and looks relatively shorter because of the abundance of hair.

Body: strong; well-sloping shoulders; thighs big and firm. Chest deep, well-sprung ribs. Level, broad back. Loin short and strong.

Tail: thickly covered with hair, and carried well up but not curled.

Forequarters: straight from elbows. Pasterns strong, slightly sprung.

Hindquarters: strong and well muscled.

Feet: large, round, compact. Well knuckled, thickly padded.

Coat: long, dense, rough, waterproof, but not wiry. Undercoat.

Colours: generally grizzle or sandy, with black and tan more or less clearly defined.

Practical information: The Otterhound makes a handsome and delightful family pet, but it can be a fearless fighter if attacked. This energetic hound has great stamina and needs ample daily exercise, and its rough, weather-resistant coat needs routine grooming.

FROM PACK PUPPY TO STARDOM

If any one dog can be credited for renewing interest in Otterhounds, the honour should surely go to *Kendal Nimrod*. As a one- and two-year-old, *Nimrod* (born May 14, 1975) hunted regularly with the Kendal and District Otterhounds in Lancashire, Cumbria, and parts of Yorkshire. In 1977 this pack starred in *Tarka the Otter,* the film based on Henry Williamson's novel, and, in 1979, *Nimrod* appeared at that most prestigious of dog shows, Crufts in London. It was the first time an Otterhound had been exhibited at Crufts and the red grizzle hound created a sensation. It not only charmed the gallery; it captured the Reserve Best of Group award, a tremendous honour in such impressive competition and doubly meaningful for a rare breed. It was a thrilling day for owner S. M. Marston of Cumbria, and for Otterhound supporters everywhere.

Papillon

Butterfly Dog

The vivacious and charming Papillon is the epitome of elegance and among the most dignified of breeds. Not surprisingly it was a popular adornment of royal courts and aristocrats' salons from the Renaissance into the eighteenth century. The breed is thought to have originated in Italy from the Dwarf Spaniel. This ancestor had droopy ears as did the original Papillons. Today, the drop-eared variety is known as Phalène, because the dropped ears resemble large, folded insect wings. (Phalène is French for moth.) The erect-eared variety, commonly seen today, was developed by Belgian breeders in the late 1800s. The flared ears create the illusion of a butterfly, hence the name. (Papillon is French for butterfly.)

Clean and odourless, the Papillon was a prized pet of noblewomen, who loved to cradle it in their fur muffs. Nobles, too, were fascinated by the animals and took the little dogs on trips. One man is even said to have carried around his neck a beribboned basket of fist-size Papillons. Historic figures associated with the breed include Madame de Pompadour, who owned two, and Marie Antoinette, who is said to have carried her pet Papillon to the guillotine.

Nowadays the Papillon is highly prized at all levels of society. It is an excellent watch-dog, giving warning of the slightest unusual sound. Tireless in play, it delights its admirers with its amusing antics. But this dog can also be calm, gentle, and patient. It is extremely affectionate and loves to be cuddled. But it tends to be possessive, even jealous.

AUS.	CAN.	S. AF.	U.K.	F.C.I.
●	●	●	●	●

ORIGINS

Paintings and tapestries confirm that the Papillon has been breeding true to type for some seven centuries. Some authorities say the breed is the most ancient in Western Europe. Others claim it is of Chinese origin. Either way it was a favourite at the courts of Europe, especially in Spain, France, and Italy, by the 1500s. Several Bolognese breeders had a thriving export trade—transferring the dogs from country to country on the backs of mules. Spaniards introduced the Papillon to South America in 1915 and the breed became known in Britain and North America soon after that. It was first exhibited in Britain in 1923 under the classification, Foreign Dogs. A year later it achieved full breed status. The Papillon has been recognized in Canada and the United States since 1935.

ARTISTS' MODEL

Even though documentary evidence about the Papillon's origins may be scanty, there are numerous works of art that clearly illustrate the breed's development. Indeed, artists have been featuring this breed in their art for centuries.

Those who have painted Papillons include Rubens (1577-1640), Van Dyck (1599-1641), Rembrandt (1606-69), Watteau (1684-1721), and Fragonard (1732-1806). A portrait of Queen Charlotte, painted in 1779 by Benjamin West, includes a Papillon.

The earliest representations of the breed show the Papillon with long hair, curled nails, and ears set at the top of the head.

Another type of Papillon is depicted in *Triumph of Death*, a 1350 fresco attributed to Orcagna, and in the Anne of Austria portrait by Pourbus (1602-66). This one's ears are clearly hanging and its eyes are round.

A third variety is seen in the works of Titian, who died in 1576. This dog is similar to that illustrated on early Flemish tiles, in the works of Clouet (1510-72), and in the Rubens painting that celebrated the birth of Louis XIII.

Although some writers maintain that the Papillon we see today was not developed before 1894, the breed is clearly distinguishable in works by portraitists Nattier (1685-1766) and Greuze (1725-1805).

Papillon

Phalène

Characteristics

General appearance: small, dainty, symmetrical. Alert, intelligent, and lively expression. Graceful, easy movement. An elegant dog distinguished by its beautiful, butterfly-like ears.

Height: 20.3 to 28 cm (8 to 11 in.).

Weight: under F.C.I. standards, 1.5 to 5 kg (3¼ to 11 lb). Elsewhere, not specified.

Head: skull slightly rounded between the ears, sometimes lightly grooved. Tapered muzzle, length from tip of nose to stop is about one-third the length of the head from tip of nose to occiput. Well-defined stop. Nose small, black, rounded, slightly flat on top. Lips black, thin, and tight. Strong, well-spaced teeth. Jaws strong. Scissor bite.

Eyes: round, medium size, well open, not protruding, dark, set fairly low, the inner core of the eyes is on a line with the stop. Eye rims dark.

Ears: heavily fringed, very large, mobile. Set on the sides towards the back of the head. In the Phalène variety, ears are considerably.above eye level, carried drooping and completely down; covered with medium-long, wavy hair. In the Papillon variety, ears are erect, set high, carried obliquely. Resemble spread wings of the butterfly. Concha faces side, is well feathered and lined with fine, wavy hair.

Neck: medium length, slightly arched at the nape.

Body: shoulders well developed. Chest rather deep. Brisket broad, well let down. Back fairly long and level, neither swayback nor flat. Loins strong. Belly slightly arched. Well-sprung ribs.

Tail: long, well fringed, set high; forms a plume. Carried arched over the back.

Forequarters: straight, slender, and fine, parallel legs. Elbows close to chest.

Hindquarters: well developed, good turn of stifle. Legs slender, fine-boned and parallel when viewed from behind. Dewclaws must be removed.

Feet: fine, long, hare-footed. Nails strong, preferably black. Toes tufted with fine hair, which may grow beyond toes and form points. Pads tough.

Coat: silky, abundant, glossy, flowing, with wavy highlights. No undercoat. Flat and short on the face, muzzle, top of the paws; of medium length on the body; frill on the neck, falling over chest. Rear of fore legs to pasterns, tail and thighs covered in long hair.

Colour: under F.C.I. and Canadian standards, white with patches of any colour. Elsewhere, liver patches not permissible.

Faults: skull flat, apple- or dome-shaped. Muzzle arched or concave. Small, protruding, light-coloured eyes. Nose not black. Poor bite. Visible tongue. Scanty, soft, or wispy coat. Straight or woolly hair. Undercoat. Discolouration of eye rims or lips. Single or double dewclaw on hind legs. Tail too short.

Practical information: Since it is a meticulously clean animal, and not particularly sensitive to cold, the Papillon can be bathed frequently. Careful, daily grooming will ensure a lustrous coat. The Papillon's teeth tend to collect tartar, so regular brushing is es- sential. This breed loves to romp in the countryside, yet makes a splendid household pet.

Pekingese

Foo Dog

This small, luxury dog with the sumptuous coat and flattened nose has a manner that is at once dignified and devil-may-care. The breed is believed to be a miniature version of the Foo Dogs, lion-like animals of old that were said to ward off evil spirits. Many Foo Dog replicas remain—some carved in ivory and jewel-studded wood, others fashioned in bronze.

The miniature breeds have existed for 1,500 years and for centuries they were the exclusive property of the Chinese Imperial Court. The animals were cherished and honoured within the royal circle but sacrificed on the deaths of their masters, whom they were said to protect in afterlife. The dogs' effigies are found on numerous works of art—on jade, lacquer ware, porcelain. Often they were painted on silk together with portraits of the master and family.

Seventh-century chronicles recount how some of the dogs rode on cushions placed in front of the mounted emperor. Certain specimens, seated thus, were credited with leading the horse by controlling the reins, and with carrying lighted torches to illuminate the pathway at night.

Veneration of the miniature dogs was such that commoners had to bow to them, and theft of a Pekingese was punishable by death.

Then in 1860 British soldiers took Peking, sacking the Summer Palace. The defenders must have determined not to let the royal dogs fall into attackers' hands, for all but five of numerous Pekingese in the palace were found slain. The survivors, pets of an imperial princess who had taken her own life, were brought to England. The Duchess of Wellington and the Duchess of Richmond received two each and the fifth was presented to Queen Victoria, who named her prize *Looty*.

Those five dogs, together with later specimens from China, were the foundation stock of all Pekingese in Britain today.

Pekingese were first exhibited in 1894 and four years later the breed was registered by the British Kennel Club. Pekingese arrived in North America in the early 1900s and the breed was registered in Canada in 1910.

This tiny dog continues to have a marked taste for silk cushions and a definite aversion to long walks. As one American writer noted irreverently: 'Once a palace pooch, always a palace pooch.'

AUS.	CAN.	S. AF.	U.K.	F.C.I.
●	●	●	●	●

ORIGINS

This breed, one of the most ancient in the world, is essentially Chinese. The miniature dogs were bred and preserved at the Imperial Palace for centuries and their popularity was at its height in the early 1800s. Even though still confined to royal circles, there were thousands in Peking at that time—and thousands of servants charged with their care. A few specimens—owned by a princess who died during the conquest—survived when Peking was overrun by the British in 1860. The dogs were brought to England and, with later imports, became the basis of Britain's present-day line. The dogs' romantic past, coupled with Queen Victoria's approval, brought instant popularity. By 1910 the breed's own dignity, loyalty, and stubborn streak had made it the most popular toy breed in the Western World.

THE PEKINGESE GAIT

All Pekingese walk with a characteristic roll, a gait induced by its shape. In profile, a Pekingese looks pear-shaped, wide in the chest and narrow at the rear. When it walks, the animal tries to distribute its weight evenly on its short legs, thus rolling along.

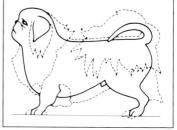

Characteristics

General appearance: small, solidly built. Alert, dignified manner.
Height: not specified.
Weight: under F.C.I. standards, 2 to 8 kg (4½ to 17½ lb). Under Canadian standards, 6.4 kg (14 lb). Elsewhere, 5 kg (11 lb) for the dog; 5.7 kg (12 lb) for the bitch.
Head: massive. Wide skull, not domed, flat between the ears, wide between the eyes. Flat profile. Deep stop. Nose short, wide, open, and black, placed high between the eyes. Wide, wrinkled muzzle. Underjaw wide and firm. Tight lips. Level mouth. Black nose, lips and eye rims.
Eyes: large, clear, dark, brilliant.
Ears: heart-shaped, set high on skull, close to the head, with long feathering. Feather not to come below level of muzzle.
Neck: short and thick. Profuse mane extends beyond the shoulders forming a frill.
Body: short. Wide chest. Ribs well sprung. Level back. Heavy in front. Distinct waist. Muscular shoulders.
Tail: set high, carried tightly, slightly arched over the back to either side. Long, straight, abundant feathering.
Forequarters: short, thick with a strong bone structure. Curved legs, solidly let into the shoulders, elbows well into the body.
Hindquarters: solid, firm, lean legs. Solid hocks.
Feet: large, flat, not round. Forefeet slightly out.
Coat: long, straight; abundant mane reaches below the shoulders. Coarse hair, thick undercoat. Long feathering on the ears, legs, tail, and toes.
Colour: all colours but albino and liver. Parti-colors evenly broken.

Practical information: This dog is prone to colds and respiratory ailments. Its eyes are sensitive. Watch for corneal ulcers and regularly clean the eye areas with cotton swabs dipped in lukewarm water.

223

Pharaoh Hound

This elegant, lightly built hound is noted for its great speed and agility. It requires a lot of exercise but fanciers find the animal's affectionate, playful nature and exceptional intelligence well worth the effort.

The Pharaoh Hound is believed to have originated in ancient Egypt, where drawings and tomb sculptures dating to 4000 B.C. show surprisingly similar animals. Indeed this resemblance to the dogs of old accounts for its name.

The Phoenicians greatly admired this hound, and introduced it to the Mediterranean region. There it became the foundation stock for several other breeds. Excellent hunters, Pharaoh Hounds were known in Malta and Gozo as Kelb-tal Fewek, or rabbit dogs. A characteristic of the breed is its excellent sense of smell; it is one of the few 'gazehounds' (hounds that hunt by sight) that also track quarry by scent.

The breed was introduced into Britain in the 1920s but failed to gain much support at that time. Reintroduced 40 years later, it met with warmer reception and in 1968 it was given official breed status by the Kennel Club. The dogs have a small following in North America, where they are a recognized breed of the Canadian Kennel Club.

AUS.	CAN.	S. AF.	U.K.	F.C.I.
●	●	●	●	●

ORIGINS

It is fairly certain that the Pharaoh Hound lived in the Maltese islands for thousands of years. But just as the other hound breeds originated in North Africa, so too did the Pharaoh Hound. It bears a strong resemblance to animals with large erect ears depicted on what is believed to be the earliest dog relic—a stone fragment showing two hounds at chase. The artefact, said to date from 3000 B.C., was discovered on the banks of the Nile. Similar dog likenessess have been found in Egyptian tombs. The link with the dead was probably Anubis, a mythical dog-god who was said to guide departed souls to the next life. The Pharaoh Hounds were likely brought to the Mediterranean region by merchants, probably Phoenicians. The breed was well established in Malta and Gozo long before the Christian era. Protected by their island location from outside influences, the dogs bred true for centuries before being introduced to other parts of the world.

Characteristics

General appearance: alert, friendly, playful, light bone structure. Fast moving, graceful, powerful.

Height: under F.C.I. standards, 46 to 50 cm (18 to 19¾ in.) for the adult dog and 42 to 46 cm (16½ to 18 in.) for the bitch. Elsewhere, 56 to 63.5 cm (22 to 25 in.) for the adult dog and 53.3 to 61 cm (21 to 24 in.) for the bitch.

Weight: under F.C.I. standards, 10 to 12 kg (22 to 26½ lb) for adult dogs; 8 to 10 kg (17½ to 22 lb) for bitches. Elsewhere, not specified.

Head: shape of blunt wedge. Long, lean, well-chiselled skull. Slight stop, sloping gently. Pointed muzzle. Lips very thin, barely covering upper teeth. Nose flesh-coloured only. Medium-size jaws.

Eyes: rather small, oval, moderately deep-set. Amber-coloured.

Ears: triangular, set medium high, narrow at the tips, carried erect.

Neck: slightly arched; long, lean, muscular. Clean throat line.

Body: lithe, nearly straight topline. Deep brisket down to elbows. Ribs well sprung. Abdomen moderately cut up. Shoulders strong, long.

Tail: rather thick and tapering. Carried high and curved when dog is in action; otherwise, hanging to the hocks.

Forequarters: Elbows well tucked in, pasterns straight and parallel.

Hindquarters: strong and muscular. Hocks well let down.

Feet: hare-footed. Toes close and arched. Pads well padded.

Coat: short, glossy, fine hair on the head, ears, and legs; moderately long elsewhere; smooth and very flat on the trunk and tail.

Colour: tan. White markings permissible; on tip of tail desirable.

Practical information: This hardy dog is not daunted by low temperatures or rainy weather. It has all the skills of a good retriever and needs lots of long runs in the countryside, whether it is being used as a hunting-dog or not. The Pharaoh Hound needs to be groomed regularly with a soft brush, and its eyes and ears should be checked often for any signs of infection.

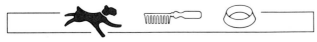

THE TESEM

Greyhounds, one of the oldest known groups of dogs, share a common ancestor—the Tesem.

The Egyptians probably acquired the Tesem from nomads journeying along the shores of the Nile, and developed it into an elegant breed. The fine, slender body perched on long, firm legs had a proud bearing; two small, pointed ears stood erect on its long, flat head; its turned-up tail spiralled over its croup. (This particular characteristic has all but disappeared in descendants such as the Pharaoh Hound, the Ibizan Hound, and the Sloughi.)

The Egyptians, enthusiasts of the chase, valued the Tesem for its hunting prowess and docility. Their artists even used the dog as a model when depicting their dog-god, Anubis.

But although the Egyptians deserve praise for their selections in breeding the Tesem, credit for introducing the dog to Europeans belongs to the Phoenicians. The greyhound varieties since developed are mostly distinguished by coat and size. The work required of the dogs and the climate where they lived have influenced those characteristics.

Pinscher

German Pinscher

With its glossy coat and solemn expression, the Pinscher is sometimes mistaken for a small Dobermann. The colouring and elegant lines of the two breeds are also similar. However, the Pinscher is the older breed, and it contributed to the development of the Dobermann in the nineteenth century. The Pinscher actually more closely resembles the Manchester Terrier. It has a terrier's instinct for hunting vermin and has been used as a ratter for centuries in Germany.

Resemblance to a small forest deer earned this breed its original name of *Reh Pinscher* (*Reh* means roe deer in German). Despite its intimidating name, the Pinscher is docile and easily trained. Its fearlessness and sensitive hearing make it a superb watch-dog, alert at the slightest disturbance.

Bright, spirited, and well suited to indoor life, the Pinscher makes a delightful companion dog. It is especially popular in Germany and Switzerland but is rarely seen elsewhere. The Miniature Pinscher is far more common in other countries.

AUS.	CAN.	S. AF.	U.K.	F.C.I.
●		●	●	●

ORIGINS

Though the Pinscher has been known in Germany for at least 300 years, its ancestry is unclear. Some authorities believe it is descended from the same ancient German breed as the Schnauzer. While the relationship between the two species has not been established, some suggest that the Pinscher compares to the Schnauzer as the Smooth-haired Fox Terrier compares to the Wire-haired Fox Terrier.

PINSCHER VARIETIES

In addition to the standard Pinscher, there exist several other varieties of the breed.

The Miniature Pinscher is hardly bigger than a Chihuahua—about 30 centimetres (12 inches) in height and weighing only three or four kilograms (about six to nine pounds). Though officially recognized in 1895, the Miniature was virtually unknown outside Germany until 1900. That year, it was presented at the Stuttgart Dog Show and immediately became a favourite with Americans.

In 1920 a number of dogs were brought to the United States, where breeders were subsequently successful in improving the strain. They dubbed it the Miniature Pinscher, rather than the Dwarf or *Zwerg* Pinscher, as it had previously been known. 'Miniature' perfectly suits the robust little dog, for it has none of the characteristics of pronounced dwarfism, such as protruding eyes and jaws.

The Miniature Pinscher Club of America was founded in 1929, and the first such association in England appeared in the 1950s. While the Miniature's popularity fell during the Second World War, it has since regained favour in English-speaking countries, especially Canada and the United States. British breeders are producing Miniatures with naturally erect ears, eliminating the need for cropping.

One of the Miniature's most attractive features is a characteristic high-stepping 'hackney' gait, evidence that the Italian Greyhound may have had a hand in the Pinscher's development. Its straight, high-set-on ears and sparkling eyes give the Miniature an animated expression. Despite its small size, it is a fine watch-dog and ratter; alert and clever, it is quick to warn of intruders and will courageously attack vermin nearly as large as itself.

The Miniature's somewhat delicate appearance masks surprisingly vigorous health and resistance to illness. It is easily trained and requires only simple grooming. Lively and self-assured, the little dog makes a devoted pet.

The Harlequin Pinscher is intermediate in size between the standard and Miniature varieties. It owes its name to a beautiful coat spotted with grey or black markings on a white or pale background. Some dogs also have flame-coloured markings. The Harlequin is especially popular in Germany, where its spiritedness and striking coat are highly regarded.

A favourite in Switzerland is the Glattharidge variety, a dog the size of a standard Pinscher, with a short coat in a salt-and-pepper shade. Though it is increasingly sought after, the Glattharidge has not yet received its own standard. These last two varieties are rarely seen outside Europe.

Miniature Pinscher

Pinscher

Characteristics

General appearance: medium size, with a muscular, squarish body. Alert, watchful, and courageous.
Height: under F.C.I. standards, 40 to 48 cm (15¾ to 19 in.). Elsewhere, 43 to 48 cm (17 to 19 in.).
Weight: under F.C.I. standards, 12 to 16 kg (26½ to 35¼ lb). Elsewhere, not specified.
Head: robust, narrow, and long. Flat skull, tapering gradually from eyes to nose tip. Wide, round nose, black, brown or red, depending on coat colour. Jaws strong and muscular. Deep muzzle, slight stop. Scissor bite.
Eyes: dark, medium size, almond-shaped, not slanting. Eye rims tight.
Ears: set high, erect or dropped. Under F.C.I. standards, the ears may be cropped symmetrically to a point.
Neck: long, lean, solidly set, gracefully curved, blending into shoulders. Slightly arched. No dewlap.
Body: sloping shoulders. Deep, moderately broad chest, reaching down to elbows. Prominent sternum. Back level, short, slightly sloping. Loin short and strong. Rounded croup. Belly moderately tucked up.
Tail: set high and carried erect. Customarily docked at third vertebra.
Forequarters: strong, straight legs.
Hindquarters: parallel, wide, and muscular. Well-defined stifles. Hocks short, set well apart, turning neither in nor out.
Feet: cat-footed; short and rounded, well-arched toes. Hard, resistant pads. Dark nails.
Coat: short, smooth, and dense, with glossy hair. No bare spots.
Colour: black, blue, or chocolate with tan markings; solid red of various shades, from deer-brown to rust; black without marks; silver-grey (salt-and-pepper); harlequin.
Faults: too heavy or light. Too high or low on legs. Domed or flat skull. Eyes too large, small, or pale. Loose skin on throat. Jaws undershot or overshot. Short, pointed muzzle. Back too long, raised, bent, or weak. Large or crooked hocks. Sparse hair. Spots or stripes.

Practical information: The Pinscher adapts easily to life in a home but must receive adequate exercise; frequent walks or romps in a garden are essential. While the Pinscher's short coat needs little care, it provides poor protection from the elements in cold climates. Regular grooming with a soft brush will make its coat glossy. Unless its nails are used often, they should be trimmed with clippers. The puppy's tail should be docked at the third vertebra before it is ten days old.

The ears can be cropped between the ages of two and three months in an indented shape slightly pointed at the tip, similar to a Dobermann's. This incision will not hold if the puppy's cartilage is still soft. Ear-cropping is performed for aesthetic reasons only; the dog's health does not suffer without it.

Pointer

English Pointer

AUS.	CAN.	S. AF.	U.K.	F.C.I.
•	•	•	•	•

The Pointer is a canine athlete developed for hunting and an outdoor life. With great concentration and stamina and a keen nose for game, it is considered the perfect gun dog.

A superb tracker of game birds, the Pointer hunts with head held high, tail extended straight behind, and upturned nose sensitive to the slightest scent. When it detects game, it freezes instantly with its leg raised as though in mid-stride. The rigid pose indicates the direction of prey to the hunter, who can then flush out his target. Some dogs have been known to remain in this stance for several hours at a time, visibly trembling with the enormous tension of the point.

Alert and graceful, the Pointer makes an excellent bird dog. With its smooth, effortless stride, it can rapidly comb the area surrounding the hunter, slowing to a stalk as it senses the presence of game. Partridge and woodcock are favourite prey on land, but snipe are its speciality in marshes.

Though it will plunge in without hesitating, the Pointer is not comfortable in water and does not retrieve after the game is shot. But these rugged dogs can tolerate extreme heat and fatigue. The Pointer is 'hare-footed,' giving it a very light step, essential for approaching game unnoticed.

The Pointer proves that a working dog can also be a handsome animal. Intelligent and obedient, it learns quickly and is easy to train. It is a hardworking dog and devoted to its master, but can nonetheless exhibit a sensitivity verging on nervousness.

While hunting lands are dwindling and the value of the Pointer's work declining, the breed is, fortunately, far from disappearing.

ORIGINS

Developed in England after the introduction of firearms, the Pointer embodied the speed and wariness essential for the new style of hunting. There is no clear evidence of its earliest ancestors, but several older varieties of this sporting breed are thought to have been involved. The old English and French pointers and the Portuguese and Italian versions are possible forerunners. But its most likely ancestor is believed to be the Spanish Pointer, which was brought back by English officers after the War of the Spanish Succession and the signing of the Treaty of Utrecht in 1713. Breeding of the Pointer probably began with the tough and speedy Foxhound, but it is uncertain which other breeds were later crossed to produce the dog we know today; both the Greyhound and Bloodhound are thought to have contributed. The Foxhound's practice of tracking at a gallop, with its nose to the ground, eventually proved to be undesirable for a bird dog, and breeders in the mid-nineteenth century eliminated the trait through selective crosses. They thus succeeded in improving the dog's gait, endurance, and tracking approach. The first recognized modern Pointers were named Bounce, Drake, Hamlet, *and* Major.

Characteristics

General appearance: graceful, strong, and muscular.
Height: under F.C.I. standards, 60 to 67 cm (23½ to 26½ in.). Else-where, 63.5 to 68.6 cm (25 to 27 in.) for the adult dog; 61 to 66 cm (24 to 26 in.) for the bitch. Under Canadian standards, not specified.
Weight: under F.C.I. standards, 20 to 30 kg (44 to 66 lb). Elsewhere, not specified.
Head: pronounced stop. Muzzle concave. Wide nostrils.
Eyes: dark. Same distance from occiput as from nostrils.
Ears: set high, close to the head, somewhat pointed at tips.
Neck: long, muscular, slightly arched. No dewlap.
Body: oblique shoulders. Deep chest. Well-sprung ribs. Level back.
Tail: medium length, tapered, straight. Carried level with back.
Forequarters: legs firm and straight.
Hindquarters: lean, muscular thighs. Well-turned stifles.
Feet: oval, with close-set, arched toes. No dewclaws.
Coat: short, fine, smooth, hard hair, with pronounced sheen.
Colour: white and lemon, orange, liver, or black; solid or tricoloured.
Faults: round skull. Indistinct stop. Roman nose. Dewlap.

Practical information: A robust and healthy dog, the Pointer needs a great deal of activity and exercise. Its ears are sensitive and should be examined regularly. It is also intolerant of cold and damp and should be dried after hunting in marshes.

TRACKING

A dog which hunts by scent tracks game by following its trail, however faint. Powerful dogs like setters and pointers, which have excellent senses of smell and hunt with their noses held high, can quickly search or 'quarter' a wide expanse of ground. The Pointer's course becomes a se-ries of zigzags as it turns fre-quently into the wind and sniffs the air on either side of its head to pinpoint the location of prey. This wide tracking is especially effi-cient in fields and open country-side. When it has spotted its quarry, the Pointer leads the hunt-er to it by freezing in a 'point.' It drops out of range of the gun when the bird is flushed.

Pomeranian

Loulou

The smallest member of the spitz breeds, the Pomeranian has a striking plumed tail that curls forward across its back. Its long, thick coat and the attractive mane encircling its face made the Pomeranian a darling of the Victorian period.

Marie Antoinette, the Empress Josephine, Mozart, and Emile Zola were proud owners of the little dogs which originated in the Baltic region of Pomerania, once a part of Germany. Gainsborough's celebrated portrait of Mrs. Robinson depicts an early version of the Pomeranian that is considerably larger than the dog we know today.

The breed did not achieve celebrity until late in the nineteenth century. In 1888, Queen Victoria noticed white Pomeranians during a trip to Florence and soon took a great interest in the breed, founding a kennel and even exhibiting her own dogs. One of these, *Gona*, won acclaim at several shows. The Queen's preference for small dogs spurred the selective breeding which resulted in the diminutive size of the modern Pomeranian.

By the turn of the century the Pomeranian had become very fashionable, particularly in Great Britain. One owner, whose dog was renowned for its beauty, refused the princely offer of 500 pounds from an American breeder, causing a sensation even greater than the dog's splendid appearance.

The Pomeranian's cleverness, natural gift for entertaining, and adeptness at learning tricks have made it a favourite circus performer. It is an excellent watch-dog with a deep bark that gives the impression of being a much larger dog. No longer the exclusive breed of royalty, the Pomeranian is an obedient and affectionate companion.

AUS.	CAN.	S. AF.	U.K.	F.C.I.
●	●	●	●	●

ORIGINS

The Pomeranian's ancestry can be traced back to the Stone Age dog Canis familiaris palustris; *this is a rare example of stability in a breed. Direct forerunners are the sled-dogs of the Middle Ages, some of which migrated to Pomerania, in the Baltic region of what today is Germany, and gave rise to the first Pomeranians. Today's dog is the product of nineteenth-century British selection, but the breed is recognized as German. In attempting to further reduce the Pomeranian's size, British breeders used intensive inbreeding, producing a number of extremely small dogs—some weighing less than three kilograms (6½ pounds)—with inherited deformities. Rounded skulls and protruding eyes—characteristics of dwarfism—soon surfaced. Dogs of an unusual colour are also the products of repeated inbreeding and are often frail and sickly.*

230

Characteristics

General appearance: a compact, short-loined spitz. Intelligent expression and docile temperament.

Height: not specified.

Weight: 1.8 to 3 kg (4 to 6½ lb). Under Canadian standards, 1.4 to 3.2 kg (3 to 7 lb).

Head: medium length, foxlike, wider at the back. Slightly flat skull. Forehead not very prominent. Muzzle small in comparison to head.

Eyes: medium size, slightly oval, bright, dark. Dark eye rims in light-coloured dogs.

Ears: small, pointed, triangular, erect, not too wide apart.

Neck: rather short, well set in.

Body: deep chest. Shoulders well laid back. Rib-cage rounded. Straight, short back. Belly slightly tucked up at the rear.

Tail: moderate length, set high, turned over back and carried flat and straight. Profusely covered with long, harsh hair.

Forequarters: legs of medium length, straight, well feathered.

Hindquarters: legs and thighs fine-boned, neither cow-hocked nor wide behind. No dewclaws.

Feet: small, round; cat-footed. Curved nails.

Coat: soft, fluffy undercoat, and long, straight, harsh outer coat. Hindquarters covered with abundant long hair or feathering from croup to hocks. Outer coat profuse around neck and forepart of shoulders and chest, forming characteristic frill or mane. Does not separate along back. Slightly airy, silky, straight, not frizzy or matted.

Colour: all solid colours, free from black or white shading; parti-coloured, with colours evenly distributed in patches.

Faults: domed skull. Eyes too wide or too pale. Long, drooping, wide-spaced ears. Pale nose. Tail too short or badly curled. Coat soft, flat, open. Poor bite.

Practical information: The Pomeranian is prone to rapid buildup of tartar on its teeth and to frequent 'weeping'; its eyes should be cleaned regularly. Its thick coat needs only occasional bathing. These dogs suffer risk of hereditary diseases, particularly hip dysplasia and dislocation of the patella, or kneecap.

MINIATURE BREEDS

Miniature, or toy, dogs are believed to have originated either in ancient Mexico or China. The Mexican Chihuahua, for instance, was for centuries the only dog that weighed less than one kilogram (two pounds).

When minimum weight requirements were removed from standards for the Pomeranian, Papillon, and Yorkshire Terrier, a few breeders decided to attempt miniaturization. They began to mate the smallest animals of their litters, producing offspring of about one kilogram in weight. This selective inbreeding met with difficulty when abnormal features and signs of weakness emerged. Among the characteristics of dwarfism which became prominent were short limbs and bulging eyes. These may still occur in miniature dogs. Other common weaknesses are missing teeth, a shrunken lower jaw, occipital dysplasia, and dislocation of the patella, or kneecap. The inbred dog's temperament can also be disagreeable. For these reasons certain breeds, such as the Toy Poodle, which measures about 25 centimetres (9¾ inches) in height, are not recognized by the Fédération cynologique internationale, although they are accepted in English-speaking countries.

Poodle

Caniche

The first Poodles were large gun dogs with a special talent for retrieving birds from water. This distinguished past has since been virtually forgotten. The Poodle's French name, *Caniche*, probably derived from a common word for young ducks and the dogs that hunted them. The similarity of Poodle to the English word 'puddle' and to the German word *Pudel* (meaning 'one who plays in the water') evokes its former career of water-dog. Now known as Standard Poodles, these were the forerunners of the smaller Miniature and Toy breeds.

Poodles are still sheared in traditional fashion to resemble lions. At one time this practice was eminently sensible: the dogs could swim more easily with their long coats trimmed, and bands of hair left on the legs and forequarters protected joints and vital organs from the cold.

The Poodle appeared in art and literature as early as the thirteenth century, eventually serving as a model for such masters as Botticelli and Rembrandt. Its trainability and sense of fun have made it a favourite with circuses for centuries.

Whatever its size, the Poodle is a bright and amusing pet whose good nature and cleverness have won it enormous popularity throughout most of the world.

AUS.	CAN.	S. AF.	U.K.	F.C.I.
●	●	●	●	●

ORIGINS

The Poodle has been claimed by many countries, including Germany, Denmark, and Italy, but France has been officially recognized as its birthplace. Its most likely ancestor is the North African Barbet, thought to be a forerunner of European water-dogs. The Poodle was widely known in France, Germany, and Russia by the sixteenth century. But several breeds were sheared in the same style, and this has caused confusion about all of the 'lion' dogs described throughout history.

THE POODLE CLIP

The Continental Clip remains the classic cut for show Poodles. In this 'Lion' style, the hindquarters and hind legs are sheared to create bracelets at the hocks, with pompons permissible on the hips. The tail is sheared, leaving a pompon at the end. The forelegs are shaved to elbow level, forming a bracelet above the foot. The muzzle, throat, and cheeks are also sheared, but hair on the ears is left long. The remainder of the coat is kept full but can be lightly contoured to create a balanced form. Another accepted style for show is the very similar English Saddle Clip. It differs from the Continental Clip only in that the hindquarters are covered with short hair and the hind legs are shaved at the stifle and hock joints. Poodles up to one year old can be shown in the Puppy Clip, in which the muzzle, throat, and feet are shaved, and the tail is sheared, except for a pompon on the tip. The rest of the coat is left long but may be shaped. The topknot can be shaped, left free, or held by bands in all of these clips.

Corded Poodle

Miniature Poodles

Standard Poodle

Toy Poodle

Characteristics

General appearance: alert and active, with smooth, springy trot. Impression of elegance and pride.

Height: under F.C.I. standards, 46 to 55 cm (18 to 21¾ in.) for the Standard Poodle. Elsewhere, at least 38 cm (15 in.). Under Canadian standards, the ideal weight for the Miniature Poodle is 38 cm (15 in.) or less; for the Toy Poodle, 25.4 cm (10 in.) or less.

Weight: under F.C.I. standards, 20 kg (44 lb) for the Standard Poodle. Elsewhere, not specified.

Head: long, fine, with slight peak. Skull oval. Brow not prominent. Broad frontal groove between eyes. Moderate stop. Muzzle long, elegant, not pointed. Nose sharp, black in white, grey, black, and apricot dogs; brown in brown or dark brown dogs.

Eyes: almond-shaped and bright. Black or dark brown in white, grey, black, and apricot dogs; dark amber in brown dogs.

Ears: long, wide, flat, hanging close to head. Long, wavy hair.

Neck: long, solid. Head carried high. No dewlap.

Body: longer than height at withers. Shoulders well muscled and sloping. Ribs rounded. Chest deep. Brisket let down. Back short, slightly hollowed behind withers. Broad, muscular loin. Rounded croup.

Tail: set high, customarily docked.

Forequarters: legs straight, parallel, well muscled.

Hindquarters: thighs muscular. Legs parallel. Well-bent stifles. Hocks well let down. No dewclaws.

Feet: small, oval. Toes compact, arched, webbed. Pads hard and thick. Nails black or brown according to dog's colour.

Coat: skin supple and pigmented according to coat colour. Characteristic frizzy coat, clipped or left hanging in tight curls of varying lengths (corded). Hair dense, fine, with woolly, harsh texture.

Colour: all solid colours.

Faults: nose hooked or discoloured. Overshot or undershot mouth. Light eyes. Flat feet. White nails. Aggressiveness. Any signs of dwarfism in the small poodle breeds.

Practical information: The animated Poodle adores human company and dislikes solitude. Nonetheless, it is sensitive and nervous and may sometimes develop minor personality problems. The Poodle has a long life expectancy—often surpassing the age of 15 years—but frequently suffers in its later years from disorders of the eyes, skin, heart, or cerebro-vascular system. Its diet should be controlled according to the dog's size. It should be brushed several times a week and clipped every month or two. The ears must be cleaned regularly and the hair that grows inside them should be removed. The Poodle puppy's tail is docked at birth to two-thirds its length in Toys and Miniatures and to half its length in Standard dogs. The tail is not docked in corded dogs.

Pug

Mopse

The origin of the Pug's name is unknown. It may derive from *pugnus*, the Latin word for fist, which its profile is said to resemble. The most likely explanation, however, is that it stems from an old English word that was used as a term of endearment to describe pets, and particularly pet monkeys.

The Pug's appearance could be described as comical: a squat body and a wrinkled black face that seems to be covered with soot. But the ungainly little dog won many hearts in the fashionable salons of eighteenth- and nineteenth-century Europe and Great Britain.

This breed had a long history in the Orient, and its image, almost identical to today's dog, can be seen on the fragile porcelain of Chinese antiquity. Brought to the West by merchants trading with China, it had become well known in Holland by the sixteenth century. King Henry II of France found his Pugs more entertaining than the royal clowns. For many years the favourite pet of Spanish royal children, it was portrayed in a number of celebrated paintings by the Old Masters.

The Pug reached the height of its popularity during the Victorian period and its stocky little form became a familiar sight as scores of pottery figurines were fashioned in its likeness.

Traditionally a companion to nobility and the wealthy, the Pug is now enjoying a well-deserved come-back. Extremely clever and mischievous, it makes an amusing companion. But it can also be gluttonous, sulky, and distant with strangers, to the point of showing outright hostility.

AUS.	CAN.	S. AF.	U.K.	F.C.I.
●	●	●	●	●

ORIGINS

The Pug's ancestry is a matter of controversy. Once thought to have come from Holland, it is now widely believed to be a smooth-coated and long-legged cousin of the Pekingese that flourished in China for many hundreds of years. But some claim it is a miniature variety of the Dogue de Bordeaux, and others say it is the product of Bulldog crosses. The breed standard was established soon after the formation of the Pug Dog Club in Britain, in 1883. It remains virtually unchanged today.

FAMOUS PUGS

Since its arrival in Europe and Britain, the charming and devoted Pug has been the preferred pet of many royal houses.

Legend has it that the life of a Dutch prince was saved one night when his brave Pug warned of the approach of enemy assassins. William III brought a collection of Pugs with him from Holland when he ascended the British throne late in the seventeenth century. In France it became the favourite of both Madame de Pompadour and Marie Antoinette.

One of the best known Pugs was *Fortune*, pet of the Empress Josephine. The dog was Josephine's constant companion and was accustomed to sleeping at the foot of her bed at night. Much to the Emperor Napoleon's consternation, it refused to leave. The obstinate animal showed its displeasure with Napoleon by biting him on the leg, thus gaining a certain notoriety. Josephine, still enchanted with her little dogs, consoled herself with their company during Napoleon's imprisonment.

The touching loyalty of the Pug which belonged to the French Duc d'Enghien illustrates one of the best qualities of the breed. Witness to its master's execution, it was inconsolable and remained for hours at the site of the tragedy. More recently, the collection of Pugs which travelled virtually everywhere with the Duke and Duchess of Windsor became a familiar sight.

Characteristics

General appearance: a solid, compact dog with a square shape. Normal proportions with hard, well-developed muscles.

Height: under F.C.I. standards, 30 to 35 cm (11⅞ to 13¾ in.). Elsewhere, not specified.

Weight: 6.4 to 8.2 kg (14 to 18 lb).

Head: massive, solid, round but not apple-headed. Lined with broad, deep wrinkles. Skull has no indentation. Muzzle short, square, and blunt, not turned up.

Eyes: large, round, prominent, protruding. Dark, lustrous, with gentle expression but fiery when excited.

Ears: set high, small and fine, soft as velvet. Rose-eared or button-eared, with the latter preferred. Flap folded forward.

Neck: short, slightly arched, blending into body.

Body: short, stocky, square. Brisket broad. Ribs deep and rounded.

Tail: high, curled tightly over hip. Double curl is considered perfect.

Forequarters: legs muscular, straight, and well under body.

Hindquarters: muscular. Legs straight, of moderate length, well under body, and very strong.

Feet: neither long nor rounded. Toes well separated. Black nails.

Coat: short, fine, smooth, and glossy hair. Neither hard nor woolly.

Colour: silver, apricot fawn, or black. Colour must be well defined to contrast with black mask and ears. Black moles on cheeks. Black thumb-mark or diamond on forehead. Black line or trace along back from occiput to tail.

Faults: too leggy or lean. Legs too short or body too long. Light bone structure.

THE PUG'S TAIL

The tail, composed of several small vertebrae, forms the final length of the spine. Characteristic of the Pug is its unusual coiled tail. Known as a curled tail, it forms a single or double spiral that is held tightly back over the hip. The double curl is considered to be ideal.

Practical information: The Pug does not tolerate heat well and has a tendency to catch cold; it should be dried briskly, if wet. Its delicate eyes are prone to frequent 'weeping,' and its short, fine coat should regularly be given a vigorous brushing. The Pug is also subject to gastric problems when overfed.

Puli

Hungarian Puli

N ow the most popular breed in Hungary, the Puli served for centuries as a sheep-dog on the plains of the Puszta region.

This dog's dense and shaggy coat is perfectly adapted for extremes of weather. Its distinctive, corded appearance results from the natural tangling of a fine-haired undercoat and long, coarse outer coat.

The Puli's lively disposition is complemented by its quick and bouncy gait. A courageous guard, the Puli also makes an affectionate and loyal companion. But it is rather independent by nature and may occasionally be obstinate.

AUS.	CAN.	S. AF.	U.K.	F.C.I.
●	●	●	●	●

ORIGINS

Descended from the Persian Shepherd or the ancient Asian Shepherd, the Puli came to Hungary with the Magyars of central Asia during the Mongol invasion, about 1,000 years ago. Brought to the United States in 1930, it was recognized in 1936.

Characteristics

General appearance: sturdy, muscular, and wiry. Active and nimble.

Height: 40.6 to 45.7 cm (16 to 18 in.) for the adult dog; 36.8 to 40.6 cm (14½ to 16 in.) for the bitch. Under Canadian standards, 35.6 to 40.6 cm (14 to 16 in.) for the bitch.

Weight: 13 to 15 kg (28½ to 33 lb) for the adult dog; 10 to 13 kg (22 to 28½ lb) for the bitch. Under Canadian standards, 12.7 to 15 kg (28 to 33 lb) for the adult dog; 10 to 12.7 kg (22 to 28 lb) for the bitch.

Head: small and fine. Slightly domed skull. Short, straight muzzle. Well-defined stop. Prominent brow. Nose large and black. Scissor bite.

Eyes: lively, dark brown. Black eyelids.

Ears: medium size, V-shaped, wide, drooping.

Neck: muscular, medium length. Appears to merge with shoulders. Held at 45-degree angle.

Body: oblique shoulders. Back of moderate length. Short, broad loin. Belly slightly tucked up. Ribs rounded. Deep, broad chest. Short, sloping croup.

Tail: tightly curled over croup and loin. Hardly distinguishable from the coat. Medium length.

Forequarters: legs long and straight, parallel when viewed from the front. Elbows tight.

Hindquarters: long, well muscled, strong. Stifles well bent. Hocks set low. Wide pelvis.

Feet: short, round, tight. Hind feet longer. Black or slate-grey nails. Elastic pads.

Coat: long, coarse outer coat; dense, fluffy undercoat. The entangled coats create narrow, tightly interwoven, rope-like cords. Shorter hair on head and feet.

Colour: under F.C.I. and Canadian standards, black, reddish black, grey, and white. Elsewhere, apricot is also permissible.

Faults: too tall or short. Tail carried low. Combed coat or excessive matting and felting. Pale brown eyes.

Practical information: The Puli is not suitable as an indoor pet. It does not need to be brushed or bathed.

Pyrenean Mountain Dog

Great Pyrenees

AUS.	CAN.	S. AF.	U.K.	F.C.I.
•	•	•	•	•

The splendid white coat of the Pyrenean Mountain Dog attests to its past as a guard of livestock in the chilly pastures of the Pyrenees.

Though its kindly expression makes it appear lethargic, the Mountain Dog is alert and quick-witted. For hundreds of years, these powerful dogs served as sentries on French estates.

The Mountain Dog is gentle, obedient, and affectionate, but is not suited to life indoors.

ORIGINS

The Tibetan Mastiff, brought to Europe from Asia, is the ancestor of the Mountain Dog. The great white dogs remained isolated in the Pyrenees for centuries, although a few puppies became French court dogs. The first standard for the breed was set in 1907.

Characteristics

General appearance: immense and strong.
Height: 70 to 81 cm (28 to 32 in.). Under Canadian standards, 68 to 81 cm (27 to 32 in.).
Weight: 50 to 57 kg (110 to 125 lb). Under Canadian standards, 45 to 57 cm (100 to 125 lb).
Head: large, wedge-shaped. Black flews. Black nose.
Eyes: amber-brown. Tight, dark eyelids.
Ears: at eye level. Small, triangular, close to head.
Neck: strong, rather short, slight dewlap.

Body: powerful. Broad, level back. Sloping croup.
Tail: long, slightly curled tip. Well plumed.
Forequarters: legs straight and well feathered.
Hindquarters: well feathered. Double dew-claws.
Feet: short, compact. Toes slightly arched.
Coat: long, thick, coarse. Straight or slightly wavy.
Colour: white; white with badger, grey, or tan patches on head, ears, base of tail, some spots on body.
Faults: too heavy or light. Tail thin or carried badly.

Practical information: The Mountain Dog should be brushed regularly and bathed several times a year.

237

Pyrenean Sheep-dog

Pyrenean Shepherd Dog
Berger des Pyrénées

AUS.	CAN.	S. AF.	U.K.	F.C.I.
		●	●	●

This smallest of the French sheep-dogs, with its mischievous chestnut eyes, resembles a little brown bear. Valiant and sure-footed, these dogs served in the First World War as guards and scouts for wounded soldiers.

The faithful Sheep-dog makes a trusty watch-dog, but its independent nature requires discipline tempered with affection from its owner.

ORIGINS

The Pyrenean Sheep-dog has long led a close existence with its larger herding partner, the Pyrenean Mountain Dog. Its numbers were greatly reduced in the First World War, but the breed recovered and was recognized in 1926.

Characteristics

General appearance: alert and active, giving the impression of great energy in a small size.
Height: 40 to 48 cm (15¾ to 19 in.) for the adult dog; 38 to 46 cm (15 to 18 in.) for the bitch.
Weight: under F.C.I. standards, 8 to 15 kg (17½ to 33 lb). Elsewhere, not specified.
Head: skull nearly flat, curving gracefully on sides. Stop not visible. Muzzle wedge-shaped. Black nose.
Eyes: dark brown, expressive. Eyelids thin, lined with black. Wall-eyes in harlequin and merle dogs.
Ears: fairly short and broad at base, set well apart at top of skull. Must not be erect.
Neck: rather long, well muscled, moving freely from shoulders.
Body: brisket descends to elbow. Long back. Loins short and slightly arched. Croup short and sloping.

Tail: well feathered, forming ring at tip. Often docked. Carried no higher than topline when dog is active.
Forequarters: legs thin, sinewy, and feathered.
Hindquarters: thighs prominent. Hocks lean, set on low, rather close. Single or double dew-claws.
Feet: oval, fairly flat. Small nails covered with hair.
Coat: long, thick, fairly straight or slightly wavy. Thicker on croup and thighs, shorter on muzzle. Swept back on face. Must not cover eyes.
Colour: tawny, solid or with black, occasionally with white on chest and feet; fairly light merle, with white on head, chest, and feet; harlequin of various shades; black with white patches rare. Solid colours preferred.
Faults: head too short, long, or narrow. Domed skull. Muzzle too long or square. Frizzy coat. Tail carried incorrectly. Erect ears.

Practical information: The robust and healthy Sheep-dog must be brushed regularly to prevent eczema.

Rhodesian Ridgeback

AUS.	CAN.	S. AF.	U.K.	F.C.I.
●	●	●	●	●

The Rhodesian Ridgeback, despite its name, hails not from Zimbabwe but from South Africa, and is the only recognized breed to have originated there. The distinctive ridge on its back is unique to this breed: hair growing in the opposite direction to the rest of the coat creates a prominent crest along the centre of the back.

In their native land, Ridgebacks are fearless hunters of lions and other big game. They track their quarry in packs, instilling panic in the animal and driving it towards the hunter with repeated feints.

The good-natured and trainable Ridgeback is a fine pet for families who enjoy large dogs.

ORIGINS

The Ridgeback is descended from a hunting-dog native to South Africa. This courageous hunter passed on its cunning as well as its characteristic 'ridge.' European pioneers brought the Ridgeback to Rhodesia and crossed it with the Great Dane and other strong breeds. The standard for the dog was set in 1922.

Characteristics

General appearance: a handsome, muscular dog.
Height: 63.5 to 68.6 cm (25 to 27 in.) for the adult dog; 61 to 66 cm (24 to 26 in.) for the bitch.
Weight: 34 to 36.3 kg (75 to 80 lb) for the adult dog; 29.5 to 31.7 kg (65 to 70 lb) for the bitch.
Head: long, deep muzzle. Nose black or brown.
Eyes: round, set well apart, dark or amber.
Ears: set high, carried close to head.

Neck: fairly long, powerful. No dewlap.
Body: muscular. Sloping shoulders. Deep chest.
Tail: strong, tapering. Carried in slight upward curve.
Forequarters: straight, strong legs.
Hindquarters: legs muscular. Hocks set on low.
Feet: compact. Well-arched toes. Pads tough, elastic.
Coat: short, dense, sleek, and glossy hair.
Colour: light to red wheaten, solid or some white.

Practical information: The Ridgeback should be brushed regularly and bathed once a year.

Rottweiler

With its broad chest and lean, muscular body, the Rottweiler gives the impression of great power. It is supple and athletic, despite its relatively large stature, and its quick trot enables it to reach astonishing speeds. This tough and rugged dog is accustomed to a life of outdoor work and can endure any climate or weather.

The Rottweiler makes a formidable guard dog, and when trained to attack and defend, it can be dangerous to intruders. Though easily trained, it must have a disciplinarian master who can earn its respect and obedience. Confident of its own strength, the Rottweiler is not suspicious or wary by nature but will react swiftly when confronted with potential danger. It displays a natural aloofness, except towards its master and his family, and does not tolerate excessive handling by strangers. But it should never be vicious.

Mobilized during the First World War, the Rottweiler served admirably as an auxiliary to the German army. It is a hard-working breed and today does duty as a guard dog for factories and businesses. In Austria, it is also employed as a police dog.

The Rottweiler is a remarkably alert and intelligent animal; indeed, it is said that this dog can remember all it has been taught. Its tranquil expression reveals both courage and devotion. A calm temperament makes the Rottweiler an agreeable pet in a family setting, where it will gently protect the children of the household.

AUS.	CAN.	S. AF.	U.K.	F.C.I.
●	●	●	●	●

ORIGINS

The Rottweiler is widely believed to be descended from the Molossian Mastiff, an enormous dog, originally from the Orient, which crossed the Alps with invading Roman legions. These powerful animals acted as guard dogs and herded cattle which accompanied the armies. Some dogs were left behind as the Romans continued on their march through Europe. These cattle dogs later spread through the Alps region and even farther afield, eventually reaching the little German market town of Rottweil. There they bred with local shepherd dogs to produce the Rottweiler. The first of these dogs arrived in North America in the early 1930s, and in Britain in 1936. By 1966, the breed was numerous enough to be recognized.

THE BUTCHER'S PAL

The Rottweiler owes its name to the village of Rottweil in the cattle-producing area of Württemberg in Germany. Hundreds of years ago, Rottweil was a prosperous market centre for grain and livestock. The butchers of Rottweil travelled the region's rough country roads with large herds of cattle and considerable sums of money. They needed a strong and trusty dog to drive their herds and accompany them on cattle-buying trips.

Highway bandits were a very real hazard in those days, and the powerful Rottweiler, with its forbidding appearance, offered protection against robbery. To guard their money, the butchers fastened their leather purses to collars around the dogs' massive necks. The Rottweiler's courage, intelligence, and vigilance made it the perfect companion for these dangerous journeys through the countryside. It became known as the 'Butcher's Dog of Rottweil' and flourished for centuries.

By the end of the last century livestock was increasingly being transported by rail, and the Rottweiler was no longer in demand as a herder. The breed entered a period of sad decline; by 1900, only one female dog could be found in Rottweil.

The breed was saved when a growing interest in unusual dogs prompted renewed appreciation of the Rottweiler's many fine qualities. It proved to be easy to train, hard-working, and very clever, making it an ideal police dog and guard. Today it plays both these roles in Germany, Austria, and many English-speaking countries. Some of these dogs are also used to control street demonstrations. In Brazil, where the breed is popular, it participates in parachute exercises with the armed forces.

Characteristics

General appearance: a solid, powerful dog of above-average height. Well proportioned and compact in build, it displays strength, suppleness, and endurance. Male dogs are bigger and heavier, with a distinctly masculine appearance.

Height: 58.4 to 68.6 cm (23 to 27 in.) for the adult dog; 53.3 to 63.5 cm (21 to 25 in.) for the bitch.

Weight: under F.C.I. standards, 50 kg (110 lb). Elsewhere, not specified.

Head: medium length. Skull broad between the ears. Forehead moderately arched. Well-defined stop. Cheeks well muscled. Fairly deep muzzle. Skin on head can form wrinkles when dog is attentive but should not be loose. Wide black nose with large nostrils. Firm black flews. Powerful scissor bite.

Eyes: of medium size, rather deep-set, almond-shaped, dark brown.

Ears: small, triangular, pendent, set high and wide apart. Inner edge of ear lies close to cheek.

Neck: robust, very muscular, slightly arched. No dewlap.

Body: long, sloping shoulders. Broad and roomy chest with well-developed sternum. Ribs well sprung.

Firm, straight back. Short, deep, and powerful loin. Wide, slightly sloping croup of medium length.

Tail: short and strong, carried horizontally. Customarily docked close to body.

Forequarters: legs straight, strongly developed, and not close together. Elbows tight.

Hindquarters: broad, well-muscled thighs. Hind legs long and robust, strong at top and sinewy lower down. Powerfully angulated hocks. Fairly well-bent stifles. No dew-claws.

Feet: round and compact. Toes well arched. Hind feet somewhat longer than the front. Hard pads. Short, dark, powerful nails.

Coat: coarse, flat, thick outer coat of medium length. Fine undercoat must not show through. Longer hair on feet, backs of legs.

Colour: black, with brown markings on cheeks, muzzle, chest, feet, over the eyes, and beneath tail.

Faults: too light or heavy. Long or curly coat. White markings. Sway or roach back. Hocks turned in or out. Abnormal hip joints. Poor bite. Missing molars or premolars. Ectropion, entropion, or slack eyelids. Eyes yellow or blue. Nervousness or viciousness.

Practical information: The hardy Rottweiler enjoys solid health. Bred for a life of work in the outdoors, it needs considerable exercise and activity; the dog's character will suffer if it is chained. Its coat must be brushed frequently and vigorously. It must receive an adequate diet to maintain proper weight, but care must be taken to avoid overfeeding.

Saint Bernard

Alpine Mastiff

AUS.	CAN.	S. AF.	U.K.	F.C.I.
●	●	●	●	●

ORIGINS

Originally a short-haired dog, the Saint Bernard is descended from the Molossian Mastiff. The monks of the ancient Hospice du Grand Saint Bernard high in the Swiss Alps began breeding dogs in the seventeenth century, intending them for work as guards and mountain guides. The Hospice offered refuge to travellers forced to find their way over the avalanche-ridden mountains, and it was natural that the great dogs would develop a talent for rescue. A long-haired variety was bred in the nineteenth century. The Saint Bernard was recognized in 1865, and in 1887 a congress in Zurich set the breed standard.

The heroic Saint Bernard carrying a cask of brandy around its neck is an image familiar to all. Since it began its rescue work in the treacherous Alps more than two hundred years ago, the Saint Bernard has saved more than 2,500 lost or injured travellers.

Gifted with extraordinary senses of smell and direction and an uncanny ability to detect approaching storms and avalanches, the Saint Bernard was once the only breed dedicated to mountain rescue. Sure-footed and confident, it can navigate perilous mountain paths and icy slopes, find its way through impenetrable fog, and detect a person buried under deep snow. And legends abound of the Saint Bernard bringing half-frozen victims back to life with the warmth of its own body.

The Saint Bernard's special task of mountain rescue is being taken over by other trained breeds, such as the German Shepherd. Now the Saint Bernard is increasingly sought after as a companion dog and is particularly popular in North America.

With its docile character, thick bear-like coat, and benevolent expression, the Saint Bernard holds a special appeal for many. Cheerful and loyal, it adapts readily to family life. It even submits patiently to the teasing of children. In fact, its gentle and unassuming nature makes one forget its enormous size.

AN INTERNATIONAL HERO

Barry, a Saint Bernard born in 1800, brought the breed great renown and spurred its development in the nineteenth century. Barry (meaning 'bear' in a dialect of Germany) rescued 40 people during its 12 years of work, and its exploits became the talk of Europe.

Barry died in Berne in 1814 after a life of devoted service. To commemorate this courageous dog, its mounted form is displayed in the natural history museum of Berne, and the best male Saint Bernards raised at the Hospice have since borne its name. Several of Barry's descendants have also gained renown for their mountain rescue skills, but their fates have been tragic: Barry II disappeared in a mountain crevasse in 1905, and Barry III died after a fall.

Characteristics

General appearance: a tall, muscular dog with a powerful build and an intelligent, kindly expression.

Height: under F.C.I. and Canadian standards, no less than 70 cm (27½ in.) for the adult dog and 65 cm (25½ in.) for the bitch. Elsewhere, not specified.

Weight: under F.C.I. standards, 55 to 60 kg (121 to 132 lb). Elsewhere, not specified.

Head: powerful. Skull massive, wide, curved towards high cheekbones. Flat cheeks. Prominent brow. Muzzle short, square at end, straight and broad from nose to stop. Pronounced, abrupt stop. Upper flews well developed and drooping. Strong scissor bite. Large black nose with wide nostrils. Pronounced wrinkles over eyes.

Eyes: dark brown. Drooping lower eyelids.

Ears: medium size, set rather high, lying close to cheeks. Slightly rounded triangular flap.

Neck: long, thick, and powerful. Pronounced dewlap.

Body: shoulders wide, oblique, muscular, powerful. Deep, wide, well-arched chest. Rounded ribs. Broad, straight back. Gently sloping croup.

Tail: long, very heavy, powerful tip. Carried low when at rest, raised during activity or excitement.

Forequarters: straight, powerful legs.

Hindquarters: well developed. Very muscular thighs and legs. Hocks well bent.

Feet: large and broad. Strong, well-arched toes. No dew-claws.

Coat: very thick. Long-haired variety has smooth or slightly wavy coat; short-haired coat is dense and flat. Longer on tail and thighs, wavier on back and between haunches and croup, short and soft on muzzle and ears.

Colour: white with various shades of red or brindle, with white on chest, forelegs, feet, tail tip, muzzle, top of head, collar; black shadings on face and ears.

Faults: light-coloured or split nose. Overshot or undershot mouth. Pointed muzzle. Wedge-shaped head. Flat skull. Ears badly set, poorly carried, or too feathered. Short neck. Curly coat. Hollow or roach back. Ring tail. Open feet or hare-footed. Cow hocks or straight hocks. Fawn or solid colour.

Practical information: The Saint Bernard is a fit, vigorous dog which needs a great deal of space and activity. Like all large dogs, it grows rapidly, and the young Saint Bernard must have a careful diet. A weekly brushing and an occasional bath will keep its coat in good condition. But the use of shampoo, which can destroy the coat's protective oils, should be avoided. Saint Bernards have sensitive eyes, can develop skin problems, and face a risk of hip dysplasia.

Saluki

Gazelle Hound, Persian Greyhound, Arabian Hound

AUS.	CAN.	S. AF.	U.K.	F.C.I.
●	●	●	●	●

The Saluki, a member of the greyhound family, is one of the oldest known breeds of dog and has remained virtually unchanged for thousands of years. A favourite of the Islamic sheikhs and tribal chieftains of North Africa, the Middle East, and Asia Minor, it is known as 'the noble one.' Long considered a gift from God, the Saluki is so highly prized by its Muslim owners that it is never sold, but is offered only as a gift of friendship or homage.

All admirers of beauty are won over by the Saluki's elegant lines and gentle, strangely sad expression. Bright almond-shaped eyes fringed with black, one of its most attractive features, also give it extraordinary sight for hunting. Its silky coat and slenderness conceal remarkable strength and tenaciousness. It is said the Saluki's appearance so enchanted the Pharaoh Antef that he enshrined his pet in his own tomb to have its spirit accompany him into the afterlife.

The Saluki is a brilliant desert hunter. Bred for speed and cunning to hunt with falcons and to course gazelle, fox, and hare, it can race over the most rugged terrain. Even today, desert tribes frequently own a number of Salukis, carrying them behind the saddle or by camel to keep their feet from burning on the scorching earth.

As wild game continues to disappear from desert sands, the sleek and graceful Saluki will become increasingly rare in its ancient homelands. Current breeding programmes in the West are paying particular attention to preserving the special qualities of this breed.

ORIGINS

The Saluki may be the oldest extant breed of domesticated dog, with a bloodline that has remained nearly pure throughout the ages—as much as 9,000 years. The breed is believed to have originated in Syria, later making its way to the rest of the Middle East and India and Afghanistan. Egyptian tomb paintings of thousands of years ago portray dogs remarkably like those we know today. Another greyhound, the Afghan, is probably closely related. Saluki puppies arrived in Britain in 1895, but not until after the First World War did the breed become popular. It was officially recognized in Britain in 1923.

DESERT HUNTING

A few active hunting Salukis can still be found in the modern Arab world. Much like thoroughbred horses, and falcons, these graceful dogs are reserved for ceremonial hunts, or as a sign of wealth and culture. While these prized dogs are sometimes carried by horse or camel to the hunting grounds, they are also transported over long distances in a style befitting their status—in cars or all-terrain vehicles.

Often accompanied by a falcon, the Salukis are used for hunting hare and the increasingly scarce gazelle. Like the falcon, its keen eyesight is more important for hunting than is its sense of smell. When a falcon spots quarry, it circles above the animal, frightening it into the open so the swift Saluki can give chase. This traditional sport is on the decline in modern Arabia.

Characteristics

General appearance: a strong and agile dog which gives the impression of grace, symmetry, and endurance. Displays speed and strength necessary to chase gazelle and other swift game over desert sand or rocky terrain. Noble and friendly expression with gentle, far-seeing glance.

Height: 58.4 to 71 cm (23 to 28 in.).

Weight: under F.C.I. standards, 14 to 25 kg (31 to 55 lb). Elsewhere, not specified.

Head: long and narrow. Skull wide between ears, not domed. Pronounced occipital crest. Slight stop. Nose black or liver. Strong teeth with scissor bite.

Eyes: oval and large, but not prominent. Luminous. Dark to hazel.

Ears: long, mobile, hanging close to head. Covered with long, silky hair.

Neck: long, supple, and muscular.

Body: shoulders sloping and set well back, muscular, but not coarse. Deep and somewhat narrow chest.

Broad back with muscles slightly arched over loin. Wide, strong hips showing prominent hip bones set well apart. Belly tucked up.

Tail: long, set low, and carried in natural curve. Underside well feathered with long, silky hair.

Forequarters: legs straight and long from elbows to wrists.

Hindquarters: thighs well muscled. Stifles moderately bent. Hocks low to ground. Legs display running and jumping power.

Feet: moderately long, supple, strong. Well feathered between toes. Toes long, well arched, not splayed.

Coat: smooth, soft, silky. Slight feathering on legs and backs of thighs. Occasionally a slight woolly feathering on thighs and shoulders. Smooth variety has no feathering.

Colour: white, cream, fawn, golden, red, grizzle, black and tan, tricolour (black, white, and tan), or variations of these colours.

Practical information: A rugged desert hunting-dog, the Saluki is accustomed to heat and open country. It adjusts easily to life as a house-dog but must have the opportunity to run freely; it should never be chained up. Its diet—a mixture of meat and vegetables—must be balanced to ensure that this lean and muscular dog does not become overweight. It needs little drinking water. The Saluki's silky coat is easy to groom: the feathering on the tail, legs, and thighs is untangled with a fine-tooth comb; a soft brush is used over the rest of the body.

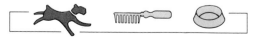

Samoyed

This rugged spitz breed has a magnificent white coat to protect it against the bitter climate in which it originated. So thick and warm is its coat that Siberian tribes often wove it into outer garments. For centuries the Samoyed lived cooperatively with man on the deserted Arctic steppes, earning the distinction of being one of the earliest domesticated animals of the north.

Bred for the arduous work of sled-dog and reindeer herder, the powerful Samoyed is known for its great endurance.

The Samoyed's master must be energetic and a disciplinarian, for this dog is quite independent by nature. Contrary to unfounded opinion, the friendly and intelligent Samoyed is not dangerous; it will attack only when driven by starvation or self-preservation.

AUS.	CAN.	S. AF.	U.K.	F.C.I.
●	●	●	●	●

ORIGINS

The Samoyed, descended from the ancestors of European spitz breeds, was named after the Samoyedes, a tribe in north-east Siberia. Fur traders dealing in sable pelts brought it to Britain late in the nineteenth century. Both Nansen and Scott used the sturdy Samoyed on their polar expeditions. Its thick, white coat was originally a variety of colours.

Characteristics

General appearance: a strong and active dog.
Height: 50.8 to 56 cm (20 to 22 in.) for the adult dog; 40.6 to 50.8 cm (16 to 20 in.) for the bitch. Under Canadian standards, 45.7 to 50.8 cm (18 to 20 in.) for bitches.
Weight: under F.C.I. standards, 20 to 30 kg (44 to 66 lb). Elsewhere, not specified.
Head: powerful, wedge-shaped. Wide, flat skull. Well-defined stop. Nose black or brown. Strong, level jaws.
Eyes: dark, almond-shaped. Eye rims black.

Ears: thick, erect, rounded, covered inside with hair.
Neck: strong, round, muscular, arched.
Body: well muscled. Chest deep and wide. Ribs well sprung. Broad, strong back of medium length.
Tail: long and profuse.
Forequarters: legs long, straight, and muscular.
Hindquarters: very muscular. Stifles well angulated.
Feet: long, fairly spread out. Pads covered with hair.
Coat: coarse, straight hair. Legs well feathered.
Colour: pure white, white and biscuit, biscuit, cream.

Practical information: The Samoyed adapts poorly to city life. Its dense coat must be brushed each day.

Schipperke

Barge Dog

As early as the fifteenth century, a tailless, mischievous black dog was described as 'the incarnation of the devil.' To those who know it, this could only be the Schipperke.

By 1700, Belgian craftsmen were displaying their Schipperkes in Sunday 'beauty contests.' These dogs were adorned with intricate brass chokers designed to prevent damage to their elegant neck ruffs.

The Schipperke was the most popular housedog in Belgium by the late nineteenth century, and was also a favourite companion of the boatmen whose barges plied the canals of Belgium and Holland. Lively and curious, the Schipperke is also suspicious of strangers, making it a fine guard dog.

AUS.	CAN.	S. AF.	U.K.	F.C.I.
●	●	●	●	●

ORIGINS

The Schipperke is thought to have descended from either the Leuvenaar, a black sheep-dog native to Belgium and now probably extinct, or the spitz family of northern dogs. Its name seems to derive from the Flemish word for 'little boatman.' Recognized in 1882, this breed is now more popular in Britain and South Africa than in its native land.

Characteristics

General appearance: a short, compact, active dog. Its expression is sharp, lively, and questioning, not mean or wild.

Height: not specified.

Weight: under F.C.I. standards, 3 to 5 kg (6½ to 11 lb). Elsewhere, 5.4 to 7.3 kg (12 to 16 lb).

Head: small, foxlike. Slight stop. Small black nose.

Eyes: dark brown, oval.

Ears: triangular, set high. Carried erect.

Neck: short, strong, full, and broad on shoulders.

Body: stocky. Deep chest. Short, level back.

Tail: customarily docked to no more than 3 cm (1 in.).

Forequarters: legs straight and well under body.

Hindquarters: powerful. Well-developed thighs.

Feet: small, catlike, tight. Short, straight nails.

Coat: abundant, harsh hair. Mane around neck, frill between forelegs, and culotte on backs of thighs.

Colour: preferably black.

Faults: ears not erect. Thin mane or culotte. A light-coloured eye. White spots.

Practical information: The solid little Schipperke enjoys excellent health. It should be brushed regularly.

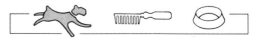

Schnauzer

Giant Schnauzer

I n German, *Schnauze* means 'muzzle,' and no name better suits this bushy-haired dog with its full moustache.

Oldest of the three Schnauzer breeds is the medium-size Standard dog. Centuries ago, this dog would accompany stage-coaches through the forests of Germany, trotting tirelessly beside the horses. It was an efficient ratter and was prized for ridding stables of vermin.

The Standard Schnauzer has been depicted in some of Europe's finest artworks. One of the earliest known representations is a statue of a watchman with lantern in hand, accompanied by his faithful dog. Both Albrecht Dürer and Lucas Cranach the Elder portrayed it in paintings and tapestries.

Clever and animated, the Standard Schnauzer is easy to instruct, and trainers find it an agreeable dog to work with. However, the dog's high spirits demand that its owner be energetic and forceful. While it is a pleasing pet, fond of children and play, the Schnauzer can occasionally be obstinate and fussy. Left outdoors on its own, it will instinctively hunt rats and other rodents.

The Giant Schnauzer is stronger and more robust than the Standard dog. A fine watch-dog, it was used to drive cattle for hundreds of years until the advent of rail transport. Though calm and quiet, the Giant Schnauzer can have a wilful temperament. It needs disciplined training.

The Miniature Schnauzer is a tiny replica of the Standard. Affectionate, obedient, and an alert guard, the Miniature makes an ideal, small companion dog.

AUS.	CAN.	S. AF.	U.K.	F.C.I.
●	●	●	●	●

ORIGINS

The Standard Schnauzer may have resulted from a cross between two extinct breeds, the Beaver Dog of the Middle Ages and a rough-coated ratting dog, or it may be descended from shepherd dogs. Whatever its origins, it probably arose in the livestock-herding regions of Württemberg and Bavaria in Germany. In 1879, it was presented at the Hanover dog show, and the breed standard was drawn up the following year. It became popular in Britain after the First World War and later in the United States. The Giant Schnauzer made its first official appearance in Munich in 1909 and won instant favour. But the breed had almost died out before it was selected for police training and service in the First World War. The Miniature Schnauzer emerged at the turn of the century, and the breed standard had been set by the early 1920s. Since then, this small dog has won hearts the world over.

Miniature Schnauzers

Standard Schnauzer

Characteristics

General appearance: the three breeds differ only in size. Of medium height, the robust and stocky Standard Schnauzer has a decidedly square shape. The Giant and Miniature are respectively larger and smaller replicas of the Standard.

Height: 45.7 to 50.8 cm (18 to 20 in.) for the adult Standard Schnauzer; 43.2 to 48.3 cm (17 to 19 in.) for the Standard bitch.

Weight: under F.C.I. standards, 15 kg (33 lb) for the Standard dog.

Head: long and robust. Prominent eyebrows. Muzzle ends in blunt wedge. Bristly moustache and whiskers. Black nose. Scissor bite.

Eyes: dark, oval, set forward. Eyelids tight. Arched bushy eyebrows.

Ears: set high, neat, V-shaped, dropping forward to temple. Under Canadian and F.C.I. standards, cropped and carried erect.

Neck: clean and moderately long; lean and arched. Strong nape.

Body: chest moderately wide. Back short and sinewy. Croup moderately rounded. Belly slightly raised. Flat, muscular shoulders.

Tail: high. Customarily docked near the third vertebra.

Forequarters: strong and straight, elbows set close.

Hindquarters: thighs muscular. Stifles well angled. Hocks well bent.

Feet: short and catlike. Tight, arched toes. Dark nails. Hard pads.

Coat: outer coat bushy, wiry, and thick. Undercoat dense.

Colour: black, or salt-and-pepper with a darker mask for contrast.

Faults: too heavy or light. Wrinkled forehead. Ears set low. Short muzzle. Roach or sunken back. Spotted coat.

Practical information: The two larger Schnauzer breeds make fine house-dogs but need plenty of exercise. While Schnauzers are usually robust and healthy dogs, when kept in an overheated house they can become susceptible to skin diseases. The dog's coat should be brushed and curried daily.

GROOMING A SCHNAUZER

All three Schnauzer breeds must be groomed in the same fashion.

As with the Fox Terrier, scissors and shears are used for shaping certain parts of the Schnauzer's coat and to trim hair in the ears and at the tip of the tail. Its silhouette must appear short and square when viewed from the side.

The eyebrows are kept bushy and the hair on the muzzle is only lightly trimmed. The rectangular shape of the head is accentuated by trimming the beard evenly. Hair on the tail is cut to give it a cylindrical appearance. To emphasize the dog's solid stance, the hair on the legs is left slightly longer, and then it is carefully combed.

Each dog is different and the quality of the coat varies from one animal to the next; some dogs require constant grooming, while others retain their cut for some time. Grooming should highlight the dog's best features and draw attention away from any faults. Schnauzers intended for show should be professionally groomed.

Scottish Terrier

Scottie

Tousled eyebrows, a bushy moustache and beard, and a tail that points towards the sky, give the Scottish Terrier a comical look which at the same time is quite dignified.

The Scottie's muscular body creates an impression of power that belies its small size. In its native Scotland, the stocky Terrier was used to hunt badger, fox, and vermin. Hardy and spirited, it was a true working dog.

The Scottie has lost nothing of its lively personality in its present career as a stylish companion dog. Familiar to many through the labels of Scotch whisky, the conceited and headstrong little Scottie still has a lot of character and exhibits considerable independence.

The Scottie can be very reserved—indeed, suspicious—with strangers, but it is unfailingly charming and amusing with its owners.

AUS.	CAN.	S. AF.	U.K.	F.C.I.
●	●	●	●	●

ORIGINS

The Scottie ranged the Highlands before the Roman invasion of the British Isles. At first known by various names—Skye, West Highland, and Aberdeen—it began to be called the Scottish Terrier towards the end of the nineteenth century. The first breed standard was established in 1883. The modern Scottie is the result of breeding intended to improve its appearance without affecting its hunting and working abilities.

Characteristics

General appearance: a short, sturdy, active dog. Keen, sharp expression.
Height: 25.4 to 28 cm (10 to 11 in.).
Weight: 8.6 to 10.4 kg (19 to 23 lb). Under Canadian standards, 8 to 10 kg (18 to 22 lb) for the adult dog.
Head: long. Slight stop. Large black nose.
Eyes: small, dark, almond-shaped, wide apart.
Ears: small, fine, pointed, erect. Set high.
Neck: thick and muscular. Moderate length.

Body: short. Deep, broad chest. Long, sloping shoulders. Short, level back. Deep, muscular loin.
Tail: carried high, tapering. Can have slight curve.
Forequarters: legs straight and well boned.
Hindquarters: powerful. Well-bent stifles.
Feet: round, with well-arched and close-knit toes.
Coat: undercoat soft. Outer coat long, thick, and wiry.
Colour: black, steel- or iron-grey, sandy, wheaten, grizzle, or brindle of any colour.

Practical information: The Scottie's grooming is similar to that of the Fox Terrier. Hair is not removed from the face but is combed towards the front. The area about the ears is sheared, and the leg areas are trimmed. The coat is left long on the chest and abdomen, to make the Scottie appear even closer to the ground, and is layer-cut on the tail. While a robust animal, the Scottie house-dog is prone to skin diseases and obesity.

Sealyham Terrier

Bred to ferret out badger and fox from their holes and to hunt for otter, the Sealyham Terrier has very short legs, a quick gait, steely courage, and powerful, square jaws. A magnificent beard as white as its coat gives this terrier a distinctive look.

Since the end of the last century, when the Sealyham was used mostly to kill vermin, it has become a quiet, even-tempered, and affectionate lap dog. It is still used for hunting in Wales, its land of origin, and occasionally reverts to its ratting instincts.

AUS.	CAN.	S. AF.	U.K.	F.C.I.
•	•	•	•	•

Characteristics

General appearance: a fast, powerful dog with an oblong shape.
Height: 25.4 to 30.5 cm (10 to 12 in.).
Weight: under Canadian standards, 10.4 to 11.3 kg (23 to 25 lb). Elsewhere, 9 kg (20 lb) for the adult dog; 8.2 kg (18 lb) for the bitch.
Head: slightly domed. Powerful, square jaws. Black nose.
Eyes: oval, medium size, dark. Well set, fairly wide apart.
Ears: medium size, folded; forward edge lies close to cheek.
Neck: rather long, thick, muscular, firmly set.
Body: shoulders well laid back. Deep, wide chest. Level topline.
Tail: set in line with the back, carried upright.
Forequarters: short, strong, and straight legs.
Hindquarters: powerful. Deep thighs. Hocks well let down.
Feet: round; cat-footed. Thick pads.
Coat: long, harsh, wiry outer coat and soft, dense undercoat.
Colour: white or white with lemon, tan or badger markings on the head and ears. Too much black and heavy ticking undesirable.

Practical information: The Sealyham does not tolerate heat well and is prone to eczema if kept in a hot, dry environment. It must be brushed and combed each day and groomed by a specialist.

ORIGINS

The Sealyham Terrier, which made its first appearance late in the nineteenth century, was the product of careful breeding planned by Captain John Edwardes of Pembrokeshire in Wales. The dog's name is taken from that of Edwardes' family estate. Captain Edwardes was a keen and somewhat eccentric hunter and gentleman farmer. Not satisfied with the hunting and ratting abilities of local terriers, he set about creating a tailor-made dog with exceptional courage and speed that could accompany his hounds for otter-hunting. He embarked on a strict breeding programme but left no records as to which breeds were selected. However, it is believed that the Sealyham's ancestry includes the Welsh Corgi and the Dandie Dinmont, the West Highland White, and the Bull Terrier. Captain Edwardes expected his dogs to meet harsh and cruel tests: if a pup failed to attack a live polecat or other vicious quarry, it was immediately shot. The surviving Sealyhams were thus by necessity a tough lot. In 1911 the British Kennel Club gave the breed official recognition.

Shar Pei

Chinese Shar Pei

The Shar Pei (pronounced *sharpay*) was originally used for fighting, hunting wild boar, protecting livestock, and guarding homes. It is a comparative newcomer to the Western canine community and was only recently preserved from extinction. The Shar Pei has a strange appearance. With a superabundance of folded flesh, the puppy looks as if it is wearing a suit of clothes several sizes too large. The mature animal fits into its coat more snugly. It is a medium-sized, but powerful dog, loyal, tranquil, and intelligent. It is particularly friendly with children, and has readily adapted to its modern role of companion and family dog.

AUS.	CAN.	S. AF.	U.K.	F.C.I.
●	●	●	●	●

ORIGINS

It is generally believed that the Shar Pei originated in southern China's Kwangtung province during the Han dynasty (202 B.C.-A.D. 220). Along with other dogs, many were slaughtered under the Communist regime. The breed would be extinct were it not that a few were smuggled into Hong Kong.

Characteristics

General appearance: strong, alert, active, compact, squarely built dog.
Height: 41-51 cm (16-20 in.).
Weight: 16-25 kg (35-55 lb).
Head: large in proportion to body, skull flat. Moderate stop. Fine wrinkles on forehead and cheeks. Distinctive 'square hippopotamus' muzzle. Large, broad nose.
Eyes: dark, small medium-sized. Almond-shaped. Should be free from entropion. Austere expression.
Ears: small, thick, triangular. Set forward, wide apart, and lying flat to head.

Mouth: blue-black tongue and flews.
Body: broad, deep chest. Short, strong back.
Tail: rounded, tightly curled, and set high.
Forequarters: muscular shoulders, well laid and sloping. Forelegs straight and moderate length.
Hindquarters: strong and muscular. Hocks well open and let down.
Feet: medium size, compact. Well knuckled toes.
Coat: distinctive feature loose skin. Single coat, short and bristly.
Colour: black, smoky, dark brown, beige, and cream.

Practical information: This dog's loose skin can cause problems. Common ailments include entropion of the eye, ear infections, and skin disorders.

Shetland Sheep-dog

Sheltie

AUS.	CAN.	S. AF.	U.K.	F.C.I.
•	•	•	•	•

The Shetland Sheep-dog is one of the world's most popular breeds. Although retaining its working dog instincts, it has easily adapted to modern city life. It is fast, alert, and responds well to training. It has an affectionate and loyal temperament, which makes it an ideal family pet and guard-dog. It can be aloof and shy with strangers.

ORIGINS

The Shetland Islands of Scotland were the original home of the Shetland Sheep-dog. Its ancestry includes the Rough Collie and the Icelandic Yakkie, which were later crossed with spaniels and small collies.

Characteristics

General appearance: a small, long-haired working dog, with a symmetrical and shapely appearance.
Height: 33 to 40.6 cm (13 to 16 in.). Under F.C.I. standards, not specified.
Weight: not specified.
Head: refined. Long and wedge-shaped, tapering from ears to nose. Top of skull flat. Skull and muzzle equal in length. Flat cheeks merge smoothly into well-rounded muzzle. Jaws clean and powerful. Tight lips. Teeth sound and level, evenly spaced. Scissor bite. Nose, lips, and the rims of the eyes, black.
Eyes: medium size, with dark, almond-shaped rims, set obliquely. Dark brown colour, with blue eyes in the case of merle dogs.
Ears: small and flexible. Set high and carried semi-erect, with tips dropping forward.
Neck: muscular, well arched, of sufficient length to carry head proudly.

Body: sloping shoulders. Level and strongly muscled back. Deep chest. Ribs well sprung. Slight arch at loin. Croup sloping gradually to rear.
Tail: set low, tapering. Long enough to reach hock joint. Abundant hair and slight upward sweep.
Forequarters: muscular and straight.
Hindquarters: thighs broad and muscular. Stifles well angled. Hocks well let down and straight when viewed from behind.
Feet: oval, compact. Toes well arched and tight. Deep, tough pads.
Coat: double-long, straight, harsh outer coat; short, dense, furry undercoat. Abundant mane and frill.
Colour: black, blue merle, sable, black and white, black and tan, tricolours.
Faults: coat smooth, short, flat, wavy, curly, soft, or silky. Lack of undercoat. Washed-out colours. Snipy muzzle.

Practical information: The Sheltie adjusts easily to apartment living, though it still requires moderate exercise. Daily brushing and grooming are essential.

253

Shih Tzu

With its small bewhiskered face and trailing coat the Shih Tzu resembles both the Lhasa Apso and the Pekingese.

Its feather-duster tail and long Mandarin beard give the Shih Tzu a beguiling appearance. An old Chinese standard solemnly describes the dog's sprightly gait as being 'like a goldfish.' Meaning 'lion dog' in Chinese and pronounced 'shid zoo,' this breed's name refers to its courage and to the collar of hair which surrounds its face, both reminiscent of the great cat. And, like the lion, it was considered a sacred animal in its native China.

The Shih Tzu was so revered in China that for many years after the country opened its doors to Western civilization the Chinese refused to sell, export, or give away the little dogs. Legend has it that crushed glass was occasionally fed to the rare dog that belonged to Westerners—to kill it.

It is easy to understand the passion aroused by this diminutive dog with its oddly dignified air. Fiercely loyal, and distant with strangers, the Shih Tzu loves luxury and the comforts of an apartment life. But its lively nature prevents it from adopting a life of complete leisure—it much prefers to romp and play.

AUS.	CAN.	S. AF.	U.K.	F.C.I.
●	●	●	●	●

ORIGINS

Little is known about the ancestry of the Shih Tzu. Its sacred status in China would appear to indicate very ancient origins. Though the Shih Tzu is variously thought to be Tibetan or Chinese in origin, it is generally believed to be a product of crossbreeding between the Tibetan temple dog, the Lhasa Apso, and the early Pekingese of China. The Tibetan temple dogs had been bred for centuries and were often presented to distinguished visitors as marks of high esteem. Both Tibet and China remained closed to Westerners for centuries, and there was thus no access to written evidence of the breed's development. An early reference to the Lhasa Apso appeared in the mid-seventeenth century when the Dalai Lama of Tibet offered temple dogs to the Manchurian emperors, rulers of China at the time. Isolated within the Forbidden City in Peking, these dogs would certainly have declined over the years had they not been bred with Pekingese. This mixing would eventually have resulted in the distinctive Shih Tzu breed. Despite the reluctance of Chinese officials, and other difficulties, the Shih Tzu was finally introduced to Britain when General Sir Douglas Brownrigg imported a pair of dogs in 1930, some ten years after he first noticed the proud little animals on a visit to China. In 1938, the Earl of Essex, captivated by the Shih Tzu, imported a few more specimens. Numbers grew slowly at first. The breed earned official recognition in Britain only in 1946 and in the United States only in 1969. Since then the Shih Tzu's popularity has soared and it has become a favourite show dog.

Characteristics

General appearance: an energetic and alert dog with a haughty carriage and bright, expressive eyes.

Height: 25.4 to 28 cm (10 to 11 in.). Under Canadian standards, considerable variations in height are permissible.

Weight: 4.5 to 7.3 kg (10 to 16 lb). Under Canadian standards, not specified.

Head: wide, round. Shock-headed with hair falling well over eyes. Good beard and whiskers. Muzzle short and square, flat and hairy, but not wrinkled. Black nose. Level or slightly undershot bite. Lips level.

Eyes: large, dark, and round, but not prominent.

Ears: large and drooping, set slightly below crown of skull. Heavily coated, appearing to blend with hair around neck.

Body: sturdy, well coupled. Level back. Length from withers to root of tail longer than height. Deep, broad chest. Shoulders well laid back.

Tail: heavily plumed, set high, and carried well over back.

Forequarters: short, muscular legs appear to be massive because of abundant hair.

Hindquarters: legs short, muscular, with profuse hair. Straight when viewed from rear. Thighs rounded and muscular.

Feet: round, well-padded, hairy.

Coat: long and dense, but not curly. Good undercoat.

Colour: all colours; white blaze on forehead and tail tip highly prized.

Faults: narrow head. Overshot jaws. Snipy muzzle. Pale pink nose or eye rims. Small or pale eyes. Legginess. Sparse coat.

Practical information: While the Shih Tzu is robust, it needs a balanced diet to avoid weight problems. Show dogs must have their coats untangled daily with a steel comb and a brush of boar bristles; a spray preparation containing mink oil helps to eliminate knots. Tie the long hair on its head in a small knot at the top of the skull to clear its vision. Never let the dog sleep near heat sources, which cause its coat to lose its lustre. Bathe the dog every five or six weeks.

ROYAL COUSINS

While the Lhasa Apso and Shih Tzu are certainly close cousins, their origins and the degree of their relationship are a matter of dispute.

They are very likely descended from the same ancestor. Some authorities believe the two breeds originated in the Byzantine Empire and were presented as tribute to the Emperor of China and the Dalai Lama more than 1,000 years ago. Archaeological excavations in Asia Minor have uncovered fossil dogs similar to both the Lhasa Apso and the Shih Tzu. These ancient dogs may also have given rise to the Maltese toy breed.

Now considered a Chinese dog, the Shih Tzu is believed to have resulted hundreds of years ago from a cross of Pekingese dogs and Tibetan Lhasa Apsos given to the Chinese Imperial court by the Dalai Lama.

But yet another opinion holds that the Shih Tzu came from western China. Just as the Dalai Lama bestowed sacred Lhasa Apsos on visiting dignitaries, so did the Emperor of China present Shih Tzus to the officials of Tibet. Thus Shih Tzus and Lhasa Apsos may have interbred often, both in China and in the temples of Tibet.

Siberian Husky

Husky

AUS.	CAN.	S. AF.	U.K.	F.C.I.
●	●	●	●	●

Though the name Husky is commonly applied to any sled-dog in the Arctic, the Siberian is the only variety officially recognized as a breed. The origin of its name is puzzling: it may refer to the dog's distinctive deep howl, but most authorities believe it derives from the Chukchi or Tuski Inuit of Siberia.

The powerful yet graceful Husky is the favourite of sled-racing enthusiasts, and with several world titles to its credit this breed is the champion of the sport. The Husky is an excellent pack dog, rarely quarrelsome with its team-mates or other dogs.

A handsome furry coat, an amiable expression, and luminous eyes make the Husky one of the most attractive dogs of the far North. Its bold head markings are especially striking. Gentle and affectionate, the Husky has the most docile nature of all sled-dogs. But it still exhibits some of the traits of its wolf ancestors, and the Husky's owner must be prepared to handle it with love and patience so as not to arouse its anger.

ORIGINS

As revealed by its name, the Husky originated in the cold and vast wastes of Siberia. It is believed that Huskies hauled the sleds and herded the reindeer of nomadic Inuit for at least 3,000 years. Isolated by the harsh northern environment, the Husky remained astonishingly pure, and the selective breeding practised by its masters resulted in an exceptionally fast, strong, and tireless dog. Nineteenth-century fur traders exploring Siberia chanced upon the breed and brought it to North America in the early 1900s. As interest mounted in sled-dog racing and the Husky began to win Alaskan competitions, increasing numbers of dogs were imported from Siberia. Some of these champion racers eventually became breeding stock in Canada and the rest of the United States. The Husky was recognized in the 1930s, and has become very popular in North America.

Characteristics

General appearance: medium size, with strong, balanced build and thick coat. Finely chiselled, foxlike face with bright expression.
Height: 53.3 to 59.7 cm (21 to 23½ in.) for the adult dog; 50.8 to 56 cm (20 to 22 in.) for the bitch.
Weight: 20 to 27.2 kg (44 to 60 lb) for the adult dog; 15 to 22.7 kg (33 to 50 lb) for the bitch.
Head: moderately round skull, tapering gradually to eyes. Muzzle of medium length. Clearly defined stop. Strong jaws with scissor bite.
Eyes: almond-shaped, set obliquely. Brown or blue, or one of each.
Ears: medium size, triangular, strongly erect. Set high.
Neck: of medium length, strong, and arched.
Body: strong, deep chest. Ribs well sprung. Strong, level back. Shoulders powerful and well laid back. Lean, muscular loin.
Tail: round, well furred. Carried over back in sickle curve when dog is running or at attention, trailing when dog is working or at rest.
Forequarters: solid, straight, muscular legs.
Hindquarters: powerful legs with good angulation. Stifles well bent. Hocks well let down. Dewclaws should be removed.
Feet: oval, furred, somewhat webbed between toes. Tough pads.
Coat: soft, dense, downy undercoat. Outer coat dense, smooth, and soft, of medium length, giving well-furred yet clean-cut appearance.
Colour: all colours and markings.
Faults: head too heavy or clumsy. Bulky muzzle. Ears too large or set low. Roach back. Bones too heavy or light. Soft or splayed feet.

Practical information: A very clean dog, the Siberian Husky is virtually odourless. Its coat does not need special care, though it should be groomed with a steel comb during shedding season.

SLED-RACING

Jack London drew vivid portraits of the Siberian Husky that will endure in adventure literature. No sooner had the first team of these dogs arrived in North America in 1909 than it was entered in the All-Alaska Sweepstake race; the new-comers won out over all the other racing breeds. The first three Husky teams selected for the sweepstake of 1914 placed first, second, and fourth, ahead of the larger and heavier Alaskan Malamutes. Leonhard Seppala, a Norwegian driver, brought celebrity to the Husky by winning several sweepstakes in a row. During the winter of 1925, he and his dogs brought diphtheria serum to Nome, Alaska, in a heroic and successful drive to prevent an epidemic. Huskies continued to prove their superiority in later years in trials such as the Iditarod, a course of 1,700 kilometres (1,050 miles) through northern wastes and considered the most difficult trial in the world. Still a fierce competitor, the Husky has become a popular companion dog.

Silky Toy Terrier

Australian Silky Terrier
Silky Terrier

T his winsome little Australian dog with British ancestry was never a working dog; it was bred to fill the role of family pet.

Yet the Silky Toy Terrier is more than a decorative animal. It is active, demanding, and occasionally aggressive. Extremely vocal, it serves as an excellent watch-dog, and its small size makes it an ideal pet for flat or apartment dwellers.

AUS.	CAN.	S. AF.	U.K.	F.C.I.
●	●	●	●	●

ORIGINS

The Silky Toy Terrier was originally known as the Sydney Terrier, and was developed in the Sydney area of New South Wales. It is the result of cross-breeding between the Australian Terrier and other terrier and toy dog varieties, including the Yorkshire Terrier, and was first shown in Australia in 1907. In the mid-1950s its name was changed to Australian Silky Terrier, which remains its official designation in Australia. Silky Toy Terriers arrived in Britain in 1928, and were exhibited there for the first time in 1930. During the Second World War, the breed gained popularity among American servicemen stationed in Australia, and they brought it to the United States. The Silky Toy Terrier was recognized by the American Kennel Club in 1959.

Characteristics

General appearance: low set, lightly built.
Height: 23 to 25.4 cm (9 to 10 in.).
Weight: 3.6 to 8 kg (8 to 18 lb). Ideal weight, 4 kg (9 lb).
Head: moderately long. Flat skull. Black nose. Tight, outlined lips.
Eyes: small, round, as dark as possible, very keen expression.
Ears: small, V-shaped, set high, pricked. No long hair.
Neck: medium length, covered with long silky hair.
Body: long in proportion to height. Chest rather wide and deep. Shoulders fairly well laid back. Straight topline. Well-sprung ribs.
Tail: customarily docked, carried erect. Free from feathering.
Forequarters: legs straight, well set under the body.
Hindquarters: thighs well developed. Hocks well set down.
Feet: small, round. Cat-footed, well padded. Nails black and strong.
Coat: fine, silky, straight, long over body, except for ears and face.
Colour: blue and tan, grey-blue and tan.
Faults: nervousness. Nose other colour than black. Coat curly, woolly, wavy, short, or rough. Nonconforming colours. White nails.

Practical information: The coat needs daily brushing and combing and should fall to either side from a centre part. After bathing it may be dried with a warm hair dryer. Some judicious trimming is required.

Skye Terrier

Early descriptions of the Skye Terrier depict an animal much smaller in size than today's lapdog. Nor was it the beautiful dog we know now. Originally a true working terrier, it was used extensively for hunting, particularly for tracking down badgers, otters, and weasels.

Although the Skye Terrier has become a companion dog, it has a strong sense of property. It is stand-offish with strangers but never overly aggressive. It is an ideal pet for the city—especially for flat or apartment dwellers.

AUS.	CAN.	S. AF.	U.K.	F.C.I.
●	●	●	●	●

ORIGINS

There are few facts available as to the origin of the Skye Terrier, despite its being one of the oldest breeds in existence. It is believed by some dog historians to be native to the Highlands of Scotland where it was originally developed for hunting small animals. Others are of the opinion that the Skye's ancestor was a long-haired basset-like dog native to the Isle of Skye. Yet another group claims it to be a descendant of the Maltese. As far back as 1842, Queen Victoria became so enamoured of this little dog that she encouraged breeding it. It was first shown in England under the name Skye Terrier at the Manchester Dog Show in 1864.

Characteristics

General appearance: a long and low body, profusely coated.
Height: 25 cm (10 in.) for adult dogs; 24 cm (9½ in.) for bitches.
Weight: 11.3 kg (25 lb). Under Canadian standards, not specified.
Head: long and powerful jaws. Slight stop. Nose black. Scissor bite.
Eyes: medium size, hazel or dark brown, close-set.
Ears: black, set high. Prick or drop. Well feathered.
Body: back level. Deep, oval chest. Well-developed flanks.
Tail: long, gracefully feathered. Carried straight or hanging.
Forequarters: legs short and muscular.
Hindquarters: strong, musuclar, well angulated. No dew-claws.
Feet: long, large. Hare-footed, with thick pads. Strong nails.
Coat: long, wiry, flat hair. Undercoat short, dense, soft, woolly.
Colour: any solid colour, preferably with dark nose and ears.

Practical information: This robust dog needs little exercise. A thorough brushing once or twice a week, along with daily combing, is sufficient to keep the coat in good condition.

Sloughi

Arabian Greyhound, Slughi

AUS.	CAN.	S. AF.	U.K.	F.C.I.
●		●	●	●

Nobleness, independence, and pride characterize the Sloughi, descended from the Egyptian Greyhound and known since the very dawn of civilization. Its coat closely hugs the fine lines of its body and is a superb example of natural adaptation: it is sand-coloured, the camouflage colour typical of gazelles, jerboas, fennecs, and other denizens of the desert.

For thousands of years nomadic Arab tribes used the Sloughi to hunt gazelle and hare. It was the only dog they treated as one of the family, allowing it into their tents. Also, it was the one dog bred and selected with the same care as given to a thoroughbred horse. Practising extreme selectivity, Sloughi breeders almost ruthlessly eliminated all mediocre, weak, or maladjusted puppies. Only the finest specimens of the breed were kept, resulting in Sloughis of rare beauty, sociability, and gentleness, and with great endurance and exceptional running speed.

The elegance of this slender, pure-bred Arabian Greyhound has inspired many a painter and poet. Gabriele D'Annunzio described it as an '... illustrious predator with its black tongue and palate, its bone structure rising out of a delicate skin, having attained the noblest pride, courage, elegance, accustomed to sleeping on beautiful rugs and drinking pure milk in an immaculate vase.' This description depicts a Sloughi far more delicate and gentle than the original hunting-dog, a creature bred for chasing gazelle, hare, and jackal.

Since 1844, gazelle-hunting has been forbidden, and the Sloughi has become a companion dog. It makes no excessive demonstrations of affection. There are no excited leaps of welcome forthcoming from this aristocrat, but it does express tenderness which can translate into a gentle lick of the hand.

The Sloughi retains from its hunting past a marked liking for independence. Indeed, it can be quite touchy on occasion, and is more likely to obey out of love for its owner than out of fear of punishment.

Unfailing vigilance also characterizes this greyhound, and it sometimes behaves aggressively towards strangers. With its high-strung temperament, it makes an objectionable household pet when there are children in the family. Devoted to its owner, it tends to be indifferent to others. This dog is happiest in a quiet atmosphere.

ORIGINS

The Sloughi's recent origins can be traced to the first nomadic tribes in the deserts of Ethiopia, Nubia, and Egypt. During the Middle Ages, Arabs invaded north-western Africa bringing their dogs with them, and it is said that the Sloughis found on the border of the Sahara and Tripolitania are the finest specimens. Tradition demands that the Sloughi count among its ancestors members of the canine family other than dogs. Aristotle felt that Sloughis in some way were related to the fox. On the other hand, the Emir Abd el Kader was convinced they were descended from the wolf: '... the Sloughis owe their name to Slouguia, in the Sahara, where they would have been born from the mating of wolves and dogs.' If one considers the derivation of the word Sloughi, this greyhound could also have come from a village in Yemen, either Saloug or Saluk. Because Arabs often mated the Sloughi with the Saluki, this perhaps lends credence to the idea of Saluk being its home territory. The breed was threatened with extinction a decade or so ago and its future remains uncertain even though its number is on the increase.

Characteristics

General appearance: elegant, racy dog. Its bone structure and musculature are clearly evident beneath its delicate skin.
Height: 60 to 70 cm (23½ to 27½ in.).
Weight: not specified.
Head: somewhat larger than the Greyhound's yet not heavy. Flat skull, rather wide. Muzzle in the shape of an elongated wedge, tapering moderately, almost the same length as the skull. Stop barely visible.
Eyes: large, set well into the orbit, triangular, slightly slanting. Burnt topaz with light coats, black with dark coats. Soft, wistful expression.
Ears: set level with the eyes or slightly above. Not very large; drooping, flat, triangular, slightly rounded.
Neck: very lean, but strong. Slight dewlap.
Body: deep chest but not too broad; in depth, reaches just to the elbows. Relatively short back. Loin lean, wide, slightly arched. Croup bony, very oblique. Hips prominent. Belly tucked up. Shoulders flat, lean, moderately oblique, clearly visible.

Tail: fine, well set, without feathering or long hair. When the dog is moving, it must not be carried higher than the level of the back. Strong curve at end.
Forequarters: legs extremely lean and flat-boned. Upright pasterns.
Hindquarters: thighs well let down, a bit flat. Hocks close to the ground and slightly angled.
Feet: thin, in a long oval shape. Hare-footed. Strong nails, if not black, at least dark.
Coat: short, tough, fine hair.
Colour: all shades of sand or fawn with or without a black mask. Sometimes coat is rather dark. Washed-out white, black brindle with tan marks or brindle marks on a fawn background on the head, paws, and sometimes the breast.
Faults: pale eyes. Gnarled muscles. Poor bite. Greyhound ears. Straight ears or with tips drooping forward. Pink pigmentation. Wiry hair. Feathering on limbs or tail. Coat black and white, balsam. Large white marks.

Practical information: The Sloughi needs regular exercise. Avoid overfeeding. It is essential to the dog's health that it not gain weight after it reaches maturity. Although it drinks little water, there should always be a fresh supply available. Regular brushing with a soft-bristled brush followed by a polishing with a chamois will keep the coat in good condition.

Staffordshire Bull Terrier

Strong and tenacious like the Bulldog, and agile like the Old English Terrier, the Staffordshire Bull Terrier was bred generations ago as a fighting dog. Though it has lost little of its original bellicosity, it is now considered a good companion animal, one that demonstrates great affection for its owners, and is particularly kind with children. These qualities, coupled with its indomitable courage and intelligence, make it a trustworthy all-purpose dog. It is not hostile with people, unless provoked, or encouraged to attack.

A medium-size dog, the Staffordshire Bull Terrier is robust, powerful, and athletic. Plenty of exercise on a regular basis is essential to its physical and mental well-being.

AUS.	CAN.	S. AF.	U.K.	F.C.I.
●	●	●	●	●

ORIGINS

The product of cross-breeding between the Bulldog and the Old English Terrier (now extinct), the Staffordshire Bull Terrier is also believed descended from the Fox Terrier. In 1952, it was recognized by the Canadian Kennel Club, and in 1974 by the American Kennel Club.

Characteristics

General appearance: intelligent and tenacious.
Height: 35.5 to 40.6 cm (14 to 16 in.).
Weight: under F.C.I. and Canadian standards, dogs 13 to 17 kg (28 to 38 lb); bitches 11 to 15.4 kg (24 to 34 lb).
Head: short, deep. Broad skull. Short muzzle.
Eyes: round, medium size, black. Rims black.
Ears: rose-shaped or half-prick, rather small.
Body: solid. Level topline. Ribs well sprung.
Tail: medium length, set low, tapering, carried low.

Forequarters: legs straight, wide apart. Well boned.
Hindquarters: thighs muscular. Hocks well down. Legs parallel when viewed from behind.
Feet: strong, medium size, well padded. Nails black in solid-coloured dogs.
Coat: smooth, short, and close.
Colour: reddish brown, beige, white, black, blue, or one of these colours with white. Brindle, or brindle and white.
Faults: tail curled. Ears drooping or erect.

Practical information: Daily brushing of the coat to eliminate dead hair and to keep it shiny is essential. Gently clean around the eyes with cotton balls that have been moistened with tepid water that has been boiled. Nails must be cut with special clippers if the dog does not have the opportunity to wear them down itself.

Sussex Spaniel

The massive and energetic Sussex Spaniel is an intelligent dog and deliberate in everything it does. Eminently trainable, it is an obedient and faithful companion. Usually calm and gentle, it gets along well with other animals. At the same time, it is a good watch-dog—without being too aggressive for a normal family situation.

The Sussex Spaniel was purposely bred in England to be a slow-moving sporting dog that hunters could follow on foot. Popular when first shown (at the Crystal Palace in 1862), the breed was later nearly decimated by disease and two world wars. It has never been particularly favoured in North America, where more stylish dogs appeal to show enthusiasts.

AUS.	CAN.	S. AF.	U.K.	F.C.I.
●	●	●	●	●

ORIGINS

The Sussex was developed in the late 1700s by a certain Mr. Fuller, who wanted a hunting-dog that could be easily followed through the dense Sussex undergrowth. Various spaniels, including the English Springer, were among the founding stock. The breed was recognized in Britain in 1885.

Characteristics

General appearance: a sturdy, strongly built dog.
Height: 38 to 40.6 cm (15 to 16 in.). Under Canadian standards, 35.6 to 40.6 cm (14 to 16 in.) for the adult dog; 33 to 38 cm (13 to 15 in.) for the bitch.
Weight: 22.7 kg (50 lb) for the adult dog; 17.7 kg (39 lb) for the bitch. Canadian standards: 20.4 kg (45 lb) for the adult dog; 18 kg (40 lb) for the bitch.
Head: well balanced. Wide skull. Occiput full but not pointed. Nostrils liver-coloured. Scissor bite.
Eyes: rather large, not too full, hazel. Soft expression.
Ears: thick, lobular, covered with soft, wavy hair. Set above eye level.
Neck: long, slightly arched. Not much dewlap.
Body: strong, level. Oblique shoulders. Deep chest.

The back and the loin are well developed. No waistline.
Tail: set low. Customarily docked. Lively action.
Forequarters: arms well boned, well muscled. Legs rather short, strong, moderately feathered.
Hindquarters: legs should not appear shorter than the forelegs. Well feathered above hocks, which are strong and muscular.
Feet: round, well feathered between the toes.
Coat: abundant, flat, smooth. Ample undercoat.
Colour: rich golden liver.
Faults: hindquarters shorter than forequarters or over-angulated at the hocks. Tail immoderately feathered or carried over the back. Curly hair. Coat too dark or too light. Head held too high. Yellow eyes.

Practical information: Brush daily. Keep ears clear of matted hair. Guard against overweight.

Swiss Laufhund

Jura Laufhund

Schweizer
Laufhund

The Swiss Laufhund is a hunting-dog native to Switzerland. In that country, and elsewhere in Europe, there are four types of Laufhund—the Jura, the Schweizer, the Lucerne, and the Berner. Although each is considered a breed, all are commonly referred to as Swiss Laufhunds. Great Britain and South Africa, however, register only Jura dogs as Swiss Laufhunds.

All are superb hunting-dogs and remarkably adroit on rocky terrain. Excellent at flushing game, they are alert, intelligent, vigorous, and brave. They have a subtle nose and will follow a trail with confidence. Their powerful, sonorous 'voice' enables the hunter to follow them easily.

Although their origin and establishment in Switzerland is considered ancient, it is difficult to recount the Swiss Laufhunds' lineage with any certainty. It is believed that Roman armies brought one type to Switzerland, and that this dog was developed into the varieties found today—varieties that are distinguished mainly by their coat colours. By the sixteenth century, Swit-

AUS.	CAN.	S. AF.	U.K.	F.C.I.
		●		●

ORIGINS

The Canis intermedium, *presumed to be the ancestor of the Swiss Laufhund, was indigenous to Italy and Austria during the Bronze Age. It probably reached the Switzerland area when the Romans arrived, but it might already have been there for some time. Laufhund skulls have been found in the ruins of some cities, and in areas near lakes. These hounds are also depicted in mosaics, specifically at Avenches. Their frequent inclusion in hunting scenes from the Middle Ages attests to their ancient origin. They have been bred continuously in Switzerland.*

Berner Laufhund

zerland was already famous for hounds bred in the eastern Alps.

During the latter half of the eighteenth century, Swiss Laufhunds were highly rated in France. In 1750, the Marquis de Foudras spoke of them at great length in his book *Contemporary Hunting*. Louis XVI also became interested in these dogs and instructed one of his ministers, Duc Etienne de Choiseul, to obtain a pair. Choiseul ordered 60, and breeding in France began in earnest.

These dogs will settle in with a family quite well, but prefer country to town life.

THE JURA LAUFHUND

Variously called the Bruno, the Arogovian Dog, and the Jura Lancer, this dog is the heaviest of all Swiss Laufhunds. Its name reflects its origins in the Jura Mountains bordering Switzerland and France. The mating of Bloodhounds with various Laufhunds is believed to account for the Jura's size and colour. It is prized for its prowess in hunting deer and fox.

Characteristics

General appearance: average-size hunting dogs, somewhat lugubrious facial expression. All variations are similar in characteristics and features, varying mainly in weight, coat colour, and hair texture. Three types—the Schweizer, the Lucerne, and the Berner— are recognized solely by the F.C.I.

Height: under F.C.I standards, 45 to 50 cm (18 to 20 in.). Under South African standards, the Jura measures 41 to 46 cm (16 to 18 in.).

Weight: under F.C.I. standards, 27 to 30 kg (59 to 66 lb). Elsewhere, not specified.

Head: lean, long, narrow, and proportioned to the dog's size. Well-defined median line. Jaws very strong. Scissor bite. Nose black, well developed.

Eyes: dark. Gentle expression.

Ears: set low and well back, narrow and flexible. Very long, and falling in folds; well rounded at tips.

Neck: rather long, muscular. No appreciable dewlap.

Body: brisket deep, not too broad. Rib cage not too rounded. Back is of a good length, compact, straight.

Tail: not too long, carried out stiffly, or slightly curved up, but never held gaily.

Forequarters: legs well balanced, of strong bone structure.

Hindquarters: thighs solid and firm. Hocks slightly bent. No dew-claws.

Coat: hair is always thick and short, sometimes wiry.

Colour: the Schweizer and the Lucerne Laufhunds are basically white with coloured markings. In the former, the marks are orange speckled with red dots; in the latter, they are dark or black with grey or blue speckles. The coat of the Berner is always tricolour; the ground is white, as in the two other dogs, with large black patches on the body, and tan over the eyes, cheeks, insides of the ears, base of the tail. The Jura dog is dark with tan markings. Under South African standards, it must be fawn or tan and may have a black or black and tan saddle.

Practical information: This dog needs plenty of daily exercise and should be allowed to run free as often as possible. In the hunting season the coat must be brushed briskly and often. Ears must be carefully examined for cuts, splinters and any other foreign matter which might have become embedded there. If unable to remove any obstruction easily with tweezers, it is advisable to seek the help of a veterinarian. Under no circumstances should you use force.

Tibetan Spaniel

AUS.	CAN.	S. AF.	U.K.	F.C.I.
●	●	●	●	●

This ancient pug-nosed breed was originally bred by Tibetan Buddhists to turn their prayer wheels and to keep watch over their monasteries. This dog was not introduced to the West until the turn of the century.

Today a delicate lap-dog, the Tibetan Spaniel is lively and affectionate with its owners, aloof and distrustful towards strangers.

Characteristics

General appearance: small, active dog, happy and even-tempered.
Height: 25.4 to 28 cm (10 to 11 in.).
Weight: under F.C.I. standards, 2 to 6 kg (4½ to 13 lb). Elsewhere, 4 to 6.8 kg (9 to 15 lb).
Head: slightly domed skull. Slight stop. Undershot jaw. Black nose.
Eyes: medium size, oval, dark brown. Bright expression.
Ears: medium size, pendent, set fairly high, well feathered.
Tail: set high, curled tightly on the back, richly plumed.
Forequarters: slightly bowed, but firm at shoulders.
Hindquarters: strong, covered with short hair.
Feet: small. Hare-footed. Covered with short hair.
Coat: double; hair rather flat. Mane on neck and shoulders.
Colour: all colours and mixtures.

Practical information: This robust dog needs daily brushing and combing, and a bath every two to three weeks. Gently remove any mucus from the eye areas with a moist cotton ball. The puppies are delicate, and only develop long hair when they are about three or four months old.

ORIGINS

Little is known about the Tibetan Spaniel, except that it is of ancient lineage. Whether it was the father of the Pekingese or whether the Pekingese was its forbear, most authorities do agree that the two breeds are linked in some way. Some experts maintain that Tibetan Spaniels were introduced into China as tributes to noblemen. These animals then mated with Pugs to produce the Pekingese. Others believe that Pekingese presented to Tibetan officials were cross-bred with Lhasa Apsos and Japanese Chins, eventually developing into the Tibetan Spaniel known today. Actually, the dog is not a spaniel; its name was selected to distinguish it from the Tibetan Terrier. Although the presence of the Tibetan Spaniel was first noted in Britain in 1905, the breed did not become established there until the mid-1940s. Since that time the Tibetan Spaniel has achieved great popularity in the West, both as a show dog and as a pet.

Tibetan Terrier

Lhasa Terrier

T his charming little dog is not a terrier at all, but is another legend-steeped Asian breed which has come down to us from ancient times. Believed to have been bred by Tibetan monks, and jealously guarded in the holy city of Lhasa, the Tibetan Terrier was treasured as a symbol of good luck.

An excellent little pet, this Terrier is easy to train. It has a loving disposition and is active and playful, but takes its time accepting strangers. Its rather loud bark makes it a good watch-dog. It does not require much exercise, though it thoroughly enjoys a romp, particularly in the country. Its undercoat usually sheds once each year and its outer coat every three years.

AUS.	CAN.	S. AF.	U.K.	F.C.I.
●	●	●	●	●

ORIGINS

Legend has it that Tibetan Terriers bred in Buddhist monasteries were given by the monks to nomadic tribes for good luck. Another legend says that those nomads stole the holy dogs. A British medical doctor practising in India is credited with introducing the breed to English-speaking countries during this century.

Characteristics

General appearance: a medium-size dog with a bushy coat. The dog bears some resemblance to the Lhasa Apso.
Height: 35.6 to 40.6 cm (14 to 16 in.). Bitches less.
Weight: under F.C.I. and Canadian standards, 8 to 14 kg (18 to 30 lb).
Head: well furnished with long hair. Skull neither domed nor flat, narrowing somewhat towards the eyes. Marked stop. Jaws forming a clean curve. Slight beard. Black nose.
Eyes: large, dark, rather wide apart. Rims black.
Ears: pendent, V-shaped, medium size, feathered.

Body: sturdy, well ribbed. Slightly arched loin.
Tail: medium length, set rather high, well feathered, curled on the back, often with a kink at the tip.
Forequarters: straight, well muscled.
Hindquarters: well muscled. Hocks set low.
Feet: big, round, well garnished with hair.
Coat: abundant, fine, long hair, neither silky nor woolly; straight or wavy. Undercoat of a fine wool.
Colour: golden, white, cream, grey, soot, black, particoloured and tricoloured. All colours are acceptable, except chocolate or liver.
Faults: overshot or undershot. Weak, pointed muzzle.

Practical information: To keep its coat free of tangles, use a fine-tooth metal comb every day. Extra combing is required when the dog is shedding. A thorough brushing with a semi-stiff brush made of rubber or natural bristle is advantageous. Gently remove any mucus from the eye area with a cotton ball moistened in tepid water that has been boiled.

Vizsla

Hungarian Vizsla, Hungarian Pointer

A hard-working hunting-dog, the Vizsla is able to track and point game, and serve as a retriever as well. It has a keen sense of smell, is calm, sensitive, and easy to train.

This large and active field dog is not suited to urban life. To burn up its tremendous energy it needs to be out working in the fields, and if confined will become a nuisance. To keep a Vizsla as a house-pet, it is essential to establish authority at the outset. The same holds true for its cousin, the Wire-haired Vizsla, a shaggy version of this smooth-coated dog.

AUS.	CAN.	S. AF.	U.K.	F.C.I.
●	●	●	●	●

ORIGINS

Some dog historians claim that the origin of the hunting-dog of Hungary, known today as the Vizsla, dates back at least to A.D. 1000. Others maintain that it is the result of cross-breeding the German Weimaraner with various pointing breeds.

Characteristics

General appearance: robust dog of average size, distinctive and aristocratic demeanor.
Height: 57 to 63.5 cm (22½ to 25 in.) for dogs; 53.3 to 59.7 cm (21 to 23½ in.) for bitches. Under Canadian standards, 56 to 58.4 cm (22 to 23 in.) for dogs.
Weight: 21.8 to 30 kg (48 to 66 lb).
Head: lean and noble. Skull broad, slightly domed, with median line. Moderate stop. Jaws strong.
Eyes: slightly oval, darker than the coat, never light. Eye rims tight. Alert expression.
Ears: rather long, set low, rounded V-shape, falling beside the head.

Neck: of average length, muscular. No dewlap.
Body: brisket deep, not too broad. Withers well defined. Back straight, short, muscular. Croup straight, sloping. Belly slightly tucked up.
Tail: set low, customarily docked to two-thirds of its length. Carried out stiffly.
Forequarters: legs straight, strong. Elbows close.
Hindquarters: strong, well muscled. Thighs developed, angle of the hock rather open. No dewclaws.
Feet: round and compact. Cat-footed. Toes close.
Coat: straight, short, thick, glossy. Greasy to touch.
Colour: russet gold.

Practical information: This dog's coat should be well brushed at least two or three times a week. When doing this, look closely for evidence of parasites on the skin and coat. Outdoor dogs are particularly susceptible to this problem. The tail should be docked at birth. If the dog is to be kept as a house-pet, have a veterinarian remove its dew-claws.

Weimaraner

AUS.	CAN.	S. AF.	U.K.	F.C.I.
•	•	•	•	•

This large, sensitive animal is an all-purpose hunting-dog of excellent quality. Used for big-game hunting in its native Germany, it was later trained as a bird dog, and as a water retriever.

The Weimaraner makes an excellent watchdog. Although not dangerous, it will make a vigorous effort to get its own way. If a Weimaraner is well trained, however, it is one of the best behaved of all breeds.

ORIGINS

It is almost certain that the Weimaraner was developed in Weimar, Germany, by crossing Bloodhounds with various pointers and local hunting-dogs. Germany's kennel club recognized the Weimaraner in 1896.

Characteristics

General appearance: well-formed dog.
Height: 61 to 68.6 cm (24 to 27 in.) for the adult dog; 56 to 63.5 cm (22 to 25 in.) for the bitch. Under Canadian standards, 63.5 to 68.6 cm (25 to 27 in.) for the adult dog; 58.4 to 63.5 cm (23 to 25 in.) for the bitch.
Weight: not specified.
Head: lean, long, and aristocratic; broader in the male. Moderate stop. Nose grey. Lips thin, pendulous, pinkish. Scissor bite.
Eyes: round, set very slightly at an angle. Shades of amber or blue-grey, Keen, intelligent expression.
Ears: set high, relatively long.
Neck: muscular, nearly round, not too short.
Body: well proportioned. Shoulders well laid and muscular. Brisket powerful, let down to elbow level. Ribs are well sprung and long. Topline level.
Tail: customarily docked to a length that is long enough to cover the anus.
Forequarters: legs very straight and strong.
Hindquarters: legs long and strong, parallel when seen from the rear. Hocks well let down, turning neither in nor out. Well-developed musculation. Stifles moderately angulated and well turned. No dewclaws.
Feet: compact and close. Toes well arched.
Coat: short and very dense.
Colour: silvery grey, roebuck, or mouse-grey and all intervening shades of grey. White patches on the paws and chest permissible if small.
Faults: too large or too small. Nose pinkish. Coat any other colour than grey. Eyes not amber.

Practical information: Since this is an active animal, it needs plenty of exercise.

Welsh Corgi

AUS.	CAN.	S. AF.	U.K.	F.C.I.
●	●	●	●	●

Both the Cardigan and the Pembroke Welsh Corgis have a somewhat cloudy lineage, with the Cardigan being the older of the two breeds. But both have made names for themselves as good working animals—rushing small game, guarding buildings, ratting, and herding. This last task is accomplished by biting the heels of the cattle, then dropping to the ground to avoid being kicked. They are tough, fearless little dogs, quick in movement despite their short legs.

The Cardigan and the Pembroke make excellent house-pets and are just as happy in an urban flat or apartment as on a country estate. They are amusing animals, extremely intelligent and loyal, affectionate, and good with children. Both types of Corgi are easy to travel with, which is a great advantage in a pet. They have a natural desire to please and they like to be included in whatever activities are going on around them. They are fine watch-dogs, are seldom quarrelsome, and are never mean. They are, however, protective of their owner's property; this trait can, on occasion, lead to confrontation. The Cardigan, particularly, is quite suspicious of strangers, and the owner should keep this characteristic in check. Training of both breeds should start early and the trainer should be firm, yet affectionate and fair.

The Pembroke Corgi is more popular than the Cardigan, perhaps because it is marginally more gentle. Naturally healthy, both types of dog require plenty of exercise.

ORIGINS

Some authorities claim separate origins for the Cardigan and the Pembroke Welsh Corgis. The Cardigan is said to have accompanied Central European Celts who invaded Wales around 1200 B.C., and has in its ancestry the Dachshund. The Pembroke is believed to have entered Britain with Flemish weavers brought to that country by Henry I in 1107, and is descended from a spitz-type dog. The two breeds probably share the Swedish Vallhund as an ancestor. Originally, both types were classed as a single breed. In 1934 the British Kennel Club gave them separate breed status.

THE PEMBROKE OF BUCKINGHAM PALACE

Somewhat smaller than the Cardigan, the Pembroke is the most popular variety of Welsh Corgi today, especially in English-speaking countries. Some experts attribute different origins to the Pembroke. They claim it is the result of a cross-breeding of spitz, Keeshond, and Schipperke. In spite of its recognition by the British Kennel Club in 1934, it is doubtful that its popularity would have received such a tremendous boost without royal patronage, which did, indeed, play a major role in the making of this star of the canine world. In 1933, the Duke of York, who later became King George VI of England, bought for his daughters, Princess Elizabeth and Princess Margaret, a Pembroke Corgi called *Roseval Golden Eagle*. This charming little dog won the heart of Princess Elizabeth, and the Welsh Corgi became her favourite breed.

Once *Roseval Golden Eagle* was established in Buckingham Palace, it was provided with a mate, and the descendants of these two dogs are pets of the Royal Family today.

Several decades have passed since the Pembroke Corgi gained royal favour. In 1975, the British Kennel Club commissioned a portrait of Queen Elizabeth II, surrounded by some of her Corgis. There are few official photographs taken of Her Majesty today in which one or more of these dogs do not appear, and this privileged position has helped immeasurably to enhance their popularity in Britain.

The United States, among other countries, did not discover the Pembroke Corgi until a few years ago. However, dog buyers are rapidly making up for lost time and the breed is now showing considerable gains in popularity throughout the world.

Cardigan Welsh Corgi

Pembroke Welsh Corgi

Characteristics

General appearance: the Pembroke and Cardigan Welsh Corgis differ essentially in the colour of their coats and eyes, the texture of their hair, and the length of their tails. Both have a long silhouette, are strongly built, are close to the ground, and are alert and lively.

Height: 25.4 to 30.5 cm (10 to 12 in.).

Weight: 9 to 11 kg (20 to 24 lb) for the adult Pembroke; 7.7 to 10 kg (17 to 22 lb) for the bitch. Not specified for the Cardigan.

Head: like a fox's. Skull flat, rather wide. Tapering muzzle. Moderate stop. Nose black. Scissor bite.

Eyes: medium size for both varieties; rather dark for the Cardigan; hazel for the Pembroke. Blue eyes permitted in Cardigan merles.

Ears: rather big and carried erect by the Cardigan; erect, not too big on the Pembroke.

Neck: muscular, wide, and long. Well developed and in proportion to the dog's build.

Body: strong and long in both varieties. Level topline. Deep chest, well-sprung ribs for the Cardigan. Deep, wide chest and rounded ribs for the Pembroke.

Tail: the Cardigan has a tail like the fox's brush, touching or nearly touching the ground. Carried low. The Pembroke has a short tail, sometimes naturally at birth; otherwise it is docked close to the body a few days after birth.

Forequarters: short for both varieties. Both dogs have level toplines.

Hindquarters: powerful on both. Dew-claws removed on the Cardigan.

Feet: Cardigan, round and rather big; Pembroke, oval with centre toes longer.

Coat: Cardigan, short, wiry hair, with good undercoat. Pembroke, thick, soft hair of medium length.

Colour: reddish brown, fawn, sand-coloured, black and tan; may have white patches on the feet, chest, and neck.

Practical information: This dog must be taken for daily walks and, as often as possible, allowed to run free in an open area. Like all dogs close to the ground, the Welsh Corgi tends to suffer from intestinal chills. Dry it well, especially the stomach and chest, after it has been out in wet weather. Brush its coat regularly. Guard against overweight.

Welsh Springer Spaniel

Welsh Spaniel

A lthough not nearly as popular as the larger English Springer Spaniel, the Welsh Springer is a delightful companion and an outstanding gun dog. It is a keen and hard worker: no outing is too long, no terrain too rough for it, and it is versatile enough to be used on any kind of game.

In fact, there is no better gun dog than a well-trained Welsh Springer. This qualification is worth noting because the Welsh has a fine nose, and is apt to become a lone hunter and difficult to handle if not properly reared. However, the breed is not at all difficult to train. A six-month-old puppy taught basic obedience and retrieving will seldom forget its early lessons.

The Welsh Springer's coat is one of the most distinctive features of the breed. The pearly white background with rich red markings is a virtual trademark—no other coloration is permitted. The coat is dense, flat, and silky, and its natural oils help keep it clean; mud, once dry on the coat, simply crumbles off and no stains remain. The soft undercoat also prevents injury from water and thorns.

The breed has a remarkable ability to withstand extremes of heat and cold. For this reason, the Welsh Springer has, in recent years, enjoyed burgeoning popularity in countries far removed from its native Wales. Indeed, India, Australia, and Thailand represent the hot climates to which this dog has adapted—thanks in large measure to its marvellous, all-weather coat.

Just as this dog can be trained for obedience and show competition, so can it be trained to work in the field on a hunt. Field work demands a dog with intelligence and keenly developed instincts—traits with which the Welsh Springer Spaniel has been amply blessed. A long string of working British champions illustrates the fact that the hunting instinct is still very much alive in the breed. Such training takes patience, of course, but if you establish a routine and spend a little time each day with your spaniel, you will be rewarded with a merry worker that will seek and flush game, and retrieve on command.

The Welsh Springer also makes an ideal housedog. Larger than the Cocker, yet smaller than the English Springer, it is equally at home on a rural estate or in an urban flat or apartment, as long as it is provided with regular exercise. The breed is amiable with children and with other animals.

AUS.	CAN.	S. AF.	U.K.	F.C.I.
●	●	●	●	●

ORIGINS

References to a dog which has been identified as the Welsh Springer Spaniel are found in the earliest extant records of the Laws of Wales—circa A.D. 1300. It is likely that for hundreds of years before that time, a breed of white spaniel with red markings had been familiar in the region. There is little doubt that it had an early shared ancestry with the Brittany Spaniel—the two are remarkably similar in their hunting prowess and physical make-up. Canine authorities maintain that in pre-Roman times, the Gauls who migrated from Brittany to Cornwall and South Wales took their dogs along with them. Eventually, the Brittany and the Welsh Springer dogs developed along different lines. In Wales, the breed first became known as the 'Starter' and was highly regarded as a gun dog. However, little was heard of the breed's fine reputation outside Wales until the late nineteenth century, when increased interest in shows and field trials led to greater breed popularity. One of its most ardent supporters was Mr. A. T. Williams, whose Welsh Springer, in 1899, won the class for working spaniels at a Birmingham show. The British Kennel Club recognized the breed in 1902. Up to that time, the name Welsh Cocker had been used; since then, it has been called the Welsh Springer. Even so, though, there were those who claimed the breed was too small and light to be a springer. Nonetheless, the non-believers were forced to reckon with Mr. Williams's Welsh Spaniel. When listed as a cocker, before 1902, it won many prizes; thereafter listed as a springer, it kept on winning.

Characteristics

General appearance: compact, strong, merry.
Height: adult dogs, 48.3 cm (19 in.); bitches, 45.7 cm (18 in.).
Weight: under F.C.I. and Canadian standards, 16 to 20 kg (35 to 45 lb). Elsewhere, not specified.
Head: skull of moderate length, slightly domed, well chiselled below eyes; clearly defined stop. Muzzle of medium length, fairly square; nose flesh-coloured, liver, or black; jaw strong. Scissor bite.
Eyes: hazel or dark, medium size, neither prominent nor sunken.
Ears: set moderately low and hanging close to the cheeks, comparatively small, covered with setter-like feathering.
Neck: long and muscular, clean in throat, neatly set into long and sloping shoulders.
Body: strong and muscular with deep brisket, well-sprung ribs; length of body proportionate to length of leg, and well balanced.
Tail: well set on and low, never carried above level of back, lightly feathered and with lively action. Customarily docked.
Forequarters: legs medium length, moderately feathered.
Hindquarters: strong and muscular. Hocks well let down.
Feet: firm and round, with thick pads. Cat-footed. Not too large, or spreading.
Coat: straight or flat and thick, of a silky texture, never wiry or wavy.
Colour: rich red and white only.
Faults: coarse skull, light bone, curly coat, loaded or poorly angulated shoulders, stilted movement, oversized.

Practical information: This dog's self-cleaning coat requires routine grooming, including regular cleansing of those heavily feathered ears—necessary for all spaniels. When brushing, look closely at the skin beneath the fur. It should be clean, supple, and a healthy pink. Regular daily exercise is essential.

TRAINING THE SPRINGER

Hunting instincts are often dormant and need to be aroused. Even if you work with a puppy for only fifteen minutes a day, you will soon be witnessing results.

Begin working in or near the house, using a training dummy and bird scent. As the dog becomes proficient, you can shift the training to the field. The same basic commands that make for good manners in the obedience ring—'come,' 'sit,' and 'stay'— are equally valued in the field. If you accustom your puppy at an early age to such household noises as the banging of metal pots and pans and the roar of the vacuum cleaner, you will be able to begin using a blank starting pistol when it is six months old without upsetting it.

By one year of age, the dog should be performing well, hunting between five and twenty metres (or yards) away from you in a semicircular fashion. It will likely pick scents from the air, flushing game carefully with few misses. Watch the tail to judge how close your Welsh Springer is to the prey. Tail action accelerates when game is found.

Welsh Terrier

One of the oldest breeds, the Welsh Terrier was bred as a sporting dog to hunt badgers, foxes, and otters, but will tackle almost anything that offers a good chase and a fight. Welsh Terriers vary in their adaptability to other animals. Most will not quarrel unless challenged. Others, however, will attack, with great gusto, every four-footed creature they meet. In spite of this, the Welsh Terrier makes an excellent family dog for town or country. It must, nonetheless, be trained to behave. Warm and affectionate, it is nevertheless wary of strangers and is a natural watch-dog. Because it is an energetic little animal, it is compatible with a young and vigorous family.

AUS.	CAN.	S. AF.	U.K.	F.C.I.
●	●	●	●	●

ORIGINS

The Welsh Terrier is believed to be a descendant of the extinct English Black and Tan Terrier. Although its origin was undoubtedly English, it was in Wales that it evolved as a sporting dog. In 1886, the British Kennel Club sanctioned the breed. The Welsh was first shown in the United States in 1901.

Characteristics

General appearance: hardy and robust.
Height: about 39.4 cm (15½ in.).
Weight: about 9 kg (20 lb). Under Canadian standards, 0.5 kg (1 lb) more or less than the standard weight is permissible.
Head: rather long. Flat skull, rather wide. Powerful jaw. Slight stop. Black nose. Strong scissor bite.
Eyes: small, deep-set, expressive, dark. Lively and intelligent.
Ears: V-shaped, small, set high, carried towards the front, next to the cheek.
Neck: rather long and thick, slightly arched.
Body: short, straight back. Well-developed ribs.

Strong loin. Oblique shoulders, well laid back. Chest deep.
Tail: well set. Customarily docked.
Forequarters: muscular. Straight, powerful pasterns.
Hindquarters: strong, muscular thighs, rather long. Hocks angled, well let down.
Feet: small, round. Cat-footed.
Coat: harsh, wiry, very dense, abundant.
Colour: black and tan; grey, black grizzle, and tan.
Faults: nose white, cherry-coloured, or spotted. Ears straight, tulip- or rose-shaped. Noticeable amount of black under the hocks. Black marks on the toes. Fine hair. Round eye.

Practical information: This dog needs exercise. Brush it regularly to keep its coat in good condition.

West Highland White Terrier

Westie

This spirited little dog will settle well into a household with children, although it is better suited to one without. It copes well with new situations as long as its family is with it. Courageous if challenged, it is nevertheless good with strangers once it has looked them over. It needs brushing everyday, but this seems to be a small price to pay for the pleasure of owning a West Highland White Terrier.

AUS.	CAN.	S. AF.	U.K.	F.C.I.
●	●	●	●	●

ORIGINS

The West Highland White Terrier shares its lineage with the Scottie, the Cairn, and the Dandie Dinmont, as well as with other rough-haired terriers of Scotland. A hardy animal, it was originally bred as a hunter to keep down fox, otter, and other vermin populations on farms. It is not an argumentative dog, but has great agility, stamina, and courage, qualities essential in its native Scotland where the generally rough terrain made nimbleness a virtual necessity in an outdoor dog. By selection and interbreeding, the white coat was purposely developed to distinguish the dog from its quarry while hunting. In 1907, the West Highland White Terrier was recognized by the British Kennel Club.

Characteristics

General appearance: small, strongly built dog.
Height: 28 cm (11 in.) for dogs; 2.5 cm (1 in.) less for bitches.
Weight: under F.C.I. standards, 7 to 10 kg (15½ to 22 lb). Elsewhere, not specified.
Head: slightly domed skull, not overly narrow between the ears. Slight stop. Straight nose bridge. Black nose. Strong teeth.
Eyes: medium size, well spaced, slightly sunken, dark, piercing look.
Ears: small, well spaced. Carried erect. No fringing.
Body: compact. Deep chest. Ribs well arched. Straight, flat back.
Tail: 13 to 15 cm (5 to 6 in.) long. Straight. Carried jauntily.
Forequarters: legs short and muscular.
Hindquarters: wide at top, thighs closer. Very muscular.
Feet: round. Black nails. Thick pads.
Coat: double-coated. Topcoat wiry, flat, without curl. Undercoat firm, soft, and close.
Colour: always pure white.

Practical information: The West Highland White should be brushed each day. Special grooming is necessary if the dog is to be shown.

Whippet

Devotees of the Whippet consider it to be one of the loveliest of all dogs. At first glance it appears to be an English Greyhound in miniature. On closer observation one discovers a particular type of greyhound, one with a shorter body, a longer and wider head—in fact, a greyhound quite different in most aspects. Terrier blood is believed to account for this dog's gameness—endurance and pluck—although some experts insist the dog exhibits no terrier-like traits.

The Whippet is a dog of great elegance and purity of line. Slender and streamlined, it gives the impression of fragility. In reality, though, it is surprisingly powerful for its slight build. When it was bred a century ago, as a sporting dog for coursing rabbits, its popularity did not reach beyond the mining areas of northern England. Indeed, in 1881, Vero Shaw wrote in his *Book of the Dog* that the Whippet was 'essentially a local dog of little value outside the limits of the Northern counties.' The Whippet of today no longer spends its energies coursing rabbits, but it is still the fastest domestic dog for its size. It can reach speeds of 55 kilometres (35 miles) an hour within seconds.

From a dog fancier's point of view, this graceful animal makes an ideal show dog. With its small size and smooth coat it is easy to transport and maintain. Its quiet deportment in the ring is an added advantage. As well as having show potential, it makes an excellent family pet. It does not shed, is neat and clean in its habits, and is easy to house-train. It enjoys being with its owners, but will show some objection to being kennelled. It likes to curl up in a blanket when it sleeps, so it is wise to give the Whippet its own blanket to avoid having to face a round of unmade beds. It is gentle and loving with children and is seldom mean. Not a yappy dog, it is nevertheless a good watch-dog.

The Whippet will live quite happily in a flat or apartment, provided it is exercised regularly. It should be taken for long walks each day, and periodically allowed to run in a wide-open area. Because of its speed, it should be carefully watched and, when it is anywhere near traffic, should be kept on a leash. Although the Whippet is hardy and durable, it does not like cold weather. It develops more slowly than most hounds and does not reach full maturity until about two years of age. By then its show quality should be apparent. Lacking that, it still makes a wonderful pet.

AUS.	CAN.	S. AF.	U.K.	F.C.I.
●	●	●	●	●

ORIGINS

The Whippet is not considered an old breed, having evolved in England a hundred or so years ago. Some authorities claim it is the result of cross-breeding the Italian Greyhound with terriers, particularly the Manchester, the Old English White, and the Bedlington Terrier. The Whippet was developed by miners in Northern England who, unable to afford the upkeep of the Greyhound for coursing hare and rabbit, developed this dog which costs less to feed and groom. The name is believed by some to have come from the Old English whappet, which means a 'small yapping dog.' Yet there are others who claim it came from whip-it, a familiar cry of Victorian gamblers. The dog's terrier blood, and presumed source of courage and stamina, has long since been bred out of the Whippet; emphasis, instead, has been placed on the dog's prowess in straight racing, a sport which had its inception in Lancashire and Yorkshire. This sport was introduced to North America by the Lancashire textile workers who took jobs in the mills of New England early in this century. The British Kennel Club recognized the breed in 1892.

Characteristics

General appearance: this dog must give an impression of sturdiness and strength, combined with great elegance. Its symmetrical proportions, muscular development, and solid gait are its principal characteristics. It is built for speed and work; any exaggerated feature is disadvantageous.

Height: 45.7 to 56 cm (18 to 22 in.) for the adult dog; 43 to 47 cm (17 to 18½ in.) for the bitch. Under Canadian standards, 48.3 to 56 cm (19 to 22 in.) for the adult dog; 45.7 to 53.3 cm (18 to 21 in.) for the bitch.

Weight: not specified.

Head: long and lean, flat on top, tapering towards the muzzle, rather wide between the eyes. Strong jaw, well outlined. Scissor bite. Black nose. For blue dogs, a bluish colour is permissible; for liver-coloured dogs, a liver nose; for white and brindle dogs, a butterfly nose is acceptable.

Eyes: oval, sparkling, very lively expression. Dark.

Ears: rose-shaped, small, of a fine texture.

Neck: long and muscular, elegantly arched.

Body: deep chest with a well-outlined rib-cage. Wide, firm back, rather long and showing a definite arch over the loin, but not humped. Loin giving an impression of strength and power. Ribs well sprung, very muscular on the back. Oblique, muscular shoulders.

Tail: long, tapering. No feathering. When in movement carried with a delicate upward curve, but not over the back.

Forequarters: straight and very solid, thrown forward and low over the ground like those of a thoroughbred horse. Front not too wide. Pasterns strong and flexible. Elbows well positioned under the body.

Hindquarters: wide and strong at the thighs, well under the body. Stifles well bent.

Feet: toes neat, well arched. Thick, strong pads.

Coat: fine, short hair of a texture as dense as possible.

Colour: all colours and mixtures are permissible.

Faults: pasterns weak, sloping, or too straight. Elbows close together. Shoulders heavy or loaded. Apple-shaped skull. Muzzle short, sagging. Straight ears, tulip-shaped. Undershot or overshot. Loin too short, too long. Straight stifles. Tail gay, curled, twisted, short, docked. Hair wiry, broken, harsh, woolly. Dewlap.

Practical information: Care must be taken to ensure that the Whippet is given a balanced diet. Too much starchy or liquid food may cause stomach problems. Avoid overfeeding. Daily walks are essential and the animal should be allowed to run free in an open area whenever possible. Brush the coat daily with a soft brush and polish it with a chamois.

Wire-haired Pointing Griffon

Korthals Griffon

AUS.	CAN.	S. AF.	U.K.	F.C.I.
	●	●		●

A rather slow, deliberate, but skilful multipurpose hunting-dog, the Wire-haired Pointing Griffon (also known as the Korthals Griffon) would certainly not take first prize in a beauty contest. But, in spite of its scruffy moustache, bushy eyebrows and generally unkempt appearance, it is a steady, positive, and intelligent animal.

The Wire-haired Pointing Griffon is a remarkable hunter, gifted with a subtle nose and keenly attentive to the slightest indication which may signal the presence of game. It hunts with an elongated trot—almost a gallop—and because of this some hunters find it too fast. However, since it does not run long distances, it is generally well suited for sportsmen who do their hunting on foot. From a good distance, the Wire-haired Pointing Griffon will sustain a long point on partridge, a feat few other Continental breeds can accomplish so well. Cornering game it has uncovered, it drops to the ground as soon as it hears its master approaching, permitting the hunter a clear view of the target. Good in undergrowth, the Griffon never hesitates to enter the densest bush, and in the woods it is very capable of flushing out pheasant or woodcock. It retrieves equally well in water or on land, and rarely loses its prey. It performs with exceptional skill on marshy ground and in very cold temperatures, thanks to its thick, weather-resistant double coat.

A bit too restless to be a perfect companion dog, it is nevertheless gentle and affectionate. There are times when it remonstrates with continuous yapping and barking—but quite gently. This happens most often when people it does not know enter the house. The Wire-haired Pointing Griffon gets along well with children. It shares in their games and patiently puts up with their pranks. However, it is not a town dog, nor is it happy living indoors. When confined it cannot be relied upon to retain its naturally calm demeanour. It needs an enormous amount of exercise to stay well and happy, and the more exposure it gets to rough terrain and hard living the happier the animal seems to be.

The Wire-haired Pointing Griffon is a dog for an active family that will regularly make demands on its boundless energy. A country house or farm with plenty of wide-open space in which it can run to heart's content is the ideal setting for this dog.

ORIGINS

This rough-coated sporting dog was first known as the Korthals Griffon, so named for Eduard Korthals, the man who standardized the breed. A Dutchman, born in Amsterdam, Korthals worked in Germany between 1865 and 1885 attempting to perfect the breed that is known today as the Wire-haired Pointing Griffon. His aim was to produce a hunting-dog that would rival the British setters, pointers, and spaniels much in fashion at that time. He purchased seven griffons from Europe and inbred them. Such inbreeding had never been applied in so systematic a way before, but it did firmly establish genetic characteristics. Korthals made a strict selection of the pups, keeping only the best of the litters. These were chosen for their emotional and physical qualities. He then bred these prime specimens with setters, spaniels, German mixed-breed dogs, and Barbets. By 1870, he had obtained a homogeneous type of wire-haired griffon to which he gave his name. The Korthals standard was established in 1887, and the breed quickly gained success not only with hunters in Germany, but in many other parts of Europe. The breed was first shown in Britain in the late nineteenth century. It was introduced to North America in 1901, where it was registered under its present name.

Characteristics

General appearance: long dog, well balanced on solid legs.
Height: under F.C.I. and Canadian standards, 55 to 60 cm (21½ to 23½ in.) for the adult dog; 50 to 56 cm (19½ to 21½ in.) for the bitch. Elsewhere, not specified.
Weight: under F.C.I. standards, about 25 kg (55 lb). Elsewhere, not specified.
Head: big, long, with harsh, bushy hair. Eyebrows pronounced.
Eyes: big, yellow or brown, not hidden by the eyebrows.
Ears: medium size, lying flat, or sometimes curled.
Neck: relatively long. No dewlap.
Body: deep chest, not too wide. Ribs slightly rounded. Strong back.
Tail: carried horizontally or with the tip slightly raised. Generally docked to one-third its length.
Forequarters: straight, strong, very solid.
Hindquarters: long and very muscular thighs.
Feet: round, solid, very tight and joined at the toes.
Coat: weather-resistant, harsh, rough outer coat, neither curly nor woolly. Undercoat fine and somewhat dense.
Colour: preferably steel-grey with brown patches, or all brown. White and brown coat, white and orange allowed.

Practical information: A generally healthy dog, it must be given a balanced diet. During the shedding season it is necessary to work on the undercoat with a stiff brush, curry-comb, and regular metal comb to eliminate the abundant, loose hair. On the outer coat the dead hair can be removed with a stripping knife, or by using the thumb and index finger as is done in the trimming of terriers. Keep a watchful eye for auricular catarrh. Examine the ears each week and clean if necessary. It is essential that the Wire-haired Pointing Griffon be given plenty of exercise each day.

A COMPLETE POINTER

Pointers are expected to have numerous and various qualities, the most important being the ability to adapt to varieties of game as well as to differences in terrain. In the hunting of snipe, which usually takes place in marshy areas, a dog must be capable of pointing from a certain distance. In heavy undergrowth, where visibility is poor and where branches obstruct long-range shooting, the dog must point close to its prey, at the same time providing the hunter with a clear view.

In the mountains, where red partridge, large grouse, and rock partridge are hunted, the pointer often has to cut across large areas to get within pointing distance of game. It must then hold a point long enough to give the hunter time to aim.

The hunting of quail and grey partridge, which are found on open terrain, requires a dog that is a fast and tireless runner. In all of these activities the Wire-haired Pointing Griffon excels, and can match even the performance of English Pointers—dogs whose reputation for adeptness has long been established.

Yorkshire Terrier

A bundle of perpetual motion is an apt description for the Yorkshire Terrier. One of the most glamorous and popular of the toy breeds, it is hard to believe that it was originally bred to control the rats in Yorkshire mines and cotton mills. It was also used by the miners as a sporting terrier in rat-killing contests. Such a gutsy little animal seems far removed from the dainty, profusely coated, pampered idol of today's show ring. However, it should be remembered that this all took place in the mid-nineteenth century when the Yorkie was bred to do the work of a terrier. Prior to 1900, it was heavier and larger. Selective breeding brought it to its current size.

When the Yorkshire Terrier first appeared as a distinct breed, there were many critics in the dog world who prophesied that it had no future, and it was often referred to disparagingly. Although not of much appeal to men once it was no longer used for sport, by 1875 it had become popular with ladies of wealth in both Britain and the United States. It was flaunted as a quintessential fashion accessory, carried in the crook of milady's arm, or peeping out from her handbag.

Gifted with a dynamic personality and a more than sufficient amount of courage, it is a delightful little animal. It is a lovable and clever dog, unstinting in its display of affection. It is alert and extremely active and the most playful member of the terrier group. Because of its small size, the Yorkie makes an ideal pet for anyone who lives in an apartment or flat.

AUS.	CAN.	S. AF.	U.K.	F.C.I.
●	●	●	●	●

ORIGINS

The Yorkshire Terrier is the product of cross-breeding several types of Scottish and English terriers, as well as the Maltese. Around 1870, when Scottish workers migrated to Yorkshire in search of work in Leeds, they brought their little dogs with them. These were bred with a local broken-haired terrier which resulted in a fearless little ratter known as the Broken-haired Scotch Terrier. This dog was then cross-bred with the long-haired Leeds Terrier. Also believed to have contributed to this breed are the Manchester Terrier, Black and Tan Terrier, and the Dandie Dinmont Terrier. It became officially known as the Yorkshire Terrier in 1886. Considered the most popular toy breed in Britain today, it is also high on the lists of many other countries.

THE MAKING OF A HANDSOME DOG

To prepare a Yorkshire Terrier for dog shows, special grooming is required. The nails must be trimmed, and hair between the toes and on the feet removed. The under-side of the belly and the anal area must also be cleaned. After washing, the coat may be gently blow-dried while being combed, to avoid the formation of knots and to ensure that the hair is straight—neither curly nor wavy. To prevent the coat from dragging on the ground and getting matted prior to showing, it should be put up loosely in curling papers. When unrolled, the hair will fall perfectly smooth and flat. To keep a Yorkshire Terrier in peak form for showing requires constant care; and the dog must be kept in excellent physical condition if it is to present a sparkling personality. Fanciers of this breed believe that the distinctive appearance this little dog presents is well worth the extra effort.

Characteristics

General appearance: very compact dog, with a straight stance.
Height: under F.C.I. standards, about 20 cm (8 in.). Elsewhere, not specified.
Weight: up to 3.2 kg (7 lb).
Head: rather small and flat. Skull neither prominent nor round. Muzzle rather short. Black nose. Level jaw, even teeth. Scissor bite. Long hair on the head of a golden-tan colour, darker on the sides, at the tip of the ears, and on the muzzle.
Eyes: medium size, must not be protruding. Eye rims dark.
Ears: small, V-shaped, covered with short, tan hair, carried erect or semi-erect.
Neck: good reach, no dewlap.
Body: very compact. Sound loin. Back level. Well laid shoulders.

Tail: customarily docked half-way, covered with abundant hair of a darker blue that the rest of the body. Carried slightly higher than the level of the back.
Forequarters: legs very straight, covered with golden-tan hair up to elbows.
Hindquarters: legs straight, covered with golden-tan hair up to stifles.
Feet: round. Black nails.
Coat: shiny and soft, long and perfectly straight.
Colour: steel-blue from the occiput to the root of the tail. A rich tan on the chest. All tan hair strands must be darker at the roots than along the length, and paler still towards the ends.
Faults: prominent eyes. Curly hair. Silver-blue coat. Tan hair on the head reaching down to the neck. Tan coat spotted with dark, or black hair, or blue mixed with fawn, bronze, or dark hair.

Practical information: It is best to choose a pup about two months old. The smallest are the most beautiful and the most expensive. but they are also the most prone to malformation. It is wise, therefore, to have your puppy examined by a veterinarian. The tail should be docked at birth to half its length. The ears straighten out between two and four months. The Yorkshire Terrier needs a balanced diet. Avoid food with a high sugar content, and do not be too liberal with meat. The dog should be taken for a walk four times a day. In winter and on wet days a raincoat is advisable. The Yorkie's long coat should be brushed daily. The hair should fall from nape to tail, dropping from a centre parting running down the back. The dog should be bathed every month. The pompon on the head, denounced by some, is essential to avoid hair getting into the eyes and causing irritation. It can be held in place by a simple slide pin, or, as is often seen, a ribbon bow. In such a small dog the teeth are soft and should be inspected regularly for tooth decay, tartar accumulation, and diseased gums.

Unofficial Breeds

An unofficial breed is any type of dog that is not formally recognized by one's national kennel club. Accordingly, a breed recognized in one, or several countries, may be unofficial in others. For example, the Canaan Dog (see opposite), an official breed (working dog category) in Canada, has no official status in Australia, Great Britain, and the U.S.A. And the Jack Russell Terrier (see p. 188), recognized by the British Kennel Club among others, has no official status in North America.

Those wanting official recognition for a breed must first agree on a breed standard—specific physical requirements—that is acceptable to the registering body. A major advantage of such recognition is that it permits breeders and owners to show their dogs for prizes.

Many breeds have not received official recognition, and the reasons are varied. The Australian Shepherd, which enjoys phenomenal popularity, is one of them. It has its clubs of avid supporters. Owners' associations in the United States maintain registries, sponsor breed shows, and function very much like national kennel clubs. But these fanciers fear that official recognition would turn their utilitarian animals into pretty but impractical mannequins.

Then there are those dogs which do not even have their own clubs, yet which are popularly considered specific breeds. In this group belongs the Lurcher. Traditionally the British Lurcher is regarded as the gypsy's and the poacher's dog, bred for catching game and providing the family's staple source of meat. A cross-breed, first mentioned as a separate type of dog in the sixteenth century, it should strictly be only a Greyhound and Collie cross, but nowadays a variety of breeds is used to produce dogs with speed, stamina, brains, courage, and a weatherproof coat. Bred to find and catch rabbit and hare, the Lurcher is slower than a Greyhound, but has more stamina and intelligence.

Still other breeds are recognized by secondary registering bodies. Of the several breeds of coonhounds popular with American hunters, only the Black and Tan Coonhound is officially recognized by the Canadian and American kennel clubs. Other coonhounds, such as the Plotthound (believed to be a cross between the American Foxhound and the Black and Tan Coonhound), are recognized by the United Kennel Club in Kalamazoo, Michigan, but are not registered in any other club's stud book. That same organization also lists as breeds dogs that have been rejected by larger clubs. Notable examples are the

AMERICAN ESKIMO DOG

The American Eskimo Dog was created from German Spitz dogs imported into the United States of America in the late 1800s. There are three varieties: standard (height 35-48 cm [14-19 in.], weight 8-16 kg [18-35 lb]); miniature (height 28-38 cm [11-15 in.], weight 4.5-9 kg [10-20 lb]); and toy (males less than 30 cm [12 in.] tall, females less than 28 cm [11 in.] tall, weighing 2.7-4.5 kg [6-10 lb]). It has a white or white-cream spitz-type coat, and is intelligent, alert, and energetic. It is a good family pet and watch-dog.

AMERICAN TOY TERRIER

The American Toy Terrier is also known as the Toy Fox Terrier, or AmerToy. It is a direct descendant of the English Smooth Fox Terrier, which was brought to North America in the 1870s. It was deliberately bred down from the runts of Fox Terrier litters to produce a miniature version, standing 25 cm (10 in.) tall and weighing 1.5 to 3.5 kg (3½-7lb). The coat is smooth and is preferably white with black or brown markings. Intelligent, inquisitive, and a delightful companion, it still retains its hunting instincts, and can be scrappy with other dogs.

American Toy Terrier, which is descended from the Fox Terrier and various toy breeds; the American Eskimo, a dog resembling a small Samoyed; and the tenacious Pit Bull Terrier, a dog now prohibited in several North American municipalities.

Some breeds are simply too rare, too few in number, to be recognized everywhere at the moment, but their speciality clubs have drawn up standards and are working hard for eventual status. To qualify for recognition there must be a sufficient number of specimens available so that breeders will not be tempted to be indiscriminate in the mating of their dogs. The powerful Tibetan Mastiff, which closely resembles the Saint Bernard, and the Blue Picardy Spaniel are recognized by some kennel clubs, but they have not, as yet, been granted complete recognition around the world—and, where they are recognized, they are seldom shown. Nevertheless, they both boast loyal supporters.

Many breeds are virtually unheard of internationally, yet popular in their native lands. Such dogs, though often listed with the Fédération cynologique internationale, are unlikely to become widely known, and thus remain 'unofficial' as breeds for showing purposes in English-speaking countries. The Dunkerstovare of Norway is a case in point, being quite rare outside its own country, where it is commonplace.

There are some countries where breeds are considered unofficial because that country's kennel club does not recognize the stud book of the dog's country of origin. In this category would fall such dogs as the Gontjaja Estonskaja, a foxhound type and one of the rarest breeds in Russia, and the Laikas, a group of spitz-type dogs found in northern Russia. Their name comes from the Russian verb 'to bark.' Laikas are used as sledge and guard dogs, and for hunting game such as bear, elk, reindeer, sable, and ermine. Medium-size dogs, they are bred for strength, agility, and endurance, and are known for their aggressive and stubborn temperament. Few people in the West are aware that Russia has quite a large canine selection, and that the dog shows, most of which are held in Moscow, are well attended.

Some breeds did, at one time, have official recognition, but because they lost popularity they were dropped from clubs' registers. Into this category falls the Clydesdale Terrier of Britain, which was a forerunner of the Skye Terrier. Differences of opinion among its breeders caused the dog to lose favour. By the mid-1930s the breed was no longer recognized and had ceased to be exhibited at dog shows.

Clearly, not all speciality breed clubs regard official kennel club recognition as a primary goal. The fanciers of these breeds are equally committed to producing quality animals that conform to certain standards, but often believe that formal kennel club status can be a mixed blessing.

CANAAN DOG

The Canaan Dog is descended from the pariah dogs found throughout the Middle and Far East. There are two types—the 'Collie' and the 'Dingo.' Both are medium-sized (48-58 cm [19-24 in.] tall) and weigh 16-25 kg (35-55 lb). The Collie type is the heavier and has a double coat. Colours range between brown, black, and white, with red, brown, or black markings. The Canaan is famous for its intelligence and endurance. It has been used for guarding and herding livestock, as a guide dog for the blind, by the Israeli army for locating wounded soldiers, and as a messenger.

TIBETAN MASTIFF

The Tibetan Mastiff is the largest of the Tibetan breeds (up to 80 cm [31 in.] at the shoulder, and weighing 100 kg [nearly 220 lb]), and is regarded as the ancestor of the modern Mastiff and flock-guarding breeds. The working dog of the Himalayas, it was developed for guarding livestock and property. It is large and heavily-boned, with a massive head, powerful neck, and strong jaws. A long, thick coat provides protection in the hardest weather, and is usually black and gold. The Tibetan Mastiff may be aggressive and unpredictable without discipline and training.

Mongrels

Cross-breeds, Mixed Breeds

Spaniel cross-breed

Pinscher cross-breed

Mongrel

Griffon cross-breed

In addition to the many pure breeds which make up the canine scene, there are literally countless combinations of breeds, and these are classified as mongrels, or cross-breeds.

Some canine authorities use the term cross-breed to refer to dogs whose sire and dam were pure-bred, but of different breeds. The mongrel, they maintain, has both parents of mixed origins. They make this distinction because many pure-bred dogs today have evolved from careful, selective interbreeding programmes—and even from the accidental yet felicitous matings of different pure breeds. A cross-bred dog, some believe, is superior to a mongrel because its genetic traits are more predictable. Indeed, such an animal may be superior to its pure-bred parents if, say, its dam's strengths compensate for its sire's deficiencies. Most dog experts, however, do not distinguish between a mongrel and a cross-bred dog, and use the terms interchangeably.

Mongrels are found in the city, in the suburbs, and in the country. Some will be given away, some sold for a pittance, and many will be destroyed. Then there are the survivors—the vagabonds—which spend their days scrounging food from rubbish bins and searching for shelter in the cold of winter. Yet another group bands together in packs, living off the farmer's young livestock and poultry and whatever wild animals they can bring down.

The fact that mongrels do not star in dog shows is far outweighed by many positive characteristics. They can be remarkably intelligent, loving, faithful, and courageous—and gentle with children. Mongrel devotees insist that mixed breeds are more quick-witted and even-tempered than pure-breds, which are sometimes genetically flawed. Furthermore, no rule of nature precludes a mongrel from being strikingly beautiful.

The problem with mongrels resides more with their owners than with the dogs themselves. When these animals are allowed to mate at random, the puppies may be hard to find homes for. It is an unfortunate fact that a large proportion of dogs in animal shelters are mongrels—and that many of them are destroyed.

You and Your Dog

Choosing a Dog
286

Sleeping Quarters
290

Feeding
292

Hygiene and Grooming
298

Canine Psychology
303

Education and Training
313

Choosing a Dog

Anyone who intends to buy a dog should be aware that this is an important decision. A dog will not only make changes in a family's everyday life, it will also, at times, cause problems. A dog is a living creature that needs its owner's presence and care; the master or mistress must accept responsibility for it on a permanent basis. In return, the dog will provide much joy as a loyal, affectionate, and faithful companion.

You must determine whether you are in a position to cater to the animal's various needs for as long as it lives—which is to say, generally from 10 to 15 years. If the millions of people who buy dogs each year carefully examined how the acquisition would disturb their routines, some would change their minds, and there would be fewer abandoned pets. You must also consider the other expenses involved apart from the purchase price: food, grooming, veterinary care.

Criteria

Your life-style, your activities, and your age should influence your choice of a dog. You must also decide what you intend the dog to be: a pet, a watch-dog, a guard dog, or a hunting-dog.

In the country, and in some suburbs, adequate space is no problem. City dwellers, however, are well advised to choose a medium-size animal since a big dog is likely to cause damage and be unhappy in a small home. A Great Dane or a Saint

Bernard, for example, needs 150 square metres (180 square yards) of space. It also needs at least an hour's walk every day, and must be allowed to play freely outdoors a minimum of one day a week.

On the other hand, even small dogs can make poor urban pets. Any type of dog that has been bred to hunt—whether for rodents, birds, or foxes—needs to run regularly. The Basset Hound, for example, is a hunter of hare by instinct. Not only is this short, stodgy-looking dog capable of great speed and endurance, it needs the space and time to exercise effectively. The Beagle as well is a deceptive pet. Beyond needing the chance to run freely off-leash, it needs to track game. Thus, a Beagle may disappear until its hunting instincts are satisfied. Toy dogs that bark zestfully, if not nervously, do not belong in thin-walled apartment buildings where footsteps in the corridor or in the upstairs unit could confuse any animal with a vigilant sense of territory. For that matter, a dog that barks too readily is a poor choice for a flat or any household where infants and children nap.

Since the owner's presence is vital to the dog's psychological well-being, you should not acquire a puppy if you intend to leave it alone all day. The fact is that in such conditions you will not be able to raise the dog properly.

The age and disposition of a pet owner must be taken into account. For a young child, there are virtual nursemaids such as the Briard, the Old English Sheepdog, the Labrador Retriever, and the Boxer. They adapt well to family life provided they are given as much exercise as necessary. And, while they play with the youngest of children, they also protect them. Older children who are able to care for the animal themselves should be given a short-haired dog, which requires a minimum of grooming. Elderly people must consider their own physical strength. High-strung animals can cause their masters to fall by leaping upon them or tugging on the leash. Yorkshire Terriers, Pekingese, Toy and Miniature Poodles, and Dachshunds are very popular because they are not bothersome and are easy to transport. But it all depends on what you are looking for. Watch-dogs and guard dogs are an effective deterrent against burglars and purse-snatchers.

All dogs are born small—but think of the future when choosing a puppy. Remember that there is no comparison between a Great Dane's needs for food and space and those of a Chihuahua.

Be sure to take into consideration the exercise area available for a dog. What amount of yard space do you have? Will you be able to let the dog run freely in a fenced-in yard or will you have to walk it on a leash? If walking is the rule, make an honest estimate as to how much time you are willing to spend accompanying the dog and where you can take it to relieve

Although they lack the select lineage of pure-breds, cross-bred dogs often make delightful and intelligent household companions.

itself and to exercise. Consider as well whether you can share this responsibility with children, a mate, or even a paid dog-walker. In some cities, dogs are forbidden in every park; other cities offer dog-runs where animals can amble if restrained by a leash. Even in cities where dogs are welcome to run freely in parks, there are likely to be laws that require owners to clean up after their pets, a chore that some people find unseemly and distasteful.

Finally, try to match the temperament of the dog with the disposition of the person it is intended for. For instance, a nervous person with limited living space might be happy to own a dog that barks readily—a Fox Terrier or a Miniature Pinscher—to alert him to every suspicious noise. An athletic person will choose a muscular animal to jog with: a Boxer or Collie, for example. A fastidious house-keeper would not be happy with a long-haired, soft-mouthed breed. Its drooling and seasonal shedding would probably prove irksome, so it would be wiser to

This modern kennel provides maximum canine comfort. It has a maternity section with 30 units, each with its own temperature control.

choose a short-haired dog with a pointed muzzle. In certain cases a dog whose temperament contrasts with the master's is a suitable choice. For instance, some parents give a sedentary child a lively animal. An overly boisterous child, on the other hand, would probably benefit from a calm, even-tempered companion.

Should you buy a mature dog—one that has been house-trained, neutered or spayed, and is past the age of chewing on chair legs and shoes? Advertisements for such dogs appear at veterinary offices and animal shelters, in newspapers and on public bulletin boards. Some dog fanciers warn against this way of obtaining a dog; the animal may have been mistreated. Others insist that you can readily tell if a dog has been poorly or maliciously handled: It will cringe or lunge or bark to excess. Few canine psychological disorders are subtle. Furthermore, these adult dogs may be cherished family pets that have to be given away—perhaps the family is leaving the country or moving to smaller

More than half of all prospective dog owners go to kennels to buy a pure-bred dog.

accommodations; perhaps a child has developed an allergic reaction to pet hairs. If you like the dog—and if the dog likes you—it is nonetheless a wise precaution to find out the name of the dog's veterinarian, then to visit his or her office to examine the animal's health records for yourself.

Should you choose a male rather than a bitch? In theory, the female is more attached to the home, while the male in some cases protects it better. To help you decide, you should remember that with modern contraceptive methods you can reduce the number of the bitch's seasons in heat and pregnancies. It is also worth remembering that males unable to satisfy their sexual needs may become habitual runaways.

Pure-bred or cross-bred?

Once you have decided you want to own a dog, the next step is to choose between a pure-bred and a cross-bred, also called a

An easy, pleasant way to obtain a puppy: adopt one from the litter of a friend's bitch.

mongrel. Some pure-bred enthusiasts contend that because their dogs are often very expensive they are seldom abandoned, but there is little proof of that theory.

The advantage of having a pure-bred is that it will develop in a predictable manner; thus the owner can determine what the puppy will look like when it is fully grown. With a cross-bred of unknown parentage, there could be some disagreeable surprises.

In any event, how people choose dogs, whether cross-breds or pure-breds, was indicated in a recent survey of 2,000 owners: One-third followed the example of a friend or relative; one-third were influenced by a dog's media image; and one-third based their decision on the average behaviour of a particular type of dog.

Although mongrels are usually chosen for economic reasons, there are nevertheless people who prefer them. They believe that because the cross-bred is not subject to the effects of inbreeding, it is healthier and more intelligent than a pure-bred (this has yet to be proved).

Many sad-eyed dogs wait in animal shelters for a master to adopt them.

Where to find a dog

Kennels that raise pure-breds must provide papers which vouch for the dog's pedigree, as well as a sales receipt which gives the purchaser recourse if he or she has been misled. In most countries, these papers consist of a registration card or certificate bearing the dog's tattoo number or noseprint (if applicable), and a birth certificate attesting to its registration in the country of its birth or its eligibility to be registered.

The best way to buy a pure-bred dog is to go to a professional breeder who sells puppies in excellent health and who can show prospective owners the parents of the pups. To find out about breeders, simply apply to a dog club that specializes in the breed you want. National kennel clubs provide lists of their affiliated breed clubs.

Next, there are the amateur breeders; the better ones are known to veterinarians. Finally, there are pet stores. When you buy a dog from one of these, make sure you obtain a grace period of 48 hours (excluding week-ends) in which to have a veterinarian examine the puppy.

Although there are many quality kennels where the animals are properly raised, some unscrupulous dealers sell mongrels with forged papers, passing them off as pure-breds. Furthermore, these animals are sometimes in such poor health that many require expensive medical treatment—or die shortly after being sold.

Another way to buy a dog is to look through the classified advertisements in specialized publications in which breeders offer puppies for sale. Breeders usually offer only one breed and refer to their registration with kennel clubs.

Acquiring a cross-bred is a relatively simple matter. There are many of them in local animal shelters. Telephone in advance to determine what identification you should take with you. Once your application has been approved, you can choose your dog from among all those abandoned.

There is one way you can acquire a cross-bred dog with minimal uncertainty: obtain it from a friend or relative who wants to find good homes for his puppies. In this case, you will probably know the parentage of the litter, so you need not fear any unpleasant surprises.

A puppy should be between two-and-a-half and four months old when you acquire it. If you are buying from a kennel, choose a puppy more than three months old. The best time of year to buy is spring Before selecting your pet, examine the entire litter carefully, and do not let your heart be melted by the runt. A healthy animal is plump and lively. It has round, sparkling eyes, a shiny coat, fresh breath, white teeth, and firm, pink gums. There are some obvious danger signals: listlessness, runny eyes, a persistent cough, a scabby nose, red skin patches, a swollen stomach, or bow-legs—a sign of rickets.

Last of all, remember that the dog will grow. Find out what its adult size will be and thereby avoid a rude awakening. Once you have finally chosen the puppy, you will want to give it a name. If the dog is a cross-bred, you may choose any name you please, but if it is a pure-bred, the choice of name is the privilege of the breeder. Tattooing and noseprinting (in countries that require such proof of identification) are the responsibility of the breeder.

Dog food is a considerable item in an owner's budget, whether store-bought or home-made.

Budgeting

Owning a dog involves expenditures that cannot be ignored: purchase or adoption expenses, equipment and grooming, and veterinary fees.

The cost of a three-month-old pure-bred puppy, for instance, does not depend on its size but on its breed. Your initial outlay can be quite large; it depends on the place of sale and the quality of the animal.

As for the equipment (collar, leash, and so forth), prices vary with the size of the dog, the sophistication of the equipment, and the materials used. Differences between minimum and maximum costs can be considerable. Nonetheless, once bought many of these items last the dog's lifetime.

Apart from the collar and leash, other essentials include: case for carrying small breeds on public transportation; indoor bed or basket; food and water dishes; grooming equipment (single comb and rubber gloves for short-haired dogs, brush and double comb for long-haired dogs).

Certain breeds require special grooming, such as stripping for Fox Terriers and Airedales, and clipping for Bedlington Terriers and Poodles. All of these dogs should be professionally groomed at least four times a year.

In addition to the above, there are the daily food costs which, naturally, rise in proportion to the size of the dog.

Veterinary expenses are difficult to anticipate since they depend on the animal's basic health. However, there are some that are definite. For instance, a puppy should be examined by a specialist once a month for the first six months. Most small dogs require dental attention twice a year. Then there are the optional operations of neutering or spaying. Cosmetic surgery, which is

To keep your dog healthy, have it examined regularly by a veterinarian.

essential for certain breeds of show dogs, may include ear-cropping or tail-docking, and sometimes both, in certain countries.

A serious step

Buying or adopting a dog is a serious step because the existence of a living creature is involved. You should never act on impulse or be swayed by pity, or you may find yourself saddled with a poor-quality puppy, or an animal that ends up being too large for its environment. Before acquiring a dog, always make sure you obtain every available guarantee, in writing. Your receipt should include the dog's date of birth, its registered name, and the registration number of the sire and the dam. In countries that require tattooing, the sequence of tattoo allocation should be included. If you have been misled about the puppy's origins or state of health, do not hesitate to make use of legal procedures. If you bought the puppy from a breeder, get in touch with the appropriate breed club.

Sleeping Quarters

You have made your decision and chosen your dog, and it is about to arrive at your house. Now you must decide where it will sleep. The options will vary according to whether you live in a house with a large or small garden or in an apartment or flat. Regardless of where you live, however, your dog must always have its own private domain where it can feel at home.

Indoors

Find a quiet place for the dog to sleep. The location should be convenient for you and suitable for your pet. Make sure your dog feels comfortable there, and do not change the location afterwards.

It is not advisable to allow a dog to sleep on an armchair or on your bed—however disarming your pet's appeal—because upholstery and blankets attract dirt, hair, and parasites.

An uncarpeted room, not too cold, with a floor that is easy to wash, is a good choice. A puppy must be well protected from draughts: beware of cold air seeping in around doors and windows. A dog will automatically settle with its back against a wall, so arrange your pet's spot next to a wall or in a corner—but not too close to a radiator or heating vent lest the dog's coat dries out and becomes brittle. The dog's place should be away from heavily travelled areas because the animal will probably need a lot of sleep, initially. But the dog should also be able to observe everyone's comings and goings so it can start taking part in family life.

Your pet can probably sleep comfortably in a crate lined with cushions, a towel,

If the dog is not too large, it can sleep in a wicker basket or in a crate lined with cushions.

or shredded newspaper. Fairly large dogs generally just sleep on a blanket. But if your dog will weigh 15 kilograms (33 pounds) or less when fully grown, you can use a wicker basket lined with a soft, easily washable cushion. The main concern is to see that the animal is well insulated from the floor, particularly a tiled one.

Air the dog's bedding every day and clean it once a week—more often if the puppy soils it. In summer, if your dog gets fleas or ticks, treat the bedding several times with the same flea and tick powder you use on the animal itself, and vacuum the floor and bottom of the walls.

You can put the dog's two bowls—one for food, the other for water—near its bed. If the dog's muzzle is pointed, use deep bowls. If its muzzle is blunt, shallow bowls are preferable. There are deep bowls specially designed for long-eared dogs. If you permit your dog to eat in the kitchen, make sure it can enter there easily at night if it becomes thirsty.

For a toy, give your dog a bone made of animal hide. It can cut its teeth safely on the hide because even if it swallows a piece, the material is digestible. You may find that your dog will choose its own plaything; if so, make sure the choice is not an old shoe. This may encourage it to start chewing new shoes.

Outdoors

Whenever possible, large heavy-coated dogs should live outdoors in a well-insulated kennel. If you buy a puppy in winter, however, keep it indoors until spring.

If you have an outbuilding, shed, laundry room, or store-room that is well ventilated but without draughts, put the dog's bed in a corner. The bed should be mounted on a wooden frame covered with a blanket to keep it off the floor.

THE FIRST NIGHT

Will you have the heart to let your little puppy spend its first night all alone in your home? No matter how distressed you may feel, this is still the best method if you want the dog to grow accustomed to its spot and not move into your room or your children's. There are, however, ways you can make the experience easier on your pet. Put a clock near its basket: The ticking will reassure it. A hot-water bottle under a cushion will provide a soothing reminder of its mother's warmth, and a light meal before bedtime will relax it.

You can build a kennel with wood (coniferous woods are best because their odours repel parasites), brick, or plastic. The kennel should be insulated; the roof and walls must be neatly joined to keep out wind and rain. The interior must be roomy enough to allow the dog free movement. Make the doorway one-and-a-half to two times the dog's width. A detachable roof permits easy access for cleaning, and you can remove it in summer.

The kennel should be well protected from wind and water runoff. Place it so that the dog can watch one of the entrances to the house and share, to some extent, in the life of the household. Disinfect it and treat it for parasites several times a year. In winter you can hang up a heavy sheet of canvas in the doorway of the kennel to ensure that warmth is retained.

Before you attach a dog to its kennel, check municipal regulations to determine what length of chain is permitted.

VERY SMALL DOGS

Very small dogs may seem to demand special treatment because of their size. If you choose such a dog, be careful not to step on its extremely delicate paws. This is especially worth noting since it is more than likely that the dog will always be close at heel.

Apart from this consideration, however, small dogs do not need any more—or any less—attention than large dogs. They can be house-trained in the same way as other dogs, and they can be taught to sleep alone, if that is your preference. Although you may be tempted to relax the rules from time to time because of the dog's smallness, it is unwise to do so. Without effective discipline, you would be inviting your pet to grow up spoiled and, possibly, ill-tempered.

A KENNEL FOR YOUR PET

If your dog is to be kept outside for any length of time, it should have a sturdy kennel where it can retreat from the heat of the midday sun and take shelter at the first sign of rain.

If you wish, you may order a kennel through most pet shops, or you can obtain plans through the numerous do-it-yourself publications that are on the market. But why not design and build one yourself? All it takes is a little ingenuity and some basic carpentry skills.

Before setting off for the wood-yard, check around your home. Is there an old packing crate, a barrel, some scrap lumber that you can use? (Plywood is excellent.)

Be sure to make the kennel big enough to allow your pet freedom of movement. The door should be 1½ to 2 times the width of the dog. If you can, build a small vestibule inside the entrance, to provide further protection from the weather. For easy cleaning, make one side—or the roof—removable. (You can use hinges for this.) Finally, cover the floor with shredded newspaper. Straw may also be used, but make sure it is clean. Unclean straw may contain fleas.

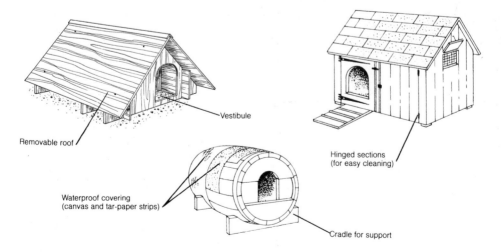

Removable roof

Vestibule

Waterproof covering (canvas and tar-paper strips)

Hinged sections (for easy cleaning)

Cradle for support

Feeding

Living as they do with people, and dependent on them for food, dogs frequently suffer the consequences of their owners' ignorance of what an animal should eat. Many pet owners simply do not know that dogs have entirely different nutritional needs from those of humans.

Although dogs have physiological and biological reactions very similar to our own, the way in which their organic needs are met is different. Unfortunately, when owners think of their pets as human and thus feed them as they would their families, they supply their dogs a diet so inappropriate that it could spell nutritional disaster for the animals.

Basics of Canine Nutrition and Proper Diet

Dogs are popularly thought to be carnivores and therefore able to subsist on diets composed entirely of meat. But such is not the case. Like most other animals, dogs are omnivores; they require a variety of foods —vegetables and grains as well as meats— to meet their daily nutrient requirements.

As an omnivore, the dog must obtain energy from carbohydrates and fats to carry out life's activities. It also requires dietary proteins to furnish amino acids, which are the 'building blocks' of muscle, skin, hair, internal organs, blood, hormones, and enzymes. Furthermore, dogs require dietary sources of minerals and vitamins, both to regulate many vital physiological reactions and to provide the necessary ele-

ments for the formation of bone and red blood cells.

The five groups of nutrients are discussed here. Most foods contain nutrients from more than one group. Only a few foods, such as sugars, pure starch, hydrogenated vegetable oils, lard, and other animal fats, provide a sole category of nutrient.

• Carbohydrates. Sugars and starches provide calories. Some, like fibre, aid greatly in maintaining normal intestinal functions, but do not contribute energy to the animal.

• Fats. These furnish a concentrated energy source and essential fatty acids. All fats contribute fatty acids to the diet, but only vegetable oils and chicken fat provide unsaturated and polyunsaturated fatty acids, the 'essential' ones.

• Proteins. These complex combinations of amino acids are essential for building and maintaining tissues and for certain biological functions. Meat, offal, and fish are high-quality (complete) proteins. Vegetables and grains are incomplete (low-quality) proteins. When combined

Most owners appreciate the time-saving benefits of using commercial dog food.

correctly, however, they form complementary proteins: for example, oatmeal and rice, or rice and corn. Crude proteins also provide calories.

• Minerals. These are substances in the diet which cannot be oxidized any further. They are recorded as 'ash' on many pet food labels. Some, such as calcium and phosphorus, which comprise the major parts of bone, are required in relatively large amounts—about 1 per cent of the total dry weight (see bottom paragraph) of the diet. Others, such as iron, a component of haemoglobin in red blood cells, are required in minute quantities—parts per million (p.p.m.).

• Vitamins. These are organic substances that promote normal metabolic functions—from the release of energy to the synthesis of normal vision. Dogs require the same vitamins as humans, except for vitamin C, which they make themselves.

• Water. Dogs cannot do without water. Humans, who often drink when they do not need to, sometimes forget that when animals want to drink it is because they are truly thirsty. A dog weighing about 30 kilograms (65 pounds) that is fed canned food drinks about a litre, or a quart, of water a day in warm weather. Those given semi-moist or dry food may drink as much as 2 litres. Be sure to provide your dog with enough clean water, and if you take it for a long walk or out hunting, remember to give it water accordingly.

Keep the supply of the various food groups carefully balanced, paying particular attention to the calorie intake in relation to the other nutrients. Every time a pet owner increases the calorie content in his dog's diet by adding too many fats or carbohydrates (bread or cakes, given supposedly as a treat for the dog but, in reality, as a treat for the owner), the proportion of proteins, minerals, and vitamins in the diet must be increased. In fact, the richer the food is in calories, the less of it the animal absorbs, and the balance of nutrients needed to meet the dog's dietary requirements may be disrupted. Furthermore, you cannot just increase the percentage of protein; you must also watch its quality. By combining high- and low-protein foods such as meat, offal, fish, cereals, and vegetables, you can provide a proper diet, in both quantity and quality.

Energy needs are influenced by the body surface area, therefore large dogs require less energy on a body weight basis than do small dogs.

The nutrient composition of dog foods is calculated on a dry weight basis—that is, the amount of protein in wet, semi-moist, and dry foods can only be compared when the quantity of moisture has been subtracted from the food's net weight. For example, if a tin of food weighs 100 units and 80 per cent of those units (80 units) is water and 10 per cent of those units (10 units) is protein, the dry weight of the tin is 20 units, 10 units of which (or half) is protein. A 100-unit sack of dry food, on the other hand, typically contains 5 per cent moisture (5 units) and 20 per cent protein (20 units). Thus, only 19 per cent of a dry-weight unit of dry food is protein compared to 50 per cent of a dry-weight unit for wet.

Quality commercial foods generally contain added vitamins to compensate for any nutrient loss during processing. For the same reason, you should be sure to provide a vitamin supplement if you prepare your dog's food yourself. When cereals or vegetables are cooked, as they must be in dog food, they can lose between 5 and 40 per cent of their vitamins. Eggs should always be given cooked since raw egg white interferes with the absorption of biotin, an important B vitamin.

Staples in Canine Diets

Dogs may become accustomed to a particular diet and refuse to eat other foods. To avoid the development of dietary 'bias,' young dogs should be exposed to a variety of foods.

Home-made food

A dog's diet is based on three foods: meats (and/or offal), cereals, and vegetables. According to the dog's weight, add a tablespoonful or a teaspoonful of sunflower or corn oil. The oil should constitute 2 to 3 per cent of the serving. Add a similar proportion of dry brewer's yeast, or, better still, lactic yeast, and, of course, a mineral and vitamin supplement.

• For meat, it is generally acceptable to buy cheap cuts for your dog. Viscera, such as beef liver or lung, can also be used. Lung provides a better quality of protein than beef cheek. Liver is an excellent source of proteins and vitamins. For sanitary reasons, meat should be served cooked.

Dogs may eat fish, provided it is cooked and the bones have been removed. If the fish is ground fine with its bones, the dog can eat it safely, while benefiting from the additional calcium. Never give fish heads or fish offal.

• For carbohydrates, use broken or whole rice, barley meal, corn, porridge oats, pasta or pasta scraps, bread, and dog biscuits. Avoid beans because dogs find them difficult to digest, and they cause flatulence. Be sparing with oats; they contain a substance that disrupts the assimilation of minerals.

• For vegetables, carrots are generally the best choice because of their low price. Cooked potatoes are another economical vegetable. Green beans, although many dogs enjoy them, are sometimes quite expensive.

Boil the vegetables, change the water at

least once, and dry them before serving. Do not give them as soup. (When soup is left standing at room temperature, it becomes a breeding ground for bacteria.)

• For fats, in addition to the sunflower or corn oil mentioned above, you can include an equal measure of lard to make the food more appetizing.

Never give your dog rancid fats or fats that have even once been heated to the smoking point.

Unlike people, dogs do not have a wide range of possible foods to help compensate for any deficiencies or dietary imbalances. Therefore make sure you choose those few foods carefully. Remember to add a mineral and vitamin supplement, and oils rich in essential fatty acids (corn or sunflower oil) to provide a balanced diet.

Commercial dog food

Pet foods are broadly classified as dry, semi-moist, or wet (canned). Wet food contains as much as 80 per cent water, semi-moist foods about 30 per cent, and dry food has as little as 5 per cent water.

Meat sources for many tinned dog foods are those parts of livestock which are no longer regarded as fit for human consumption. Lungs, hearts, livers, spleens, tracheae, and oesophagi are added.

The vegetables included are generally carrots, sometimes leeks, and finally a small amount of onion, which adds flavour. Some authorities think that onions have other useful properties as well, including natural antibiotics, although heating tends to render these properties inactive.

Rice, porridge oats, and in some cases wheat, accompany the vegetables. Manufacturers include a low percentage of lactic or hydrolysed yeasts. Other ingredients include various mineral substances, bone and grain meals, and fat- and water-soluble vitamins. Sometimes fresh pork fat, sunflower oil, or corn oil are added to the product.

Apart from the dry foods, a dog eats food that is, for the most part, soft in consistency. As a result, the animal's teeth may suffer from tartar buildup and decay. The most efficient way to control tartar is by regularly brushing or scaling your pet's teeth. Contrary to popular belief, giving the dog a bone to gnaw will not really result in cleaning its teeth, except for the incisors and the canines.

How to Feed Your Dog

Adults

Although it may seem logical to feed your adult dog at the same time as you feed yourself, avoid the temptation. A full-grown dog should have only two meals a day, and these should be six or seven hours apart. Be sure to serve food that is no hotter than 38°C (100°F), and make the morning meal smaller than the evening meal. Regular feedings are important for your pet's digestion—and for your routine. Remember, dogs must not be walked after eating.

Approximate quantity of food needed by adult dogs according to body weight								
			Daily Food Ration					
Size of breed	Weight of dog		90% dry		75% dry		25–35% dry	
	kg	lb	g	oz	g	oz	g	oz
Small and very small dogs	1	2¼	35	1¼	48	1¾	118	4
	2	4½	58	2	80	2¾	195	7
	3	6½	79	2¾	109	3¾	262	9¼
	4	8¾	97	3½	133	4¾	323	11½
	5	11	114	4	155	5½	380	13½
	6	13¼	130	4½	177	6¼	433	15¼
	7	15½	146	5	201	7	487	17¼
	8	17½	161	5½	223	7¾	537	19
	9	19¾	175	6	238	8½	583	20½
	10	22	190	6¾	257	9	630	22¼
Medium-size dogs	20	44	313	11	442	15½	1040	36¾
	30	66	423	15	567	20	1410	49¾
Large and very large dogs	40	88	523	18½	725	25½	1740	61½
	50	110	613	21¾	832	29¼	2043	72

'Dry' refers to the dry weight of the dog food after its moisture content has been subtracted. Thus, commercial dry food is 90 per cent dry; semi-moist food to which porridge, oats, and vegetables have been added is 75 per cent dry; and canned food that is similar in composition to the formula at the bottom of page 296 is 25 to 35 per cent dry.

Most veterinarians will gladly advise you on what to feed your dog. For your convenience, however, we have incorporated an established formula below. The formula was devised by Professor Raymond Ferrando, a veterinarian. One kilogram, or 2¼ pounds, of this food will provide your dog with approximately 1500 kilocalories of metabolizable energy, 70 grams (2½ ounces) of proteins, and a balanced amount of fatty acids and B complex vitamins. The following figures represent weight units, thus the proportion of ingredients is constant whether you measure in the metric or imperial system. Be sure to stick consistently to one unit of weight—grams or ounces. Units of volume, either liquid or dry, are not appropriate.

Boiled carrots 27
Cooked, broken or whole rice 35
Cooked meat 30
Lard and (or) corn or sunflower oil 4
Dry brewer's yeast 3
Mineral and vitamin supplement 1

While it is possible to concoct your own vitamin and mineral supplement, most dog owners today find this practice both time-consuming and impractical given the wealth of commercially manufactured supplements available. Your veterinarian will be able to help you choose a specific brand. A typical mix will be as follows:

Calcium phosphate .... 60 g
Dipotassium phosphate .... 10 g
Sodium chloride .... 10 g
Magnesium sulphate .... 3 g
Iron citrate .... 1.50 g
Copper sulphate .... .15 g
Cobalt acetate .... .01 g
Zinc sulphate .... .01 g
Manganese dioxide .... .10 g
Potassium iodide .... .01 g
Coated vitamin A .... 100 000 IU*
Coated vitamin B3 .... 10 000 IU
Vitamin E .... 500 mg
Methionin .... 15 g
Enough calcium lactate to make up
    100 grams

* International units

In terms of nutritional value, this supplement corresponds to a commercial, tinned dog food that is between 25 and 30 per cent dry.

Special diets

We will not deal here with the various diets needed to treat obese, nephritic, or diabetic dogs. For these conditions, consult your veterinarian. (Veterinarians today have access to a variety of special, commercially made diet foods that are used for treating dogs with kidney disease, dogs with delicate stomachs, and dogs recovering from illnesses, as well as for bitches nursing puppies.)

You can protect your dog from obesity by keeping it on a strict diet, and not feeding it table scraps. Indeed, in a recent article on diets, it was emphasized that the greatest number of obese dogs are those that are fed on table scraps or whose rations are prepared at home by owners with little or no knowledge of canine dietetics. Such dogs grow accustomed to begging for—and receiving—bread, chocolate, sugar, and a host of other undesirable foodstuffs, both at mealtime and at other hours of the day. As a result of their owners' indulgence, these dogs fall prey to a variety of deficiency-related diseases, not the least of which is chronic eczema. Although we ourselves sometimes deviate from sound eating habits, we should not cause our dogs to do likewise. Proper feeding is one important way of caring for your pet.

Pregnant and lactating dogs

If your dog is in gestation, you may feed it the diet suggested for adult dogs, but increase the quantity by 10 per cent.

The day after the dog whelps, increase its usual ration (already raised by 10 per cent during pregnancy) and let it eat all it wants for four or five days more. It is generally agreed that the nutritional requirements for a bitch during lactation will at least double—some even say triple—par-

Approximate quantity of food needed by lactating dogs							
Dog's weight		week 1		weeks 2 to 5		Pre-weaning	
kg	lb	g	oz	g	oz	g	oz
3.5–5	7½–11	280–400	10–14	450–800	16–28	200–250	7–9
5–6	11–13	400–450	14–16	800–900	28–32	250–300	9–11
6–10	13–22	450–800	16–28	900–1200	32–42		
10–12	22–26	800–850	28–30	1200–1500	42–53	500–550	18–19
12–20	26–44	850–1300	30–45	1500–2500	53–88		
20–22	44–48	1300–1500	45–53	2500–2700	88–95	950–1000	33–35
22–27	48–59	1500–1800	53–63	2700–3200	95–112		
27–32	59–70	1800–2200	63–78	3200–3700	112–130	1100–1300	39–46
32–40	70–88	2200–3000	78–106	3700–4800	130–169	1500–1700	53–60
45–50	99–110	3500–4000	123–141	5200–6000	183–212	1800–2000	63–70

ticularly for bitches that nurse large litters. (Actually, it is difficult, if not impossible, to meet the needs of a lactating dog in such cases.)

As is the case for most special-purpose dog foods, food for lactating dogs can usually be obtained commercially. Your veterinarian will be able to advise you. If such food is difficult to obtain, however, or if you intend to prepare food for a lactating dog yourself, the following formula will serve as a guide. The figures represent weight units and are proportionally correct in metric and imperial dimensions.

Boiled carrots 8
Cooked, broken or whole rice 23
Cooked meat 55
Equal parts of lard and
   corn or sunflower oil.............................. 6
Dry brewer's yeast.. 5
Mineral and vitamin supplement............ 3

To determine the amount of food needed for your dog, see the table at the bottom of the previous page.

Besides these rations, you could give a bitch a little milk—up to about 50 millilitres (¼ cup) per day. Large bitches may be given twice this amount.

Puppies

Start weaning the puppy at the end of its fourth week. It should be weaned completely by the time it is six weeks old. Separate the puppies from their mother gradually, and feed them the same food as that recommended for the mother during lactation.

You can add a small supplement of vitamins A and D3 to these rations and, depending on the puppy's size, a little milk each morning as well.

When you start weaning the puppy, feed it four times a day, and then three, so that gradually you accustom it to the two daily feedings it will receive as an adult. Refrain from giving the dog so-called fancy foods, and make sure that feeding utensils are kept clean. During weaning, particularly in cold weather, puppies should be kept in a relatively

warm, draft-free place that is particularly easy to keep clean.

Of course, you should always keep an eye on the puppy's growth. Let it drink as much water as it wishes. Refrain from giving it bones other than large beef or veal bones or sliced marrow bones on which it can cut its teeth while playing. Animal-hide bones are also suitable.

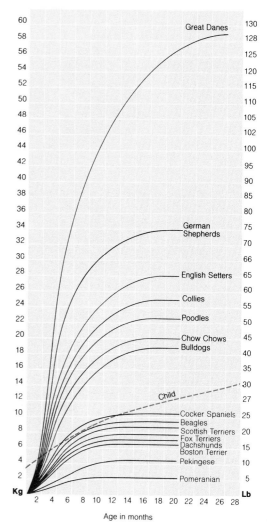

GROWTH CURVES FOR THE HUMAN CHILD AND VARIOUS BREEDS OF DOG

Age in months

Formula for home-made dog food								
	From weaning to 3 months		From 3 to 6 months		From 6 to 12 months		Adult	
Meals per day*	4		3		2 to 3		2	
	g	oz	g	oz	g	oz	g	oz
Boiled carrots	200	7	250	9	250	9	280	10
Cooked rice	280	10	300	10½	320	11¼	350	12¼
Cooked meat	400	14	350	12¼	350	12¼	300	10½
Lard and/or oil	50	1¾	50	1¾	30	1	40	1½
Dry brewer's yeast	50	1¾	30	1	20–30	¾–1	10–20	½–¾
Mineral and vitamin supplements	20	¾	20	¾	10–20	½–¾	5–10	¼–½

*Quantities vary according to size of breed. See next chart.

Dog's daily food requirements after weaning

Age	Size	Weight		Food	
		kg	lb	g	oz
Weaning to 3 months,	Very small	0.5–1.5	1–3½	90–150	3–5
4 meals a day	Small	1.5–3	3½–6½	200–350	7–12
(7–8 a.m., 12–1 p.m.,	Medium	3–6	6½–13	350–600	12–21
5–6 p.m., 10 p.m.)	Large	6–10	13–22	600–850	21–30
	Very large	7–12	15–26	750–950	26–33
3 to 6 months,	Very small	1.5–5	3½–11	200–600	7–21
3 meals a day	Small	2.5–7.5	5½–16½	350–800	12–28
(8–9 a.m., 12–1 p.m.,	Medium	6–13	13–29	700–1000	25–35
6 p.m.)	Large	8.5–18	19–40	800–1600	28–56
	Very large	12–27	26–60	1000–2000	35–70
6 to 12 months,	Very small	2–7	4½–15	300–800	11–28
2 or 3 meals a day	Small	7–12	15–26	750–950	26–33
depending on dog's size	Medium	10–18	22–40	850–1600	30–56
(9 a.m., 6 p.m.)	Large	18–27	40–60	1600–2000	56–70
	Very large	27–50	60–110	2000–3000	70–105

BOTTLE-FEEDING PUPPIES

Bitches can become ill or even die after whelping. In other cases, they are simply unable to give milk. Thus it often happens that young pups must be bottle-fed.

Having another bitch or a female of another species adopt the puppies may cause problems, while a diet of cow's milk or goat's milk alone may not provide enough energy and minerals. You can minimize this disadvantage by mixing 100 millilitres (½ cup) of water with 50 grams (1¾ ounces) of powdered milk, one egg yolk, and a teaspoonful of calcium phosphate. As well, give a weekly dose of 1000 to 5000 International Units of vitamin A and 300 to 1200 International Units of vitamin D3, according to the young dog's size.

It is also worth noting that there are a number of good commercial formulas on the market today. The formula opposite provides excellent nourishment, although it is a little more complicated.

The mineral and vitamin supplement is similar to the one recommended for adult dogs, but it should not contain calcium and dipotassium phosphates or sodium chloride.

Bottles and nipples must be kept very clean. Boil them before use.

Milk diet (Ferrando formula)

	g	oz	
Hydrolysed brewer's yeast	20	¾	Combine 300 g (10½ oz) of this mixture with 1 L (1 quart) of uncarbonated mineral water. Heat the formula to 39°C (102°F).
Powdered skim milk	370	13	
Powdered whole milk	430	15	
Powdered egg	150	5¼	
Lactose	3	1 tsp.	
Calcium phosphate	2	1 tsp.	
Mineral and vitamin supplement	25	1	

Yield: approximately 1 kilogram (2¼ pounds) of formula

The twenty-four-hour feeding schedule in the table below was developed several years ago in France by Professor Marcel Jean-Blain. It is based on years of experience and takes into account both the puppy's age and its breed. There are acceptable alternatives.

Around the third week the puppies will be able to lap their milk. Be sure to keep the plates clean. Begin feeding solids when the puppy is around 40 or 45 days old. It should be weaned gradually between the ages of 45 and 60 to 70 days.

Bottle-feeding schedule for puppies
Bottles per 24 hours and amount per feeding (in household units*) by breed size

Age	Small breeds: Pekingese, Pomeranians, Griffons Bruxellois, etc.		Medium-size breeds: Fox Terriers, Dachshunds, Cockers, etc.		Large and very large breeds: Shepherds, Setters, Pointers, Mastiffs, etc.	
	Milk	No. of feedings	Milk	No. of feedings	Milk	No. of feedings
Week 1	2 tsp.	8	1½ tbsp.	8	4½ tbsp.	8
Week 2	3 tsp.	8	2⅓ tbsp.	8	7⅓ tbsp.	8
Week 3	4 tsp.	8	2½ tbsp.	8	8 tbsp.	8
Week 4	4 tsp.	8	2½ tbsp.	8	8 tbsp.	8
Month 2	5 tsp.	7	3 tbsp.	7	9⅓ tbsp.	7

*Given this way for convenience. (Units are approximate.) Allow 5 mL per tsp.; 15 mL per tbsp.

Hygiene and Grooming

Keeping Your Dog Clean

Proper hygiene is essential if your dog is to enjoy good health and a long life. The first requirement of hygiene is cleanliness. To keep your dog clean, you will need to brush and bathe it and clean various parts of its body. Some of these tasks should be done daily, others weekly, and still others every month. But remember that dogs cannot be healthy unless they have exercise—this, too, is an aspect of hygiene.

Brushing

Depending on its breed, your dog will need to be brushed anywhere from once a week to once a day. Brushing removes dust, traces of dirt or soil, and dead hair. Dogs must be brushed more frequently while they are shedding—in spring and autumn. Large dogs with thick, heavy undercoats will shed copious amounts of hair per day for a month so do not be alarmed if the hair comes out by the handful.

This is the equipment you will need for brushing:
• a brush made of nylon, horsehair, or boar bristle for long-haired dogs; a metal brush for medium-length coats; and either type for short-haired dogs;

• a fine-tooth comb, a wide-tooth dressing comb, or a standard comb with a handle;
• a metal-tooth curry-comb to brush out the undercoat when your dog is shedding.

Put the dog on a table and start by brushing it vigorously, always in the direction of the nap of the coat. First, work from head to tail, then do the sides, and finally the paws. Be careful not to remove the undercoat. If your dog has very long hair (Afghan Hound or Collie, for instance), the coat may become matted and you will have trouble untangling it. This matting often occurs behind the ears, and looks somewhat like a growth. If you are unable to remove it with a brush, use scissors, but take care not to cut the skin. Once you have brushed the dog, use a fine-tooth metal comb on the whole body except for the whiskers and ears.

A curry-comb is the best tool when a dog is shedding. Used instead of the brush and comb, it massages the skin and this helps stimulate growth of the new coat and shortens the shedding period. Dogs kept indoors should be brushed more often than those that live in the country and sleep outdoors. After brushing the coat, you can use a light oil to give it a gloss.

BASIC GROOMING EQUIPMENT

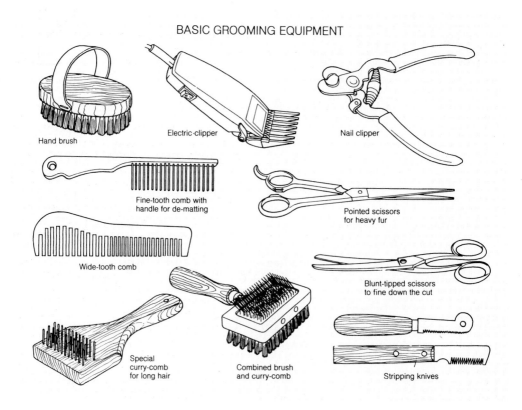

Hand brush

Electric-clipper

Nail clipper

Fine-tooth comb with handle for de-matting

Pointed scissors for heavy fur

Wide-tooth comb

Blunt-tipped scissors to fine down the cut

Special curry-comb for long hair

Combined brush and curry-comb

Stripping knives

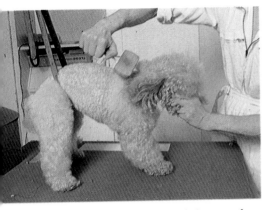

Always brush along the nap of the coat: from head to tail, from back to belly.

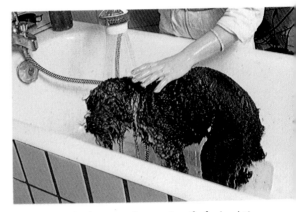

When you bathe your dog, put opthalmic ointment in the eyes, and cotton wool in the ears.

Baths

Puppies can be bathed when quite young (three months old), and any puppy arriving from a kennel should be given a bath. For dogs this age, the room temperature must be at least 20°C (68°F). You may use an alcohol-base lotion sometimes, but avoid powders that can soil the coat. Only sick animals should be given a dry shampoo.

How often you bathe your dog depends on its life-style (urban or rural), breed, and above all its type of coat. If it spends most of its time in the garden and rarely comes into the house, three or four baths a year are enough. Certain breeds with very thick, wiry coats, or medium-length coats with heavy undercoats (Bouviers des Flandres, for example) need two baths a year. Dogs kept indoors will need baths more often— once every month or two—since their owners will have to be more careful about hygiene. Dirt carried indoors via a pet's coat can ultimately infiltrate the home.

After a dog is bathed it takes six weeks for the natural oil to return to the skin and coat. Thus it is wise to use a special dog shampoo, preferably one that contains parasite repellents. There are also cosmetic shampoos for 'furry' dogs and those with very long hair, seborrhoea shampoos for animals with excessively oily skins, and dandruff shampoos. Avoid shampoos made for humans, and toilet soaps. A pH-balanced baby shampoo that does not sting the dog's eyes may be used, but only occasionally.

Before bathing a dog, brush and comb it, and if it has long hair make sure there are no matted sections.

If your dog is not too big, it can be bathed in your bathtub. Put a rubber mat in the tub to prevent slipping, and add a little warm water. Toy breeds can be bathed in a large bowl. The water temperature should be around 35°C (95°F). First, wet the dog all over from head to tail. Then apply the shampoo with a sponge or by hand, making sure to keep the shampoo out of the dog's eyes and ears. If necessary, put cotton wool in the ears to protect them. Use a small, soft brush on its paws, in the space between its toes, and on its nails. Next, rinse its whole body with warm water, making sure that you remove all the shampoo. If necessary, repeat the entire process.

Once you have finished this operation, take the dog out of the bathtub without delay and wrap it in a warm towel, unless the dog is too large. Rub it vigorously and dry it with a hair blower set at medium. Comb out its coat with a metal brush or a comb, working gently so you do not pull out tufts of hair. See that the dog does not catch cold after its bath. Its skin is naturally covered with a layer of sebum (grease, from the sebaceous glands) that serves to regulate its body temperature, and soap removes this protective film. After its bath, even if the dog looks dry, it has lost its main protection from the cold. Therefore, it is important that you dry it thoroughly. In cold weather, you should wait several hours before allowing the dog outside. You should also take the precaution of dressing it in a coat or raincoat.

In hot weather, dry the dog by hand and let it shake itself outdoors.

Ears

Check your dog's ears every week. Start by removing any hairs blocking the canal, using your thumb and index finger or tweezers to pull them out. There are antiseptics and detergents for cleaning ears. You can also use 60 per cent alcohol or ether. Never use soap and water. Remove any secretions with cotton swabs or balls of cotton wool. When a dog too frequently shakes or scratches its head, you will often find blackish scabs in its ears. This is ear mange, and needs special treatment. If you notice a foul smell, or a brownish or whitish fluid that persists in spite of your treatment, consult your veterinarian. In summer, tufts of hair often lodge deep in the ear canal. They are very painful and should be removed without delay. To avoid this problem, have the under-sides of the ears shaved. Long-eared dogs are particularly predisposed to ear ailments.

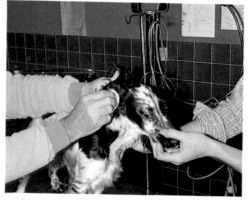

At least once a week, use cotton wool to remove any discharge that gathers in your dog's ears.

Clean each eye with a fresh swab of cotton wool. Perform this operation gently.

Eyes

About once a week, remove the discharge that gathers in the inner corner of the eye. Use cotton wool soaked in sterile water. If your dog's eyes are slightly red, try opthalmic eye drops or ointment. If persistent 'weeping' discolours the hair under the eyes, consult your veterinarian. Many dogs, particularly toy breeds, suffer from this complaint.

Teeth

Check the condition of your dog's teeth once a week. If the dog lets you, and if you have the patience, try to rub the teeth with a damp cloth soaked in a baking soda solution or lemon juice. There are toothpastes for dogs as well, but they are not necessarily any easier to use. Dogs' teeth are particularly vulnerable to tartar, a calcareous deposit that gradually covers molars and canines. It causes bad breath and encourages gum infections and gum shrinkage. If your dog shows symptoms of this ailment, call your veterinarian without delay.

Nails

If your dog walks on hard surfaces, such as sidewalks, every day, its nails will be worn down naturally.

To cut nails, hold the paw firmly and be sure not to injure the fleshy part, or quick.

If your dog does not walk often, or walks mostly on rugs or carpets, make sure that its nails do not grow too long. Clipping nails is not always as simple as it sounds; there is a risk of causing bleeding. Be sure not to cut the quick. If your dog has 'white' nails, the quick is easy to see, and you can trim them with clippers. If your dog's nails are dark, they should be trimmed by a groomer or a veterinarian. Check the dew-claws each month to make sure that they are not becoming ingrown. Use clippers, but be careful not to injure the dog. If you should cause bleeding, disinfect the cut immediately.

Paws

Clean your dog's paws often—every day if the dog lives in the city. Make sure there is no gravel lodged in the pad, no thorns between the toes, and no chewing gum stuck on the sole of the paw. If your dog spends hours licking a paw, check the sole and between the toes, and remove the cause of the discomfort.

Physical hygiene

All dogs need regular exercise. This keeps their muscles and joints in good condition. In the city, a dog should have some exercise each time you take it out to relieve itself—a minimum of three or four times a day. At least one of these walks should last more than half an hour. Once or twice a week, your pet should be allowed to exercise freely for several hours.

Protect your dog with a warm garment in cold weather and a raincoat in wet weather, particularly if the dog has long hair. If your dog returns home wet, dry it immediately.

If your dog is apathetic, force it to run and exercise—play ball with it, for instance. For owners of hunting-dogs there is always a danger that the animals could be overworked during the hunting season and underactive during spring and summer. Regulate your dog's feedings according to its activity.

Grooming

The purpose of grooming is to emphasize a dog's natural beauty. The procedure involves three main steps: clipping (all dogs with heavy coats are clipped), stripping (done by hand or with a serrated stripping knife), and trimming (a finishing touch, to help the dog look its best).

You can, of course, groom your dog yourself. If it is pure-bred, certain rules should be observed to accentuate the characteristics of the breed. If you enter the dog in a show, it will have to be meticulously groomed. In this case, it is usually best to engage a professional.

Equipment

For brushing you need brushes, combs, and slickers and rakes. You also need a table with a grooming post and restraining straps, a dryer, clippers (each with several heads), small and large hairdressing scissors, thinning scissors, stripping knives, hound gloves, and nail clippers.

How often to groom and when to start

A dog should have its initiation into grooming as early as possible. Five to six months is a good age for this. How often you groom depends on the breed—once a month, or as rarely as twice a year. Whatever kind of dog you own, brush it and bathe it regularly between groomings.

Grooming sheep-dogs

Sheep-dogs should be groomed two or three times a year. This is more a 'tidying up' than a complete grooming—the hair is not clipped or trimmed, or only one area of the body is clipped or trimmed.

• Belgian Shepherd Dogs, Kelpies, Kuvaszok, and Welsh Corgis: Brush and remove matted hair using whatever brushes and combs are best suited to the length of the coat. Trim the nails and hair between the toes. Clean and pluck the ears. Bathe the dog and dry the coat with a blower.

• Bouviers des Flandres, Pulis, Collies, Shetland Sheep-dogs, Old English Sheep-dogs, and Briards: Use a slicker and rake on parts that are difficult to get to. Clip hair around the anal region no shorter than 2 centimetres (1 inch). Shave the belly from pubis to navel. Trim the hair of the ears, eyebrows, whiskers, and paws (to make the paws look round). Clip stray hairs on the back. Comb the dog all over, bathe it, and dry it.

• Komondors, Corded Pulis: The coat starts to cord when the dog is about a year and a half old. After bathing the dog, wring out the cords by hand, and separate them from the skin, one by one. Trim those that touch the ground.

Grooming working dogs

The main requirement for these mainly guard and draught dogs is a bath and check-up of the various parts of the body two or three times a year.

• Short-haired dogs (Boxers, Dobermanns, and Great Danes): Brush the coat with a stiff, short-bristled brush or a hound glove. Give the same treatment for nails and ears. Clean the folds of skin and the wrinkles beneath the eyes and jowls. Check the elbows and hocks to see whether calluses have formed. Bathe and dry the dog.

• Long-haired dogs (Newfoundlands, Saint Bernards, Pyrenean Mountain Dogs, Leon-

To groom a Kerry Blue Terrier, you will need thinning scissors to keep the coat soft, silky, and slightly wavy.

bergers): Brush the coat with a slicker and rake. Check the nails and ears. Clean the jowls. Trim the hair around the legs and feet. Bathe and dry the dog.

• Heavy coats with a thick undercoat (Alaskan Malamutes, Akitas, and Siberian Huskies): Do not bathe this kind of dog too often or you will soften its hair.

• Wire-haired coats (Schnauzers): You need fine-tooth stripping knives for the top of the head, wide-tooth ones for the body, and thinning scissors. Strip two to four times a year, and groom as for Fox Terriers. Strip close on the top of the head, and blend to the neck. Strip cheeks short, cut eyebrows, cut the beard straight, and strip the ears. Strip short on the belly, and on the inside and rear of the thighs. Strip moderately and in blended layers on the top of the back, neck, withers, loin, ribs, flanks, and outside of the thighs. The tail should be cylindrical, rounded at the tip. Comb the hair on the legs, do not clip it. Trim the feet so they look rounded. Remove any hair that is between the toes.

Grooming hunting-dogs

• Wire-haired terriers: Some terriers must be groomed according to requirements of their standards. This is the case for such

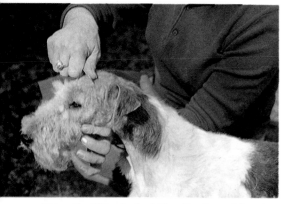

Trim the Wire-haired Fox Terrier with a fine stripping knife.

breeds as Wire-haired Fox Terriers, Scottish Terriers, Cairns, and Airedales. These terriers are not clipped; they are stripped lock by lock, by hand or with a knife. If you are not a dog-show enthusiast, you can use clippers on the dog, although the result may be slightly less attractive. The new hair will be less stiff after clipping than after stripping. You will need a stiff metal brush, a metal comb with a handle, stripping knives, a soft brush, and a metal slicker. To groom the dog, brush it with the slicker, de-mat its coat, and bathe it. Strip as for Schnauzers.

• Other hunting-dogs: Brush the coat to remove dead hair, bathe the dog, and trim a little with scissors. Trim the hair on the ears evenly. Trim the feet.

For Wire-haired Pointing Griffons, use the slicker and stripping knife as for terriers. Trim the whiskers, eyebrows, cheeks, and top of the head evenly.

For Cocker Spaniels, pay particular attention to the ears. American Cocker Spaniels are groomed in a special way. Clip the forehead, the cheeks, the outside of the ears (upper part only), the under-sides of the ears, and the under-side of the neck down to the breastbone. Trim the eyelashes and eyebrows. With scissors, trim the rest of the body where necessary to enhance the dog's appearance and gait.

Grooming pet dogs

• Poodles: There are two main clips—the traditional 'Lion,' or English Saddle, clip, which until recent years was compulsory for participation in dog shows, and the more modern 'Town and Country,' or Continental, clip.

For the Lion clip, the hindquarters are clipped completely to show off the shape of the muscles. The hind legs are also clipped completely, but bracelets, in proportion to the size of the dog, are left at the hocks. The lower part of the tail is shaved, leaving a pompon at the tip. The forelegs are shaved to the elbow, and they also have a bracelet above the foot. Clip the upper and under-sides of the muzzle, then the cheeks from the ear to the corner of the mouth, but leave the whiskers between the nose and the corner of the mouth. Do not touch the hair on the ears. After clipping, trim the rest of the coat evenly with thinning scissors.

For the Town and Country clip, do not clip the hair on the legs. Clip the feet and muzzle in the same way as for the lion clip. The back, belly, neck, and chest are close-shaven. You may dispense with the pompon on the tail. The head is clipped, leaving a topknot or a ball, and the whiskers are sometimes removed. Additional pompons and bracelets can give a Poodle an original appearance.

• Yorkshire Terriers: Brush the whole body with a soft boar-bristle brush, cut the nails, and remove the hair between the pads with scissors. Trim the hair in the perineal region and on the underbelly. Bathe the dog and dry it. Trim the hair of the ears and feet evenly with scissors. Comb the coat downwards, on both sides of the body, starting from the middle of the back, from head to tail. Gather the topknot of hair and fasten it with a small elastic. Tie a small ribbon around it.

• Bichons Frises: Their coats should not be trimmed or cut with scissors. The only equipment used is a short-bristled brush, a rake, and sometimes a slicker.

The two main clips for Poodles are the Lion (left) and the Town and Country (right). But *there are other, more unusual clips such as the Lamb and Dutch clips.*

Canine Psychology

To understand your dog, you should know the basics of canine psychology and ethology (animal behaviour).

An animal's psychology is determined largely by its instincts. The dog is a predator, and its hunting instinct runs strong. Its instinct to defend its territory makes it a born sentinel. Because it is naturally gregarious, it is sociable. Its sexual and maternal instincts also dictate many aspects of its behaviour.

Dogs also have a certain form of intelligence, for they store their visual, auditory, gustatory, and tactile experiences in their memories. This enables them to moderate the effects of their instincts.

Throughout their lives, dogs will remember some of the things that happen to them. These remembered experiences—with people, other dogs, or in situations—determine their day-to-day behaviour. Although memory plays a role in conditioning their behaviour, dogs cannot think as people do, in the abstract or reasoning mode. Dogs' intelligence is on the level of immediate perception only.

Besides memory and instinct, emotions affect a dog's attitude, particularly towards people.

Although a dog's nature is determined by its heredity, it is also influenced by what the dog has learned and how it relates to its own species and to the humans that train and care for it.

Territorial Instincts

Dogs lay claim to a certain zone or territory for their own exclusive use or—if they live in groups—for the use of their pack. A dog marks out its territory with scent signals secreted by its anal glands. Every dog leaves its own particular scent.

Setting boundaries

When dogs are allowed to run free in the countryside, they stake out their territory daily, leaving their scent and sniffing carefully at the scents of others. Among wolves, this behaviour is a way of establishing the boundaries of the hunting territory to be defended against intruders.

To a certain extent, scent marks are a sign that a territory is occupied. When a strange male 'reads' them with its nose, it knows that it must keep away. These marks also help a bitch in heat to find the male that made them.

Marking with urine has a different significance. Dogs spray tree trunks and street corners to give notice of their presence on common ground.

Some dogs, both male and female, roll in stool or decomposing bodies, or urinate nearby. When they do so, they may perhaps be trying to mask a particularly strong odour with their own. But this practice can also indicate a dietary deficiency of some sort, particularly alkaline.

Defending boundaries

Dogs, as we have said, instinctively defend their territories against intrusion by other dogs or by humans. A domesticated dog, however, views people as members of its family, just as it would view its puppies. In most cases, therefore, it does not react if an animal of a different species (a horse or other mammal other than a cat) encroaches on its domain. Studies of Eskimo Dogs indicate that in villages adult males form packs. Each pack has a territory which it defends against the members of all other packs. The dominant dog, usually a male, takes responsibility for this defence. The adult males are fully aware of the boundaries and do not cross them. Young dogs, however, seem to be ignorant of them. When they stray into another pack's territory they are punished.

The dog's abilities as a sentinel stem from this instinct to defend its territory. The dog keeps a careful watch over the grounds, the garden, or the house, and barks a warning at the slightest hint of danger. Some specific breeds are reputed to be particularly fine watch-dogs, but you will find excellent ones in every breed.

Unlike sexual aggressiveness, aggressiveness that stems from the dog's territorial instinct is not affected by castration.

When a dog sniffs the ground, it finds scent marks—messages—from other dogs.

If a dog's owners have accustomed it to visits from other humans, it will probably not react aggressively towards guests, particularly if its owner is in full command. For the dog, the family is its pack and its owner is the pack leader. Therefore it is up to the owner to take the initiative in defending the territory.

A dog feels sheltered in an enclosed garden or its owner's car. If someone opens the gate or car door, it no longer feels safe; it feels threatened on its home turf. Depending on its temper, the dog will growl or attack right away. If the intruder does not take to his heels when the dog barks and looks threatening, the animal often becomes disconcerted and less aggressive. But if the person retreats, the dog thinks its behaviour has had an effect—it barks more aggressively and bares its teeth.

Welsh Corgis, a Great Dane, and a Brittany Spaniel sniff one another. Once acquainted, they will either play, fight, or lose interest in one another.

Never hit your dog if any show of hostility towards intruders is linked to defence of its territory. Just scold it and shut it away in another room each time it growls or barks at guests. Remember, a dog that attacks an intruder believes it is doing its duty. It is the dog's instinct to defend its—and your—territory.

The people who are most often bitten by watch-dogs are children. Statistics show that half of the people bitten in the United States, for example, are under the age of 20 and only 10 per cent of the cases are serious bites. When a child comes close to a dog's territory, he or she runs the risk of arousing the dog's instinct to defend it. Since the child does not realize this, the dog attacks. All too often dogs are accused of being aggressive; in fact, they almost never attack without a reason.

Canine Hierarchies

All animals living in a group on a permanent basis establish a hierarchy to regulate relations between individuals. Dominant animals are aggressive and the dominated

German Shepherds are traditionally considered reliable watch-dogs for the home.

AGGRESSIVE BEHAVIOUR

From time to time we hear or read of incidents in which an otherwise good-natured dog suddenly acts wholly out of character and, without provocation, attacks a human. The causes for such behaviour are often rooted deep in the dog's psyche. Aggressiveness cannot always be explained by the instinct to attack and defend, sharpened by training. Other instincts come into play—maternal, sexual, and hunting.

In France in 1982, two Great Danes, one male and one female, known for their even tempers, escaped from an enclosure and attacked an eight-year-old child, who later died of the injuries. How can we explain such an occurrence? Perhaps the

dogs were overcome by frenzy when they suddenly found themselves free. Or perhaps the scents of the countryside awakened the hunting instinct, and brought out the underlying nature of the predator within.

One possible explanation is that the male's aggressive behaviour was brought on by the instinct to protect its female companion. Another factor may have come into the equation: emulation. The meeker dog followed the example of the dominant dog. Aggressiveness rooted in the sex drive cannot be ruled out either. Any dog that cannot satisfy its impulses will react in one of two ways: repression and neurosis, or aggression.

ones are submissive, with varying degrees between the two extremes. Dogs' behaviour in groups, which is inherited from their wild ancestors, arises from this social structure.

Dominant dogs

If you watch puppies at play, performing their mock battles, you can already pick out which ones will be dominant. Dominant puppies are aggressive—they jostle the others, gripping them by the throat, and are the first to rush headlong towards their food. Generally, however, the mother continues to rule over her young even when they reach adulthood. It is rare for a young dog to subjugate its mother, even if it is the bigger and stronger of the two.

Dominance is an integral part of a puppy's character. It has nothing to do with size, strength, or sex. As puppies grow older, however, it is generally the strongest males that assert themselves and become dominant in a group. You can observe this phenomenon by watching a pack of dogs—the strongest takes the initiative, heads the excursions, and acts as leader. But this supremacy can be challenged. Struggles can occur within a group because of shortages of food, or because a

bitch in heat has joined the pack. If the leader loses, the social order is called into question.

The instinct that causes dogs to imitate the leader of their pack is extremely strong. If the leader starts to gnaw a bone, play, or race about wildly, the others will follow suit. This means that individuals in a pack will act together and, when hunting, the pack follows the dog in the lead.

When two strange dogs meet, you can spot the dominant one by the aggressive behaviour it displays (see p. 309). If the other dog submits when it sees these signals, nothing happens. If, however, it is also dominant and responds aggressively, battle is inevitable. The fight will not end until one of the dogs has managed to conquer the other.

An adult dog will never hurt a puppy; it may even play with it.

Some breeds of dog have very strong dominating tendencies. The trait is most evident in large breeds such as Great Danes, Pyrenean Mountain Dogs, and sled dogs, but smaller dogs such as Fox Terriers and Dachshunds also have these tendencies. Such dogs must be firmly controlled. They need a master stronger than themselves, who can impose his will. Even so, owners should not terrify them, or the dogs may turn into fearful, excessively submissive animals. Every time a dog tries to dominate its master, shows aggressiveness, or is not submissive, the master must immediately call it to order and discipline it. With breeds such as Poodles, Beagles, and other hunting-dogs, the problem does not arise: The master's authority is clearly established. The dominant Beagle in a pack has no problems with the other dogs for they do not try to dispute its authority.

When two dogs live under the same roof, they establish between themselves a hierarchy which, in principle, does not cause problems as long as the dominant dog's position is stable. But if one dog becomes injured or sick, the other may try to assert itself and take its place.

CATS AND DOGS

'To fight like cat and dog' is an old expression, but it does not necessarily reflect the true picture. When a dog meets a cat, even on its own territory, it often is friendly and wags its tail. The cat, for its part, spits, shows its claws, arches its back, and runs away.

It seems to be a law of nature that cats have a natural tendency to run away and that dogs, the eternal rascals, are ever willing to give chase. It is as if their behaviour patterns were designed to complement each other.

Nonetheless, cats and dogs often share the same territory—their owner's home—living together without difficulty (as far as the dog is concerned, the cat belongs to the family pack). The two creatures get along harmoniously, and each one respects the other's favourite spots. This does not prevent them from chasing each other playfully to maintain the age-old status quo.

Despite 'communication' problems, cats and dogs can become friends.

This dog, lying on its side with its belly exposed, is signalling total submission.

Leadership conflicts

When faced with two rival dogs, owners should hide their feelings for the 'underdog' and refrain from protecting the weaker one in the presence of the stronger. The stronger would view such an action as a failure to respect the rule of submission and might attack the other dog. Instead, you should reassure the dominant dog and lavish it with affection. In this way, the 'rules' will be clear and the hierarchy will be respected: master first, dominant dog next, dominated dog last.

Human domination

Some submissive dogs display an infantile type of subjugation to humans and even have parent-child relationships with their owners. (Behavioural scientist Konrad Lorenz described these dogs as 'jackal types.') Others have social relations with humans ('wolf-type' dogs, according to Lorenz) and consider the owner as a pack leader, provided the owner has sufficient authority to assert himself as such. If he has not, the dog will tend to take the dominant role that the owner has left vacant. This happens more often than is generally realized, particularly with large dogs that have timid owners. When a dog makes rules, refuses to obey orders, and is generally hostile, it is difficult to live with. In some cases, the dog can rule a whole family. In others, it decides that it is superior to one member of the family only.

If you do not want to risk being dominated by your dog, adopt it when it is still a puppy, at about eight weeks of age. During this period, called the 'socialization' stage, a young dog is ready to establish the closest contacts with people. This is the time when owners must impose their wills firmly, give orders that are to be obeyed without question, and refuse to tolerate any attempt at rebellion from their dog. Nonetheless, you should always reward your dog for being obedient.

While still very young, a dog will try at least once to bite its master to attempt to achieve dominance. Never let it do so, though, for according to the law of the pack this will acknowledge that the dog is the stronger in the relationship. It is vital to discipline the dog immediately.

Generally, another trial of strength occurs when a male dog reaches sexual maturity, at the age of about 12 months. A dog which in its youth was submissive to its owner simply pretends to bite; however, a dog which has been able to dominate will bite for real.

Although a dog's dominant nature is inborn, it is not irreversible. Proper education and firm but not brutal training will, in most cases, overcome this tendency.

Sexuality

Manifestations of sex instincts

Dogs show their sexual desires as early as seven weeks of age by simulating copulation. They reach sexual maturity between the age of seven and twelve months for males, and between seven and ten months for bitches. The time varies considerably according to the breed.

Females, in principle, come into heat, or estrus, every six months (although this may vary from four to eight months). Estrus lasts between 15 and 20 days, and corresponds with ovulation. Bitches can be impregnated between the seventh and fourteenth day of ovulation. During this period, they become restless and on the look-out for males. The male is attracted by chemicals present in the urine of a bitch in heat. Males can smell these secretions from a considerable distance.

The female dog shows her acceptance by holding her tail aside and presenting her vulva to the male. Before coupling, the dogs perform ritual games and smell each

Before coupling, the male sniffs its mate. The bitch, in turn, may remain impassive or invite the male to play.

other thoroughly. The coupling itself lasts from 15 to 20 minutes. Afterwards, the male may either lose interest in the female immediately or remain restless for a day or two. The male may even run away in an effort to rejoin the female. But dogs are polygamous and do not form couples.

When several males spot a bitch in season, they fight among themselves to determine hierarchy. The victor mates first. Sometimes the mere presence of this 'top dog' inhibits the others.

Emotional factors can alter the male's behaviour: if it is frightened or on unfamiliar territory, it may refuse to couple. This is why, if you want to mate a bitch with a dog of the same breed, it is always wise to bring the bitch to the male.

Canine sexual problems

The male's sex drive is strong and continuous. It does not have periods of 'pursuit'; it becomes excited when near a female in heat. Ninety per cent of all dogs in cities are frustrated, and this causes such disorders as sexual confusion (improperly termed homosexuality) or masturbation. A dog may simulate sexual intercourse with a chair or a person's leg. Do not let this continue—punish the dog if necessary. When frustrated, some pure-breds refuse to couple.

Repressed sexuality can result in aggressiveness, particularly among dogs around age two. This can be treated with injections. In extreme cases, castration is a remedy.

Frustrated dogs tend to run away. Bitches are less likely to do so, but they may become over-excited. Nerve sedatives and certain neuroleptics used in psychoanalysis can help in such circumstances.

Bitches that have not mated frequently may have hysterical pregnancies. Folliculin is administered to halt the production of milk, and tranquillizers are given to relieve the attendant stress.

Neuroses resulting from sexual frustration may take other forms as well: dogs may suffer from bulimia (abnormal craving for food) or lose their appetites.

The Maternal Instinct

A few days before it whelps, the bitch starts to plan for the safety of its litter. It looks for a quiet place to make its 'nest,' frequently choosing a cupboard or closet.

Immediately after the birth, the maternal instinct impels the bitch to perform actions without which the puppy will not survive. The mother licks the puppies' bellies firmly, and thus stimulates their first reactions. This is often the moment when the puppy makes its first sound. A little later, the mother licks the urogenital and anal areas, which makes the puppy urinate and defecate. During the early days, the mother eats these excretions.

Like many animals in the wild, the bitch eliminates deformed or sick puppies. It seems to have a very sharp awareness of the slightest deformities in its litter. Cases have been reported of females killing puppies born with a crooked tail, bandy legs, or even missing toes.

Maternal lapses

Sometimes a mother is indifferent to her litter, particularly after the first pregnancy. The whelping can leave the bitch exhausted and bewildered. The maternal instinct seems to have been caught short and the mother watches the care given to the puppies with grateful interest. If the mother has trouble cutting the umbilical cord, sever it, but not too close to the navel. Remove the placental sack and rub the puppy briskly where the bitch can see what you are doing. With luck, she will do the same. If the bitch seems weak or indifferent, place the young beneath the mother's teats. Supervise these first contacts carefully lest the mother smother the pups or even eat them.

Sometimes a bitch may mutilate or devour one or more of the litter, particularly when the umbilical cord is being handled. In principle, the mother will stop as soon as the puppy starts to make a noise. The sound acts as a signal. If the sound does not come, or if the bitch is excited by the sight of blood, it will continue, disembowelling the infant and eating it as if it were part of the placenta. This phenomenon represents a deviation from the maternal instinct, and some specialists think a bitch that kills its litter probably does so because of deficiencies in its diet. This behaviour may also be linked with errors in training or with physical, psychological, or emotional constraints imposed on the animal.

In most cases, bitches are good mothers that see to the education of their young until the pups are completely weaned.

A bitch that has had a Caesarean section may, when the puppies are brought to it, associate them with the 'mistreatment' it has received, and kill them. Sometimes, if many puppies in a litter have been destroyed, the mother eats the survivors.

A good mother

As a rule, the bitch is a good mother, even to the point of taking care of whelps from another litter.

Some males, but not many, take care of puppies. It cannot reasonably be said that dogs have a paternal instinct. Generally, males pay little attention to newborn puppies and may even be frightened of them. Nevertheless, they never harm them. Unless an adult is starving, it will never attack a puppy less than six months old.

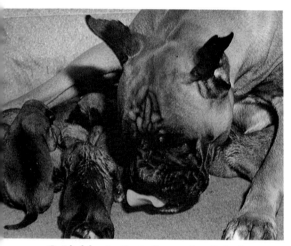

Guided by instinct, the mother licks her puppies to clean them and stimulate their physiological functions.

After a bitch whelps, it becomes uneasy and will go to any lengths to defend its litter. Aggressiveness rooted in the maternal instinct is common among all animals, even those that are gentle at all other times. Dogs almost always show threatening attitudes before they take action. A mother, however, will attack without warning if she considers her young to be in danger. If disturbed too often, she may move the litter to a safer place.

If the mother feels safe, on the other hand, she will allow members of the 'family pack' to pet the puppies. But she will still be wary of strangers and will bare her teeth, even bite if they come close. Some mothers have a phobia of young children, even of youngsters they normally play with. Such mothers realize instinctively that children, unintentionally, can hurt newborn puppies.

A system of communication is established early on between the mother and her puppies. If a puppy gets lost or gives calls of distress, the mother will pick it up by the scruff of the neck and bring it back to the others. If necessary, the mother will discipline it with a nip. A bitch licks its puppies one by one not just to wash them, but to make them feel secure.

To an extent, bitches take care of educating the puppies until they are weaned, a process which occurs gradually. After three or four weeks, some mothers start to regurgitate half-digested food for the puppies. In this way, the bitch is preparing them to give up their milk diet. Towards the end of the fifth week, when the puppies are weaned, the mother begins to leave the litter more frequently; she becomes less watchful, refusing to nurse them as often as in the past, and bites them to stop them from suckling. (Their milk teeth hurt her teats.) Little by little, she becomes wholly indifferent.

For physiological and psychological reasons, it is always advisable to leave the mother at least two puppies. If a mother loses a whole litter, she becomes upset—even if she does not appear to be hunting very earnestly for her offspring. 'Milk fever' is not particularly serious in itself, but it is one symptom of the disturbance caused by the puppies' disappearance. Removing the litter can also cause more serious problems such as eclampsia (convulsions). This said, though, if you cannot keep the puppies, it is better to take them away from the mother immediately.

Language

Dogs 'speak'—and not just by barking or other vocal communications. They use olfactory and visual signals, as well as gestures and mime patterns or rituals. They learn this elaborate language when they are three to four weeks old.

Olfactory communication

A dog's sense of smell, which is highly developed, plays a vital part in its communication with other dogs. When a dog urinates at street corners or on tree trunks, it leaves urinary and glandular secretions which mark its presence and send messages to other dogs. Although we do not yet fully understand how this code works, it is thought that when a dog scratches the ground vigorously after urinating or defecating, the sweat glands on its pads may produce a smell apparently intended to command respect.

When two dogs meet, they initiate communications by using their noses. They sniff each other nose to nose, then smell each other's bodies all over, particularly the genital and anal areas. Dogs identify each other by smell. They start acquiring this behaviour during the very first days of life from their mothers.

The sense of smell is also important in dogs' sex lives. A male can smell an 'avail-

When two dogs meet, they use their most developed sense—smell—to explore each other.

able' female several kilometres away and does not hesitate to run off to join it, following the olfactory messages the female leaves in her wake.

The sense of smell also plays a role in a dog's relations with other animals, especially in locating and recognizing game. As a rule, however, a dog will not touch cats or small animals sharing its home—they give off a particular odour which it recognizes as being the 'family' scent.

Vocal communication

Dogs communicate vocally as well as through the sense of smell. The sounds they produce complement their other forms of communication. Barking can give a warning. If the threat is not defined, the dog howls. If the threat is clear, the bark is dry and short. As soon as a dog bays or howls desolately, all the others in the neighbourhood gradually join in. The meaning of this message? It is thought that a special contact is established during these twilight and nocturnal concerts—perhaps, even, a rallying cry for pack animals which have become prisoners in a territory imposed by humans.

Howling is also associated with sexuality. Males separated from females in heat may howl continuously, while the bitches answer in kind.

Each time it barks, a dog modulates its voice to fit its feelings. A dog at liberty, when facing a rival, does not bark to express itself. It uses rituals of greeting or intimidation. On the other hand, if it is on a leash or behind a fence, a dog will bark to assert itself, to feel safe. Barking becomes a way of compensating for the 'escape gap,' the space which, in nature, a dog would normally keep between itself and a potential enemy. (Every animal being threatened attempts to maintain a critical distance between itself and its pursuer—a gap that supplies precious time while the animal figures out its best means of escape.)

The volume of a dog's barking corresponds to the nature of the message being transmitted. A sharp, staccato bark ex-

presses a threat and warns the other dog, animal, or person to leave the territory. In doing this, the dog voices its strength, but will not necessarily attack. Exuberant barking, on the other hand, may indicate a master's return or the prospect of a walk. In hunting, dogs use special barks to announce that they have flushed game, that they are giving chase, and so forth.

Dogs, of course, do not merely bark. They whimper, whine, howl, yelp, yap, and growl. All these sounds have precise meanings in a dog's social relationships. When puppies yap, their mother is immediately alerted and comes to help them. One puppy's whimpers and whines are often taken up by the whole group. A whine may express a puppy's discomfort or pleasure, and a yelp expresses pain.

Growling is often linked to protection of territory. A dog growls to show its hostility to an intruder. This is the final warning. The next step is attack.

A dog's stare is another form of communication. If a dog stares it is either frightened or hostile. Dogs stare at animals they intend to attack. If you stare into a dog's eyes, there is a good chance you are provoking it. Sheep-dogs know very well how to command obedience with a look—this is the way they get sheep or cows to obey. To keep a flock or herd from straying the dog lies down and stares at the lead animals.

Posture and rituals

Dogs also convey messages with their postures. The happy, wagging tail means welcome. A tail between the legs means fear. Wagging the tail timidly indicates humility, lack of confidence. Dogs use their whole bodies to signal their intentions to other dogs, animals, and people.

A dog that wants to look aggressive will stand in such a way that it appears larger than it really is. It straightens up, raises its hindquarters, moves forward with its tail in the air, shoulders wide, ears pricked, hackles almost on end, lips curled, and teeth bared. Conversely, an animal showing submission tries to look smaller. It crouches, lays its head on its paws, crawls with its tail between its legs, its ears lowered. To show utter humility, it may go as far as lying on its side, exposing its genitals, and even urinating.

When a dog is inviting another dog to play, it lowers its head and forepaws, keeping its tail and hindquarters high. Another way of extending the overture is to nibble the other dog's tail, while prancing around and presenting the flank as a sign of good intentions. A male wishing to play with a female dances on its hind legs, then places its forepaws on the bitch's chest. A big dog lies supine in front of a smaller one to indicate this desire.

Dogs are also capable of making an eloquent array of facial expressions. Greeting

SOME MEANINGFUL POSTURES

As you can see from the sketches below, dogs use specific postures to convey their intentions. Other dogs understand these gestures and rituals instantly, and respond accordingly.

1. Dog is on its feet and on the alert.
2. It asks to play.
3. This posture indicates that the dog is friendly and means no harm.

4 to 6. Successive stages of submission. The last posture is typical of total submission: the dog lies on its side, raises a hind leg, and exposes its genitals.

7 to 9. Development of aggressiveness: first the dog is on the alert, then it becomes frightened and on the defensive, then it becomes plainly aggressive.

other dogs, they become deferential, lower their ears and the corners of their mouths, smooth out their foreheads, and become caricatures of politeness.

Wrinkling the face expresses aggressiveness. If the dog also pricks up its ears, it is not afraid; it may attack. When afraid, it draws its ears back and down, making a 'grinning' expression similar to the 'welcome' expression. Other dogs understand these rituals instinctively.

Communication with humans

The sense of smell is particularly important in a dog's relations with people. Among thousands of smells, a dog will recognize its master's scent and those of other members of the family.

Dogs 'talk' to people by barking in various tones—joyful, sad, furious, or uneasy, according to the circumstances. Dogs are also very sensitive to words and intonations. Remember this when training a dog. Never shout. Always use the same word to give the same order.

Dogs are sentient to the fact that people stand upright. Presumably, they consider this a sign of our superiority. If people go on all fours to play, or if they fall, a dog may attack.

Physical contact is one of the most effective means of communication between people and dogs. A caress from the master means a reward. When training your pet, never use your hand to discipline it—the master's hand should always be associated with gratification. Use a separate object such as a rolled-up newspaper. When a dog licks and nibbles its master it is expressing sympathy and affection. When it places a paw on its owner's knee, it is saying it wants something or that it shares the

owner's worries. (Apparently the owner's personal odour changes when he is unhappy, which may explain the second reaction.) A dog that wants to play prods gently with its nose or pats firmly with a paw. It whines sadly to indicate that it needs to go outside or it wants to be untied.

The feats of performing dogs can be explained by the fact that animals are highly receptive to the slightest change in the master's behaviour.

It also whines this way when waiting for its owner.

Some dogs 'smile' at people, and this usually implies submission. This smile of welcome can easily be distinguished from the grimaces of intimidation and submission directed towards other animals. Is it a result of imitation? Conceivably. The longer it lives with humans, the more the dog refines its own language.

Intelligence

Although abstract thought, ethics, and creative thinking remain exclusively human attributes, dogs have a form of intelligence above and beyond instinct. It enables them to make associations between ideas and, consequently, to perform deliberate actions, such as obey orders.

The most gifted dogs can understand about fifty words. The majority of dogs, however, just obey simple orders such as 'up,' 'lie down,' and 'sit,' or react to words such as 'food' and 'walk.' Although dogs know what certain words mean, sentences are beyond them. The word and the tone of voice are what counts for them.

Association of ideas

Dogs are capable of associating ideas. If a dog wants to go out, it will bring its leash to its owner. If it wants to be included in a trip, it will lie on the suitcases. Some dogs take the initiative so far as to open doors when they need to go for a walk.

It is difficult to determine which of dogs' 'intelligent' actions—those performed for reasons other than thirst, hunger, or fear—result from what combinations of instinct, heredity, education, and training. A dog confronted with a problem can often devise a practical solution such as trying to find an opening in a barrier, using its paws to catch an object, or gnawing a rope to free itself from restraint.

Present and future

Many researchers think that a dog's intelligence relates only to an occurrence as it is happening, never to the future. A dog uses its experience to solve an immediate problem, but does not anticipate difficulties. Yet there are contradictions to this theory. For instance, when a dog is boarded in a kennel for the first time, it howls and refuses to eat. Then its owner returns. The next time the dog is boarded, it calmly waits for the owner to return even though his arrival is clearly in the future.

Genetics and aptitudes

It has been said that human intelligence depends 51 per cent on genetic ancestry and 49 per cent on environment. It appears that this is also the case for dogs.

A Beauceron has a definite genetic advantage over a Fox Terrier when it comes to herding a flock, and conversely the Fox Terrier is better 'programmed' for hunting. Genetically, German Shepherds are bred to guard and protect, and Greyhounds for hunting by sight and racing. Dogs of some breeds are, genetically, better suited than others to certain forms of training. As a result they are often used as 'performing dogs' in circuses. These dogs—Poodles,

Poodles are one of the breeds best able to learn to perform circus tricks.

Dachshunds, and especially cross-breeds—do not really know how to read or count. They merely obey the slightest signals which the audience cannot see: a hand gesture, a tiny nod from their trainer. They are no more intelligent than any other dogs, but they have a particular receptivity for training. They are extremely attentive and have a fine associative memory.

The way a dog is educated has a profound influence on how intelligently it behaves. A puppy that spends the first four months of its life in a kennel has little chance of reaching the level of understanding of a puppy that joins a family at six weeks of age, when it is very receptive. Compared to a guide dog, a laboratory Beagle seems stupid. This is because the guide dog has been educated and trained, whereas the Beagle has been deprived of every experience, often even of affection.

The more attention you give a dog, the more it learns. Training develops the memory, hones the instincts, gives the animal useful experience, and enables the owner to put the dog to work. Keeping watch over a flock and finding a fugitive are elaborate canine activities which require not only instinctive abilities, but mental ones as well.

Some dog behaviour cannot be explained by intelligence alone, or just instinct, or mere perception. What psychic factors are involved, for example, when a dog travels across an entire country to find its owner? There are many examples of long treks. Novelist Victor Hugo gave his dog, *Baron,* to a friend living near Moscow. One day, *Baron* disappeared. Two months later, thin, filthy, and exhausted, it appeared at the door of the writer's home in Paris. It had crossed the whole of Europe to find him.

Doctor Axel Munthe, author of the book *The Story of San Michele,* attributed such feats to a telepathic link between dog and man. It is this bond that allows a dog to 'know' some hours in advance that its master will come home from a trip. Other authors explain the phenomenon by saying that the dog employs a sensory form of orientation that we have not yet discovered.

Puppy Psychology

During the first days of its life, a puppy spends 90 per cent of its time sleeping and the rest seeking its mother's teat to feed. After this period, it grows very quickly. At three and a half weeks, it begins exploring its surroundings. Then comes a critical stage—socialization—which will have a strong influence on its future development. It is by playing with its siblings that a puppy becomes fully and finally aware that it belongs to the canine species.

At four or five weeks, puppies already show group behaviour, tumbling over one another to chase after a ball. The hierarchy that will prevail later in the pack is already developing. The young animals show their aggressiveness by growling at anything they consider unusual or alien.

Importance of play

As with children, play is an essential part of a puppy's development. Play begins with activities that lead the puppy to discover smells, sights, and tastes. Gradually almost all aspects of adult behaviour appear in the play: stalking, chasing game, guarding, shaking a rag held between the teeth to imitate the killing of prey. These games are accompanied by yelping and barking, which helps the group act as a coordinated unit. Some experts say that a puppy that does not get enough play may not develop its hunting aptitude and consequently will be unable to defend itself when it reaches adulthood.

Contacts with children and adults

Ideally, puppies should be between six and eight weeks old when they start having contact with people. If they are deprived of these contacts, or if they have only short, intermittent relationships, they will have little chance of becoming domesticated. They may well remain timid. It has been noted that puppies fed and cared for in a

A healthy puppy adores playing, and play is vital for its development.

laboratory, with no other contact with the outside world, are three times more likely to develop viral illnesses than those left with the mother. This underscores the importance of contact, not only with people but with other dogs as well.

When the behaviour of guide dogs in training was analysed, it was discovered that young dogs that had stayed in the litter for over twelve weeks without human contact were not good subjects for training. However, if a puppy is separated from the litter too soon—at four or five weeks, say—and left solely in the company of humans, it will become exclusively attached to its owner. When it grows up, it will find it difficult to relate to other dogs and may even be difficult to train.

Children and puppies get along easily. Their play is spontaneous, natural—and educative.

Relationships between children and puppies—and even adult dogs—are, as a rule, excellent. Babies and puppies are at approximately the same stage of development and they communicate with each other through play. When a puppy plays with a child, it matures quickly and adjusts readily to life with humans.

However, you should ensure that your child never torments the dog or treats it like a toy. A dog is a living creature which the child must learn to respect.

Socialization

Some breeds have particular socialization problems in puppyhood. Puppies that mature slowly should not be weaned until they are six or seven weeks old. Nonetheless, make sure that they are able to have sustained contact with humans.

A puppy weaned too early or too late will not necessarily adapt poorly. If a puppy weaned too early has frequent contact with other dogs, or one weaned too late is exposed to attentive people, it can still learn healthy social behaviour. Always try to bring out the best in your pup's natural qualities. If you have an alert puppy, for example, encourage it to play.

Education and Training

There are many theories on how best to train a dog—some more controversial than others. The recommendations that follow, however, represent one training method that is tried and true. If you heed the instructions carefully, your dog will develop into a well-disciplined animal.

Proper training, it should be understood from the outset, is not only necessary for a dog—it is also good for it. Accustomed throughout their history to living in packs, dogs accept, and even seek, a hierarchy. In a group of dogs, one will always impose itself as leader. In a dog's relations with people, it is the owner who must be the leader. Do not hesitate to set rules for your dog—and do not hesitate to insist that the dog respect them. The dog will be grateful to you, and you will in turn be helping your pet, by keeping it in good psychological health. No dog suffers if it is properly controlled—that is to say, with kindness.

Basic Education

Teacher-trainer qualities

To succeed in educating a dog and, later, in training it (to guard or hunt, for example), an owner needs certain personal qualities. Some, such as understanding, fairness, and authority, are essential. Others are nearly as important—self-control, patience, and gentleness, among others.

Training creates a bond of mutual trust between pupil and master. Therefore, get to know your dog well; the rest, with a little experience, will follow naturally. Be fair, because a dog will not understand an undeserved reprimand or one given because you are in a bad mood. Be firm in the orders you give and show your authority without being brutal. If you want to obtain a specific result, perform the same exercise five or six times a day for several days running, consistently. Reward the dog often, always making your approval absolutely clear, and be sparing with punishments.

Pavlov's dog

Dogs do not reason the way we do. They act instinctively, and by association. You will be able to train your dog if you apply Pavlov's theory of conditioned reflex. Each order well carried out, every action properly performed, should lead automatically to an appropriate reward. The reward must be accompanied by obvious signs that you are pleased. Bear in mind that the sound of your voice is very important in emphasizing this attitude. The next time, your dog will outdo itself—not because it wants to perform that specific action, but to obtain the reward. Similarly, of course, punish any misconduct or mistake without delay. Your 'pupil' will lose any desire to disobey you just by awareness of the consequences.

DOGS AND SPORT

A dog's sporting abilities depend to a great extent on its size and physical make-up. A Whippet, for example, can reach speeds of about 50 kilometres (30 miles) an hour over a short distance. German Shepherds, on the other hand, are excellent jumpers and are known to be able to scramble over vertical obstacles as high as three metres (ten feet). A dog kept indoors travels little more than one or two kilometres—about a mile—on an average day, while a sheep-dog may cover fifty times as much ground in the same period. Some dog breeds are especially good at pulling heavy burdens. Arctic sled dogs, for instance, can haul double their own weight as far as 32 kilometres (20 miles) for eight hours a day, despite temperatures well below freezing.

Whippets, noted for their sleek lines, are traditional favourites at dog races.

German Shepherds are naturally gifted for jumping competitions.

Rewards

The simplest reward is to stroke the dog and say in a pleased voice: 'well done,' 'very good,' 'good dog,' 'yes.' You might give it a treat—a dog biscuit, a piece of cheese, for example. Be careful not to give it too much sugar, however, or your dog may develop health problems by the end of its training.

Punishment

Punish as little as possible, and always progressively and with subtle distinctions. For any dog, a clear show of disapproval is already a punishment. You need only to raise your voice and say 'bad dog,' 'no,' and so forth. Raising your voice again, give the dog an order it will consider unpleasant: 'go lie down,' 'go to your box.'

Depriving a dog of its freedom is a more serious punishment. Tie the dog up or shut it away in a room (after removing all breakables in case the dog tries to rebel). This rebellious attitude, which may reveal itself early in training, should not show up later. Muzzling can be used to punish a dog that tends to bite. You can also give the dog a light smack with a rolled-up newspaper while scolding it loudly. Sometimes the threat of a slap will be sufficient.

Always punish the dog immediately. If you wait until later, it may not associate the cause with the chastisement. When a dog relieves itself in the house, scold it only if you catch it in the act. Do not take it to the scene of the 'crime' two hours later and tell it that it is a 'bad dog.'

Speak your dog's name clearly, often, and with every order, and always emphasize the same syllable. If the dog's name is long, use a nickname.

Vocabulary with the dog should be simple and limited to about fifty words. Repeat these words slowly and often so that the association between the word and the meaning becomes automatic.

General Training

Start training your puppy as early as possible, when it is about two months old. The younger it is, the more patience you will need, but the time spent now will pay off as the dog grows older. A dominant dog will try to assert itself almost from infancy. Indeed, if such a dog is left with its siblings, it will display its leadership traits just after it has been weaned, and a weak master will have difficulty imposing discipline by the time the puppy has turned six months old.

Although it is easy to be swayed by the 'cute' protestations of a young puppy, avoid the temptation to give in to the animal's whims. If you do not, the dog will eventually act in your home as though it were leader of the pack in its own territory, and you will then find yourself complaining that the animal is hopelessly disobedient. If you do not want the dog to sleep in your room, for example, be firm: put the dog out the very first night.

You can train a full-grown dog, but only to the extent that the animal is willing to let you. If you try to break habits the dog has had for years, you will traumatize it. It is best to begin with simple exercises.

House-training

House-training demands a great deal of patience and attention. It is pointless to shout at your pet once the damage is done—the puppy will not understand.

Until the dog is three months old and able to have booster injections, it should not be taken outside lest it pick up an infection. During this period, try to keep it in a room with a washable floor, and block the entrance with a board. Put the dog's bed and food dishes in the room, arm yourself with a floor cloth—and wait. When the puppy relieves itself, wipe up the mess with a cloth, rinse the cloth, and put it back in a corner of the room. The cloth will retain its smell and the dog will soon understand that this is where it must go. Dogs generally relieve themselves just after being fed. As soon as your pet has finished eating, carry it to the place you have chosen as its toilet. The animal will soon start to go there of its own accord. In summer, you can teach the dog to 'go' outside, using the same procedure so that your pet learns to restrict itself to a particular area. Remember to pat your animal and speak affectionately to it as soon as it does what it is supposed to do.

Start taking the puppy outside when it is three months old. Even if you have just spent a full half-hour encouraging it, the dog will no doubt relieve itself the moment it returns home. This is understandable—the house, after all, is a more private and familiar place.

You can break this habit by taking the dog out again right away (with its floor-cloth if necessary). The dog should be taken out six to eight times a day. Choose quiet places with greenery and earth. Until a dog is six months old, it cannot control itself for more than a few hours. When older, it will be able to do so for a whole night. Adult dogs, nonetheless, must be taken out at least four times a day.

You will know that your dog is properly trained when it yelps at the door to warn you that it cannot wait any longer.

Collar and leash

The first time you take your pet for a walk, put a collar and leash on it. The collar should be of sturdy leather. Fasten it around the puppy's neck tightly enough to

MUZZLING YOUR DOG

Generally, not even large dogs should be muzzled. However, since dogs are obliged to wear muzzles in certain public places, it is a good idea to have a muzzle and to know how to put it on for exceptional situations: to transport the dog, to punish it, to stop it from licking an injury or a bandage. Accustom the dog to wearing the muzzle at about the age of seven or eight months and make sure you know how to adjust the holding straps so that they fit properly around the dog's head.

Metal muzzle.

Traditional leather muzzle.

prevent the puppy from escaping as soon as it tugs backwards. For small dogs such as Dachshunds and Yorkshire Terriers, you may prefer a cat-collar or a harness. If the dog has a thick, heavy ruff, like a Chow Chow's, use a leather harness instead of a collar. Hounds and Whippets should be equipped with a broad collar specially designed for them. For a large dog, use a single- or double-choke collar, especially if your pet tends to tug hard on the leash. Choose a collar that will fit the dog when it is seven or eight months old.

The leash must be strong, flexible, and light. It should attach to the collar with clips that will not break or bend under stress.

Begin to accustom your dog to the collar at the age of two and a half months. You can do this by putting it on the dog at each feeding. The first walks on a leash should take place at home. Initially, the dog will probably pull backwards. Later, try taking it outside. If another dog or a car frightens it, reassure it with a pat and change direction. The leash must always represent the pleasure of going for a walk—it should never be used for punishment.

Earliest orders and obedience exercises

Successful training depends greatly on the way you speak to your dog. Your orders should be simple; they should not consist of more than one or two words spoken clearly, emphasizing only one syllable each. Do not say 'please lie down, Mickey' or 'sit down right now, Gertie.' Say 'Mickey, lie down' or 'Gertie, sit,' accentuating the operative word in each case. Do not become annoyed if your dog carries out the order in reverse. On the other hand, do not show amusement if the animal sits when you order it to lie down!

● Sit. This is the simplest and easiest of all commands given to dogs, be they pets or guard dogs. Take your dog to a quiet place, along with its leash. Position the dog on your left and hold the leash in your right hand. With your left hand, press down on its hindquarters, while your right hand holds the leash close to the collar and pulls the dog backwards and slightly upwards to prevent it from lying down. Pat the dog and praise it. Repeat the exercise several times until the dog no longer needs pressure from your left hand to make it under-

Dogs can be taught to respond to a variety of gestures—subtle and obvious—particularly by professionals. Here, the left arm is lowered, palm down: the dog lies down.

stand. You can then do the same exercise without the leash. Train the dog to sit each time you stop moving. The animal should not move its forepaws. It should simply tuck its hindquarters under, to move from a standing to a sitting position.

• Lie down. This is a logical extension of the exercise above. Once the dog sits, order it to lie down, pulling downwards on the leash with the right hand and pressing on the withers with the left. The dog may show some resistance, because lying down puts it in a weak position. If it does, pull the forepaws to the front or step on the leash with your left foot and pull on it with your right hand. As soon as the dog has performed the manoeuvre, stroke and encourage it. The dog is in the correct position if your leg is just behind its shoulder at the rib level. Repeat the 'sit' and 'lie down' orders several times before continuing.

• Sit, stay; lie down, stay. These commands are intended to make the dog remain in the same position even when you are not there. Once you have given the order 'stay,' go away—but keep within sight. Walk backwards at first, saying 'stay.' Then return and stroke the dog. Move farther and farther away, gradually, until the dog is out of sight. Do not let the dog try to crawl in your direction, and do not remain absent for more than a minute. When you return, give the dog a reward and signal the end of the exercise: 'that's all' or 'go play,' or whatever expression you have decided to use.

• Walking a dog on or off a leash. This exercise is intended to teach your dog to follow you without pulling. In this way, the walk will not become a tiring contest between you and the animal. The dog's forepaws should be level with your legs. Hold the loop of the leash in your right hand, and regulate the length with your left. If the dog moves too far away, tell it to 'heel' and yank the leash with your left hand. Repeat this instruction as often as necessary, but pat your dog when it follows

TEACHING A DOG TO SIT AND LIE DOWN ON COMMAND

To make a dog sit, put it on the leash and place it on your left, holding the leash in your right hand. Press down on its hindquarters with your left hand, using the leash to keep the dog's head up. Hold it in the sitting position with your left hand, and reward it for its obedience by patting and praising it, or by giving it a treat. Repeat the exercise without using the leash.

To teach the dog to stay seated, stand up, keeping the leash taut, and raise your right hand in front of the animal. Keep your hand up as you tell the dog to 'stay.' Still holding the leash, start to move away. If the dog tries to stand up, scold it. Once the dog has understood the exercise, take the leash off, keep your hand raised, and repeat 'stay.' Repeat the exercise as often as necessary, going farther and farther away each time, until the dog has learned to 'stay.' Reward the dog at the end of the exercise.

To teach the dog to lie down, tell it to sit. Then slide its forepaws forward with your right hand while your left hand puts pressure on the dog's back. As you make it lie down, give it the order 'lie down.' If the dog tries to get up, repeat the order and say 'stay.' When the dog is lying down, gradually move back, keeping your hand raised in front of it. Back away from it at first, repeating 'stay.' Repeat until you are sure the dog understands. When the dog has successfully completed the exercise, reward it with a pat or a treat.

TEACHING A DOG TO HEEL

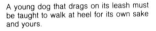

A young dog that drags on its leash must be taught to walk at heel for its own sake and yours.

When the dog strays from your side, give a sharp tug on the leash and firmly order it to 'heel.' Do this consistently.

The dog is in the proper position when it matches your pace, keeping its forelegs in line with you.

your paces. It is difficult to walk a dog without a leash; thus you should not start this exercise until the animal clearly understands and carries out the orders above. Begin by using a light rope about three metres, or ten feet, long and then let go of the rope. Talk to your dog and pat it often during its first few steps alone.

● Heel. This exercise goes with the one above, teaching the dog to walk while off the leash. Attach the dog to a rope about five metres, or fifteen feet, long to give it the impression that it is free. As you make the command gesture, order the dog to 'heel.' If it does not respond, tug sharply on the rope. Never move towards the dog if it halts before reaching you. Repeat the order and tug on the rope until the animal obeys. As soon as the dog comes to heel, pat it and instruct it to sit or lie down.

Correcting shortcomings

● Unjustified barking. Your dog may bark at the slightest sound outside—a ring from a neighbour's doorbell, a door closing, and so on. This behaviour is quite natural within certain limits, for the dog's instincts to guard make it react to any suspicious

sound. However, this is less acceptable if the dog does not distinguish between everyday sounds (such as a telephone ringing or a car starting) and unusual ones (creaks, footsteps, scratching noises). Each time your dog barks unacceptably, call it to order with a 'heel,' 'quiet,' or 'lie down.' Although you should not beat the dog you must nevertheless not give in to it. If you let the dog have its own way once in a while, barking will become a habit.

● Dislike of solitude. Dogs do not like being alone, but this is no reason to allow your pet to disturb your neighbours each time you go out. If you want to train the dog not to bark, begin when the animal is young. Before you go out, settle the dog comfortably in its basket with a hot-water bottle under the blanket. Give it food and water and put a few of its toys close by. Start by going away for a few minutes, then gradually increase the time. Listen at the door. If the dog whimpers for more than five minutes, go back and scold it. Return it to its basket and go out again. Do not let your determination waver because the dog makes a show of looking miserable, and keep in mind that many people have had to give up their dogs because of neighbours who

To teach a dog to walk to heel, start training it on a long, flexible leash. Then progress to exer- *cises off the leash. This demands patient teaching, preferably in a secluded place.*

complained about excessive barking. You will not always be able to take your dog with you everywhere you go, so if you train it to stay by itself without barking you will not have to resort to such drastic measures as giving it sedatives every time you leave.

• Pilferage. Unlike cats, dogs do not usually steal food. If a dog is well fed and properly trained, the smell of a steak or a leg of lamb should not present more than a minor temptation, easily resisted. If your dog does steal food, however, leave some meat 'booby-trapped' with hot mustard or hot peppers within its reach, and scold the dog if you catch it in the act. You can also watch carefully and spray the dog's muzzle with a scented aerosol mist at the exact moment it goes for the meat. Nonetheless, do not tempt the dog unnecessarily by leaving food lying around.

• Running away. Some dogs are born runaways. They disappear for several hours and come back in a sorry state, sometimes with injuries. Often a dog runs away because its hunting instinct is frustrated, or because it does not get enough walks, or, most often of all, because it has scented a bitch in heat. Try to find an appropriate solution. But if nothing works, you may have to resign yourself to the situation. Even castration is not always completely effective. When the dog comes home, your impulse will be to scold it. Try not to. Doing so will only make it stay away even longer the next time, and it will be afraid of you without understanding the reason for your annoyance. Punish your pet only if you catch it running away, or if you recapture it. If it comes home by itself, reward it with affection.

• Aggressiveness. Watch-dogs and guard dogs are trained to be aggressive towards strangers, but there is no justification for your dog to behave that way with you. If it feels safe, it should not bare its teeth, much less bite you, when you pat it or go near its dish. Biting is the most serious crime your dog can commit, and it deserves the most serious punishment. If you do not discipline the dog, it may become uncontrollable and dangerous. If you are afraid to punish your pet, ask a trainer to give you a demonstration. Dogs are rarely vicious from birth. If by chance yours is, the only solution is to get rid of it. If, though, your dog was mistreated by a previous owner, try patiently to build up its trust in you.

Dogs sometimes behave aggressively towards each other, and small dogs often show aggressiveness towards large dogs. This may stem from a bad early experience with another dog, or can arise between two over-sexed males. In the latter case, tranquillizers or castration may be a remedy.

A leashed dog is always more aggressive towards a dog running free than it would be if it too were off the leash itself.

When a fight between dogs erupts, the dogs are usually so agitated that any order to heel tends to be futile. It is best not to try to separate the animals by hand, or you may be severely bitten. You can, however, pull hard on the leash, or throw a bucket of water over the combatants. Each owner should call his dog and punish it if it started the fight. Afterwards, attend to the dog's wounds.

As soon as the dog has learned to walk to heel with a leash and without one, repeat these exercises when other dogs are present. Your dog should not be permitted to react when it sees another dog. If it does, order it to 'sit' or 'lie down.' If the dog becomes aggressive, muzzle it and punish it.

A dog may be aggressive because it is instinctively defending its territory, or because it is over-sexed, traumatized, or scared.

When a dog behaves aggressively towards everyone except its owner, it is an excessively timid and wary animal. And dogs that systematically avoid being patted, even by a friendly hand, tend to be fearful and hypertensive. If your dog exhibits either of these symptoms, be patient with it and help it become accustomed to meeting people. Be sure to take the animal out often, and treat it reassuringly.

• Over-exuberance. This can be a problem when your dog is so delighted to see you that it cannot help leaping at you and leaving paw marks all over your clothes. If the dog does not obey when you say 'down,' step lightly on its hind paws until it understands what is required of it.

• Sexual arousal. Some males—Poodles and Pinschers in particular—cannot help rubbing themselves against your leg in a way that leaves no room for misunderstanding. Do not allow this. Ask your veterinarian to recommend tranquillizers to treat this condition, and always indicate your disapproval.

• Vandalism. A vandal dog is one that cannot be left alone without tearing cushions, chewing books or shoes, or clawing doors

---

TRAVELLING WITH YOUR DOG

Just like people, some dogs enjoy travelling; others hate it. Thus, it may be wise to board your pet at a kennel rather than subject it to a long and stressful journey.

Trips by automobile, however, can be pleasurable for a dog if you accustom it to car travel before your holiday. Take the dog for short drives at first, and gradually increase the distance driven. Bring along a passenger who will hold the dog to assuage its nervousness. Never allow it to lean out the window; the rush of air may harm its ears or eyes. On a long drive, make sure the dog is exercised at least four times a day.

If you are travelling by train or plane, your dog will likely be transported in a carrier. If so, start to accustom the animal to the container at least a week in advance. On the day the dog is to travel, do not feed or water it within two hours of departure. Sedatives or tranquilizers should be administered only if the animal is excitable.

Before transporting a dog abroad, be sure to investigate quarantine regulations and vaccination requirements. Documentation—import permits, for example—may have to be arranged in advance. A live-cargo shipping agency can offer helpful advice.

---

and furniture. This behaviour appears very early and you must act at once to curtail it. Punish the dog if you catch it in the act. To prevent such behaviour in the first place, though, give the dog something to play with—a ball or a toy. Join in when you see the dog playing.

• Excessive fear. Although a dog must respect and obey its master, it is dismaying to have a dog that is so afraid that it starts to tremble and urinate whenever it is scolded. Such a dog needs to be made to feel safe, and to be trained without shouts or threats. Otherwise it may become aggressive out of fear, or completely inhibited.

• Laziness. Some dogs seem to be naturally lazy. This shortcoming, however, is often

A frightened dog can become dangerous, so train it gently and with lots of patience. Be sure to lavish it with encouragement.

encouraged by owners who make little or no effort to provide activity for the dog. As a result, the animal becomes obese. If your dog is lazy, use every possible tactic to encourage it to go outdoors—change the route of its walks, for example. Playing is also good therapy for a lazy dog. Play with the dog yourself, and bring it into contact with other dogs.

• Tyranny. Tyrannical, overly dominating dogs like to rule the roost. This is more a social trait than a psychological one, for the dog behaves as if it were the leader of the pack. If you do not display enough authority to put your dog in its place, try rewarding the animal with food or patting whenever it shows a hint of docility. A dog will eventually submit to the person who protects it.

• Jealousy. A jealous dog wants to be the centre of its owner's attention. If a rival appears on the scene—another dog or a baby, for example—your pet may become sick with jealousy to attract attention, or become hyperactive. Some dogs pretend to limp or refuse to eat. To make sure that a jealous dog does not become aggressive, give it more attention than usual. Make it feel that it is part of the family and that its place is not threatened.

• Dogs and traffic. Dogs are often involved in traffic accidents, so it is wise to train them not to cross streets or roads alone. To do this, wait in hiding until your dog tries to cross and then call it to heel. Repeat this exercise until it makes no further attempts. A dog's excellent hearing is its best protection against the dangers of traffic. Most dogs are quite able to hear cars coming from far off.

• Chasing livestock and poultry. Some dogs cannot resist chasing anything that moves—other animals, livestock, poultry, even bicycles and motorcycles. This habit is not only bothersome and costly, it is also potentially dangerous. Each time the dog commits this offence, it must be called to heel. Punish it every time it acts aggressively towards other animals.

Remote control

Canine hearing is infinitely better developed than human hearing, and thus dogs can be called to heel with an ultrasonic whistle when out of voice range. A series of short or long blasts can call the dog back. You can also use the whistle to tell the dog to sit or lie down if you want the animal to stay where it is.

Dogs trained to guard objects often instinctively watch over children.

Training Guard Dogs

Dogs have natural instincts to guard and to protect their owners. There are approximately twenty formidable breeds which respond particularly well to training. The best known are German Shepherds, Dobermann Pinschers, Beaucerons, and Belgian Shepherds. If you are planning to own a guard dog, choose a puppy which is neither fearful nor vicious and has good parents. Introduce obedience exercises when it is young, and begin specialized training when it matures. You will almost always need help from a professional trainer who knows dogs well—their psychology, their strengths, and their weaknesses. He may be able to tell immediately why a dog refuses to obey an order correctly, something that might take you months to puzzle out by yourself. He can give private lessons, but you can also join a training club where experienced instructors will teach you and other dog enthusiasts how to understand, and therefore educate, your dogs. Do not hesitate to call on a professional trainer if you find you cannot carry out the training program you have set for yourself.

Guard exercises

To teach a dog to guard an object, ask a friend—whom the dog does not know—to pretend to be a prowler or thief. Tie the dog up near the object (a suitcase, baby carriage, or garment), and show how important you think the object is by making the dog sniff it carefully. As you move away, tell the dog to 'watch.' Next, the thief appears, concealing a crop or switch behind his back. He approaches the object but does not touch it. If the dog does not react, he pretends to take the object and strikes the dog with the crop. As soon as the dog reacts by growling or barking, the thief runs away and the master comes to praise and pet the pupil. If the dog does not react after two or three attempts, suspend the training until the next day. Remember that a good guard dog is never vicious.

GUARD DOG CERTIFICATES

To become a certified guard dog, an animal must pass a demanding test that includes seven exercises: heeling on leash; the 'heel-free' (that is, without a leash but with a muzzle); the 'long sit' (remaining stationary for one minute in the master's absence); protection of its master (vigilance, defence of master, cessation of attack); reaction to gunshot; attacking skills; and general comportment.

If the dog is gun-shy, afraid of sticks, or does not hold the 'long sit' position for one minute, it will be eliminated. Success in the trial wins the title of certified guard dog. A well-trained guard dog will disarm an assailant and keep him cornered without savagely attacking him.

A dog-training club is a good place to teach obedience. Here, the dogs are heeling on leash.

Use the same technique to teach your dog to guard a car. Leave the dog in the car with the order to 'watch.' You can either stay with it and encourage it to react when a stranger approaches by repeating 'look out, watch him,' or you can leave the car and train the dog to react as soon as a 'prowler' tries to open the car door.

To train a dog to guard a house, make the animal lie down in front of the door, and then walk away. Your helper appears and, if the dog does not react, he strikes it with the crop as he did when the dog was being trained to guard an object.

Retrieval

Put a familiar object in the dog's mouth to accustom the animal to picking things up and giving them back on the order 'give.' Extend the exercise by moving away and then saying 'fetch.' Finally, throw the object farther off and give the same order.

Refusing bait

Have a helper offer your dog some food, then strike the dog with a crop as soon as it touches the offering. Repeat the exercise with several helpers. You can also take the dog for a walk on the leash, passing close to a tempting piece of meat you placed there beforehand. If, after sniffing it, the dog prepares to eat the meat, give the animal a scolding and a sharp tug on the leash, and muzzle it. For this exercise, some owners use collars that inflict a small electric shock at the appropriate moment.

Dogs find it difficult to remember not to take food from strangers, so test often to see whether your pet still reacts correctly.

Attack

Only dogs required to defend their masters should do this exercise. The assistant, or 'attacker,' wears specially padded clothing.

The master gives the order to 'attack,' either after an assault has been attempted or after the object being guarded has been

This Poodle 'paper boy' is a fine product of successful training.

Final phase of the attack exercise: the man pivots and the dog must not loose its hold.

stolen. The attacker waves his arms threateningly to incite the dog to bite. Then he pivots to test the dog's grip. On the order 'stop, heel' or 'stop,' the dog must let go and you must congratulate it.

TRAINING A DOG TO GUARD AN OBJECT

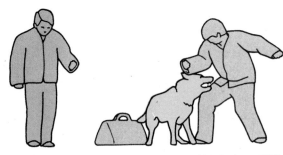

Leave the dog alone with the object it knows it must guard.

The attacker approaches and tries to take the object.

Without being told to, the dog must then assault the attacker.

Training Hunting-dogs

Every variety of hunting-dog—pointer, hound, retriever, or terrier—receives different, specialized training. But the basic education, which includes all the obedience exercises, is the same for all. Among the exercises are: tolerating the collar; heeling on and off the leash; and 'sit' and 'heel.' The decisive exercise for a hunting-dog occurs when the animal walks behind the master, and its indifference to gunshot is tested. This is a demanding test, and any hunting-dog that proves gun-shy is automatically disqualified from field trials.

Motionless, a Braque Français points, signalling the location of game it has found.

A German Short-haired Pointer in the 'down' position: one of the basics of hunt training.

The down

The 'down' is the key to special hunt training. Once the dog can perform this manoeuvre correctly, it will be easy to teach it the other skills needed. The dog lies flat on the ground with its head between its forepaws and holds this position until it hears the countermand 'go.' The order can be given verbally, or by a long blast on the whistle, or by waving your arm in the air. Make the dog lie down in front of you, and with both hands put its head and paws in the proper position, repeating 'down.' With each training session, move gradually farther and farther away.

Pointing

Most hunting-dogs have an innate talent for pointing, that is to say signalling, the location of game. A dog may do this by standing rigid (the dog stiffens with one forepaw raised, nose in the wind), refusing to advance, sitting down, or adopting the 'down' position (the dog flattens itself against the ground). However, sometimes a dog needs to be trained to 'stand on point,' or to hold the position longer.

Tracking and flushing

Hunting-dogs are born with a well-honed 'quartering' instinct (the search-pattern by which the dog locates game), but it is best not to begin training until the age of ten months. Take your dog into the country and it will start to pick up the scent of game by itself. It will flush game by quartering—scenting the wind, making 'casts' (tracing visually and instinctively) to the right and the left and across the wind. The owner gives the order 'go find' with his outstretched arm indicating the direction of the hunt. The example of an experienced dog is useful in early training. Pack hounds are more easily trained under the aegis of a canine role-model.

This Pointer is scenting the wind. It will sniff all the odours and then set off seeking game.

HUNTING DOGS

Dog at heel.

Tracking game.

Down in front of flushed game.

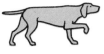
Pointing at game.

Going down as hunter shoots.

Chasing game.

Retrieving game in mouth.

Presenting game to master.

Retrieving

Although all hunting-dogs are capable of retrieving, this activity is primarily the speciality of particular breeds such as the Golden, Labrador, and Flat-coated retrievers. A retriever does not hunt game; it fetches it after the game has been downed. To train a retriever, employ the same technique required for training a guard dog to bring back an object. Use a rabbit skin or a dead game animal. The orders used are 'fetch' and 'give.'

Special Training

Guide dogs

Although German Shepherds have won renown for this discipline, other breeds such as the Labrador and Golden retrievers have also proved excellent. Specialized centres provide basic education and advanced training. The dog selected must be obedient. After exercises to increase the dog's adaptability, the instructor puts a

Retrieving game without damaging it is easy for this Brittany Spaniel, a fine hunting-dog.

The guide dog gives warning of obstacles and helps to negotiate or avoid them.

harness on its back with a U-shaped handle attached to its shoulder. The animal will wear this harness throughout its life as a guide dog. Once fitted with a harness, the dog is then taught how to alert its master to obstacles either by making a detour around them or by stopping and sitting

down to warn of danger ahead—a flight of stairs, for example. The instructor, who carries a white cane, refuses to negotiate the obstacle until the dog acknowledges it by stopping.

Other training

There are many other activities for which dogs can be trained that employ some of their special attributes. Their keen sense of smell makes them especially valuable for finding victims of avalanches and earthquakes. The Saint Bernard, once the very symbol of the alpine rescue dog, has now been replaced by the German Shepherd, which has better tracking skills. Similarly, police, customs, and army tracking dogs often help look for missing persons, contraband drugs, and even criminals. Truffle hounds put their noses at the service of gourmets, uncovering this delicacy beneath oaks in certain regions of Europe. Sheep-dogs, circus dogs, racing dogs, sled dogs—all are fine examples of the dog's capacity to adapt to human objectives.

SHEEP-DOG TRAINING

Choose a dog whose nature will allow it to adapt to the work required of it. Sheep-dogs must be obedient, brave, watchful, gentle, and intelligent. High-strung or aggressive dogs are not suitable. When your dog is between six and eight months old, it should be taught all the basic obedience exercises, including walking on and off the leash. After it has thoroughly mastered these basics, the dog should be put into a sheep pen and taught how to hold a sheep gently on the neck, hock, or ear, and then release it on command. Continue the training with an experienced dog that will teach your fledgling how to herd a flock.

Sheep-dogs can be specialized. The herder brings strays and laggards back into the flock. The line dog protects crops by dexterously guiding the flock around them when the sheep are being moved from one place to another. A third type of sheep-dog stays at the shepherd's side. It is trained to intervene only on command.

During sheep-dog trials, the dog is judged on a variety of exercises: entering and leaving the pen, coping with a difficult gate, moving and controlling the flock at a good pace, displaying intelligence in its performance, and halting the flock. Shepherds accompany their dogs on foot or by vehicle and issue orders in various ways: by shouting commands, by gesturing with their caps, by whistling, or by hand signals.

TYPICAL TRIAL COURSE

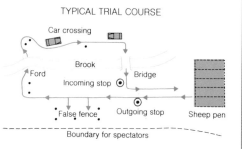

Because of their sense of smell, dogs often replace pigs in hunting for truffles. Truffle-hound competitions are held regularly in Europe.

Dogs are used to hunt for illicit drugs, and many drug smugglers owe their arrests to a dog's acute sense of smell.

Health

Your Dog's Anatomy
326

Your Dog's Physiology
332

Medical Care
338

Your Dog's Anatomy

THE SKELETON

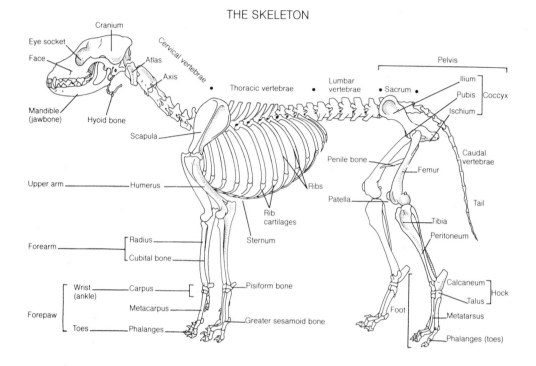

Skeleton

The skeleton is a jointed structure of bones controlled by muscles. It supports the whole anatomy and contains the central nervous system. It also stores minerals and marrow for the body's use.

The bones are living organisms whose form, structure, and composition vary during the animal's life.

A dog has approximately 320 bones. The axial skeleton consists of 134 bones, including the skull, spinal column, breastbone, ribs, and hyoid bone. The appendicular skeleton consists of 186 bones, including those of the limbs, and in male dogs the penile bone.

There are four types of bones: long bones such as the femur and tibia in the leg; flat bones such as the scapula (shoulder-blade) and cranium (skull); irregular bones such as the vertebrae; short bones such as the phalanges (bones of the paws); and sesamoid bones, which are really ossified portions of tendons.

A dog's spinal column runs horizontally between the shoulders and the pelvis. It consists of 7 cervical, 13 thoracic, and 7 lumbar vertebrae, as well as 3 sacral vertebrae fused to form the sacrum. There are also caudal vertebrae which vary in number according to the breed and the individual dog. At the level of the thorax, the spinal column joins the ribs and the sternum (breastbone).

The skeleton of the head is made up of two sets of bones: the cranial bones, which protect the brain (cerebrum, cerebellum, and brain stem), and the facial bones around the mouth and nose cavities. The proportions of these bones vary from one breed to another.

The limbs are connected to the axial skeleton by girdles. The shoulder girdle consists solely of two scapulae, one on each side of the body, since dogs, like other running animals, have no clavicles (collarbones). The pelvic girdle links the hind legs to the spine. Together with the sacrum it forms the pelvis.

The bones of the limbs correspond to those in humans. In the foreleg (arm) the upper part is supported by the humerus; the lower part is supported by the radius and the ulna; the forepaw (hand) is supported by the carpus, the metacarpus, and five toes (fingers) of three phalanges each, except for the dew-claw (thumb), which has only two. The hind leg consists of the thigh, supported by the femur; the leg, supported by the tibia and fibula; the foot, containing the tarsus and metatarsus; and four toes, each having three phalanges.

The dog is a digitigrade animal—that is, it walks on its toes. Its third phalanges rest on the ground, protected by the pads on the sole of the foot. When a dog runs, its feet are straight and elongated. When a dog is at rest, the bones of its limbs are at angles to each other.

Joints

Joints enable the bones to move in relation to each other. There are three kinds: fixed, mobile, and semi-mobile.

The fixed joints, such as those of the cranium, are called sutures.

The most mobile joints are those of the limbs. The surfaces of these bones are covered with cartilage and lubricated by synovial fluid so that they can glide smoothly over each other. The bones are held in place by a fibrous envelope called the articular capsule, which encloses the joint and is reinforced with ligaments. Muscles and tendons surround each joint to direct and control their actions.

The semi-mobile joints, as their name indicates, permit only limited movement. There are semi-mobile joints after each vertebra in the spinal column.

Muscles

There are three types of muscle: the striated (striped), or skeletal muscles, which make movements of the skeleton, the skin, and certain organs possible; the cardiac muscle, which is also striated but is controlled by the nervous system; and the smooth muscles of the digestive tract and other internal organs.

The muscles of the skin are well developed in dogs. Their contraction allows the animal to shake itself dry after a bath. Among the head muscles, however, only the muscles of the ears and eyelids have an important role; the other muscles do not enable the animal to alter its facial expressions as we do. The skeletal muscles vary a great deal in their form. They may be long or short, and their attachment to the bones may be direct or by way of a tendon. Dogs, like other mammals, also have a muscle called the diaphragm. This separates the thoracic and abdomino-pelvic cavities.

Digestive System

The digestive system consists of all the organs needed to ingest food and transform it by mechanical and chemical means into energy. The system comprises the digestive tract proper, beginning with the mouth (buccal cavity) and the glands linked to it.

The dog, a meat-eating mammal, uses its mouth—specifically, its canine teeth—to seize prey. The flesh of the prey is then masticated through the movements of the lower jaw, or mandible. The premolar and the carnassial teeth (the last upper premolar and first lower molar, which are particularly developed) tear the meat to pieces, and the molars crush the bones. A young dog has only 28 milk-teeth, which consist of incisors, canines, and premolars, but no molars. At the age of about six or

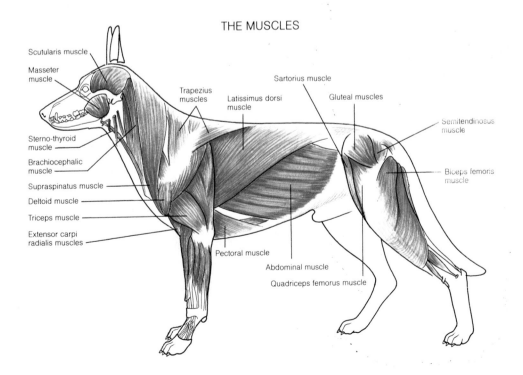

THE MUSCLES

Scutularis muscle
Masseter muscle
Trapezius muscles
Sartorius muscle
Latissimus dorsi muscle
Gluteal muscles
Semitendinosus muscle
Sterno-thyroid muscle
Brachiocephalic muscle
Supraspinatus muscle
Deltoid muscle
Triceps muscle
Biceps femoris muscle
Extensor carpi radialis muscles
Pectoral muscle
Abdominal muscle
Quadriceps femorus muscle

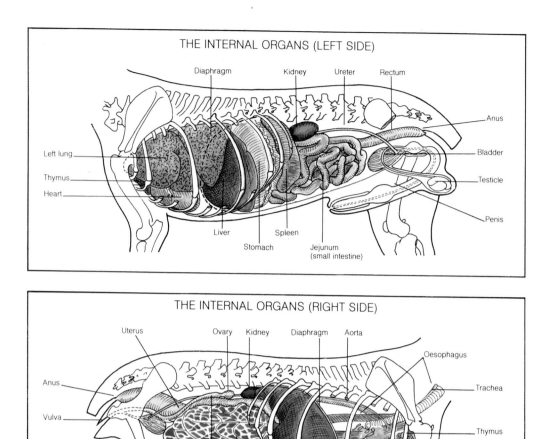

THE INTERNAL ORGANS (LEFT SIDE)

Diaphragm · Kidney · Ureter · Rectum · Anus · Bladder · Testicle · Penis · Left lung · Thymus · Heart · Liver · Stomach · Spleen · Jejunum (small intestine)

THE INTERNAL ORGANS (RIGHT SIDE)

Uterus · Ovary · Kidney · Diaphragm · Aorta · Oesophagus · Anus · Vulva · Trachea · Thymus · Heart · Duodenum · Stomach · Liver · Omentum, covering the intestines

seven months these are replaced by a full set of 42 teeth (this process may occur even earlier in certain breeds such as Rough Collies and Boxers).

All of a dog's teeth become worn with age. Examining the incisors and canines can sometimes give a good idea of how old a dog is. However, the food given to domestic animals, and consequently the wear on their teeth, varies a great deal. Saliva is secreted by means of glands in the mouth. The saliva's function is mainly mechanical, to help the dog to swallow.

A dog's tongue is broad, thin, and very dexterous. It helps the animal take food into its mouth and, by means of taste-buds, to perceive its flavour.

Solid food is shaped by the tongue into a lump, or bolus, which passes from the mouth through the oesophagus. The oesophagus runs down the throat, past the trachea and the heart, between the lungs, past the diaphragm, and empties into the stomach.

The stomach is a pocket of muscle with a capacity of from one to nine litres (about one quart to two gallons), depending on the size of dog. Its shape depends on how full it is. The internal surface of its wall is covered with glands which secrete gastric juices. These juices, together with the stomach muscles, convert the bolus into a whitish fluid mass called chyme, which enters the small intestine.

There are two parts to the intestine: the small intestine (called the jejunum), and the large intestine (called the duodenum). The large intestine is where the digestive process ends and where the waste accumulates to become excrement.

Unlike humans, the dog has no appendix. In most respects, however, the dog's digestive system closely resembles ours.

Glands of the digestive tract

Both in size and function, the liver is the most important gland of the digestive system. It accounts for about three per cent of the dog's total weight, though it shrinks with age. It acts on food, fats, proteins, and food-nutrients such as glucosides; neutralizes toxic substances; and regulates the hormonal system. The liver also secretes bile, which accumulates in the gall-bladder and then is discharged into the small intestine to aid digestion. In addition to this, the liver stores vitamins and iron, plays an essential part in maintaining the body's internal temperature, and contributes to the production of certain components of blood. Another gland of the digestive tract, the pancreas, secretes pancreatic juice into the small intestine. This juice plays an important part in the digestion of proteins and glucosides.

Respiratory System

This system consists of the respiratory tracts and the two lungs, which convey oxygen to the blood. Air enters through the nostrils at the tip of the nose, a hairless area that is usually pigmented and normally cool and moist. The tip of the nose is surrounded by bone and cartilage. The large nasal cavity, divided into right and left sides, is separated from the buccal cavity by the palate. The air is purified in the nasal cavity since dust and other particles are trapped in mucus secreted by the nasal lining. The air is also warmed and humidified as it passes through the nose. Two bones on each side help to increase the surface area of the nasal cavity. Rolled back upon themselves, these two turbinate bones are covered by a mucous tissue with an extensive vascular system.

The sense of smell is provided by the olfactory mucous membrane, which covers the ethmoid bone at the root of the nose. Dogs have a particularly acute sense of smell. Their olfactory mucous membrane occupies a much larger surface than ours: 120 square centimetres (18½ square inches) in dogs, compared to 5 square centimetres (¾ square inch) in humans.

Air passes through the pharynx and enters the larynx, which is in front of the trachea. The vibrations of the vocal cords in the larynx produce barking. The sound is amplified in the pharynx and the nasal cavity, which act as a resonating chamber. The air is channelled to the lungs along the trachea, which is held open by rings of cartilage and divides into two bronchial tubes.

In the lungs, the bronchial tubes themselves divide into bronchioles, very fine tubes that lead to small air cells, the alveoli, where the exchange of gases takes place. It is here that the

blood rids itself of carbon dioxide and replenishes its store of oxygen. The lungs are relatively large because the dog is an animal adapted for running. The lungs are encased in a two-layer sac made up of the pulmonary and the costal pleura, which enables the lungs to make the same movements as the rib cage.

Urinary and Genital Systems

The urinary system has the task of eliminating waste products and excess water. It consists of the kidneys and the urinary tract proper. The kidneys purify the blood by filtering it. They weigh from 40 to 60 grams (1½ to 2 ounces). The toxic substances which they retain are diluted into urine, which is discharged through two tubes called ureters, which in turn empty into the bladder. From the bladder, the urine is discharged through another duct, the urethra, which is longer in male dogs than in females.

The genital system consists of the reproductive glands, or gonads, which produce

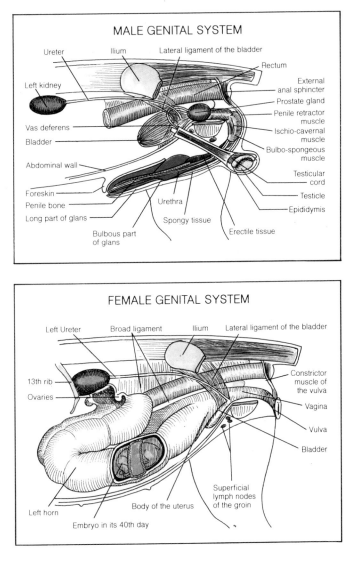

MALE GENITAL SYSTEM

Ureter — Ilium — Lateral ligament of the bladder — Rectum — External anal sphincter — Prostate gland — Penile retractor muscle — Ischio-cavernal muscle — Bulbo-spongeous muscle — Testicular cord — Testicle — Epididymis — Left kidney — Vas deferens — Bladder — Abdominal wall — Foreskin — Penile bone — Long part of glans — Bulbous part of glans — Urethra — Spongy tissue — Erectile tissue

FEMALE GENITAL SYSTEM

Left Ureter — Broad ligament — Ilium — Lateral ligament of the bladder — Constrictor muscle of the vulva — Vagina — Vulva — Bladder — 13th rib — Ovaries — Left horn — Embryo in its 40th day — Body of the uterus — Superficial lymph nodes of the groin the procreative cells; the genital tracts, which transport them; and the copulatory organs, which make it possible for the reproductive cells, or gametes, to meet.

Male genital system

This system consists of two spherical testicles contained in a pouch, the scrotum, situated under the anus and between the thighs. The testicles produce the male gametes, or spermatozoa. Each testicle is topped by its epididymis, of which the continuation is the *vas deferens*. These two tubes discharge into the urethra after passing the prostate gland, which produces the fluid that carries the spermatozoa. Dogs have neither vesicular nor bulbo-urethral (Cowper's) glands, as humans do. In the penis, the urethra is surrounded by tissue capable of being inflated by an influx of blood into its vessels. The dog's penis has a penile bone; a groove along its length contains the urethral duct.

Female genital system

In this system, the two ovaries are the gonads. They are small and flattened, and lie slightly below and behind the kidneys. A bitch generally reaches puberty at between four and six months (but this may vary considerably), after which the ovaries function intermittently. In theory, there are two cycles per year, at six-month intervals. The period when the bitch is in heat (the estrus), during which she can couple, lasts from four to eight days. Ovulation (the production of ova, or reproductive cells) begins about a third of the way into this period. The ovum is caught in the pavilion, or fringed opening, of the Fallopian tube, and passes into it, where it can be fertilized by the spermatozoa.

Each Fallopian tube leads into one 'horn,' or innermost end, of the uterus; the two horns meet in the main body of the uterus. The vagina is very long and offers access from the outside through the vulva. The egg which results from the fusion of an ovum and a spermatozoon can only be implanted in the uterine wall two weeks after fertilization. During this period gestation can be aborted.

A litter generally consists of from four to ten puppies, and gestation lasts about sixty-three days. After whelping, the bitch cuts their umbilical cords with her teeth. The puppies, whose eyes are closed at birth, suckle at eight to ten teats arranged in two rows running from the thorax along the mother's underbelly.

Circulatory System

The circulatory system is composed of the heart, the blood vessels (both arteries and veins), as well as the lymphatic ducts and glands.

The heart is the pump which sends blood through the body. It is quite round and weighs from 10 grams (less than half an ounce) in small breeds to 500 grams (slightly more than a pound) in the largest. A vital organ, the heart constitutes less than one per cent of total body weight.

As in other mammals, the dog's heart is divided into two halves and four cavities (two auricles and two ventricles) which

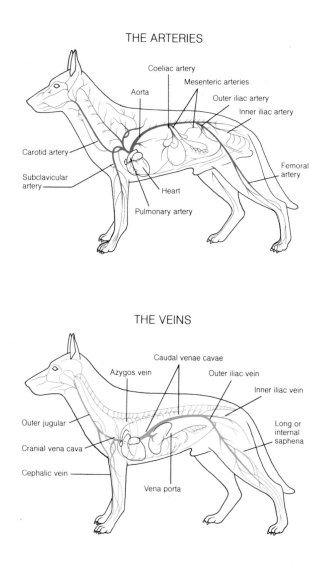

THE ARTERIES

Coeliac artery
Mesenteric arteries
Aorta
Outer iliac artery
Inner iliac artery
Carotid artery
Femoral artery
Subclavicular artery
Heart
Pulmonary artery

THE VEINS

Caudal venae cavae
Azygos vein
Outer iliac vein
Inner iliac vein
Outer jugular
Long or internal saphena
Cranial vena cava
Cephalic vein
Vena porta

are connected vertically but not horizontally. This ensures a double system of circulation: general circulation throughout the whole body, and pulmonary circulation (of the lungs).

The arteries of the pulmonary system consist of one single vessel, the pulmonary trunk, which begins in the right half of the heart and divides into two pulmonary arteries, which carry blood heavily loaded with carbon dioxide. The arteries for general circulation all rise from the aorta, which comes from the left ventricle.

The veins of pulmonary circulation (the pulmonary veins) bring oxygenized blood from the lungs to the left auricle. The veins of the general circulatory system open into the two *venae cavae* which carry the blood loaded with carbon dioxide into the right auricle.

The lymphatic system ensures the defence of the organism; it consists of lymph ducts, which meet in the swellings known as the lymph nodes. Lymph drains the spaces between cells and helps protect the animal against infection.

Nervous System

The nervous system monitors variations in the dog's physical condition (body) and in its environment, and it triggers appropriate reactions. It keeps the dog in touch with the world around it and co-ordinates the activity of its organs.

The nervous system includes the central (neuraxial), peripheral, and autonomic (sympathetic and parasympathetic) nervous systems.

The central nervous system consists of the brain and the spinal cord. The brain includes the brain stem, the cerebellum, and the cerebrum.

The spinal cord, from which come the spinal stalks or rachides and the sensory and the motor nerves, lies within the vertebral column.

The brain stem is essential to life. The command and regulatory centres for the major functions (respiratory, cardiac, digestive, reproductive, and thermoregulatory) are situated in this small area.

The cerebellum is concerned with balance, posture, and movement. It coordinates voluntary muscular contractions.

The cerebrum consists of two hemispheres of convoluted masses of nerve tissue. It controls conscious sensation, voluntary movement, and mental activity.

The whole central nervous system is enclosed in three envelopes which protect and nourish it, called the meninges. Their names (from the outermost inwards) are the *dura mater*, the *arachnoid*, and the *pia mater*.

The autonomic nervous system controls the vegetative life of the dog, directing it to expend energy, through the sympathetic system, or to recuperate energy, through the parasympathetic system.

Sensory Organs

The dog's eye is composed of three concentric envelopes: the sclera, the choroid, and the retina. The first of these is the white of the eye, on which rests the transparent cornea. Underneath is the choroid coat, or coloured iris, pierced by the pupil. The retina provides light-sensitive backing. Inside the eye is the lens. Though its purpose is to focus sight, it is not capable of much adjustment; this explains the dog's near-sightedness. Dogs' eyes are also not very mobile.

These two handicaps are slightly offset by a reflecting surface at the back of the eye, behind the retina. This surface provides better vision as the light gets poorer, since the light registers twice on the retina. This explains why a dog's eyes reflect the light of an automobile headlamp so luminously. Certain breeds see far better at night than during the day. Dogs are probably not able to distinguish colours, merely different shades of grey.

The dog's ear has a structure like that of the human ear. The auditory passage is very long and curved, and ends in a very mobile outer ear supported by cartilage. The middle and inner ear have the same parts as in human ears: the eardrum, the bones of the inner ear, the cochlea, and the auditory canal.

Dogs have a very highly developed sense of touch (tactile sense) in the paws and tongue.

THE NERVES

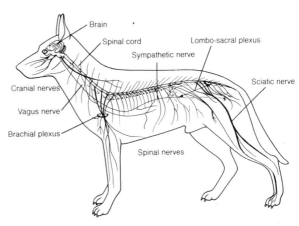

Brain
Spinal cord
Lombo-sacral plexus
Sympathetic nerve
Sciatic nerve
Cranial nerves
Vagus nerve
Brachial plexus
Spinal nerves

Your Dog's Physiology

The physiology of the dog—the way its body works—is like ours in some ways, but not in others. Its respiratory and excretory functions are similar to a human's, but its digestive, reproductive, and body-temperature controls are quite different.

Digestion

Digestion is a complex process which takes place in several stages.

Ingestion

To hold and chew solid food the dog has to use its jaws, which are very powerful. Large pieces of food, especially bones, are held in place by the front paws, which the dog uses much like hands. The dog manoeuvres food into its mouth by jerking its head backwards and forwards. Chewing is not thorough since the jaws do not move sideways, so the morsels swallowed are large in proportion to the size of the dog. Saliva is secreted in response to the stimuli of taste and smell of the food, or by conditioned reflex—when the dog knows, for example, that its meal is being prepared.

Water forms a very high proportion of a dog's body, as it does of all mammals' bodies. To balance the loss of water due to urination, excretion, and evaporation via the respiratory tract, a dog has to drink water every day. The dog laps the liquid; it moves its tongue rapidly backwards and forwards, and folds it like a spoon to throw the water into its mouth.

Gastric digestion

The stomach hardly ever contracts, except after meals. When it does, it works vigorously, mixing the food. From two to three litres (two to three quarts) of gastric juice are secreted each day. Gastric juice contains hydrochloric acid and enzymes, which digest the proteins and separate the connective tissues in meat. Gastric secretions are stimulated by the ingestion of food and its arrival in the stomach, and also by conditioned reflex. This is why it is so important to give the dog its meals at fixed times.

Intestinal digestion

The bolus is carried farther by intestinal contractions, and acted upon by various digestive juices. The pancreatic juice contains enzymes which attack fats, proteins, and starches. The dog secretes bile which assists the action of the pancreatic juice, and also allows certain wastes to be eliminated.

The intestinal juices do their work of digestion by means of their enzymes. Puppies digest milk partly in the stomach and partly in the intestines, by means of an enzyme which disappears after weaning. (This is why so many adult dogs cannot tolerate milk.) All the products of digestion are absorbed from the small intestine or, to a lesser extent, from the large intestine. Some nutrients pass into the blood (water, mineral salts, glucose, amino-acids, and some fats) while others (mainly fats) pass into lymph. The digestive scheme for each type of food is as follows:

- Proteins (meat, fish, casein from milk). Partial digestion in the stomach is completed in the small intestine by enzymes from the pancreatic and intestinal juices.
- Lipids, or fats (meat, fish, milk). These are digested entirely in the intestine by the enzymes in the pancreatic juice, helped by the presence of bile.
- Glucosides (cereals, starchy foods). The starch is digested by the pancreatic juice. For puppies, lactose (milk sugar) is digested by a special enzyme.

Reproduction

In both male and female, the genital system has two functions. It produces not only the reproductive cells but also the sex hormones which control the reproductive process by acting upon the dog's anatomy, physiology, and behaviour. The whole phenomenon of reproduction is controlled, in a complex but precise manner, by a ductless gland called the pituitary, or hypophysis.

How the male genital system works

A tiny amount—a cubic millimetre, say—of sperm contains between 100,000 and 200,000 spermatozoa. The volume and the concentration, however, are greatly reduced if the dog mates too often. It is advisable not to have the dog mate more than once every two days. The male hormone, mainly testosterone, is produced by the Leydig cells in the testicles. The suprarenal glands can also produce small quantities of hormone. These secretions must occur if the dog is to produce spermatozoa. They also determine secondary sexual characteristics and reproductive behaviour. A dog's sexual activity begins at puberty, between six and eleven months of

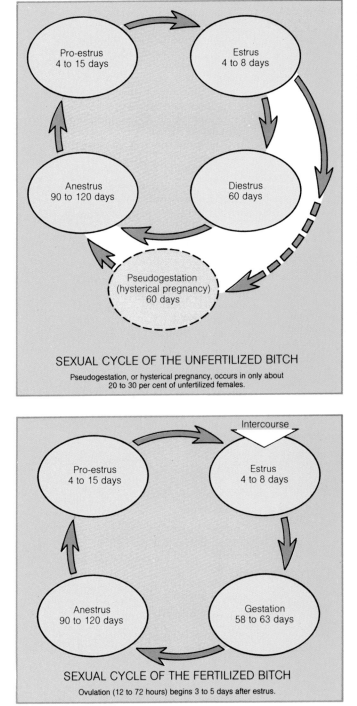

SEXUAL CYCLE OF THE UNFERTILIZED BITCH

Pseudogestation, or hysterical pregnancy, occurs in only about
20 to 30 per cent of unfertilized females.

SEXUAL CYCLE OF THE FERTILIZED BITCH

Ovulation (12 to 72 hours) begins 3 to 5 days after estrus.

cles, a certain number of which grow during each cycle. These follicles rupture at the moment of ovulation, freeing the ova to reach the uterus. The ovaries secrete the sexual hormone oestrogen during the first part of the cycle. These hormones cause the animal to come into heat. Another hormone, progesterone, is secreted by the yellow *corpus luteum* which forms around the Graafian follicles in the ovaries.

The bitch's sexual cycle falls into four periods, the pro-estrus, the estrus, the diestrus, and the anestrus. In theory, the cycles have an average length of six months, so there should be two periods of sexual activity every year. In practice, however, the cycles vary because of differences in the length of the anestrus (the period when the genital system is inactive) for different breeds, different ages, and different bitches.

The pro-estrus lasts from four to fifteen days (nine on average) and is the period when Graaffian follicles grow in the ovaries. The vulva swells and emits a mucous discharge which later contains blood, the visible sign of how congested the genital system has become.

The estrus lasts for from four to eight days. This is the time when the bitch will accept the dog; she is now in heat. The discharge from the vulva stops. At this time the animal gives many signs of nervousness and often runs away. Ovulation begins from three to five days after the onset of estrus (from one to seven days at the extreme). From one to more than 20 ova may be released and the period of ovulation lasts from 12 to 72 hours.

Matings with males of different breeds at intervals of 24 or 48 hours can therefore result in a mixed litter.

The diestrus generally lasts for a period of about two months. It does not occur, however, if the bitch is pregnant. The changes brought about in the genital system are not visible; they mainly affect the uterus, whose wall thickens. They are linked with the secretion of progesterone by the yellow *corpus luteum*.

age, and continues to the age of ten or twelve years, or even later. But, in any case, a progressive reduction in the reproductive instinct becomes obvious from the age of ten onwards. Unlike that of the female, the male reproductive system is active all through the year.

How the female genital system works

The bitch's genital system is more complex than that of the male, and is marked by sexual cycles. The ova, secreted in the ovaries, are enclosed in the Graafian folli-

The anestrus is of variable length (several months, but three and a half on average). In basic terms, this is a period of rest for the reproductive system. For bitches, the anestrus is controlled by a number of different hormones secreted by the pituitary gland, which itself is to some extent controlled by the nervous system through the hypothalamus, a part of the brain.

Mating and gestation

The act of coitus enables the spermatozoa and the ova to be brought into contact in the bitch's genital tract. When bitches are in heat, they attract males by the odour of the pheromones that they secrete. The bitch will only accept the male during the estrus period.

The success of the mating requires that the male have an erect penis. The insertion of this organ is made easier by its rigidity, which is partly due to the penile bone, and also by the distention and lubrication of the vulva and the vagina.

Penetration sets off a reflex contraction of the muscles of the vagina while the tip of the penis swells. This makes it impossible to separate the two animals. This phase, called the 'tie,' can last 20 or 30 minutes—even an hour or more in small breeds—after which the male usually dismounts from the female and the two animals may end up side by side or, more commonly, back to back, until the contraction of the vaginal muscles lessens, freeing the penis.

At this stage the animals should not be frightened, nor should any attempt be made to separate them, as this can result in severe lesions on the male's genitals.

During the tie the sperm is ejaculated into the vagina in three successive spurts; the first and last of these spurts contain very few spermatozoa. Ejaculation usually takes place after about two or three minutes. In the bitch's genital tract the spermatozoa will not survive longer than three or four days.

The fusion of a spermatozoon with an ovum marks the beginning of gestation. The bitch shows very little sign of this, which explains why it is so difficult to be certain about it. However, after three weeks, certain changes should become evident in the bitch's behaviour.

A clinical examination carried out by a veterinarian can provide a more exact judgement, although small litters (one to two puppies) may escape detection until the last days of gestation. The bitch becomes calmer and her belly swells, but this may not be visible if the animal happens to be fat. It is only towards the end of the gestation period that development of the teats can be observed.

The time of whelping is usually near when the bitch goes off on her own to prepare a 'nest.' The preparatory phase lasts several hours.

Each pup is ejected after its amnion, or caul, has broken and its 'water' (amniotic fluid) has spilled. This additional matter is expelled at the same time as the puppy, or just afterwards.

The bitch frees the puppy from the caul if it is still encased in it, and then licks its own genital opening very carefully, swallowing the placenta (also known as the afterbirth). When there are several puppies, the intervals between their births are usually anywhere from 10 to 30 minutes. There are from five to seven puppies on average—although there have been some instances of litters containing more than 20—and even up to 27—puppies.

Lactation, which begins after delivery, allows the mother to nourish her young. Normally, the teats are small, but they become larger in the days just before whelping. Secretion of milk begins immediately after this and stops if the milk is not removed by suckling.

The mammary glands need the mechanical stimulus of sucking and of pressure from the puppies' paws if the pituitary gland is to continue producing the hormones which stimulate milk production. Lactation lasts from 35 to 42 (sometimes 50) days. After this the pups can be weaned.

Bitch's milk is particularly rich. Although cow's milk is similar, it contains lower levels of some nutrients and thus is a poor substitute.

Modification of the bitch's sexual cycle

A bitch's heats can be suppressed in either of two ways: by preventing their onset completely or by interrupting them after they have begun.

To prevent heats, synthetic hormones such as medroxyprogesterone can be administered. This treatment must be carried out during the anestrus, or the period of sexual inactivity; that is, from approximately three to five months after the last heat, or from 20 to 30 days after the puppies have been weaned.

A single intramuscular injection of medroxyprogesterone is usually sufficient. Regular treatment every five or six months prevents further heats. However, there are many other factors involved, so it is always prudent to have the bitch examined by a veterinarian prior to each injection. Only a person with professional experience can determine the correct dosage for a particular dog, and the appropriate length of time between injections.

It is worth noting that there are potential drawbacks to this treatment. These include possible increase in infections of the uterus, which could well jeopardize future pregnancies, and pose a risk of sterility. For these reasons it is important that the treatment be interrupted every two or three cycles to prevent problems in the functioning of the genital system.

Heats can be interrupted rather than prevented altogether, but this is much less satisfactory since it is sometimes difficult to determine precisely at what point of the cycle the dog may be. The treatment must be carried out in the first three days of pro-estrus, so it is absolutely necessary to have the bitch examined by a veterinary surgeon who will decide what substance—in what dosage, and administered in what manner—should be used to interrupt the estrous cycle.

Pregnancy can be interrupted when the bitch has already mated and the owner does not want her to have puppies, or the male is not of the breed desired. Hormone treatment by a veterinary surgeon is then required.

To be effective, this treatment must be carried out as soon as possible after the mating has occurred—that is, from 24 to 72 hours later.

Best period for mating

For best results, a bitch should not become pregnant too early in life. She should not be mated during her first, or even her second, estrus.

Because of the short time that the spermatozoa and the ova survive, and the time pattern of ovulation, the bitch should couple twice to give the greatest chance of fertilization. If at all possible, therefore, she should have the first coitus 24 hours after going into heat, and the second after another 48 hours.

Circulation and Respiration

Circulation and respiration are essentially similar in dogs and humans. The volume of blood is about 80 millilitres per kilogram (1.5 fluid ounces per pound) of body weight. Thus a haemorrhage of more than 150 millilitres (a quarter-pint) is a serious matter for a medium-size dog. Just as with man, dogs are of different blood groups.

A dog has a relatively large heart, but it works much like a human's, although the pulse rate varies considerably from one animal to another (from 70 to 120 beats per minute). In general, very small dogs have a much faster pulse than do members of larger breeds. Again like humans, dogs that are in physical training have slower pulses than less fit dogs.

Blood circulates in the following manner: oxygenized (bright red) blood leaves the left ventricle of the heart, passes into the aorta, and from there is distributed throughout the body by the other arteries and the arterial capillaries. These lie close to the venous capillaries. After the blood in the muscles and the various organs has been charged with carbon dioxide, it passes

---

COMPOSITION OF THE BLOOD
OF THE ADULT DOG

Volume of blood: 80 mL/kg
Corpuscle count (number of corpuscles per mm³ of blood):
   red corpuscles: 5,000,000 to 7,000,000
   white corpuscles: 7,000 to 10,000
Proportions of different types of white corpuscles:
   neutrophiles: 60 to 75%
   esinophiles: 1 to 10%
   basophiles: 0 to 1%
   lymphocytes: 10 to 30%
   monocytes: 2 to 9%
Haematoblast (blood platelet) count:
   150,000 to 600,000
Volume of constituents:
   haemoglobin: 10 to 15 g/L
   glucose: 0.8 to 1.0 g/L
   urea: 0.2 to 0.5 g/L
   total protein: 40 to 60 g/L

---

into the venous capillaries, which connect with the veins. At this stage it is dark red, and it flows back to the heart through the *venae cavae*. It runs through the right auricle to the right ventricle, then to the lungs. There, it gives up its carbon dioxide and is recharged with oxygen. It returns through the left auricle to the left ventricle to begin a fresh tour of the body. Thus venous and arterial blood are separate.

Thermoregulation

Dogs are warm-blooded mammals, so their internal temperature is constant. The normal temperature of an adult dog is 38.5°C (101.3°F) but for the puppy just a few days old, the mechanism which maintains this temperature at its normal level is still not fully developed. That is why, if a newborn puppy is left exposed to cold air, its internal temperature falls rapidly until the animal succumbs to hypothermia.

After the age of one to three months, control of internal temperature becomes stable, but the rectal temperature of a young dog is always slightly higher than that of an adult animal.

A dog has two ways of defending itself against the cold. It can reduce the loss of heat or increase the production of heat. To reduce heat loss, the peripheral blood vessels (of the limbs, the ears, and the skin) may contract. This reduces the amount of heat brought to these parts, and thus the amount lost to the surrounding air.

The dog's coat increases the body's insulation by trapping a fairly deep layer of air—air being an excellent insulator. It is in winter that the dog's coat is at its thickest, and usually at its longest. Certain breeds that are well adapted to cold climates have particularly profuse coats—the Saint Bernard and the Pyrenean Sheepdog, for example. Furthermore, the coat provides even more effective protection because of small cutaneous muscles at the base of the follicles which contract, making the hairs stand on end, thereby deepening the insulating layer of air. The dog also protects itself from the cold by changing positions: It curls up in a ball, exposing less of its body surface to the cold, or, if in the company of other animals, it snuggles up against them.

When these methods of defence are not enough, the dog produces more heat by shivering. Dogs that have become acclimatized generate heat by increasing the metabolic rate of the liver and the fatty tissues. This requires additional food to supply the extra calories used up in this way.

When the air temperature rises, or when the dog produces more heat by exercising vigorously, mechanisms to expedite heat loss come into play. This is accomplished to some extent by bringing more blood to the surface of the body by dilating the blood vessels and so warming the skin. The surplus calories then escape into the atmosphere. This transfer of heat will be greater if the ventilation is good and the air in contact with the skin is quickly renewed; it also helps if the dog's body is in contact with water or cool ground, both of which are good conductors of heat. That is why in the summer we see dogs stretched out full length on a shady slab or looking for a moist place to lie.

When the air temperature rises sharply, the need to lose heat becomes urgent. Some mammals lose heat when sweat evaporates from the surface of the body. But dogs have only a few sweat glands, and these are at the ends of the paws, located on the pads. Being so few, and placed as they are, they are virtually useless in the struggle against overheating.

The lack of the ability to sweat is balanced by the evaporation of water from the mucous tissues of the mouth, the trachea, and the bronchial tubes. This is most effective when the movement of the air surrounding these surfaces is increased by acceleration of the breathing rate to as many as 300 breaths per minute, and the dog is said to be panting. One often sees dogs panting in the summer or after a long spell of running. Much water may be lost, and, if this is not replaced, the dog may become dehydrated. It is important to make sure your dog has an adequate supply of water at all times.

Because a dog's coat offers such an effective protection against cold, owners should observe certain rules. Dogs should not be clipped at the beginning of winter, and in cold weather the dog's coat should not be left damp. This is because there is no insulating cushion of air when the coat is flattened, and the dog loses heat much more rapidly. Furthermore, since the wind greatly increases loss of heat, dogs living permanently outdoors should be provided with shelter from air currents. The insulation of the kennel can be improved by putting shredded newspaper inside it and changing it frequently.

The heat of the body is largely due to chemical reaction in the muscles and the glands, especially the liver, and to the activity of the heart.

Even when the dog is at rest the muscles produce heat, since they are never completely relaxed. This permanent, slight tension is called the 'muscle tone.'

Seeing, Hearing, and Smelling

The dog's relationship to its environment depends on how it perceives the world around it through its sense organs, and on its power to react to the information that they provide. Abilities in this area vary with age and from one breed to another.

A dog's ability to smell is the most highly developed of its senses, as numerous experiments have shown. It is so keen as almost to defy human imagination. (It has even been suggested, albeit without clear evidence, that it is precisely because of this unique sense of smell that abandoned dogs are often able to find their way back home over phenomenal distances.) For example, a dog can detect acetic acid (vinegar) in a concentration obtained by mixing one drop of vinegar with 1000 litres (220 gallons) of water, and then putting one drop of the mixture thus obtained in a further 1000 litres of water!

The German Shepherd has 225 million olfactory cells, compared with about 125 million for the Basset Hound and 147 million for the Fox Terrier. Humans, on the other hand, have only about 500,000 such receptors in their nasal cavities. It has been established that dogs are extremely sensitive to the odours of fatty acids; they can register the smell of butyric acid in a concentration a million times weaker than that required for human recognition. A suitably trained dog can thus find the owner of an object or can pick up the trail of a person upon smelling a piece of old clothing that belonged to him. It is equally due to its keen sense of smell that a hunting-dog discovers and tracks game. Lastly, it is through this sense that a male dog can locate—from a great distance—a bitch in heat.

The sense of hearing is equally well developed in dogs. They hear low-pitch sounds about as keenly as humans do, and medium- and high-pitch sounds even better. They can also hear sounds in what for us is the ultrasonic range. This is why dog handlers use ultrasonic whistles, which enable the trainer to issue commands silently (to the human ear) from a distance.

Dogs have far weaker eyesight than humans. Some breeds—specifically the gazehounds, such as the Borzoi—do make great use of their sight in following game across open country, but even if they can distinguish variations in the intensity of light, as we can, they do not recognize shapes nearly as well. It is widely believed that dogs cannot perceive colours, although there is little precise data to confirm that hypothesis.

Gait

The dog, as we have said, is a digitigrade animal, walking with only its toes on the ground rather than the whole foot. Movement is propelled by the hind legs, while the front legs act as supports and shock-absorbers. The speed of movement (action) and the pattern of footfall together determine what is called a dog's gait, of which there are four principal types.

The walk is the slowest gait and the least tiring. The dog starts by moving its right front paw, then the left hind paw, the left front and the right hind, and so on. The dog has taken one complete pace when it has left four footprints on the ground.

The trot is the usual gait of huntingdogs, for it is well suited to uneven ground and long pursuits. The animal puts the diagonally opposed legs down at the same time: right front and left hind, then left front and right hind. No one paw works more than another. The dog controls its balance by putting the hind leg down an instant before the front one.

The amble is a natural gait for all dogs and is typical of certain breeds such as the Old English Sheepdog. It is as effective as trotting and less tiring. It is the gait for the end of the day, and for young dogs, that use it before their muscles will allow them to trot. The two feet on one side of the body move together, first the right front and hind feet, then both the left ones.

The gallop is a jumping gait in a threebeat rhythm. The dog moves its front and hind feet at the same time. The hind legs are placed outside the forelegs with a slight time-lag in their touching the ground. This interval is greatest for greyhound breeds.

There is also the irregular gait of a dog that limps. The weight of the body is concentrated on the good side, and the neck and tail work together to help the dog keep its balance.

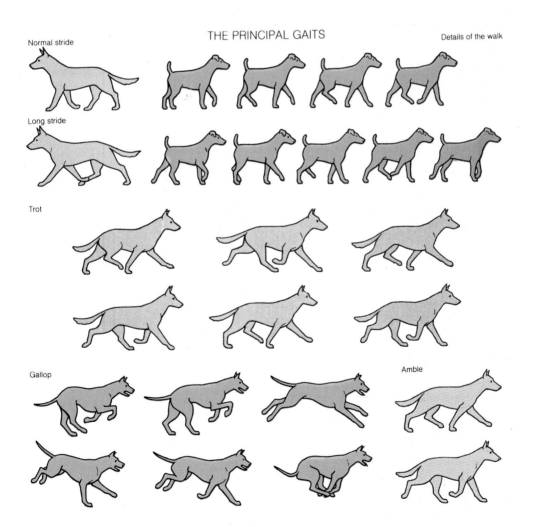

THE PRINCIPAL GAITS

Normal stride

Details of the walk

Long stride

Trot

Gallop

Amble

Medical Care

Your Veterinarian and You

Even in prehistoric times animals received medical care. We know this because modern scientists have discovered ancient trepanned skulls and fractured bones wrapped in makeshift casts of clay. But between the first fumbling efforts of cavemen and the clinical techniques of the contemporary veterinary hospital team stand many centuries of trial and error, ingenuity and concern.

A short history of veterinary medicine

The word 'veterinarian' comes from the Latin *veterinarius*, meaning 'doctor for beasts of burden.' Before there were genuine doctors, animals were cared for by people as various as an Egyptian priest practising exorcism in a society which believed in reincarnation; a Greek soothsayer; and a Roman freeman who tended the wild beasts and slaves at the Colosseum. The medieval scholars tried to avert plagues and sicknesses among animals by calling on patron saints: Saint Hubert for protection from rabies, Saint Ely to mend broken bones, and Saint Cosmas and Saint Damian to ward off other physiological disorders.

The first scientific work on veterinary care was written during the Italian Renaissance. Titled *L'Anatomica del Cavallo*

('The Anatomy of the Horse'), it was published in 1598, and was inspired by the minutely detailed dissections of animals by the scientist, inventor, and artist, Leonardo da Vinci. But it took the rigorous teaching methods of Claude Bourgelat, founder of the world's first veterinary college (in Lyons, France, in the mid-eighteenth century) and the discoveries of Louis Pasteur to provide veterinary medicine with its scientific precision.

Today the profession is diversified. Some veterinary surgeons continue to be all-round practitioners, treating horses, sheep, cows, pigs, and chickens, while other members of the profession specialize exclusively in the care of pets.

Modern veterinary medicine

Stimulated by the canine 'population explosion' of recent years, the doctoring of dogs has become a vast discipline with many branches, even including the psychology of canine behaviour.

Man's best friend can now receive as sophisticated treatment as its master does. Homeopathy and physiotherapy both have their veterinary practitioners, and other therapeutic methods have been grafted on to Western treatments. Chinese veterinarians, for example, have counted

Treatments being given to dogs. From the fourteenth-century hunting treatise of Gaston Phoebus.

two hundred different pulses in the same dog. They have also mapped the dog's 'meridian points' for use in acupuncture. But the future lies with prevention and early diagnosis of cardiac, renal, and other illnesses, by laboratory analyses of the blood and the urine, by electrocardiography, and through other procedures.

Nowadays, you can take your dog to a veterinarian's consulting room, to a clinic, or even to a hospital which has medical teams, equipment, intensive-care units—and everything else needed for complete care of the sick animal. You can also make use of consulting facilities at veterinary colleges.

Modern animal clinics have sophisticated diagnostic resources such as X-ray machines, electrocardiographs, microscopes, and laboratories. Bacterial cultures, biopsies, and blood analyses have become routine diagnostic tools. At the surgical level,

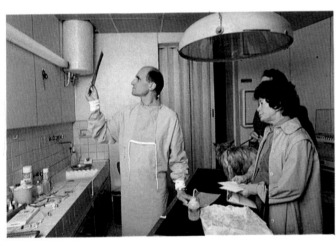

more and more treatments are carried out on operating tables, with anaesthesia by gas, cardiac monitoring, and hygiene control comparable to those used on human patients. Removal of cataracts and insertion of artificial bones or suture plates held in place by screws are other forms of surgery now carried out on dogs.

Choosing a veterinarian

Choose your veterinarian carefully, making sure that you have found one who meets your specific needs. All veterinary surgeons are schooled in accredited colleges and receive the same basic training, but some have a natural fondness for dogs, and others prefer treating cats or horses. A veterinarian with forty years of practice behind him will have acquired a great deal of experience. A novice, on the other hand, may make up for lack of experience with a thoroughgoing knowledge of the latest techniques and equipment.

Before selecting your veterinarian, seek advice from dog breeders and owners in your district. Consider whether the veterinarian's office is nearby, and whether you can reach it quickly in an emergency. What equipment does he or she have? Are the premises clean and well organized? Is the staff polite? How much real interest has he or she in dogs?

In many countries, animal clinics and hospitals are governed by a national or regional regulating body which sets norms for equipment and quality of care. These bodies often issue certificates of approval to establishments that meet their standards. If there is such a certificate on your veterinarian's wall, it is more than likely a point in his or her favour.

The cost of veterinary care varies in proportion to its quality. The price of the same operation can vary according to whether the surgical equipment employed (gloves,

The veterinary surgeon examines the dog by palpating (feeling) its muscles and joints.

Dogs, like humans, are X-rayed to help diagnosis of complaints.

masks, overalls, instruments) is totally sterile, whether the dog is hospitalized, and so on. Unlike farm animals, which have an economic value, domestic dogs have a purely subjective, sentimental value (with the exception of a few 'professionals' such as stud-dogs, guide dogs for the blind, and police dogs). Treatment for an international show champion costs the same as for a friendly mongrel. The extent of treatment depends upon one's personal commitment to the animal.

How to help the veterinarian

If there is one major difference between the medical care of dogs and that of humans, it is in the area of symptomatology. Like very small children, dogs do not talk, so to help the veterinarian make his diagnosis, you should give him as much relevant information as possible. Where does the dog live (indoors or in a kennel, for example)? What are its eating habits? Does it have any 'eccentricities?' Does it steal bones? Have you taken it hunting? When was your bitch last in heat? All these pieces of information will help the veterinarian assess the animal.

Other signs you notice may be important: skin parasites, worms in the stool, or vomiting, for instance. If you have to provide a sample of your dog's urine, get the dog to urinate into a bowl that has been immersed in boiling water, then transfer the contents into a sterilized jar. To obtain a more complete diagnosis, take a sample of the stool (about two teaspoonfuls in a jar) if the dog has diarrhoea. This should also be done as a matter of course whenever you take the dog for its annual immunization.

Some dogs have aggressive or nervous temperaments. For routine visits to the veterinarian it may be a good idea to give such a dog a tranquillizer or to muzzle it. Keep your pet on a leash during the visit so as not to disrupt the calm of the waiting room. Treating a rebellious animal can be a gruelling ordeal for even the most seasoned professional, so you should assist the veterinarian as much as possible. Remain cool-headed, learn to control the dog on the operating table, and be on time.

Medical instructions should be followed faithfully. A treatment of antibiotics planned to last eight days must not be stopped after three, even if the dog seems completely well again. There is always a risk of relapse.

Some veterinarians will accept emergency calls at night. Try not to use this service unnecessarily. Unless you are dealing with a special night clinic, think twice before waking the veterinarian for a minor problem at three o'clock in the morning. Endeavour to distinguish between real emergencies and your own anxieties.

Do the fees seem prohibitive? Keep in mind that the veterinary surgeon has to give a dog treatment of the same quality as a doctor would give a human being, at fees that the owner can afford, without any government subsidy. The high calibre of treatment has to be paid for.

Psychology and the patient

The same illnesses that afflict humanity also occur in dogs, but the symptoms express themselves differently. You can tell your doctor all about your latest attack of liver trouble; if your dog suffers from hepatitis, however, the infection may do considerable damage before it is detected. As a result, many animals are brought to the veterinarian too late. The best way to counteract this problem is to be extremely vigilant—watch for the slightest hint of illness in your dog.

A dog must be held firmly so that it cannot bite while being examined.

Be on the look-out for any of the following signs: lack of vitality; changes in character; tendency to hide; unusual thirst or appetite; dull coat or itchy skin; eyes sad and weepy; unusually coloured urine or stool; vomit with blood in it; constipation; diarrhoea; difficulty in urinating; temperature more than 38.5°C (101.3°F); rapid pulse and rate of breathing when at rest; whining and restlessness.

Any of these symptoms indicate that the dog's condition is not normal. For further information, see the table on pages 356 and 357. If in doubt, consult your veterinarian.

Sometimes symptoms are deceptive. A dog rubs its rear end on the floor, for example, and its well-meaning owner gives it a treatment for worms. But this will not empty its anal glands, which may be what is needed. Some dogs scratch the base of the ear, not as a sign of otitis but as a way of relieving the agony of toothache.

Every dog has its own level of sensitivity. Some dogs continue to hunt when their bodies are riddled with gunshot; others cannot bear the slightest change in temperature. There are anxious dogs prone to stomach ulcers, and there are hypochondriacs, natural actors who limp to attract attention and affection. There are even dogs that develop psychosomatic illnesses: hysterical pregnancies when the maternal instinct is frustrated; obesity arising out of boredom; chewing and grinding of teeth (bruxism) as a nervous release.

Because of the values inculcated in training, a dog that is a good companion is accustomed to being rewarded or punished according to how it behaves. Thus, when a dog suddenly gets a toothache, the four-footed patient is most probably stupefied. It must wonder what terrible thing it has done to deserve all this pain.

A sick dog expecting comfort may snap or even bite when it is given a painful injection at the clinic. The wound to its morale must be 'bandaged' (as you would any wound to its body). Gentleness and compassion are the prescription. Otherwise the dog will have to be muzzled.

Emergencies

Animals sometimes incur injuries that require immediate treatment. The veterinarian must be reached as soon as possible. While waiting for professional help, however, you may be able to save your pet's life or relieve its suffering.

The general advice set out below is followed by a description of common emergencies, signs to look for, and first-aid treatment. Keep in mind that all such treatments should be referred to a veterinarian at the earliest opportunity.

EMERGENCY FIRST AID

To alleviate symptoms of the trouble:
- Unblock the respiratory tracts (apply artificial respiration if necessary)
- Deal with cardiac arrest
- Stop any haemorrhages
- Disinfect and bandage any wounds
- Keep the animal warm
- Do not move it unnecessarily
- Treat it for shock, if required

When you call the veterinarian, explain the problem before moving the dog; he or she will make the necessary preparations while waiting for you.

Car accidents and falls

Internal bleeding is common, usually from a rupture of the spleen or other organ. Do not move the dog more than necessary. Lift a small dog by the skin of its neck. Seek the help of two or three people to lift a large dog. Carry the animal in a blanket or on a board to a veterinarian as quickly as you can. Perform artificial respiration if needed (see pp. 346–47). Emergency treatments for broken bones, a state of shock, or coma, as the case may be, are described in the pages that follow.

Coma

A number of different types of accident can cause a dog to lose consciousness: electrocution, car accidents, poisoning, or heat-stroke, for example. Make certain that the dog is still alive (check for breathing, eyelid reflexes, dilation of the pupils, sign of pulse). Urinary or fecal incontinence or a body temperature of less than 27°C (80.6°F) may indicate death. If the dog is still alive, treat it for shock (see p. 342) and take it to a veterinarian.

Foreign objects

A dog may accidentally swallow an indigestible object when it is at play—a bone, for example, or a rubber ball.

Symptoms: These depend on where the object has lodged.

- In the mouth (a bone jammed against the palate, for example). The dog scratches, and rubs its jaws in an effort to dislodge the object. It salivates a great deal.
- In the oesophagus. The animal tries to bark and vomit, but merely produces a kind of scum.
- In the stomach or the intestine. Touching with the hand produces a sharp pain in the abdomen. The dog seeks contact with a cold surface, and vomits. In the last stages it may go into shock.
- In the rectum. The dog has difficulty voiding its bowel (constipation). The stool may contain blood.

Treatment: Take action as soon as possible, while the object is still in place. Try to remove it. If a fish-hook has pierced the cheek, push it through until the point emerges. Then cut the barb off with pliers.

If the dog has swallowed a needle, feed it bread, leeks, or cotton wool soaked in milk (or Bovril, or another liquid it likes). Check carefully that the needle is passed with the stool in the next few days.

If the end of a piece of string or elastic comes out through the anus, do not pull it, or you will risk twisting the intestine. Feeding the dog cooking oil usually helps to make foreign objects slip out more easily from the intestinal tract.

Heat-stroke

Heat can kill a dog that has been left too long in a hot place without water—in a car parked in the sun with all its windows closed, for example.

Symptoms: Suffocation, a sharp rise in temperature, gasping, heavy salivation. If action is not taken quickly, the dog may slip into a coma and die.

Treatment: The dog must be put in a cool, shady spot immediately and sprinkled with cold water. Perform artificial respiration if needed and, if the dog is conscious, give it little sips of very strong coffee or water. Take it to a veterinarian.

Poisoning

Be sure to identify the poison before treating a sick dog.

Symptoms: The dog vomits and salivates profusely. If it has inhaled poisonous gas, it gags and coughs.

Treatment: Move the dog away from the source of poisoning. Get it to drink as much liquid as possible, thereby eliminating the toxins by urination. Give water, milk, or tea, or, if the dog is very feeble, strong coffee. If the poison is an acid, an alkali, or a petroleum-based product, give the dog milk or vegetable oil to drink and do not try to make it vomit. If the poison is a noncorrosive, such as strychnine, induce vomiting (see pp. 344–45). If an antidote is specified on the container of poison, give it that; if not, contact the nearest poison control centre. Several substances which may make the dog feel better are: activated charcoal, water, milk, kaolin, vegetable oil, and bismuth. Specific antidotes against acids are: bicarbonate of soda or milk of magnesia. Lemon juice and water with vinegar both act against alkalis. While waiting for the veterinarian, keep the dog warm, and apply artificial respiration if it is having difficulty breathing.

Shock
Third-degree burns, prolonged bouts of diarrhoea, car accidents, poisoning, internal bleeding, or heart attacks can put a dog into a state of shock. In this condition the dog's constitution offsets the reduction in the volume of the blood by increasing the heartbeat and the rate of breathing and constricting the peripheral blood-vessels so that as much blood as possible can be supplied to the essential organs, particularly the brain.

Symptoms: Coldness of the extremities and the skin, and a weak, rapid pulse (at least 130 beats per minute). The rate of breathing rises to between 35 and 40 breaths per minute, the eyes are immobile, and the pupils dilated. The mucous tissues (gums, conjunctivae, tongue) are pale. The dog may even slip into a coma if the supply of blood to the brain is not adequate, or should suddenly drop.

Treatment: Eliminate the cause, whether it is electrocution, lack of air, haemorrhage, poison, and so forth. Massage the heart. Raise the temperature with blankets or hot-water bottles (40°C, or 104°F, maximum). Put the dog on an inclined plane, head down, to supply blood to the brain. Give artificial respiration.

Take the dog to a veterinarian immediately. If it is conscious, give it a teaspoonful of salt and half a teaspoon of bicarbonate of soda in a litre (3½ cups) of water, to drink in sips.

Frostbite
Short-haired dogs are very sensitive to the cold, especially on the pads, scrotum, ears (especially breeds with long, pendulous ears), and tip of the tail.

Treatment: Warm the frozen part, either with a warm cloth, warm water, or with a hair-dryer (temperature not above 38°C, or 100°F). Apply antibiotic cream to the damaged parts. Protect the dog from secondary wounds caused by scratching or nibbling by applying bandages or an Elizabethan collar (see p. 344). Treat for shock if necessary (see above). If the animal is completely frozen, put its body in a hot bath (40°C, or 104°F). Massage the affected parts and give the animal hot milk to drink, or the following mixture: half a teaspoonful of salt and half a teaspoonful of bicarbonate of soda in a litre (3½ cups) of water. Dry the dog with towels or a hair-dryer, and wrap it in a blanket.

Travel sickness
Travelling is rarely a pleasure for an animal. After all, what living creature could possibly want to have motion sickness to contend with—as well as the inevitable hardship of being shut up for a long period of time in a cage?

Dogs invariably like fresh air, coolness, and water. They are often suspicious of the unknown and of new places. Your own dog may even be sensitive to changes in temperature or atmospheric pressure. A wise safeguard, therefore, is to consult your veterinarian. He or she can best tell you how to treat your dog on the journey, according to its temperament and medical history.

Treatment: If the dog suffers from motion sickness or tends to become very excited in the car, your veterinarian will prescribe a suitable sedative or antivomit medicine. On the journey the dog must have adequate drinking water, and you should stop regularly to let it have a short run. It is never advisable to leave a dog in a car parked in the sun, not even with the windows open.

Insect bites and stings
Insect bites and stings can be just as irritating and painful to dogs as to humans—and could be allergenic as well.

Treatment: Try to remove the sting by pressing gently on the swollen part and drawing it out with eyebrow tweezers. Bee stings are barbed and particularly difficult to pull out. Bicarbonate of soda relieves the discomfort of bee stings, while vinegar does the same for the sting of the wasp. As a general rule, a cold-water compress or a cube of ice will relieve pain. If the dog has an abnormal degree of swelling, or difficulty in breathing, it may be suffering an allergic reaction.

THE EMERGENCY KIT

It is a good idea to keep the following items close at hand in a box:
- A rectal thermometer, cotton-tipped swabs
- Ready-cut gauze, cotton wool
- Bandages
- Adhesive tape, 90% alcohol
- Hydrogen peroxide (3%)
- An antibiotic skin ointment
- An antibiotic eye lotion, without corticosteroids
- Kaolin pectate, animal black
- Milk of magnesia
- A 3 cm³ syringe, a size 22 needle

A number of items normally found in the house may be useful:
- String, scissors, blanket, towels
- Nail clippers, eyebrow tweezers
- Mineral oil, mild soap, petroleum jelly
- Bicarbonate of soda, Aspirin

Surgery

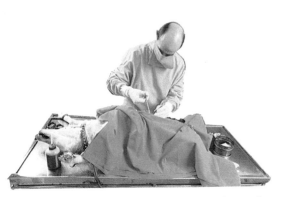

Operations on dogs are carried out under modern anaesthetics. Conditions in the operating room are similar to those required for humans.

Surgical conditions for dogs these days are almost identical to those for humans. Many operations are preceded by blood tests and heart monitoring. After a preoperative injection, the animal is anaesthetized with gas. Masks, gloves, and a sterile operating theatre are prerequisites for all major operations. Even for minor surgery, good antisepsis (disinfection) and antibiotic protection are provided.

Some surgery is carried out as a matter of routine. In some countries, ear-cropping or tail-docking is intended, rightly or wrongly, to bring the dog into line with official breed standards or dictates of fashion.

Here is a brief description of the various types of elective surgery, with an explanation of the advantages and disadvantages.

Sterilization of bitches
Several operations are possible.
• Ovariectomy. This consists of removing only the ovaries. The bitch will no longer go into heat or bear puppies.
• Tying the Fallopian tubes. By suturing the tubes which connect the ovaries to the corners of the uterus, the ovum is prevented from descending into the uterus and becoming fertilized. The bitch will still go into heat, however.
• Ovario-hysterectomy. The surgeon removes the ovaries and the uterus. This has the advantage of eliminating heats with absolute certainty, completely sterilizing the animal, preventing hysterical pregnancy, and removing all possibility of uterine infections such as metritis or pyometritis. If performed on a young bitch (less than three years old) it prevents the development of breast tumours, which occur commonly after the age of eight.

Sterilization of dogs
• Tying off the vas deferens (the narrow tube that allows the passage of spermatozoa). This sterilizes the dog but does not reduce its sexual instincts. It obviates the hormonal imbalances which sometimes follow castration.

• Castration. This is the removal of both testicles. It eliminates sexual urges and thus any tendency to roam in search of bitches. Castration greatly reduces the excess canine population and is recommended for dogs that are chronic masturbators.

After sterilization by removing the ovaries or testicles, the animal should be fed in moderation.

Cropping the ears
In the past it was considered useful to cut the ears of sheep-dogs, dogs used to hunt wolves, and those used in dogfights. These days the operation's function tends to be aesthetic, and its appropriateness is hotly contested in many countries. In broad terms, ear-cropping is not practised in Great Britain, Australia, and South Africa; it is, however, common in Canada, Europe, and the United States (although it is forbidden in some U.S. states).

Aesthetic value apart, there is some feeling that the operation may be useful in ventilating the ear passages and in helping to avoid the development of ear infections, especially yeast-based otitis. Ironically, the breeds most susceptible to this—the English and American Cocker Spaniels, for example—are those whose ears tend not to be cropped.

Docking the tail
Cutting the tail has no more practical purpose than cutting the ears. Nevertheless, the operation is traditionally performed on certain breeds, and kennel club standards usually stipulate the number of vertebrae or the length of tail to be left or docked.

For hyperactive dogs, the operation could pose the advantage of preventing bruising and fractures. The procedure is simple and should be carried out the first few days after the puppy's birth.

In some countries tail-docking is illegal, or is allowed only under strict veterinary control.

Apparatus used for anaesthesia in veterinary practice. On the left is a cardiac monitor, a machine that surveys and registers the condition of the heart.

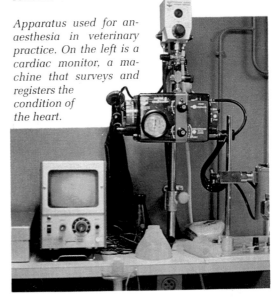

First Aid

If worried about the state of your dog's health, you should always consult a veterinarian. Nonetheless, though, it is useful to know how to deal with minor accidents, to judge for yourself whether your dog is healthy, and to be able to carry on treatment started by a veterinarian. Here are some techniques for basic health care.

Cleaning off poisonous substances
• Spray from a foul-smelling animal. A skunk's anal secretions irritate and inflame a dog's eyes. Rinse the eyes well with water, then apply eye ointment, or, failing that, olive oil. Wash the dog, preferably outdoors, in tomato juice, then give it a thorough shampoo. Repeat if necessary.
• Petroleum products (fuels and solvents). Cover the soiled parts of the coat with vegetable oil and wash with soap.
• Tar. This sticks stubbornly to the coat and pads. Cut the affected hair with scissors. Rub the affected pads with vegetable oil. Bandage, and 24 hours later wash off remaining tar with a mild shampoo.
• Paint. Take off as much as you can by rubbing with a damp cloth, then wash the affected area with soapy water. Cut any patches of coat that are badly stuck together. Get rid of the remaining paint with rubbing alcohol or vodka. Never use any paint solvents or removers.
• Oil paints and motor oil. Coat the affected parts with vegetable oil, then wash several times with soap and plenty of water. Do not use benzine-based paint solvents, which burn the skin. Shave the coat where there are any obstinate patches.

Improvising splints
If your dog breaks a leg when you are a long way from help, being able to put on a splint may temporarily prevent displacement of parts of the bones, with all the attendant complications. You can make the splints from small wooden boards or from branches of trees. Cleanse the wound and protect it with a clean cloth. Use pieces of wood the same length as the injured limb and hold them in place with string or adhesive tape.

Making an Elizabethan collar
To prevent a dog from licking its wounds, biting stitches, or scratching its ears, eyes, or nose, the Elizabethan collar, or ruff, is a useful device. This is a type of cone put around the dog's head. You can obtain one ready-made from your veterinarian.

To make one yourself, use a cardboard box or an old plastic bucket. Cut a hole in the bottom the right size for your dog's neck. Make three or four short slits radiating from the hole to allow the opening to expand wider and to avoid hurting your pet as the collar is fitted over its head. Punch holes (half a dozen or so) in the base, through which a tie-cord to the dog's collar can be threaded.

Making a dog vomit
Never try to induce vomiting if the dog has swallowed anything pointed, such as a

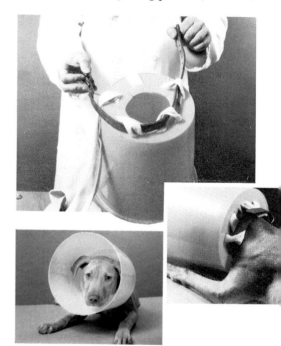

An Elizabethan collar prevents the dog from licking its wounds and scratching itself. You can make one with household items.

To improvise a splint from newspaper, cut the paper to the length of the limb and hold it in place with adhesive tape. Then wrap some of the tape around the animal's shoulders.

fish-hook, a piece of glass, or a corrosive substance. Nor should you make it vomit if it is unconscious or if its throat or oesophagus is blocked.

It should be made to vomit, however, if it has eaten too much food, rotten food, a wild animal, a foreign object, or a non-corrosive poison such as strychnine. Make it swallow one or two teaspoonfuls of dilute hydrogen peroxide every 15 minutes until it vomits, or a teaspoonful of salty water (equal parts of salt and water), or put half a teaspoonful of salt right at the back of its throat and then make it drink.

Giving an enema
This means injecting a suitable solution through the anus to help a constipated dog evacuate fecal matter. This is necessary when a dog has eaten too many bones, for example, or has swallowed an object likely to cause blockage of the intestine. There are ready-mixed solutions on the market. To prepare an enema solution yourself, dissolve two tablespoonfuls of liquid soap in a litre (3½ cups) of warm water. Administer the mixture with an enema bag or through a funnel connected to a narrow rubber tube.

If your dog has a long coat, shave the area around the anus and lightly lubricate the rim of the anus. Hold the dog upright (muzzled, if it is a biter), preferably in a place that can be easily cleaned. Grease the tube, and insert it gently and slowly, well into the rectum. Hold the funnel high, and pour in the liquid—six tablespoonfuls for small dogs, up to a litre (1¾ pints) for very large ones. If necessary, repeat two or three times at one-hour intervals. If the treatment is unsuccessful, see your veterinarian.

Disinfecting, cleaning, and bandaging a wound
For superficial injuries without heavy bleeding, clean the affected area thoroughly with mild soap and water. Disinfect with 90 per cent alcohol, hydrogen peroxide, or a commercial antiseptic. Apply antibiotic cream to the wound, and bandage. The dressing should be changed daily. Deep wounds require stitches.

Antibiotic pills and an antitetanus injection should be administered if the dog was injured outdoors.

Giving medicine
Dog owners should know how to administer medicine at home so as to continue treatments started by the veterinarian.
● Injections. Some remedies can be absorbed quickly only if given as injections. Check the bottle carefully to see what type of injection is required: subcutaneous (s.c.), intramuscular (i.m.), or intravenous (i.v.). Always use sterilized equipment and disinfect the site of the injection (the skin, not the coat) with 90 per cent alcohol. You will need an assistant to hold the animal's head.

Before administering an injection, go over the procedure with your veterinarian to be sure you have been thoroughly instructed.

Subcutaneous injections: These are the simplest type, and owners of diabetic dogs, for example, need to know how to give them. The needle must be inserted in the neck. With thumb and index finger, pinch the skin to form an inverted V. Insert the needle perpendicularly, through the skin, and inject the medication slowly.

Intramuscular injections: These are useful for injecting oily suspensions. They should be given in the loin or the inside of the thigh. Injecting in the back of the thigh can be dangerous, for you could damage

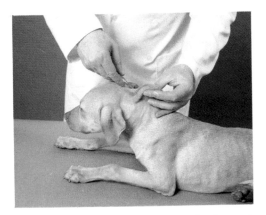

Subcutaneous injections are given in the neck by pinching the skin firmly.

the sciatic nerve. Insert the needle one centimetre (½ inch) for small breeds, two centimetres (1 inch) for larger dogs. Before injecting the medication, make sure that you have not entered a blood vessel—or you could kill your dog.

Intravenous injections: These are more difficult, and best left to a specialist. You should attempt one only in extreme emergency and after proper instruction.

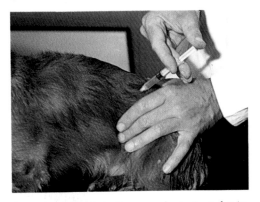

Intramuscular injections are best given by inserting the needle into the loin.

● Applying ointments. Lotions, creams, and drops can be tricky to administer.
On the skin: If you apply ointment to your dog's skin, it may lick it off. To pre-

vent this, make an Elizabethan collar for it (see p. 344) or cover the affected area with a protective cloth, stocking, or any other clean garment.

In the eyes: To put drops in the eyes, pull gently on the upper and lower eyelids towards the nose so that the third (or inner) eyelid covers the pupil. The dog will not be able to see what you are doing, and will remain calm. In the same movement, draw down on the lower eyelid to form a small pocket. Insert about ten drops, depending on the dog's size. Shut the lids and rub them with a circular motion. Administer the drops several times a day, as necessary.

In the ears: Before you put ointment or drops in the ears, make sure that the ear passage is free of any accumulated material. If necessary, clean it with cotton swabs and a few drops of mineral oil. Do not be timid: the auditory canal turns at a right angle, so you are not likely to damage the ear-drum. Put 10 to 20 drops of solution in each ear. Rub the ear to ensure maximum penetration by the medication (otitis drops have to seep right up to the ear-drum). Plug the ear for at least 15 minutes with cotton wool.

• Powders and granules. Some medicines can be mixed into the dog's food. If the dog refuses to eat, put it on a fast for at least a day, then give it the medicine in a one-quarter portion of its usual daily allowance of food. When the dog has licked its bowl clean, give it another quarter of its usual ration.

Wait until the end of the day before giving it the balance of the food.

• Pills. Feed your dog a light meal before giving it a pill. The mucous tissue of the stomach will then be protected and the pill will not cause irritation. Put your hand on the dog's muzzle and press with your thumb and middle finger on each corner of the jaw to make the animal open its mouth. Tilt the head upwards and put the pill as far back on the tongue as possible. If the dog tries to bite, it will bite its own cheeks. Shut the mouth quickly and massage the throat to help the dog swallow. Now watch the animal carefully for a good 15 minutes to make sure that it does not reject the pill.

• Liquids. Fill a plastic bottle with the appropriate dosage. Tilt the dog's head upwards by about 45 degrees. Make a pocket of the cheek by drawing the skin of the mouth towards you. Hold the muzzle with one hand, and with the other insert the spout of the bottle into the pocket.

Pour the liquid slowly, in several stages, to allow it to be swallowed completely and to avoid having any of the liquid enter the trachea.

Artificial respiration

This technique can save your dog's life. It must be carried out if the dog has stopped breathing.

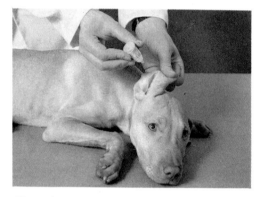

To put drops in the eye, draw the eyelids towards the muzzle, pull down on the lower lid, and insert the drops. Then close the lids and massage with a circular movement.

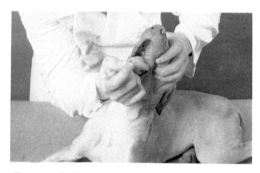

Clean the ear, put in the drops, then massage the ear so that the medication is absorbed.

Press on both corners of the lips and place the pill right at the back of the tongue.

Pull out the edges of the lips to form a pocket and pour the liquid in.

Lay the animal down. Open its mouth to make sure that there is no foreign object lodged within. If there is, take it out. Remove the dog's collar and let the tongue hang to one side to avoid its getting caught at the back of the throat. Place your palms between the scapula (shoulder-blade) and the ribs. Push down hard and let go abruptly at five-second intervals. This pumping action on the thoracic cavity will fill the lungs with air. Continue until the dog is breathing on its own.

Another effective method of reviving a dog is mouth-to-nose resuscitation. To do this, hold the dog's mouth firmly shut and inflate its lungs by blowing air into its nostrils for three seconds. Stop for two seconds to let the dog breathe out, then repeat the process.

With newborn puppies you can use the swing method. This is simply a matter of taking the puppy in your cupped hands and swinging it vigorously up and down a dozen times.

If an animal's chest has been pierced, try to seal the wound temporarily using a piece of bandage held in place by adhesive tape. In this situation, mouth-to-nose resuscitation is advised.

A dog that has been drowning must be lifted up by its hind legs to empty the water from its lungs. If the dog is too heavy, put it on an inclined board, with the head downwards. Apply artificial respiration until the dog starts to breathe on its own.

If the heart has stopped, strike the dog two or three times, solidly, behind the shoulder on the centre ribs.

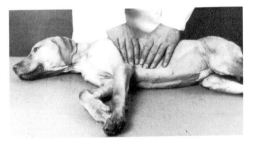

To apply artificial respiration, place your hands flat between the dog's scapula and ribs.

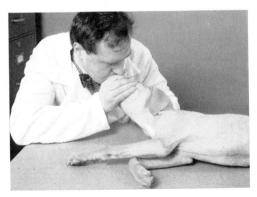

For mouth-to-nose resuscitation, hold the dog's mouth shut and blow air into its nostrils.

Bandages and dressings

Wounds are dressed with gauze and tape for a variety of reasons—to stop haemorrhaging, immobilize a limb, prevent exposed flesh from becoming contaminated, absorb discharges of blood or pus, and relieve pain. They also prevent a dog from scratching or biting its wounds.

Before applying a bandage, wash the wound with a mild soap and disinfect it well, with Mercurochrome, for example. If the bandage is needed to cover a paw, put balls of cotton wool between the toes and beneath the pads to prevent humidity from building up and creating an environment susceptible to infection. It is best to change dressings daily.

Put a piece of sterile gauze on the wound and cover it with thick cotton wool. Wrap a strip of gauze around the whole bundle. Finally, to prevent the bandage from slip-

Before bandaging a paw, place balls of cotton wool between the toes and around the pads.

ping, stick a wide strip of adhesive tape over the edge of the bandage and the dog's coat. Bitches that have had abdominal operations and dogs with stomach injuries have a tendency to lick themselves, which may delay or prevent healing. Make a protective covering from an old towel by cutting four circular openings for the legs, and cutting strips two by six centimetres (one by six inches) to tie around the dog's back.

Taking your dog's pulse

Press with the index and middle fingers on the femoral artery. A normal pulse is from 70 to 120 beats per minute. A weak, rapid pulse is typical of a dog in shock. The smaller the breed, the faster its pulse.

The rate of breathing

Various factors, ranging from body and room temperature to nervousness, influence the rate of breathing. An animal adjusts its breathing rate to cool itself by drawing as much air as possible over its tongue and mouth. Dogs do not sweat except through their pads and nose. The normal breathing rate is from 10 to 30 breaths a minute.

Taking the rectal temperature

Lubricate the thermometer with petroleum jelly, and shake it to ensure that the column of mercury is at its lowest. Have an assistant hold the dog's head. Lift the animal's tail and put the thermometer half-way into the anus, turning it gently as you do so. Leave it in for three minutes. A dog's normal temperature is 38.5°C (101.3°F).

Treating injuries

• Abdomen. A dog may impale itself while jumping over a fence or it might be bitten in a fight with another dog.

Symptoms: If the injury is deep, the pain will be considerable. Disembowelment, the falling out of internal organs, could result from a severe abdominal cut.

Treatment: Muzzle the animal (unless it needs to vomit). Wrap a bandage around the stomach to stop the organs from coming out further. Take the dog to a veterinarian as quickly as possible.

• Thorax. Any number of accidents could damage the chest.

Symptoms: A dog with chest injuries and whose ribs are broken will instinctively reduce its breathing to relieve the pain. It will take rapid, shallow breaths.

Treatment: Even if the dog tries to bite, do not muzzle it. Bandage the injury lightly and lay the dog on its injured side (this is less painful) with its head raised. If the chest cavity has been pierced, administer artificial respiration (see pp. 346-47). Take the animal to a veterinarian.

• Eyes. A dog's eyes are vulnerable to many hazards—dust and solid particles when it rides in a car with its nose out the window, branches of bushes when it romps in the park, even the claws of the neighbour's cat.

Treatment: Keep the animal still and gently remove the cause of the trouble using your fingers, a pair of tweezers, or a piece of gauze. Then apply an antibiotic ointment. Do not use an anti-inflammatory ointment. This will inhibit the healing process if there is damage to the cornea.

For serious bleeding in the eye, apply a bandage and take the animal to a veterinarian. If the eye is out of its socket, sprinkle it with water to prevent drying. You can also use an aqueous solution made for contact lenses or, failing this, olive oil.

Improvising a muzzle

If an injured dog wants to bite, fit it with a makeshift muzzle made from a stocking or a bandage. Make a large slip-knot. Put the dog's jaw through the loop, and tighten the loop. Pass the two free ends around the mouth and tie them behind the nape of the neck. If the dog has a short nose, wrap a blanket or a large towel around its neck and hold the dog firmly in your arms.

Preventing ingrowing toe-nails

Your dog's nails should be trimmed regularly. The older it gets, the less opportunity it will have to wear them down, especially if it lives in the city. Sometimes, especially with older dogs, the nails begin

to grow into the leg (this is particularly true of the dew-claws). The nails are so long that they penetrate deep into the flesh, usually the pads. Unless the dog starts limping, this will pass unnoticed at first, especially with long-haired breeds.

Symptoms: The dog limps and licks the pad, which festers and begins to smell.

Treatment: A veterinarian uses a special cutter to cut an ingrowing toe-nail. If you do not own one, you can use stout nail-clippers. Be careful not to cut into the quick. Remove the nail part that has en-

To improvise a muzzle, make a large, open knot in a bandage.

Wrap a long bandage around the dog's jaw and tie the knot snugly above the mouth.

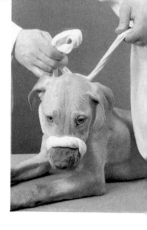

Twist the ends of the bandage loosely and pass them around the dog's neck, tying them firmly behind the nape of the neck.

tered the flesh, and clean and disinfect the wound thoroughly. Apply an antibiotic ointment to the sore.

You can avoid this problem altogether by simply trimming your dog's nails regularly. If you cut one of the nails too short so that the dog bleeds, rub in some soap.

Keeping a dog from licking its wounds

You can prevent this by fitting the dog with an Elizabethan collar (see p. 344) or by covering the wound with a bandage. You may also smear the wound with an unpalatable ointment.

Diseases

Now we come to deal with actual illnesses. The following pages list, in alphabetical order, the diseases most likely to occur in a dog. For each disease there is an explanation of the sickness itself and of its cause, an account of the symptoms that characterize it, and a recommended treatment. A table on pages 356 and 357 allows you to identify the disease by its symptoms. If in doubt, consult a veterinarian.

Abscesses

An abscess is a pocket of pus, caused by inflammation, which accumulates in a sac or cavity. It may appear in various places. Those infections you can most easily notice are:

● Abscesses under the skin. These develop where bacteria have entered (a scratch from the claws of a cat, or a bite, for example).

Symptoms: A painful, inflamed mass forms. The dog may even run a high fever in serious cases.

Treatment: Bring the abscess to a head by applying lukewarm compresses, which will dull the pain. Now lance the abscess with a well-disinfected razor-blade, and let the pus flow out. Disinfect with an antiseptic solution or a one-percent solution of permanganate, and then apply an antibiotic powder. If the dog is feverish give it antibiotic tablets for at least a week.

Some abscesses are cold or dry, a condition that often accompanies infection after an insect bite. The pus has become hard and granular and is packed into a fibrous membrane. These abscesses can easily be punctured by applying pressure.

● Dental abscesses. After a large buildup of tartar on the teeth, the gums become highly susceptible to abscesses. Only a veterinarian should treat this malady. One of the most severe abscesses develops at the root of the fourth premolar. The tooth must be extracted under anaesthetic.

● Abscesses of the anal glands. These abscesses occur frequently if the anal glands are not emptied regularly. The organs should be evacuated by whoever grooms the dog or by the veterinarian during a routine visit.

Symptoms: The dog rubs its hindquarters excessively. This painful abscess often bursts of its own accord.

Treatment: Clean the abscess thoroughly with water and a disinfectant soap, rub in an antibiotic cream well, three times a day, and apply cold-water compresses to relieve the pain. Sometimes surgical removal is the only effective treatment.

Acanthosis nigricans

This is a skin disease that affects Dachshunds, especially between the ages of six and nine years. It is a result of hormonal imbalance precipitated by lack of thyroxin in the blood.

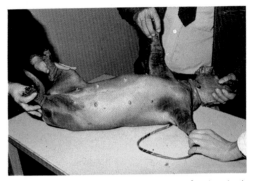
A Dachshund suffering from Acanthosis nigricans, the result of a hormonal imbalance.

Symptoms: The skin becomes black and thickens under the arms.

Treatment: Mix a thyroid hormone supplement into the food.

Agalaxia

Some bitches have no milk after whelping. A hormone injection (oxytocin) will stimulate milk production. If not, put the pups out to nurse, or feed them commercial or home-made formula (see p. 297).

BAD BREATH

No carnivore has a pleasant-smelling breath. But when the odour is very marked, there is often an accumulation of tartar (a mixture of hardened food and bacteria) on the teeth.

To prevent this, brush your dog's teeth regularly with a soft toothbrush, using bicarbonate of soda as a toothpaste. If the trouble is sufficiently advanced a specialist can remove the tartar ultrasonically under anaesthesia. If this is not done the gums will become inflamed (a condition known as gingivitis), the roots of the teeth will rot, the dog will suffer from severe toothache, and the teeth will work loose. They will eventually fall out.

Tartar is a problem that results from domestication. Dogs still have carnassial teeth designed for killing and eviscerating prey. Most commercial dog foods, however, offer little of the exercise necessary to the health of teeth and gums of the modern dog. Hard biscuits are not a complete remedy, but they help to clean the teeth.

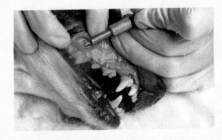
Ultrasonic removal of tartar, carried out by the veterinarian, cleans the teeth effectively.

Aggravated pads

This is an inflammation of the pads that occurs when a dog has exercised excessively on hard or pebbly ground and its pads are unaccustomed to such rough terrain. This condition is common during the hunting season.

Symptoms: The pads are swollen and painful. The dog treads gingerly with stiffened paws.

Treatment: Bathe the pads in lukewarm water to which you have added two per cent copper sulphate, apply some anti-inflammatory ointment (cortisone), and let the dog rest. If the dog is suffering greatly, give it an Aspirin.

Allergies

Allergies result from physiological reactions to substances the dog cannot tolerate. These substances are called allergens.

Symptoms: They vary, appearing a few minutes after contact with the allergen. Coughing, sneezing, and choking occur in respiratory allergies due to pollen (hay fever), dust, aerosols, and so forth; vomiting and chronic diarrhoea are exhibited when the dog cannot tolerate certain foods; urticaria, appearing as skin eruptions, with swelling of the nose, ears, and skin, shows up after an injection of penicillin or a vaccine, or after eating foods to which the dog is sensitized. Eczema appears when the skin has been in contact with grass or synthetic textiles, or after being bitten by a flea. All such reactions are usually benign.

The most serious reaction is anaphylactic shock, which strikes suddenly. The dog lapses into violent spasms and convulsions, and may die a few minutes later.

Treatment: Take the animal to the veterinarian immediately. During the acute phase, only antihistamines administered at once have any effect. Render artificial respiration on the way if necessary. In its chronic forms (eczema, asthma), antihistamine tablets or long-acting (six weeks) injections of corticosteroids will inhibit the reactions. Prevention is accomplished by identifying the substances to which the dog is allergic and avoiding all contact with them.

The best remedy is to have the dog undergo immunological tests to identify precisely the allergen or allergens that affect it. You can then have the dog desensitized by weekly injections. This treatment yields a success rate of up to 75 per cent. The process is long, however, lasting several months, and thus discourages many owners from initiating it.

Anaemia

This disease of the blood is characterized by a reduction in the number of red corpuscles or in the quantity of haemoglobin available for the exchange of gases in the lungs. It can be caused by parasites, malnutrition, or bone-marrow damage.

Symptoms: An anaemic dog has pale mucous tissues and is weak and lazy. It also breathes rapidly. When there has been a massive destruction of the red corpuscles, signs of jaundice appear.

Treatment: Only your veterinarian can determine the cause of the anaemia and, thus, the appropriate treatment. You can help by giving your dog ferrous sulphate supplements and B complex vitamins, as well as feeding it a diet rich in liver or another raw-meat source of iron.

Anuria

This is the inability to urinate. It may be due to stones blocking the urethra, an infection, tumours, or a ruptured bladder resulting from a fall or traffic accident. These are serious conditions that require a veterinarian's expertise.

Arthritis

This is a painful inflammation or infection of the joints.

Symptoms: When suffering from the inflammatory form of the disease, the dog walks with difficulty, and its joints become deformed. The infectious form is similar, but more acute.

Treatment: The degeneration must be slowed down and the pain relieved with anti-inflammatory and analgesic treatments (phenylbutazone, corticosteroids, or Aspirin). Selenium capsules, combined with vitamin E, slow down the degeneration. The infectious form should be treated with antibiotics.

Bladder stones

The bladder is often blocked by stones obstructing the urethra. (See also Kidney stones.)

Symptoms: Unable to urinate, the dog starts to suffer. It licks its genitals and strains to urinate, producing at best only a few drops.

Treatment: If this happens, take the dog at once to a veterinary surgeon, who will catheterize the urethra. (If this is not done, the bladder may burst and the dog will die of uraemia.)

Afterwards, keep the animal on a suitable diet, to avoid relapse. Your veterinarian will advise you.

Burns

• Heat burns. These are painful, prone to infection, and slow to heal. If no more than 15 per cent of the skin is burnt, the prognosis is good. If, however, more than 50 per cent of the skin has been destroyed, the dog will die. (See also Sunburn.)

Treatment: The pain of mild burns can be relieved by applying a cold-water compress or an ice-pack. Dry the wound, then apply Mercurochrome or an antibiotic ointment. Protect the wound with a bandage (changed daily) and give Aspirin as an analgesic. To be certain of the optimum dosage for your pet, consult your veterinarian.

Do not apply greasy medications to wide or deep wounds. Instead, cover the burn with a cloth soaked in cold water and get the dog to a veterinarian as soon as possible. In the interim, cover the dog with a blanket to keep it warm and prevent it from going into shock, which can be fatal. If the dog is conscious try to make it drink the following solution: half a teaspoonful of salt and half a teaspoonful of bicarbonate of soda in a litre (3½ cups) of water.

• Chemical burns. Many household products that we use freely (detergents, herbicides, paint) can badly burn the skin or eyes of a curious dog.

Treatment: Remove the corrosive agent by dousing the affected area with water, or by administering the specific antidote printed on the label. If a caustic substance with a soda or alkaline base is involved, rinse the skin with water and vinegar or water and lemon juice. Use a solution of bicarbonate of soda and water (one teaspoonful per litre, or 3½ cups) to treat burns caused by acids. If the skin is seriously damaged, apply an antibiotic ointment or, failing this, petroleum jelly. Do not let the dog lick or scratch itself, and take it to a veterinarian as soon as possible.

Cataracts

A cataract is an eye lens that has hardened and become opaque, causing varying degrees of blindness. It is prevalent among old or diabetic dogs.

Treatment: Cataract removal is a routine operation performed by specialists. It improves the animal's vision, quite often dramatically.

Constipation

Dogs often have difficulty defecating after they have swallowed bones or foreign objects. Pieces of wood and bits of plastic are among the main culprits.

Treatment: Put the dog on a 48-hour fast. Give it fresh water and make it swallow a good dose of mineral oil (up to two-thirds of a cup, according to the dog's size). If there is no result after 48 hours, give an enema (see p. 345) or consult your veterinarian. Constipation can be a symptom of more serious illness: prostatitis, an abscess of the anal glands, or even a tumour, for example.

Dogs suffering from chronic constipation should eat a very liquid mash. Brewer's yeast, milk, liver, and fresh fruit all have laxative effects.

Convulsions

Many illnesses bring on convulsions: viral diseases (rabies), epilepsy, tetanus, eclampsia, and poisoning.

Symptoms: Often disturbing. The dog shakes its head, foams at the mouth, and barks erratically. Its eyes are wild, it breathes rapidly, it cannot control its bowels. Often, it lies on one side and makes pedalling movements. Spasms of the jaw prevent it from swallowing, which is why it foams at the mouth.

Do not try to talk to a dog in this state; it cannot hear you. Even more important, do not let it bite you. Protect the animal by wrapping it in a good, thick blanket and putting it in a room where there are no objects for it to bump into. Keep the lights dim. Bright light only aggravates the spasms.

Get to your veterinary surgeon as soon as possible. Epilepsy is a common sickness in certain breeds, such as Cocker Spaniels, Miniature Poodles, and setters. It appears suddenly, between the ages of one and three years. The attacks at first are at wide intervals. Sometimes, however, they occur several times a week. They generally last one or two minutes.

Treatment: Preventive treatment is the only way to control epileptic convulsions. The dog must be given a daily dose of phenobarbital for the rest of its life. Your veterinarian will determine what dosage to administer.

Coprophagy

Eating its own excrement, or that of other dogs, is a tendency sometimes displayed by a bored puppy, or a puppy that has been confined in too small a space. It may also be a reaction to poor diet; occasionally, it is

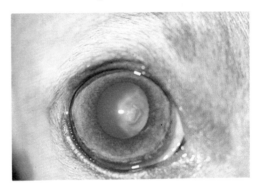

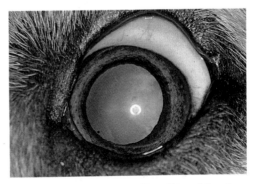

Although cataracts usually afflict older dogs, they also occur in young animals. Above, inflammatory cataract in a three-year-old Italian Greyhound. In some cases, a cataract is congenital, as with the Golden Retriever below.

the result of a bitch's re-enacting the eating of her pups' stool.

Treatment: Add vitamin and mineral supplements to the dog's food. Avoid enclosing the animal in a confined space. Discourage the dog from eating excrement by sprinkling the stool with an unpalatable substance, such as strong curry sauce.

Cough

If your dog is coughing, look carefully inside its mouth and down its throat to see if a foreign object is stuck there. If the animal has no fever, you can give it codeine syrup, which is a temporary palliative for benign cases. If the cough persists, get in touch with your veterinarian since this could be a symptom of a more serious illness.

Dermatitis

Bacteria invade and infect the skin, causing various infectious skin diseases. (See also Eczema.)

Symptoms: Pustules, sores, boils, and acne. All of these become aggravated when the dog scratches and licks them.

Treatment: The coat must be shaved to allow the dog to be thoroughly cleansed with a disinfectant soap. Then apply an antibiotic ointment to the infected area.

Systemic antibiotics in the form of pills are recommended in serious cases.

Diabetes

• Sugar diabetes (diabetes mellitus). This illness is marked by an abnormal rise in

Treatment: Regular injections of insulin. Your veterinarian will show you what to do after he or she has determined the appropriate dosage. In the event of an overdose (hypoglycaemic coma) the dog should be given sugar, honey, or jam to swallow. The animal must be put on a special diet. Avoid starches and sugars, and increase the amount of meat and fat.

• Diabetes insipidus. Even though this condition resembles sugar diabetes in its general symptoms, it is the result of a hormonal deficiency in the pituitary gland. The pituitary fails to secrete an antidiuretic hormone responsible for controlling the elimination of water by the kidneys. Diabetes insipidus is a debilitating disease that attacks mainly old dogs.

Symptoms: The sick dog drinks enormous quantities of water and suffers from polyuria (copious urination) and urinary incontinence. Its breath does not have the odour of acetone (which occurs with sugar diabetes), nor is there an abnormal amount of sugar in the urine.

Treatment: Hormone treatment is often chancy and disappointing. The animal usually has to be destroyed.

Diarrhoea

Liquid stool can arise from viral infections, parasites, poison, or an intestinal imbalance resulting from an antibiotic treatment.

Treatment: If the dog suffers from non-specific diarrhoea, give it water but no

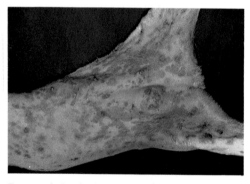

Bacterial dermatitis (pyoderma) on a Pointer, showing pustules, sores, and boils.

Solar dermatitis on a Collie's nose. Unpigmented nose tips are very prone to sunburn.

the amount of sugar in the blood and urine. It is caused by faulty metabolization of carbohydrates (sugars and starches) due to an acutely low production of insulin by the pancreas.

Symptoms: A diabetic dog eats and drinks a great deal but nonetheless loses weight. It is weak, sluggish, and urinates frequently. Its breath sometimes smells of acetone (an odour like that of nail varnish). Sometimes the illness causes ulceration of the cornea or cataracts. In extreme cases the dog falls into a diabetic coma. Exact diagnosis is through a biochemical blood examination.

food for 48 hours. You should also give the dog a solution of kaolin and pectin (two teaspoonfuls for each 5 kilograms, or 11 pounds, of body weight, every six hours) or phosphate of codeine (8 milligrams, or 12 grains, per 10 kilograms, or 22 pounds, of weight, twice a day). If the problem continues, consult a veterinarian.

Unflavoured yoghurt helps to remedy mild intestinal disorders. Therapeutic diets, which your veterinarian can obtain, will cure chronic diarrhoea where the intestine is sensitive. Rice (20 per cent of daily diet) and rice water (water in which rice is cooked) are also effective.

THE DIFFERENT PHASES
OF DYSPLASIA OF THE HIP JOINT

In a normal hip the head of the femur is spherical. It is smooth, and sits snugly in the cotyloid cavity (hip socket). When movement occurs at the joint, the parts in contact rub together and can become worn. In dysplasia the head of the femur is irregular in shape. It does not fit its cavity (1), and no longer covers the head of the femur (2). The cavity is almost a plane surface and the head of the femur is nearly completely out. Osteophytes (bony excrescences) appear (3). The head of the femur comes completely out of the cavity and the hip is dislocated (4).

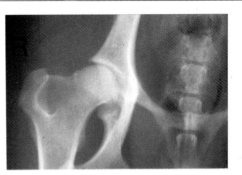

X-ray of a normal hip showing how the head of the femur fits into the cotyloid cavity.

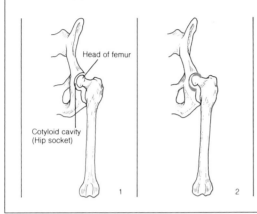
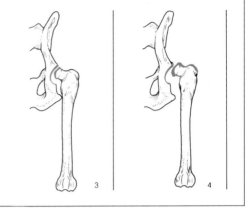

Head of femur

Cotyloid cavity
(Hip socket)

1   2   3   4

Distemper

This is a viral illness which affects young dogs mainly, though older ones sometimes suffer from it.

Symptoms: The illness takes three forms—*digestive*, with high fever, vomiting, diarrhoea, loss of appetite, and severe dehydration; *respiratory*, with the same general symptoms but also coughing; and *nervous* (sometimes the final form of the sickness), with symptoms of meningitis, nerve spasms, muscle contractions, and even paralysis, usually ending in death of the animal.

Distemper may be carried on the nose or the pads (hard-pad disease).

The incubation period is from 7 to 12 days. The illness can last several weeks.

Treatment: Specific serums (antibiotics, anticonvulsants, rehydrating serum) are usually disappointing. Preventive vaccination is the only effective way to control this disease. As a general rule, the older the dog is, the less likely it is to die from distemper.

Dysplasia of the hip joint

This painful hip affliction is one of the commonest forms of arthritis. A deformity of the coxa-femoral joint, it shows up in large breeds at one year of age or older.

Symptoms: Pain, limping on one or both sides, complaining, difficulty in getting up from a sitting or lying position, unsteady gait.

Treatment: Different treatments are possible. They can be medical, as indicated for arthritis, or surgical—cutting the pectineal muscle or cutting the head of the femur (arthroplasty). At the onset of the illness there is also the possibility of putting in a prosthesis (artificial limb).

Since this sickness is hereditary, a sufferer should not be mated. Before you buy a dog of a large breed, have the breeder guarantee that its ascendants have been X-rayed and shown to be free from this debilitating illness.

Eclampsia

This sometimes attacks small bitches when they bear their first litter. It also occurs in a bitch that gives birth to a large litter (12 to 14 pups). It arises from a shortage, or imbalance, of calcium and phosphorus (the bitch has expended too much of these minerals in pregnancy). It is likely to be preceded by a more benign ailment, milk fever, a febrile condition some lactating bitches are susceptible to.

Symptoms: The bitch lies on its side, moans, and has spasms. Sometimes it falls into a coma. It cannot stand up and its temperature runs very high: 40°C (104°F).

Treatment: The dog must have an intravenous injection of calcium gluconate as soon as possible.

Until the bitch has recovered its health, feed the puppies artificially.

Add calcium, phosphorus, and vitamin D supplements to the mother's diet all the time that she is producing milk and before the next pregnancy.

Ectropion

This is a deformity of the eyelids which affects some breeds more than others.

Symptoms: The lower eyelid folds back and outwards, increasing the tendency to chronic conjunctivitis.

Treatment: Cortisone ointment relieves mild cases. In serious cases only surgery will go to the root of the matter.

Eczema

This term covers a group of skin inflammations accompanied by pruritis, or violent itching. Nowadays, however, many people speak of eczema in specific terms. Contact dermatitis, allergenic dermatitis, and neurodermatitis are particular types of eczema, and no one treatment cures all.

DEFORMITIES OF THE EYELID

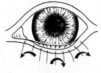

ECTROPION
The lower eyelid turns outwards.

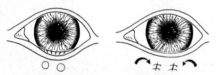

To correct a mild ectropion, the surgeon cuts two small circular holes in the skin. He then draws the eyelid together with vertical stitches and puts it back in place.

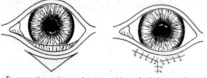

To correct a serious ectropion, a triangular hole must be cut in the skin and the incision drawn together with a suture.

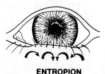

ENTROPION
The lower eyelid turns inwards.

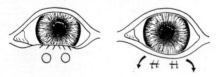

To correct a mild entropion, two small circular holes must be cut in the skin, then drawn together horizontally to pull on the eyelid and thus unroll it.

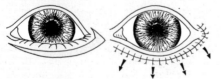

To correct a serious entropion, a 'lance-head' of skin is removed and sutures applied along its whole length.

There are two forms of eczema, the dry and the wet. They are accompanied by irritation, redness, itching, and thickening of the skin; and the dog licks itself. Sometimes there is suppuration and formation of scabs in the final stage of a wet eczema. Spring and summer are the seasons when eczemas develop most easily. The environment, the animal's temperament, and its diet must all be taken into account.

Eczema may have several causes. It can be a contact dermatitis not caused by an allergy. This occurs when the skin first comes into contact with an irritant (a detergent, tar, chemical, corrosive, or insecticide, for example). The irritation appears in the less hairy areas of the skin. In a more localized and more specific form, it can be an irritation of the lips of a dog that feeds from a bowl made of plastic. This is because the plastic often contains antioxidizing agents. Flea-collars, although generally harmless, must also be counted among the possible sources of irritation; the villain here may be dichlorvos, the active agent in the collar. This form of inflammation is common when the flea-collar is too tight. The resulting itch often spreads over the whole skin of a small dog. Bacteria, fungi, mange, and other microorganisms that invade the skin, produce endopeptides that sometimes cause serious irritations.

Even the animal's own physical make-up can be a cause, especially among breeds where the tip of the nose sometimes lacks pigmentation (Collies and German Shepherds, for example). The sun's rays irritate the skin causing sunburn, sometimes with ulcers and suppuration. Parasites can also cause eczema, in the area of the perineum and the insides of the thighs.

There are other frequent causes of eczema. Common among them are allergic reactions to certain proteins found in the saliva of fleas and in wool, pollen, and feathers. Food allergies can cause urticaria (blisters on the skin). This happens to dogs that are allergic to eggs, horse-meat, salmon, wheat, and other substances. Even respiratory allergies caused by pollen or dust can affect the skin. In this case the eczema is limited to the face.

Nervousness and dietary deficiencies (lack of vitamin A or B) also play a key role in eczema.

Symptoms: Eczema begins with redness and itching in the irritated area. Itching occurs locally or generally. Sometimes the skin bleeds and the coat falls out. Secondary infections easily set in under such circumstances, then scabs and festering sores develop.

Treatment: The basic principle of treatment is removal of the cause of the trouble: a synthetic rug on which the animal sleeps, the fleas that have invaded its coat, or food such as horseflesh, if the dog is sensitive to it. In the case of sunburn, keep the dog in the shade, apply a cortisone ointment, and, when the dog is better, have the unpigmented part of the tip of the nose tattooed black. Deal with any dietary deficiencies. Long-acting corticosteroid pills and injections are useful on a short-term basis. Antihistamine tablets are moderately effective. If the eczema is localized, an application of 2.5 per cent hydrocortisone ointment will comfort the animal.

Since dry skin is a predisposing factor, it is a good idea to add wheat germ oil to the diet of an eczematous dog to remedy the lack of fatty acids. If allergic reaction recurs, ask your veterinarian to carry out immunological tests. The results may enable the dog to be desensitized by means of vaccines, although this treatment is not always completely effective.

Entropion
This deformity of the eyelid is the opposite of ectropion.
Symptoms: The eyelid turns in upon itself. The eyelashes rub and irritate the cornea, causing a chronic condition of purulent conjunctivitis. The dog scratches its eye to relieve the itching.
Treatment: Surgery is the only effective remedy for this uncomfortable affliction.

Feminization syndrome in male dogs
A tendency to feminization can appear between the ages of five and ten years. It is caused by cancer of the testicles, which raises the level of oestrogen in the blood.
Symptoms: The dog shows no sexual interest, yet attracts other males. Its penis atrophies, its teats become enlarged, and its coat sheds.
Treatment: Castration. The symptoms disappear within a month.

Fractures
Fractures may be closed, as when the skin has not been broken; or open, as when a bone has pierced the skin. In the latter case, there is a risk of infection.
Symptoms: Pain, limping, and haematoma. Little by little the limb will atrophy. When the animal walks, the fractured limb goes askew.

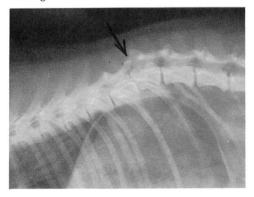

Fracture of the spine. An operation should be carried out within six hours of the accident.

Treatment: As much as possible, avoid moving the broken bone. Immobilize it temporarily with a splint (see p. 344).

With any fracture, move the dog as little as possible. Take it to a veterinarian on an improvised stretcher. Act quickly. A spinal fracture must be operated on within six hours of the accident if the surgery is to be successful.

Glaucoma
This extremely painful illness is marked by increased pressure of the fluids inside the eyeball. As a result, the eyeball enlarges and becomes hard to the touch. The causes are not yet fully known. The disease, however, may be congenital in origin —primary glaucoma—or due to dislocation of the lens—secondary glaucoma. (See also Luxation of the eye lens). Some breeds, such as the Cocker Spaniel, the Beagle, and the Miniature Poodle, are especially vulnerable to secondary glaucoma.

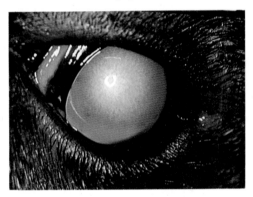

Secondary glaucoma arising from dislocation of the lens. The eyeball hardens and enlarges.

Symptoms: The eyeball increases in size and the cornea becomes opaque. The pupil dilates and vision is reduced because the membranes covering the base of the eye atrophy. The dog suffers, scratching the bad eye. A veterinarian will make the diagnosis with an instrument called a tonometer, which is applied to the cornea to measure orbicular pressure.
Treatment: There are several veterinary treatments designed to reduce the production of, or help to eliminate, the fluids in the eyeball. Surgical treatment is hardly ever satisfactory, except when the glaucoma is due to luxation of the lens.

Haemorrhages
A pressure bandage firmly applied to a simple wound will make the blood coagulate. For a serious haemorrhage of a leg or of the tail, press on the artery serving that limb while you wait for the veterinarian. For a foreleg haemorrhage, press on the brachial artery where the leg joins the trunk; for a hind leg haemorrhage, press on the femoral artery; and for a tail haemorrhage, press on the coccygeal artery.

355

HOW TO RECOGNIZE DISEASES

The symptoms along the top of the page indicate the diseases listed down the left-hand side. The accuracy of diagnosis depends on the number of symptoms.

- ● very significant symptom for this disease
- ◐ fairly significant symptom for this disease
- ○ non-specific symptom for this disease

DISEASES	ABDOMINAL DISTENSION (ascites)	ABDOMINAL PAIN	BAD BREATH	BLOOD IN THE URINE	CHANGES IN BEHAVIOUR	COMA	CONSTIPATION	CONVULSIONS	COUGH	CYANOSIS (low blood oxygen)	DIARRHOEA (WITH BLOOD)	DIARRHOEA (NORMAL)	DICUBITUS (BEDSORES)	DIFFICULTY MOVING	DIFFICULTY SWALLOWING	DIFFICULT OR NO URINATION	FEVER	FREQUENT-URINATION	HEAVY SALIVATION
ABCESSES (according to site)			○							○				●	○		●		○
ARTHRITIS					○								○				○		
BURNS	○					○				○							○		○
CYSTITIS (inflammation of the bladder)		◐		●									○			◐	○	◐	
DERMATITIS (skin inflammation)																			
DIABETES INSIPIDUS								○				○	○					●	
DIABETES MELLITUS (sugar diabetes)			◐		●			○					○					◐	
DISTEMPER		◐						◐	●		●		○		○		●		●
ECLAMPSIA					◐	○		●					●				●		
ECZEMA																			
ENTERITIS (inflammation of the intestines)		◐	○					○	○		○	●					○		○
EXTERNAL PARASITES																			
FOREIGN BODIES		◐					●		◐	○	◐	○		●					◐
GASTRITIS (inflammation of the stomach)		◐	◐							○	○				○		○		○
HAEMORRHAGE				○		○							○				○		
HEART DISEASE	●					○		◐	◐				○					○	
HEAT STROKE					◐	●		○	○				●				●		○
INFECTIOUS HEPATITIS	○	◐						○		○	●	○	○				●		
INTERNAL PARASITES		○							◐		◐	●							○
INTESTINAL BLOCKAGE		◐				○	●	◐		○			○						○
LEPTOSPIROSIS		◐		◐								◐	○			◐	●	◐	
LEUKAEMIA										○			○						
METRITIS (inflammation of the uterus)	○	◐						◐		◐			○				○		
NEPHRITIS (inflammation of the kidneys)	◐	◐		◐						◐						◐	◐	◐	
OTITIS								◐											
PARA-INFLUENZA (kennel cough)									●								○		
PARVOVIRUS								◐		○	●	●	○				●		
POISONING	○	○	○	○	◐	○		◐		◐	◐		○		○				
RABIES				●				●					○		○		◐		●
RINGWORM																			
STONES (bladder, or other)		◐		●	○								○			●		◐	
TARTAR			●																●
TONSILLITIS									●							◐	◐	◐	○
TOOTHACHE			◐													◐	○		
TORSION OF THE STOMACH		●			●	◐		◐					◐	●					●
TUBERCULOSIS	○	○							●			○	○						○
TUMOURS (according to site)	◐	○		○	○		○	○	○		○	○				○			○

INTENSE THIRST | JAUNDICE | LETHARGY | LOSS OF APPETITE | LOSS OF BALANCE | LOW SPIRITS (depression) | MUCOUS TISSUES PALE | NICTITATING MEMBRANE (conspicuous inner eyelid) | PAINFUL BREATHING | PAINFUL TO TOUCH | PAINFUL URINATION | POOR APPETITE | PUS | RAPID BREATHING | SCRATCHES THE EARS | SHEDDING COAT | SHOCK | SKIN IRRITATION | SWELLING OF THE ABDOMEN | TREMBLING | ULCERATION | URINARY INCONTINENCE | VOMITING | VORACIOUS APPETITE | WEIGHT LOSS

MISALLIANCES AND ABORTIONS

If your bitch has just coupled, and you do not want it to whelp, take it to the veterinarian within eight days for an oestradiol injection. The hormone interrupts pregnancy by preventing the fertilized ova from becoming implanted. This does not affect the quality of future litters, but the bitch will stay in heat another ten days.

Stop the pressure when the haemorrhage has ceased. While waiting for the veterinarian, you can apply a tourniquet, but this could be dangerous. It must be just tight enough—and no more—to stop the bleeding. If it is left on too long, there is risk of cutting off the circulation entirely and causing gangrene. Do not make a tourniquet out of string, which will damage the tissues, but out of a broad ribbon or strip of cloth, or even a soft belt.

The blood which flows out will be blue if a vein has been damaged, bright red if from an artery. Tie the tourniquet five centimetres (two inches) from the wound in the direction of the heart. To judge how much pressure to use, tie a pencil to the tourniquet as shown to the right and turn it just until the blood stops flowing. Then attach the other end of the pencil to the limb.

Heart disease

Many dogs are 'cardiac cases' without their masters knowing it. Like us, they suffer from valvular insufficiency, myocarditis, arteriosclerosis, and a number of other heart conditions.

Symptoms: Shortness of breath, oedema of the lungs, and ascites (an accumulation of liquid in the abdomen). Electrocardiograms are used more and more to assist diagnosis.

Treatment: Low-sodium diet, and certain other treatments, including diuretics.

Puppies may show a number of hereditary cardio-vascular diseases. Surgery can sometimes deal with these problems. But such animals should not be allowed to reproduce.

Hernia

This is a protrusion commonly found at the umbilicus (navel) or the scrotal areas, caused by rupture of an organ or intestine which has escaped the cavity lining. Some hernias are congenital, therefore insignificant, although any that increases in size should be reported to your veterinarian. Surgical treatment may be necessary if a vital organ has become strangled by the herniary bulge.

Hypoglycaemia

This attacks adult, generally small dogs (Chihuahuas and Yorkshire Terriers, for example) and young puppies which have exercised strenuously or are under stress.

In effect, they expend too much energy too quickly, and no longer have enough glucose in their blood.

Symptoms: Moaning and lack of muscular co-ordination (pedalling movements).

Treatment: Put honey or jam on the tongue or gums immediately and take the dog to a veterinarian. If your dog suffers chronically from this problem, keep a constant supply of energy supplements (glucose tablets and tubes of high-calorie supplements) on hand.

To make a tourniquet when there is haemorrhaging, make a loose, open knot in a bandage.

Pass it over the animal's limb and tighten the bandage, putting a pencil inside the knot.

Turn the pencil. This lets you control the degree of pressure on the bleeding blood vessel.

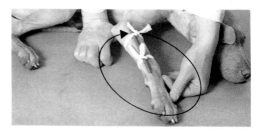

Tie a second bandage to fix the pencil and maintain the exact degree of pressure required.

Hysterical pregnancy

False motherhood can occur several weeks after the bitch has been in heat but has not in fact coupled.

Symptoms: The 'mother' will show all the signs of a normal pregnancy, including the development of breasts and an increased appetite. She will even go through an *accouchement*, complete with dilation of the vulva and contractions. She will collect all sorts of objects (socks, slippers, balls of wool) and press them to her teats, which she licks to bring down the milk.

Treatment: Give less food and water, to dry up the milk, and give the bitch more exercise. To cut off milk production entirely a veterinarian will inject hormones (oestrogens or testosterones) and antibiotics to prevent breast inflammation. If the condition recurs, ovario-hysterectomy (removal of the ovaries and the uterus) is recommended as a radical treatment. This condition makes a bitch more likely to develop breast ulcers when older.

Incontinence (urinary)
Among old dogs, incontinence may be due to relaxing of the sphincter muscle of the bladder. However, there are many other causes: chronic interstitial nephritis, bladder infections (cystitis), diabetes, or corticosteroid (cortisone) treatments.

Symptoms: The animal urinates involuntarily, in normal or large quantity.

Treatment: This depends on the cause, and should be diagnosed by the veterinary surgeon. Old dogs are sometimes treated with hormone supplements.

Infectious hepatitis (Rubarth's disease)
This illness, transmitted through urine, is particularly common among male dogs in their first year.

Symptoms: High fever, loss of appetite, intense thirst, and severe pains (cramps) occur suddenly. The dog is very weak. It vomits and has diarrhoea with blood in the stool. Its mucous tissues are saffron yellow and congested. In some cases the whole cornea turns bluish; this colour disappears when the animal is well again. There is a high survival rate for dogs which survive the first forty-eight hours.

Treatment: This is carried out by the veterinarian. It is supportive in nature, consisting of serum, antibiotics, and vitamin supplements, particularly the B complex. Vaccines are the best prevention.

Inflammation of the nictitating membrane
The third eyelid is in the inside corner of the eye, and is affected by such conditions as fatigue and debilitating illnesses.

Symptoms: Under the nictitating membrane there is a gland which sometimes swells and covers much of the eye.

Treatment: Surgical removal of the gland is the only treatment that provides an effective remedy.

Kennel cough, see Para-influenza.

Keratitis
This inflammation of the cornea (the transparent covering of the front of the eye) may be due to an injury, such as a blow to the eye, or irritating objects or substances lodged in the eye.

Symptoms: To relieve this painful irritation the dog weeps copiously, blinks its eyelids nervously, rubs and scratches instinctively, and shakes its head and complains. The animal tends to be reluctant to let you examine its eyes.

If the trouble is neglected, the surface of the cornea clouds over, is sometimes even ulcerated, inviting secondary infections.

Treatment: Do not apply just any eyewash. Beware of those that contain cortisone. If the keratitis is accompanied by a deep lesion of the cornea, such a lotion may impede healing. The eye should be washed thoroughly in distilled water to remove the cause of irritation.

Eye ointment should be applied if it contains only an antibiotic, and has no anti-inflammatory substances in it. Only your veterinarian should prescribe an anti-inflammatory lotion.

If the dog begins scratching its eyes, apply a protective bandage and take it to a veterinarian.

Kidney stones
Stones are formed by a buildup of minerals (usually phosphates) in the bladder or the kidneys. The stones vary in size but can become as large as hen's eggs. The cause of this is still unknown. We do know, however, that a diet too rich in minerals, a lack of uric acid, and certain infections are factors. Some breeds—Dalmatians and Miniature Schnauzers in particular—are more susceptible than other dogs to stones.

Symptoms: The dog shows pain, its back is arched, and there is blood in the urine.

Urination is generally slight. There may be total retention of the urine, however, if the urethra is blocked by a stone. This constitutes an emergency. Veterinary diagnosis is by means of palpation or X-ray.

EUTHANASIA

When your dog is suffering from an incurable illness it is often better to cut the suffering short than to carry on an anguished and—finally—useless struggle. The most humane method is the injection of an overdose of barbiturates. Death comes to the dog at once, without pain or struggle.

Treatment: Usually surgical. The stone is removed by opening the kidneys, or the bladder, and treating the secondary infection.

One form of prevention is to encourage the dog to drink copiously. You can do this by adding 0.5 to 10 grams (up to ½ teaspoonful) of salt to the dog's daily food. Maintain the acidity of the urine by giving the dog acidifying agents (orally) and keeping it on a diet low in minerals.

Leptospirosis

This is a bacterial disease. It is usually transmitted in the urine of infected dogs, and is sometimes passed from dog to man. Because of their way of urinating, male dogs are more often affected than females because the penis sometimes makes contact with other dogs' urine.

Symptoms: Low spirits, loss of appetite, pain in the stomach and kidneys. The dog walks very little, the mucous tissues of the eyes and tongue becomes almost yellow. Diarrhoea and vomiting occur.

Treatment: Antibiotics are given, particularly streptomycin. If treated in time, the illness is quickly cured. When symptoms of jaundice are present, treatment takes much longer. The best prevention is an annual vaccination.

Leukaemia

This cancer of the blood is marked by an excessive increase in the number of leucocytes, the white corpuscles whose function is to defend the organism. Studies

---

VACCINATION SCHEDULE

Orphaned puppies and those weaned very early should be vaccinated against measles before they reach the age of two months. This inoculation also provides immunity against distemper.

• At two months of age puppies should be vaccinated simultaneously against distemper, leptospirosis, hepatitis, para-influenza, and parvovirus.

• A month and a half later, the puppy needs a booster shot of all of these.

• At five months of age puppies should be given a vaccination against rabies.

• Once a year ensure that your dog undergoes booster shots against rabies, leptospirosis, and parvovirus.

• Every three years your dog should be given a booster shot against distemper. If a dog dies of a viral infection on your premises, wait at least two months before bringing in another dog. Make sure that the new dog has already been vaccinated.

It is essential to disinfect a breeding establishment after a viral illness with a solution of chlorhedixine acetate.

---

indicate that about 0.5 per cent of dogs in veterinary hospitals are kept there to receive treatment for this ailment.

Symptoms: Weakness, lack of vitality, diarrhoea, occasional constipation, vomiting, coughing, difficulty in breathing, loss of appetite, and nausea. The lymph nodes become enlarged. The illness can last from six months to a year. In the final stage there may be pallor of the mucous tissues, loss of weight, and nasal discharge.

Treatment: Examining an enlarged lymph node under the microscope will confirm the diagnosis. A blood test alone is not sufficient. The dog's life can be prolonged by certain treatments which it finds hard to bear—chemotherapy or radiotherapy, for instance. A lasting cure has not yet been found. Euthanasia is the course which causes the least suffering.

Luxation (dislocation) of the eye lens

In this rare illness, the eye lens slips across the pupil into the front or back eye-chamber. This condition may arise from an injury, or from an inflammation of the iris. It is often accompanied by secondary glaucoma, and reduces the dog's vision.

Symptoms: Those of glaucoma.

Treatment: Surgery is the only effective remedy for this illness.

Mammitis

This is an infection of the mammary glands. It can follow a hysterical pregnancy, or be caused by scratches from the puppies' toe-nails.

Symptoms: The teats become hard, and are painful when touched. They yield a greenish-yellow discharge.

Treatment: To relieve the pain, apply petroleum jelly and cold-water compresses. Take the pups from the bitch and have your veterinarian give her a general course of antibiotics. Feed the litter with artificial bitch's milk (see p. 297).

Milk fever, see Eclampsia.

Nephritis

This is an inflammatory disease of the kidneys. It can be acute or chronic.

• Acute nephritis. This may be caused by an infection (leptospirosis, after-effects of cystitis) or by poisoning.

Symptoms: The animal passes small quantities of urine, very frequently, and it suffers. Its back tends to dip, its mucous tissues darken, and its urine may show signs of blood. An acute attack of uraemia (increase of urea in the blood) is likely to prove fatal.

Treatment: This consists of boosting detoxification of the blood, of assisting the elimination of urine (with serum and diuretics), and of fighting infections by giving antibiotics which will pass through the urinary tract until normal kidney function is re-established.

• Interstitial chronic nephritis. This develops slowly and then strikes suddenly. It is particularly prevalent in older dogs. It can arise from acute nephritis or lifelong poor nutrition. The kidneys do not properly eliminate the wastes that accumulate in the blood.

Symptoms: There is a large amount of very clear urine. The animal suffers from nausea and drinks copiously. Urine and blood analyses confirm the diagnosis.

Treatment: Diet is vitally important. The animal must be given high-quality food, with a minimum of nitrogenous wastes, and must always have access to fresh water.

Nymphomania
A bitch with cysts on the ovaries shows excessive sexual excitement.

Symptoms: There is increased production of oestrogen, and the animal seems to be constantly in heat (with loss of blood from the vulva), but does not conceive.

Treatment: Progesterone injections will bring temporary relief. Ovariectomy provides a permanent solution.

Obesity
In the Western world many dogs suffer from malnutrition arising, not from poverty, but from excess of food. Overweight is a disease of civilization that carries many other problems in its wake, such as hypertension and kidney failure.

Treatment: There are three ways of reducing the weight of an obese dog:

1. Give it more exercise so that it uses up additional calories.

2. Limit its meals.

3. Put it on a low-calorie reducing diet. Your veterinarian will be able to recommend some appropriate ready-to-use diet foods. These are available as dry and wet (canned) products. If you prefer, however, you can use the following recipe, prepared by canine nutritionists.

DAILY RATIONS FOR AN OBESE DOG

Weight of dog		Approximate ration	
2.5 kg	5½ lb	150 g	5¼ oz
5 kg	11 lb	300 g	10½ oz
10 kg	22 lb	450 g	1 lb
20 kg	44 lb	800 g	1¾ lb
30 kg	66 lb	1,125 g	2½ lb
40 kg	88 lb	1,250 g	2¾ lb
50 kg	110 lb	1,450 g	3 lb

110 grams (14½ ounces) of lean, chopped or minced beef

½ cup of white cheese made from skim milk

2 cups of carrots cooked in water and well drained

2 cups of green beans cooked in water and well drained

½ teaspoon of dicalcic phosphate.

Fry the meat until it is lightly browned. Drain off the fat and let the meat cool. Better yet, broil the meat slowly, without burning, and mince it after it has been drained of fat and cooled. Add the other ingredients and sprinkle with mineral and vitamin supplements. Mix well. Makes about 750 grams (1½ pounds).

This is the only food that should be given while the dog is on the diet.

Obstruction of the tear duct
Normally, tears flow from the inner corners of the eyes along the tear ducts to the nose (which they keep moist). After an infection, or because of hereditary degeneration or deformity occurring in some breeds (Poodles, Pekingese, Pomeranians, for example) the tear ducts may be blocked.

Symptoms: Tears run down the cheeks, the coat is dirty, and the skin is irritated.

Treatment: The only really satisfactory treatment is to have the ducts catheterized.

Otitis
The ear can be the site of many troubles, any of which is loosely called otitis.

• Inflammation. This has many origins: infections, foreign bodies, parasites, for example.

Symptoms: The dog scratches the ear that is making it suffer. Brown or blackish deposits accumulate in the ear passage and give off a foul smell. The dog inclines its head towards the side that hurts.

Treatment: Before treating the dog, the cause of the trouble must be found. A veterinarian will examine the ear with an otoscope and then take a bacterial culture (to find out what germs are involved) and an antibiogram (to know which specific antibiotic to use). Nowadays there are so many antibiotic-resistant strains of infection that it is highly impractical to choose an antibiotic at random.

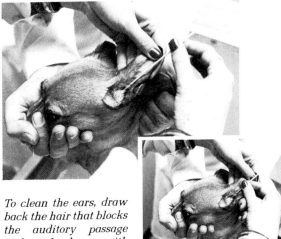

To clean the ears, draw back the hair that blocks the auditory passage and gently cleanse with a cotton swab.

Some dogs whose ears are folded over (Cocker Spaniels, for example) have permanently damp ear passages, and they have a tendency to develop yeast infections there. To relieve the symptoms, rinse the ear passages regularly with a solution of water and a drop of vinegar.

• Foreign bodies in the ear. Such objects as seeds, gravel, and bits of chaff can enter a dog's ear. The animal then scratches ferociously, in great pain. Remove such matter gently, with tweezers, before they pierce the ear-drum.

Otitis can become chronic, since the dog's ear passages bend at right angles to themselves and are difficult to clear. The only remedy is for a veterinarian to carry out La Croix's operation (also known as Hinz's operation) in which the outer wall of the ear passage is removed.

• Haematoma of the ear. If the dog is bitten, or scratches itself violently, the blood vessels of the external part of the ear (the pavilion) may be broken.

Symptoms: A pocket of blood forms between the skin and the cartilage.

Treatment: A veterinary surgeon will have to make a long incision into the skin and the cartilage to drain the blood. Then the ear must be protected with a bandage. Until the wound is completely healed it must be kept covered to prevent the dog from scratching it.

Para-influenza (Kennel cough)

This virus is the cause of serious tracheobronchitis, and usually affects dogs cloistered in large groups (in kennels and grooming establishments, for example).

Symptoms: A dry, noisy cough, easily triggered by pressing on the throat. The illness develops gradually, over the course of several weeks.

Treatment: Sulphonamides stop the cough within two or three weeks. Codeine syrup eases the discomfort.

In some countries a vaccine is available. The serum used against distemper may also be administered. It often contains antibodies which fight against influenza.

Paralysis

Paralysis is characterized by a loss of feeling and movement in one or several muscles after nerve tissue has been crushed or has degenerated. It can be temporary or permanent, in which case the limb atrophies. Among the commonest causes of paralysis are accidents, bandages applied too tightly; tumours, injections, infections, and slipped discs. Physiotherapy is the key to effective healing.

Dachshunds are particularly susceptible to paralysis. The condition occurs when the spinal cord is compressed by a slipped disc or when bony excrescences form.

Treatment: Surgery (laminectomy), undertaken right at the start of the affliction, gives satisfactory results. Drug treatment may also be effective.

Parasites

EXTERNAL PARASITES

• Fleas. These are very common in the summer, and they spread easily from one dog to another. Brownish in colour, they infest the skin rapidly.

Symptoms: The dog scratches to relieve its discomfort. It is the fleas' excrement, however, that provides the strongest evidence of infestation. Check for tiny black dots at the root of the dog's tail.

Treatment: Antiflea shampoo works well, but it must be applied several times. Flea-collars or medallions can be helpful. Their effect, however, is too localized to protect a large dog. Certain aerosols are a radical treatment, but their 'whistling' sound upsets most dogs. Powders are less effective.

The after-effects of having fleas must be carefully treated. These are eczema (because even after the fleas have gone the dog still itches) and tapeworms, an internal parasite transmitted by fleas.

• Ticks. Greyish, oval in shape, from 2 to 10 millimetres (up to $\frac{1}{3}$ inch) in diameter, they adhere to the dog's skin with a sort of beak, through which they suck the dog's blood. Ticks are often discovered while the animal is being groomed. They can transmit piroplasmosis, a serious blood disease.

Treatment: Do not try to pull a tick violently off your dog with eyebrow tweezers; you will not be able to do it. First you must numb the tick with insecticide or a drop of ether, wait until it lets go, then lift it off gently. If the tick's head is still affixed to the dog, disinfect the skin thoroughly and work the head out with a needle, as though you were taking out a splinter. Afterwards, carry out a general de-infestation treatment with an antitick shampoo or aerosol.

A dog-flea magnified

Ticks transmit piroplasmosis

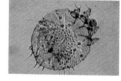

Sarcoptes scabiei, a mange-producer

Trichodectis canis, a blood-sucker

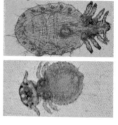

Linognatus setosus, a biting louse

It is a good idea to put a specimen in a bottle of alcohol and have a veterinarian confirm your identification of it.

Ticks are common in the countryside. To prevent attacks, spray the dog regularly with an antitick vapour, or have it wear a protective collar.

• Mange. There are three forms:

1. Otodectic mange, a microscopic parasite transmitted by dogs and cats.

Symptoms: A brownish secretion accumulates in the ear passage.

This infestation produces a great deal of

irritation. The dog scratches violently, and this may cause haematoma of the ear (see Otitis). The problem may result in the dog's losing its balance if the inner ear is damaged. The dog may even go deaf.

Treatment: Clean the ear thoroughly with mineral oil and give ear-drops of benzyl benzoate for two weeks. Antibiotic ear-drops given at the same time will eliminate secondary infection.

2. Demodectic mange does not infest humans. It is usually transmitted by the mother dog and only infests dogs less than one year old. It is best not to become the owner of an infected puppy.

Symptoms: The dog bites itself and scratches violently. Its skin becomes red and scabby, and hair falls out.

Treatment: This is a long and unpredictable condition, often complicated by purulent secondary bacterial infections (*staphylococci*). It is an ordeal for both dog and owner. Recovery comes of its own accord when the dog matures sexually.

3. Sarcoptic mange is very contagious to animals and humans.

Symptoms: Very similar to those of demodectic mange.

Treatment: An ointment to treat the condition should be obtained from your veterinarian.

Note that only an examination under the microscope can distinguish between the second and third types of mange.

• Lice. These are little insects one to three millimetres (1/64 to 3/64 inch) long. There are two types, biters and blood-suckers. Lice prefer the parts of the body where the skin is folded, particularly the ears.

Symptoms: Light infestations cause itching. More serious cases involve loss of hair, sores, anaemia, redness, and physical and nervous exhaustion.

Treatment: Consult your veterinarian for a medicinal aerosol spray. If the dog has a very long coat, it is better to shave it before using the aerosol.

Wherever there are external parasites (fleas, ticks, lice, or mites) you should disinfect the furniture, the carpets, and rugs thoroughly to ensure that the animal does not become reinfested.

INTERNAL PARASITES

If you think your dog has worms, take a sample of its stool to a veterinarian to have the parasites identified by microscopic inspection. Since parasite eggs will not be passed in every bowel movement, supply several stool samples.

A systematic examination of the stool every spring and autumn is a good general rule, as no one medicine will expel all worms. The following are the main types of worm:

• Threadworms (roundworms, ascarids). Adult dogs pick these up by eating grass or dirt. The infestation can propagate itself in the mother's womb towards the end of pregnancy, and then her pups become victims.

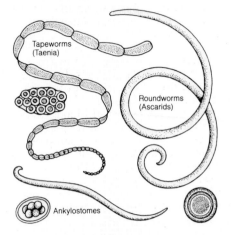

THE PRINCIPAL WORMS
AND THEIR EGGS FOUND IN DOGS

Tapeworms (Taenia)

Roundworms (Ascarids)

Ankylostomes

Symptoms: Threadworms pass through the lungs as they develop. Their journey gives the dog a cough. They become adult in the stomach and digestive system, causing vomiting (often passing spaghetti-like worms), diarrhoea, swelling and hardening of the abdomen, a voracious or irregular appetite, and poor physical development. Children can become infected by contact with the dog's stool.

Treatment: Specific worm-killers (piperazine) to be repeated after two weeks.

• Ankylostomes. These are very difficult to find with the naked eye. The adults are one millimetre (1/64 inch) long. They are acquired from eating on contaminated ground.

Symptoms: They can kill young puppies, which are infected from the womb or by their mother's milk. They cause haemorrhagic diarrhoea, anaemia, weakness, and loss of weight. The dog's environment should be treated, as well as the dog.

Treatment: Specific worm-killers administered at one- to six-week intervals. A vaccine has been developed, and is recommended in heavily infested areas. It is advisable to treat contaminated surfaces with salt and hot water. To understand how virulent this parasite is, consider that the female can lay from 15,000 to 30,000 eggs a day. If the puppy has several hundred worms to start with, it can end up with tens of millions of them in its system.

• Whipworms (trichuris). These are so named because they have a long, thin tail (like the lash of a whip) and a short, thick head (like the rod). They are very tiny, and particularly prevalent in towns and cities. They infest dogs that eat stool or contaminated grass. The whipworm's eggs are covered by a hardy membrane and can remain potentially dangerous for years.

Symptoms: Diarrhoea (black, or with blood), intermittent nausea with abdominal cramps.

Treatment: Specific worm-killers. The main problem is that the eggs live so long, thus the dog must be removed from the infested area and treated for several months.

• Tapeworms (taenia). These look like very long, flat ribbons. Fleas and lice which the dog ingests when it bites itself are common carriers of the infestation.

Symptoms: Irregular appetite, a dry, prickly coat, and occasional diarrhoea. You will notice segments of dried worms, similar in size and shape to grains of rice, near the anus or in the faeces. When these are visible they can be seen to squirm around. Tapeworms can be transmitted to humans.

Treatment: Your veterinarian will prescribe pills or give an injection. It is very important to get rid of the lice and fleas that act as intermediary hosts.

• Heartworms (filaria). These are very thin, spaghetti-like worms which can measure up to 30 centimetres (12 inches). They install themselves in the heart, develop in the blood vessels, and end their adult phase in the right ventricle and the pulmonary artery. They cause serious damage to the lungs and liver, sometimes resulting in death. This is a disease of hot climates, transmitted from one dog to another by mosquitoes.

Symptoms: Breathing difficulties, accumulation of fluid in the abdomen (ascites), and chronic cardiac insufficiency. Diagnosis is made by means of blood analysis.

Treatment: Intravenous injections of arsenical solutions (but there is danger of embolism). In extreme cases open-heart surgery is required. Nothing can equal preventive injections of diethyl carmabenzyle (D.E.C.) given every day and continued until two months after the dog has been exposed to infection. Begin the treatment thirty days before the onset of the mosquito season.

• Coccidia. These are minute parasites, detectable only with a microscope, which infest the digestive system. The illness is picked up at poorly maintained kennels and breeding establishments. It attacks mainly young puppies.

Symptoms: Violent diarrhoea, blood and mucus in the stool, dehydration, and a depressed condition.

This illness ceases of its own accord when the dog becomes adult, but the animal will continue to show coccidia eggs in its stool for months.

Treatment: Sulphonamide pills for several weeks.

Parvovirus

This serious disease has come to attention only in recent years.

Symptoms: A profuse brownish or haemorrhagic diarrhoea, loss of appetite, and rapid dehydration. If the dog is not treated very quickly it may die within 24 hours.

Treatment: The sick dog may recover if it receives good supportive treatment: plenty of serum, antibiotics, and so on. Various vaccines have appeared on the market. The best seems to be an attenuated live virus of canine derivation. Yearly vaccinations are recommended.

Prolapse

Two organs can sometimes slip out of their proper locations: the uterus, after an *accouchement*, and the intestines, during violent contractions.

Treatment: Do not let the organ become dry; coat it with petroleum jelly. Try to replace it section by section into the abdomen, and hold it in place with gauze and bandages.

Take the animal to a veterinarian right away. Surgical treatment is nearly always needed.

Prostatitis

This is an inflammation and swelling of the prostate gland which often results from hormonal imbalance. It affects male dogs five or more years old.

Symptoms: Abdominal pain, difficulty urinating, and even constipation. Diagnosis is made by palpating the rectum. Sometimes the condition is discovered when it is difficult to insert the thermometer into the anus.

Treatment: Hormone (oestradiol) injections. Obviously, castration is a radical solution which prevents any recurrence.

Rabies

This terrible, dangerous scourge for all warm-blooded animals, including man, can be found virtually throughout the world. Rabies exists in two forms:

• The raging form. The dog bites everything, even inedible things such as wood, stone, and metal. It attacks anything that moves, and mutilates itself. The least sound excites it and makes it bark.

• The dumb or paralytic form. The animal's jaw muscles are paralysed. It neither eats nor drinks. Since it cannot swallow its saliva, it foams at the mouth. It is racked by spasms, always agitated, and experiences frenzied genital activity.

A rabid animal must be terminated. But it is difficult to know in advance whether the animal is rabid or not. Certainly it must be isolated, but the decision to have it destroyed can be made only after seeing the illness evolve. The final diagnosis can be made after the brain has been examined during the autopsy. It is best to confirm the diagnosis before treating humans bitten by the sick dog because rabies vaccines can be dangerous.

Symptoms: Ten to 60 days after being bitten by a rabid animal, the dog shows an obvious change of character (the virus attacks the nervous system). A usually agitated, aggressive dog may become calm and timid, or a gentle animal may become an unpredictable biter.

Treatment: If your animal is bitten by an animal suspected of having rabies, wash the wound with soap and disinfect it. Take the dog as soon as you can to a veterinarian to be vaccinated (if it has not already been) or to have a booster shot. The vaccine is very effective if it is administered at once.

If it is shown that the animal that bit the dog was rabid, the infected dog will be destroyed, unless it can be proved that it has been vaccinated.

Antirabies vaccination is carried out after the age of three months. It involves two injections from two to four weeks apart, and a regular booster shot. This is legally compulsory in afflicted areas, for crossing international borders, and in boarding kennels.

Rickets (Rachitis)
This disease occurs in young, growing dogs suffering from a shortage of minerals, vitamin D, or both.

Symptoms: The limbs are deformed and twisted at the joints.

Treatment: Large doses of vitamin D, phosphorus, and calcium. The deformities are permanent. The best prevention is a mineral supplement given to puppies and gestating bitches.

Ringworm (Tinea)
Ringworm develops on the skin after contact with an infected dog or human.

Symptoms: Loss of the coat in small round patches, starting on the face and then little by little spreading over the whole body.

Treatment: Antifungal and antibiotic pills for 40 days and daily application of tolnaphtate ointment to the affected areas.

It is important to prevent humans and other animals from coming into contact with the afflicted dog; a sick animal can remain contagious for several months or even years.

Rubarth's disease, see Infectious hepatitis.

Ringworm, caused by Microsporum canis, *develops on the skin and is highly contagious.*

Sunburn (Solar dermatitis)
Some dogs, such as Collies, are prone to sunburn on the tips of their noses because they lack protective pigmentation there to block out ultraviolet rays.

Symptoms: A scab forms because the dog scratches, and this sore can become infected.

Treatment: Disinfect the sore, and then apply an antibiotic and cortisone ointment. Keep the dog out of the sun. Have the unpigmented part of the tip of the nose tattooed black.

Torsion and distention of the stomach
After a meal followed by vigorous exercise, a large dog's stomach may undergo a torsion-like constriction, twisting as much as 180 degrees—in some cases more.

Symptoms: Intense abdominal pain, exhaustion, acute swelling of the abdomen (which fills with gas), salivation, panting, and then shock. The illness develops quickly and the animal may die within hours.

Treatment: The animal must be rushed to a veterinarian, who will put the stomach back in place surgically. Prevention is essential—don't let large dogs romp after a big meal.

Tuberculosis
This is caused by Koch's bacillus. It is rare in dogs, although humans or cattle can serve as transmitters, and vice versa.

Symptoms: This illness appears in several forms:
• Tuberculosis of the skin. Chronic ulceration, deep and often festering, on the skin of the head and neck.
• Tuberculosis of the lungs. Loss of weight, difficulty in breathing, chronic cough, and swelling of the lymph nodes.
• Tuberculosis of the abdomen. Abdominal pain, accumulation of fluid in the abdominal cavity (ascites), and sometimes symptoms of hepatitis. This illness may turn into a diffused peritonitis.

Treatment: Diagnosis is only possible through chest X-rays, bacterial cultures, or positive reactions to laboratory tests. Because of the danger to public health, tubercular dogs have to be destroyed. Their owners should be examined by a doctor.

Tumours
There are two sorts of tumour:
• Benign tumours. These are mainly on the skin, like warts. Their edges are well defined. They have little tendency to spread to other tissues (they are non-transferring). If observed early, they can be removed surgically without danger.
• Malignant tumours. These develop at the expense of the organs, and can metastasize (that is, spread themselves throughout the organism). If they are diagnosed in time they can be contained within limits and removed surgically (breast cancers, for example).

The other common methods of treatment (chemotherapy, radiotherapy) can be applied to dogs with the same degree of success as on humans, but are not in everyday use. Early detection is essential.

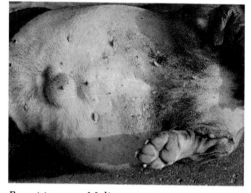

Breast tumour. Malignant tumours can metastasize, or spread. When diagnosed very early, they can be removed by surgery.

Warts. These are benign tumours whose edges are clearly defined. They can be removed without danger by surgery.

Vaginal discharges

A bitch can lose blood or mucus through the vulva, usually when in heat. There may be suppurating discharges in cases of vaginitis, cystitis, or uterine infections, any of which requires a veterinarian's care.

Vomiting

Throwing up food enables a dog to eliminate bones, poisons, and rotten food from its stomach. Sometimes a dog will even eat grass as an emetic. There are many causes of vomiting: indigestion, sudden changes in diet, poisoning, foreign bodies, infectious illnesses, nephritis, travel sickness, peritonitis, liver upsets, pharyngeal inflammmation, tonsillitis, parasites, tumours, or pressure on the oesophagus.

Treatment: To alleviate non-specific vomiting that is clearly not a symptom of poisoning, put the dog on a 36-hour fast. Give it milk of bismuth (one teaspoonful for each 10 kilograms, or 22 pounds, of body weight every 15 minutes) or even a few teaspoonfuls of sodium citrate. Make it drink very small quantities so as not to irritate the stomach. Keep the dog warm and calm. When the vomiting stops, feed it on small quantities of boiled, lean meat six times a day, then return it gradually to its normal diet. If the vomiting persists, get in touch with your veterinarian. Some dogs vomit and foam at the mouth on car journeys. Have the dog fast in this case and, two hours before setting out, give it a tranquillizer.

Radical treatment for rabies. *Sixteenth-century engraving. 'Herbs of Dioscorides.'*

Kennel Clubs

Overview of Kennel Clubs

Wherever dogs work for man or keep him company there are organizations set up to protect the interests of both animal and owner. These are kennel clubs—variously known as kennel unions, councils, dog clubs, and canine societies. Although the characters of these organizations, from the Australian National Kennel Council to the Fédération cynologique internationale, differ somewhat, their functions are similar. Their duties include:

Recognizing breeds. Each kennel club publishes a register of breeds that are eligible for prizes at dog competitions. Criteria for gaining official kennel club recognition vary greatly from country to country.

Maintaining breed registries. Owners of pedigreed dogs file papers that delineate their dogs' parentage. If the application is approved, the owner is issued a certificate of registration. It is often more difficult to register a dog than it is to register a baby.

Compiling stud books. This record of the breeding particulars of a country's recognized breeds traces ancestries from generations ago to the present.

Establishing breed standards. These detailed descriptions of the ideal dog, breed by breed, are the basis for choosing winners at dog competitions.

Sponsoring dog shows and trials. Strict procedures and skilled judging at championship shows and outdoor competitions ensure that the titles awarded are meritorious—and merited. Dogs awarded championship titles can command high stud fees, and considerable prices for their litters.

Approving of judges. Judges at any competition must be thoroughly knowledgeable about the breed or breeds they are judging. To qualify as a judge, an individual must generally attend training sessions, take a written or verbal examination, act as an observer at shows, and also judge at non-championship shows, such as open shows in Great Britain and sanction matches in Canada.

Each national kennel club accepts as members or affiliates canine clubs devoted to one or several breeds, which in turn sponsor their own competitions. The Great Joint Dachshund Association in Britain, for example, offers numerous cups and trophies at its championship shows, enabling Dachshund owners to gain many more awards for their dogs than would be possible at all-breed shows. Some independent breed clubs, such as for Harriers and for Jack Russell Terriers in Britain, set their own breed standards.

Although most competitions under kennel club auspices are the championship (also called conformation) shows where a dog's appearance is paramount, outdoor competitions are increasingly popular. These test dogs' skills at hunting (in field trials), at following commands (obedience trials), at working (herding trials), at following scents (tracking), and in gamesmanship (lure-coursing and scent hurdle-racing). Here, only performance counts, and dogs are not examined for conformity to breed standards.

Judging Steps at Championship Shows

Several thousand dogs may be entered at one championship show to be judged on their conformity to breed standards in order to win prestigious titles. To winnow out one dog for 'Best in Show' requires a high degree of organization and a number of judging steps. The largest championship shows in English-speaking countries subscribe to the following order:

Step one is to take all the entries for a given breed and subdivide them by sex and class (generally, age).

Step two is to choose a Best of Class, by sex.

Step three is where the best dogs from each class, per breed, compete for the title Best of Sex.

Step four brings the best male and female of a breed together in a run-off for Best of Breed. In some countries, this is where champions of record first compete directly with aspiring champions. At this point, too, dogs in Australia, Britain, and South Africa are entitled to be promoted for Challenge Certificates.

Step five sees the best of all breeds within a given group challenge each other for Best of Group.

Step six pits the best dogs of their groups against each other for the prestigious accolade, Best in Show.

Fédération cynologique internationale

The Fédération cynologique internationale, better known as the F.C.I., is a worldwide federation of national dog clubs. Its objective is to bring international uniformity to the breeding, exhibiting, and judging of pure-bred dogs.

Founded in May, 1911, the original F.C.I. was wholly European. Membership consisted of dog organizations representing France, Belgium, Germany, Austria, and Holland. Headquarters were in Belgium, as they still are:

Fédération cynologique internationale
Rue Leopold-II
14B-6530 Thuin
Belgium

Since then, the F.C.I. has grown, spreading to every continent. Today its membership includes delegates from 19 European countries, 12 Latin American, 2 Asian, and 1 from Africa. An additional 11 countries (among them, Great Britain and South Africa) are affiliated as associate members, while others maintain informal contacts.

Over 300 breeds are on the F.C.I.'s official roster—twice the number of breeds recognized by either Canada or Australia. This is because the F.C.I. automatically recognizes all the registered breeds of its member countries. Its list, therefore, includes many dogs known only within their countries of origin. The Fila Brasileiro, for example, is a breed developed in Brazil by Portuguese settlers several centuries ago. Thought to be a mixture of Mastiff, Bloodhound, and Bulldog, and reputed to be an aggressive guard dog, it is seldom seen outside its homeland.

Unique to the F.C.I. is that the breed standards it approves are those drawn up in a dog's country of origin. This assures uniformity among competing specimens at shows, making it far easier for a dog from, say, France to win at a show held in Germany. Another unique feature is that member countries may refuse to register any dog showing genetic flaws or any animal which does not conform to approved breed standards. This feature obliges breeders to eliminate hereditary defects and serves to heighten the value of any registered dog.

Two types of shows are held under F.C.I. auspices: the national and the international. It is the country where the show or trial is held that determines the judging system—that is, the rules for selecting and rating winners.

The federation's two international titles are International Working Trial Champion and International Beauty Champion, both based on accumulating either one or two types of *certificats d'aptitude* (aptitude certificates) and prizes in several countries under several judges. To become a national champion, a dog must be awarded a third type of certificate, three times, under at least two different judges.

Despite its size and prominence, the F.C.I. is little known in English-speaking countries, where long-standing and prestigious canine organizations are firmly established. Furthermore, strict quarantine laws in some English-speaking nations— a dog is quarantined for six months in Great Britain and sometimes up to nine months in Australia—discourage all but the most determined and wealthy dog owners from crossing borders to exhibit their dogs. And some of the F.C.I.'s regulations are controversial: Although the principle of making country-of-origin breed standards universal may seem to be sensible and straightforward, innumerable breeders with large investments in their breeding stock would find themselves with dogs too big, or too small, or wrongly coloured to qualify for F.C.I. registration. Many dog fanciers, moreover, disapprove of the F.C.I.'s lengthy registry list, saying that it includes too many dogs of doubtful or disputed lineage.

F.C.I. GROUPS

Dogs recognized by the F.C.I. are categorized by groups and then as to whether they must undertake working trials to qualify for championship titles. Here are the names of those groups and of familiar breeds within each:

Herding and Shepherd Dogs: Old English Sheepdog (non-working).

Watch-dogs and Working Dogs: Boxer (working); Newfoundland (non-working).

Terriers: Airedale (working); Staffordshire Bull (non-working).

Dachshunds: Miniature; Standard (all working).

Hounds for Big Game: Bloodhound (working); Norwegian Elkhound (non-working).

Hounds for Small Game: Beagle (working); Basenji (non-working).

Pointers (except British breeds): Weimaraner; Brittany (all working).

British Gun Dogs: English Setter (working); American Cocker Spaniel (non-working).

Companion Dogs: Chow Chow; Mexican Hairless (all non-working).

Coursing Dogs: Deerhound; Whippet (all non-working).

Australian National Kennel Council

Each of the eight Australian states and territories has its own canine society, but the controlling body is the Australian National Kennel Council (A.N.K.C.), established in 1958. It is this organization's mandate to propose uniform policies and procedures for all Australia, although member societies are not compelled to adopt any resolutions. On the whole, however, there are only minor administrative variations among the societies, and reciprocal agreements ensure that champion dogs within one state are recognized in the others.

Australian National Kennel Council
Royal Agricultural Society
Epsom Road, Ascot Vale
Victoria, Australia 3032

The Melbourne Royal Show, held each September, is the country's most prestigious dog show. It attracts some 7,000 entries and ranks among the world's largest conformation shows. Another championship show, the Royal Easter Show, held in Sydney, is also one of the world's biggest, accepting some 4,500 entries. Both have been staged since the late 1800s.

A dog competing at a championship show is initially entered in a class for its particular breed, age, and sex. When classes overlap, exhibitors can enter their dogs where the animals are most likely to win. The major show classes are:

Baby puppies: 4 to 6 months old.
Minor puppies: 6 to 9 months old.
Puppy class: 6 to 12 months old.
Junior class: 6 to 18 months old.
Intermediate class: 18 months to 3 years old.
Australian-bred class: 6 months and over, born in Australia.
Open class: any eligible dog, generally a mature one.

Ear-cropping is illegal in Australia, and the A.N.K.C. publicizes the fact that dogs with cropped ears are not eligible for registration or exhibition.

The judging system in Australia is based on points, and these are accrued when a dog wins Best of Sex, and thereon up. The number of points reflects the number of competitors over which a dog has won, although minimum and maximum limits are set. Dogs are judged by breed standards approved by the Kennel Club (Britain), except for breeds of Australian origin whose standards have been established by the A.N.K.C. The highest championship title is that of breed champion. To attain it, a dog must accumulate a total of 100 points and earn four Challenge Certificates (C.C.s), which are awarded to each breed's two Best of Sex winners at championship shows. Each certificate includes a statement, signed by the judge, that the dog warrants the title Champion. Yet the awarding of C.C.s is discretionary; winning Best of Sex does not assure a dog a C.C.

THE NEW ZEALAND KENNEL CLUB

The New Zealand Kennel Club operates almost identically to the A.N.K.C. Its breed standards are the same and its shows, although much smaller, follow virtually the same rules. Australian dogs may enter New Zealand and vice versa without going into quarantine whereas dogs from the United Kingdom are quarantined for two months; dogs from most other countries remain in quarantine for nine months. The largest New Zealand show, attracting some 3,000 entries, is the Fido Show, in Wellington.

New Zealand Kennel Club
Private Bag, Porirua
New Zealand

Official Breeds

The following list is a reproduction—by name and by group—of the A.N.K.C. breed registry. A total of 166 breeds are recognized by this club.

TOY GROUP
Affenpinscher
Australian Silky Terrier
Bichon Frise
Cavalier King Charles Spaniel
Chihuahua (Long coat)
Chihuahua (Smooth coat)
Chinese Crested Dog
English Toy Terrier (Black & Tan)
Griffon Bruxellois
Italian Greyhound
Japanese Chin
King Charles Spaniel
Lowchen
Maltese
Miniature Pinscher
Papillon
Pekingese
Pomeranian
Pug
Tibetan Spaniel
Yorkshire Terrier

TERRIER GROUP
Airedale Terrier
American Staffordshire Terrier
Australian Terrier
Bedlington Terrier
Border Terrier
Bull Terrier
Bull Terrier (Miniature)

Cairn Terrier
Dandie Dinmont Terrier
Fox Terrier (Smooth)
Fox Terrier (Wire)
Glen of Immal Terrier
Irish Terrier
Jack Russell Terrier
Kerry Blue Terrier
Lakeland Terrier
Manchester Terrier
Norfolk Terrier
Norwich Terrier
Parson Jack Russell Terrier
Scottish Terrier
Sealyham Terrier
Skye Terrier
Soft-coated Wheaten Terrier
Staffordshire Bull Terrier
Welsh Terrier
West Highland White Terrier

GUN DOG GROUP
Brittany
Chesapeake Bay Retriever
Clumber Spaniel
Cocker Spaniel
Cocker Spaniel (American)
Curly Coated Retriever
English Setter
English Springer Spaniel
Field Spaniel
Flat-Coated Retriever
German Short-haired Pointer
German Wire-haired Pointer
Golden Retriever
Gordon Setter
Hungarian Vizsla
Irish Red and White Setter
Irish Setter
Irish Water Spaniel
Italian Spinone
Labrador Retriever
Large Munsterlander
Nova Scotia Duck Tolling Retriever
Pointer
Sussex Spaniel
Weimaraner
Welsh Springer Spaniel

HOUND GROUP
Afghan Hound
Basenji
Basset Hound
Beagle
Bloodhound
Borzoi
Dachshund (Long-haired)
Dachshund (Smooth-haired)
Dachshund (Wire-haired)
Dachshund (Miniature Long-haired)
Dachshund (Miniature Smooth-haired)
Dachshund (Miniature Wire-haired)
Deerhound
Elkhound
Finnish Spitz
Foxhound
Greyhound
Hamiltonstövare
Harrier
Ibizan Hound
Irish Wolfhound
Otterhound
Petit Basset Griffon Vendeen
Pharaoh Hound
Rhodesian Ridgeback

Saluki
Sloughi
Whippet

WORKING GROUP
Anatolian Shepherd Dog
Australian Cattle Dog
Australian Kelpie
Bearded Collie
Belgian Shepherd Dog (Groenendael)
Belgian Shepherd Dog (Laekenois)
Belgian Shepherd Dog (Malinois)
Belgian Shepherd Dog (Tervueren)
Border Collie
Bouvier des Flandres
Briard
Collie (Rough)
Collie (Smooth)
German Shepherd Dog
Hungarian Puli
Maremma Sheep-dog
Norwegian Buhund
Old English Sheepdog
Polish Lowland Sheep-dog
Shetland Sheep-dog
Stumpytail Cattle Dog
Swedish Vallhund
Welsh Corgi (Cardigan)
Welsh Corgi (Pembroke)

UTILITY GROUP
Akita
Alaskan Malamute
Bernese Mountain Dog
Boxer
Bullmastiff
Dobermann
German Pinscher
Komondor
Leonberger
Mastiff
Neapolitan Mastiff
Newfoundland
Portuguese Water-dog
Pyrenean Mountain Dog
Rottweiler
St. Bernard
Samoyed
Schnauzer
Schnauzer (Giant)
Schnauzer (Miniature)
Shiba Inu
Siberian Husky
Tibetan Mastiff

NON-SPORTING GROUP
Boston Terrier
British Bulldog
Chow Chow
Dalmatian
French Bulldog
German Spitz
Great Dane
Japanese Spitz
Keeshond
Lhasa Apso
Poodle (Miniature)
Poodle (Standard)
Poodle (Toy)
Schipperke
Shar Pei
Shih Tzu
Tibetan Terrier

Canadian Kennel Club

The first North American dog show took place in Québec City, Canada, in 1867. Twenty years of exhibitions followed, all locally run, until 1884, when the American Kennel Club (A.K.C.) was formed. Its rules and regulations prevailed in North America for four years until Canadian dog owners determined to set up their own club. Since that time, the Canadian Kennel Club (C.K.C.) has had a good working relationship with the A.K.C. The two clubs recognized then, as they do to this day, each other's judges and stud books. They share similar judging systems, many of the same regulations, and most of the same breed standards.

The Canadian (and American) judging system is based on points. To be a Canadian Champion, a dog must accumulate ten points under at least three different judges at shows held under C.K.C. regulations. Points are awarded according to the number of dogs in competition and are handed out to each Best of Sex winner. Additional points may be earned, to a limit of five at any one show, should the dog then place first, second, third, or fourth in its group or go on to win Best in Show. The C.K.C. co-ordinates some 1,500 dog events

yearly, and local clubs flourish throughout Canada.

Unique among canine clubs, the C.K.C. is responsible to the federal government for the registering of pedigreed animals. Stringent regulations penalize, by law, anyone who sells a 'pure-bred' puppy which is not registered or eligible for registration with the C.K.C. Pedigreed dogs, moreover, must be identified on their registration forms either by tattoo or by microchip implant.

Canadian Kennel Club
100 Skyway Avenue
Etobicoke, Ontario M9W 6R4

It is more difficult in Canada than in many countries to gain official recognition for a particular breed. For the federal Minister of Agriculture's approval, the C.K.C. must prove that both its members and Canadian breeders of the specific breed have been consulted in writing. Ministerial approval will depend on a majority of breeders voting for recognition of the breed, and proof that at least 25 percent of C.K.C. members responded to the poll and that two out of three respondents wanted the breed recognized.

Official Breeds

The following list shows the breeds registered with the C.K.C. Some of the more than 160 miscellaneous breeds recognized by the C.K.C. are listed at the end.

SPORTING GROUP
Braque Français
Griffon (Wire-haired Pointing)
Pointer
Pointer (German Long-haired)
Pointer (German Short-haired)
Pointer (German Wire-haired)
Pudelpointer
Retriever (Chesapeake Bay)
Retriever (Curly-coated)
Retriever (Flat-coated)
Retriever (Golden)
Retriever (Labrador)
Retriever (Nova Scotia Duck Tolling)
Setter (English)
Setter (Gordon)
Setter (Irish)
Spaniel (American Cocker)
Spaniel (American Water)
Spaniel (Brittany)
Spaniel (Clumber)
Spaniel (English Cocker)
Spaniel (English Springer)
Spaniel (Field)
Spaniel (French)
Spaniel (Irish Water)
Spaniel (Sussex)
Spaniel (Welsh Springer)
Tahltan Bear Dog
Vizsla (Smooth)
Vizsla (Wire-haired)
Weimaraner

HOUND GROUP
Afghan Hound
Basenji
Basset Hound
Beagle
Bloodhound
Borzoi
Coonhound (Black & Tan)
Dachshund (Miniature Long-haired)
Dachshund (Miniature Smooth)
Dachshund (Miniature Wire-haired)
Dachshund (Standard Long-haired)
Dachshund (Standard Smooth)
Dachshund (Standard Wire-haired)
Deerhound (Scottish)
Drever
Finnish Spitz
Foxhound (American)
Foxhound (English)
Greyhound
Harrier
Ibizan Hound
Norwegian Elkhound
Otterhound
Petit Basset Griffon Vendeen

Pharaoh Hound
Rhodesian Ridgeback
Saluki
Whippet
Wolfhound (Irish)

WORKING GROUP
Akita
Alaskan Malamute
Bernese Mountain Dog
Boxer
Bullmastiff
Canaan Dog
Canadian Eskimo Dog
Dobermann Pinscher
Great Dane
Great Pyrenees
Karelian Bear Dog
Komondor
Kuvasz
Leonberger
Mastiff
Newfoundland
Portuguese Water-dog
Rottweiler
St. Bernard
Samoyed
Schnauzer (Giant)
Schnauzer (Standard)
Siberian Husky

TERRIER GROUP
Airedale Terrier
American Staffordshire Terrier
Australian Terrier
Bedlington Terrier
Border Terrier
Bull Terrier
Bull Terrier (Miniature)
Cairn Terrier
Dandie Dinmont Terrier
Fox Terrier (Smooth)
Fox Terrier (Wire)
Irish Terrier
Kerry Blue Terrier
Lakeland Terrier
Manchester Terrier
Norfolk Terrier
Norwich Terrier
Schnauzer (Miniature)
Scottish Terrier
Sealyham Terrier
Skye Terrier
Soft-coated Wheaten Terrier
Staffordshire Bull Terrier
Welsh Terrier
West Highland White Terrier

TOY GROUP
Affenpinscher
Cavalier King Charles Spaniel

Chihuahua (Long-coat)
Chihuahua (Short-coat)
Chinese Crested
English Toy Spaniel
Griffon (Brussels)
Italian Greyhound
Japanese Spaniel
Maltese
Mexican Hairless
Papillon
Pekingese
Pinscher (Miniature)
Pomeranian
Poodle (Toy)
Pug
Silky Terrier
Toy Manchester Terrier
Yorkshire Terrier

NON-SPORTING GROUP
Bichon Frise
Boston Terrier
Bulldog
Chinese Shar Pei
Chow Chow
Dalmatian
French Bulldog
Japanese Spitz
Keeshond
Lhasa Apso
Poodle (Miniature)
Poodle (Standard)
Schipperke
Shih Tzu
Shiba Inu
Tibetan Spaniel
Tibetan Terrier

HERDING GROUP
Australian Cattle Dog
Australian Shepherd
Bearded Collie
Belgian Sheepdog
Berger des Pyrénées
Berger Picard
Bouvier des Flandres
Briard
Collie (Rough)
Collie (Smooth)
German Shepherd Dog
Old English Sheepdog
Puli
Shetland Sheep-dog
Welsh Corgi (Cardigan)
Welsh Corgi (Pembroke)

MISCELLANEOUS CLASS
Border Collie
Irish Red and White Setter
Soft-Coated Griffon
Tyrolean Hound

AMERICAN KENNEL CLUB

Known familiarly as the A.K.C., the American Kennel Club is the largest canine organization in the world. From its headquarters in New York City, the club licenses and oversees championship shows, field trials, and obedience tests in all 50 states. More than 2,000 championship shows are held annually under A.K.C. auspices.

Like Canada, the United States is one of the few Western countries where quarantines are seldom imposed on imported dogs. Thus it is in North America that breeds verging on extinction stand a particularly good chance of being revived. The A.K.C., however, imposes such rigorous criteria before a breed can be recognized that its official list of dogs numbers only 132.

American Kennel Club
51 Madison Avenue
New York, New York 10010

Kennel Club (Great Britain)

The Kennel Club of Great Britain was founded in 1873. Its impact on the British dog world was immediate, and its influence has never waned since.

The Kennel Club's mandate has been to bring canine societies under a central authority that sets uniform rules for dog shows and trials; to maintain a register for all recognized breeds; to approve the standards by which they are judged; to establish procedures for the future recognition of additional breeds; and to promote the ongoing well-being of Britain's dogs.

Today, more than 1,700 dog clubs and organizations fall under the Kennel Club's jurisdiction, and these in turn sponsor some 7,800 shows and trials.

Its most famous show by far is the Crufts Show, held in Birmingham. Some 20,000 dogs—all previous prize-winners—compete for awards under the gaze of as many as 85,000 spectators, including breeders from around the world.

The Kennel Club has reciprocal arrangements with more than 40 national dog clubs and is an associate member of the Fédération cynologique internationale.

The Kennel Club
1-5 Clarges Street
London WlY 8AB

Most dog fanciers prize the British title Champion above all other countries' titles because it is the most difficult to obtain. To become a breed champion, a dog must earn three Challenge Certificates (C.C.s) from three different judges. And although there are thousands of shows each year, C.C.s—one for the best male and one for the best female of its breed—are won only at a limited number of shows.

Furthermore, the total number of C.C.s available during a show year is based on the number of dogs registered for a given breed during the previous year. The most popular breed, therefore, has the greatest number of C.C.s offered; the least popular, the fewest. For some breeds there may not be enough specimens to warrant any C.C.s. What is more, if a judge believes that a dog is not of championship calibre—despite winning Best of Breed at the show—he or she may withhold the C.C.

To make things even more difficult for the aspiring champion, British shows have no special classes for champions only. This means that title seekers compete with title holders for the Best of Sex award and the coveted C.C. Thus, if a truly superior specimen is shown at every event where C.C.s are offered in its breed, it could take years for a new breed champion to be confirmed.

Official Breeds

The following list is a reproduction—by name and by group—of the Kennel Club breed registry. A total of 192 breeds are recognized by this club.

HOUND GROUP
Afghan Hound
Basenji
Basset Fauve de Bretagne
Basset Hound
Bavarian Mountain Hound
Beagle
Bloodhound
Borzoi
Dachshund (Long-haired)
Dachshund (Miniature Long-haired)
Dachshund (Smooth-haired)
Dachshund (Miniature Smooth-haired)
Dachshund (Wire-haired)
Dachshund (Miniature Wire-haired)
Deerhound
Elkhound
Finnish Spitz
Foxhound
Grand Bassett Griffon Vendéen
Grand Bleu de Gascogne
Greyhound
Hamiltonstovare
Ibizan Hound
Irish Wolfhound
Norwegian Lundehund
Otterhound
Petit Basset Griffon Vendeen
Pharaoh Hound
Rhodesian Ridgeback
Saluki
Segugio Italiano
Sloughi
Whippet

GUN DOG GROUP
Bracco Italiano
Brittany
English Setter
German Long-haired Pointer
German Short-haired Pointer
German Wire-haired Pointer
Gordon Setter
Hungarian Vizsla
Hungarian Wire-haired Vizsla
Irish Red & White Setter
Irish Setter
Italian Spinone
Kooikerhondje
Large Munsterlander
Nova Scotia Duck Tolling Retriever Pointer

Pointer
Retriever (Chesapeake Bay)
Retriever (Curly Coated)
Retriever (Flat Coated)
Retriever (Golden)
Retriever (Labrador)
Small Munsterlander
Spaniel (American Cocker)
Spaniel (American Water)
Spaniel (Clumber)
Spaniel (Cocker)
Spaniel (English Springer)
Spaniel (Field)
Spaniel (Irish Water)
Spaniel (Sussex)
Spaniel (Welsh Springer)
Weimaraner

TERRIER GROUP
Airedale Terrier
Australian Terrier
Bedlington Terrier
Border Terrier
Bull Terrier
Bull Terrier (Miniature)
Cairn Terrier
Cesky Terrier
Dandie Dinmont Terrier
Fox Terrier (Smooth)
Fox Terrier (Wire)
Glen of Imaal Terrier
Irish Terrier
Jack Russell Terrier
Kerry Blue Terrier
Lakeland Terrier
Manchester Terrier
Norfolk Terrier
Norwich Terrier
Scottish Terrier
Sealyham Terrier
Skye Terrier
Soft-coated Wheaten Terrier
Staffordshire Bull Terrier
Welsh Terrier
West Highland White Terrier

UTILITY GROUP
Boston Terrier
Bulldog
Canaan Dog
Chow Chow
Dalmatian
French Bulldog
German Spitz (Klein)
German Spitz (Mittel)
Japanese Akita
Japanese Shiba Inu
Japanese Spitz
Keeshond
Leonberger
Lhasa Apso
Mexican Hairless
Miniature Schnauzer
Poodle (Miniature)
Poodle (Standard)
Poodle (Toy)
Schipperke
Schnauzer
Shar Pei
Shih Tzu
Tibetan Spaniel
Tibetan Terrier

WORKING GROUP
Alaskan Malamute
Anatolian Shepherd Dog

Australian Cattle Dog
Australian Kelpie
Bearded Collie
Belgian Shepherd Dog (Groenendael)
Belgian Shepherd Dog (Laekenois)
Belgian Shepherd Dog (Malinois)
Belgian Shepherd Dog (Tervueren)
Bergamasco
Bernese Mountain Dog
Border Collie
Bouvier des Flandres
Boxer
Briard
Bullmastiff
Collie (Rough)
Collie (Smooth)
Continental Landseer
Dobermann
Eskimo Dog
Estrela Mountain Dog
Finnish Lapphund
German Shepherd Dog (Alsatian)
Giant Schnauzer
Great Dane
Hovawart
Hungarian Kuvasz
Hungarian Puli
Komondor
Lancashire Heeler
Maremma Sheep-dog
Mastiff
Neapolitan Mastiff
Newfoundland
Norwegian Buhund
Old English Sheepdog
Pinscher
Polish Lowland Sheep-dog
Portuguese Water-dog
Pyrenean Mountain Dog
Pyrenean Sheep-dog
Rottweiler
St. Bernard
Samoyed
Shetland Sheep-dog
Siberian Husky
Swedish Lapphund
Swedish Vallhund
Tibetan Mastiff
Welsh Corgi (Cardigan)
Welsh Corgi (Pembroke)

TOY GROUP
Affenpinscher
Australian Silky Terrier
Bichon Frise
Bolognese
Cavalier King Charles Spaniel
Chihuahua (Long Coat)
Chihuahua (Smooth Coat)
Chinese Crested
Coton du Tulear
English Toy Terrier (Black & Tan)
Griffon Bruxellois
Italian Greyhound
Japanese Chin
King Charles Spaniel
Lowchen
Maltese
Miniature Pinscher
Papillon
Pekingese
Pomeranian
Pug
Yorkshire Terrier

Kennel Union of Southern Africa

The Kennel Union of Southern Africa (K.U.S.A.) was the brain-child of regional dog club representatives who saw the need to organize their country's proliferating canine organizations under one umbrella group. To this end, delegates from dog clubs in Cape Town, Cradock, East London, Grahamstown, Port Elizabeth, and the Transvaal formed an affiliation in 1895 known as the South African Kennel Club. This was later renamed the Kennel Union of Southern Africa.

Today, K.U.S.A. oversees the operations of some 150 affiliated clubs. These clubs in turn sponsor more than 200 shows and trials. Most of K.U.S.A.'s approved breed standards are those issued by Britain's Kennel Club. Where the Kennel Club publishes no standards, or does not recognize a breed, K.U.S.A. usually follows standards set by the Fédération cynologique internationale.

> Kennel Union of Southern Africa
> Box 2659
> Cape Town 8000
> South Africa

A champion South African dog wins its title by accumulating Challenge Certificates (C.C.s) awarded at the Best of Sex judging stage to both the winning dog and the runner-up (called Reserve Best of Sex). To this extent, South Africa's judging system resembles that of Great Britain. It differs, however, in that the title Champion (Ch.) is earned on points, not on the number of C.C.s. Awarded at the judge's discretion, a C.C. can be worth one or two points; the Reserve C.C. is worth one-third of a point. Five points are needed in order to become a champion. It is, thus, somewhat easier to win the 'Ch.' prefix in South Africa than in Britain.

K.U.S.A. specifies 4 classes as compulsory for championship shows and another 16 as optional. Mandatory classes divide entries by age, except for the Open class, which any dog can enter. The addition of optional classes to a show gives an exhibitor the opportunity to place his or her dog in the division that offers the least competition. In this way, an unexceptional animal stands a chance to, at least, place in the show. There may well be several options. For example, the exhibitor of a dog that has never been shown may enter that dog in the Local class, for dogs domiciled in the environs of the show; the Maiden class, for dogs that have not won a prize at a championship show; and the Members' class, when the exhibitor is a member of the show-holding club. Dogs are frequently entered in several classes.

Official Breeds

The following list is a reproduction—by name and by group—of the K.U.S.A. breed registry. A total of 186 breeds are recognized by this club.

HOUND GROUP
Afghan Hound
Basenji
Basset Fauve de Bretagne
Basset Griffon Vendeen
Basset Hound
Beagle
Bloodhound
Borzoi
Dachsbracke
Dachshund (Long-haired)
Dachshund (Miniature Long-haired)
Dachshund (Smooth-haired)
Dachshund (Miniature Smooth-haired)
Dachshund (Wire-haired)
Dachshund (Miniature Wire-haired)
Deerhound
Elkhound
Finnish Spitz
Foxhound
Greyhound
Hamiltonstovare
Ibizan Hound
Irish Wolfhound
Otterhound
Petit Basset Griffon Vendeen
Pharaoh Hound
Portuguese Warren Hound
Rhodesian Ridgeback
Saluki
Sloughi
Swiss Laufhund (Jura)
Whippet

GUN DOG GROUP
Brittany
English Setter
German Long-haired Pointer
German Short-haired Pointer
German Wire-haired Pointer
Gordon Setter
Hungarian Vizsla
Hungarian Wire-haired Vizsla
Irish Red & White Setter
Irish Setter
Irish Water Spaniel
Italian Spinone
Large Munsterlander
Nova Scotia Duck Tolling Retriever
Pointer

Pointing Wire-haired Griffon
Retriever (Chesapeake Bay)
Retriever (Curly Coated)
Retriever (Flat Coated)
Retriever (Golden)
Retriever (Labrador)
Small Munsterlander
Spaniel (American Cocker)
Spaniel (American Water)
Spaniel (Clumber)
Spaniel (Cocker)
Spaniel (English Field)
Spaniel (English Springer)
Spaniel (Irish Water)
Spaniel (Sussex)
Spaniel (Welsh Springer)
Weimaraner

TERRIER GROUP
Airedale Terrier
Australian Terrier
Bedlington Terrier
Border Terrier
Bull Terrier
Bull Terrier (Miniature)
Cairn Terrier
Dandie Dinmont Terrier
Fox Terrier (Smooth)
Fox Terrier (Wire)
Glen of Imaal Terrier
Irish Terrier
Kerry Blue Terrier
Lakeland Terrier
Manchester Terrier
Norfolk Terrier
Norwich Terrier
Parson Jack Russell Terrier
Scottish Terrier
Sealyham Terrier
Skye Terrier
Soft-coated Wheaten Terrier
Staffordshire Bull Terrier
Welsh Terrier
West Highland White Terrier

UTILITY GROUP
Boston Terrier
Bulldog
Canaan Dog
Chow Chow
Dalmatian
French Bulldog
Giant Schnauzer
Japanese Akita
Japanese Shiba Inu
Japanese Spitz
Keeshond
Leonberger
Lhasa Apso
Mexican Hairless
Miniature Schnauzer
Poodle (Miniature)
Poodle (Standard)
Poodle (Toy)
Schipperke
Schnauzer
Shar Pei
Shih Tzu
Tibetan Spaniel
Tibetan Terrier

WORKING GROUP
Alaskan Malamute
Anatolian (Karabash) Dog
Appenzeller

Australian Cattle Dog
Australian Kelpie
Bearded Collie
Beauceron
Belgian Shepherd Dog (Groenendael)
Belgian Shepherd Dog (Laekenois)
Belgian Shepherd Dog (Malinois)
Belgian Shepherd Dog (Tervueren)
Bernese Mountain Dog
Border Collie
Bouvier des Flandres
Boxer
Briard
Bullmastiff
Collie (Rough)
Collie (Smooth)
Dobermann
Eskimo Dog
Estrela Mountain Dog
Finnish Lapphund
German Shepherd Dog (Alsatian)
Great Dane
Hovawart
Hungarian Kuvasz
Hungarian Puli
Komondor
Lancashire Heeler
Maremma Sheep-dog
Mastiff
Neapolitan Mastiff
Newfoundland
Norwegian Buhund
Old English Sheepdog
Pinscher
Polish Lowland Sheep-dog
Portuguese Water-dog
Pyrenean Mountain Dog
Pyrenean Sheep-dog
Rottweiler
St. Bernard
Samoyed
Shetland Sheep-dog
Siberian Husky
Swedish Lapphund
Swedish Vallhund
Tibetan Mastiff
Welsh Corgi (Cardigan)
Welsh Corgi (Pembroke)

TOY GROUP
Affenpinscher
Australian Silky Terrier
Bichon Frise
Bolognese
Cavalier King Charles Spaniel
Chihuahua (Long Coat)
Chihuahua (Smooth Coat)
Chinese Crested Dog (Hairless)
Chinese Crested Dog (Powderpuff)
English Toy Terrier (Black & Tan)
Griffon Bruxellois
Italian Greyhound
Japanese Chin
King Charles Spaniel
Lowchen
Maltese
Miniature Pinscher
Papillon
Pekingese
Pomeranian
Pug
Yorkshire Terrier

Glossary

A

Action. The way a dog moves.

Almond eye. Almond-shaped eye rim.

Angulation. The angle formed by joints; particularly at the shoulder, upper arm, elbow, stifle, and hock.

Anus. The outlet of the rectum.

Apple head. A skull that is unusually domed or rounded.

Apron. Long chest hair beneath the neck. Frill.

Arched loin. Prominent musculature at loin.

B

Babbler. A hound that barks though off-trail.

Badger. A fine blend of brown, black, grey, and white hair.

Bad mouth. Any incorrect bite, depending on the breed standard.

Balanced. The appearance of structural harmony for any part of the dog; overall proportions.

Barrel chest. Rounded rib-cage.

Barrel hocks. Outward-turning hocks, causing the feet to turn in.

Basset. A low-set hound (from French, *bas set*).

Bat ear. An erect ear with a broad base; rounded at the top and facing forward.

Bay. The characteristic bark of a hound on the trail.

Beard. Thick, long hair on the under-side of the muzzle.

Beefy. Overdeveloped body.

Belton. A mixture of white and coloured hair.

Benched show. A dog show at which the dogs are restrained to sitting on benches.

Berger. French for sheep-dog.

Best in Show. Top award at dog shows.

Best of Breed. Award at dog shows given to the best specimen of each breed in competition.

Best of Group. Award at dog shows given to the winner of a group competition.

Bird dog. A dog that tracks birds by air scent.

Bitch. A female dog.

Bitchy. A male dog with feminine characteristics.

Bite. The way upper and lower teeth meet.

Blaze. White marking between the eyes and down the nose.

Blocky. A cube-like head.

Bloom. Sheen characteristic of a healthy coat.

Blue. Nearly black.

Blue merle. A mixture of blue, grey, and black hairs.

Bobtail. A dog that has either no tail or one that is docked very short.

Bodied up. Well developed.

Bone. A reference to the substance of a dog's legs: well boned.

Bouvier. French for cattle-dog.

Brace. A pair of dogs.

Bracelets. Rings of hair on a dog's legs left after trimming.

Braque. French for pointer.

Breastbone. Chest bone at front of dog. Sternum.

Breeching. Tan hair on the inner thighs.

Breed standards. Detailed descriptions of breeds against which dogs are judged at dog shows.

Breeding particulars. Background of a dog: sire, dam, date of birth, sex, colour, etc.

Brindle. An even mixture of black hair in lines or bands covering a tan, brown, or grey coat.

Brisket. Breastbone or sternum. Often used synonymously with chest.

Broken colour. Solid colour intersected with another colour.

Broken-up face. Foreface characterized by a receding nose, deep stop, and wrinkles.

Brush. A bushy tail.

Bull neck. Short, thick neck.

Burr. The inside of the ear.

Butterfly nose. A dark nose with some light pigmentation.

Button ear. A short ear that folds forward to cover the burr.

C

Camel back. Arched back. Humped or roached.

Canines. Pointed molars in the upper and lower jaw.

Carpus. Bone just above the foot, similar to the human wrist.

Casting. See Moulting.

Cat-footed. Having short, round, arched foot.

Champion. Title awarded to a show dog which has accumulated a certain amount of points or Championship Certificates, or both, at several dog shows.

Championship Certificate. An award given to Best of Breed winners if a judge considers them worthy of the title Champion.

Championship show. A show at which Championship Certificates or champion points are awarded.

Character. A reference to the individuality of a particular breed: its appearance and temperament.

Cheeky. Round, prominent cheeks that appear thick and protruding.

Chest. Section of the body between the neck and abdomen. Thorax. Brisket.

China eye. A clear blue eye.

Chippendale front. See Fiddle front.

Chiselled. A head that is particularly clean-cut between the eyes.

Chops. Jowls.

Cloddy. Heavy, low, thick-set.

Coarse. Unrefined.

Cobby. Comparatively short between the withers and the hips.

Collar. A marking around the neck.

Conformation show. See Championship show.

Corky. Lively and active.

Couplings. The body from the withers to the hips.

Coursing. Hunting, usually of hare.

Cow hocks. Hocks that turn inwards.

Crank tail. Tail carried down, slightly bending upwards.

Crest. The upper neck where it arches.

Cropping. The trimming of ears.

Cross-breed. A mixed breed. Mongrel.

Croup. The back, from the loin to the hind legs.

Culotte. Longer hair on thighs.

Cushion. The thickness of the upper lip.

Cut up. Arch of the underbelly.

D

Dam. The female parent.

Dappled. Coloured, mottled markings.

Deadgrass. Tan.

Dentition. Number and arrangement of teeth.

Dew-claw. Extra toe on the inside of the leg; virtually useless, it is often removed.

Dewlap. Loose, pendulous skin beneath the throat.

Digits. Toes.

Dish-faced. A type of face characterized by an upward-slanting or concave nasal bone.

Dock. To shorten a tail by cutting.

Dogue. French for mastiff.

Domed. A rounded, convex skull.

Down-faced. Foreface with down-curved nasal bone from the stop to the nose.

Down in pasterns. Pronounced angulation at the pasterns, resulting from weak joints, tendons, or muscles.

Drop ear. A folded, drooping ear; the opposite of an erect ear.

Dry neck. Taut neck skin.

Dudley nose. Flesh-coloured nose.

E

East-west feet. Feet that toe out. Slew feet.

Ectropion. An ailment resulting in outward-turning eyelids.

Entropion. An ailment resulting in inward-turning eyelids.

Épagneul. French for spaniel.

Estrus. The mating period for bitches.

Even bite. When upper and lower teeth meet without overlap.

Ewe neck. Concave curvature of the neckline.

Expression. The impression created by the colour, size, and positioning of the eyes.

Eyeteeth. The upper canines.

F

Fall. Hair that falls over the face.

Fallow. Pale colour, varying from cream to light fawn.

Fangs. The canine teeth.

Fault. Any trait that conflicts with the breed standard.

Fawn. Red-yellow with a brownish cast, of medium brilliance.

Feathering. Fringe.

Femur. The thigh bone—from the hips to the stifle.

Fiddle front. Stance resulting from poor angulation at elbows whereby forefeet turn out, creating violin-like outline. French front. Chippendale front.

Field trial. Outdoors competition for hunting-dogs in which dogs are judged for their tracking, pointing, or retrieving abilities.

Flag. A long tail, carried vertically.

Flare. A blaze that widens towards the skull.

Flat bone. An elliptical rather than round leg bone.

Flat-sided. Ribs that are too flat.

Flecked. Lightly ticked coat.

Flews. Pendulous upper lips.

Flush. To drive birds or other game from cover and force them to take flight.

Flying ears. Any type of ear that sticks out wing-like from the face.

Flying trot. A fast gait when all feet are briefly off the ground.

Forearm. The foreleg between the elbow and pastern.

Foreface. Front of the head. Muzzle.

Forefoot. Front foot.

Foreleg. Front leg from elbow to foot.

Forequarters. Front part of the dog, excluding head and neck.

Foxy. Alert, keen expression. Pointed nose on short foreface and erect ears.

French front. See Fiddle front.

Frill. See Apron.

Frontal bone. Bone over the eyes. Forehead.

Furnishings. Long hair on the head, legs, breechings, and tail.

Furrow. An indentation along the centre of the skull to the stop. Median line.

G

Gait. The manner and rhythm of forward motion —walking, trotting, or running.

Game. Hunted wild birds or animals. Spirited: a game dog is an enthusiastic hunter.

Gay tail. A tail carried particularly high.

Gazehound. A hound that tracks game by sight. Sight-hound.

Gestation. Period from conception to birth; usually about 60 days.

Greyhound. A type of hunting-dog with keen eye-sight and a swift gait.

Griffon. A coarse-haired, terrier-like type of dog.

Grizzle. A mixture of coloured hair with a grey cast.

Grooming. Trimming, combing, and brushing of a dog's coat.

Guard dog. Watch-dog.

Guard hairs. Stiff, long hairs which extend beyond the undercoat.

Gun dog. A dog trained to work with a hunter, usually to find live game and retrieve shot game.

H

Hackney action. Forefeet that lift high.

Hare-footed. Having a long, narrow foot with tight toes.

Hare-pied. A predominantly tan pied coat, resembling the colour of a hare.

Harlequin. Patched or pied coat, usually black on white coloration.

Haunches. Buttocks. Croup.

Haw. The membrane in the inside corner of the eye. Third eyelid. Inner eye.

Haw-eyes. Drooping lower eyelid that exposes conjunctiva or third eyelid.

Hazel. Light brown.

Heat. See Estrus.

Heel. See Hock.

High standing. Tall, long-legged.
Hind foot. Rear foot.
Hip dysplasia. Abnormal hip joint.
Hock. The joint between the second thigh and the pastern. Heel.
Hocks well let down. Relatively short hocks that are close to the ground.
Honourable scars. Scars earned from work.
Hound. A dog that hunts by scent or sight.
Hound-marked. White, tan, and black coloration.
Hund. German for dog.
Husky. A cross-bred sled dog.

I

Inbreeding. The mating of close relatives.
Incisors. Upper and lower front teeth.
Interbreeding. The cross-breeding of dogs of different varieties.
Isabella. Fawn.

K

Kink tail. A tail that is sharply bent.
Knee. See Stifle.

L

Layback. The angle of the shoulder blade when seen from the side. A face with a receding nose.
Leather. Lobe of the outer ear.
Leggy. Legs that are too long.
Level bite. When the upper front teeth meet the lower, edge to edge. Pincer bite.
Level gait. Movement whereby the withers neither rise nor fall.
Linty. Soft-textured coat.
Lion. Tawny.
Lippy. Pendulous or ill-fitting lips.
Liver. Deep brown.
Loaded shoulders. Shoulders that project from the body because of over-developed muscles.
Loin. The portion of the body that straddles the spine between the ribs and the hindquarters.
Long coupled. A long loin.
Lower thigh. See Second thigh.
Lumber. Superfluous flesh.
Lumbering. A ponderous gait.

M

Mane. Long, profuse neck hair.
Mantle. Dark hair on the shoulders, back, and sides.
Markings. Colouring on the coat.
Mask. Dark shading on the face.
Mastiff. A large, strong type of dog with drooping ears and pendulous lips.
Median line. See Furrow.
Merle. Blue-grey with black flecks.
Merle eyes. Brown and blue eyes with a black iris.
Metacarpus. See Pastern.
Metatarsus. See Pastern.
Milk-teeth. First teeth.
Miscellaneous class. A group of dogs where no regular classification is provided.

Mismarks. Coat markings that do not conform to the coloration of the breed.
Mongrel. A dog whose parents are of different breeds.
Moulting. Seasonal shedding of the coat.

O

Oblique shoulders. Shoulders that slope rearwards; well laid back.
Occipital protuberance. A prominent occiput.
Occiput. Top of the skull, located towards the back.
Oestrus. See Estrus.
Open show. A dog show where championship rating is given only to certain breeds.
Otter tail. A round tail coated with short, thick hair that tapers towards the tip from a thick root.
Out at shoulders. When shoulder-blades are pronounced and jut from the body.
Oval chest. A chest more deep than wide.
Overhang. A pronounced brow.
Overshot. A jaw whose upper incisors overlap the bottom incisors. Pig jaw.

P

Pads. Soles of the feet.
Paper foot. A flat foot with thin pads.
Parti-colour. Patches of at least two colours.
Pastern. The region between the carpus and the foot; metacarpus. Rear pastern is the region between the hock and foot; metatarsus.
Pedigree. The written record of a pure-bred dog's lineage.
Pencilling. Black lines.
Pied. Patches of white and another colour.
Pigeon-breast. Protruding breastbone in a narrow chest.
Pig-eye. Small, steely eye.
Pig jaw. See Overshot.
Pile. Dense, soft undercoat.
Pincer bite. See Level bite.
Pluck. See Strip.
Plume. Long fringe on the tail.
Point. The immobile stance taken by a hunting-dog to indicate the location of game.
Pointer. A hunting-dog that points.
Points of the dog. Body parts and joints.
Prick ear. An erect, pointed ear.
Prognathism. Undershot or overshot jaws.
Pump handle tail. See Crank tail.
Pure-bred. A dog whose sire and dam are of the same breed.

R

Racy. Tall, lightly built.
Rat tail. A tail that has a thick root covered with curls and a bare tip.
Retriever. A hunting-dog that can be trained to pick up shot game.
Ribbed up. Long, angular ribs.
Ridge. A streak of hair growing in reverse direction to the main coat.
Ring tail. A tail that is carried up and around.
Roach back. Back with a convex curve.

Roan. Coloured hair finely mixed with white.

Roman nose. A nose with a high bridge.

Rose ear. A small, drop ear that folds back to expose the burr.

Ruff. Long, thick hair around the neck.

Rump. See Croup.

S

Sable. Black hair over a sandy background. Golden to mahogany brown.

Sabre tail. Curved, sabre-like tail.

Saddle. Contrasting hair (colour, texture, or length) that forms a saddle-like shape over the back.

Saddle back. A back that is long and dips behind the withers.

Scapula. Shoulder blade.

Scissor bite. When the upper teeth closely overlap the lower teeth.

Screw tail. Short, twisted tail.

Season. See Estrus.

Second thigh. Hindquarters from stifle to hock. Lower thigh.

Sedge. See Deadgrass.

Self colour. One (whole) colour, and maybe lighter shadings.

Semi-prick ears. Erect ears with tips breaking forwards.

Septum. Vertical line between nostrils.

Service. Use of a stud dog.

Setter. A type of long-haired dog that 'freezes' in the presence of game and flushes the game upon command.

Sheep-dog. A dog trained to guard and herd sheep. Shepherd dog.

Shelly. Weak, narrow, insubstantial body.

Shepherd dog. See Sheep-dog.

Sickle hocks. When the hock joints are under-extended, resulting in a sharp hock angle.

Sickle tail. A tail that is carried out and up in a sickle shape (semi-circle).

Single tracking. When footprints fall on a single line.

Sire. The male parent.

Skully. Thick and coarse through skull.

Slab-sided. Flattened ribs.

Slew feet. Feet turned out.

Sloping shoulders. Shoulder-blades set obliquely.

Smooth coat. Short, close hair.

Snipy. A pointed, weak muzzle.

Snowshoe feet. Slightly webbed toes.

Spaniel. A type of sporting dog characterized by drooping ears and a silky coat.

Spectacles. Dark markings around the eyes.

Spike tail. Short, straight, tapering tail.

Spitz. A type of northern dog, distinguished by a wedge-shaped head, erect ears, thick coat, and a powerful build. The spitz family comprises several breeds.

Splay foot. A flat foot with spreading toes.

Spring of ribs. A reference to the rib contours.

Squirrel tail. A tail that is carried up and back over the topline.

Stern. The tail of a sporting dog.

Sternum. Breastbone. Brisket.

Stifle. The hind leg joint located between the thigh and second thigh. Knee.

Stop. The depression beneath the eyes at the junction of the nasal bone and the skull.

Straight-hocked. Hocks that are insufficiently bent.

Straight shoulders. Shoulder-blades that are truly straight up and down, rather than sloping.

Strip. To remove hair on a wire-coated dog. Pluck.

Stud book. A registry of the breeding particulars of pedigreed dogs.

Swayback. A topline that is concave between the withers and hips.

Sword tail. A tail that hangs straight down.

T

Tail set. The way the tail is positioned on the croup.

Team. A group of at least three dogs.

Terrier. A type of small and hardy dog bred to go to ground after rodents, rabbits, and other small game.

Terrier front. Straight, narrow front.

Texture. Feel (nature) of a coat.

Thigh. The region between the hip and the stifle.

Thorax. See Chest.

Throat. The front of the neck, below the muzzle.

Throatiness. An excess of skin on the throat.

Thumb marks. Black spots on the pasterns or on the head.

Ticked. Flecks of black or coloured hair interspersed on a white coat.

Tied at the elbows. Elbows that are too close together beneath the body.

Timber. Bone.

Topknot. A tuft of hair on the head.

Topline. The top of the back.

Tuck up. A reference to the body depth at the loin. Waist.

Tulip ears. Wide, stiffly upright ears whose outer edges curve slightly forward to resemble a tulip petal.

Tricolour. Three colours. Frequently the black, white, and tan coloration of hounds.

U

Undercoat. A dense second coat that is hidden by a longer topcoat.

Undershot. A jaw whose lower incisors overlap the upper incisors.

W

Waist. A narrowing of the body at the loin.

Wall-eye. Light blue eye.

Weedy. Light in bone, insubstantial.

Well laid back shoulders. See Oblique shoulders.

Well let down. Short, upright metatarsals.

Well-sprung ribs. Sound, round ribs.

Wet neck. A neck with dewlap.

Wheaten. Pale yellow, or fawn.

Wheel back. A topline that arches over the loin.

Whelping. The act of giving birth to puppies.

Whip tail. Pointed, stiff, straight tail.

Whiskers. Long hair on the muzzle and the jaw.

Whole colour. Solid colour. Self colour.

Withers. The highest point of the body, excluding the head; located behind the neck.

Wrinkle. Folded skin.

Wrist. See Carpus.

Wry mouth. A mouth whose lower and upper jaws are not aligned.

Index to Album of Dogs

A

Affenpinscher, 45, 166
Afghan Hound, 46, 126, 244
African Lion Hound. *See* Rhodesian Ridgeback
Airedale Terrier, 48
Akita, 50
Akita Prefecture. *See* Akita
Alaskan Malamute, 51, 142, 257
Alpine Mastiff. *See* Saint Bernard
Alpine Montano, 119
Alsatian. *See* German Shepherd
Alsatian Wolf Dog. *See* German Shepherd
American Eskimo Dog, 282
American Foxhound. *See* Foxhound
American Toy Terrier, 282
Anglo-Français, 52
Appenzell, 70
Arabian Greyhound. *See* Sloughi
Arabian Hound. *See* Saluki
Arogovian Dog, 265
Asian Shepherd, 236
Aussie. *See* Australian Terrier
Australian Cattle Dog, 53
Australian Collie. *See* Australian Kelpie
Australian Heeler. *See* Australian Cattle Dog
Australian Kelpie, 53, 54
Australian Shepherd, 282
Australian Silky Terrier. *See* Silky Toy Terrier
Australian Terrier, 55

B

Barb. *See* Australian Kelpie
Barbet (North African Barbet), 232, 278
Barenbeiszer, 86
Barge Dog. *See* Schipperke
Barkless Dog. *See* Basenji
Basenji, 56
Basset Artésien-Normand, 75
Basset Bleu de Gascogne, 74, 75
Basset d'Artois, 58
Basset Fauve de Bretagne, 168
Basset Hound, 58, 60, 76, 119, 120, 124
Beagle, 60, 150, 172, 173
Beagle-Harrier, 60
Bearded Collie, 116, 216
Beauceron, 62, 84, 92, 128
Beaver Dog, 248
Bedlington Terrier, 64, 78, 124, 192, 200, 215, 276
Belgian Sheep-dog. *See* Belgian Shepherd Dog
Belgian Shepherd Dog, 66
Bengali Braque, 122
Berger de Beauce. *See* Beauceron
Berger des Pyrénées. *See* Pyrenean Sheep-dog
Berger Picard, 68, 84
Berner Laufhund. *See* Swiss Laufhund
Bernese Mountain Dog, 70
Bichon Frise, 72
Billy, 73
Black and Tan Coonhound, 282, 283
Black and Tan King Charles Spaniel, 194, 195
Black and Tan Terrier (Old English Black and Tan Terrier), 48, 138, 150, 200, 206, 274, 280
Blenheim King Charles Spaniel, 194
Bleu de Gascogne, 74, 169
Bloodhound, 58, 74, 76, 170, 171, 172, 218, 228
Blue Heeler. *See* Australian Cattle Dog
Bluetick Coonhound, 74
Bobtail. *See* Old English Sheepdog
Border Collie, 78, 116, 117
Border Terrier, 78, 124, 200, 214

Borzoi, 80, 116, 126, 176
Boston Bulldog, 82
Boston Terrier, 82
Bouledogue Français. *See* Bulldog (French)
Bouvier des Flandres, 84
Boxer, 86, 130
Bracco Italiano, 88, 90, 170
Braque Charles X, 90
Braque d'Auvergne, 89
Braque Français, 89, 90, 91, 122
Braque Saint-Germain, 91
Breton Spaniel. *See* Brittany
Briard, 62, 92, 216
British Bulldog. *See* Bulldog (English)
Brittany, 94, 272
Brussels Griffon. *See* Griffon Bruxellois
Bulldog (English), 82, 86, 87, 96, 98, 100, 102, 130, 149, 150, 234, 262
Bulldog (French), 82, 98
Bullenbeiszer, 86
Bullmastiff, 100
Bull Terrier, 82, 102, 122, 251
Butterfly Dog. *See* Papillon

C

Cà Eivessenc, 175
Cairn Terrier, 55, 104, 124, 214, 275
Canaan Dog, 283
Canadian Eskimo Dog. *See* Eskimo Dog
Cane de Pelo Duro, 186
Cane Griffone, 186
Caniche. *See* Poodle
'Cantab Terrier 215
Cardigan Welsh Corgi. *See* Welsh Corgi
Carpex Spaniel, 194
Cavalier King Charles Spaniel, 195
Céris, 73
Charlie, 194
Charnique. *See* Ibizan Hound
Chesapeake Bay Retriever, 106
Chien d'Oysel, 88, 94, 114, 139
Chihuahua, 108, 226
Chin. *See* Japanese Chin
Chinese Crested Dog, 208, 209
Chinese Hairless. *See* Mexican Hairless
Chow Chow, 110, 144, 145
Clumber Spaniel, 112
Clydesdale Terrier, 283
Coach Dog. *See* Dalmatian
Cocker Spaniel (American), 113
Cocker Spaniel (English), 113, 114, 136, 272
Collie, 53, 54, 116, 148, 160, 161
Congo Terrier. *See* Basenji
Continental Spaniel, 176
Cu, 182
Curly Coated Retriever, 106, 118, 180, 181, 198

D

Dachsbracke, 119, 120
Dachshund, 79, 119, 120
Dalmatian, 53, 102, 122
Dandie Dinmont Terrier, 55, 64, 78, 124, 192, 200, 251, 275, 280
Deerhound, 84, 116, 126, 182, 183
De Montemboeuf, 73
Deutsche Dogge, 162
Dingo, 53, 54
Dobermann Pinscher, 45, 63, 128, 226, 227
Dogue de Bordeaux, 130, 211, 234
Drahthaar. *See* German Wire-haired Pointer
Drever, 119
Dunkerstovare, 283
Dutch Barge Dog. *See* Keeshond
Dwarf Spaniel, 220

E

Elkhound, 132, 190
English Bulldog. *See* Bulldog (English)
English Foxhound. *See* Foxhound
English Greyhound. *See* Greyhound
English Mastiff. *See* Mastiff
English Pointer. *See* Pointer
English Setter, 94, 134, 160, 176
English Springer Spaniel, 114, 136, 176, 263, 272
English Toy Spaniel. *See* King Charles Spaniel
English Toy Terrier, 102, 108, 138, 166
Entlebuch, 70
Épagneul de Pont-Audemer, 139
Épagneul Fougères, 94
Épagneul Français, 94, 140
Épagneul Picard, 141
Eskimo Dog, 142
Espainhalz, 114
Eurasier, 144

F

Finnish Spitz, 146, 190
Firehouse Dog. *See* Dalmatian
Flat-coated Retriever, 148, 198
Foo Dog. *See* Pekingese
Foxhound, 52, 60, 149, 169, 172, 173, 228, 282
Fox Terrier, 48, 150, 178, 179, 188, 193, 200, 226, 250, 262, 282
Français Blanc et Noir, 152
French Basset, 172
French Bulldog. *See* Bulldog (French)
Frenchie. *See* Bulldog (French)
French Pointer. *See* Braque Français
French Spaniel. *See* Épagneul Français

G

Galgo, 126, 153
Gascon, 152
Gazelle Hound. *See* Saluki
German Mastiff. *See* Great Dane
German Shepherd Dog, 154, 242
German Short-haired Pointer, 94, 156
German Wire-haired Pointer, 158, 186
Giant Schnauzer, 248, 249
Glattharidge, 226
Golden Retriever, 148, 159
Gontjaja Estonskaja, 283
Gordon Setter, 134, 160, 176
Grand Bleu de Gascogne, 74, 75
Grand Fauve de Bretagne, 168
Grand Loulou, 190
Grand Spitz, 190, 191
Great Dane, 122, 130, 162, 239
Greater Swiss Mountain Dog, 70
Great Pyrenees. *See* Pyrenean Mountain Dog
Greyhound, 126, 128, 164, 183, 184, 185, 228, 261, 276
Griffon Belge. *See* Griffon Bruxellois
Griffon Boulet, 186
Griffon Bruxellois, 45, 166, 167
Griffon Fauve de Bretagne, 168, 170
Griffon Nivernais, 169
Griffon Vendéen, 169, 170
Groenendael, 66, 67
Grönlandshund. *See* Eskimo Dog
Gypsy Dog. *See* Bedlington Terrier

H

Hanoverian Schweisshund, 171
Harlequin Pinscher, 226
Harrier, 60, 73, 172
Hungarian Kuvasz. *See* Kuvasz
Hungarian Pointer. *See* Vizsla
Hungarian Puli. *See* Puli
Hungarian Vizsla. *See* Vizsla
Husky. *See* Siberian Husky

I

Ibizan Hound, 126, 153, 174, 225
Irish Blue Terrier. *See* Kerry Blue Terrier
Irish Setter, 134, 160, 176, 180, 181
Irish Sheep-dog, 182
Irish Spaniel, 176
Irish Terrier, 55, 178, 192, 214
Irish Water Spaniel, 106, 118, 139, 176, 180
Irish Wolfhound, 126, 182, 192
Istrian Pointer, 122
Italian Greyhound, 126, 182, 184, 226, 276
Italian Griffon. *See* Italian Spinone
Italian Pointer. *See* Bracco Italiano and Italian Spinone
Italian Spinone, 186

J

Jack Russell Terrier, 188
Japanese Akita. *See* Akita
Japanese Chin, 189, 266
Japanese Spaniel. *See* Japanese Chin
Japanese Spitz, 190
Jura Lancer, 265
Jura Laufhund. *See* Swiss Laufhund

K

Keeshond, 190, 270
Kelpie. *See* Autralian Kelpie
Kerry Blue Terrier, 192
King Charles Spaniel, 114, 194
King's White Dog (Chien Blanc du Roy), 73, 76, 173
Komondor, 196
Korthals Griffon. *See* Wire-haired Pointing Griffon
Kurzhaar. *See* German Short-haired Pointer
Kuvasz, 197

L

Labrador Retriever, 107, 148, 178, 198, 212
Laekenois, 66, 67
Laïka, 144, 190, 283
Lakeland Terrier, 78, 200
Landseer. *See* Newfoundland
Laverack Setter, 134
Leeds Terrier, 280
Leonberger, 201, 212
Leuvenaar, 247
Lhasa Apso, 202, 254, 255, 266
Lhasa Terrier. *See* Tibetan Terrier
Long-coat Chihuahua, 108, 109
Loulou. *See* Pomeranian
Lurcher, 282

M

Malamute. *See* Alaskan Malamute
Malinois, 66, 67
Maltese, 72, 204, 259, 280
Manchester Terrier, 128, 138, 206, 226, 276, 280
Maremma, 197
Mastiff, 86, 100, 207
Mastino Napolitano. *See* Neapolitan Mastiff
Melita. *See* Maltese
Mexican Hairless, 208
Miniature Bull Terrier, 102
Miniature Pinscher, 226
Miniature Poodle, 232, 233
Miniature Schnauzer, 248, 249
Molossus (Molossian Mastiff), 96, 130, 207, 210, 240, 242
Mongrels, 284
Monkey Dog. *See* Affenpinscher
Monkey Terrier. *See* Affenpinscher
Mopse. *See* Pug

N

Neapolitan Mastiff, 210
Newfoundland, 106, 116, 118, 148, 176, 201, 212
Norfolk Terrier, 214, 215

Normandy Spaniel, 139
Norwegian Elkhound. *See* Elkhound
Norwich Terrier, 214, 215

O

Old English Sheepdog, 216
Old English Terrier, 102, 262
Old English White Terrier, 276
Otterhound, 48, 124, 200, 218
Owtchar (Russian Owtchar), 216

P

Papillon, 109, 220, 231
Pekingese, 109, 205, 222, 234, 254, 266
Pembroke Welsh Corgi. *See* Welsh Corgi
Perras de Presa, 211
Persian Greyhound. *See* Saluki
Persian Shepherd, 236
Petit Basset Griffon Vendeen, 170
Petit Bleu de Gascogne, 74, 75
Petit Brabançon, 166, 167
Phalène, 220, 221
Pharaoh Hound, 21, 22, 126, 175
Picardy Spaniel. *See* Épagneul Picard
Pinscher, 45, 128, 226
Pit Bull Terrier, 283
Plotthound, 282
Plum Pudding, 122
Podenco Ibicenco. *See* Ibizan Hound
Podengo Hound (Portuguese Podengo Hound),175
Pointer, 89, 91, 94, 122, 176, 228, 279
Poitevin, 52
Pomeranian, 109, 190, 230
Pont-Audemer Spaniel. *See* Épagneul de Pont-Audemer
Poodle, 64, 72, 180, 181, 232
Porcelaine, 173
Portuguese Water-dog, 181
Prince Charles Spaniel, 194
Pug, 78, 190, 234, 266
Puli, 216, 236
Pyrenees Mountain Dog, 197, 212, 237, 238
Pyrenean Sheep-dog, 238

Q

Queensland Heeler. *See* Australian Cattle Dog

R

Redesdale Terrier, 78
Red Setter. *See* Irish Setter
Red Pinscher, 226
Rhodesian Ridgeback, 239
Rothbury Terrier, 64
Rottweiler, 128, 240
Rough Collie. *See* Collie
Roulers, 84
Round Head. *See* Boston Terrier
Ruby King Charles Spaniel, 194, 195
Russian Wolfhound. *See* Borzoi

S

Saint Bernard, 201, 212, 242, 283
Saint Hubert, 58, 76, 77
Saint Louis Grey Dog (Chien Gris de Saint-Louis), 76, 170
St John's Dog. *See* Labrador Retriever
Saintongeois, 152
Saluki, 126, 244
Samoyed, 142, 246, 283
Schipperke, 247, 270
Schnauzer, 226, 248
Schweizer Laufhund. *See* Swiss Laufhund
Scottie. *See* Scottish Terrier
Scottish Terrier, 55, 104, 124, 250, 275
Sealyham Terrier, 251
Ségusien, 169
Segusium, 76
Shar Pei (Chinese Shar Pei), 252

Sheltie. *See* Shetland Sheep-dog
Shetland Sheep-dog, 116, 253
Shih Tzu, 254
Shishi Inu. *See* Akita
Siberian Husky, 142, 190, 256
Silky Terrier. *See* Silky Toy Terrier
Silky Toy Terrier, 258
Skye Terrier, 104, 124, 259, 283
Sloughi, 126, 153, 182, 225, 260
Slughi. *See* Sloughi
Smithfield, 53
Smooth Collie, 116, 117
Smooth-haired Fox Terrier. *See* Fox Terrier
Smooth-haired Terrier, 150
Somerset Harrier, 172, 173
Southern Harrier, 218
Spanish Greyhound. *See* Galgo
Spanish Pointer, 90, 156, 228
Spinone. *See* Italian Spinone
Staffordshire Bull Terrier, 96, 102, 215, 262
Staghound (English Staghound), 149, 173
Suomenpystykorva, 146
Sussex Spaniel, 263
Swiss Laufund, 264
Swiss Mountain Dog, 70
Sydney Terrier. *See* Silky Toy Terrier

T

Talbot Hound, 172
Tazi. *See* Afghan Hound
Tchin. *See* Japanese Chin
Teckel. *See* Dachshund
Teneriffe. *See* Bichon Frise
Tervuren, 66, 67
Tesem, 175, 225
Tibetan Apso. *See* Lhasa Apso
Tibetan Mastiff, 98, 130, 202, 237, 283
Tibetan Spaniel, 202,266
Tibetan Terrier, 202, 266, 267
Timmins Biter, 53
Toonie, 252
Toy Black and Tan Terrier. *See* English Toy Terrier
Toy Bulldog, 82
Toy Manchester Terrier. *See* English Toy Terrier
Toy Poodle, 109, 231, 232, 233
Tweed Water Spaniel, 198

UV

Unofficial Breeds, 282
Vallhund (Swedish Vallhund), 270
Vizsla, 268
Volpino, 190

W

Weimaraner, 268, 269
Welsh Corgi, 251, 270
Welsh Spaniel. *See* Welsh Springer Spaniel
Welsh Springer Spaniel, 136, 272
Welsh Terrier, 188, 274
West County Harrier, 173
West Highland White Terrier, 104, 206, 251, 275
Westie. *See* West Highland White Terrier
Westphalian Basset, 119
Whippet, 64, 102, 184, 206, 276
Wire-haired Fox Terrier. *See* Fox Terrier
Wire-haired Pointing Griffon, 186, 278
Wire-haired Vizsla, 268
Wolfhound. *See* Irish Wolfhound
Wolf-Spitz, 190

XY

Xolo. *See* Mexican Hairless
Xoloizcuintle. *See* Mexican Hairless
Yakki, 252
Yorkie. *See* Yorkshire Terrier
Yorkshire Terrier, 55, 109, 231, 258, 280

Credits and Acknowledgments

The editors are grateful for the assistance provided by the following individuals: Brandi Becker, Natasha Burns, Antoine Dubois, Raymond Ferrando, Léonard Ginsburg, François Lubrina, Francis Petter, Pierre Rousselet-Blanc; and Marc Buzzini and Gérard Lacz-Lemoine.

To identify a photograph or illustration on its page, the following referencing has been used: *r*, right-hand column; *l*, left-hand column; *t*, top of the page; *b*, bottom of the page; *c*, centre.

Illustrations

JOËL BLANC: pages 8, 10, 13 *b*, 50, 51, 52, 73, 90, 95, 118, 119, 120, 121, 123, 127, 148, 149, 155, 157, 159, 160, 161, 162, 172, 173, 174, 183, 197, 213, 216, 236, 239, 241, 244, 245, 261, 265, 269.
FRANÇOISE BONVOUST: pages 189, 194, 195, 227, 228, 229.
JOSIANE CAMPAN: pages 69, 79, 145, 251, 254, 255, 274, 310, 316, 317, 321, 323, 333, 337.
JEAN COLADON: pages 67, 71, 101, 103, 106, 112, 113, 114, 115, 131, 171, 206, 207, 211, 215, 223, 224, 225, 235, 238, 242, 243, 246, 247, 258, 262, 274, 275.
LOUISE DELORME: page 291.
MAURICE ESPÉRANCE: pages 12, 13 *t*, 34, 35, 36, 37, 38, 39, 40, 41, 99, 222, 296, 298, 324, 326, 327, 328, 329, 330, 331, 353, 354, 363.
PHILIPPE GOSSENT: pages 83, 98, 105, 264.
MICHEL JANVIER: pages 63, 65, 74, 85, 86, 87, 93, 97, 99, 110, 111, 153, 175, 182, 210, 217, 235, 256, 257, 280.
OLENA KASSIAN: pages 54, 258.
BRENDA KATTÉ: pages 66, 89, 124, 125, 138, 178, 179, 196, 199, 250, 266, 267.
JEAN-MARIE LE FAOU: pages 45, 48, 49, 88, 91, 92, 93, 165, 184, 185, 191, 208, 209, 237, 271, 277.
LINE MAILHÉ: page 96.
GUY MICHEL: pages 53, 54, 55, 58, 59, 62, 72, 82, 84, 85, 108, 109, 116, 120, 121, 128, 133, 134, 135, 139, 140, 143, 168, 169, 180, 181, 188, 193, 200, 201, 203, 204, 205, 218, 221, 230, 231, 232, 233, 248, 249, 253, 259, 272, 281, 284, 297.
PHILIPPE SAUNIER: pages 60, 61, 64, 65, 141, 170.

JEAN-CLAUDE SENNE: pages 116, 117, 166, 167, 187.
GRÉGOIRE SOBIESKI: pages 46, 47, 76, 77, 80, 81, 152, 268.
FRANÇOIS VITALIS: pages 129, 158.
JEAN-PIERRE WEINTZEM: pages 56, 57, 136, 137, 146, 147, 150, 177, 263.

Contributing persons and organizations: Bran-Mar, p. 252; A. Cumbers, p. 82; J.-P. Ferrero, p. 210, 229, 281, 321; Foto-Mauritius, p. 171, 119; Jacana/R. Dulhoste, p. 284 *tl*; Pictor, p. 88; Pitch/Bel-Vienne, p.155; Rebouleau, p. 157; A. Schmidecker, p. 201, 221; Thompson Animal Photography, p. 120, 134, 138, 148, 174, 206, 207, 262; G. Trouillet, p. 80, 111, 205; Vloo/Staincq, p. 284 *br*; Zefa/Rötzel, p. 86; Dr. V. Ziswiler, p. 265 *br*; Yves Lignereux, p. 38 and 326 to 331.

The following illustrations originated in, or were based on, other publications: p. 36, 99, 337: *le Chien, morphologie, extérieur, esthétique*, M. Luquet; Maloine; p. 39, 41, 337: *le Chien*, Pierre Rousselet-Blanc; Larousse; p. 363: *les Chiens*, J. Palmer; Nathan; p. 324: *les Chiens de berger français*, M. Luquet; de Vecchi; p. 182, 323: *le Grand Livre du chien*, Édito-Service, S.A., Geneva; p. 296: *Handbook of Veterinary Procedures and Emergency Treatment*, R. Kirk and S. Bithner; W. B. Saunders; p. 353: *le Praticien vétérinaire*, no. 164; p. 37 *r*, 354: *Revue Chiens 2000*, no. 53, 1981; p. 222: *Revue Chiens 2000*, no. 59, September 1981; p. 337: *The Dog in Action*, McDowell Lyon, ©1978, 1950; Howell Book House Inc. with special authorization from the editor; p. 217: *The Old English Sheepdog*, A. Davis, Popular Dogs.

Photographs

Bibliothèque nationale, Paris: 26 *c* • M. Bruggmann: *10, 11* • Bulloz: *17 tr* • Cairo Museum: *19 t* • M. Buzzini: *35* (1), *36* (2, 4), *37, 41, 286, 300, 301, 306 b, 315 tr, 320 t, 321 t, 322 b* • J.-L. Charmet/Bibliothèque nationale: *27 t* • Condé Museum, Chantilly, France: *338* • École nationale vétérinaire d'Alfort/Department of Parasitology: *349 t, 352, 362* (1, 3, 4, 5), *365*; Department of Medicine: *353* • Edimages/Goldner: *24 t* • Elveca, Orgeval (Yvelines): *287 b* • Et-Archive/Bibliothèque nationale, Paris: *25 c* • National Gallery: *26 b, 29 bl* • J.-P. Ferrero: *320 b, 322 t, 339, 343 l, 349 b* • Giraudon: *31 c* • With special authorization from the city of Bayeux, France: *24 b* • M. Holford/National Museum of Turkey: *16* • British Museum: *17 tl, 18 bl* • Jacana/G.Trouillet: *35* (3), *291* • J.-P. Thomas: *310* • Varin-Visage: *318* • Lorne: *362* (2) • H. Josse/Cernuschi Museum: *17 b* • Louvre Museum: *19 bl, 28 t* • Musée des Antiquités nationales, Paris: *23 b* • Musée de la Chasse, Paris: *30 tl* • Lacz-Lemoine: *35* (2, 4, 5, 6), *36* (1), *287 c, 288 t, 289 r, 290, 300 tl & b, 302, 303, 306 t, 309, 312, 315 tl, 319, 321 c, 322 c, 324 bl, 366 l & r* • Lauros-Giraudon/Louvre Museum: *20 b* • Naples Museum: *23 t* • Angiers Museum: *28 b* • F. Lubrina: *340, 344, 345 t, 346, 347, 348, 358, 361* • Michigan State University: *366 b* • Cairo Museum: *19 br* • Musée national d'Histoire naturelle/Department of Paleontology: *9* • Nature/Samba: *304 r* • Pitch/J.-L. Patel: *313* • Provincial Archives of British Columbia: *31 t* • Rapho/Condé Museum, Chantilly, France: *25 tl* • Bibliothèque nationale, Paris: *26 t* • L. Frédéric: *22 c* • H. Donnezan: *305 b* • Réunion des musées nationaux/Louvre Museum: *29 br* • Drs. Robin and Anfrye: *343 r, 355 l* • Roger-Viollet: *31 b* • Scala/Palermo Museum: *21 c, 22 t* • Marciana Library, Venice: *25 tr, 27 c*; Scuola San Giogio dei Schiavoni, Venice: *27 b* • Prado Museum: *29 tl* • Free Library, Philadelphia: *30 tr* • Dr. M. Simon: *351, 355 r* • Snark: *25 b* • Carnavalet Museum, Paris: *30 b* • S.R.D./J.-P. Germain: *288 b, 292, 299, 316 b, 318, 345 b* • R. Mazin: *324 t* • A.D.A.G.P., 1982: *32 tr* • Tapabor/Kharbine: *32 tc* • G. Trouillet: *36* (3), *304 l, 305 t, 308, 323* • Vloo/C. Elinguel: *287 t* • Mery: *289 l, 307* • M. Laval: *311* • M. Gile: *313 r* • Montferrand: *324 bl* • Ziolo/Agraci, Louvre Museum: *29 tr* • A. Held: *18 br, 211* • Musée d'Art et d'Histoire, Geneva: *21 b* • Nimatallah/Athens National Museum: *20 t*.

40/071/6